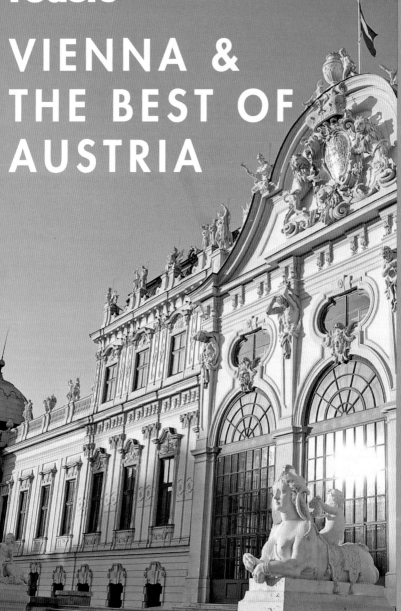

Fodor's

VIENNA & THE BEST OF AUSTRIA

WELCOME TO VIENNA & THE BEST OF AUSTRIA

From Vienna to the Alps, Austria celebrates the elegance of the past yet also embraces the pleasures of contemporary culture and the outdoors. Sophisticated Vienna buzzes with former imperial palaces and striking modern structures, traditional coffeehouses and chic locavore restaurants. Beyond the capital, you can hike the Salzkammergut with its cool blue lakes, ski the fashionable slopes of Innsbruck, or soak in the enduring charms of Salzburg's classical music scene. In this fascinating intersection of old and new, you'll find plenty to savor.

TOP REASONS TO GO

★ **Vienna:** Baroque and art nouveau architecture, cool boutiques, top-tier concert halls.

★ **Scenery:** Stunning views of alpine passes, the Danube Valley, and lowland vineyards.

★ **Music:** The land of Mozart and Strauss entertains fans with performances galore.

★ **Historic Palaces:** From Mirabell to Schönbrunn, Austria flaunts its imperial past.

★ **Museums:** The Kunsthistorisches, MuseumsQuartier, and Museum der Moderne, for a start.

★ **Skiing:** Posh resorts and world-class runs at Kitzbühel, St. Anton, and more.

12
TOP EXPERIENCES

Vienna offers terrific experiences that should be on every traveler's list. Here are Fodor's top picks for a memorable trip.

1 Schönbrunn Palace

Play royalty for a day in Vienna by visiting the summer residence of the Habsburgs with its elegant gardens, fountains, fake Roman ruins, a hilltop café, and Europe's oldest zoo. *(Ch.2)*

2 Sachertorte

Indulge in a slice of Sachertorte, a dense chocolate cake layered with apricot jam. It was invented in the early 19th century by one of Austria's court confectioners. *(Ch. 2)*

3 Grossglockner High Alpine Highway

In the Alps, you can ascend to Austria's tallest peak and view the Pasterze glacier from 12,470 feet. See it while you can; it shrinks 30 feet every year. *(Ch. 9)*

4 The Ringstrasse
Streetcars travel full circle along Vienna's best-known avenue, lined with monumental buildings that recall the city's imperial splendor. *(Ch. 2)*

5 Thermal Spas
Soak in hot springs at one of several thermal spas that dot small towns throughout Austria. Then brag that you've experienced the country's unofficial leisure sport. *(Ch. 11)*

6 Heurigen
Visit a wine tavern where owners serve new wines from their own vineyards. In September, sample *Sturm*, a drink made from the first pressing of the grapes. *(Ch. 3)*

7 MAK Museum
In Vienna, this gorgeous collection of Austrian art objects and contemporary works also includes a fascinating display devoted to the Wiener Werkstätte. *(Ch. 2)*

8 The Salzkammergut

Enjoy a hike in this rural paradise in Upper Austria with 76 lakes and the Dachstein Mountain range. The opening scenes from *The Sound of Music* were filmed here. *(Ch. 10)*

9 The Viennese Ball

As many as 400 black-tie balls are held every year during Vienna's *Fasching*, or carnival season, which lasts from New Year's Eve through Mardi Gras. *(Ch. 5)*

10 Fortress Hohensalzburg

Evening classical music concerts take place in the prince's chamber of this mighty castle overlooking Salzburg's skyline. *(Ch. 8)*

11 Hofbibliothek

Browse the stacks at Vienna's National Library, a cathedral of books and one of the world's most ornate Baroque libraries. *(Ch. 2)*

12 Kitzbühel

This 16th-century village with a medieval town center has carved out a reputation as one of Europe's most fashionable winter ski resorts. *(Ch. 12)*

CONTENTS

**1 EXPERIENCE VIENNA AND
THE BEST OF AUSTRIA. 13**
Vienna and Austria Today 14
What's Where. 16
Vienna Planner 18
Quintessential Vienna
and Austria 20
Flavors of Austrian Cuisine. 22
If You Like 24
Great Itineraries 26
When to Go. 29
Festivals in Austria. 30
Notable Austrians 31
Skiing in Austria 32

2 EXPLORING VIENNA 35
Exploring Vienna 44

3 WHERE TO EAT. 91
Dining Planner 92
Restaurant Reviews 94
Best Bets for Vienna Dining 95

4 WHERE TO STAY. 113
Planning 115
Hotel Reviews. 116
Best Bets for Vienna Lodging . .117

**5 NIGHTLIFE AND
PERFORMING ARTS. 125**
Planning 126
Nightlife 128
Performing Arts. 131

6 SHOPPING. 139

**7 VIENNA WOODS,
LAKE NEUSIEDL, AND
THE DANUBE RIVER 153**
Vienna Woods 160
The Weinviertel. 164
Neusiedl Lake Area 168
Along the Danube River 174

Linz: "Rich Town of the
River Markets" 183

8 SALZBURG. 195
Exploring Salzburg 200
Where to Eat 216
Best Bets for Salzburg Dining . .218
Where to Stay. 225
Best Bets for
Salzburg Lodging. 227
Nightlife and Performing Arts . .230
Shopping. 235
Excursions from Salzburg. 238

9 EASTERN ALPS 241
Across the
Grossglockner Pass 246
Mountain Spas and
Alpine Rambles. 255

10 SALZKAMMERGUT 263
Fuschlsee, St. Wolfgang,
and Bad Ischl. 267
Gosau and Hallstatt 276

11 CARTHINA AND GRAZ 281
Klagenfurt toward
the Gurktal Region. 286
Graz. 295

**12 INNSBRUCK, TYROL,
AND VORARLBERG 309**
Innsbruck 319
Tyrol. 336
Vorarlberg 353
Bregenz 360

UNDERSTANDING AUSTRIA . .367
Austria at a Glance 368
Chronology 369
Words and Phrases 373
Menu Guide 376
Conversions 380

CONTENTS

TRAVEL SMART
VIENNA AND AUSTRIA 381

INDEX 403

ABOUT OUR WRITERS 416

MAPS

Exploring Vienna
Historic Heart 46–47

The Hofburg (Imperial Palace). . .61

Schönbrunn Palace and Park . . .88

Where to Eat in Vienna 96–97

Where to Stay in Vienna . .118–119

Lower Danube Valley 161

Upper Danube Valley 176

Salzburg 202

Where to Eat and Stay
in Salzburg. 220–221

Eastern Alps. 248–249

Salzkammergut/
The Lake District 268

Carinthia 287

Styria 294

Graz 297

Ski Areas 316–317

Innsbruck 323

Where to Eat and Stay
in Innsbruck 329

Eastern Tyrol 337

Western Tyrol 347

Vorarlberg 354

ABOUT THIS GUIDE

Fodor's Ratings

Everything in this guide is worth doing—we don't cover what isn't—but exceptional sights, hotels, and restaurants are recognized with additional accolades. Fodor's Choice★ indicates our top recommendations, and **Best Bets** call attention to notable hotels and restaurants in various categories. Care to nominate a new place? Visit Fodors.com/contact-us.

Trip Costs

We list prices wherever possible to help you budget well. Hotel and restaurant price categories from **$** to **$$$$** are noted alongside each recommendation. For hotels, we include the lowest cost of a standard double room in high season. For restaurants, we cite the average price of a main course at dinner or, if dinner isn't served, at lunch. For attractions, we always list adult admission fees; discounts are usually available for children, students, and senior citizens.

Hotels

Our local writers vet every hotel to recommend the best overnights in each price category, from budget to expensive. Unless otherwise specified, you can expect private bath, phone, and TV in your room.

Top Picks	Hotels &
★ **Fodor's** Choice	**Restaurants**
	🏨 Hotel
Listings	⤴ Number of
✉ Address	rooms
✉ Branch address	⫽⊙⫽ Meal plans
☎ Telephone	✗ Restaurant
🖷 Fax	⇖ Reservations
⊕ Website	🏛 Dress code
✐ E-mail	▭ No credit cards
✑ Admission fee	$ Price
⊙ Open/closed	
times	**Other**
Ⓜ Subway	⇨ See also
⊹ Directions or	☞ Take note
Map coordinates	🏌 Golf facilities

Restaurants

Unless we state otherwise, restaurants are open for lunch and dinner daily. We mention dress code only when there's a specific requirement and reservations only when they're essential or not accepted. To make restaurant reservations, visit Fodors.com.

Credit Cards

The hotels and restaurants in this guide typically accept credit cards. If not, we'll say so.

EUGENE FODOR

Hungarian-born Eugene Fodor (1905–91) began his travel career as an interpreter on a French cruise ship. The experience inspired him to write *On the Continent* (1936), the first guidebook to receive annual updates and discuss a country's way of life as well as its sights. Fodor later joined the U.S. Army and worked for the OSS in World War II. After the war, he kept up his intelligence work while expanding his guidebook series. During the Cold War, many guides were written by fellow agents who understood the value of insider information. Today's guides continue Fodor's legacy by providing travelers with timely coverage, insider tips, and cultural context.

1

EXPERIENCE
VIENNA AND THE
BEST OF AUSTRIA

VIENNA AND AUSTRIA TODAY

In today's Austria, the old exists alongside the new. Austria has, at various times, been the seat of an empire, the hub of artistic expression, an occupied territory during wartime, and the lone neutral ground of the Cold War. All of Vienna's distinctive eras, from the 18th-century age of the great composers to the Vienna Secession Art Nouveau period at the turn of the 20th century to the present day—with skyscrapers like the newly built DC Towers soaring above the banks of the Danube—can be found in this remarkable city of 1.7 million residents. For centuries, the country has attracted artists, musicians, writers, athletes, actors, and doctors hoping to make a name for themselves.

Austria has been under the control of emperors, kings, dictators, presidents, and Caesars. At its height a century ago, the Austro-Hungarian Empire covered most of central and eastern Europe with about 53 million people living under the rule of the House of Habsburg. The country's present-day boundaries put it at roughly the size of South Carolina with a population of 8.5 million, comparable to that of New Jersey.

Move over Mozart

Austria is synonymous with classical music almost to the point of obsession; therefore, changes in the musical landscape often take time. After more than 500 years in existence, the famed Vienna Boys' Choir only recently received their first theater all to themselves: the 400-seat MuTh (Music & Theater) concert hall, where classical enthusiasts can hear this world-renowned choir, founded in 1498 by Holy Roman Emperor Maximillian I, perform music by Mozart, Schubert, and more. The theater, which opened in 2012, mixes Baroque and contemporary architecture enriched with distinctive seating and panels to create some of the best acoustics in Vienna. In addition to calling on MuTh, classical devotees can listen to music (free in many cases) at Vienna's often overlooked University of Music and Performing Arts, where students from across the globe come to study.

Perhaps more than any other genre except for Austria's beloved classical, electronic music has grabbed national—and, increasingly, international—attention. Since the 1990s when Austrian duo Kruder & Dorfmeister began popularizing downtempo, which is more mellow than house or trance, Vienna has been the unofficial international capital of the cozy groove genre; visitors will find it playing in clubs, bars, and cafés throughout the city. Popular techno lounges frequently change up their playlists to keep things fresh for eager crowds, while more and more outdoor parties like the aptly named Kein Sonntag ohne Techno (No Sunday Without Techno) dot the city's new musical terrain. Record stores are also filled with electronic music produced by small labels, which have helped fuel the movement. Beyond Vienna, the Ars Electronica Festival, held every September in the northern city of Linz, focuses on digital culture with the final day devoted to electronic music, while the southeastern city of Graz—a UNESCO World Heritage Site—hosts the urban electronic arts and music Springfestival in May, drawing international crowds that bear witness to the growing popularity of electronica.

Weathering the Storm

Unlike its Italian neighbors to the south, Austria survived the euro crisis (when a group of 10 central and eastern European

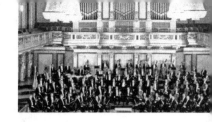

banks asked for a bailout) in much better shape than many other EU countries. From 2008 through 2012, Austria was one of a handful of EU countries to maintain a healthy GDP and a lower-than-average unemployment rate through fiscal stimulus plans. The export-heavy country is seeing only a slow growth in its economy and a creeping rise in the unemployment rate; still, if the continent's fiscal woes have taught Austria anything, it's that its citizens are now much more aware of the strength of their economy and the value of their own products. Chocolate, pistachio, and marzipan "Mozart balls," originally produced by Salzburg confectioner Paul Furst in 1890 and named in honor of the great composer, are now as much a draw for visitors as they are exports that provide valuable bits of tasty Austrian marketing.

To the Right, to the Right

As with any large economic shakeup, change affects politics. The country's two main political parties, the center-left Social Democratic Party and the center-right Austrian People's Party still hold much of the power (the two make up the coalition government) but new contenders are emerging from the right. Led by the simultaneously charismatic and reviled (depending on whom you ask) Heinz-Christian Strache, the right-wing nationalist Austrian Freedom Party (FPÖ) has seen a resurgence in recent years, gaining 20% of the vote in the most recent parliamentary elections. The FPÖ is critical of the European Union, believing that integration weakens Austria's "cultural identity"; the party also takes a strict stance on immigration. This has resonated with many younger voters (Strache's support is strongest among those under 30) and small groups on the right have sprung up, more or less echoing the FPÖ's positions. The FPÖ has been the only party to see consistent gains in elections since 2005, when Strache became FPÖ leader. However, though many FPÖ voters are defectors from other parties, Strache's propaganda machine still hasn't managed to convince Austrians that they're in need of the drastic change he claims.

Farm-to-Table Is a Way of Life

The modern sustainable food movement commonly called "farm-to-table" didn't begin in Austria, but it may as well have. The country's small size, distinct seasons, aversion to processed food, and varied growing areas from mountains to vineyards to grassy flatlands provide the perfect setting for getting food quickly from its source, something that has been normal practice in Austria since the years immediately following World War II, when the country struggled to provide enough food within its borders for its citizens. Only recently has farm-to-table been promoted as such. Austrian farms and vineyards have been known to practice "biodynamic agriculture," a holistic approach that treats the farm as an entire organism, a concept developed by Austrian thinker Rudolf Steiner. Austria is considered one of the pioneers of organic farming with one-fifth of the agricultural land in the country being farmed organically, the highest percentage in the European Union. The country also has more organic farmers than all of the other EU countries together. Many restaurants have gotten into the habit of publishing the source of each ingredient, both to appease picky diners and excite foodies, with products derived from organic farming and humane animal keeping.

WHAT'S WHERE

The following numbers refer to chapters.

2 **Vienna.** Vienna mixes old-world charm with elements of a modern metropolis. The city's neighborhoods offer a journey thick with history and architecture, and the famous coffeehouses are havens for an age-old coffee-drinking ritual.

7 **Vienna Woods and the Danube Valley.** Vienna is surrounded with enticing options such as hiking in the Vienna Woods and exploring the nearby towns of Marchegg and Carnuntum. The famously blue Danube courses through Austria past medieval abbeys, fanciful Baroque monasteries, verdant pastures, and compact riverside villages. A convenient base is Linz, Austria's third-largest city, and probably its most underrated.

8 **Salzburg.** Salzburg is an elegant city with a rich musical heritage that also draws visitors for its museums and architecture, the Trapp family history, old-fashioned cafés, and glorious fountains.

9 **The Eastern Alps.** Farther south and into the Alps, panoramic little towns, spas, and an array of sports highlight this section of Austria. No road in Europe matches the Grossglockner High Alpine Highway, the most spectacular pass through the Alps.

10 Salzkammergut.
The Salzkammergut stretches across three states—from Salzburg through Styria to Upper Austria—and includes Austria's Lake District. Hallstatt is touted as one of the world's prettiest lakeside villages.

11 Carinthia and Graz.
Carinthia is the country's sunniest (and southernmost) province. Here you'll find the Austrian Riviera, a blend of mountains, valleys, and placid blue-green lakes with lovely resorts, while Graz, the capital of Styria, is the country's second-largest city.

12 Innsbruck, Tyrol, and Vorarlberg. The Tyrol is a region graced with cosmopolitan cities and monuments, but with the glorious Alps playing the stellar role, Nature steals every scene. Nearby, Vorarlberg's big draw is its powdery skiing regions.

VIENNA PLANNER

When to Go

Late spring to early fall are the best times to visit Austria, when the weather is nice enough to spend most of the day outdoors. Restaurants begin setting up outdoor seating as early as March, though some years this amounts to wishful thinking when the winter lasts longer than anticipated. The summer months usually feature plenty of outdoor festivals in the major cities. The eastern half of the country has hot summers and only somewhat cold winters. In the western Alpine half, summers are shorter and winters are longer and colder. Austria's tourist season peaks in July and August, so expect to pay more for accommodations during these months.

Getting Here

Nearly all the air traffic into the country comes through Vienna International Airport (VIE), which recently opened a new terminal. Salzburg (SGZ), Innsbruck (INN), and Graz (GRZ) airports handle regional flights. Austria is highly accessible by train, and the country's national railway system recently upgraded certain lines to accommodate high-speed train travel. Vienna is also in the process of building the largest train station in the country, Vienna Central Station, which is slated for completion in December 2015. The new station will offer increased railway links with improved international service and will include as many as 100 shops and restaurants.

Getting Around

Austria's size and high quality of train travel mean you can get by without renting a car, though it may be convenient if you plan a trip to the more rural parts of the country. If visiting Vienna, the public transit system is the best way to get around within the city. Smaller Austrian cities also have reliable intra-city bus services.

Travel Times

FROM VIENNA TO	BY CAR	BY TRAIN
Salzburg	3 hours	2.5 hours
Linz	2 hours	1.5 hours
Graz	2 hours	2.5 hours
Innsbruck	4.5 hours	4.5 hours
Budapest	2.5 hours	3 hours
Munich	4 hours	4 hours
Prague	3.5 hours	5 hours
Bratislava	1 hour	1 hour

Getting Oriented

Moving around Austria is not without its idiosyncrasies. Most public restrooms charge €0.50, so make sure to always carry change with you. The right-hand side of escalators are for standing, the left for walking. Most shops are closed all day on Sunday and are closed after 6 pm on weekdays. Be sure to allow passengers to exit public transit before getting on. If a restaurant, museum, or theater has a coat check, you are expected to use it.

Visitor Information

Austrian Tourism Office. For more information, contact the Austrian Tourism Office. ☎ 212/944–6880 ⊕ www.austria.info.

Eating Out: The Basics

Restaurants and cafés move at a leisurely pace, so waiters won't chase you out if you want to sit and talk for a few hours. Prices in all restaurants, grocery stores, and markets include tax, so what you see is what you pay. Tipping is usually rounded up to the next euro or two and usually done when you pay your bill, which you must specifically request. For a bill of €28.50, it's appropriate to say "make it 30." When paying as part of a group, waiters and waitresses are able to easily split the bill at the table, even if some customers want to pay cash and some by card.

WHAT IT COSTS IN EUROS

	$	$$	$$$	$$$$
Restaurants	under €18	€18–€23	€24–€31	over €31
Hotels	under €120	€121–€170	€171–€270	over €270

Restaurant prices are per person for a main course at dinner. Hotel prices are for a standard double room in high season, including taxes and service.

Sav

Make v with 20

Take Vier (look for the red sig of the green CAT train. It will take you slightly longer (only by 15 minutes) but will cost you about €10 less.

Buy a daily or weekly pass for the Vienna public transit system.

Many museums have a free admission day once a month; some are free once a week.

Grocery stores will often have a deli for cheap lunchtime sandwiches, making it an easy way to sample the local meats and cheeses.

The €21.90 Vienna Card offers unlimited public transit rides for 72 hours and discounts at museums, restaurants, and cafés.

Free Wi-Fi is available in many restaurants, cafés, hotels, and shops.

Wurstelstands (the Austrian equivalent of hot dog stands), selling all types of sausages, provide cheap, walking-around food.

TESSENTIAL
NNA AND AUSTRIA

The Viennese Coffeehouse

Twice the Ottoman armies stood at the gates of Vienna (in the 16th and 17th centuries), and twice they were turned back after long, bitter sieges. Although the Turks never captured the city, they left a lasting legacy: the art of preparing and consuming coffee. Emotions about coffee tend to run high throughout Austria: ask anyone on the street where you can get a good cup of coffee or homemade *Apfelstrudel,* and you're likely to get a lengthy and passionate exposition on why you must try a certain coffeehouse. Many Austrians spend a good part of the day sitting over a single cup of coffee in their favorite coffeehouse while reading the newspaper, discussing business or politics, or just catching up on the local gossip. As any Austrian will tell you, many of the world's great cultural moments had their genesis in coffeehouse discussions in Vienna. You'll hear about where Leo Trotsky regularly played chess while working out the subtleties of communist theory (at Café Central), where Gustav Klimt and Egon Schiele worked out their ideas for modern art (Café Museum), and where Sigmund Freud spent Wednesday evenings laying the foundation for modern psychoanalytic theory (Kaffeehaus Korb). Although more and more generic Italian espresso bars and even Starbucks coffee shops (gasp!) are cropping up in urban areas, these fulfill another purpose entirely and cannot begin to compete with the role the traditional Viennese coffeehouse has in defining Austrian identity.

The Outdoors

"Land der Berge, Land am Strome" ("Land of mountains, land on the river") is the first verse of the Austrian national anthem, and it sums up what Austrians treasure most about their country: the breathtaking and diverse landscapes.

If you want to get a sense of contemporary Austrian culture and indulge in some of its pleasures, start by familiarizing yourself with the rituals of daily life. These are a few highlights—things you can take part in with relative ease.

The mania for the outdoors transcends all age groups. Ten-year-olds, determined to follow in the footsteps of great Austrian skiers like Hermann Maier, will overtake you on the ski slope. And on a warm summer day when you reach that mountain hut in an Alpine meadow near the peak, out of breath after a five-hour hike, you'll find a score of 70-year-olds who beat you there. Austrian Alpine skiing is as legendary as the Olympic athletes it has produced (See Notable Austrians). The country holds the third most Winter Olympic medals, (behind only Norway and the United States), an impressive feat given Austria's small size. Austria has hosted two Winter Olympics, both in Innsbruck.

Classical Music

Austrians are serious about their classical music. Cities vie to put their venue or festival in the limelight. Top of the bill is, of course, Vienna, with the Vienna State Opera and the Vienna Philharmonic Orchestra. But even the Viennese are prepared to make the seven-hour journey to Bregenz, where opera productions on a giant stage overlooking Lake Constance occur every summer. Summer evenings in the Alps can be chilly and wet, but music-hungry Austrians will brave a downpour, sitting on blankets and wearing parkas. Other events, such as the annual Salzburg festival, provide the perfect backdrop for society-conscious Austrians who gather in opulent evening attire to admire each other. However, many Viennese dressed only in jeans and a pullover will go several times a week to the opera. They won't pay the high price for a seat but instead pay a few euros for a spot in the standing room (where acoustics are better anyway).

FLAVORS OF AUSTRIAN CUISINE

The phrase "meat and potatoes" describes the bare essentials, as well as the core components of Austrian cuisine. Nearly every typical dish in the country consists of some variation of pork, beef, or chicken with the go-to hearty vegetable, though Austrian food is frequently so much more.

The focus on "just the basics" can be seen in breakfasts that usually feature a roll topped with butter and jam alongside coffee and slices of cheese and meat and sometimes a hard-boiled egg. Lighter, lunchtime meals consisting of crusty bread, holey Alpine cheese, and ham resemble the British Ploughman's Lunch.

Thanks to Austria's small size, it's not hard to find fresh, local food. Most neighborhoods in cities big and small will have some sort of outdoor market full of produce, cheeses, and meats alongside small restaurants and fast-food stands. Chief among these is Vienna's *Naschmarkt* (literally: snack market), an outdoor food extravaganza that stretches for nearly a mile.

New Trends

Of course, not all Austrian food boils down to meat and potatoes. Influences from nearby former imperial holdings like Hungary and Poland pepper the palate (goulash from the east, Mediterranean spices from the south, and pastries from Poland helped shape those found in Austria). The influx of immigrants from Turkey over the last few decades helped the *doner* kebab, a sandwich of sorts similar to a Greek gyro that featured meat sliced from a rotating vertical spit, rise to the level of fast food usually reserved for pizza and french fries.

In the world of haute cuisine, you can find several restaurants in Vienna and Salzburg boasting Michelin stars and menus that are anything but traditional. At Steirereck in Vienna's Stadtpark, you'll see Austrian ingredients like alpine beef, locally grown citrus, and vegetables mixed with French cheese and South American herbs. A six-course meal at Restaurant Konstantin Filippou will expose you to foods as varied as lamb's tongue, mackerel, and pigeon.

Austria has also seen a growing "bread trend." Josepf Brot von Pheinsten boutique bakery recently expanded from its single location in Vienna's center to an elegant bistro on one of the city's popular shopping streets. Not to be outdone, the country's chain bakeries are rebranding themselves as hipper and homier. One chain, Strück, is opening a line of breakfast and bistro locations that serve wine, cocktails, cheese plates, and risotto in addition to a selection of breads, rolls, and pastries.

Sausage

A good portion of the country's pork consumption comes in the form of the ever-present *Wurstelstand,* where sausages of all varieties can be found. The lowly hot dog is called a frankfurter here (just don't call it wiener, the name for a Viennese person) and usually served sliced on its own with a side of mustard and bread or stuffed lengthwise into a bun for easier carrying. There is also *Burenwurst,* a pork sausage similar to kielbasa, and *Bosna,* a wurst served with onions. For those who like smoked meat, there's the *Waldviertler,* which is smoked wurst, and the more elaborate *Beinwurst,* made of smoked pork, a selection of herbs and wine. *Bockwurst* is a white pork sausage,

and *Weisswurst* is simple boiled white sausage. The *Nürnberger* is a small spicy pork wurst, and the *Blutwurst* is—are you sitting down?—a sausage with congealed blood. Other varieties include the paprika-spiced *Debreziner* and the cheese-filled *Käsekrainer*.

Coffee

Austrian writer Stefan Zweig called the Viennese coffeehouse "a sort of democratic club, open to everyone for the price of a cheap cup of coffee." The types of drinks available are as varied as the coffeehouses that serve them. Most common is the *Melange,* the Austrian version of the cappuccino featuring steamed milk and milk foam. A *Kleiner Brauner* consists of a shot of dark coffee with a bit of milk mixed in. The *Einspänner* is a strong black coffee served in a glass and topped with whipped cream. Ask for a *Maria Theresia* and your drink will come with shot of orange liqueur inside. The *Schwarzer Mokka* is a straight espresso while *Schale Gold* is coffee with a small shot of cream, and *Kapuziner* is coffee with a splash of sweet cream (though not a cappuccino, despite the similar-sounding name.)

Cakes

Naschkatze, or those with a sweet tooth, have their choice of cakes and sweets to go with their many coffee options.

Sachertorte. The famous chocolate cake with a layer of apricot jam and dark chocolate icing is associated with Vienna so much that it was featured as a lyric in a Beatles song. Developed in the 18th century, the Hotel Sacher lays claim to the "original" recipe, supposedly known only to a few individuals and kept under lock and key.

Linzer torte is the famous Austrian torte with a lattice design made of pastry, cinnamon, hazelnuts, and red currant jam, often served at Christmastime.

Apfelstrudel. Often served with a dollop of whipped cream, the Austrian apple strudel gained popularity in the 1700s throughout many of the areas under the empire's control and is today considered a national dish.

Kaiserschmarrn. Literally, the "emperor's folly," these shredded pancakes are served with fruit, nuts, and whipped cream. The dish took its name from Emperor Franz Josef, who took such a liking to it that people joked it would be his folly.

Traditional dishes

Wiener schitzel. Veal, pork, or sometimes turkey is hammered flat, breaded and deep-fried. A spritz of freshly squeezed lemon and a side of potato salad or french fries completes this quintessential Austrian meal.

Tafelspitz. Boiled beef in broth is served with horseradish and sliced and fried potatoes. Ever the foodie, it was Emperor Franz Josef who popularized the dish, which became so synonymous with Austrian cuisine that one famous restaurant hands patrons a card detailing the proper way *Tafelspitz* should be eaten.

Leberknödel is a beef liver dumpling that is breaded, spiced, and boiled, usually served in a thin soup. Some varieties feature spleen mixed in with the dumpling.

Fiedermaus (pork) is another cut that Austrian butchers supply, named after the batlike shape of the cut. And then, of course, there is Speck, which is essentially Austrian bacon, and *Leberkäse,* which is a loaf of corned beef, pork and bacon.

IF YOU LIKE

Wine

Although not as well known as regional varieties in France and Italy, Austrian wines, particularly whites, are now recognized by wine experts around the world for their excellent quality. The center of wine production in Austria is found in northern and eastern Lower Austria, in Burgenland, in Styria, and on the hilly terraces overlooking Vienna. Whites account for nearly 70% of production, but the quality of Austrian reds continues to improve. The most popular white variety is Grüner Veltliner, followed by Riesling, Sauvignon Blanc, and Pinot Blanc (often labeled as Weissburgunder). The major red varieties are Zweigelt and Blaufränkisch. Wines to look for include:

■ **Wieninger.** Some of the best wine in the Vienna region comes from this winery—and at reasonable prices. Look for Sauvignon Blanc and Grüner Veltliner, but also a very complex Chardonnay.

■ **Bründlmayer.** This house in Kamptal in Lower Austria produces some of Austria's most acclaimed whites, especially Grüner Veltliner and Riesling.

■ **Umathum.** Austrian reds are drawing more and more attention from the wine press, including those produced in south Burgenland at this winery known for its full-bodied Pinot Noirs and a very interesting St. Laurent.

Beer

Beer in Austria doesn't have the storied brewing tradition as its Bavarian neighbors to the north, but a number of microbreweries have cropped up around Vienna featuring seasonal bocks and experimental hemp beers, which offer a nice alternative to canned Austrian beer (the four big ones are Gösser,

Ottakringer, Stiegl, and Puntigamer). Lagers, ales, and pilsners are common enough, but for a distinctive local taste, try one of the several varieties of the light, hoppy *Märzen* lager, which is caramel in color and slightly sweeter than its German counterpart, and a cloudy *Weissbier* (wheat beer) common to the Salzburg area. *Radler*, a mix of beer and lemonade is a popular summertime refreshment in Austria.

Skiing

Austria is synonymous with great skiing. Aside from world-class runs, the close proximity of the many ski areas to one another and an excellent infrastructure make moving around from one place to another quick and easy. The action is concentrated on the big ski regions of the Arlberg, Tyrol, and Land Salzburg for good reason—here, many individual ski areas span and connect multiple mountains and valleys, and they are linked together with common ski passes. The question, then, is where to begin? The answer depends on what you're looking to do. Posh resorts such as Lech and Kitzbühel are popular with the society crowd—and usually come with the price to match. Nearby villages, however, are often much less expensive, and their lifts serve the same large ski domain.

Here are some classics to get you started:

■ **Lech and St. Anton, Vorarlburg.** Exclusive, and a paradise for purists.

■ **Kitzbühel, Tyrol.** The elegant resort in the heart of Tyrol has well-groomed pistes.

■ **Sölden, Tyrol.** The snow conditions are excellent, and so are the spa facilities.

Castles, Palaces, and Abbeys

It seems that if you travel a few miles in any direction in Austria, you are confronted with a fairy-tale castle, an ostentatious palace, or an ornate Baroque abbey. It's easy to be overwhelmed by all of the architectural splendor, the fanciful decorations, and the often impossibly intricate mythical lore attached to these sites. The secret to overcoming the "not-another-castle" syndrome is to take your time at each, and not to limit yourself to the site alone.

Discover how rewarding it can be to leave the palace grounds or castle walls and to explore the surroundings, whether a city, small village, or mountainside. Around the corner might be a lovely chapel, a spectacular view, or an excellent local restaurant that, because it is somewhat off the beaten path and perhaps not (yet) in any guidebook, is yours alone to appreciate.

■ **Schönbrunn Palace, Vienna.** You could spend an entire day here (and still not see all the rooms in the palace), or choose from several shorter tours of one of Austria's premier attractions, the palace built by Empress Maria Theresa.

■ **Melk, Lower Austria.** Perched on a hill overlooking the Danube and the Wachau, the giant abbey of Melk features imposing architecture, lovely gardens, and one of Europe's most resplendent Baroque libraries.

■ **Fortress Hohensalzburg, Salzburg.** The medieval fortress, central Europe's largest, towers over Salzburg and offers lavish state rooms, a collection of medieval art, a late-Gothic chapel, and magnificent views of the entire region.

Biking

Over the last decade or so, Austria has invested a lot in the construction and maintenance of thousands of kilometers of cycle routes along its rivers and through its lush valleys. The close proximity of many sites of interest means that cycling is often the best means of leisurely exploration. Many hotels now provide bikes to their guests for a nominal fee, or your hotel can direct you to a nearby bike-rental shop. It helps to have a Radkarte (a map with the local bike routes), available at hotels or at the local tourist office. Here are some of the best routes that combine cultural attractions with stimulating landscapes:

■ **The Wachau, Lower Austria.** The Donauradweg—or Danube bike route—follows the Danube all the way from Passau to Vienna. The Wachau is not far from Vienna, and it offers one of the most spectacular landscapes along Austria's stretch of the Danube. Very well-maintained bike paths take you past the abbey of Melk and through Krems and other charming wine-making towns. The best time to go is spring, when the apricot trees are in glorious blossom, or in early fall, when grapes hang ripe and heavy on the vines of the terraced slopes.

■ **Mozart Radweg, Salzburg.** The Mozart Route is a circuit around Salzburg, the city where the great musician was born. Leaving Salzburg, the route passes through stations associated with Mozart's life and work, and continues through an arrestingly beautiful landscape of mountain lakes, castles, and small villages.

GREAT ITINERARIES

VIENNA TO VORARLBERG

This itinerary travels the country from end to end, hitting the heights and seeing the sights—all in a one-week to 14-day trip.

Days 1–3: Vienna

Austria's glorious past is evident everywhere, but especially where this tour begins, in Vienna. Get to know the city by trolley with a sightseeing tour of the Ringstrasse. Take in the Kunsthistoriches Museum (the incredible detail of the famous Brueghel paintings could keep you fascinated for hours), walk along Kärntnerstrasse to magnificent St. Stephen's Cathedral, and spend an afternoon in one of the city's cozy coffeehouses. Devote a half day to Schönbrunn Palace, and set aside an evening for a visit to a jovial *Heurige* wine tavern. ⇨ *Chapter 2: Vienna Exploring.*

Day 4: Danube River from Vienna to Linz

To zoom from Vienna to Linz by autobahn would be to miss out on one of Austria's most treasured sights, the blue Danube. To tour some quaint wine villages, follow the "Austrian Romantic Road" (Route 3), along the north bank of the river, instead of the speedier A1 autobahn. Cross to the south side of the Danube to the breathtaking Baroque abbey at Melk, and along the way visit the 1,000-year-old town of Krems and picture-perfect Dürnstein, in the heart of the Wachau wine region. ⇨ *Chapter 7: Vienna Woods, Lake Neusiedler, and the Danube River.*

Days 5 and 6: Linz

Fast-forward into Austria's future with a stop in progressive Linz, the country's third-largest city. Linz is a busy port on the Danube and an important center for

> ### TIPS
>
> For a more romantic kickoff, travel by a Blue Danube Schiffahrt/DDSG riverboat from Vienna to Linz (departs from Vienna three times a day between mid-April and September).

trade and business. Techno geeks will enjoy the Ars Electronica Museum; others can wander the beautifully restored medieval courtyards of the Altstadt (Old Town). For great views, ride the city's Pöstlingbergbahn, the world's steepest mountain railway, or opt for a Danube steamer cruise to Enns. ⇨ *Chapter 7: The Danube Valley.*

Days 7 and 8: Salzkammergut

For Austria in all its Hollywood splendor, head to the idyllic Salzkammergut, better known as the Lake District, where *The Sound of Music* was filmed. The town of Bad Ischl—famous for its operetta festival and pastries—makes a good base. Travel south on Route 145 to Hallstatt, one of Austria's most photographed lakeside villages. Return to Bad Ischl, then head west to St. Wolfgang for swimming and sailing. ⇨ *Chapter 10: Salzkammergut.*

Days 9 and 10: Salzburg

This is a city made for pedestrians, with an abundance of churches, palaces, mansions, and—as befits the birthplace of Mozart—music festivals. Stroll through the old city center with its wrought-iron shop signs, tour the medieval Fortress Hohensalzburg, and relax in the Mirabell Gardens (where the von Trapp children "Do-Re-Mi"-ed). Children of all ages will adore the famed Marionettentheater. ⇨ *Chapter 8: Salzburg.*

Days 11 and 12: Innsbruck and Tyrol

Tour Innsbruck's treasures—including the famous Golden Roof mansion and the Hofburg—but do as the Tyroleans do and spend time reveling in the high-mountain majesty. After all, Innsbruck is the only major city in the Alps. For a splendid panorama, take the cable railway to the Hafelekar, high above the Inn Valley. For a trip through the quaint villages around Innsbruck, ride the Stubaitalbahn, a charming old-time train, or head by bus to the Stubai Glacier for year-round skiing. ⇨ *Chapter 12: Innsbruck, Tyrol, and Vorarlberg.*

Days 13 and 14: Bregenz

Taking the Arlberg Pass (or the much more scenic Silvretta High Alpine Road), head to the city of Bregenz, capital of Vorarlberg. Bregenz owes its character as much to neighboring Switzerland and Germany as to Austria, and is most appealing in summer, when sun-worshippers crowd the shores of Lake Constance to enjoy an opera festival set on the world's largest outdoor floating stage. Take a lake excursion and explore Bregenz's medieval streets. ⇨ *Chapter 12: Innsbruck, Tyrol, and Vorarlberg.*

MOUNTAIN MAGIC

This is a trip where Alpine glory is all around you: meadows and forests set against a backdrop of towering craggy peaks, and gentle wooded rambles that lead to clear mountain lakes and storybook castles. Let go of your worries and let the natural beauty of the countryside work its magic.

Days 1 and 2: Bad Ischl/St. Wolfgang

The villages and lakes of the Salzkammergut region extend south from Salzburg like a string of pearls. Base yourself in Bad Ischl, a first-class spa in the heart of the Lake District. From there, head west to St. Wolfgang, one of the most photo-friendly villages in Austria. For the most scenic surroundings, park in nearby Strobl and hop one of the lake ferries to the pedestrian-only village, where you can relax with a coffee on the terrace of the famous Weisses Rössl (White Horse Inn), marvel at the 16th-century Michael Pacher altarpiece in the parish church, and take the railway up the 5,800-foot Schaftberg peak for gasp-inducing vistas. ⇨ *Chapter 10: Salzkammergut.*

Day 3: Hallstatt

Set on fjordlike Hallstättersee, this jewel is an optical illusion perched between water and mountain—a tight grouping of terraced fishermen's cottages and churches offering, at first glance, no apparent reason why it doesn't tumble into the lake. On a sunny day the views of the lake and village, considered the oldest settlement in Austria, are spectacular, and on a misty morning they are even more so. Consider a canoe outing, or tour the Hallstatt salt mine, the oldest in the world. ⇨ *Chapter 10: Salzkammergut.*

Day 4: Werfen

Take in the birds-of-prey show at the formidable Burg Hohenwerfen, a castle built in the 11th century, tour the Eisriesenwelt ("World of the Ice Giants")—the largest collection of ice caves in Europe—and cap the day with dinner at Obauer, one of Austria's finest restaurants. ⇨ *Chapter 9: Eastern Alps.*

Day 5: Zell am See

Southwest of Werfen, the charming lake resort of Zell am See is nestled under the 1,829-meter (6,000-foot) Schmittenhöhe mountain. Ride the cable car from the center of town for a bird's-eye view, then take the narrow-gauge Pinzgauer railroad through the Salzach river valley to famous Krimmler waterfalls. ⇨ *Chapter 9: Eastern Alps.*

Day 6: Heiligenblut

Head skyward over the dizzying Grossglockner High Alpine Highway to one of Austria's loveliest villages, Heiligenblut, which fans out across the upper Möll Valley with fabulous views of the Grossglockner, at 3,801 meters (12,470 feet) the highest mountain in Austria. ⇨ *Chapter 9: Eastern Alps.*

Day 7: Kitzbühel

Travel to the glamorous resort town of Kitzbühel for a bit of window-shopping and celebrity-spotting. On the road headed west, the sunny valley has plenty of snow in winter and golf in summer. End your trip in Innsbruck, 91 km (57 miles) west. ⇨ *Chapter 12: Innsbruck, Tyrol, and Vorarlberg.*

WHEN TO GO

Austria has two main tourist seasons. The weather usually turns glorious around Easter and holds until about mid-October, sometimes later. Because much of the country remains "undiscovered," you will usually find crowds only in the major cities and resorts. May and early June, September, and October are the most pleasant months for travel; there is less demand for restaurant tables, and hotel prices tend to be lower. A foreign invasion takes place between Christmas and New Year's Day and over the long Easter weekend, and hotel rooms in Vienna are then at a premium.

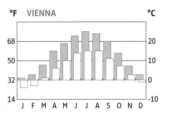

Climate

Austria has four distinct seasons, all fairly mild. But because of altitudes and the Alpine divide, temperatures and dampness vary considerably from one part of the country to another; for example, northern Austria's winter is often overcast and dreary, while the southern half of the country basks in sunshine. The eastern part of the country, especially Vienna and the areas near the Czech border, can become bitterly cold in winter. The *Föhn* is a wind that makes the country as a whole go haywire. It comes from the south, is warm, and announces itself by clear air, blue skies, and long wisps of cloud. Whatever the reason, the Alpine people (all the way to Vienna) begin acting up; some become obnoxiously aggressive, others depressive, many people have headaches, and (allegedly) accident rates rise. The Föhn breaks with clouds and rain.

FESTIVALS IN AUSTRIA

Austria's changing seasons and countless holidays mean something is always afoot. Check out www.austria.info, the website for the Austrian Tourism Office for a comprehensive list of festivals and events.

Winter

Christkindlmarkt (⊕ *www.christkindl-maerkte.at* ⊘ *Nov. and Dec.*). Practically every open space in cities and towns across the country is devoted to end-of-the year Christmas markets. Sweets, meats, gifts, and trinkets are available at these pop-up festivals that also feature mulled wine and the fruit-and-liquor infused *punsch*.

Ball season (⊕ *www.austria.info* ⊘ *Dec.– Feb.*). What better place to dance the waltz than in the country where it was invented? Nearly 500 balls are staged throughout the city for those who need to satisfy their inner Cinderella.

Spring

Fasnacht (⊕ *www.fasnacht-nassereith.at* ⊘ *Feb. and Mar.*). Venice has its Carnival, Tyrol has its Fasnacht. Arriving just before Ash Wednesday, this Alpine festival features costumes, parades, and hand-carved masks. One of the most famous is the Schellerlaufen pageant in the small Tyrolean town of Nassereith, which depicts the symbolic fight between a bear and his keeper.

Oestermarkt (⊕ *www.austria.info* ⊘ *Mar. and Apr.*). Like the Christmas markets before it, Easter markets pop up in public plazas everywhere and feature a range of regional meats, cheeses, butter, and, of course, decorative eggs.

Festwochen (⊕ *festwochen.at* ⊘ *May and June*). Theaters, museums, galleries, and concert spaces across Vienna offer special programs over the course of five weeks to celebrate the city's "will to survive" after World War II.

Summer

Salzburg festival (⊕ *www.salzburgerfest-spiele.at* ⊘ *July and Aug.*). Opera's elite flock to Salzburg for six weeks of opera, concerts, and stage plays in one of the world's premiere events of the art form.

Donauinselfest (⊘ *June*). For three days, thousands of fans pack a 4-mile stretch of the Vienna's Danube Island for the annual music festival billed as the largest open air event in Europe.

Fall

Long Night of the Museums (⊕ *www.wien. info* ⊘ *Oct.*). More than 100 museums in Vienna and other parts of Austria open their doors from 6 pm until 1 the next morning in a cultural free-for-all that attracts thousands each year. Comfortable shoes not included.

National Day (Oct. 26). Marking the day in 1955 when Austria declared its neutrality, the city takes a day off to take a tour of the parliament, see a free museum or two, or to check out the military's giant display on Heldenplatz in the center of Vienna.

NOTABLE AUSTRIANS

Everyone knows where the Governator is from and, like Arnold Schwarzenegger, many well-known actors, artists, writers, and historical figures have found international fame after their Austrian beginnings. Movie stars Hedy Lamaar, Maximilian Schell, directors Billy Wilder, Erich Von Stroheim, Fritz Lang, and Michael Hanake all found fame in the United States, as did Quentin Tarantino's two-time Oscar-winning character actor Christoph Waltz.

Most people don't realize Marie Antoinette was originally an Austrian princess, the 15th child of Empress Maria-Theresa and Francis I. Children of Habsburg royalty were often married as teenagers, as she was to Louis XVI, to other royal houses to strengthen political ties.

The country also produced its share of well-known athletes such as multiple Olympic gold medalist skier Hermann Maier, three-time Formula 1 champ Niki Lauda, Peter Habler (who made the first co-ascent of Mt. Everest without oxygen). Of course, there's also Felix Baumgartner, who became the first person to break the sound barrier while skydiving during his 2012 "space jump" from a hot air balloon in the stratosphere.

The list of famous Austrian composers and musicians plays more like a who's who of classical music itself: Mozart, Joseph Hayden, Johann Strauss II, Richard Strauss, Franz Schubert, Gustav Mahler, Franz Schubert, Franz Lehár, and Arnold Schoenberg. Anyone who has seen *The Sound of Music* knows that Maria von Trapp and the Trapp Family Singers originated from Salzburg. More recently, Austria produced pop musicians such as Falco and the cross-dressing Conchita Wurst, winner of the 2014 Eurovision Song Contest.

The turn of the 20th-century Vienna Secession branch of the Art Nouveau movement gave Gustav Klimt, Egon Schiele, Oscar Kokoschka, and architect Otto Wagner to the world. Austria's famous authors include Arthur Schnitzler (*La Ronde,* adapted into two movies), playwright Johann Nestroy (*Einen Jux will er sich machen,* adapted into *Hello, Dolly!*), Ludwig Bemelmans (author of the *Madeline* children's books), and Stefan Zweig, a writer who was known mainly in Europe until Wes Anderson's recent film *The Grand Budapest Hotel* revived American interest in his work.

Austria also has its share of famous humanitarians. The Nobel Peace Prize was awarded to Baroness Berta Kinsky von Suttner, founder of the Austrian Society of Peace Lovers and author of *Lay Down Your Arms!,* in 1905; and to Alfred Hermann Fried, a proponent for the cause of international peace, in 1911. Austrian Theodor Herzl, founder of the Zionist movement, was an early advocate of creating a Jewish state in Palestine, while writer Simon Wiesenthal, a concentration-camp survivor, has searched for Nazi war criminals around the world.

Sigmund Freud is synonymous, of course, with psychoanalysis. There are also several Austrian scientists and researchers who've gained fame and have concepts and theories named after them including Hans Asperger (Asperger syndrome) and Christian Andreas Doppler (Doppler effect).

SKIING IN AUSTRIA

SKIING AND SNOWBOARDING

In Austria, skiing is not just a popular pastime; it's a national obsession, a way of life. Images of Alpine ski villages conjure fairy-tale fantasies of heavily timbered houses, onion-domed churches, welcoming locals, schnapps, and gluhwein. Add to the mix some of the world's highest, treeless slopes and the liveliest après-ski scene and you have a winter sport destination of extraordinary allure.

American skiers are often amazed to find how big European skiing is, in every sense of the word. The entire country embraces skiing, and the sport is deeply woven into the patterns of daily life in the Austrian countryside. In most cases, Alpine ski resorts are the result of the evolution of an Alpine village, where individual ski areas are linked together with a common ski pass and a spider web network of lifts spanning and connecting different valleys and multiple mountains. The trend of late has been resorts joining forces, creating "ski circuses" of stunning size.

Guides, Lifts, and Costs

To take full advantage of the promise of so much snowy terrain, American skiers should consider hiring a ski-instructor/guide for a day or two. Private instructors are less expensive in Austria than in the United States, and the upper levels of Austrian ski-school classes are more about guiding than actual teaching.

It's often possible to ski the whole day without using the same lift twice, as lift systems in Austria are astonishingly sophisticated. You'll find double-decker cable cars and eight-person chairlifts. In some resorts nearly every chairlift has a weather protection bubble, and many have heated seats. Magic carpet loading aids efficiency, and nearly every lift has electronic entry, so you'll rarely see an attendant checking a ticket or marshalling the line-ups. Equally, there are no ski area boundaries so you may see experienced skiers going *off-piste* (the French term for off-trail), skiing until they reach a village in the valley or the snow runs out.

Expect costs to balance up with America. Lift tickets and rental equipment in Austria are generally cheaper than in the United States, while eating out is more expensive. Lunch isn't a quick refueling stop here; the slopes abound with unique little huts welcoming skiers with hearty Austrian fare.

Best Slopes

There are so many choices when it comes to Austrian skiing that you're not going to see it all, or ski it all, in one lifetime. Foreign ski enthusiasts and newcomers to Austrian slopes would do well to focus first on the biggest ski regions of the Arlberg, Tyrol, and Land Salzburg. These mega-ski regions showcase what makes Alpine skiing so special: an astonishing variety of slopes and lifts that allow the visitor to ski, day after day, often from one village to the next. True, there are many tiny and delightful ski villages in Austria, real discoveries for adventurous skiers, but it makes more sense to sample the feast of a major *Skigebiet* (interconnected ski region, sometimes called a ski arena) first. Here, to get you started, are some of the finest.

THE ARLBERG

This is a capital of Austrian skiing: a double constellation of ski-resort towns—Zürs, Lech, and Oberlech, in the Vorarlberg; and, just across the Arlberg Pass to the east and thus technically in the Tyrol, St. Anton, St. Christoph, and Stuben. These classic Arlberg resorts are interconnected by ski lifts and trails and share more than 260 km (160 miles) of groomed slopes (and limitless off-piste possibilities), 83 ski lifts, snowboard parks, carving areas and permanent race courses, and, significantly, a common ski pass.

St. Anton, part of the fabulous Arlberg area, is the cradle of skiing, where ski pioneer Hannes Schneider opened the world's first ski school back in 1921. A skier here can feel like a character out of a 1930s Luis Trenker ski film: from enjoying Jaeger tea after skiing to dinner at the Post Hotel. St. Anton links with elegant Lech, in Vorarlberg (once a favorite of Princess Diana) and secretive Zurs, where royalty and celebrities discreetly vacation. In turn, Lech has recently been linked by lift with the villages of Warth and Schrocken in the next valley. St. Christoph is a spartan resort for skiing purists, a handful of handsome hotels lost in a sea of white, high above timberline, and the permanent home of the Austrian National Ski School's training and certification courses.

The pièce de résistance of Arlberg skiing is the all-day round-trip, on skis, from Zürs to Lech, Oberlech, and back. This ski epic starts with a 5-km (3-mile) off-piste run from the Madloch down to Zug and ends, late in the afternoon, many lifts and many thousands of vertical feet later, high on the opposite side of Zürs, swinging down the slopes of the Trittkopf.

THE TYROL/INNSBRUCK

Austria boasts resorts throughout the country but the western province of Tyrol is the heart of Austrian skiing, chock full of world-class skiing—about a third of all Austrian ski resorts are found in this province.

After St. Anton and the Arlberg, Kitzbühel, in the heart of the Tyrol, is Austria's best-known ski destination, and although not as exclusive as Lech or Zürs, certainly one of Austria's most elegant. "Kitz" is picture-perfect and posh—all medieval, cobbled streets, wrought-iron signs, and candles flickering in the windows of charming restaurants.

For an altogether different sort of ski vacation, especially for groups of skiers and nonskiers, consider staying in downtown Innsbruck and making day trips to the six ski areas of Olympia Ski World Innsbruck. Innsbruck has twice hosted the winter Olympics, and boasts a stunning collection of medium-size ski areas with grand views.

In ever-increasing numbers, skiers are attracted by the excellent snow conditions and après-ski nightlife of Ischgl, in the Paznaun (Valley) southwest of Innsbruck, where you can cross-border ski into the village of Samnaun, Switzerland.

In Salzburgerland, serene Zell am See overlooks a lake and Bad Gastein dramatically sits astride a raging torrent. In Carinthia, mystical Heiligenblut broods at the foot of the Grossglockner, Austria's highest mountain, and Nassfeld extends into Italy.

EXPLORING
VIENNA

Updated
by Patti
McCracken

When six-year-old Mozart arrived in Vienna with his parents, he strode into the Hofburg Imperial Palace, sat down at the piano awaiting him, and played gloriously for Empress Maria Theresa, then crawled into her lap and smothered her face with kisses. She was smitten.

Maria Theresa ruled the Habsburg kingdom when the mighty empire was at its zenith, and though it is long gone, many reminders of its imperial heyday remain, carefully preserved by the tradition-loving Viennese. The glories of its artistic past are particularly evergreen, thanks to the cultural legacy of the many artistic geniuses nourished here.

They were gilt-covered, halcyon decades of symphonies and sonatas, concertos and operas. Mozart, Haydn, and Beethoven were soon followed by Schubert, Strauss, Brahms, and Mahler, all of whom lived in the city during the peaks of their careers. Their music resounded in the grand halls of newly built Baroque edifices, erected as art their flamboyant facades ornamented with madonnas and cherubs, with soaring columns reaching upward to graceful domes, perched atop like an elegant gentleman's hat. It was a time of wealth and enlightenment. Literati crowded the cafés, and the ballroom became the centerpiece of culture, both patrician and peasant, as all took to a waltzing craze that would forever define the capital city. Vienna was a stage for opulence and cheer, the air tinged with zephyrs of refinement and joy.

Vienna had been founded as a Roman military encampment around AD 50, and remained so for some 300 years. By the 13th century new city walls encompassed further development to the south. According to legend, the walls were financed by the huge ransom paid by the English for their king, Richard I (the Lion-Hearted), kidnapped en route home from the Third Crusade in 1192 by the local duke.

Vienna's third set of walls dates from 1544, courtesy of the Habsburg dynasty, which ruled the Austro-Hungarian Empire for an astonishing 645 years. These walls stood until 1857, when Emperor Franz Josef decreed that they be replaced by the series of boulevards that make up the tree-lined Ringstrasse. Outlying villages were brought into Vienna's fold, and Vienna's urban planning was revolutionized, becoming a model for other European cities.

Vienna's heyday as a European capital did not begin until 1683, after a huge force of invading Turks laid siege to the city for two months before being ousted. Among the supplies they left behind were sacks of coffee beans, and, so the story goes, this gave birth to the kaffeehaus culture that remains one of the city's most prized customs.

The 19th century brought with it a somber sky. Napoleon twice captured the city, denting what seemed an invincible empire. This mood was reflected in the more subdued and stately Biedermeier architecture, but the era also ushered in a splash of cutting-edge artists and architects—Gustav Klimt, Egon Schiele, Oskar Kokoschka, Joseph

Hoffmann, Otto Wagner, and Adolf Loos ("form follows function") among them. They brought an unprecedented artistic revolution that set the stage for the radically experimental art of the 20th century.

Today's Vienna, with a multicultural population of 1.7 million, is as vibrant and stunning as was Maria Theresa's Baroque wonderland. Side streets teem with buskers playing to appreciative crowds. Churches and halls resound with the notorious strains of Strauss on summer days, while the city's nightlife and the fabulous music scene it nurtures is one of Europe's best-kept secrets. *Fast Company* magazine recognizes Vienna as the World's Smartest City, for its innovation and sustainability. All these are among the reasons why Vienna has for five consecutive years been voted "The World's Most Livable City" in a competition pitting it against more than 220 international rivals.

But it is for her grace and refinement that Vienna will forever stand alone from her peers—London, Paris, and Rome.

ORIENTATION AND PLANNING

GETTING ORIENTED

The Eastern City Center: Stephansdom and Medieval Vienna. Time seems to stand still in this part of Vienna, where hidden architectural treasures await discovery down narrow lanes and cobbled streets. One of the quaintest parts of town, it is a mythical place where the city's legends originated.

The Inner City Center: Baroque Gems and Vienna's Shopwindows. Sip a *mélange* from a splendid café while admiring the rich facades of the palatial homes of former Viennese aristocrats. Waiters, dressed as if they're off to a ball, serve coffee and cakes to the regulars.

The Hofburg: an Imperial City. The huge former Habsburg winter abode for seven centuries now houses many of the belongings the family left behind. The Imperial Treasury advertises with the slogan "We don't have the emperors, but we do have their jewels."

The Western City Center: Burgtheater and Beyond. Hobnob with the city's most celebrated thespians at Café Landtmann after catching a performance at one of Europe's largest and oldest theaters; or stroll past the Mölker Bastei, where Beethoven wrote his one and only opera, *Fidelio*.

East of the Ringstrasse: Stadtpark and Karlsplatz. Home to the Musikverein, the city's top concert hall, and the modernist Wien Museum, dedicated to the city's history, Karlsplatz is a destination on its own. Relax in the manicured green expanses of the Stadtpark, or take the tram up to Belvedere Palace to marvel at Klimt's Kiss.

South of the Ringstrasse: the MuseumsQuartier. The MuseumsQuartier is on the site of former Hapsburg stables and is among Europe's most respected museum complexes. Visit the Naturhistorisches museum to view the world's largest meteorite collection, and the Kunsthistorisches museum to see the Hapsburg sizable collection of Flemish and Italian painters.

West of the Ringstrasse: Parliament and City Hall. The Rathaus, the Ringstrasse's most photographed building, beckons with free outdoor concert recordings throughout the summer and a sprawling Christmas market in the winter.

Schönbrunn Palace, Park, and Zoo. Rococo romantics and Habsburg acolytes should step back in time and spend a few hours experiencing the imperial family's former summer home.

PLANNING

WHEN TO GO

Vienna is warm and sunny in spring and autumn; July and August can be hot and stormy, with temperatures reaching well above 32°C (90°F). From November through March, winter can get cold, with snow falling in January and February; lows of -12°C (10°F) are frequent. Culturally, high season in Vienna is May, June, and September, when festivals, marathons, concerts, and operas are in full swing. In winter, the glittering Christmas markets attract international crowds and during the Ball Season, December through February, nearly 500 balls take place, hosted by nearly every profession or trade; the Coffee House Owners Ball is the biggest, the Opera Ball the most internationally famous. Many Viennese leave the city in July and August, so the city tones down some, though it fills with tourists.

Christkindlmarkt (Christmas Market). In Vienna the biggest Christmas market goes up in mid-November in the plaza in front of the city's Rathaus (town hall); there are more than 30 smaller ones dotted around town, including outside Schönbrunn and the Belvedere Palace, in the Spittelberg Quarter on the Freyung square, and in front of Karlkirche on Karlsplatz.

Donauinselfest (Danube Island Festival). Held in late June, this is Europe's largest open-air music fest, attracting 3 million visitors each year. Entrance is free. ⊠ *Donauinsel* ⊕ *www.donauinselfest.at.*

Fasching. In February, Fasching (or Fasnacht, as it's called in the western part of the country), the Carnival period before Lent, can get very wild, with huge processions of disguised figures and the occasional unwilling participation by spectators.

Hofburg New Year's Ball. Vienna's Ball Season, in January and February, kicks off on New Year's Eve with this glittering—and expensive—event (formerly known as Kaiserball), held in the elegant rooms of the Hofburg. ☎ *01/58736–66214* ⊕ *www.hofburg.com.*

Wiener Festwochen. This festival of theater, music, film, and exhibitions takes over Vienna from mid-May to mid-June. ☎ *01/589–220* ⊕ *www. festwochen.at.*

Wiener Opernball (*Vienna Opera Ball*). One of the year's biggest society events is the Vienna Opera Ball, held the Thursday before Ash Wednesday at the magnificent Staatsoper. ☎ *01/5144–42250, 01/514–44–2606* ⊕ *www.staatsoper.at*

TOP REASONS TO GO

Ride the Ringstrasse. Hop on streetcar No. 1 or No. 2 and travel full circle along Vienna's best-known avenue. No. 1 will take you from Staatsoper to Schwedenplatz, No. 2 from Schwedenplatz to Staatsoper. Those monumental buildings along the tree-lined boulevard reflect the imperial splendor of yesteryear.

World of Music. Delight your eyes and ears with a night out at the State Opera or Musikverein to experience what secured Vienna the title "heart of the music world."

Kunsthistorisches Museum. Enjoy the classic collection of fine art, including the best of Breughel, Titian, Rembrandt, and Rubens, at Austria's leading museum.

Schönbrunn Palace romantics and Habsbu.., should step back in time and spend a half day experiencing the Habsburgs' former summer home.

An extended coffee break. Savor the true flavor of Vienna at some of its great café landmarks. Every afternoon around 3 the coffee-and-pastry ritual of *Kaffeejause* takes place from one end of the city to the other, a tradition so storied that UNESCO recognizes it as an "intangible cultural heritage." For historical overtones, head for the Café Central or the opulent Café Landtmann. Intellectuals flock to Café Bräunerhof, known for its free chamber music concerts on weekends. Café Hawelka is the contrasting seat of the smoky art scene.

Wiener Philharmoniker. The New Year in Vienna is greeted with a concert by the Vienna Philharmonic. Reserve a year, or even more, in advance. ☎ *01/505–6525* ⊕ *www.musikverein.at.*

Volksoper. The opera season runs from September through June. If you can't get into the Philharmonic concert, try for one of the performances of the Franz Lehar operetta *Die lustige Witwe*, or another light delight. ☎ *01/5144–43670* ⊕ *www.volksoper.at.*

GETTING HERE AND AROUND

AIR TRAVEL

Vienna International Airport is at Schwechat, about 19 km (12 miles) southeast of the city. Austrian Airlines flies nonstop from several cities in North America. Many other major carriers make a change in Europe.

AIRPORT TRANSFERS

The fastest way into Vienna from Schwechat Airport is the sleek, double-decker **City Airport Train.** From the airport to the center of the city, the CAT takes only 16 minutes, and trains operate daily every 30 minutes between 6 am and 11 pm. The cost is €12 one way and €19 round-trip. Tickets can also be purchased online at ⊕ www.cityairporttrain.com for a reduced price. But the cheapest way to get into town from the airport is the **S7 train,** called the *Schnellbahn,* which shuttles twice an hour between the station beneath the airport and the Wien-Mitte/Landstrasse station; the one-way fare is €4.40, and it takes about 20 minutes. Your ticket is also good for an immediate transfer to your destination within the city on streetcar, bus, or U-Bahn.

Another cheap option is the fleet of buses operated by **Vienna Airport Lines,** which has separate routes to the city center at Schwedenplatz (20 minutes) and to the Westbahnhof (45 minutes). Buses operate every 30 minutes between 5 am and 12:30 am, and the fare is €8 each way and €13 round-trip.

If convenience is your priority, **Airport Driver** has private cars to the airport; one way is €35, and you must reserve at the Tourist Info desk, open 7 am to 10 pm. A regular taxi between the airport and the city center will charge around €40.

BICYCLE

Citybike rents bicycles at public stations. Payment is by credit card, with a €1 registration fee. The first hour is free; the second is €1, third €2, and fourth €3. Bikes can be picked up or returned to any of the 110 locations around town. A flat fee for exceeding the time limit or loss of the bike is a hefty €600. Bicycle Rental Pedal Power offers a special service for tourists in which several bikes can be rented at the same time.

BOAT AND FERRY TRAVEL

When you arrive in Vienna via the Danube, the Blue Danube Steamship Company/DDSG will leave you at Praterlände near Mexikoplatz. It's a two-block walk to the U1/Vorgartenstrasse subway station, or you can take a taxi directly into town.

CAR TRAVEL

Vienna is 300 km (187 miles) east of Salzburg, 200 km (125 miles) north of Graz. Main routes leading into the city are the A1 Westautobahn from Germany, Salzburg, and Linz and the A2 Südautobahn from Graz and points south. Rental cars can be arranged at the airport or in town. Buchbinder is a local firm with particularly favorable rates.

On highways from points south or west or from Vienna's airport, "Zentrum" signs clearly mark the route to the center of Vienna. From there, however, finding your way to your hotel is a challenge, because traffic planners have installed a devious scheme limiting through traffic in the city core. Traffic congestion within Vienna is not as bad as in some places, but driving to in-town destinations generally takes longer than does public transportation.

PARKING

The entire 1st through 9th districts, and most of the rest of the city, are limited-parking zones and require a Parkschein, a paid-parking chit that can be purchased at tobacconists (AustriaTabak), gas stations and, oddly, from cigarette machines. They must be filled out and displayed on the dash during the day, and the procedure is maddening and laborious. At this writing, a Parkscheine costs €1 for 30 minutes, €2 for one hour, €3 for 90 minutes, and €4 for two hours. These are required from 8 am until 10 pm in districts 1 to 9, and a maximum parking time of two hours is permitted, at which point the procedure must be repeated in full. You can park for 15 minutes free of charge, but you must get a violet "gratis" sticker to put in your windshield. You can also park free in the 1st District from noon on Saturday until Monday at 8 am.

PUBLIC TRANSIT TRAVEL

Overseen by Wiener Linien, Vienna's public transportation system is fast, clean, safe, and easy to use. Vienna's subway system, called the U-Bahn, services the core of the inner city. Several apps are available to ease travel, offering timetables, ticket purchase, information about service disruptions, and more. Visit ⊕ *www.wieninfo.at* and look under "Public Transport & Taxis" for a list and links.

Five subway lines, whose stations are prominently marked with blue "U" signs, crisscross the city. Track the main lines of the U-Bahn system by their color codes on subway maps: U1 is red; U2 purple, U3 orange, U4 green, and U6 brown. The last subway runs at about 12:30 am.

The main city-center subway stops in the 1st District are Stephansplatz, Karlsplatz, Herrengasse, Schottenring, and Schwedenplatz. Stephansplatz is the very heart of the city, at St. Stephen's cathedral. You can reach the amusement park of the Prater from Stephansplatz by taking the U1 to Praterstern. Near the southern edge of the Ringstrasse, the major Karlsplatz stop is right next to the Staatsoper, the pedestrian Kärntnerstrasse, and the Ringstrasse, with an easy connection to Belvedere Palace via the D Tram. You can also take the U4 from Karlsplatz to Schönbrunn Palace (Schönbrunn stop). Schottenring is on the Ringstrasse, offering quick tram connections. Schwedenplatz is a 10-minute walk to St. Stephen's through some of Vienna's oldest streets. Karlsplatz is serviced by the train lines U1, U2, and U4, while U3 goes to Herrengasse. There are handy U-Bahn stops along the rim of the city core, such as Stadtpark, MuseumsQuartier, Volkstheater, and Rathaus.

Streetcars (*Strassenbahnen*) run from about 5:15 am until about midnight. Where streetcars don't run, buses—*Autobusse*—do. Should you miss the last streetcar or bus, special night buses with an "N" designation operate at half-hour intervals over several key routes; the starting (and transfer) points are the Opera House and Schwedenplatz. These night-owl buses accept all normal tickets.

Tickets are valid for all public transportation—buses, trams, and the subway. Although there are ticket machines on trams and buses, there is a surcharge of €0.50. You'll need to punch your ticket before entering the boarding area at U-Bahn stops, but for buses and trams you punch it on board. If you're caught without a ticket you'll pay a hefty fine.

Buy single tickets for €2.20 from dispensers on the streetcar or bus, from ticket machines in subway stations, or online at ⊕ *shop. wienerlinien.at*. At tobacco shops, newsstands, or U-Bahn offices you can buy a 24-hour ticket for €7.60, a three-day ticket for €16.50, or an eight-day ticket for €38.40. An inexpensive option is the €16.20 *Wochenkarte* (week card), valid from Monday to Sunday. Children under six travel free on public transit, and children under 15 travel free on Sunday and public holidays.

The Vienna Card, in addition to providing an array of deep discounts at sites, can be used on all public transportation. It costs €19.90 and is good for 72 hours.

RICKSHAWS

Two companies, Velocityline and Faxi, operate canopied rickshaws and have enough space for two passengers, three at a squeeze. Prices range from €3 per km (0.5 miles) to get you to the nearest U-Bahn station; €10 for anywhere within the 1st District.

TAXI TRAVEL

Taxis in Vienna are relatively reasonable. The initial charge is €2.50, and about 5% more from 11 pm until 6 am. They also may charge for each piece of luggage in the trunk. It's customary to round up the fare to cover the tip. Several companies offer chauffeured limousines.

TRAIN TRAVEL

Vienna's railroad system is nearing the end of an extensive overhaul. By 2015, the former Südbahnhof will have been converted into the city's main train station, called Hauptbahnhof Wien (or Vienna Central Station) for national and international travel.

TOURS

BUS TOURS

When you're pressed for time, a good way to see the highlights of Vienna is through a sightseeing bus tour, which gives you a speedy tour around the heart of the city and allows a closer look at the Schönbrunn and Belvedere palaces. You can cover almost the same territory on your own by taking either streetcar No. 1 or No. 2 around the Ring. (Streetcar No. 1 runs from Staatsoper to Schwedenplatz, and streetcar No. 2 runs from Schwedenplatz to Staatsoper.) For tours, there are a couple of reputable firms: Vienna Sightseeing Tours and Cityrama Sightseeing. Both run daily "get-acquainted" tours lasting about three hours (€39), including visits to the Schönbrunn and Belvedere palace grounds. Both firms provide hotel pickup for most tours.

You can tour at your own pace with Vienna Sightseeing's Hop On, Hop Off bus tour. There are 15 stops, and a day ticket purchased after 3 pm is valid for the whole next day, too. The short city tour costs €15 and does a run around the major sites in about an hour. The day ticket for €25 allows far more freedom. All tickets can be purchased at hotels, at the bus stops, and on the bus. The first bus leaves the Opera stop at 9:30 am and every 15 minutes until 7 pm.

FIAKER (HORSE CARRIAGE) TOURS

A *Fiaker*, or horse carriage, will trot you around to whatever destination you specify, but this is an expensive way to see the city. A short tour of the inner city takes about 20 minutes and costs €55; a longer one including the inner city and part of the Ringstrasse lasts about 40 minutes and costs €70; and an hour-long tour of the inner city and the whole Ringstrasse costs €80. The carriages accommodate four (five if someone sits next to the coachman). Starting points are Heldenplatz in front of the Hofburg, Stephansplatz beside the cathedral, and across from the Albertina, all in the 1st District.

WALKING TOURS

Guided walking tours are a great way to see the city highlights. The tourist office offers around 40 tour topics, ranging from "Unknown Underground Vienna" to "Hollywood in Vienna" to "Jewish Families and Their Past in

Vienna." Vienna Walks and Talks offers informative walks through the old Jewish Quarter and a *Third Man* tour about the classic film starring Orson Welles. Tours take about 1½ hours, are held in any weather provided at least three people turn up, and cost €15, plus any entry fees. No reservations are needed. Ask for the monthly brochure "Walks in Vienna," which details the tours, days, times, and starting points.

If you can, try to get a copy of Henriette Mandl's "Vienna Downtown Walking Tours" from a bookshop. The six tours take you through the highlights of central Vienna, with excellent commentary and some entertaining anecdotes that most of your Viennese acquaintances won't know.

Cityrama Sightseeing. There's a variety of options for being guided around the city (and beyond): a classic city tour including Schönbrunn, nighttime tours, tours including a boat trip on the Danube, and tours including dinner and a show or classical concert. ⊠ *Opernpassage, 1st District* ☎ *01/504–7500* ⊕ *www.cityrama.at* ▧ *From €44.*

Vienna Sightseeing Tours. Tours of historical sites of the city, including Schönbrunn Palace, are offered, plus themed tours, bus/boat ride tours, and a hop-on, hop-off service with 37 stops. Tours beyond the city are also available, including the Vienna Woods and the Danube Valley. ⊠ *Weyringergasse 28A, 4th District/Wieden* ☎ *01/7124–6830* ⊕ *www. viennasightseeing.at* ▧ *Tours from €10; hop-on, hop-off bus €15–39.*

Vienna Walks and Talks. Tailor-made and scheduled tours of "Classical Vienna," "Third Man," "Jewish Vienna," neighborhood walking tours, bike tours, and others are offered. ⊠ *Werdertorgasse 9/2, 1st District* ☎ *01/774–8901* ⊕ *www.viennawalks.com* ▧ *From €14.*

VISITOR INFORMATION

The main center for information is the Vienna City Tourist Office, open daily 9–7 and centrally located on Albertinaplatz between the Hofburg and Kärntnerstrasse. Ask about an €18.90/€21.90 Vienna Card that combines 48/72 hours of public transportation and more than 210 discounts at museums, galleries, theaters, and concert halls, as well as bars, cafés, and restaurants. The cards are also available at hotel and train stations.

ESSENTIALS

Airport Contacts **Airport Driver** ☎ *01/22822* ⊕ *www.airportdriver.at.* **City Airport Train** ☎ *01/25250* ⊕ *www.cityairporttrain.com.* **Vienna Airport Lines** ☎ *01/7007–32300* ⊕ *www.postbus.at.* **Vienna International Airport** (*VIE*). ☎ *01/7007–22233 for flight information* ⊕ *www.viennaairport.at.*

Public Transporation Contacts **Wiener Linien** ☎ *01/790–9100* ⊕ *www.wienerlinien.at.*

Taxi Companies **60160 Taxi** ☎ *01/60160.* **31300 Taxi** ☎ *01/31300.* **40100 Taxi** ☎ *01/40100.*

Train Contacts **Central Train Station (Hauptbahnhof)** ☎ *05/1717* ⊕ *www.hauptbahnhof-wien.at.* **Franz-Josef Bahnhof** ⊠ *Julius-Tandler-Platz 3, 9th District/Alsergrund.* **Meidling Bahnhof** ⊠ *Eichenstrasse 27, 12th District/ Meidling.* **Westbahnhof (Bahnhof City)** ⊠ *Europaplatz 2, 15th District/ Fünfhaus.* **Wien-Mitte/Landstrasse** ⊠ *Landstrasser Hauptstrasse 1c,*

3rd District/Landstrasse ☎ *01/05711.* **Wien Praterstern Bahnhof** ✉ *Lassall-estrasse, 2nd District/Leopoldstadt* ☎ *05/1717 ÖEBB.*

Tourist Information **Vienna City Tourist Office** ✉ *Am Albertinaplatz 1, at Maysedergasse, 1st District* ☎ *01/24555* ⊕ *www.wien.info.*

EXPLORING VIENNA

Most of Vienna lies roughly within an arc of a circle with the straight line of the Danube Canal as its chord. The most prestigious address of the city's 23 *Bezirke,* or districts, is its heart, the **Innere Stadt** ("Inner City"), or 1st District, bounded by the Ringstrasse (Ring). It's useful to note that the fabled 1st District holds the vast majority of sightseeing attractions and once comprised the entire city. In 1857 Emperor Franz Josef decided to demolish the ancient wall surrounding the city to create the more cosmopolitan Ringstrasse, the multilane avenue that still encircles the expansive heart of Vienna. At that time several small villages bordering the inner city were given district numbers and incorporated into Vienna. Today the former villages go by their official district numbers, but sometimes they are also referred to by their old village or neighborhood names.

The circular 1st District is bordered on its northeastern section by the Danube Canal and 2nd District, and clockwise from there along the Ringstrasse by the 3rd, 4th, 6th, 7th, 8th, and 9th districts. The 2nd District—Leopoldstadt—is home to the venerable Prater amusement park with its *Riesenrad* (Ferris wheel), as well as a huge park used for horseback riding and jogging. Along the southeastern edge of the 1st District is the 3rd District—Landstrasse—containing the Belvedere Palace and the fabulously quirky Hundertwasser Museum (Kunsthauswien). Extending from its southern tip, the 4th District, Wieden, is firmly established as one of Vienna's hip areas, with trendy restaurants, art galleries, and shops, plus Vienna's biggest outdoor market, the Naschmarkt, which is lined with dazzling Jugendstil buildings.

The southwestern 6th District, Mariahilf, includes the largest shopping street, Mariahilferstrasse, which the city has recently designated a pedestrian-friendly zone. Independent stores compete with international chains, smart restaurants, movie theaters, bookstores, and department stores. Directly west of the 1st District is the 7th District, Neubau. Besides the celebrated Kunsthistorisches Museum and headline-making MuseumsQuartier, the 7th District also houses the charming Spittelberg quarter, its cobblestone streets lined with beautifully preserved 18th-century houses. Moving up the western side you come to the 8th District, Josefstadt, which is known for its theaters, upscale restaurants, and antiques shops. Completing the circle surrounding the Innere Stadt on its northwest side is the 9th District, Alsergrund, once Sigmund Freud's neighborhood and today a nice residential area with lots of outdoor restaurants, curio shops, and lovely early-20th-century apartment buildings.

The other districts—the 5th, and the 10th through the 23rd—form a concentric second circle around the 2nd through 9th districts. These are mainly residential and only a few hold sights of interest for tourists. The 11th District, Simmering, contains one of Vienna's architectural wonders, Gasometer, a former gasworks that has been remodeled into a housing and shopping complex. The 13th District, Hietzing, with the fabulous Schönbrunn Palace as its centerpiece, is also a coveted residential area. The 19th District, Döbling, is Vienna's poshest neighborhood and also bears the nickname the "Noble District" because of all the embassies on its chestnut-tree-lined streets. The 19th District also incorporates several other neighborhoods within its borders, in particular the wine villages of Grinzing, Sievering, Nussdorf, and Neustift am Walde. The 22nd District, Donaustadt, now called Donau City, is a modern business and shopping complex that has grown around the United Nations center. The 22nd District also has several grassy spots for bathing and sailboat watching along the Alte Donau (Old Danube).

It may be helpful to know the neighborhood names of other residential districts: the 5th/Margareten; 10th/Favoriten; 12th/Meidling; 14th/Penzing; 15th/Fünfhaus; 16th/Ottakring; 17th/Hernals; 18th/Währing; 20th/Brigittenau; 21st/Floridsdorf; and 23rd/Liesing. For neighborhood site listings *below*—except the 1st District—both the district and neighborhood name will be given.

■ TIP➜ For hard-core sightseers, the tourist office has a booklet called "Vienna from A–Z" (€3.60) that gives short descriptions of some 250 sights around the city, all numbered and keyed to a fold-out map at the back.

Vienna is a city to explore and discover on foot. Above all, *look up* as you tour Vienna: some of the most fascinating architectural and ornamental bits are on upper stories or atop the city's buildings.

THE EASTERN CITY CENTER: STEPHANSDOM AND MEDIEVAL VIENNA

For more than eight centuries, the commanding Stephansdom cathedral has remained the nucleus around which the city has grown. Vienna of the Middle Ages is encapsulated behind it, and you could easily spend half a day or more just prowling the narrow streets and passageways. Stephansplatz is the logical starting point from which to explore Vienna's past and present. Streets here are named after medieval trades: while Bäckerstrasse was the street of the bakers, weavers peddled their wares on Wollzeile. Legend has it that several Knights Templar were murdered in Blutgasse, or "Blood Alley."

TOP ATTRACTIONS

Griechenbeisl (*Greeks Tavern*). If you want to find a nook where time seems to be holding its breath, head to the heart of the old town, where the Fleischmarkt (Meat Market) meets the hilly Griechengasse. Commanding the cobblestone lane is a 14th-century watchtower, Vienna's oldest, and an ivy-covered tavern called the Griechenbiesl, which has been serving customers for 500 years. Half a millennium ago, this quarter was settled by Greek and Levantine traders (there are still many rug dealers here) and many of them made this tavern their "local." The wooden carving on the facade of the current restaurant

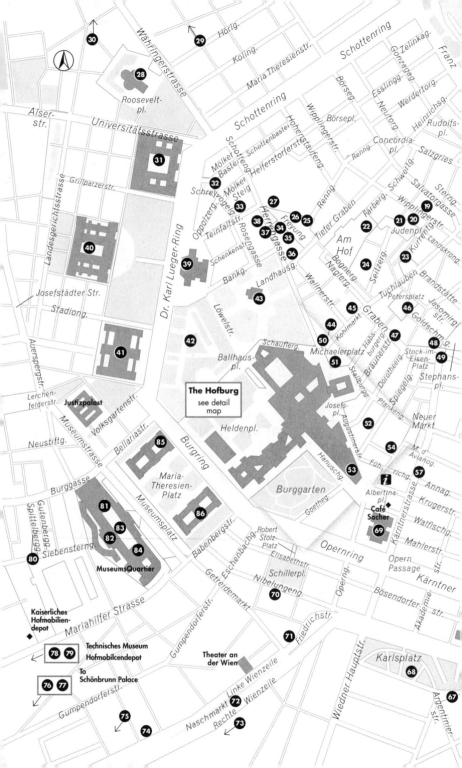

Exploring Vienna:
The Historic Heart

TO PRATER

Danube Canal

Stadtpark

Musikverein

Konzerthaus

0   1/4 mi

0   1/4 km

21er Haus **61**

Akademie der Bildenen Künste **70**

Albertina Museum **53**

Altes Rathaus **19**

Am Hof **22**

Basiliskenhaus **9**

Belvedere Palace **62**

Blutgasse District **2**

Bohemian Court Chancery **20**

Burgtheater **39**

Café Central **36**

Demel **44**

Dominikanerkirche **6**

Dorotheum **52**

Dritte Mann Museum **73**

Fälshermuseum **63**

Finanzministerium **56**

Freud Haus **28**

The Freyung **25**

Globe Museum **37**

The Graben **47**

Griechenbeisl **12**

Haas-Haus **48**

Haus der Musik **58**

Heiligenkreuzerhof **11**

Himmelpfortgasse **55**

Hofmobiliendepot (Furniture Museum) **78**

Hoher Markt **18**

Hollmann Salon **10**

Hundertwasserhaus **65**

Joseph Haydn House **75**

Jüdisches Museum der Stadt Wien **64**

Judenplatz Museum **21**

Kaisergruft **54**

Karlskirche **67**

Karlsplatz **68**

Kärntnerstrasse **57**

Kirche Am Hof **24**

Kirche Am Steinhof **77**

Kohlmarkt **45**

Kriminalmuseum **15**

Kunsthalle Wien **82**

Kunsthaus Wien **59**

Kunsthistorisches Museum **86**

Leopold Museum **84**

Looshaus **50**

Michaelerplatz **51**

Minoritenkirche **43**

Mozarthaus **3**

Museum für Angewandte Kunst (MAK) ... **7**

Museum Moderner Kunst Stiftung Ludwig **81**

MuseumsQuartier **83**

Naschmarkt **72**

Naturhistorisches Museum **85**

Otto Wagner Houses **74**

Palais Ferstel **35**

Palais Harrach **34**

Palais Kinsky **38**

Parlament **41**

Pasqualatihaus **32**

Peterskirche **46**

Postsparkasse **8**

Prater **14**

Rathaus **40**

Römermuseum **17**

Ruprechtskirche **16**

Schönbrunn Palace **76**

Schönlaterngasse **4**

Schottenhof **26**

Schottenkirche **27**

Schubert's Birthplace **30**

Schwarzenbergplatz **60**

Schweizerhaus **13**

Secession Building **71**

Spittelberg Quarter **80**

Staatsoper **69**

Stephansdom **1**

Stock-im-Eisen **49**

Technisches Museum **79**

Third Man Portal **33**

Uhrenmuseum **23**

Universität **31**

Universitätskirche **5**

Volksgarten **42**

Votivkirche **29**

Wien Museum Karlsplatz **66**

KEY

i *Tourist Information*

commemorates Marx Augustin—best known today from the song "Ach du lieber Augustin"—an itinerant musician who sang here during the plague of 1679. A favored Viennese figure, he fell into a pit filled with plague victims but survived, presumably because he was so pickled in alcohol. In fact, this tavern introduced one of the great pilsner brews of the 19th century and everyone—from Schubert to Mark Twain, Wagner to Johann Strauss—came here to partake. Be sure to dine here to savor its low-vaulted rooms adorned with engravings, mounted antlers, and bric-a-brac; the Mark Twain room has a ceiling covered with autographs of the rich and famous dating back two centuries. Adjacent to the tavern is a Greek Orthodox church co-designed by the most fashionable neoclassical designer in Vienna, Theophil Hansen. ⊠ *Fleischmarkt 11, 1st District* ☎ *01/533–1977* ⊕ *www.griechenbeisl.at* Ⓜ *U1 or U4/Schwedenplatz.*

FAMILY
Fodor's Choice
★

Haus der Musik (*House of Music*). You could spend an entire day at this ultra-high-tech museum, housed on several floors of an early-19th-century palace near Schwarzenbergplatz. Pride of place goes to the rooms dedicated to each of the great Viennese composers—Haydn, Mozart, Beethoven, Schubert, Strauss, and Mahler—complete with music samples and manuscripts. Other exhibits trace the evolution of sound (from primitive noises to the music of the masters) and illustrate the mechanics of the human ear (measure your own frequency threshold). There are also dozens of interactive computer games. You can even take a turn as conductor of the Vienna Philharmonic—the conductor's baton is hooked to a computer, which allows you to have full control over the computer-simulated orchestra. ⊠ *Seilerstätte 30, 1st District* ☎ *01/513–4850* ⊕ *www.hausdermusik.at/en/2.htm* 🎟 *€11* ⊘ *Daily 10–10* Ⓜ *U1, U2, or U4/Karlsplatz, then Tram D/Schwarzenbergplatz.*

Himmelpfortgasse. The maze of tiny streets surrounding Himmelpfortgasse (literally, "Gates of Heaven Street") conjures up the Vienna of the 19th century. The most impressive house on the street is the Ministry of Finance. The rear of the Steffl department store on Rauhensteingasse now marks the site of the house in which Mozart died in 1791. There's a commemorative plaque that once identified the street-side site, together with a small memorial corner devoted to Mozart memorabilia, which can be found on the sixth floor of the store. ⊠ *1st District* Ⓜ *U1 or U3/Stephansplatz.*

■ NEED A
BREAK?

Kleines Cafe. This landmark café, owned by Austrian actor Hanno Poschl, is on one of the most charming squares in Vienna, between Himmelpfortgasse and Singerstrasse. It's open daily for coffee, cocktails, and light snacks, and few places are more delightful to sit in and relax on a warm afternoon or evening. In summer, tables are set up outside on the intimate cobblestone square where the only sounds are the tinkling fountain and the occasional chiming of bells from the ancient Franciscan monastery next door. If you have time, take a stroll up the very quaint and pleasant Ballgasse, the tiny 18th-century street opposite the café. ⊠ *Franziskanerplatz 3, 1st District.*

Mozarthaus. This is Mozart's only still-existing abode in Vienna, with three floors of displays about his life and the masterworks that he composed here. Equipped with an excellent audio guide and starting out on the third floor of the building, you can hear about Mozart's time in Vienna: where he lived and performed, who his friends and supporters were, and his passion for expensive attire—he spent more money on clothes than most royals at that time. The second floor deals with Mozart's operatic works. The first floor focuses on the 2½ years that Mozart lived at this address (he moved around a lot in Vienna), when he wrote dozens of piano concertos, as well as *The Marriage of Figaro* and the six quartets dedicated to Joseph Haydn (who once called on Mozart here, saying to Mozart's father, "Your son is the greatest composer that I know in person or by name"). For two weeks in April 1787, Mozart took on a 16-year-old pupil from Germany named Ludwig van Beethoven. Concerts are staged here, and there are activities for children. Save on the entrance fee by purchasing a combined ticket for Mozarthaus Vienna and Haus der Musik for €17. ⊠ *Domgasse 5, 1st District* ☎ *01/512–1791* ⊕ *www.mozarthausvienna.at* 🎫 *€10* 🕐 *Daily 10–7* Ⓜ *U1 or U3/ Stephansplatz.*

Postsparkasse (*Post Office Savings Bank*). One of modern architecture's greatest curiosities, the Post Office Savings Bank was designed in 1904 by Otto Wagner, whom many consider the father of 20th-century architecture. In his manifesto *Modern Architecture,* he condemned 19th-century revivalist architecture and pleaded for a modern style that honestly expressed modern building methods. Accordingly, the exterior walls of the Post Office Savings Bank are mostly flat and undecorated; visual interest is supplied merely by varying the pattern of the bolts used to hold the marble slabs in place. Later architects embraced Wagner's beliefs wholeheartedly, although they used different, truly modern building materials: glass and concrete rather than marble. To see how Wagner carried his concepts over to interior design, check out the building's museum, which contains a permanent exhibition with over 200 photographs, plans, models, and documents. ⊠ *Georg-Coch-Platz 2, 1st District* ☎ *01/59905* 🎫 *€5* 🕐 *Museum: weekdays 9–5, Sat. 10–5* Ⓜ *U1 or U4/Schwedenplatz, then Tram 1 or 2/Julius-Raab-Platz.*

Schönlaterngasse (*Street of the Beautiful Lantern*). Once part of Vienna's medieval Latin Quarter, Schönlaterngasse is the main artery of a historic neighborhood that has blossomed in recent years, thanks in part to government *Kulturschillinge*—or renovation loans. Streets are lined with beautiful baroque town houses (often with colorfully painted facades), now distinctive showcases for art galleries, boutiques, and coffeehouses. At No. 5 you'll find a covered passage that leads to the historic **Heiligenkreuzerhof** courtyard. The picturesque street is named for the ornate wrought-iron wall lantern at Schönlaterngasse 6. Note the Baroque courtyard at Schönlaterngasse 8—one of the city's prettiest. ⊠ *1st District* Ⓜ *U3/Stubentor, U3/Stephansplatz, U4/Schwedenplatz.*

Basiliskenhaus (*House of the Basilisk*). The quarter's most famous house is the Basiliskenhaus. According to legend, on June 26, 1212, a foul-smelling basilisk (half rooster, half toad, with a glance that could kill) took up residence in the courtyard well, poisoning the water. An enterprising apprentice dealt with the problem by climbing down the well armed with a mirror; when the basilisk saw its own reflection, it turned to stone. The petrified creature can still be seen in a niche on the building's facade. Be sure to peek into the house's miniature courtyard for a trip back to medieval Vienna. ⊠ *Schönlaterngasse 7, 1st District.*

Alte Schmiede (*Old Smithy*). A former blacksmith's workshop, this is now a center for literature, art, and music. Entry is free for all events. ⊠ *Schönlaterngasse 9, 1st District* ☎ *01/512–8329* ⊕ *www.alte-schmiede.at* Ⓜ *U1 or U3/Stephansplatz.*

Stephansdom. Vienna's soaring centerpiece, this beloved cathedral enshrines the heart of the city—although when first built in the 12th century it stood outside the city walls. Vienna can thank a period of hard times for the Catholic Church for the cathedral's distinctive silhouette. Originally the structure was to have had matching 445-foot-high spires, a standard design of the era, but funds ran out, and the north tower to this day remains a happy reminder of what gloriously is not. The lack of symmetry creates an imbalance that makes the cathedral instantly identifiable from its profile alone. Like the Staatsoper and some other major buildings, it was very heavily damaged in World War II, but reconstruction loans have been utilized to restore the cathedral's former beauty. Decades of pollution have blackened the exterior, which is being painstakingly cleaned using only brushes and water, so as not to destroy the facade with chemicals.

It's difficult now to tell what was original and what parts of the walls and vaults were reconstructed. No matter: its history-rich atmosphere is dear to all Viennese. That noted, St. Stephen's has a fierce presence that is blatantly un-Viennese. It's a stylistic jumble ranging from 13th-century Romanesque to 15th-century Gothic. Like the exterior, St. Stephen's interior lacks the soaring unity of Europe's greatest Gothic cathedrals, much of its decoration dating from the later Baroque era.

■ TIP➔ **The wealth of decorative sculpture in St. Stephen's can be overwhelming to the layman, so if you want to explore the cathedral in detail, buy the admirably complete English-language booklet describing the works, sold in the small room marked "Dom Shop."** One particularly masterly work should be seen by everyone: the stone pulpit attached to the second freestanding pier on the left of the central nave, carved by Anton Pilgram between 1510 and 1550. The delicacy of its decoration would in itself set the pulpit apart, but even more intriguing are its five sculpted figures. Carved around the outside of the pulpit proper are the four Church Fathers (from left to right: St. Augustine, St. Gregory, St. Jerome, and St. Ambrose), and each is given an individual personality so sharply etched as to suggest satire, perhaps of living models. There is no satire suggested by the fifth figure, however; below the pulpit's stairs Pilgram sculpted a fine self-portrait, showing himself peering out

a half-open window. Note the toads, lizards, and ot
ing the spiral rail alongside the steps up to the pul

As you stroll through the aisles, remember that n
occurred here, including Mozart's marriage in 17℄
December 1791. The funeral service was conducte
beneath the Heidenturm, to the left of the cathedra.
The funeral bier on which his casket was placed stan
Chapel, which marks the entrance to the crypt and ⌐⌐⌐ ⌐⌐
from outside the church. His body rested at a spot not far from the
open-air pulpit—near the apse, at the other end of the cathedral—
named after the monk St. John Capistrano, who, in 1450, preached
from it to rouse the people to fight the invading Turks. Continuing
around the cathedral exterior, at the apse you'll find a centuries-old
sculpted torso of the Man of Sorrows, known irreverently as Our
Lord of the Toothache because of its agonized expression. Inside,
nearly every corner has something to savor: the Marienchor (Virgin's
Choir) has the Tomb of Rudolph IV, the Wiener Neustadt altar is a
masterpiece of woodcarving, and the catacombs, where the internal
organs of the Habsburgs rest.

The bird's-eye views from the cathedral's beloved **Alter Steffl** (Old
Stephen Tower) will be a highlight for some. The south tower is 137
meters (450 feet) high and was built between 1359 and 1433. The
climb up the 343 steps is rewarded with vistas that extend to the rising slopes of the Wienerwald. The north steeple houses the big Pummerin bell and a lookout terrace (access by elevator). For a special
treat, take the 90-minute Saturday-evening tour including a roof walk.
⊠ *Stephansplatz, 1st District* ☎ *01/5155–23767* ✉ *Guided tour €4.50*
(€10 on Sat.); catacombs €4.50; stairs to south tower €3.50; eleva-
tor to Pummerin bell €4.50; combined ticket €14.50 ⊘ *Mon.–Sat. 6*
am–10 pm, Sun. 7 am–10 pm. English-language guided tour, Apr.–
Oct. at 3:45; catacombs tour, Mon.–Sat. every half hr 10–11:30 and
1:30–4:30, Sun. every half hr 1:30–4:30; Pummerin bell, Apr.–June,
Sept., and Oct., daily 8:30–5:30; July and Aug., daily 8:30–6; Nov.–
Mar., daily 8:30–5; evening tours, June–Sept., Sat. at 7 pm Ⓜ *U1 or*
U3/Stephansplatz.

NEED A BREAK?

Zanoni & Zanoni. Between Rotenturmstrasse and Bäckerstrasse, this place
dishes up 25 or more flavors of smooth, Italian-style gelato, including
mango, caramel, and chocolate chip, and has frozen yogurt and vegan ice
cream too. It's open 365 days a year and has tables, too. ⊠ *Am Lugeck 7,*
1st District ☎ *01/512-7979.*

Universitätskirche (*Jesuit Church*). The church was built around 1630. Its
flamboyant Baroque interior contains a fine trompe l'oeil ceiling fresco
by Andrea Pozzo, the master of visual trickery, who was imported from
Rome in 1702 for the job. You might hear a Mozart or Haydn Mass
sung here in Latin on many Sundays. ⊠ *Dr.-Ignaz-Seipl-Platz, 1st Dis-*
trict ☎ *01/5125–2320* Ⓜ *U3 Stubentor/Dr.-Karl-Lueger-Platz.*

WORTH NOTING

Blutgasse District. Today this block, bounded by Singerstrasse, Grünangergasse, and Blutgasse, is a splendid example of city renovation and restoration, with cafés, shops, and galleries tucked into the corners. Nobody knows for certain how its gruesome name originated—*Blut* is German for "blood"— but one legend has it that Knights Templar were slaughtered here when their order was abolished in 1312. (There are roads named "Blutgasse" in villages surrounding Vienna, so many believe the name to be in remembrance of massacres suffered at the two Turkish invasions.) In later, pre-pavement, years the narrow street was known as Mud Lane. You can look inside the courtyards to see the open galleries that connect various apartments on the upper floors, the finest example being at Blutgasse 3. At the corner of Singerstrasse sits the 18th-century **Neupauer-Breuner Palace,** with its monumental entranceway and delicate windows. Opposite, at Singerstrasse 17, is the **Rottal Palace,** attributed to Hildebrandt, with its wealth of classical wall motifs, a contrast to the simple 18th-century facades on Blutgasse. ⊠ *1st District* Ⓜ *U1 or U3/Stephansplatz.*

Dominikanerkirche (*Dominican Church*). The Postgasse, to the east of Schönlaterngasse, introduces this unexpected visitor from Rome, built in the 1630s, some 50 years before the Viennese Baroque building boom. Its facade is modeled after the Roman churches of the 16th century. The interior illustrates why the baroque style came to be considered the height of bad taste during the 19th century and still has many detractors today. "Sculpt till you drop" seems to have been the motto here, and the viewer's eye is given no respite. This sort of Roman architectural orgy never really gained a foothold in Vienna, and when the great Viennese architects did pull out all the decorative stops at the Belvedere Palace, they did it in a very different style and with far greater success. ⊠ *Postgasse 4, 1st District* ☎ *01/512–9174* Ⓜ *U3/Stubentor/ Dr.-Karl-Lueger-Platz.*

Finanzministerium (*Ministry of Finance*). The architectural jewel of Himmelpfortgasse, this imposing abode—designed by Fischer von Erlach in 1697 and later expanded by Hildebrandt—was originally the town palace of Prince Eugene of Savoy. The Baroque details here are among the most inventive and beautifully executed in the city. The delightful motifs are softly carved, as if freshly squeezed from a pastry tube. Such baroque elegance may seem inappropriate for a finance ministry, but the contrast between place and purpose could hardly be more Viennese. ⊠ *Himmelpfortgasse 8, 1st District* Ⓜ *U1 or U3/Stephansplatz.*

BIRD'S-EYE VIEW

A good introduction to Vienna is a view high above it, and the city's preeminent panoramic lookout point is the observation platform of Vienna's mother cathedral, the Stephansdom. The young and agile will make it up the 343 steps of the south tower in 8 to 10 minutes; the rest will make it in closer to 20. There's also an elevator to the terrace of the north tower, which gives pretty much the same view. From atop, you can see that St. Stephen's is the veritable hub of the city's wheel.

Heiligenkreuzerhof (*Holy Cross Court*). Off the narrow streets and alleys behind the Stephansdom is this peaceful spot, approximately 0.5 km (a quarter mile) from the cathedral. The beautiful Baroque courtyard has the distinct feeling of a retreat into the 18th century. Visit on a Sunday morning and you'll find a craft fair in full swing. ⊠ *1st District* Ⓜ *U1 or U3/Stephansplatz.*

NEED A BREAK?

Hollmann Salon. At last someone was wise enough to open up an eatery so weary wanderers could spend time appreciating the wonders of this Baroque court. The fare is as good a reason to come to Hollmann Salon as the tranquility of the place. Smoke-free air pairs well with the organic ingredients used in the delicious, wallet-friendly, weekday three-course lunch for a mere €19; or choose "Eat the Menu" for €64. Actor-chef Robert Hollmann also runs the nearby boutique hotel Hollmann Bele-tage. ⊠ *Grashofgasse 3/Heiligenkreuzerhof, 1st District* ☏ *01/961-1960* ⊘ *Closed Sun.* Ⓜ *U1 or U4/Schwedenplatz.*

THE INNER CITY CENTER: BAROQUE GEMS AND VIENNA'S SHOPWINDOWS

The compact area bounded roughly by the back side of the Hofburg palace complex and Staatsoper, the Kohlmarkt, the Graben, and Kärntnerstrasse belongs to the oldest core of the city. Remains of the Roman city are just below the present-day surface. This was and still is the city's commercial heart, dense with shops and markets for various commodities. Today, the Kohlmarkt and Graben in particular offer the choicest luxury shops.

The area is marvelous for its visual treats, from the decorated squares to the varied art-drenched architecture to shop windows. The evening view down Kohlmarkt from the Graben is an inspiring classic, and the gilded dome of Michael's Gate, illuminated at night, shines its light into the palace complex, creating a glittering backdrop. Sights in this area range from the sacred—the Baroque Peterskirche—to the more profane pleasures of Demel, Vienna's beloved pastry shop, and the modernist masterwork of the Looshaus.

Dorotheergasse is home to two Baroque masterpieces. Palais Eskeles draws visitors to the newly restored Jewish Museum, and the former palace of Duke Albert of Saxony-Teschen is now the Albertina Museum and harbors one of the world's largest collections of drawings and prints.

TOP ATTRACTIONS

Albertina Museum. This not-to-be-missed collection is home to some of the greatest old-master drawings in Vienna—including Dürer's iconic *Praying Hands* and beloved *Alpine Hare.* The collection of nearly 65,000 drawings and almost a million prints was begun by the 18th-century Duke Albert of Saxony-Teschen. All the names are here, including Leonardo da Vinci, Michelangelo, Raphael, and Rembrandt. The Batliner Collection includes excellent examples of French and German impressionism and Russian avant-garde. The mansion's early-19th-century salons—all gilt boiserie and mirrors—provide a jewel-box setting.

The excellent Do & Co restaurant, with a patio long enough for an empress's promenade, offers splendid vistas of the historical center, and the Burggarten is the perfect place to take a break. ☒ *Augustinerstrasse 1, 1st District* ☏ *01/534–830* ⊕ *www.albertina.at* ☑ *€9.50* ☉ *Thurs.– Tues. 10–6, Wed. 10–9* Ⓜ *U3/Herrengasse.*

Am Hof. In the Middle Ages, the ruling Babenberg family built its castle on what today is Vienna's oldest square, the Am Hof (which means "at court"). The grand residence hosted such luminaries as Barbarossa and Walter von der Vogelweide, the minnesinger who stars in Wagner's *Tannhäuser*. The Baroque **Column of Our Lady** in the center dates from 1667, marking the Catholic victory over the Swedish Protestants in the Thirty Years' War (1618–48). The onetime **Civic Armory** at the northwest corner has been used as a fire station since 1685 (the high-spirited facade, with its Habsburg eagle, was "baroqued" in 1731). The complex includes a firefighting museum that's open on Sunday mornings. Presiding over the east side of the square is the noted Kirche Am Hof (*kirche* means church), adjacent to the newly opened Park Hyatt, which took over the former grand headquarters of a bank. At No. 13 is the fairly stolid 17th-century Palais Collalto, famous as the setting for Mozart's first public engagement at the age of six. This was but the first showing of the child prodigy in Vienna, for his father had him perform for three Viennese princes, four dukes, and five counts in the space of a few weeks. This new arrival from Salzburg set Vienna on its ear, and he was showered with money and gifts, including opulent children's clothing from Empress Maria Theresa. In Bognergasse, to the right of the church, is the **Engel Apotheke** (pharmacy) at No. 9, with a Jugendstil mosaic depicting winged women collecting the elixir of life in outstretched chalices. At the turn of the 20th century, the inner city was dotted with storefronts decorated in a similar manner; today this is the sole survivor. Around the bend from the Naglergasse is the picturesque Freyung square. Am Hof hosts one of Vienna's celebrated Christmas markets. ☒ *Am Hof, 1st District* Ⓜ *U3/Herrengasse.*

FodorsChoice
★

Demel. Vienna's best-known pastry shop, Demel offers a dizzying selection, so if you have a sweet tooth, a visit will be worth every euro. And in a city famous for its tortes, its almond-chocolate Senegaltorte takes the cake. Demel's shopwindows have some of the most mouthwatering and inventive displays in Austria. ☒ *Kohlmarkt 14, 1st District* ☏ *01/5351–7170* ⊕ *www.demel.at* Ⓜ *U1 or U3/Stephansplatz.*

Dorotheum. The narrow passageway just to the right of St. Michael's leads into the Stallburggasse, an area dotted with antiques stores attracted by the presence of this famous Viennese auction house, which began as a state-controlled pawnshop in 1707. Merchandise coming up for auction is on display at Dorotheergasse 17. The showrooms—packed with everything from carpets and pianos to cameras, jewelry and postage stamps—are well worth a visit. On the second floor the goods are not for auction but for immediate sale; the same goes for the terrific, mainly late-19th- to early-20th-century glass, wood, and art objects in the glass-roofed court just opposite the reception area on the ground floor. ☒ *Dorotheergasse 17, 1st District* ☏ *01/51560* ⊕ *www. dorotheum.com* ☉ *Weekdays 10–6, Sat. 9–5* Ⓜ *U1 or U3/Stephansplatz.*

The Graben. One of Vienna's major crossroads, the Graben's unusual width gives it the presence and weight of a city square. Its shape is due to the Romans, who chose this spot for the city's southwestern moat (Graben literally means "moat" or "ditch"). The Graben's centerpiece is the effulgently Baroque **Pestsäule**, or Plague Column. Erected by Emperor Leopold I between 1687 and 1693 as thanks to God for delivering the city from a particularly virulent plague, today the representation looks more like a host of cherubs doing their best to cope with the icing of a wedding cake wilting under a hot sun. Protestants may be disappointed to learn that the foul figure of the Pest also stands for the heretic plunging away from the "true faith" into the depths of hell. ⊠ *Between Kärntnerstrasse and Kohlmarkt, 1st District* Ⓜ *U1 or U3/Stephansplatz.*

Jüdisches Museum der Stadt Wien. The former Eskeles Palace, once an elegant private residence, now houses the Jewish Museum Vienna. Permanent exhibits tell of the momentous role that Vienna-born Jews have played in realms from music to medicine, art to philosophy, both in Vienna and in the world at large. Changing exhibits add contemporary touches. The museum complex includes a café and bookstore. ⊠ *Dorotheergasse 11, 1st District* ☎ *01/535–0431* ⊕ *www.jmw.at/en* 🎫 *€10, includes admission to Judenplatz Museum* ☉ *Sun.–Fri. 10–6* Ⓜ *U1 or U3/Stephansplatz.*

Judenplatz Museum. In what was once the old Jewish ghetto, construction workers discovered the fascinating remains of a 13th-century synagogue while digging for a new parking garage. Simon Wiesenthal (a former Vienna resident) helped to turn it into a museum dedicated to the Austrian Jews who died in World War II. Marking the outside is a concrete cube whose faces are casts of library shelves, signifying Jewish love of learning, designed by Rachel Whiteread. Downstairs are three exhibition rooms devoted to medieval Jewish life and the synagogue excavations. Also in Judenplatz is a statue of the 18th-century playwright Gotthold Ephraim Lessing, erected after World War II. ⊠ *Judenplatz 8, 1st District* ☎ *01/535–0431* ⊕ *www.jmw.at/museum-judenplatz* 🎫 *€10; includes admission to Jewish Museum Vienna* ☉ *Sun.–Thurs. 10–6, Fri. 10–2.*

Kärntnerstrasse. Vienna's leading central shopping street is much maligned—too commercial, too crowded, too many tasteless signs—but when the daytime tourist crowds dissolve, the Viennese arrive regularly for their evening promenade, and it is easy to see why. Plebeian the street may be, but it is also alive and vital, with an energy that the more tasteful Graben and the impeccable Kohlmarkt lack. For the sightseer beginning to suffer from an excess of art history, classic buildings, and museums, a Kärntnerstrasse window-shopping respite will be welcome. ⊠ *1st District* Ⓜ *U1, U4/Karlsplatz, or U1, U3/Stephansplatz.*

Kohlmarkt. Aside from its classic view of the domed entryway to the imperial palace complex of the Hofburg, the Kohlmarkt is best known as Vienna's most elegant shopping street, and fronts the area being refashioned the Goldenes Quartier (Golden Quarter). All the big brand names are represented here: Gucci, Louis Vuitton, Tiffany, Chanel, and

Armani, to name a few. The shops, not the buildings, are remarkable, although there is an entertaining odd-couple pairing: No. 11 (early 18th century) and No. 9 (early 20th century). The mixture of architectural styles is similar to that of the Graben, but the general atmosphere is low-key, as if the street were consciously deferring to the showstopper dome at the west end. The composers Haydn and Chopin lived in houses on the street and, indeed, the Kohlmarkt lingers in the memory when flashier streets have faded. ⊠ *Between Graben and Michaelerplatz, 1st District* Ⓜ *U3/Herrengasse.*

Looshaus. In 1911 Adolf Loos built the Looshaus on imposing Michael-erplatz, facing the Imperial Palace, and it was considered nothing less than an architectural declaration of war. After 200 years of Baroque and neo-baroque exuberance, the first generation of 20th-century archi-tects had had enough. Loos led the revolt; *Ornament and Crime* was the title of his famous manifesto, in which he inveighed against the conventional architectural wisdom of the 19th century. He advocated buildings that were plain, honest, and functional. The city was scan-dalized by Looshaus. Emperor Franz Josef, who lived across the road, was so offended that he ordered the curtains of his windows to remain permanently shut. Today the building has lost its power to shock, and the facade seems quite innocuous. The interior remains a breathtaking surprise; the building now houses a bank, and you can go inside to see the stylish chambers and staircase. To really get up close and personal with Loos, head to the splendor of his Loos American Bar, about six blocks east at No. 10 Kärntnerdurchgang. ⊠ *Michaelerplatz 3, 1st Dis-trict* Ⓜ *U3/Herrengasse.*

Michaelerplatz. One of Vienna's most historic squares, this small plaza is now the site of an excavation revealing Roman plus 18th- and 19th-century layers of the past. The excavations are a latter-day distrac-tion from the Michaelerplatz's most noted claim to fame—the eloquent entryway to the palace complex of the Hofburg.

Mozart's *Requiem* debuted in the **Michaelerkirche** on December 10, 1791. More people stop in today due to a discovery American soldiers made in 1945, when they forced open the crypt doors, which had been sealed for 150 years. Found lying undisturbed for centuries were the mummified remains of former wealthy parishioners of the church—even the finery and buckled shoes worn at their burial had been preserved by the perfect temperatures contained within the crypt.

Bilingual tours are offered from Easter to October, Monday–Saturday, at 11 am and 1 pm. The cost is €7. You're led down into the shad-owy gloom and through a labyrinth of passageways, pausing at several tombs (many of which are open so you can view the remains) for a brief explanation of the cause of death. On Wednesday at 3 pm, free tours of the church are held in English. ⊠ *Herrengasse, Reitschulgasse, and Schauflergasse, 1st District* ☎ *0676/503–4164* Ⓜ *U3/Herrengasse.*

Peterskirche. Considered the best example of church Baroque in Vienna—certainly the most theatrical—the Peterskirche was con-structed between 1702 and 1708 by Lucas von Hildebrandt. Accord-ing to legend, the original church on this site was founded in 792 by

Charlemagne, a tale immortalized by the relief plaque on the right side of the church. The facade has angled towers, graceful turrets (said to have been inspired by the tents of the Turks during the siege of 1683), and an unusually fine entrance portal. Inside, the Baroque decoration is elaborate, with some fine touches (particularly the glass-crowned galleries high on the walls on either side of

> **EURO TOUR**
>
> The more important churches, such as Stephansdom, Peterskirche, Minoritenkirche, and Michaelerkirche, have coin-operated (€1–€2) tape machines that give an excellent commentary in English on each structure's history and architecture.

the altar and the amazing tableau of the martyrdom of St. John Nepomuk). Just before Christmas each year the basement crypt is filled with a display of nativity scenes. The church is shoehorned into tiny Petersplatz, just off the Graben. ⊠ *Petersplatz, 1st District* Ⓜ *U1 or U3/Stephansplatz.*

Ruprechtskirche. North of the Kornhäusel Tower, this is the city's most venerable church, founded, according to legend, in 740; the oldest part of the present structure (the lower half of the tower) dates from the 11th century. Set on the ancient ramparts overlooking the Danube Canal, it is serene and unpretentious. ⊠ *Ruprechtsplatz, 1st District* Ⓜ *U1 or U4/Schwedenplatz.*

Staatsoper (*State Opera House*). Vying with the cathedral for the honor of emotional heart of the city—the opera house is a focus for Viennese life and one of the chief symbols of resurgence after World War II. Its directorship is one of the top jobs in Austria, almost as important as that of the president of the country, and one that draws even more public attention. The first of the Ringstrasse projects to be completed (in 1869), the opera house suffered disastrous bomb damage in the last days of World War II—only the outer walls, the front facade, and the main staircase survived. The auditorium is plain when compared with the red-and-gold eruptions of London's Covent Garden or some of the Italian opera houses, but it has an elegant individuality that it shows off beautifully when the stage and auditorium are turned into a ballroom for the great Opera Ball.

The construction of the opera house is the stuff of legend. When the foundation was laid, the plans for the Opernring were not yet complete, and in the end the avenue turned out to be several feet higher than originally planned. As a result, the opera house lacked the commanding prospect that its architects, Eduard van der Nüll and August Sicard von Sicardsburg, had intended. Even Emperor Franz Josef pronounced the building a bit low to the ground. For the sensitive van der Nüll (and here the story becomes a bit suspect), failing his beloved emperor was the last straw. In disgrace and despair, he committed suicide. Sicardsburg died of grief shortly thereafter. And the emperor, horrified at the deaths his innocuous remark had caused, limited all his future artistic pronouncements to a single immutable formula: *"Es war sehr schön, es hat mich sehr gefreut"* ("It was very nice, it pleased me very much").

Renovation could not avoid a postwar look, for the cost of fully restoring the 19th-century interior was prohibitive. The original design was followed in the 1945–55 reconstruction, meaning that sight lines from some of the front boxes are poor at best. These disappointments hardly detract from the fact that this is one of the world's half-dozen greatest opera houses, and experiencing a performance here can be the highlight of a trip to Vienna. If tickets are sold out, some performances are shown live on a huge screen outside on Karajanplatz. Tours of the opera house are given regularly, but starting times vary according to rehearsals; the current schedule is posted under the arcades on both sides of the building. Under the arcade on the Kärntnerstrasse side is an information office that also sells tickets to the main opera and the Volksoper. ⊠ *Opernring 2, 1st District* ☎ *01/514–44–2606* ⊕ *www.staatsoper.at* ⊠ *€5* ⊙ *Tours year-round* Ⓜ *U1, U2, or U4 Karlsplatz.*

Uhrenmuseum (*Clock Museum*). At the far end of Kurrentgasse, which is lined with appealing 18th-century houses, the appealing Uhrenmuseum's three floors display clocks and watches—more than 3,000 timepieces—dating from the 15th century to the present. The ruckus of bells and chimes pealing forth on any hour is impressive, but for the full cacophony try to be here at noon. Enter to the right on the Schulhof side of the building. ⊠ *Schulhof 2, 1st District* ☎ *01/533–2265* ⊠ *€4* ⊙ *Tues.–Sun. 10–6* Ⓜ *U1 or U3/Stephansplatz.*

WORTH NOTING

Altes Rathaus (*Old City Hall*). Opposite the Bohemian Chancery stands the Altes Rathaus, dating from the 14th century but displaying 18th-century baroque motifs on its facade. The interior passageways and courtyards, which are open during the day, house a Gothic chapel (open at odd hours); a much-loved baroque wall fountain (Georg Raphael Donner's **Andromeda Fountain** from 1741); and display cases exhibiting maps and photos illustrating the city's history. ⊠ *Wipplingerstrasse 6–8, 1st District* Ⓜ *U1 or U4/Schwedenplatz.*

Böhmische Hofkanzlei (*Bohemian Court Chancery*). This architectural jewel of the Inner City was built between 1708 and 1714 by Johann Bernhard Fischer von Erlach. He and his contemporary, Johann Lukas von Hildebrandt, were the reigning architectural geniuses of baroque-era Vienna. They designed their churches and palaces during the building boom that followed the defeat of the Turks in 1683. Both had studied architecture in Rome, and both were deeply impressed by the work of the great Italian architect Francesco Borromini, who brought to his designs a freedom of invention that was looked upon with horror by most contemporary Romans. But for Fischer von Erlach and Hildebrandt, Borromini's ideas were a source of triumphant architectural inspiration, and when they returned to Vienna they produced between them many of the city's most beautiful buildings. Alas, narrow Wipplingerstrasse allows little more than an oblique view of this florid facade. The rear of the building, on Judenplatz, is less elaborate but gives a better idea of the design concept. The building first served as the offices of Bohemia's representatives to the Vienna-based monarchy, and still houses government offices today. ⊠ *Wipplingerstrasse 7, 1st District* Ⓜ *U1 or U4/Schwedenplatz.*

Haas-Haus. Designed by the late Hans Hollein, one of Austria's best-known contemporary architects, who died in 2014, the Haas-Haus is one of Vienna's more controversial buildings. It's impossible to miss the modern lines of the glass-and-steel complex, which contrast sharply with the venerable walls of St. Stephen's, just across the way. ⊠ *Stephansplatz 12, 1st District* Ⓜ *U1 or U3/Stephansplatz.*

Hoher Markt. Crowds gather at noon each day to see the huge mechanical timepiece at the east end of this square in action, when the full panoply of mechanical figures representing Austrian historical personages parades by. The Anker Clock took six years (1911–17) to build and survived the World War II artillery fire that badly damaged the square. The graceless buildings erected around the square since 1945 do little to show off the square's lovely baroque centerpiece, the St. Joseph Fountain (portraying the marriage of Joseph and Mary), designed in 1729 by Joseph Emanuel Fischer von Erlach, son of the great Johann Bernhard Fischer von Erlach. ⊠ *1st District* Ⓜ *U1 or U4/Schwedenplatz)*

Kaisergruft (*Imperial Burial Vault*). On the southwest corner of the Neuer Markt, the Kapuzinerkirche, or Capuchin Church, is home to one of the more intriguing sights in Vienna: the Kaisergruft, or Imperial Burial Vault. The crypts contain the partial remains of some 140 Habsburgs (most of the hearts are in the Augustinerkirche and the entrails in St. Stephen's) plus one non-Habsburg governess ("She was always with us in life," said Maria Theresa, "why not in death?"). Perhaps starting with their tombs is the wrong way to approach the Habsburgs in Vienna, but it does give you a chance to get their names in sequence, as they lie in rows, their pewter coffins ranging from the simplest explosions of funerary conceit—with decorations of skulls, snakes, and other morbid symbols—to the huge and distinguished tomb of Maria Theresa and her husband. Designed while the couple still lived, their monument shows the empress in bed with her husband—awaking to the Last Judgment as if it were just another morning, while the remains of her son (the ascetic Josef II) lie in a simple copper casket at the foot of the bed as if he were the family dog. In 2011, 98-year-old Otto Habsburg, the eldest son of the last emperor, was laid to rest here with as much pomp as is permissible in a republic. ⊠ *Tegetthofstrasse 2, 1st District* ☎ *01/512–6853* 💲 *€5* 🕙 *Daily 10–6* Ⓜ *U1, U3/Stephansplatz; U1, U4/Karlsplatz.*

Kirche Am Hof. On the east side of the Am Hof, the Church of the Nine Choirs of Angels is identified by its sprawling baroque facade designed by Carlo Carlone in 1662. The somber interior lacks appeal, but the checkerboard marble floor may remind you of Dutch churches. ⊠ *Am Hof 1, 1st District* Ⓜ *U3/Herrengasse.*

Römermuseum. The Hoher Markt harbors one wholly unexpected attraction: underground ruins of a Roman military camp dating from the 2nd and 3rd centuries. You'll see fragments of buildings, pieces of pottery, children's toys, and statues, idols, and ornaments. Kids can learn about everyday life with interactive games. ⊠ *Hoher Markt 3, 1st District* ☎ *01/535–5606* 💲 *€4* 🕙 *Tues.–Sun. 9–6* Ⓜ *U1 or U4/Schwedenplatz.*

Stock-im-Eisen. Set into the building on the west side of Kärntnerstrasse is one of the city's odder relics, the Stock-im-Eisen, or the "nail-studded stump." Chronicles first mention the Stock-im-Eisen in 1533, but it is probably far older, and for hundreds of years any apprentice metal-smith who came to Vienna to learn his trade hammered a nail into the tree trunk for good luck. During World War II, when there was talk of moving the relic to a museum in Munich, it mysteriously disappeared; it reappeared, perfectly preserved, after the threat of removal had passed. ⊠ *Stock-im-Eisen-Platz, Kärntnerstrasse and Singerstrasse, 1st District* Ⓜ *U1 or U3/Stephansplatz.*

THE HOFBURG: AN IMPERIAL CITY

A walk through the Imperial Palace, called the Hofburg, brings you back to the days when Vienna was the capital of a mighty empire. You can still find in Viennese shops vintage postcards and prints that show the revered and bewhiskered Emperor Franz Josef leaving his Hofburg palace for a drive in his carriage. Today you can walk in his footsteps, gaze at the old tin bath the emperor kept under his simple iron bedstead, marvel at his bejeweled christening robe, and, along the way, feast your eyes on great works of art, impressive armor, and some of the finest Baroque interiors in Europe.

Until 1918 the Hofburg was the home of the Habsburgs, rulers of the Austro-Hungarian Empire. Now it is a vast smorgasbord of sightseeing attractions, including the Imperial Apartments, two imperial treasuries, six museums, the National Library, and the famous Winter Riding School. One of the latest Hofburg attractions is a museum devoted to "Sisi," the beloved Empress Elisabeth, wife of Franz Josef, whose beauty was the talk of Europe and whose tragic assassination (the murder weapon is one of the various exhibits) was mourned by all. The entire complex takes a minimum of a full day to explore in detail.

■ TIP➔ If your time is limited (or if you want to save most of the interior sightseeing for a rainy day), omit all the museums mentioned below except for the Imperial Apartments and the Schatzkammer. An excellent multi-lingual, full-color booklet, describing the palace in detail, is for sale at most ticket counters within the complex; it gives a complete list of attractions, and maps out the palace's complicated ground plan and building history wing by wing.

Vienna took its imperial role seriously, as evidenced by the sprawling Hofburg complex, which is still today the seat of government. While the buildings cover a considerable area, the treasures lie within, discreet. Franz Josef was beneficent—witness the broad Ringstrasse he ordained and the panoply of museums and public buildings it hosts. With few exceptions (Vienna City Hall and the Votive Church), rooflines are on an even level, creating an ensemble effect that helps integrate the palace complex and its parks into the urban landscape without overwhelming it. Diplomats still bustle in and out of high-level international meetings along the elegant halls. Horse-drawn carriages still traverse the Ring and the roadway that cuts through the complex. Ignore the cars and tour buses, and you can easily imagine yourself in a Vienna of a hundred or more years ago.

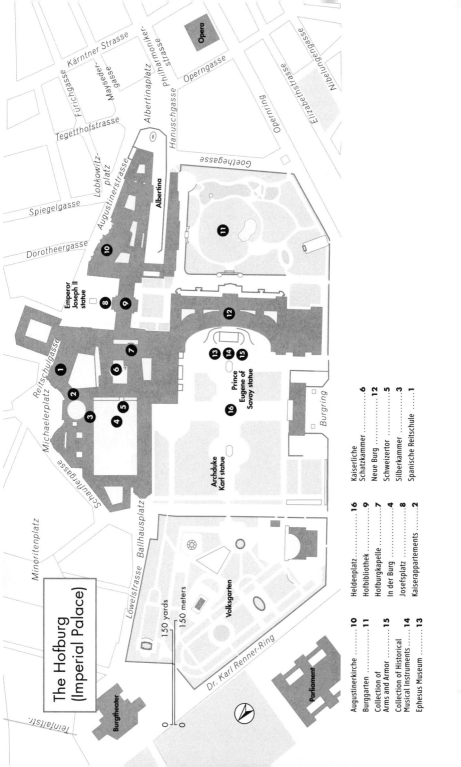

The Hofburg (Imperial Palace)

Augustinerkirche **10**
Burggarten **11**
Collection of
Arms and Armor **15**
Collection of Historical
Musical Instruments **14**
Ephesus Museum **13**

Heldenplatz **16**
Hofbibliothek **9**
Hofburgkapelle **7**
In der Burg **4**
Josefsplatz **8**
Kaiserappartements **2**

Kaiserliche
Schatzkammer **6**
Neue Burg **12**
Schweizertor **5**
Silberkammer **3**
Spanische Reitschule **1**

150 yards
150 meters

Architecturally, the Hofburg—like St. Stephen's—is far from refined. It grew up over a period of 700 years (its earliest mention in court documents is from 1279, at the very beginning of Habsburg rule), and its spasmodic, haphazard growth kept it from attaining a unified identity. But many individual buildings are fine, and the National Library is a tour de force. ■TIP➡ Want to see it all without breaking the bank? A €23 Sisi Ticket includes admission to the Kaiserappartements, the Silberkammer, the Imperial Furniture Depot, Vienna Furniture Museum, and a Grand Tour of the Schönbrunn Palace.

TOP ATTRACTIONS

Augustinerkirche (*Augustinian Church*). Built during the 14th century and presenting the most unified Gothic interior in the city, the church is something of a fraud—the interior dates from the late 18th century, not the early 14th—though the view from the entrance doorway is stunning: a soaring harmony of vertical piers, ribbed vaults, and hanging chandeliers that makes Vienna's other Gothic interiors look earthbound by comparison. Note on the right the magnificent **Tomb of the Archduchess Maria-Christina,** sculpted by the great Antonio Canova in 1805 (his own tomb was to look just like this), with mourning figures trooping into a pyramid. The imposing baroque organ sounds as heavenly as it looks, and the Sunday-morning high Mass (frequently works by Mozart or Haydn) sung here at 11 can be the highlight of a trip. To the right of the main altar, in the small Loreto Chapel, stand silver urns containing some 54 hearts of Habsburg rulers. This rather morbid sight is viewable after Mass on Sunday or by appointment. ✉ *Josefsplatz, 1st District* ☎ 01/533–7099–0 Ⓜ *U3/Herrengasse.*

Burggarten. The intimate Burggarten in back of the Neue Burg is a quiet oasis that includes a statue of a contemplative Franz Josef and an elegant statue of Mozart, moved here from the Albertinaplatz after the war, when the city's charred ruins were being rebuilt. Today the park is a favored time-out spot for the Viennese; an alluring backdrop is formed by the striking former greenhouses, now the gorgeous Palmenhaus restaurant and the **Schmetterlinghaus.** Enchantment awaits you at Vienna's unique Butterfly House. Inside are towering tropical trees, waterfalls, a butterfly nursery, and more than 150 species on display (usually 400 winged jewels are in residence). The park also has entrances on Hanuschgasse and Goethegasse. ✉ *Opernring, 1st District* ⊕ *www.schmetterlinghaus.at* ✉ €5.50 ☉ *Apr.–Oct., weekdays 10–4:45, weekends 10–6:15; Nov.–Mar., daily 10–3:45* Ⓜ *U2/MuseumsQuartier; Tram: 1, 2, and D/Burgring.*

Fodor's Choice
★
Hofbibliothek (*formerly Court, now National, Library*). This is one of the grandest Baroque libraries in the world, a cathedral of books, its centerpiece the spectacular Prunksaal—the Grand Hall—which probably contains more book treasures than any comparable collection outside the Vatican. The main entrance to the ornate reading room is in the left corner of Josefsplatz. Designed by Fischer von Erlach the Elder just before his death in 1723 and completed by his son, the Grand Hall is full-blown High Baroque, with trompe l'oeil ceiling frescoes by Daniel Gran. Twice a year, special exhibits highlight some of the finest and rarest tomes, well documented in German and English. From 1782 Mozart

performed here regularly at the Sunday matinees of Baron Gottfried van Swieten, who lived in a suite of rooms in the grand, palacelike library. Four years later the baron founded the Society of Associated Cavaliers, which set up oratorio performances with Mozart acting as conductor. Across the street at Palais Palffy, Mozart reportedly first performed *The Marriage of Figaro* before a select, private audience to see if it would pass the court censor. ⊠ *Josefsplatz 1, 1st District* ☎ *01/534–100* ⊕ *www.onb.ac.at* 🖾 *€7* ⊙ *Tues., Wed., and Fri.–Sun. 10–6, Thurs. 10–9* Ⓜ *U3/Herrengasse.*

Hofburgkapelle (*Chapel of the Imperial Palace*). Fittingly, this is the main venue for the beloved Vienna Boys' Choir, since the group has its roots in the Hofmusikkapelle choir founded by Emperor Maximilian I five centuries ago (Haydn and Schubert were both participants as young boys). The choir sings Mass here at 9:15 on Sunday from mid-September to June (tickets, ranging in price from €7 to €35, are sold to hear the choir). Be aware that you *hear* the choirboys but don't see them: soprano and alto voices peal forth from a gallery behind the seating area. In case you miss out on tickets to the Sunday performance, note that just to the right of the chapel entrance a door leads into a small lobby. Here a television screen shows the whole Mass for free. ⊠ *Hofburg, Schweizer Hof, 1st District* ☎ *01/533–9927* ⊕ *www. hofburgkapelle.at* Ⓜ *U3/Herrengasse.*

In der Burg. This prominent courtyard of the Hofburg complex focuses on a statue of Francis II and the noted **Schweizertor** gateway. Note the **clock** on the far upper wall at the north end of the courtyard: it tells time by a sundial, also gives the time mechanically, and even, above the clock face, indicates the phase of the moon. ⊠ *off Löwelstrasse, 1st District* Ⓜ *U3/Herrengasse.*

Josefsplatz. Many consider this Vienna's loveliest courtyard and, indeed, the beautifully restored imperial style adorning the roof of the buildings forming Josefsplatz is one of the few visual demonstrations of Austria's onetime widespread power and influence. The square's namesake is represented in the equestrian **statue of Emperor Joseph II** (1807) in the center. ⊠ *Herrengasse, 1st District* Ⓜ *U3/Herrengasse.*

Kaiserappartements (*Imperial Apartments*). From the spectacular portal gate of the Michaelertor—you can't miss the four gigantic statues of Hercules and his labors—you climb the marble Kaiserstiege (Emperor's Staircase) to begin a tour of a long, repetitive suite of 18 conventionally luxurious state rooms. The red-and-gold decoration (19th-century imitation of 18th-century rococo) tries to look regal, but much like the empire itself in its latter days, it's only going through the motions, and ends up looking merely official. Still, these are the rooms where the ruling family of the Habsburg empire ate, slept, and dealt with family tragedy—in the emperor's study on January 30, 1889, Emperor Franz Josef was told about the tragic death of his only son, Crown Prince Rudolf, who had shot himself and his soulmate, 17-year-old Baroness Vetsera, at the hunting lodge at Mayerling. Among the few signs of life are Emperor Franz Josef's spartan, iron field bed, on which he slept every night, and Empress Elisabeth's wooden gymnastics equipment (obsessed with her looks, Sisi suffered from anorexia and was fanatically devoted to exercise). In the Sisi Museum, part of the regular tour, five rooms display many of her treasured possessions, including her jewels, the gown she wore the night before her marriage, her dressing gown, and the opulent court salon railroad car she used. There is also a death mask made after her assassination by an anarchist in Geneva in 1898, as well as the murder weapon that killed her: a wooden-handled file. ⊠ *Hofburg, Schweizer Hof, 1st District* ☎ *01/533–7570* ⊕ *www.hofburg-wien.at* 🖃 *€10.50, includes admission to Silberkammer* ⊙ *Sept.–June, daily 9–5:30; July and Aug., daily 9–6* Ⓜ *U3/Herrengasse.*

Fodor's Choice   **Kaiserliche Schatzkammer** (*Imperial Treasury*). The entrance to the Schatz-
★   kammer, with its 1,000 years of treasures, is tucked away at ground level behind the staircase to the Hofburgkapelle. The elegant display is a welcome antidote to the monotony of the Imperial Apartments, and the crowns and relics fairly glow in their surroundings. Here you'll find such marvels as the Holy Lance—reputedly the lance that pierced Jesus's side—the Imperial Crown (a sacred symbol of sovereignty once stolen on Hitler's orders), and the Saber of Charlemagne. Don't miss the Burgundian Treasure, connected with that most romantic of medieval orders of chivalry, the Order of the Golden Fleece. ∎ TIP→ The €20 combined ticket that includes admission to the Kunsthistorisches is a great deal. ⊠ *Hofburg, Schweizer Hof, 1st District* ☎ *01/525–240* 🖃 *€12* ⊙ *Wed.–Mon. 10–6* Ⓜ *U3/Herrengasse.*

Silberkammer (*Museum of Court Silver and Tableware*). Fascinating for its behind-the-scenes views of state banquets and other elegant affairs, there are more than forks and finger bowls here. Stunning decorative pieces vie with glittering silver and gold for your attention. Highlights include Emperor Franz Josef's vermeil banqueting service, the jardinière given to Empress Elisabeth by Queen Victoria, and gifts from Marie-Antoinette to her brother Josef II. The fully set tables give you a view of court life. ⊠ *Hofburg, Michaelertrakt, 1st District* ☎ *01/533–7570* 🖃 *€10.50, includes admission to Kaiserappartements* ⊙ *Sept.–June, daily 9–5:30; July and Aug., daily 9–6* Ⓜ *U3/Herrengasse.*

Spanische Reitschule (*Spanish Riding School*). The world-famous Spanish Riding School, between Augustinerstrasse and the Josefsplatz, has been a favorite for centuries, and no wonder: who can resist the sight of the stark-white Lipizzaner horses going through their masterful paces? For the last 300 years they have been perfecting their *haute école* riding demonstrations to the sound of baroque music in a ballroom that seems to be a crystal-chandeliered stable. The interior of the riding school, the 1735 work of Fischer von Erlach the Younger, makes it Europe's most elegant sports arena.

The performance schedule is fairly consistent throughout the year. From August to June, evening performances are held mostly on weekends and morning exercises with music are held mostly on weekdays. Booking months ahead is good idea. If you do so, pick up tickets at the office under the Michaelerplatz rotunda dome. Otherwise tickets are available at the visitor center in Michaelerplatz (Tuesday–Saturday 9–4), and at Josefsplatz on the day of the morning exercise, 9–5. ⊠ *Michaelerplatz*

1, 1st District ☎ *01/533–9031* ⊕ *www.srs.at* ✉ *€23–€130; morning training €12* ⊙ *Aug.–June* Ⓜ *U3/Herrengasse.*

WORTH NOTING

Collection of Historical Musical Instruments. See pianos that belonged to Brahms, Schumann, and Mahler, along with the rest of the world-renowned collection in this Neue Burg museum. An acoustic guided tour allows you to hear the various instruments on headphones as you move from room to room. ✉ *Neue Burg, Heldenplatz, 1st District* ⊕ *www.khm.at/en* ✉ *€12, includes Collection of Arms and Armor, Ephesus Museum, and the Kunsthistorisches Museum* ⊙ *Wed.–Mon. 10–6* Ⓜ *U2/MuseumsQuartier.*

Collection of Arms and Armor. Rivaling the armory in Graz as one of the most extensive arms and armor collections in the world is this Neue Burg museum. Enter at the triumphal arch set into the middle of the curved portion of the facade. ✉ *Neue Burg, Heldenplatz, 1st District* ⊕ *www.khm.at* ✉ *€12, includes Collection of Ancient Musical Instruments, Ephesus Museum, and the Kunsthistorisches Museum* ⊙ *Wed.– Mon. 10–6* Ⓜ *U2/MuseumsQuartier.*

Ephesus Museum. One of the museums in the Neue Burg, the Ephesus Museum contains exceptional Roman antiquities unearthed by Austrian archaeologists in Turkey at the turn of the century. ✉ *Neue Burg, Heldenplatz, 1st District* ⊕ *www.khm.at* ✉ *€12, includes Collection of Ancient Instruments, Collection of Arms and Armor, and Kunsthistorisches Museum* ⊙ *Wed.–Sun. 10–6* Ⓜ *Tram: 1, 2, and D/Burgring.*

Heldenplatz. The Neue Burg was never completed and so the Heldenplatz was left without a discernible shape, but the space is punctuated by two superb equestrian statues depicting Archduke Karl and Prince Eugene of Savoy. The older section on the north includes the offices of the federal president. ✉ *Hofburg, 1st District* Ⓜ *Tram: 1, 2, and D/Burgring.*

Neue Burg. Standing today as a symbol of architectural overconfidence, the Neue Burg was designed for Emperor Franz Josef in 1869, this "new château" was part of a much larger scheme that was meant to make the Hofburg rival the Louvre, if not Versailles. The German architect Gottfried Semper planned a twin of the present Neue Burg on the opposite side of the Heldenplatz, with arches connecting the two with the other pair of twins on the Ringstrasse, the Kunsthistorisches Museum (Museum of Art History) and the Naturhistorisches Museum (Museum of Natural History). But World War I intervened, and with the empire's collapse the Neue Burg became the last in a long series of failed attempts to bring architectural order to the Hofburg. (From its main balcony, in March 1938, Adolf Hitler told a huge cheering crowd below of his plan for the new German Empire, declaring that Vienna "is a pearl! I am going to put it into a setting of which it is worthy!") Today the Neue Burg houses four specialty museums: the **Collection of Arms and Armor,** the **Collection of Historical Musical Instruments,** the **Ephesus Museum,** and the **Ethnological Museum.** For details on these museums, see separate listings. ✉ *Heldenplatz, 1st District* ☎ *01/525–240* Ⓜ *U2/ MuseumsQuartier.*

Schweizertor (*Swiss Gate*). Dating from 1552 and decorated with some of the earliest classical motifs in the city, the Schweizertor leads from In der Burg through to the oldest section of the palace, a small courtyard known as the Schweizer Hof. The gateway is painted maroon, black, and gold, giving a fine Renaissance flourish to the building's facade. ⊠ *Hofburg, 1st District* Ⓜ *U3/Herrengasse.*

ACROSS THE DANUBE: THE SECOND DISTRICT

Walk across the Danube Canal on Schwedenbrücke or Marienbrücke and you'll reach the 2nd District, the home of Vienna's famous Prater amusement park.

Fälschermuseum (*Museum of Art Fakes*). This museum is a must-see for those who like a bit of cunning cloak and dagger—an utterly unique collection that includes a myriad of magnificent forgeries in both arts and letters, and offers captivating backstories on how the faked pieces came to be. On display are fakes of Chagall and Rembrandt, as well as the infamous "Hitler Diaries" that were front-page news in the 1980s. ⊠ *Löwengasse 28, 3rd District* ⊕ *www.faelschermuseum.com* ⧉ *€5* ⊙ *Tues.–Sun. 10–5* Ⓜ *Tram 1 to Hetzgasse.*

Johann Strauss the Younger's House. The most popular composer of all, waltz king Johann Strauss the Younger, composed the "Blue Danube Waltz" at this house in 1867. Standing in the huge salon of this Belle Epoque building, you can well imagine what a sumptuous affair a Strauss soirée would have been. Artifacts include Strauss's Amati violin. ⊠ *Praterstrasse 54, 2nd District/Leopoldstadt* ☎ *01/214–0121* ⧉ *€4* ⊙ *Tues.–Sun. 10–1 and 2–6* Ⓜ *U4/Nestroyplatz.*

Kriminalmuseum (*Criminal Museum*). This might be the strangest museum in the city, and it's certainly the most macabre. The vast collection is entirely devoted to Viennese murders of the most gruesome kind, with the most grisly displays situated, appropriately, in the cellar. Murderers and their victims are depicted in photos and newspaper clippings, and many of the actual instruments used in the killings are displayed, axes seeming to be the most popular. The Criminal Museum is across the Danube Canal from Schwedenplatz, about a 15-minute walk from the Ruprechtskirche, the Hoher Markt, or the Heiligenkreuzerhof. ⊠ *Grosse Sperlgasse 24, 2nd District/Leopoldstadt* ☎ *01/664–300–5677* ⊕ *www.kriminalmuseum.at* ⧉ *€5* ⊙ *Thurs.–Sun. 10–5* Ⓜ *U2/Taborstrasse.*

Prater. In 1766, to the dismay of the aristocracy, Emperor Josef II decreed that the vast expanse of imperial parklands known as the Prater would henceforth be open to the public. East of the inner city between the Danube Canal and the Danube proper, the Prater is a public park to this day, notable for its long promenade (the Hauptallee, more than 4½ km [3 miles] in length), the traditional amusement-park rides, a planetarium, and a small but interesting museum devoted to the Prater's long history. If you look carefully, you can discover a handful of children's rides dating from the '20s and '30s that survived the fire that consumed most of the Volksprater in 1945. The best-known attraction is the 200-foot Ferris wheel that figured so prominently in the 1949 film *The Third Man.*

2

It was one of three built in Europe at the end of the 19th century (the others were in England and France, but have long since been dismantled); the wheel was badly damaged during World War II, but restored shortly thereafter. Its progress is slow and stately (a revolution takes 10 minutes), the views from its cars magnificent, particularly toward dusk. ⊠ *Riesenradplatz, 2nd District/Leopoldstadt* 🖘 *Park free, Ferris wheel €8.50* ☉ *Mar., Apr., and Oct., daily 10–10; May–Sept., daily 9 am–midnight; Nov.–Feb., daily 10–8* Ⓜ *U1/Praterstern.*

NEED A BREAK?

Schweizerhaus. When you're at the Prater, try to eat at Schweizerhaus, which has been serving frothy mugs of beer, roast chicken, and *Stelze* (a huge hunk of crispy roast pork on the bone) for more than 100 years. The informal setting, with wood-plank tables indoors or in the garden in summer, adds to the fun. Credit cards are not accepted. ⊠ *Strasse des 1. Mai 116, 2nd District* ☎ *01/728–0152* ☉ *Closed Nov.–Feb.*

THE WESTERN CITY CENTER: BURGTHEATER AND BEYOND

Hailed as one of the most prestigious stages in the German-speaking world, the Burgtheater is home to a highly venerated ensemble of 80 actors. Always keen on stargazing, the Viennese flock to the elegant Café Landmann to observe thespians eating linzer torte. In the warmer months, students from Vienna University across the Ringstrasse stroll through Volksgarten to smell its fragrant rose garden. From here it's a short walk to the Freyung, a sumptuous square graced by the neo-Renaissance Palais Ferstel and its 19th-century shopping arcade.

TOP ATTRACTIONS

Burgtheater (*National Theater*). One of the most important theaters in the German-speaking world, the Burgtheater was built between 1874 and 1888 in the Italian Renaissance style, replacing the old court theater at Michaelerplatz. Emperor Franz Josef's mistress, Katherina Schratt, was once a star performer here, and famous Austrian and German actors still stride across this stage. The opulent interior, with its 60-foot relief *Worshippers of Bacchus* by Rudolf Wyer and lobby ceiling frescoes by Ernst and Gustav Klimt, makes it well worth a visit. ⊠ *Dr. Karl Lueger-Ring 2, 1st District* ☎ *01/514–4441–40* ⊕ *www.burgtheater. at* 🖘 *€5.50* ☉ *Guided tours daily at 3; also Sept.–June, Fri.–Sun. at 2* Ⓜ *Tram: 1, 2, and D/Burgtheater, Rathaus.*

Café Central. Part of the Palais Ferstel complex, this is one of Vienna's more famous cafés, its full authenticity blemished only by complete restoration in recent years. In its prime (before World War I), the café was "home" to some of the most famous literary figures of the day, who dined, socialized, worked, and even received mail here. The denizens of the Central favored political argument; indeed, their heated discussions became so well known that in October 1917, when Austria's foreign secretary was informed of the outbreak of the Russian Revolution, he dismissed the report with a facetious reference to a well-known local Marxist, the chess-loving (and presumably harmless) "Herr Bronstein from the Café Central." The remark was to become famous all over

CLOSE UP

Mozart, Mozart, Mozart!

The composer Wolfgang Amadeus Mozart (1756–91) crammed a prodigious number of compositions into the last 10 years of his life, of which he spent in Vienna. It was in Vienna that he experienced many of the high points of his life, both personal and artistic. He wed his beloved Constanze Weber (with whom he would have six children) at St. Stephen's Cathedral in August 1782, and led the premieres of several of his greatest operas. But knowing his troubled relations with his home city of Salzburg makes his Vienna sojourn an even more poignant one.

From the beginning of Mozart's precocious and prolific career, his father, frustrated in his own musical ambitions at the archbishopric in Salzburg, looked beyond the boundaries of the Austro-Hungarian Empire to promote the boy's fame. At the age of six, his son caused a sensation in the royal courts of Europe with his skills as an instrumentalist and impromptu composer. As Mozart grew up, however, his virtuosity lost its power to amaze and he was forced to make his way as an "ordinary" musician, which then meant finding a position at court. Not much more successful in Salzburg than his father had been, he was never able to rise beyond the level of organist (allowing him, as he noted with sarcasm, to sit above the cooks at table). In disgust, he relocated to Vienna, where despite the popularity of his operas he was able to obtain only an unpaid appointment as assistant Kapellmeister at St. Stephen's mere months before his death. By then, patronage subscriptions had been taken up in Hungary and the Netherlands that would have paid

him handsomely. But it was too late. Whatever the truth about the theories still swirling around his untimely death, the fact remains that not only was he not given the state funeral he deserved, but he was buried in an unmarked grave (although most Viennese were at that time) after a hasty, sparsely attended funeral.

Only the flint-hearted can stand in Vienna's Währingerstrasse and look at the windows behind which Mozart wrote those last three symphonies in the incredibly short time of six weeks in the summer of 1788 and not be touched. For this was the time when the Mozart fortunes had slumped to their lowest. "If you, my best of friends, forsake me, I am unhappily and innocently lost with my poor sick wife and my child," he wrote. And if one is inclined to accuse Mozart's fellow countrymen of neglect, they would seem to have made up for it with a vengeance. The visitor to Vienna and Salzburg can hardly ignore the barrage of Mozart candies, wine, beer, coffee mugs, T-shirts, baseball caps—not to mention the gilt statues and all the other knickknacks. Mozart, always one to appreciate a joke, would surely see the irony in the belated veneration. Today, places with which he is associated are all reverently marked with memorial plaques.

—Gary Dodson

Austria, for Herr Bronstein had disappeared and was about to resurface in Russia bearing a new name: Leon Trotsky. Today things are a good deal more yuppified: the overpriced coffee now comes with a little chocolate biscuit, and the pianist is more likely to play Sinatra ballads than Strauss. But you can linger as long as you like over a single cup of coffee and a newspaper from the huge international selection provided. ⊠ *Herrengasse 14, 1st District* ☎ *01/533–3763–24* ⊕ *www.palaisevents.at* Ⓜ *U3/Herrengasse.*

The Freyung. This square, whose name means "freeing"—so called, according to lore, because for many centuries monks at the adjacent Schottenkirche had the privilege of offering sanctuary for three days to anyone on the lam. In the center of the square stands the allegorical **Austria Fountain** (1845), notable because its Bavarian designer, Ludwig Schwanthaler, had the statues cast in Munich and then supposedly filled them with cigars to be smuggled into Vienna for black-market sale. Around the sides of the square are some of Vienna's greatest patrician residences, including the Ferstel, Harrach, and Kinsky palaces. ⊠ *Am Hof and Herrengasse, 1st District* Ⓜ *U3/Herrengasse.*

Palais Ferstel. Not really a palace, this commercial complex dating from 1856 is named for its architect, Heinrich Ferstel. The facade is Italianate, harking back in its 19th-century way to the Florentine palazzi of the early Renaissance. The interior is unashamedly eclectic: vaguely Romanesque in feel and Gothic in decoration, with a bit of renaissance or baroque sculpted detail thrown in for good measure. Such eclecticism is sometimes dismissed as derivative, but here the architectural details are so respectfully and inventively combined that the interior is a pleasure to explore. The 19th-century stock-exchange rooms upstairs are now gloriously restored and used for conferences, concerts, and balls. ⊠ *Freyung 2, 1st District* Ⓜ *U3/Herrengasse.*

Schottenhof. This shaded courtyard typifies the change that came over Viennese architecture during the Biedermeier era (1815–48). The Viennese, according to the traditional view, were so relieved to be rid of the upheavals of the Napoleonic Wars that they accepted without protest the iron-handed repression of Prince Metternich, chancellor of Austria. Restraint also ruled in architecture; baroque license was rejected in favor of a new and historically "correct" style that was far more controlled and reserved. Kornhäusel led the way in establishing this trend in Vienna; his Schottenhof facade is all sober organization and frank repetition. But in its marriage of strong and delicate forces it still pulls off the great Viennese-waltz trick of successfully merging seemingly antithetical characteristics. ⊠ *Freyung, 1st District* Ⓜ *U2/Schottentor.*

NEED A BREAK?

Zattl. In a delightful tree-shaded courtyard, this *Biergarten* has quickly become immensely popular. Zattl is the owner and he loves his beer, and the secret to his success is to have huge tanks of Bohemia's best brew, unpasteurized Pilsner Urquell, delivered to the cellar to be tapped directly into the glass. Good local dishes like veal goulash and grilled chicken are inexpensive and well prepared. ⊠ *Freyung 6, 1st District* ☎ *01/533–7262* ⊕ *www.zattl.at* ⊙ *Daily* Ⓜ *U2/Schottentor.*

Schottenkirche. From 1758 to 1761, Bernardo Bellotto did paintings of the Freyung looking north toward the Schottenkirche; the pictures, which hang in the Kunsthistorisches Museum, are shockingly similar to the view you see today. A church has stood on the site of the Schottenkirche since 1177, when the monastery was established by monks from Ireland—Scotia Minor, in Latin, hence the name "Scots Church." The present edifice dates from the mid-1600s, when it replaced its predecessor, which had collapsed because of weakened foundations. The interior, with its ornate ceiling and a surplus of cherubs and angels' faces, is in stark contrast to the plain exterior. The adjacent **Museum im Schottenstift** includes the celebrated late-Gothic high altar dating from about 1470. The winged altar is fascinating for its portrayal of the Holy Family in flight into Egypt—with the city of Vienna clearly identifiable in the background. ⊠ *Freyung 6, 1st District* ☎ *01/534–98–600* ⊕ *www.schottenstift.at* ☒ *Church free, museum €5* ☉ *Tues–Sat. 11–5* Ⓜ *U2/Schottentor.*

WORTH NOTING

Beethoven Pasqualatihaus. Beethoven lived in the Pasqualatihaus while he was composing his only opera, *Fidelio,* as well as his Seventh Symphony and Fourth Piano Concerto. Today his apartment houses a small commemorative museum (in distressingly modern style). After navigating the narrow and twisting stairway, you might well ask how he maintained the jubilant spirit of the works he wrote there. Note particularly the prints that show what the window view out over the Mölker bastion was like when Beethoven lived here and the piano that dates from his era—one that was beefed up to take the banging Beethoven made fashionable. ⊠ *8 Mölker Bastei, 1st District* ☎ *01/535–8905* ⊕ *www.wienmuseum.at* ☒ *€2* ☉ *Tues.–Sun. 10–1 and 2–6* Ⓜ *U2/Schottentor.*

Globe Museum. Across the street from the Café Central, the beautifully renovated Palais Mollard has a rare collection of more than 400 terrestrial and celestial globes on display in its second-floor museum—the only one of its kind in the world open to the public. The oldest is an earth globe dating from 1536, produced by Gemma Frisius, a Belgian doctor and cosmographer. On the ground floor is a small but fascinating exhibition of the history of Esperanto, including a film. ⊠ *Herrengasse 9, 1st District* ☎ *01/534–10–710* ⊕ *www.onb.ac.at/ev/globe_museum.htm* ☒ *€5* ☉ *Tues., Wed., and Fri.–Sun. 10–6, Thurs. 10–9* Ⓜ *U3/Herrengasse.*

Minoritenkirche (*Minorite Church*). Minoritenplatz is named after its centerpiece, the Minoritenkirche, a Gothic affair with a strange stump of a tower, built mostly in the 14th century. The front is brutally ugly, but the back is a wonderful, if predominantly 19th-century, surprise. The interior contains the city's most imposing piece of kitsch: a large mosaic reproduction of Leonardo da Vinci's *Last Supper,* commissioned by Napoléon in 1806 and later purchased by Emperor Francis I. ⊠ *Minoritenplatz 2A, 1st District* ☎ *01/533–4162* ☉ *8–6* Ⓜ *U3/Herrengasse.*

Palais Harrach. Mozart and his sister Nannerl performed here as children for Count Ferdinand during their first visit to Vienna in 1762. The palace, next door to Palais Ferstel, was altered after 1845 and severely damaged during World War II. Many of the state rooms have lost their historical luster, but the Marble Room, set with gilt boiseries, and the Red Gallery, topped with a spectacular ceiling painting, still provide grand settings for receptions. ⊠ *Freyung 3, 1st District* Ⓜ *U3/Herrengasse.*

Palais Kinsky. Just one of the architectural treasures that comprise the urban set piece of the Freyung, the Palais Kinsky is the square's best-known palace, and is one of the most sophisticated pieces of Baroque architecture in the whole city. Built between 1713 and 1716 by Hildebrandt, it now houses Wiener Kunst Auktionen, a public-auction business offering artworks and antiques. If there's an auction viewing, try to see the palace's spectacular 18th-century staircase, all marble goddesses and crowned with a trompe-l'oeil ceiling painted by Marcantonio Chiarini. ⊠ *Freyung 4, 1st District* ☎ *01/532–4200* ⊕ *www.imkinsky. com* Ⓜ *U3/Herrengasse.*

Third Man Portal. This doorway (up the incline) was made famous in 1949 by the classic film *The Third Man*. It was here that Orson Welles, as the malevolently knowing Harry Lime, stood hiding in the dark, only to have his smiling face illuminated by a sudden light from the upper-story windows of the house across the alley. To get to this apartment building from the nearby Schottenkirche, follow Teinfaltstrasse one block west to Schreyvogelgasse on the right. ⊠ *Schreyvogelgasse 8, 1st District* Ⓜ *U2/Schottentor.*

Volksgarten. Just opposite the Hofburg is a green oasis with a rose garden, a shining white 19th-century Greek temple, and a rather wistful white-marble monument to Empress Elisabeth, Franz Josef's Bavarian wife, who died of a dagger wound inflicted by an Italian anarchist in Geneva in 1898. If not overrun with latter-day hippies, these can offer spots to sit for a few minutes while contemplating Vienna's most ambitious piece of 19th-century city planning: the Ringstrasse. ⊠ *Burgring 1, 1st District* Ⓜ *Tram: 1, 2, or D/Rathausplatz, Burgtheater.*

EAST OF THE RINGSTRASSE: STADTPARK AND KARLSPLATZ

Next to Stephansplatz, Karlsplatz is the inner city's busiest hub. It sprawls across the Ringstrasse to encompass the magnificent Baroque Karlskirche and an exquisite Jugendstil pavilion designed by Otto Wagner, the architect of the partly elevated tram system to the outer boroughs (now part of the U4 and U6 subway lines). From Karlsplatz, you can travel eastward on the Ringstrasse to visit the stunning Museum for Applied Arts and the romantic Stadtpark with its gilded statue of Johann Strauss, or head in the other direction to Prince Eugene's Belvedere Palace, a treasure trove of art spanning the centuries.

TOP ATTRACTIONS

Fodor'sChoice **Belvedere Palace.** One of the most splendid pieces of Baroque architec-
★ ture anywhere, the Belvedere Palace—actually two imposing palaces separated by a 17th-century French-style garden parterre—is one of the masterpieces of architect Lucas von Hildebrandt. Built outside the city

Tracking Down The Third Man

Nothing has done more to create the myth of postwar Vienna than Carol Reed's classic 1949 film *The Third Man*. The bombed-out ruins of this proud, imperial city created an indelible image of devastation and corruption in the war's aftermath. Vienna was then divided into four sectors, each commanded by one of the victorious armies—American, Russian, French, and British. But their attempts at rigid control could not prevent a thriving black market.

Reed's film version of the Graham Greene thriller features Vienna as a leading player, from the top of its Ferris wheel to the depth of its lowest sewers—"which run right into the Blue Danube." It was the first British film to be shot entirely on location.

Joseph Cotten plays Holly Martins, a pulp-fiction writer who comes to Vienna in search of his friend Harry Lime (Orson Welles). He makes the mistake of delving too deeply into Lime's affairs, even falling in love with his girlfriend, Anna Schmidt (Alida Valli), with fatal consequences.

Many of the sites where the film was shot are easily visited. Harry Lime appears for the first time nearly one hour into the film in the doorway of Anna's apartment building at No. 8 Schreyvogelgasse, around the corner from the Mölker-Bastei (a remnant of the old city wall). He then runs to Am Hof, a lovely square lined with Baroque town houses and churches, which appears much closer to Anna's neighborhood than it actually is.

The scene between Lime and Martins on the Ferris wheel was filmed on the Riesenrad at the Prater, the huge amusement park across the Danube Canal. While the two friends talk in the enclosed compartment, the wheel slowly makes a revolution, with all Vienna spread out below them.

In the memorable chase at the end of the movie, Lime is seen running through the damp sewers of Vienna, hotly pursued by the authorities. In reality, he would not have been able to use the sewer system as an escape route because the tunnels were too low and didn't connect between the different centers of the city. A more feasible, if less cinematic, possibility of escape was offered by the labyrinth of cellars that still connected many buildings in the city.

Lime's funeral is held at the Zentralfriedhof (Central Cemetery), reachable by the No. 71 streetcar. This is the final scene of the movie, where Anna Schmidt walks down the stark, wide avenue, refusing to acknowledge the wistful presence of Holly Martins.

After touring sewers and cemeteries, treat yourself to a stop at the Hotel Sacher, used for a scene in the beginning of the movie when Holly Martins is using the telephone in the lobby. The bar in the Sacher was a favorite hangout of director Carol Reed, who left a signed note to the bartender, saying: "To the creator of the best Bloody Marys in the whole world."

The film is screened on Tuesday, Friday, and Sunday in the Burg Kino, and a memorabilia museum open on Saturday is near the Naschmarkt.

fortifications between 1714 and 1722, the complex originally served as the summer palace of Prince Eugene of Savoy; much later it became the home of Archduke Franz Ferdinand, whose assassination in 1914 precipitated World War I. Though the lower palace is impressive in its own right, it is the much larger upper palace, used for state receptions, banquets, and balls, that is acknowledged as Hildebrandt's master-piece. The upper palace displays a wealth of architectural invention in its facade, avoiding the main design problems common to palaces: monotony on the one hand and pomposity on the other.

Hildebrandt's decorative manner here approaches the rococo, that final style of the baroque era when traditional classical motifs all but disap-peared in a whirlwind of seductive asymmetric fancy. The main interiors of the palace go even further: columns are transformed into muscle-bound giants, pilasters grow torsos, capitals sprout great piles of sym-bolic imperial paraphernalia, and the ceilings are aswirl with ornately molded stucco. The result is the finest rococo interior in the city. On the garden level you are greeted by the Sala Terrena, whose massive Atlas figures shoulder the marble vaults of the ceiling and, it seems, the entire palace above. The next floor is centered around a gigantic Marble Hall covered with trompe l'oeil frescoes. In the Lower Belvedere (entrance is at Rennway 6), there are more 17th-century salons, including the Grotesque Room painted by Jonas Drentwett and another Marble Hall (which really lives up to its name).

Both the upper and lower palaces of the Belvedere are museums devoted to Austrian painting. The Belvedere's main attraction is the collection of 19th- and 20th-century Austrian paintings, centering on the work of Vienna's three preeminent early-20th-century art-ists: Gustav Klimt, Egon Schiele, and Oskar Kokoschka. Klimt was the oldest, and by the time he helped found the Secession movement he had forged an idiosyncratic painting style that combined realis-tic and decorative elements in a way that was revolutionary. *The Kiss*—his greatest painting—is here on display. Schiele and Kokoschka went even further, rejecting the decorative appeal of Klimt's glitter-ing abstract designs and producing works that ignored conventional ideas of beauty. ⊠ *Prinz-Eugen-Strasse 27, 3rd District/Landstrasse* 📞 *01/795–57–134* ⊕ *www.belvedere.at* 💶 *€16* 🕓 *Daily 10–6* Ⓜ *U1, U2, or U4/Karlsplatz; then Tram D or Tram 71.*

Karlskirche. Dominating the Karlsplatz is one of Vienna's greatest build-ings, the Karlskirche, dedicated to St. Charles Borromeo. Before you is a giant Baroque church framed by enormous freestanding columns, mates to Rome's famous Trajan's Column. These columns may be out of keeping with the building as a whole, but were conceived with at least two functions in mind: one was to portray scenes from the life of the patron saint, carved in imitation of Trajan's triumphs, and thus help to emphasize the imperial nature of the building; and the other was to symbolize the Pillars of Hercules, suggesting the right of the Habsburgs to their Spanish dominions, which the emperor had been forced to renounce. The end result is an architectural tour de force.

The Karlskirche was built in the early 18th century on what was then the bank of the River Wien. The church had its beginnings in a disaster. In 1713 Vienna was hit by a brutal outbreak of plague, and Emperor Charles VI made a vow: if the plague abated, he would build a church dedicated to his namesake, St. Charles Borromeo, the 16th-century Italian bishop who was famous for his ministrations to Milanese plague victims. In 1715 construction began, using an ambitious design by Johann Bernhard Fischer von Erlach that combined architectural elements from ancient Greece (the columned entrance porch), ancient Rome (the Trajanesque columns), contemporary Rome (the baroque dome), and contemporary Vienna (the baroque towers at either end). When it was finished, the church received decidedly mixed press. History, too, delivered a negative verdict: the Karlskirche spawned no imitations, and it went on to become one of European architecture's curiosities. Notwithstanding, seen lighted at night, the building is magical in its setting.

The main interior of the church utilizes only the area under the dome and is conventional despite the unorthodox facade. The space and architectural detailing are typical High Baroque; the fine vault frescoes, by J. M. Rottmayr, depict St. Charles Borromeo imploring the Holy Trinity to end the plague. If you are not afraid of heights, take the panorama elevator up into the sphere of the dome and climb the top steps to enjoy an unrivalled view to the heart of the city. ⊠ *Karlsplatz, 4th District/ Wieden* ☎ *01/504–6187* ⊕ *www.karlskirche.at* ◨ *€6* ⊗ *Daily 9–12:30 and 1–6, Sun. noon–5:45* Ⓜ *U1, U2, or U4 Karlsplatz.*

Karlsplatz. As with the Naschmarkt, Karlsplatz was formed when the River Wien was covered over at the turn of the 20th century. At the time, architect Otto Wagner expressed his frustration with the result—too large a space for a formal square and too small a space for an informal park—and the awkwardness is felt to this day. The buildings surrounding the Karlsplatz, however, are quite sure of themselves: the area is dominated by the classic Karlskirche, made less dramatic by the unfortunate reflecting pool with its Henry Moore sculpture, wholly out of place, in front. On the south side of the Resselpark, that part of Karlsplatz named for the inventor of the screw propeller for ships, stands the Technical University (1816–18). In a house that occupied the space closest to the church, Italian composer Antonio Vivaldi died in 1741; a plaque marks the spot. On the north side, across the heavily traveled roadway, are the Künstlerhaus (built in 1881 and still in use as an exhibition hall) and the Musikverein. The latter, finished in 1869, is now home to the Vienna Philharmonic. The downstairs lobby and the two halls upstairs have been restored and glow with fresh gilding. The main hall has what may be the world's finest acoustics.

Some of Wagner's finest Secessionist work can be seen two blocks east on the northern edge of Karlsplatz. In 1893 Wagner was appointed architectural supervisor of the new Vienna City Railway, and the matched pair of small pavilions he designed, the Otto Wagner Stadtbahn Pavilions, at No. 1 Karlsplatz, in 1898 are among the city's most ingratiating buildings. Their structural framework is frankly exposed (in keeping with Wagner's belief in architectural honesty), but they are also lovingly decorated (in keeping with the Viennese fondness for architectural finery). The result is Jugendstil at its very best, melding plain and fancy with grace and insouciance. ✉ *4th District/Wieden* Ⓜ *U1, U2, or U4/Karlsplatz.*

Museum für Angewandte Kunst (MAK) (*Museum of Applied Arts*). This fascinating museum contains a large collection of Austrian furniture, porcelain, art objects, and priceless Oriental carpets. The Jugendstil display devoted to Josef Hoffman and his Secessionist followers at the Wiener Werkstätte is particularly fine. The MAK also showcases changing exhibitions of contemporary works, and the museum shop sells furniture and other objects (including great bar accessories) designed by young local artists. ✉ *Stubenring 5, 1st District* ☎ *01/711–36–0* ⊕ *www.mak.at* 🎫 *€7.90; free Sat.* ☉ *Tues. 10 am–midnight; Wed.–Sun. 10–6* Ⓜ *U3/Stubentor.*

Schwarzenbergplatz. The center of this square is marked by an oversize equestrian sculpture of Prince Schwarzenberg—he was a 19th-century field marshal for the imperial forces. See if you can guess which building is the newest—it's the one on the northeast corner (No. 3) at Lothringer Strasse, an exacting reproduction of a building destroyed by war damage in 1945 and dating only from the 1980s. The military monument occupying the south end of the square behind the fountain is the **Russian War Memorial,** set up at the end of World War II by the Soviets; the Viennese, remembering the Soviet occupation, call its unknown soldier the "unknown plunderer." South of the memorial is the stately **Schwarzenberg Palace,** designed as a summer residence by Johann Lukas von Hildebrandt in 1697 and completed by Fischer von Erlach, father and son. ✉ *3rd District/Landstrasse* Ⓜ *Tram: Schwarzenbergplatz.*

Wien Museum Karlsplatz (*Museum of Viennese History*). Housed in an incongruously modern building at the east end of the Karlsplatz, this museum possesses Viennese historical artifacts and treasures: everything from 16th-century armor to paintings by Schiele and Klimt to the preserved facade of Otto Wagner's *Die Zeit* offices. ✉ *Karlsplatz, 4th District/Wieden* ☎ *01/505–8747–0* ⊕ *www.wienmuseum.at* 🎫 *€6* ☉ *Tues.–Sun. 9–6* Ⓜ *U1, U2, or U4 Karlsplatz.*

WORTH NOTING

21er Haus. Vienna's newest museum of contemporary art is housed in the structure originally built for the 1958 World Expo, the design of which won architect Karl Schwanzer the Grand Prix d'Architecture that year. The structure was modified and reopened in 2011 as a space to showcase the best of Austrian modern art. The museum houses the largest collection and archive of renowned Austrian sculptor Fritz Wotruba. ✉ *Arsenalstrasse 1, 3rd District* ⊕ *www.21erhaus.at* 🎫 *€7* ☉ *Wed. and Thurs. 11–9, Fri.–Sun. 11–6* Ⓜ *U1/ SüdTyrolerplatz; Tram D, 18 or O (station Quartier Belvedere).*

OFF THE BEATEN PATH

Hundertwasserhaus. To see one of Vienna's most architecturally intriguing buildings, travel eastward from Schwedenplatz or Julius-Raab-Platz along Radetzkystrasse. Here you'll find the Hundertwasserhaus, a 52-apartment public-housing complex designed by the late Austrian avant-garde artist Friedensreich Hundertwasser, arguably Austria's most significant post-modernist artist. The complex looks like a colorful patchwork of gingerbread houses strung precariously together, and was highly criticized

CLOSE UP

Jugendstil Jewels

From 1897 to 1907, the Vienna Secession movement gave rise to one of the most spectacular manifestations of the pan-European style known as Art Nouveau. Viennese took to calling the look *Jugendstil*, or the "young style." In such dazzling edifices as Otto Wagner's Wienzeile majolica-adorned mansion, Jugendstil architects rebelled against the prevailing 19th-century historicism that had created so many imitation Renaissance town houses and faux Grecian temples. Josef Maria Olbrich, Josef Hoffman, and Otto Schönthal took William Morris's Arts and Crafts movement, added dashes of Charles Rennie Mackintosh and flat-surface Germanic geometry, and came up with a luxurious style that shocked turn-of-the-20th century Viennese traditionalists (and infuriated Emperor Franz Josef). Many artists united to form the Vienna Secession—whose most famous member was painter Gustav Klimt—and the Wiener Werkstätte (Vienna Workshop), which transformed the objects of daily life into works of art, paving the way for 20th-century modernism. Today Jugendstil buildings are among the most stunning structures in Vienna. The shrine of the movement is the Secession Building, the "architectural manifesto" of Klimt and his peers.

when it opened in 1985. Time heals all wounds, even imaginary assaults to the senses, and now the structure is a beloved thread of the Viennese architectural tapestry. ✉ *Löwengasse and Kegelgasse, 3rd District/Landstrasse* Ⓜ *U1 or U4/Schwedenplatz, then Tram N to Hetzgasse.*

Kunsthaus Wien. This art museum mounts outstanding international exhibits in addition to showings of the vibrant works by avant-garde artist Friedensreich Hundertwasser. (He designed this building, along with the nearby apartment building called Hundertwasserhaus.) The building itself is pure Hundertwasser, a crayon box of colors, irregular floors, windows with trees growing out of them, and sudden architectural surprises, all of which make a wholly appropriate setting for modern art. ✉ *Untere Weissgerberstrasse 13, 3rd District/Landstrasse* ☎ *01/712–0491–0* 🌐 *www.kunsthauswien.com* 🎫 *€9* 🕒 *Daily 10–7* Ⓜ *U1 or U4/Schwedenplatz, then Tram N or O to Radetzkyplatz.*

OFF THE BEATEN PATH

Zentralfriedhof (*Central Cemetery*). Austrians take seriously the pomp of a funeral, brass bands and all, and nowhere is that more evident than the Central Cemetery. A streetcar from Schwarzenbergplatz takes you to the front gates of the cemetery that contains the graves of most of Vienna's great composers: Ludwig van Beethoven, Franz Schubert, Johannes Brahms, the Johann Strausses (father and son), and Arnold Schönberg, among others. Find your way around with the help of an audio guide, which can be rented for a small fee. For a hefty fee, Fiakers are on standby for a carriage ride around the beautiful grounds. The monument to Wolfgang Amadeus Mozart is a memorial only; the approximate location of his unmarked grave can be seen at the now deconsecrated St. Marx-Friedhof at Leberstrasse 6–8. ✉ *Simmeringer Hauptstrasse, 11th District/Simmering* Ⓜ *Tram: 71 to St. Marxer Friedhof, or on to Zentralfriedhof Haupttor/2.*

SOUTH OF THE RINGSTRASSE: THE MUSEUMSQUARTIER

Late in 1857 Emperor Franz Josef issued a decree announcing the most ambitious piece of urban redevelopment Vienna had ever seen. The inner city's centuries-old walls were to be torn down, and the *glacis*—the wide expanse of open field that acted as a protective buffer between inner city and abutting villages—was to be filled in. A wide, tree-lined, circular boulevard was to be constructed in the open field, and an imposing collection of new buildings reflecting Vienna's status as the political, economic, and cultural heart of the Austro-Hungarian Empire would be erected. During the 50 years of building that followed, many factors combined to produce the Ringstrasse as it now stands, but the most important was the gradual rise of liberalism after the failed Revolution of 1848. By the latter half of the Ringstrasse era, support for constitutional government, democracy, and equality—all the concepts that liberalism traditionally equates with progress—was steadily increasing. As the Ringstrasse went up, it became the definitive symbol of this liberal progress; as Carl E. Schorske put it in his *Fin-de-Siècle Vienna*, it celebrated "the triumph of constitutional *Recht* (right) over imperial *Macht* (might), of secular culture over religious faith. Not palaces, garrisons, and churches, but centers of constitutional government and higher culture dominated the Ring."

As an ensemble, the collection is astonishing in its architectural presumption: it is nothing less than an attempt to assimilate and summarize the entire architectural history of Europe. The centerpiece of Ringstrasse is Heldenplatz, the huge square in front of the Hofburg. Emperor Franz Josef had two monumental museums built as an extension of Heldenplatz: the Kunsthistorisches Museum (filled with centuries of art) and Naturhistorisches Museum (focusing on natural history). Vienna's most cutting-edge art complex lies just beyond the two sandstone giants. The MuseumsQuartier is made up of several galleries showing art ranging from expressionist to modern art to avant-garde. There's even a breathtaking museum for children. Hipsters flock to the cafés and restaurants in and around the former 18th-century riding stables.

When you exit MuseumsQuartier, walk up Burggasse to Spittelberggasse, where you will find the Spittelberg Quarter and its Baroque and Biedermeier buildings. Emperor Josef II supposedly frequented the neighborhood's "houses of pleasure." A plaque at the Witwe Bolte restaurant on Gutenberggasse reminds strollers that his majesty was thrown out of one establishment during a clandestine visit.

TOP ATTRACTIONS

Fodor'sChoice **Kunsthistorisches Museum** (*Museum of Fine Art*). However short your ★ stay in Vienna, you'll want to come here, to visit one of the greatest art collections in the world, standing in the same class with those of the Louvre, the Prado, and the Vatican. This is no dry-as-dust museum illustrating the history of art, as its name might imply, but rather the collections of old-master paintings that reveal the royal taste and style of many members of the mighty House of Habsburg, which, during the 16th and 17th centuries, ruled over the greater part of the Western world. Today you can enjoy what this great ruling house assiduously (and in most cases, selectively) brought together through the centuries.

The museum is most famous for the largest collection of paintings under one roof by the Netherlandish 16th-century master Pieter Brueghel the Elder—many art historians say that seeing his sublime *Hunters in the Snow* is worth a trip to Vienna. Brueghel's depictions of peasant scenes, often set in magnificent landscapes, distill the poetry and magic of the 16th century as few other paintings do. Room 10 is the Brueghel shrine—on its walls hang *Children's Games,* the *Tower of Babel,* the *Peasant Wedding,* the *Nest-Robber,* and eight other priceless canvases. There are also hundreds of other celebrated old-master paintings here. Even a cursory description would run on for pages. The large-scale works concentrated in the main galleries shouldn't distract you from the equal share of masterworks in the more intimate side wings.

The Flemish wing also includes Rogier van der Weyden's *Crucifixion Triptych,* Holbein's *Portrait of Jane Seymour, Queen of England,* a fine series of Rembrandt portraits, and Vermeer's peerless *Allegory of the Art of Painting.* The grand style of the 17th century is represented by Rubens's towering altarpieces and his *Nude of Hélène Fourment.* In the Italian wing are works by Titian, including his *Portrait of Isabella d'Este,* whose fiercely intelligent eyes make you realize why she was the first lady of the Renaissance, and Giorgione's *The Three Philosophers,* an enigmatic composition in uniquely radiant Venetian coloring. Other highlights include Raphael's *Madonna in the Meadow,* Correggio's *Jupiter Embracing Io,* Parmigianino's *Cupid Cutting a Bow,* Guercino's *Return of the Prodigal Son,* and Caravaggio's *Madonna of the Rosary.*

One level down is the remarkable, less-visited **Kunstkammer,** displaying priceless objects created for the Habsburg emperors. These include curiosities made of gold, silver, and crystal (including Cellini's famous salt cellar "La Saliera"), and more exotic materials, such as ivory, horn, and gemstones. In addition, there are rooms devoted to Egyptian antiquities, Greek and Roman art, sculpture (ranging from masterworks by Tilmann Riemenschneider to Italian Mannerist bronzes, which the Habsburgs collected by the roomful) and numerous other collections. When your feet are ready to call a sit-down strike, repair to a comfy armchair in the café on the museum's second floor.

■ **TIP→ One of the best times to visit the Kunsthistorisches Museum is Thursday, when you can enjoy a sumptuous gourmet dinner (€44) in the cupola rotunda. Just across from the seating area, take a leisurely stroll through the almost-empty gallery chambers. Seating starts at 6:30 pm and the museum galleries close at 9 pm, so make sure you get your fill of art.** ✉ *Maria-Theresien-Platz, 7th District/Neubau* ☎ *01/525–240* ⊕ *www. khm.at* ▣ *€12* ☉ *Tues., Wed., and Fri.–Sun. 10–6, Thurs. 10–9* Ⓜ *U2/ MuseumsQuartier; U2 or U3/Volkstheater.*

FAMILY **MuseumsQuartier** (*Museum Quarter*). One of the largest of its kind in the world, the MuseumsQuartier—or MQ, as many call it—is a sprawling collection of galleries housed in what was once the Imperial Court Stables, the 260-year-old baroque complex designed by Fischer von Erlach. Between the Kunsthistorisches Museum and the Spittelberg neighborhood, it's in one of Vienna's hippest enclaves.

Where once 900 cavalry horses were housed, now thousands of masterworks of the 20th and 21st centuries are exhibited, all in a complex that is architecturally an expert and subtle blending of historic and cutting-edge: the original structure (adorned with pastry-white stuccoed ceilings and rococo flourishes) was retained, while ultramodern wings were added to house five museums, most of which showcase modern art at its best.

The Architekturzentrum, Kunsthalle, Leopold Museum, Museum Moderner Kunst Stiftung Ludwig, and the ZOOM Kinder Museum are all part of the MuseumsQuartier complex. In addition, the Quartier21 showcases up-and-coming artists and musicians in the huge Fischer von Erlach wing facing the Museumsplatz. Lovers of modern art will find it easy to spend at least an entire day at MuseumsQuartier, and with several cafés, restaurants, gift shops, and bookstores, won't even need to venture outside. ⊠ *Museumsplatz 1, 7th District/Neubau* ☎ *01/523–5881* ⊕ *www.mqw.at* ✉ *Combination tickets range from €17 to €25* ⊙ *Daily 24 hrs* Ⓜ *U2/MuseumsQuartier; U2 or U3/Volkstheater.*

Leopold Museum. Filled with the pieces amassed by Rudolf and Elizabeth Leopold, this square, white museum contains one of the world's greatest collections of Austrian painter Egon Schiele, as well as impressive works by Gustav Klimt and Oskar Kokoschka. Other artists worth noting are Josef Dobrowsky, Anton Faistauer, and Richard Gerstl. Center stage is held by Schiele (1890–1918), who died young, along with his wife and young baby, in the Spanish flu pandemic of 1918. His colorful, appealing landscapes are here, but all eyes are invariably drawn to the artist's tortured depictions of nude mistresses, orgiastic self-portraits, and provocatively sexual couples, all elbows and organs. ⊠ *Museums-Quartier, Museumsplatz 1, 7th District/Neubau* ☎ *01/525–700* ⊕ *www.leopoldmuseum.org* ✉ *€11* ⊙ *June–Aug., Fri.–Wed. 10–6, Thurs. 10–9; Sept.–May, Wed. and Fri.–Mon. 10–6, Thurs. 10–9* Ⓜ *U2 Museums-Quartier; U2 or U3/Volkstheater.*

Museum Moderner Kunst Stiftung Ludwig (*Museum of Modern Art Ludwig Foundation*). In a sleek edifice constructed of dark stone, this museum—known to locals by the slightly odd acronym MUMOK—houses the national collection of 20th-century art. Spread over eight floors, the collection is largely a bequest of Peter Ludwig, a billionaire industrialist who collected modern art that was the cream of the crop. The top works here are of the American pop-art school, but all the trends of the last century, from Nouveau Réalisme to Viennese Actionism, vie for your attention. Names include René Magritte, Max Ernst, Andy Warhol, Jackson Pollock, Cy Twombly, and Nam June Paik, to name a few. Kids will make a beeline for Claes Oldenburg's walk-in sculpture in the shape of Mickey Mouse. ⊠ *MuseumsQuartier, Museumsplatz 1, 7th District/Neubau* ☎ *01/525–000* ⊕ *www.mumok.at* ✉ *€9* ⊙ *Tues., Wed., and Fri.–Sun. 10–7, Mon. 2–7, Thurs. 10–9* Ⓜ *U2/MuseumsQuartier; U2 or U3/Volkstheater.*

Kunsthalle Wien (*Vienna Art Gallery*). The gigantic rooms here are used for temporary exhibitions of avant-garde art, including photography, video, film, and new-media projects. The museum prides itself on finding artists who break down the borders between the genres. ⊠ *Museums Quartier, Museumsplatz 1, 7th District/Neubau* ☎ *01/521–8933* ⊕ *www.kunsthallewien.at* 🎫 *€8.50* ☉ *Fri.–Wed. 10–7, Thurs. 10–10* Ⓜ *U2 MuseumsQuartier; U2 or U3/Volkstheater.*

Architekturzentrum Wien (*Vienna Architecture Center*). Besides the permanent show of Austrian architecture in the 20th and 21st centuries, the center holds major exhibitions presenting the breadth of architecture history and visions of what is to come. ⊠ *MuseumsQuartier, Museumsplatz 1, 7th District/Neubau* ☎ *01/522–3115* ⊕ *www.azw.at* 🎫 *€7* ☉ *Daily 10–7* Ⓜ *U2/MuseumsQuartier; U2 or U3/Volkstheater.*

ZOOM Kinder Museum. Kids of all ages can enjoy various areas of this museum. In the lab, they can experience the fine line between the real and virtual worlds, making screenplays come to life by becoming directors, sound technicians, authors, and actors. For the little ones there's an "ocean" where kids and parents enter a play area inhabited by magical underwater creatures. You must reserve at least one hour ahead. ⊠ *MuseumsQuartier, Museumsplatz 1, 7th District/Neubau* ☎ *01/524–7908* ⊕ *www.kindermuseum.at* 🎫 *€5* ☉ *By reservation only* Ⓜ *U2/MuseumsQuartier; U2 or U3/Volkstheater.*

Naschmarkt. The area between Linke and Rechte Wienzeile is home to the Naschmarkt, Vienna's largest and most famous outdoor produce market. It's certainly one of Europe's—if not the world's—great open-air markets, where packed rows of polished and stacked fruits and vegetables compete for visual appeal with braces of fresh pheasant in season. Also here are fragrant spices, redolent of Asia or the Middle East. In winter, many stalls shorten their hours. On Saturdays, a lively flea market takes place at the tail end of the market. Be sure you get the correct change and watch the scales when your goods are weighed. ⊠ *Between Linke and Rechte Wienzeile, 4th District/Wieden* ⊕ *www. wienernaschmarkt.eu* ☉ *Mon.–Sat. 7–6:30* Ⓜ *U1, U2, or U4/Karlsplatz (follow signs to Secession).*

FAMILY   **Naturhistorisches Museum** (*Natural History Museum*). The palatial 19th-century museum, twin of the celebrated Kunsthistorisches Museum, is the home of, among other artifacts, the *Venus of Willendorf,* a tiny statuette (actually, a replica—the original is in a vault) thought to be some 20,000 years old. This symbol of the Stone Age was originally unearthed in the Wachau Valley, not far from Melk. The reconstructed dinosaur skeletons draw the most attention, especially among kids. Tours are Friday at 4 and Saturday at 3. ⊠ *Maria-Theresien-Platz, 1st District* ☎ *01/52177* ⊕ *www.nhm-wien.ac.at* 🎫 *€10* ☉ *Wed. 9–9, Thurs.–Mon. 9–6:30* Ⓜ *U2 or U3/Volkstheater.*

▌ NEED A
BREAK?

There are so many enticing snack stands in the Naschmarkt that it's hard to choose. A host of Turkish stands offer juicy *Döner* sandwiches—thinly sliced, pressed lamb, turkey, or veal with onions and a yogurt sauce in a freshly baked roll. A number of Asian noodle and sushi stalls offer quick meals, and many snack bars offer Viennese dishes. At the Karlsplatz end of the Naschmarkt is the Nordsee glass-enclosed seafood hut.

CLOSE UP

The Neue City

Early one day in 1911, Emperor Franz Josef started out on a morning drive from the Hofburg, when he was stunned to come upon the defiantly plain Looshaus, constructed just opposite the Michaelerplatz entrance to the imperial palace. Never again, it was said, did the royal carriage use the route, so offensive was this modernist building to His Imperial Highness. One can only imagine the emperor's reaction to the Haas-Haus, built in 1985 on Stephansplatz. Here, across from the Gothic cathedral of St. Stephen's, famed architect Hans Hollein designed a complex whose elegant curved surfaces and reflecting glass interact beautifully with its environment. The architecture proved an intelligent alternative to the demands of historicism on the one hand and aggressive modernism on the other.

This balancing act has always been a particular challenge in Vienna. For a few critics, the Gaudíesque eccentricities of the late Friedensreich Hundertwasser did the trick (besides the Kunsthaus museum he is also responsible for the multicolor, golden-globe-top central heating tower that has become almost as much a part of the skyline as St. Stephen's spire). But for all their charm, they have now been overshadowed by the Viennese modernism of today. By far the most exciting urban undertaking has to be the Spittelau Viaducts, just across from the Hundertwasser power plant. This revitalization plan for the Wiener Gürtel, perhaps Vienna's busiest thoroughfare, includes public-housing apartments, offices, and artists' studios that interact with the arched bays of the viaduct, a landmarked structure

built by Otto Wagner. Responsible for the staggering three-part complex, partly perched on stilts, is star architect Zaha Hadid. A pedestrian and bicycle bridge connects the whole project to the University of Business, the North Railway Station, and the Danube Canal.

A discreet example of Vienna's new architecture is the vast Museums-Quartier. Hidden behind the Baroque facade of the former imperial stables, the design by Laurids and Manfred Ortner uses its enclosed space to set up a counterpoint between Fischer von Erlach's riding school and the imposing new structures built to house the Leopold Museum and the Modern Art Museum. From the first, old and new collide: to enter the complex's Halle E + G, you pass below the Emperor's Loge, whose double-headed imperial eagles now form a striking contrast to a silver-hue steel double staircase. Other important projects—notably the underground Jewish history museum on Judenplatz (look for a stark cube memorial by English sculptor Rachel Whiteread); the Gasometer complex, a planned community recycled from the immense brick drums of 19th-century gasworks; the ellipse-shape Uniqa Tower on the Danube Canal designed by Heinz Neumann, and the ecologically responsible Donau City—are among the architectural highlights on tours now organized by the Architecture Center (AZW) of the MuseumsQuartier; its maps and brochures can be used for self-guided tours.

—Gary Dodson

Otto Wagner Houses. The apartment houses that line the Wienzeile are an attractive, if rather ordinary, lot, but two stand out: **Linke Wienzeile 38 and 40**—the latter better known as the "Majolica House"—designed (1898–99) by the grand old man of Viennese fin-de-siècle architecture, Otto Wagner. A good example of what Wagner was rebelling against can be seen next door, at **Linke Wienzeile 42,** where decorative enthusiasm has blossomed into baroque-revival hysteria. Wagner banished classical decoration and introduced a new architectural simplicity, with flat exterior walls and plain, regular window treatments meant to reflect the orderly layout of the apartments behind them. There the simplicity ended. For exterior decoration, he turned to his younger Secessionist cohorts Joseph Olbrich and Koloman Moser, who designed the ornate Jugendstil patterns of red-majolica-tile roses (No. 40) and gold stucco medallions (No. 38) that gloriously brighten the facades of the adjacent house—so much so that their baroque-period neighbor is ignored. The houses are privately owned. ⊠ *Linke Wienzeile, 6th District* Ⓜ *U1, U2, or U4/Karlsplatz.*

Secession Building. If the Academy of Fine Arts represents the conservative attitude toward the arts in the late 1800s, then its antithesis can be found in the building immediately behind it to the southeast: the Secession Pavilion, one of Vienna's preeminent symbols of artistic rebellion. Rather than looking to the architecture of the past, like the revivalist Ringstrasse, it looked to a new antihistoricist future. It was, in its day, a riveting trumpet-blast of a building, and is today considered by many to be Europe's first example of full-blown 20th-century architecture.

The Secession began in 1897, when 20 dissatisfied Viennese artists, headed by Gustav Klimt, "seceded" from the Künstlerhausgenossenschaft, the conservative artists' society associated with the Academy of Fine Arts. The movement promoted the radically new kind of art known as Jugendstil, which found its inspiration in both the organic, fluid designs of Art Nouveau and the related but more geometric designs of the English Arts and Crafts movement. The Secession building, designed by the architect Joseph Olbrich and completed in 1898, was the movement's exhibition hall. The lower story, crowned by the entrance motto *Der Zeit Ihre Kunst, Der Kunst Ihre Freiheit* ("To Every Age Its Art, To Art Its Freedom"), is classic Jugendstil: the restrained but assured decoration (by Koloman Moser) complements the facade's pristine flat expanses of cream-color wall. Above the entrance motto sits the building's most famous feature, the gilded openwork dome that the Viennese were quick to christen "the golden cabbage" (Olbrich wanted it to be seen as a dome of laurel, a subtle classical reference meant to celebrate the triumph of art). The plain white interior—"shining and chaste," in Olbrich's words—was also revolutionary; its most unusual feature was movable walls, allowing the galleries to be reshaped and redesigned for every show. One early show, in 1902, was a temporary exhibition devoted to art celebrating the genius of Beethoven; Klimt's *Beethoven Frieze* was painted for the occasion, and the fragments that survived can be admired in the basement. Guided tours are given weekends at 11. ⊠ *Friedrichstrasse 12, 1st District* ☎ *01/587–53–070* ⊕ *www.secession.at* ⊡ *€5, €8.50 including the Beethoven Frieze* ⊙ *Tues.–Sun. 10–6* Ⓜ *U4/Karlsplatz.*

WORTH NOTING

Akademie der Bildenen Künste (*Academy of Fine Arts*). If the teachers here had admitted Adolf Hitler as an art student in 1907 and 1908 instead of rejecting him, history might have proved very different. The Academy was founded in 1692, but the present Renaissance Revival building dates from the late 19th century. The idea was conservatism and traditional values, even in the face of a growing movement that scorned formal rules. The Academy includes a museum focusing on Old Masters. The collection is mainly of interest to specialists, but Hieronymus Bosch's *Last Judgment* triptych hangs here—an imaginative, if gruesome, speculation on the hereafter. ⊠ *Schillerplatz 3, 1st District* ☎ *01/588–16–2222* ⊕ *www.akademiegalerie.at* 🎫 *€8* ⊙ *Tues.–Sun. 10–6* Ⓜ *U1, U2, or U4 Karlsplatz.*

Dritte Mann Museum (*Third Man Museum*). Close to the Naschmarkt, this shrine for film-noir aficionados offers an extensive private collection of memorabilia dedicated to the classic film, *The Third Man,* directed by Carol Reed and shot entirely on location in Vienna. Authentic exhibits include cinema programs, autographed cards, movie and sound recordings, and first editions of Graham Greene's novel, which was the basis of the screenplay. Also here is the original zither used by Anton Karas to record the film's music, which started a zither boom in the '50s. In the reading corner, you can browse through historic newspaper articles about the film. ■ **TIP➔ A visit is a good complement to the walking tour.** ⊠ *Pressgasse 25, 4th District* ☎ *01/586–4872* ⊕ *www.3mpc.net* 🎫 *€7.50* ⊙ *Sat. 2–6* Ⓜ *U4/Kettenbrückengasse.*

Joseph Haydn House. In commemoration of the 200th anniversary of Joseph Haydn's death, his last residence has been completely redone and now holds an exhibition worthy of the great master. There is also a Brahms memorial room. ⊠ *Haydngasse 19, 6th District/Mariahilf* ☎ *01/596–1307* 🎫 *€4* ⊙ *Tues.–Sun. 10–1 and 2–6* Ⓜ *U4/Pilgramgasse or U3/Zieglergasse.*

OFF THE BEATEN PATH

Hofmobiliendepot (Furniture Museum). In the days of the Habsburg Empire, palaces remained practically empty if the ruling family was not in residence. Cavalcades laden with enough furniture to fill a palace would set out in anticipation of a change of scene, while another caravan accompanied the royal party, carrying everything from traveling thrones to velvet-lined portable toilets. Much of this furniture is on display here, allowing a glimpse into everyday court life. The upper floors contain re-created rooms from the Biedermeier to the Jugendstil periods, and document the tradition of furniture making in Vienna. Explanations are in German and English. ⊠ *Mariahilferstrasse 88, entrance on Andreasgasse, 7th District/Neubau* ☎ *01/524–3357* 🎫 *€7.90* ⊙ *Tues.– Sun. 10–6* Ⓜ *U3 Zieglergasse/follow signs to Otto-Bauer-Gasse/exit Andreasgasse.*

Spittelberg Quarter. The Spittelberg is like a slice of Old Vienna, a perfectly preserved little enclave that allows you to experience the 18th century by strolling along cobblestone pedestrian streets lined with pretty baroque town houses. The quarter—one block northwest of Maria-Theresien-Platz off the Burggasse—offers a fair visual idea of the Vienna that existed outside the city walls a century ago. Most buildings have been replaced, but the engaging 18th-century survivors at Burggasse 11 and 13 are adorned with religious and secular decorative sculpture, the latter with a niche statue of St. Joseph, the former with cherubic work-and-play bas-reliefs. Around holidays, particularly Easter and Christmas, the Spittelberg quarter, known for arts and handicrafts, hosts seasonal markets offering unique and interesting wares. Promenaders will also find art galleries and lots of restaurants. ⊠ *Off Burggasse, 7th District/Spittelberg* Ⓜ *U2 or U3/Volkstheater.*

WEST OF THE RINGSTRASSE: PARLAMENT AND CITY HALL

From her pedestal in front of Austria's National Parliament, Athena, the gold-helmeted Greek goddess of wisdom, looks sternly over the Ringstrasse. Locals hope that her good judgment rubs off on the legislators inside the templelike building. Nearby is the Rathaus, or City Hall, a negolithic masterpiece that's one of the city's most photographed buildings. During the summer months, the surrounding park is the setting for an international food and film festival; in winter there's a delightful Christmas market. The mood is a little more somber at the Votivkirche, an imposing cathedral that the royal family built after a thwarted assassination attempt on Emperor Franz Josef. Travel up Währingerstrasse and Liechtensteinstrasse to visit Sigmund Freud's apartment and the city's new-old dazzler, the Liechtenstein Museum, with its fabled collection of paintings by Peter Paul Rubens.

TOP ATTRACTIONS

Freud Haus. Not far from the historic Hofburg district, the marvels and pains of the 20th century come into focus at the Freud House museum. Sigmund Freud's residence from 1891 to 1938, this apartment has five rooms of memorabilia. It's mostly a photographic record of Freud's life, with some documents, publications, and a portion of his collection of antiquities also on display. The waiting-room furniture is authentic, but the consulting room and study furniture (including the famous couch) can be seen only in photographs. Chilling is the collection of telegrams (photocopies of the originals) from the State Department, which chronicle frantic efforts to help the Freud family escape Austria after the Nazi Anschluss in 1938. The apartment is one flight up, which is well marked with signs. ⊠ *Berggasse 19, Apt. 6, 9th District/Alsergrund* ☎ *01/319–1596* ⊕ *www.freud-museum.at* ☙ €7 ☉ *Jan.–June and Oct.–Dec., daily 9–5; July–Sept., daily 9–6* Ⓜ *U2/Schottentor.*

OFF THE BEATEN PATH

Kirche Am Steinhof. Otto Wagner's most exalted piece of Jugendstil architecture lies in the suburbs—the church on the grounds of the Vienna City Psychiatric Hospital. Wagner's design here unites functional details (rounded edges on the pews to prevent injury to the patients) with a soaring, airy dome, with stained glass by Koloman Moser. Guide tours in English are available by appointment. ⊠ *Baumgartner Höhe 1, 13th District/Hütteldorf* ☎ *01/91060* ☙ €6 for guided tour ☉ *Sat. 3–5* Ⓜ *U4/ Unter-St.-Veit; then Bus 47A to Psychiatrisches Krankenhaus. U2/Volkstheater; then Bus 48A.*

Parlament. Reminiscent of an ancient Greek temple, this sprawling building is the seat of the country's elected representative assembly. An embracing, heroic ramp on either side of the main structure is lined with carved marble figures of ancient Greek and Roman historians. Its centerpiece is the Pallas-Athene-Brunnen, a fountain designed by Theophil Hansen that is crowned by the Greek goddess of wisdom and surrounded by water nymphs symbolizing the executive and legislative powers governing the country. Call ahead, because tours are not given when the legislature is in session. ✉ *Dr. Karl Renner-Ring 3, 1st District* ☎ *01/401–1024–00* ⊕ *www.parlament.gv.at* ✆€5 ⊗ *Tours mid-Sept.–mid-July, Mon.–Thurs. at 11, 2, 3, and 4, Fri. at 11, 1, 2, 3, and 4, and Sat. 11–4 on the hour; mid-July–mid-Sept., Mon.–Sat. 11–4 on the hour* Ⓜ *Trams 1, 2, or D/Stadiongasse, Parlament.*

Rathaus (*City Hall*). Designed by Friedrich Schmidt and resembling a Gothic fantasy castle with its many spires and turrets, the Rathaus was built between 1872 and 1883. The facade holds a lavish display of standard-bearers brandishing the coats of arms of the city of Vienna and the monarchy. Guided tours include the banqueting hall and various committee rooms. A regally landscaped park graces the front of the building, and is usually brimming with activity. In winter it's the scene of the most famous Christmas market in Vienna, and after the New Year, it is transformed into a gigantic ice skating rink. In summer, folks can enjoy good food and piped music nightly. The building is open by guided tour only. ✉ *Rathausplatz 1, 1st District* ☎ *01/52550* ✆ *Free* ⊗ *Guided tours Mon., Wed., and Fri. at 1* Ⓜ *Trams 1, 2, or D/Rathaus.*

WORTH NOTING

Schubert's Birthplace. Unlike most of Vienna's composers, Schubert was a native of Vienna. You can visit this modest two-floor house where he was born. ✉ *Nussdorferstrasse 54, 9th District/Alsergrund* ☎ *01/317–3601* ⊕ *www.wienmuseum.at* ✆€4 ⊗ *Tues.–Sun. 10–1 and 2–6* Ⓜ *Streetcar 37 or 38 to Canisiusgasse.*

Universität (*University of Vienna*). The oldest university in the German-speaking world (founded in 1365), the main section of the university is a massive block in Italian Renaissance style designed by Heinrich Ferstel and built between 1873 and 1884. Statues representing 38 important men of letters decorate the front of the building, while the rear, which encompasses the library (with nearly 2 million volumes), is adorned with sgraffito. English-language guided tours costing €5 are given on Thursday and Saturday at 11:30 am (reservations not required). Audio guides are available for €3 (ID required). ✉ *Dr. Karl Lueger-Ring 1, 1st District* ☎ *01/4277–17676, 01/4277–176–01 guided tours* ⊕ *www.univie.ac.at* Ⓜ *U2/Schottentor.*

Votivkirche (*Votive Church*). When Emperor Franz Josef was a young man, he was strolling along the Mölker Bastei, one of the few remaining portions of the old city wall, when he was taken unawares and stabbed in the neck by a Hungarian revolutionary. He survived, and in gratitude his family ordered that a church be built exactly at the spot he was gazing at when he was struck down. The neo-Gothic church was built of gray limestone with two openwork turrets between 1856 and 1879. ✉ *Rooseveltplatz, 9th District/Alsergrund* ☎ *01/406–1192* ⊙ *Tues.–Sat. 9–1 and 4–6, Sun. 9–1* Ⓜ *U2/Schottentor.*

SCHÖNBRUNN PALACE, PARK, AND THE ZOO

The glories of imperial Austria are nowhere brought together more convincingly than in the Schönbrunn Palace (Schloss Schönbrunn) complex. Imperial elegance, interrupted only by tourist traffic, flows unbroken throughout the grounds. This is Vienna's primary tourist site, although few stay long enough to discover the real Schönbrunn (including the fountain with the little maiden carrying the water jar, after whom the complex is named). The outbuildings served as entertainment centers when the court moved to Schönbrunn in summer, accounting for the zoo, the theater, the fake Roman ruins, the greenhouses, and the walkways. In Schönbrunn you step back three centuries into the heart of a powerful and growing empire and follow it through to defeat and demise in 1918.

TOP ATTRACTIONS

Gloriette. At the crest of the hill, topping off the Schönbrunn Schlosspark, sits a baroque masterstroke: Johann Ferdinand von Hohenberg's Gloriette, now restored to its original splendor. Perfectly scaled, the Gloriette—a palatial pavilion that once offered royal guests a place to rest and relax on their tours of the palace grounds and that now houses a welcome café—holds the vast garden composition together and at the same time crowns the ensemble with a brilliant architectural tiara. This was a favorite spot of Maria Theresa's, though in later years she grew so obese—not surprising, given that she bore 16 children in 20 years—it took six men to carry her in her palanquin to the summit. ✉ *Schönbrunn Palace, Schönbrunner-Schloss-Strasse, 13th District/ Hietzing* ⊕ *www.schoenbrunn.at* Ⓜ *U4/Schönbrunn.*

Hofpavillon. The restored imperial subway station known as the Hofpavillon is just outside the palace grounds (at the northwest corner, a few yards east of the Hietzing subway station). Designed by Otto Wagner in conjunction with Joseph Olbrich and Leopold Bauer, the Hofpavillon was built in 1899 for the exclusive use of Emperor Franz Josef and his entourage. Exclusive it was: the emperor used the station only once. The exterior, with its proud architectural crown, is Wagner at his best, and the lustrous interior is one of the finest examples of Jugendstil decoration in the city. ✉ *Schönbrunner-Schloss-Strasse, 13th District/Hietzing* ☎ *01/877–1571* 🎫 *€4* ⊙ *Weekends 10–6* Ⓜ *U4/Hietzing.*

Palmenhaus. On the grounds of Schönbrunn Palace is this huge greenhouse filled with exotic trees and plants. ✉ *Schönbrunn Palace, Schönbrunner-Schloss-Strasse, 13th District/Hietzing* ☎ *01/877–5087* ⊕ *www. schoenbrunn.at* 🎫 *€4; €14 for combination ticket with Tiergarten* ⊙ *May–Sept., daily 9:30–6; Oct.–Apr., daily 9:30–5* Ⓜ *U4/Schönbrunn.*

Fodor's Choice ★ **Schönbrunn Palace.** Originally designed by Johann Bernhard Fischer von Erlach in 1696 and altered considerably for Maria Theresa 40 years later, Schönbrunn Palace, the huge Habsburg summer residence, lies within the city limits, just a few metro stops west of Karlsplatz on

A Hop Through Hip Vienna

Paris has the Latin Quarter, London has Notting Hill, and the bohemian district in Vienna is the **Freihaus** sector in the 4th District (Wieden), Vienna's trendiest neighborhood.

In the 17th century, Freihaus provided free housing to the city's poor, hence the name "Freihaus," which means Free House. The complex was destroyed in the Turkish siege of 1683, then rebuilt on a much larger scale, becoming arguably the largest housing project in Europe at the time. It was a city within a city, including shops and the old Theater auf der Wieden, in which Mozart's *The Magic Flute* premiered. A slow decline followed, spanning Franz Josef's reign from the mid-19th century to the early 20th century, with some of the area razed to the ground before World War I. During World War II, bombing raids practically finished it off.

But in the late 1990s a group of savvy local merchants revitalized the area, opening funky art galleries, antiques shops, espresso bars, trendy restaurants, and fashion boutiques. Freihaus is small, stretching from Karlsplatz to Ketten-brückengasse, which encompasses part of the Naschmarkt, the city's largest open-air market. Two of the best streets are Operngasse and Schleifmühlgasse.

What do you do with four immense gasometers more than 100 years old? Turn them into a cool, urban complex combining living and shopping, naturally. Looming large on the Vienna horizon, the **Gasometers** (⊕ *www.gasometer.org*) have generated a lot of publicity. Just to give an idea of their size, Vienna's giant Ferris wheel (the Riesenrad) at the Prater Amusement Park would fit easily inside each one. Top architects were hired to accomplish the sleek and modern interior renovations, creating more than 600 modern apartments and a huge shopping mall with movie theaters and restaurants. It's in Simmering, Vienna's 11th District, and is eight minutes from the heart of the city on the U3 subway.

A visit to Vienna during the summer months would not be complete without a few hours spent on the Donauinsel (Danube Island), more popularly known as the **Copa Kagrana.** ("Kagrana" is taken from the name of the nearby local area known as Kagran.) It was originally built as a safeguard against flooding, but now this 13-square-mile island is where the Viennese head for bicycling, skateboarding, jogging, swimming, or just a leisurely stroll and dinner by the water. There are dozens of stalls and restaurants, offering grilled steaks, fried chicken, or freshly caught fish to go along with a mug of ice-cold draft beer or Austrian wine. Every year, 2 million visitors converge on the island for three days in June for an admission-free summer festival, the Donauinselfest (⊕ *www.donauinselfest.at*). The Copa Kagrana can be reached by subway: either the U1 to Donauinsel or the U6 to Handelskai.

2

Gloriette **7**
Hofpavillon **1**
Palmenhaus **4**
Schönbrunn
Schlosspark **3**
Tiergarten **5**
Tyroler
House **6**
Wagenburg **2**

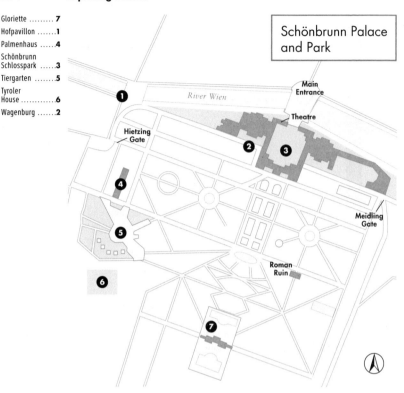

Schönbrunn Palace and Park

the U4. Bus trips to Schönbrunn offered by the city's tour operators cost several times what you'd pay if you traveled by subway; the one advantage is that they get you there with a bit less effort. Travel independently if you want time to wander through the grounds, which are open dawn to dusk.

The most impressive approach to the palace and its gardens is through the front gate, set on Schönbrunner Schloss-Strasse halfway between the Schönbrunn and Hietzing metro stations. The vast main courtyard is ruled by a formal design of impeccable order and rigorous symmetry: wing nods at wing, facade mirrors facade, and every part stylistically complements every other. The courtyard, however, turns out to be a mere appetizer; the feast lies beyond. The breathtaking view that unfolds on the other side of the palace is one of the finest set pieces in all Europe and one of the supreme achievements of baroque planning. Formal *Allées* (promenades) shoot off diagonally, the one on the right toward the zoo, the one on the left toward a rock-mounted obelisk and a fine false Roman ruin. But these, and the woods beyond, are merely a frame for the composition in the center: the sculpted marble fountain; the carefully planted screen of trees behind; the sudden, almost vertical rise of the grass-covered hill beyond, with the **Gloriette** a fitting crown.

Within the palace, the state salons are quite up to the splendor of the gardens, but note the contrast between these chambers and the far more modest rooms in which the rulers—particularly Franz Josef—lived and spent most of their time. Of the 1,441 rooms, 40 are open to the public on the regular tour, of which two are of special note: the Hall of Mirrors, where the six-year-old Mozart performed for Empress Maria Theresa in 1762 (and where he met seven-year-old Marie Antoinette, developing a little crush on her), and the Grand Gallery, where the Congress of Vienna (1815) danced at night after carving up Napoléon's collapsed empire during the day. Ask about viewing the ground-floor living quarters (Berglzimmer), where the walls are painted with palm trees, exotic animals, and tropical views.

As you go through the palace, glance occasionally out the windows; you'll be rewarded by a better impression of the formal gardens, punctuated by hedgerows and fountains. These window vistas were enjoyed by rulers from Maria Theresa and Napoléon to Franz Josef. ⊠ *Schönbrunner-Schloss-Strasse, 13th District/Hietzing* ☎ *01/811–13–239* ⊕ *www. schoenbrunn.at* 🖭 *€13.50, €15.50 for guided tour* ☉ *Apr.–June, Sept., and Oct., daily 8:30–5; July and Aug., daily 8:30–6; Nov.–Mar., daily 8:30–4:30* Ⓜ *U4/Schönbrunn.*

Schönbrunn Schlosspark (*Palace Park*). The palace grounds entice with a bevy of splendid divertissements, including a grand zoo (the Tiergarten) and a carriage museum (the Wagenburg). Climb to the Gloriette for a panoramic view out over the city as well as of the palace complex. If you're exploring on your own, seek out the intriguing Roman ruin. The marble *schöner Brunnen* ("beautiful fountain") gave its name to the palace complex. Then head over the other side of the gardens to the playground and the newly grown maze. ⊠ *Schönbrunner-Schloss-Strasse, 13th District/Hietzing* ⊕ *www.schoenbrunn.at* ☉ *Apr.–Oct., daily 6–dusk; Nov.–Mar., daily 6:30–dusk* Ⓜ *U4/Schönbrunn.*

OFF THE BEATEN PATH

Technisches Museum. About a 10-minute walk from Schönbrunn Palace is the Technical Museum, which traces the evolution of industrial development over the past two centuries. On four floors you'll find actual locomotives from the 19th century, a Tin Lizzie, airplanes from the early days of flying, as well as examples of factory life, how electric lighting took the place of gas lamps, and how mountain highway tunnels are constructed. ⊠ *Mariahilferstrasse 212, 14th District/Penzing* ☎ *01/899–98–0* ⊕ *www.tmw.at* 🖭 *€8.50* ☉ *Weekdays 9–6, weekends 10–6* Ⓜ *U3 or U6/Westbahnhof, then Tram 52 or 58/ Penzingerstrasse.*

FAMILY **Tiergarten.** Claimed to be the world's oldest, this zoo has retained its original baroque design, but new settings have been created for both the animals and the public. In one case, you gaze out over a natural habitat from inside one of the former animal houses. The zoo is constantly adding new attractions and undergoing renovations, so there's plenty to see. A 25-year-old John Irving, living in Vienna at the time, used the Tiergarten as the setting for his first novel, "Setting Free the Bears." ⊠ *Schönbrunner Schlosspark, Schönbrunner-Schloss-Strasse, 13th District/Hietzing* ☎ *01/877–92–940* ⊕ *www.zoovienna.at* 🖭 *€14;*

combination ticket with Palmenhaus €18 ⊙ *Nov.–Jan., daily 9–4:30; Feb., daily 9–5; Mar. and Oct., daily 9–5:30; Apr.–Sept., daily 9–6:30* Ⓜ *U4/Schönbrunn.*

Tyroler House. This Tyrolean-style building to the west of the Gloriette was a favorite retreat of Empress Elisabeth; it now includes a restaurant. ⊠ *Schönbrunner Schlosspark, Schönbrunner-Schloss-Strasse, 13th District/Hietzing* Ⓜ *U4/Schönbrunn.*

Wagenburg (*Carriage Museum*). Most of the carriages are still roadworthy, and in fact Schönbrunn dusted off the black royal funeral carriage for the burial ceremony of Empress Zita in 1989. Today a special Sisi trail leads through the museum; on show are some of her famous gowns, carriages, personal objects and paintings, highlighting the empress's life from marriage to tragic death. ⊠ *Schönbrunner Schlosspark, Schönbrunner-Schloss-Strasse, 13th District/Hietzing* ☎ *01/877–3244* ⊕ *www.khm.at* ⊠ *€6* ⊙ *May–Oct., daily 9–6; Nov.– Apr., daily 10–4* Ⓜ *U4/Schönbrunn.*

WHERE TO EAT

Updated
by Patti
McCracken

Vienna has tried hard to shed its image of a town locked in the 19th century, and nowhere is that more evident than in the kitchens of the top-notch Austrian chefs who dominate the culinary scene here. They have turned dining from a mittel-*europäisch* sloshfest of *Schweinsbraten*, *Knödeln*, and *Kraut* (pork, dumplings, and cabbage), into an exquisite feast of international flavors.

No one denies that such courtly delights as *Tafelspitz*—the blush-pink boiled beef famed as Emperor Franz Josef's favorite dish—is delicious, but these traditional carb-loaded meals tend to leave you stuck to your seat like a suction cup.

The dining scene of today's Vienna has transformed itself, thanks in part to a new generation of chefs, such as Heinz Reitbauer Jr. and Christian Petz, who've worked hard to establish an international brand of Viennese cooking, *Neue Wiener Küche* (New Vienna cuisine). They have stepped onto the stage, front and center, to create signature dishes, such as fish soup with red curry, which have rocketed to fame; they have fan clubs, host television shows and publish top-selling cookbooks, such as *Neue Cuisine: The Elegant Tastes of Vienna;* there are star Austrian chefs the way there are in New York and Hollywood, and these chefs want to delight an audience hungry for change.

Schmaltzy schnitzels have been replaced by prized Styrian beef—organic meat from farm-raised cattle—while soggy *Nockerl* (small dumplings) are traded in for seasonal delights like Carinthian asparagus, Styrian wild garlic, or the zingy taste of common garden stinging nettle. Wisely, Vienna has also warmly welcomed into its kitchens chefs from around the world, who give exotic twists to old favorites.

DINING PLANNER

Where should you eat? With hundreds of restaurants to choose from, it may seem like a daunting question. But fret not—our expert writers and editors have done most of the legwork. The selections here represent the best the city has to offer. Scan "Best Bets" on the following pages for top recommendations by price and experience. Or find a review quickly in the listings. Search by neighborhood, then alphabetically.

CUSTOMS
In Vienna, the basket of bread put on your table is not free. Most of the older-style Viennese restaurants charge €0.70–€1.70 for each roll that is eaten.

DISCOUNTS
In Vienna, dining out doesn't always have to break the bank. For lunch, look for cafés and bistros offering a *Mittagsmenü*, or a set lunch menu. Two courses will usually cost less than €12. The bakery

chains Anker, Mann, Ströck, and Felber are found everywhere in the city. Grab a pastry filled with jam or *Topfen* (a rich ricotta cheese) to tide you over until dinner.

In late February and early March, a few dozen restaurants offer reduced-price lunches and dinners during Restaurantwoche (Restaurant Week). For more details, see ⊕ *www.restaurantwoche.at*.

DRESS

The Viennese are keenly aware of how people are dressed. As a general rule, people try to look their best in public. Showing up at a restaurant wearing jogging pants, T-shirts, or other extremely casual clothing is a definite no-no. That said, jeans and a nice shirt will be fine at most places. A jacket and tie for men would be necessary in only the most formal establishments.

FOOD FESTIVALS

Taking place over a weekend in May, the **Genuss Festival** (Gourmet Festival) is held in the Stadtpark on the Ringstrasse. The event aims at preserving Austria's rich and varied culinary traditions by highlighting delicacies from different regions. Food producers from all over the country present their creations, from poppy-seed oil to ox sausage. For more, see ⊕ *www.kulinarisches-erbe.at*.

In April, the province of Styria, known for its dishes involving pumpkinseed oil, showcases its culinary skills in Rathausplatz during **Steiermarkdorf** (⊕ *www.steiermarkdorf.at*). At the end of August, Austria's northernmost region of Waldviertel draws many visitors to Heldenplatz for **Waldviertelpur** (⊕ *www.waldviertelpur.at*). Servers wearing traditional dirndls serve dumplings to the sounds of brass music.

MEALTIMES

Lunch typically starts at 11:30 or noon, and dinner service begins around 5:30 or 6. Many restaurants close between lunch and dinner (roughly 2:30 to 5:30). On weekdays, kitchens usually close around 11 pm.

RESERVATIONS

Reservations are always a good idea; we mention them only when they're essential or not accepted. Book as far ahead as you can. (Large parties should always call to check the reservations policy.)

SMOKING

Smoking is still allowed in the city's restaurants, but smokers are required to be in separate rooms. Smaller restaurants are not required to make special provisions for nonsmokers, so it's a good idea to check ahead.

TIPPING AND TAXES

In Austria, tipping is customary. In cafés, bistros, and other less expensive eateries, the Viennese usually round up to the nearest euro. If they are very happy with the service in a fancier restaurant, they will give the waiter anywhere from €1 to €3. They never tip 15% to 20% of the total bill, as is customary in the United States. Tipping so much can be insulting to the wait staff.

WHAT IT COSTS IN EUROS			
$	$$	$$$	$$$$
AT DINNER　under €18	€18–€23	€24–€31	over €31

Prices are per person for a main course at dinner or, if dinner is not served, at lunch.

RESTAURANT REVIEWS

Listed alphabetically within neighborhoods.

THE EASTERN CITY CENTER: STEPHANSDOM AND MEDIEVAL VIENNA

$　✕ **Café Frauenhuber.** Repair here to find some peace and quiet away
CAFÉ　from the busy shoppers on Kärntnerstrasse. The original turn-of-
the-20th-century interior, with its obligatory red velvet seating and
somewhat tired upholstery (if you don't suffer from back problems
you'll be fine), is a visual treat. Breakfast Frauenhuber style is a going-
for-broke affair and includes, among other variants, a pot of tea (or
a pot of coffee), a glass of prosecco, fresh-squeezed orange juice,
toast, and fresh salmon with a dash of horseradish. Although billed as
Vienna's oldest café (and Mozart's favorite), you'll find fewer tourists
here than in other typical cafés, and more of a local feel, which it's had
since it opened its doors in 1824. $ *Average main: €14* ✉ *Himmelp-
fortgasse 6, 1st District* ☎ *01/512–5323* ⊕ *www.cafe-frauenhuber.at*
Ⓜ *U1 or U3/Stephansplatz.*

$　✕ **Café Schwarzenberg.** A bright-yellow facade and a large terrace wel-
CAFÉ　come all to this café across from the Hotel Imperial. The location is
perfect if you want a snack after a concert at the Musikverein or the
Konzerthaus, both just a couple of minutes away. Wall-to-wall mirrors reflect the elegant clientele perched on dark-green leather seats.
Open until midnight, it has a good choice of food and pastries. Even
though the waiters can be a little condescending, the overall atmosphere is still nice enough to encourage longer stays. Piano music can
be heard until late on Wednesday and Friday and from 5 until 7 on
weekends. Sit outside when the weather allows and appreciate the
lights on Schwarzenbergplatz. $ *Average main: €15* ✉ *Kärntnerr-
ing 17, 1st District* ☎ *01/512–8998* ⊕ *www.cafe-schwarzenberg.at/
en* Ⓜ *U2/Schottentor.*

$　✕ **Figlmüller.** This Wiener schnitzel institution is known for breaded
AUSTRIAN　veal and pork cutlets so large they overflow the plate, and it's always
packed. The cutlet is so large because it's been hammered (you can
hear the mallets pounding from a block away). The schnitzel winds
up wafer-thin but delicious, because the quality, as well as the size,
is unrivaled (a quarter kilo for each). As the Viennese say, "Schnitzel
should swim," so don't forget the lemon juice. Their potato salad
is the best in town, and if you want to try the recipe at home, you
can even buy their cookbook. If this location is full, try the one just

BEST BETS FOR VIENNA DINING

Fodor's Choice ★	Konstantin-Filippou, p. 98	$$$$
DO & CO Albertina, $$, p. 102	Weibels Wirtshaus, p. 99	Restaurant Edvard, p. 110
Ice Dream Factory, $, p. 109		Steirereck, p. 108
Restaurant Edvard, $$$$, p. 110	$$	**By Cuisine**
Steirereck, $$$$, p. 108	Café Mozart, p. 101	
Zum Schwarzen Kameel, $$$, p. 103	Do-An, p. 109	AUSTRIAN
	DO & CO Albertina, p. 102	Figlmüller, $, p. 94
By Price	Mayer am Pfarrplatz, p. 110	Griechenbeisl, $, p. 95
	Vestibül, p. 107	Steirereck, $$$$, p. 108
		Weibels Wirtshaus, $, p. 99
$	$$$	
Café Central, p. 105	Fabios, p. 102	CONTEMPORARY
Figlmüller, p. 94	Julius Meinl am Graben, p. 103	Konstantin-Filippou, $, p. 98
Gmoa Keller, p. 107	Zum Schwarzen Kameel, p. 103	DO & CO Albertina, $$, p. 102
Griechenbeisl, p. 95		
Hansen, p. 106		

around the corner on Bäckerstrasse 6. $ *Average main: €14* ✉ *Wollzeile 5, 1st District* ☎ *01/512–6177* ⊕ *www.figlmueller.at* Ⓜ *U1 or U3/Stephansplatz.*

$ ✕ **Gasthaus zur Oper.** Vienna's famous Plachutta chain has added another
AUSTRIAN   restaurant to its stable of eateries. Located in a side street near Kärntnerstrasse, this restaurant focuses on traditional Austrian dishes (the "Best Schnitzel in Vienna"). Other favorites on the menu include pork roast with cabbage and dumplings covered in a light caraway sauce, and roasted veal liver with marjoram gravy over buttered rice. (The beef used here is obtained from small Austrian farms.) The decor is stark white, the interior long and narrow, the perfect contrasting canvas for the warm, comfort food it serves up. The proximity to the opera house, in case its name doesn't give it away, should be a clue that among the dinner guests will be many of the city's regular operagoers, sitting for a meal before the show. $ *Average main: €15* ✉ *Walfischgasse 5–7, 1st District* ☎ *01/512–2251* ⊕ *www.plachutta.at.*

$ ✕ **Griechenbeisl.** Mozart, Beethoven, and Schubert all dined here—so
AUSTRIAN   how can you resist? Neatly tucked away in a quiet and quaint area of the Old City, this ancient inn goes back half a millennium. You can hear its age in the creaking floorboards when you walk through some of the small, dark-wood panel rooms. Yes, it's touristy, yet the

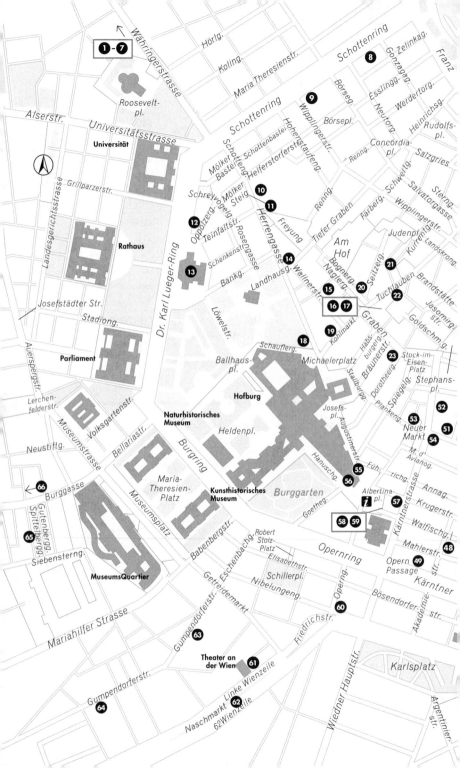

Where to Eat in Vienna

Amerlingbeisl	**65**
Anna Sacher	**58**
Augustinerkeller	**55**
Bizi Pizza	**24**
Café Central	**14**
Café Frauenhuber	**51**
Café Griensteidl	**18**
Café Hawelka	**23**
Café Landtmann	**12**
Café Mozart	**57**
Café Museum	**60**
Café Sacher	**59**
Café Schwarzenberg	**46**
Cafe Sperl	**63**
Cantino	**50**
Corns 'n Pops	**64**
Demel	**19**
DO & CO Albertina	**56**
Do-An	**62**
Esterházykeller	**15**
Fabios	**22**
Figlmüller	**37**
Gasthaus Wild	**38**
Gasthaus zur Oper	**48**
Gerstner	**52**
Gmoa Keller	**45**
Gösser Bierklinik	**21**
Griechenbeisl	**33**
Haas & Haas Colonial Teahouse	**47**
Hansen	**9**
Heiner	**36, 54**
Hofzeile 27	**6**
Ice Dream Factory	**66**
Joseph Genuss	**40**
Julius Meinl am Graben	**16**
Karlsplatz Mall	**49**
Kim Kocht	**7**
Konstantin Filippou	**34**
Le Loft	**31**
Mayer am Pfarrplatz	**5**
Meinl am Graben	**17**
Melker Stiftskeller	**11**
Motto am Fluss	**30**
Oberlaa	**53**
Osterreicher im MAK	**42**
Radatz	**10**
Restaurant Edvard	**8**
Schöne Perle	**28**
Skopik & Lohn	**29**
Steirereck	**43**
Ströck	**41**
The Dining Room	**44**
Theatercafe Wien	**61**
Urania	**32**
Vestibül	**13**
Walter Bauer	**35**
Weibels Wirtshaus	**39**
Weingut Reinprecht	**2**
Weinhof Zimmermann	**3**
Wieninger	**1**
Wolff	**4**
Wrenkh	**25**
Würstelstand	**26**
Zum Finsteren Stern	**27**
Zum Schwarzen Kameel	**20**

KEY

i Tourist Information

food, including all the classic hearty dishes like goulash soup, Wiener schnitzel, and *Apfelstrudel,* is as good as in many other *Beisln* (pub). The Mark Twain room has walls and ceiling covered with signatures of the famed who have been served here. $ *Average main: €17* ✉ *Fleischmarkt 11, 1st District* ☎ *01/533–1977* ⊕ *www.griechenbeisl. at* Ⓜ *U1 or U4/Schwedenplatz.*

$ ✕**Konstantin Filippou.** This newly opened establishment has quickly

INTERNATIONAL

become a go-to place in Vienna's Altstadt. The dining room alone is an invitation to stay a while; crisp, ice-blue walls are a cool complement to warm, blond wood floors and pine tables. An abundance of natural light further softens the ambience during daylight, which is when many of Filippou's customers come to enjoy a business lunch of pork-filled ravioli or chicken ragout. In the evening, guests seated in the main dining room can watch as well-honed chefs prepare the restaurant's specialties, including their famous escargot seasoned with horseradish and watercress. Dine outside in the garden in spring and summer and you won't regret it. $ *Average main: €16* ✉ *Dominikanerbastei 17, 1st District* ☎ *01/51 22 229* ⊕ *www.konstantinfilippou.com* ⊘ *Weekdays noon–5, 6:30–midnight* ⊘ *Weekends, last 3 wks of August.*

$ ✕**Motto am Fluss.** Even though night owls flock to Motto am Fluss

CONTEMPORARY

until the wee hours, this sleek eatery serves an inspired selection of dishes when the sun is up, including herbal beef tartare with mushroom sauce, or spinach ravioli topped with a warm, creamy butternut sauce. Breakfast delights at the sister café include the "Full Speed Ahead," (scrambled eggs on whole wheat bread, with slices of ham and salami and a selection of cheeses, including Camembert). The building overlooks the Danube and resembles an ocean liner, with a retro 1950s interior of checkerboard floors below and gigantic globe-mirrored lamps above. Chairs and tables are of a heavy varnished, dark timber. The dining room is sprawling and has huge windows through which you can watch the city's twinkling lights. $ *Average main: €17* ✉ *Franz-Josefs Kai, 1st District* ☎ *01/25255* ⊕ *www.motto. at/mottoamfluss* ⊘ *Closed 2:30–6 daily.*

$ ✕**Ströck.** Everything old is new again at one of Austria's iconic institu-

AUSTRIAN

tions. Long known as a reliable haunt for breads and strudels, Stroeck is giving itself a makeover and is launching its brand of bistros around town. Open for evening and weekend meals, the eateries will serve only organic, locally grown goods, such as beef tartare, marinated with a house dressing and seasoned with a red onion and yellow pepper chutney. For a light dessert try the vegan chocolate-dipped cherries with brown sugar. Breakfast and lunch served only on weekends. $ *Average main: €10* ✉ *Landstrasser Hauptstrasse 82, 3rd District/Landstrasse* ☎ *01/204 39 99 93 057* ⊕ *www.stroeck-feierabend.at* ⊘ *Mon.–Fri., 4–midnight; weekends, 7 am–midnight.*

$$$ ✕**Walter Bauer.** Hidden away in one of the quietest quarters of his-

AUSTRIAN

toric Vienna, this charming and unpretentious Michelin-starred restaurant serves the very best in traditional cuisine. Even the everyman *Leberkäse*—an artery-blocking loaf of pork, bacon, corned beef, and onions—is turned into a delectable delight (and served with a dash of mustard). More modern and international fare, such as foie gras with

Munch on the Run

CLOSE UP

If you don't have time for a leisurely lunch, or you'd rather save your money for a splurge at dinner, here's a sampling of the best places in the city center to grab a quick, inexpensive, and tasty bite to eat.

✕ **Bizi Pizza.** Most people are drawn in by the thick aroma of buttered garlic wafting down the street, though for some, the attraction is watching the bakers toss the pizza pies in the air before popping them into the oven. Bizi Pizza is arguably one of the best slices of New York–style pizza you'll find anywhere on the Continent. There is also a buffet at this casual restaurant serving fresh salads and pasta dishes. It is standing room only, which is fine for grabbing a bite on the run, but a bit chilly under the Austrian winter's grip when the line extends outside. $ *Average main: €5* ✉ *Rotenturmstrasse 4, 1st District* ☎ *01/513–3705.*

✕ **Meinl am Graben.** The main draw is the location on the ground floor of Vienna's premier gourmet grocery store, with fabulous views out the panoramic windows onto the historic Graben, a people-watching mecca. The food is on the light side, as this is a café (not to be confused with

the full-service restaurant upstairs). Expect to find an array of soups and salads including pumpkin cream soup and tomato and mozzarella with pine-nut pesto. A wee bit pricey, but you're paying for the view. $ *Average main: €11* ✉ *Graben 19, 1st District* ☎ *01/532–3334* ⊙ *Closed Sun.*

A sure way to spike a lively discussion among the Viennese is to ask which *Würstelstand* serves the most delicious grilled sausages. Here are three that are generally acknowledged to be the best:

✕ **Würstelstand am Hohen Markt.** Hot on the trail of the "Best Sausage" appellation, Würstelstand am Hohen Markt is a stall serving the best *Bürenwurst* and American-style hot dogs. As with most of the Würstelstands, or *Imbiss* kiosks, there is a surprising amount of foodstuffs on offer. *Käsekrainer,* fried sausage, is a popular choice for locals, as is a *Bosna,* bratwurst with onions and a mustard/ketchup concoction served on a roll. Open until the wee hours, and you can also pick up a beer, wine, or even a bottle of champagne. $ *Average main: €3* ✉ *Hoher Markt, corner of Marc-Aurel-Strasse, 1st District* ▭ *No credit cards.*

confits and brioche, are specialties not to be missed. The quality-crazy owner has over the years encouraged some of Austria's greatest chefs, including Christian Domschitz and Michael Feuerbrand, to perform their very best in his kitchen, using only the finest ingredients. The best Austrian wines—including reds Gradenthal and Blaufrankisch, and white Grüner Veltliner—and friendly service make this a winner. $ *Average main: €30* ✉ *Sonnenfelsgasse 17, 1st District* ☎ *01/512–9871* ⊕ *www.restauranttester.at* ⌔ *Reservations essential* ⊙ *No lunch Mon. Closed weekends and mid-July–mid-Aug.* Ⓜ *U1 or U3/Stephansplatz.*

$ ✕ **Weibels Wirtshaus.** Down an old cobbled lane between Singerstrasse
AUSTRIAN   and Schulerstrasse and a stone's throw from the cathedral, Weibels Wirtshaus is one of the coziest places to have a lazy lunch or a delightful dinner. Try to reserve a table upstairs in the Galerie: with just a couple

of tables, it soon feels like home. The dinner menu changes with the season; in summer try the cold cucumber soup with cilantro shrimp, and strawberry-rhubarb mousse for dessert. On sunny days, opt for outside seating in the delightful garden. In winter, Wiener schnitzel with beer is about as cozy as it gets. ■ TIP➜ Ask the staff for wine recommendations, as owner Hans Weibel, a wine buff, keeps some of the best local vintages in stock. $ *Average main: €17* ⊠ *Kumpfgasse 2, 1st District* ☎ *01/512–3986* ⊕ *www.weibel.at* ⌒ *Reservations essential* Ⓜ *U1 or U3/Stephansplatz.*

THE INNER CITY CENTER: BAROQUE GEMS AND VIENNA'S SHOPWINDOWS

$$$$
AUSTRIAN

✕ **Anna Sacher.** The Sachertorte is the culmination of a family saga that began with Franz Sacher, Prince von Metternich's pastry chef. Franz's son and his wife, Anna, Vienna's hostess with the mostest, opened the 19th-century hotel. The restaurant Anna Sacher, with sparkling chandeliers casting a warm glow on green walls hung with gilt frames, offers a lighter version of traditional Austrian cuisine. The restaurant has two menus—one with traditional Austrian fare, and an "innovative" menu, with star chef Werner Pilchmaier serving up tasty dishes, such as yellow bell pepper soup with lamb and sage. The slightly less formal Rote Bar, at the front of the hotel, always has classics on offer, including Tafelspitz (boiled beef), the favorite dish of Emperor Franz Josef. $ *Average main: €33* ⊠ *Hotel Sacher, Philharmonikerstrasse 4, 1st District* ☎ *01/514– 56840* ⊕ *www.sacher.com* ⌒ *Reservations essential* ⊘ *Closed Mon. and July and Aug.* Ⓜ *U1, U2, or U4/Karlsplatz/Opera.*

$
CAFÉ

✕ **Café Griensteidl.** Once the site of one of Vienna's oldest coffeehouses and named after the pharmacist Heinrich Griensteidl—the original dated back to 1847 but was demolished in 1897—this café was resurrected in 1990. Karl Kraus, the sardonic critic, spent many hours here writing his feared articles, and it's also here that Hugo von Hofmannsthal took time out from writing libretti for Richard Strauss. Although this establishment is still looking for the patina needed to give it real flair, locals are pleased by the attempt to re-create the historic atmosphere. Numerous newspapers and magazines hang on the rack (many are in English). It's also entirely no-smoking. $ *Average main: €12* ⊠ *Michaelerplatz 2, 1st District* ☎ *01/535–2692* ⊕ *www.cafegriensteidl. at* Ⓜ *U3/Herrengasse.*

$
CAFÉ

✕ **Café Hawelka.** Practically a shrine—indeed, almost a museum—the beloved Hawelka was the hangout of most of Vienna's modern artists, and the café has acquired quite an admirable art collection over the years. The city grieved openly when its founder Leopold Hawelka died at the age of 100 four years ago. As you enter the rather dark interior, wait to be seated—which is unusual in Vienna—but then you can ask to have a look at the guest book, itself a work of art, with entries including some very illustrious names (Elias Canetti, Andy Warhol, Tony Blair et al.). Back in the 1960s, the young John Irving enjoyed the atmosphere here, too, as you can see when reading *The Hotel New Hampshire*. The Hawelka is most famous for its *Buchteln*, a baked bun with a sweet filling, served fresh from the oven after 10 pm. $ *Average main: €10*

Vienna's Sweetest Vice

Many think that the chief contribution of the people who created the Viennese waltz and the operetta comes with the dessert course in the form of rich and luscious pastries, and in the beloved and universal *Schlagobers* (whipped cream).

✕ **Demel.** The display cases are filled to the brim at the world-renowned Demel, a 200-year-old confectioner famous for sweetmeats that make every heart beat faster (and eventually slower). All you have to do is point at what you want and then take a seat. Don't forget to watch the pastry chef at work in the glassed-in courtyard. Beyond the shop proper are stairs that lead to dining salons where the decor is almost as sweet as the goods on sale. Chocolate lovers will want to try the Viennese Sachertorte (two layers of dense chocolate cake, with apricot jam sandwiched between, and chocolate icing on top) and compare it with its competition at Café Sacher. Can get crowded with tourists. $ *Average main: €10* ✉ *Kohlmarkt 14, 1st District* ☎ *01/535–1717* ⊕ *www.demel.at.*

✕ **Oberlaa.** You'll find irresistible confections such as the Oberlaa Kurbad cake, truffle cake, and chocolate-mousse cake here. The lemon torte is filled with a light, fruity lemon cream and a thin layer of almond paste. The Maroni Obers

Torte is a dark chocolate cake, filled with chestnut and milk chocolate mousse, garnished with maraschino cherries. Popular with the locals and a great value, there are many Oberlaa branches to choose from, including Landstrasser Hauptstrasse 1 and Babenbergerstrasse 7. Included among their tasty delights are gluten- and lactose-free treats. Candy can also be wrapped as a lovely gift to take home. $ *Average main: €8* ✉ *Neuer Markt 16* ☎ *01/513–2936* ⊕ *www.oberlaa-wien.at.*

✕ **Cafe Sperl.** Coffee in Vienna is designed to be savored and enjoyed and one of the most splendid places in Vienna to do just that is at the Sperl. Featured in Hollywood films *A Dangerous Method* and *Before Sunrise,* the venerable café—commandeered way back when as the café for artists—is more than just a fantastically pretty face. The Old Vienna ambience is not merely preserved here but vibrantly alive. Get a table by the window to ensure a captivating street view, and be sure to enjoy the piano music Sunday afternoon. It's in the 6th District not far from the MuseumsQuartier and the Naschmarkt. $ *Average main: €12* ✉ *Gumpendorferstrasse 11, 6th District/Mariahilf* ☎ *01/586–4158* ⊕ *www.cafesperl.at* ⊙ *Closed July and August.*

3

✉ *Dorotheergasse 6, 1st District* ☎ *01/512–8230* ⊕ *www.hawelka.at* Ⓜ *U1 or U3/Stephansplatz.*

$$ ✕ **Café Mozart.** When he stayed at the adjacent Hotel Sacher, Graham
CAFÉ Greene loved having his coffee here while working on the script for *The Third Man.* (Greene included the café in the film, and Anton Karas wrote a waltz for the place.) The café, named after the monument to Mozart (now in the Burggarten) that once stood outside, is overrun with sightseers, but the waiters are charming and manage to remain calm even when customers run them ragged. Crystal

chandeliers, a brass-and-oak interior, comfortable seating, and delicious food—the excellent Tafelspitz here has to be mentioned—add to its popularity. With the opera just behind the café, this is a fine place for an after-performance snack; be on the lookout for opera divas here for the same reason. [$] *Average main: €18* ✉ *Albertinaplatz 2, 1st District* ☎ *01/24–100–200* 🌐 *www.cafe-mozart.at* [M] *U1, U2, or U4/Karlsplatz/Opera.*

$ CAFÉ

🍴 **Café Sacher.** This legend began as a *Delikatessen* opened by Sacher, court confectioner to Prince von Metternich, the most powerful prime minister in early-19th-century Europe. It was for this fervent chocoholic that the Sachertorte was created. War-weary Metternich must have been amused to see a battle break out between Sacher and Demel—a competing confectioner—as to who served the real Sachertorte. Sacher puts its apricot jam in the cake middle, while Demel puts it just below the icing. If you're not a sweets person, try a savory alternative: *Sacher Würstl* (slim sausages served with fresh horseradish, mustard, and home-baked bread). Mirrors and chandeliers add glitter, and there is live piano music every day from 4:30 until 7 pm. [$] *Average main: €12* ✉ *Hotel Sacher, Philharmonikerstrasse 4, 1st District* ☎ *01/514560* 🌐 *www.sacher.com* [M] *U1, U2, or U4/Karlsplatz/Opera.*

$$ CONTEMPORARY
Fodor's Choice ★

🍴 **DO & CO Albertina.** When you're ready to collapse after taking in all the art at the fabulous Albertina, fall into the museum eatery's high-back, camel-color leather seating. For something exotic, try the Thai-style steamed rice, oysters, and sweet chili sauce that can be served with vegetables, prawns, or beef. If you fancy just a snack, sit at the bar and enjoy the Baguette Albertina, stuffed with juicy smoked salmon, cream cheese, arugula, and sundried tomatoes. DO & CO is open every day, 9 am to midnight. In summer you can sit outside on one of the city's nicest terraces and enjoy the view of the Burggarten. [$] *Average main: €19* ✉ *Albertina Museum, Albertinaplatz 1, 1st District* ☎ *01/532–9669* 🌐 *www.doco.com* ✍ *Reservations essential* [M] *U1, U2, or U4/Karlsplatz/Opera.*

$ WINE BAR

🍴 **Esterházykeller.** The origins here go back to 1683, when this spot opened as one of the city's official *Stadtheuriger* (wine taverns), to provide Turk-fighting soldiers with wine before going off to battle. Below the Esterházy palace, the atmosphere is like that of a cozy cave, with low-hanging vaults and alpine wooden booths. The maze of rooms offers some of the best wines of any cellar in town, plus a typical Viennese menu noontime and evenings. Ordering seems back to front: food orders are taken at the counter, while a waiter comes to the table to take your order for drinks. The best choice for meat lovers is roast pork with dumplings and cabbage. [$] *Average main: €10* ✉ *Haarhof 1, 1st District* ☎ *01/533–3482* 🌐 *www.esterhazykeller.at* [M] *U1 or U4/Stephansplatz.*

$$$ MEDITERRANEAN

🍴 **Fabios.** The easiest way for Viennese to experience sleek, suave, New York–style power dining—short of paying for a round-trip plane ticket—is to book a table at this Italian hot spot in the heart of Vienna. If they can, that is. Wait-listed weeks in advance, this modernist extravaganza has brought a touch of big-city glamour to Alt Wien, and everyone from foodies to fashionistas loves it. Seafood is so fresh it's flown in daily for the kitchen to prepare specialties, such as shrimp marinated in lemon and served on a bed of Tuscan beans, or roasted sea bass in a couscous salad of cucumber and avocado. For beef eaters, the chef prepares a special piquant sauce poured over a rib-eye steak. $ *Average main: €29 ⊠ Tuchlauben 4–6, 1st District ☎ 01/532–2222 ⊕ www. fabios.at ⊲ Reservations essential ⊘ Closed Sun.*

$ ╳**Gösser Bierklinik.** Dating back four centuries, this engaging old-world

AUSTRIAN house sits in the heart of Old Vienna. One of the country's top addresses for beer connoisseurs, it serves brews, both draft and bottled, *Dunkeles* (dark) and *Helles* (light), from the Gösser brewery in Styria. Of the four eating areas, many diners opt for the covered courtyard, where beer tastes better no matter the weather. Besides the obligatory (but first-class) Wiener schnitzel with potato salad, you shouldn't miss the whole-wheat sandwiches stuffed with ham, cheese, and vegetables. Another good choice is the *Kas'nocken* (pasta dumplings topped with melted Tyrolean mountain cheese). $ *Average main: €15 ⊠ Steindlgasse 4, 1st District ☎ 01/533–7598 ⊕ www.goesser-bierklinik.at ⊘ Closed Sun. No lunch weekdays July and Aug. Ⓜ U3/Herrengasse.*

$$$ ╳**Julius Meinl am Graben.** A few doors down from the Hofburg Palace,

AUSTRIAN Julius Meinl am Graben opened as a caterer to the Habsburgs in 1862 and has remained Vienna's most posh grocery store. On the first floor up is a cozy salon, all dark wood and deep-orange banquettes. The window tables have stunning views over the Kohlmarkt. Allow the excellent staff to guide you through the daily changing menu with their expertise and charm. Note: after 7 pm you enter via an outdoor elevator on Naglergasse. $ *Average main: €28 ⊠ Graben 19, 1st District ☎ 01/532–3334 ⊕ www.meinlamgraben.at ⊘ Closed Sun. and first 3 wks in Aug. Ⓜ U3/Herrengasse.*

$ ╳**Wrenkh.** Vienna's vegetarian pioneer extraordinaire Christian Wrenkh

VEGETARIAN prefers teaching evening cookery classes to standing in the kitchen every day. His two sons run the show, and roughly two-thirds of the menu is vegetarian, with delightful dishes like wild-rice risotto with mushrooms, Greek fried rice with vegetables, or tofu, tomato, and basil tarts. The minimalist-style bistro, with mid-century modern decor that looks a tad like a modish hotel, offers affordable lunches and dinners. Customers who sign up for the culinary classes can learn to cook Wrenkh's cuisine themselves. $ *Average main: €13 ⊠ Bauernmarkt 10, 1st District ☎ 01/533–1526 ⊕ www.wiener-kochsalon.com ⊘ Closed Sun. Ⓜ U1 or U3/Stephansplatz.*

$$$ ╳**Zum Schwarzen Kameel.** Back when Beethoven dined at "the Black

AUSTRIAN Camel," it was already a foodie landmark. Since then, it has split into

Fodor'sChoice a *Delikatessen* and a restaurant. Try the former if you're in a hurry—

★ fresh sandwiches are served at the counter. If time is not an issue, dine in the elegant, intimate Art Nouveau dining room. Let the head waiter, the one with the Emperor Franz Josef mustache, rattle off the specials of the day in almost-perfect English; the *Beinschinken* (Viennese ham) is the specialty of the house and is renowned throughout Austria. $ *Average main: €30 ⊠ Bognergasse 5, 1st District ☎ 01/533–8125 ⊕ www.kameel.at ⊲ Reservations essential ⊘ Closed Sun. Ⓜ U3/Herrengasse.*

Coffeehouse 101

Is it the coffee they come for or the coffeehouse? This question is one of the hot topics in town, as Vienna's café scene has become overpopulated with Starbucks branches and Italian outlets. The ruckus over whether the quality of the coffee or the *Atmosphäre* is more important is not new, but is becoming fiercer as competition from all sides increases. The result is that the landmark *Wiener Kaffeehäuser*—the cafés known for centuries as "Vienna's parlors," where everyone from Mozart and Beethoven to Lenin and Andy Warhol were likely to hang out—are smarting from the new guys on the block. On the plus side, their ageless charms remain mostly intact (not to mention their numbers: there are some 1,600 coffeehouses in Vienna), including the sumptuous red-velvet padded booths; the marble-top tables; the rickety yet indestructible Thonet bentwood chairs; the waiters, dressed in Sunday-best outfits; the pastries, cakes, strudels, and rich tortes; the newspapers, magazines, and journals; and, last but not least, a sense that here time stands still. To savor the traditional coffeehouse experience, set aside a morning or an afternoon, or at least a couple of hours, and settle down in the one you've chosen. Read a while, catch up on your letter writing, or plan tomorrow's itinerary: there's no need to worry about overstaying your welcome, even over a single small cup of coffee—though don't expect refills. (Of course, in some of the more opulent coffeehouses your one cup of coffee may cost as much as a meal somewhere else.)

In Austria coffee is never merely coffee. It comes in countless forms and under many names. Ask a waiter for *ein Kaffee* and you'll get a vacant stare. If you want a black coffee, you must ask for a *kleiner* or *grosser Schwarzer* (small or large black coffee, small being the size of a demitasse cup). If you want it strong, add the word *gekürzt* (shortened); if you want it weaker, *verlängert* (stretched). If you want your coffee with cream, ask for a *Brauner* (again *gross* or *klein*); say *Kaffee Creme* if you wish to add the cream yourself (or *Kaffee mit Milch extra, bitte* if you want to add milk, not cream). Others opt for a *Melange*, a mild roast with steamed milk (which you can even get *mit Haut*, with skin, or *Verkehrter*, with more milk than coffee). The usual after-dinner drink is espresso. Most delightful are the coffee-and-whipped-cream concoctions, universally cherished as *Kaffee mit Schlag*, a taste that is easily acquired and a menace to all but the very thin. A customer who wants more whipped cream than coffee asks for a *Doppelschlag*. Hot black coffee in a glass with one knob of whipped cream is an *Einspänner* (literally, "one-horse coach"—as coachmen needed one hand free to hold the reins). Or you can go to town on a *Mazagran*, black coffee with ice and a tot of rum, or *Eiskaffee*, cold coffee with ice cream and whipped cream. Or you can simply order *eine Portion Kaffee* and have an honest pot of coffee and jug of hot milk. Most coffeehouses offer hot food until about an hour before closing time.

ACROSS THE DANUBE: THE SECOND DISTRICT

$$$$ ✕ **Le Loft.** Dine at Vienna's most posh restaurant while taking in the
FRENCH stunning, 360-degree panoramic vistas of the city's skyline from the
18th floor of the Sofitel Stephansdom. The gourmet meals are just as
fabulous, offering Vienna's finest in French cuisine. A four-course tasting menu may include roasted foie gras, fresh pan-fried pike perch
from nearby Neusiedler Lake, and crispy lamb crown, with a dessert
of raspberry and pistachio sorbet. The ambience is accentuated by the
ceiling, designed by Swiss multimedia artist Pipilotti Rist. She has created a magnificent visual feast, which is best viewed at sunset, as the
changing colors outside have a lovely dance with the colors playing
out on the ceiling above you. $ *Average main: €40* ✉ *Praterstrasse 1,
Leopoldstadt* ☎ *1906160* ⚓ *Reservations essential.*

$ ✕ **Schöne Perle.** This "beautiful pearl" is one of the most popular dining
AUSTRIAN spots for locals in Leopoldstadt. It offers traditional Austrian comfort
FAMILY food, including Tafelspitz—boiled beef, the favored dish of Emperor
Franz Joseph—and Wiener schnitzel, but its real palate-pleasers are the
vegetarian dishes, of which there is a wide selection: avocado salad,
pumpkin cream soup, spinach ravioli, and red lentil soup are among
the top favorites. The interior is surprisingly spacious, so the restaurant can get crowded but not cramped. The staff is friendly, and seems
to tolerate well the children who can't resist roaming the vastness.
Come with cash, as credit cards are a no-go; reservations recommended
for dinner. $ *Average main: €17* ✉ *Grosse Pfarrgasse 2, Leopoldstadt*
☎ *664–2433–593* ▭ *No credit cards.*

$ ✕ **Skopik & Lohn.** Many restaurants have set up shop in former stalls on
AUSTRIAN the market square in the artsy neighborhood that has sprung up around
Karmelitermarkt, just across the Donaukanal, including Skopik &
Lohn. The owner originally intended to open in New York, but fate
landed it a few footsteps from the square and to great acclaim. The
menu features international fare, such as roast chicken with figs and
chestnuts, and linguini with fresh chanterelle mushrooms (which grow
only two months out of the year). The interior is rather minimalist and
modern, except for artist Otto Zitko's massive doodling spree on the
ceiling. The black-and-white art creeps like a vine onto the walls and
you want to get out your markers and color it in. $ *Average main:
€17* ✉ *Leopoldsgasse 17, 2nd District/Leopoldstadt* ☎ *01/219–8977*
⊕ *www.skopikundlohn.at* ☉ *Closed Sun.* Ⓜ *U2/Taborstrasse.*

THE WESTERN CITY CENTER: BURGTHEATER AND BEYOND

$ ✕ **Café Central.** Made famous by its illustrious guests, the Café Central is
CAFÉ right up there with Florian's in Venice. With soaring ceiling and gigantic
columns giving it the look of an apse strayed from St. Stephen's, Café
Central provided a rather sumptuous home-away-from-home for Leon
Trotsky, who mapped out the Russian Revolution beneath portraits of
the Imperial family. There is more than the standard café fare here, with
the kitchen serving up salmon fillet sprinkled with roasted pine nuts;
or try the *Mohr im hemd* for dessert, chocolate hazelnut cake dusted
with powdered sugar and served with hot chocolate sauce and whipped

cream. Piano music fills the marble pillared hall in the afternoon; it can get packed with tourists, but it's worth the crowds. [$] *Average main: €14* ✉ *Herrengasse 14, at Strauchgasse, 1st District* ☎ *01/533–3764–24* [M] *U3/Herrengasse.*

A STRUDEL STEAL

Why not take your afternoon coffee break in one of the very best restaurants in town, for less than you would pay in most Viennese cafés? At around 2 pm weekdays, head to the Steirereck's "Meierei" in Stadtpark and savor the freshest *Apfelstrudel* around, when it comes out hot from the oven. It doesn't last long, though, so if you don't make it in time for this fruitiest and juiciest of Apfelstrudel, you can try for the 3 pm revelation of the creamy *Topfenstrudel*—a strudel with a creamy cheese filling, rather than apples. Both are best served warm and accompanied by a smooth, aromatic coffee.

$ CAFÉ 🍴 **Café Landtmann.** A century-old favorite of politicians and theater stars (the Burg is next door), this was Sigmund Freud's favored café. Burt Lancaster, Hillary Rodham Clinton, and Paul McCartney are just a few of the famous who have patronized this esteemed establishment, whose glass-and-brass doors have been open since 1873. During Ball Season, you'll spot tired but chatty groups of gowned and tuxedoed Viennese repairing here for breakfast after their night of dancing. If you want a great meal at almost any time of day, there are few places that can beat this one. An air-conditioned glass veranda has added contemporary flair to this venerable location. [$] *Average main: €13* ✉ *Dr.-Karl-Lueger-Ring 4, 1st District* ☎ *01/24–100–100* 🌐 *www.landtmann.at* [M] *U2/Schottenring.*

$ MEDITERRANEAN 🍴 **Hansen.** This fashionable establishment, in the basement of the 19th-century Vienna Stock Exchange, shares an enormous space with the flower shop Lederleitner, and the air is mixed with the sweet perfume of tuberoses and the tantalizing whiff of truffle. Although this eatery is named after Theophil Hansen—the ornament-crazy architect of the Börse—the decor is sleek and modern; note the superb contemporary artwork adorning the walls. Chef Tom Frötsch and his team create a new menu of Mediterranean specialties each week. If you have a light appetite, ask for a smaller-size portion. Their brand new feature is a summer special: brunch on Saturday from 9 to 2. [$] *Average main: €15* ✉ *Wipplingerstrasse 34, 1st District* ☎ *01/532–0542* 🌐 *www.hansen.co.at/en/restaurant* ✍ *Reservations essential* ⏲ *Closed Sun. No dinner Sat.* [M] *U2/Schottenring.*

$ WINE BAR 🍴 **Melker Stiftskeller.** Down and down you go, into one of the friendliest cellars in town, where *Stelze* (roast pork) is a popular feature, along with outstanding regional wines—Grüner Veltliner among them—by the glass or, rather, mug. Part of the Melkerhof complex—dating from 1438 but rebuilt in the 18th century—this was originally the storehouse for wines from the Melk Abbey in the Danube Valley. It's a complex of six cavernous rooms, and the most atmospheric has low-arched vaults right out of a castle dungeon. [$] *Average main: €14* ✉ *Schottengasse 3, 1st District* ☎ *01/533–5530* 🌐 *www.melkerstiftskeller.at* ⏲ *Closed Sun. and Mon. No lunch* [M] *U2/Schottentor.*

$$ AUSTRIAN 🍴 **Vestibül.** Attached to the Burgtheater, this was once the carriage vestibule of the emperor's court theater. Today, the dining room with marble Corinthian columns, coffered arcades, and flickering candlelight adds romance, but don't expect high drama. An example of Ringstrasse architecture, the Burgtheater offers splendor at its most staid. Christian Domschitz, one of Austria's best chefs—and of the same family who owns Hansen—took over the kitchen in 2010. The menu changes frequently, but often includes Domschitz's famous *Hummerkrautfleisch,* a Viennese creamy cabbage dish, to which Domschitz adds one of his specialties: lobster. [$] *Average main: €22* ✉ *Universitätsring 2, 1st District* ☎ *01/532 49 99 10* 🌐 *www.vestibuel.at* 🕒 *Closed Sun. and 3 wks in Aug. No lunch Sat.* [M] *Tram: 1 or 2.*

EAST OF THE RINGSTRASSE: STADTPARK AND KARLSPLATZ

$ AUSTRIAN 🍴 **Gasthaus Wild.** Gasthaur Wild is the best dining option near the Kunsthaus Wien and the Hunderwasser House. Formerly a wine tavern, it's now a down-to-earth Beisl (the equivalent of a pub, also called a *Gasthaus*). The menu changes regularly but almost always features local dishes and *Schinkenfleckerl* (delicious pasta squares stuffed with ham and cabbage), and, most importantly, a selection of wild game when in season. The restaurant also serves a selection of fine wines and an extensive desert menu. [$] *Average main: €12* ✉ *Radetzkyplatz 1, 3rd District/Landstrasse* ☎ *01/920–9477* [M] *Tram: O/Radetzkyplatz.*

$ AUSTRIAN 🍴 **Gmoa Keller.** One of the friendliest places in Vienna, this wonderful old cellar—just across the street from the Konzert Haus—offers some of the heartiest home cooking in town. Come here to enjoy dishes that hail from Carinthia, one of the best being the *Kas'nudeln* (potatoes and spinach pasta filled with cheese and onion), best served with green leaf salad. Another favorite is the *Tafelspitzsulz mit Kernoel und Zwiebeln* (cold cut of beef in aspic served with onions). You'll want to use the *Semmel* (white bread roll) to sop up that last drop of dark-green pumpkinseed-oil dressing. [$] *Average main: €12* ✉ *Am Heumarkt 25, 3rd District/Landstrasse* ☎ *01/712–5310* 🌐 *www.gmoakeller.at* 🕒 *Closed Sun.* [M] *U4/Stadtpark.*

$$$$ AUSTRIAN 🍴 **Hofzeile 27.** With an intimacy often lacking in larger restaurants, Hofzeile 27 seats just a dozen guests. Sibylle Fellner-Kisler opened up her elegant home in Döbling (Vienna's most affluent district), cooking classic Austrian dishes with creativity and flair. Dinner is a fabulous five courses of outstanding fare. Each menu is prepared nightly, but can include an octopus salad for an appetizer, vichyssoise, and for the main course halibut with fennel, and Jerusalem artichokes topped with a lemon sauce. For dessert, crème brûlée, all rounded out with a glass of champagne. She also serves brunch and lunch. There's a comprehensive wine list, a stylish bar, and terrace to boot. Reservations are accepted by phone and email. [$] *Average main: €79* ✉ *Hofzeile 27, 19th District* ☎ *0664/527–7929* 🌐 *www.hofzeile27.at* ✍ *Reservations essential* 🕒 *Closed 3 wks: end July–mid-Aug.*

$ AUSTRIAN 🍴 **Joseph Genuss.** This new bistro/patisserie is quickly becoming known around town as "the bread place." Each morning, the bread is baked fresh—kneaded by hand—using what the owners call an ancient recipe with only organic ingredients. All of their breads are whole grain, and include varieties such as honey lavender, sourdough walnut, and sourdough pumpkinseed. The ambience is like pristine factory meets Old Europe: a floor of Styrian stone with chandeliers dangling from the ceiling, alongside sleek, modern baking ovens. A must-try for meat lovers is the burger, using fresh lamb meat on a sourdough poppy bun, which comes with a side dish of fat toasted bread fingers. $ *Average main: €6* ✉ *Landstrasser-Hauptstrasse 4, 3rd District* ☎ *1710–2881* ⊕ *www.joseph.co.at.*

$$
AUSTRIAN
✗ **Österreicher im MAK.** Chef Bernie Rieder learned his craft from his father and brings the flare of the Austrian countryside to the kitchen. The restaurant is a destination in itself, but also a great way to extend your museum visit. The decor is modern, and dark hardwood floors soften the chic. For such a large space, it is surprisingly quiet. The contemporary Austrian culinary creations include entrées such as roasted rack of lamb with deep-fried sweetbread, smoked ricotta cheese, wild garlic and parsley. $ *Average main: €22* ✉ *Museum of Applied Arts, Stubenring 5, 1st District* ☎ *01/714–0121* ⊕ *www.oesterreicherimmak. at* Ⓜ *U3/Stubentor.*

$$$$
AUSTRIAN
Fodor's Choice
★
✗ **Steirereck.** Considered one of the world's 50 best restaurants, this eatery is definitely the most raved-about place in Austria. It's in the former Milchhauspavilion, a grand Jugendstil-vintage dairy overlooking the Wienfluss promenade in the Stadtpark, the main city park on the Ringstrasse. Winning dishes include delicate wild boar's head with "purple haze" carrots, turbot in an avocado crust, or char in beeswax, yellow turnips, and cream. At the end of the meal, an outstanding selection of more than 120 cheeses awaits. If you don't want the gala Steirereck experience, opt for a bite in the more casual lower-floor Meierei, which is still stylish, with its hand-painted floor and furniture in shades of milky white. $ *Average main: €45* ✉ *Stadtpark, Am Heumarkt 2A, 3rd District/Landstrasse* ☎ *01/713–3168* ⊕ *steirereck.at* ✎ *Reservations essential* ⊘ *Closed weekends* Ⓜ *U4/Stadtpark.*

SOUTH OF THE RINGSTRASSE: THE MUSEUMSQUARTIER

$
AUSTRIAN
✗ **Amerlingbeisl.** If you're lucky, you can snag a table in the idyllic garden of this low-key pub, hidden away inside a delightful Biedermeyer cobbled courtyard. Vines and ivy provide cover from the intense summer sun, and the decor inside is minimalist. The walls of the passageway leading from the courtyard are lined floor to ceiling with concert placards, which may leave the over-thirties feeling a tad obsolete. Fish with pumpkin sauce is a popular menu choice, as is the chicken schnitzel. The staff is young, fly, and carefree, and will gladly serve you breakfast—both traditional Viennese-style and vegetarian—until 3 pm. On Sunday, the large breakfast buffet is a big draw. In winter, there's nothing more cozy than to sit inside and sip the ginger apricot punch. $ *Average main: €6* ✉ *Stiftgasse 8, 7th District* ☎ *1526–1660* ⊘ *Daily 9–2.*

$
CAFÉ
✗ **Café Museum.** The controversial architect Adolf Loos (famed for his pronouncement "Ornament is a sin") laid the foundation stone for this coffeehouse in 1899. Throughout the 20th century, this was a top rendezvous spot for Wien Secession artists, along with actors, students, and

professors, because of its proximity to the Academy of Fine Arts, the Theater an der Wien, and Vienna's Technical University. Gustav Klimt, Egon Schiele, and Josef Hoffmann all enjoyed sipping their Melange here. Apart from the eye-catching 1930s-style steel globes, the ambience is much like that of other cafés in town, with red upholstery, marble-topped tables, and black bentwood chairs. On weekdays at noon, a tasty daily special, such as rucola salad with potato puffs seasoned with a creamy garlic sauce, guarantees a full house. $ *Average main: €10* ✉ *Operngasse 7, 1st District* ☎ *01/241–00–620* ⊕ *www.cafemuseum. at* Ⓜ *U1, U2, or U4/Karlsplatz/Opera.*

$
INTERNATIONAL
FAMILY

✗ **Corns 'n Pops.** The dining area looks a bit like the set of a modern sitcom. Dining tables are simple and white, and chairs are in white plastic. This ensemble complements the white walls, which are lined with white shelves filled with candy-color pillows and other candy-color household items for sale. Within sight is the white, home-style refrigerator dotted with magnets. This vegan/vegetarian breakfast nook—which also offers takeout—serves up an abundance of healthful cold cereal, or "muesli," which can be topped with fresh fruits. Bagels (still a rarity in Vienna) are also available, as are various hot breakfasts including scrambled eggs with tomatoes and feta cheese. Lunch offerings include pasta and salads. $ *Average main: €5* ✉ *Gumpendorferstrasse 37, 2nd District* ☎ *664* �Cosed *Sun.*

$$$$
AUSTRIAN

✗ **The Dining Room.** The pioneer of private dining in Vienna, Angelika Apfelthaler prepares and serves a gourmet dinner three times a week in her lovely Mediterranean-color dining room. This is a one-woman show from start to finish. Her effortless presentation of subtly flavored dishes—such as tomato stuffed with mackerel and seasoned with pine nuts and raisins—is available for a maximum of 14 guests. Toward the end of the meal comes the fantastic cheese plate, with Apfelthaler's homemade *mostarda* (a blend of melon, pineapple, and ginger), and then the grand finale, her signature "chocolate heaven" cake. The price for six courses is €55. $ *Average main: €55* ✉ *Maygasse 31, 13th District/Hietzing* ☎ *01/804–8586* ⊕ *www.thediningroom.at* ⚑ *Reservations essential.*

$
INTERNATIONAL

✗ **Do-An.** This bustling restaurant in a stall along the Naschmarkt is a prime place to stop for a bite and watch the crowds go by. The menu is as diverse as the customers, and includes various Turkish mainstays, such as tzatziki and falafel, and a variety of international choices, including chicken and avocado salad, pumpkin curry with vegetables and cashew nuts over rice, and lemon Moroccan chicken with couscous. The prices are easy on the wallet and the customers tend toward the young and citified, so bring your hipster self. $ *Average main: €10* ✉ *Naschmarkt Stand 412–415, 6th District* ☎ *01/585 8253* ⊕ *www.doan.at.*

$
AMERICAN
FAMILY
Fodor'sChoice
★

✗ **Ice Dream Factory.** This hopping little spot popped onto the Burggasse last year, and it's the best thing that's happened to the sweet tooth since cake was invented. The decor is ice-cream parlor meets relaxed coffeehouse, the menu a delirious smorgasbord of delectable American-style ice creams and hot-from-the-oven pies. Everything is homemade, from the cherry cobbler (yum!) to the waffle cones the ice cream is served up in, and only organic ingredients are used. Try the Nerd's Favorite: vanilla ice cream with brownies, candied walnuts, and caramel sauce (remember: all homemade), or go all in for Mother's Nightmare: chocolate ice cream with brownies, peanut butter, chocolate fudge and hazelnuts. Finish with a refreshing drink of homemade ice tea. $ *Average main: €3* ⊠ *Burggasse 69, 7th District* ☎ *699–82–4697* ⊕ *www.icedreamfactory* ☯ *Weekdays noon–9, weekends 10–9.*

WEST OF THE RINGSTRASSE: PARLAMENT AND CITY HALL

$$$$ ✕ **Kim Kocht.** Korean-born Sohyi Kim has established herself as Aus-
ASIAN   tria's most inventive Asian chef. Every night in her cozy, wood-paneled dining room she dreams up a five-course "surprise dinner" (€70, seating at 7 pm), which might include mixing ingredients such as mussels with local porcini mushrooms. Dinner reservations should be made weeks in advance. In case you don't make it to dinner, Kim also runs a "shop and studio" on Naschmarkt, where she sells simpler dishes like rice and vegetables topped with beef bulgogi—thin slices of grilled sirloin marinated in a melange of soy sauce, garlic, and sesame. $ *Average main: €70* ⊠ *Lustkandlgasse 4, 9th District* ☎ *01/319 02 42* ⊕ *www.kimkocht.at* ⟜ *Reservations essential* ☯ *Closed weekends and Mon.; closed for lunch* Ⓜ *Tram: 37 or 38 to Spitalgasse/Währinger Strasse from Schottentor.*

$$$$ ✕ **Restaurant Edvard.** This gourmet establishment at the Palais Hansen
INTERNATIONAL   Kempinski Hotel earned a Michelin star within months after open-
Fodor's Choice   ing last year. Chef Philipp Vogel prepares his creative, contemporary
★   masterpieces only from foods grown locally and in season. The menu changes frequently, and includes daring dishes, such as pikeperch with spinach and anchovies, seasoned with lemon, bacon, and focaccia; deer loin with strawberries and white asparagus seasoned in a balsamic vinaigrette. The interior is elegant, not opulent, with ivory walls and ebony-covered chairs complementing the stark white table linens. There are two entrances, one from the hotel lobby and one at the street, a nod to locals that this restaurant is for them, too. $ *Average main: €35* ⊠ *Schottenring 24* ☎ *1236–1000* ⟜ *Reservations essential.*

OUTSIDE THE CITY CENTER

$$ ✕ **Mayer am Pfarrplatz.** Heiligenstadt is home to this *Heurige* (wine tav-
WINE BAR   ern) in one of Beethoven's former abodes; he composed his 6th Symphony, as well as parts of his Ninth Symphony ("Ode to Joy") while staying in this part of town. The à la carte offerings and buffet are abundant, and include traditional Viennese dishes, such as Wiener schnitzel and Tafelspitz (with roasted chive potatoes); goulash with chanterelle mushrooms, and dumplings with apricots, a regional specialty; the Riesling house wines are excellent. You'll find lots of Viennese among the tourists here. $ *Average main: €19* ⊠ *Pfarrplatz 2, 19th District/ Grinzing* ☎ *01/370–7373* ⊕ *www.pfarrplatz.at* ☯ *No lunch weekdays* Ⓜ *Tram: D/Nussdorf from the Ring.*

CLOSE UP

Wine-Wien-Wein-Vienna

For a memorable experience, sit at the edge of a vineyard in the outskirts of the city with a tankard of young white wine and listen to the *Schrammel* quartet playing sentimental Viennese songs. The wine taverns in this region sprang up in 1784 when Joseph II decreed that owners of vineyards could establish their own private wine taverns, with the provision that the vintners rotated their opening times among them; soon the Viennese discovered it was cheaper to go out to the wine than to bring it inside the city walls, where taxes were levied.

These taverns in the wine-growing districts vary from the simple front room of a vintner's house to ornate settings. Named after the "new" wine, the true *Heurige* is open for only a few weeks a year to allow vintners to sell a certain quantity of their production, tax-free, when consumed on their own premises. The choice is usually between a "new" and an "old" wine, but you can also ask for a milder or sharper wine according to your taste. Most *Heurigen* are happy to let you sample the wines before you order. You can also order a *Gespritzter*, half wine and half soda water. If you visit in the fall, be sure to order a glass of *Sturm*, a cloudy drink halfway between grape juice and wine, with a delicious yeasty fizz. Don't be fooled by its sweetness; it goes right to your head.

Tourist traps still abound in Grinzing, where for years busloads descended on the picturesque wine village on Vienna's outskirts to drink new wine, but there are also worthy Heurigen destinations in Stammersdorf, Sievering, Nussdorf, or Neustift. And these days you can usually find fine dinners to accompany the excellent wine.

3

$ WINE BAR 🍴 **Weingut Reinprecht.** The grandest Heurige in Grinzing (the town has more than 30 of them), Reinprecht is *gemütlichkeit* heaven: Tyrolean wood beams, Austrian-eagle banners, portraits of army generals, globe lanterns, marble busts, trellis tables, and what is probably the greatest collection of corkscrews in Austria. The building—a former monastery—is impressive, as is the garden, which can hold up to 700 people (to give you an idea of how popular this place is). The menu relies on what is in season, and offers up wild garlic soup, and sweet white asparagus with ham (or eggs, if you prefer). If you ignore the crowds, get a cozy corner table and focus on the archetypal *atmosphäre*, you should have a great time. [$] *Average main: €16* ✉ *Cobenzlgasse 22, 19th District/Grinzing* ☎ *01/320–1471* 🌐 *www.heuriger-reinprecht.at* 🕒 *Closed Dec.* [M] *U2/Schottentor; Tram: 38/Grinzing.*

$ WINE BAR 🍴 **Weinhof Zimmermann.** A winding walk up a tree-lined lane brings you to the garden of one of the city's most well-known Heuriger. Here you will find one of the finest, most peaceful views around. The tables in the ample garden overlook Vienna's vineyards, from which part of the cityscape can be viewed beyond. Inside is cozy, though a small labyrinth of rooms. The specialty wine is the Grüner Veltliner, but a Malvasier (also a Viennese white) and Chardonnay are among a host of others served up. Most Austrians go for the heuriger hallmark drink spritzer—wine mixed with sparkling water. The buffet is a bounty of traditional dishes, including Wiener schnitzel, fried chicken, vegetable strudel, and cheese and meat platters. [$] *Average main: €12* ✉ *Mitterwurzergasse 20, 19th District/Grinzing* ☎ *01/440–1207* ⏲ *No lunch* [M] *U2/Schottentor; Tram: 38/Grinzing.*

$ WINE BAR 🍴 **Wieninger.** The driving force behind the WienWein group, this vintner knows his business better than many. He exports his Vienna wines to the United States and elsewhere, but luckily there are some left to be savored in this pleasant, tree-shaded inner courtyard and tavern. The food is not typical heuriger fare, instead they cater to more contemporary tastes, à la roasted scampi burgers with mango avocado dip. It's across the Danube in Stammersdorf, one of Vienna's oldest Heurige regions. [$] *Average main: €14* ✉ *Stammersdorferstrasse 78, 21st District/Floridsdorf* ☎ *01/292–4106* ⏲ *Thu.–Sun.* ⏲ *Closed late Dec.–Apr. No lunch Thu.–Fri.* [M] *U2, U4/Schottenring; Tram: 31/Stammersdorf.*

$ WINE BAR 🍴 **Wolff.** In the heart of the vine village of Neustift am Walde, this inn dating from 1609 sticks to tradition. The selection of white wine includes Grüner Veltliner, Riesling, and Chardonnay, and reds of Blauburger and Zweigelt. All to wash down the traditional Viennese dishes served, including pork schnitzel and fried chicken. Every Wednesday, Friday, and weekends from mid-April to mid-September, a local singing group performs well-known arias from favorite operettas. It's €48 for a three-course meal including drinks and show, starting at 8:15 pm. [$] *Average main: €14* ✉ *Rathstrasse 44–46, 19th District/Grinzing* ☎ *01/440–2335* [M] *U4/U6/Spittelau; Bus: 35A/Neustift am Walde.*

WHERE TO STAY

Updated
by Patti
McCracken

The luxury hotel market has surged in Vienna in recent years, bringing top rivals to the revered landmark lodgings that have dominated the city for well over a century. The grand old five-star dames of the Ringstrasse still stand supreme with their gilt mirrors, red velvet, and crystal chandelier opulence. The service, as ever, tends toward impeccable, bringing to mind the valets who served the medley of Imperial Highnesses who once lived in these palaces.

For those with more modest requirements and purses, ample rooms are available in less costly but no less alluring hotels. A number of new hotels have opened in this category, as well, making for an array of affordable and enticing choices.

Our lower-price options offer the best in location, value, and, in many instances, a quaint echo of Alt Wien (Old Vienna) atmosphere.

If you have only a short time to spend in Vienna, you'll probably choose to stay in the inner city (the 1st District, or 1010 postal code), to be within walking distance of the most important sights, restaurants, and shops. Outside the 1st District, though, there are many other delightful neighborhoods in which to rest your head. The "Biedermeier" quarter of Spittelberg, in the 7th District of Neubau, has cobblestone streets, rows of 19th-century houses, a wonderful array of art galleries and restaurants, and, increasingly, some good hotel options. Just to its east is the fabulous MuseumsQuartier, an area that has some very nice hotel finds. Schwedenplatz is the area fronted by the Danube Canal—a neighborhood that is one of the most happening in the city, although just a stroll from the centuries-old lanes around Fleischmarkt. Other sweet hotel options can be found in the 8th District of Josefstadt, an area noted for antiques shops, good local restaurants, bars, and theater.

Because of the Christmas markets, the weeks leading up to the holidays are a popular time to visit, as is the week around New Year's (*Silvester*), with its orchestral concerts. Expect to pay accordingly, and, at the very top hotels, a lot (around €300–€600 a night). Summer months are not as busy, perhaps because the opera is not in season. You'll find good bargains at this time of year, especially in August. Air-conditioning is customary in the top-category hotels only, so don't be surprised if you have to do without. On the plus side, nights are generally cool.

PLANNING

Where should you stay? With hundreds of Vienna hotels, it may seem like a daunting question. But fret not—our expert writers and editors have done most of the legwork. The selections here represent the best the city has to offer—from the best budget B&Bs to the sleekest boutique hotels.

RESERVATIONS

Hotel reservations are a necessity—rooms fill up quickly, so book as far in advance as possible. WienTourismus (⊕ *www.wien.info/en/travelinfo*), the Viennese Tourist Board, lets you reserve accommodations in all categories online.

FACILITIES

Unless otherwise noted in individual descriptions, all the hotels listed have private baths, central heating, and private phones. Almost all hotels have Wi-Fi and phones with voice mail.

Bringing a car to Vienna can be a headache unless your hotel provides free parking. Considering the city's parking restrictions and the intricate web of one-way streets, it makes more sense to rely on public transportation.

WITH KIDS

Many hotels offer free stays for kids under 12, but make sure to inquire when making reservations. In the listings, look for the family icon, which indicates a property that we recommend for when you're traveling with children.

DISCOUNTS AND DEALS

When booking, remember first to ask about discounts and packages. Even the most expensive properties regularly reduce their rates during low-season lulls and on weekends. If you're a member of a group (senior citizen, student, auto club, or the military), you may also get a deal.

PRICES AND PRICE CHART

The lodgings we list are the cream of the crop in each price category. Properties are assigned price categories based on the price of a standard double room during high season, which in Vienna runs from September to June, when the Staatsoper is in season.

WHAT IT COSTS IN EUROS			
$	**$$**	**$$$**	**$$$$**
FOR TWO PEOPLE	under €120	€120–€170	€171–€270	over €270

Prices are for two people in a standard double room.

HOTEL REVIEWS

Listed alphabetically within neighborhoods.

THE EASTERN CITY CENTER: STEPHANSDOM AND MEDIEVAL VIENNA

$$
RENTAL
Adagio Wien Zentrum. These inexpensive and convenient one- and two-room apartments with fully fitted kitchens are a much-need addition to the city's lodging scene. **Pros:** good for longer stays; central location. **Cons:** space is sometimes tight; maid service only if you stay for more than four days. $ *Rooms from: €124* ⊠ *Uraniastrasse 2, 1st District* ☎ *01/908–303* ⊕ *www.adagio-city.com* ↝ *124 apartments* ⦿ *No meals.*

$$$
HOTEL
Am Stephansplatz. You aren't likely to find a better location than this serene hotel, which sits directly across from the front entrance of St. Stephen's Cathedral. **Pros:** top location; great breakfast-bar views; excellent staff. **Cons:** busy location; noisy area at night. $ *Rooms from: €230* ⊠ *Stephansplatz 9, 1st District* ☎ *01/534–050* ⊕ *www. hotelamstephansplatz.at* ↝ *48 rooms, 8 suites* ⦿ *Breakfast.*

$$$$
HOTEL
Ambassador. Franz Lehár, Marlene Dietrich, the Infanta Isabel of Spain, and Mick Jagger are just a few of the celebrities who have stayed at this old dowager (from 1866). **Pros:** excellent last-minute deals; great location for shopaholics and casino lovers. **Cons:** very busy neighborhood; outdated. $ *Rooms from: €332* ⊠ *Kärntnerstrasse 22, 1st District* ☎ *01/961–610, 01/961–61157 reservations* ⊕ *www.ambassador. at* ↝ *71 rooms, 14 suites, 4 apartments* ⦿ *No meals.*

$$$$
HOTEL
Fodor'sChoice
★
Grand Hotel Wien. With one of the great locations on the Ringstrasse, just across from the Musikverein and a minute on foot from the Staatsoper, the Grand (the first luxury hotel in Vienna) has risen to new splendor. **Pros:** two superb restaurants; good shopping next door. **Cons:** desk staff can seem haughty; check-in can be slow. $ *Rooms from: €425* ⊠ *Kärntnerring 9, 1st District* ☎ *01/515–800* ⊕ *www.grandhotelwien. com* ↝ *194 rooms, 11 suites* ⦿ *No meals.*

$$$
HOTEL
Hollmann Beletage. Tucked away in the center of town just a short walk from the cathedral, this intimate boutique hotel has a quiet but convenient location. **Pros:** in the heart of the city; marvelous staff; great breakfast. **Cons:** hotel entrance is hard to spot from the street. $ *Rooms from: €189* ⊠ *Köllnerhofgasse 6, 1st District* ☎ *01/961–1960* ⊕ *www. hollmann-beletage.at* ↝ *25 rooms, 1 suite* ⦿ *Breakfast.*

$$$
HOTEL
Fodor'sChoice
★
Hotel Lamée. Guests here are transported back to the 1930s Vienna of the imagination, a glamorous center for café culture that longed to be the "European Hollywood." **Pros:** minibar is complimentary; triple-glazing keeps street noise at street level; many rooms have stunning views of the cathedral. **Cons:** not all rooms have cathedral views. $ *Rooms from: €178* ⊠ *Rotenturmstrasse 15, 1st District* ☎ *01/532–2240* ⊕ *hotellamee.com* ↝ *22 rooms, 10 suites* ⦿ *Multiple meal plans.*

$$$
HOTEL
König von Ungarn. In a 16th-century house in the shadow of St. Stephen's Cathedral, this dormered hotel began catering to court nobility in 1746 and today lets you choose between "classic" and "modern"

BEST BETS FOR VIENNA LODGING

Fodor's Choice ★

25hours Hotel Wien, $$$, p. 123
Das Triest, $$$$, p. 122
Grand Hotel Wien, $$$$, p. 116
The Guesthouse, $$$, p. 120
Hotel Lamée, $$$, p. 116
Hotel Sacher, $$$$, p. 120
Palais Hansen Kempinski Vienna, $$$$, p. 117
Park Hyatt, $$$$, p. 122
Radisson Blu Style Hotel, $$, p. 120
Sofitel Vienna Stephansdom, $$$$, p. 122
Topazz, $$$, p. 117

By Price

$$

Radisson Blu Style Hotel, p. 120
Rathaus Wine & Design, p. 124
Spiess & Spiess, p. 123

$$$

25hours Hotel Wien, p. 123
Altstadt, p. 123
Das Tyrol, p. 123
The Guesthouse, p. 120
Hotel Lamée, p. 116
Topazz, p. 117
Wandl, p. 121

$$$$

Das Triest, p. 122
Do&Co, p. 120
Grand Hotel Wien, p. 116
Hotel Sacher, p. 120
Le Méridien Vienna, p. 123
Palais Hansen Kempinski Vienna, p. 117
Park Hyatt, p. 122
The Ring, p. 123
Sofitel Vienna Stephansdom, p. 122

rooms. **Pros:** staff very helpful, accommodating, and friendly; great location. **Cons:** a tad old-fashioned; tour buses pass regularly. [$] *Rooms from: €225* ✉ *Schulerstrasse 10, 1st District* ☎ *01/515–840* 🌐 *www.kvu.at* 🛏 *35 rooms, 9 suites* 🍴 *Breakfast.*

$$$$ HOTEL **Palais Coburg.** In this 19th-century regal residence, the lobby is sleek white stone and plate glass, embodying the hotel's philosophy of "preserving the past—shaping the future." **Pros:** luxurious atmosphere; excellent dining. **Cons:** interior design can feel a bit over the top; pricey. [$] *Rooms from: €695* ✉ *Coburgbastei 4, 1st District* ☎ *01/518–180* 🌐 *www.palais-coburg.com* 🛏 *35 suites* 🍴 *No meals.*

$$$$ HOTEL Fodor's Choice ★ **Palais Hansen Kempinski Vienna.** This Renaissance Revival-style structure, built in 1873 as an exhibition hall, was transformed 140 years later into a luxe hotel, which pays homage to the grand beginnings while also incorporating modern-day amenities. **Pros:** central location; historic site; popular on-site dining and nightlife; extensive spa. **Cons:** posh prices. [$] *Rooms from: €320* ✉ *Schottenring, 24, 1st District* 🌐 *www.kempinski.com/en/vienna/palais-hansen/* 🛏 *98 rooms, 54 suites* 🍴 *No meals.*

$$$ HOTEL Fodor's Choice ★ **Topazz.** Opened in 2012, and already one of the top hotel showstoppers in town, the Topazz should win every design award in the book: it's an extraordinary homage to the Wiener Werkstätte style that took Vienna by storm in the early 1900s. **Pros:** a designer's dream; "green" sustainability is the rule here; complimentary minibars; views out those oval windows! **Cons:** some rooms on the snug side. [$] *Rooms from: €198* ✉ *Lichtensteg 3, 1st District* ☎ *01/532–2250* 🌐 *www.hoteltopazz.com* 🛏 *33 rooms* 🍴 *No meals.*

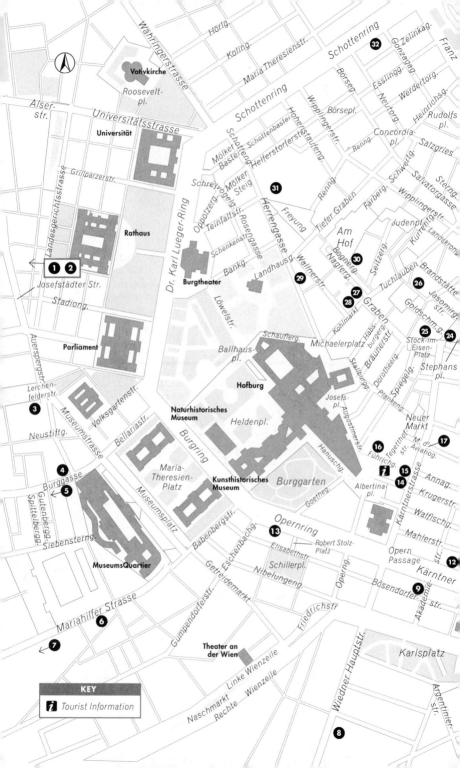

Where to Stay in Vienna

25hours Hotel Wien **3**
Adagio Wien Zentrum **38**
Altstadt **5**
Ambassador **17**
Am Stephansplatz **24**
Astoria.............................**15**
Benediktushaus **31**
Das Triest **8**
Das Tyrol **6**
Do&Co **25**
Gal Apartments Vienna **36**
The Guesthouse **16**
Grand Hotel Wien **12**
Hollmann Beletage **21**
Hotel Lamée **22**
Hotel Sacher **14**
Hotel Vienna Downtown Franz **33**
Hotel Vienna Downtown Sissi **34**
Imperial **10**
König von Ungarn **20**
Le Méridien Vienna **13**
Palais Coburg **18**
Palais Hansen Kempinski Vienna **32**
Park Hyatt **30**
Park Royal Palace Vienna............**7**
Pension Nossek **27**
Pension Zipser **1**
Pertschy Hotel **28**
Radisson Blu Style Hotel **29**
Rathaus Wine & Design **2**
The Ring **9**
Ritz-Carlton **11**
The Rooms **35**
Sans Souci Hotel **4**
Sofitel Vienna Stephansdom **37**
Spiess & Spiess **19**
Topazz **23**
Wandl **26**

THE INNER CITY CENTER: BAROQUE GEMS
AND VIENNA'S SHOPWINDOWS

$$$$ 🏨 **Astoria.** Built in 1912 and still retaining the outward charm of that
HOTEL era, the Astoria is one of the grand old Viennese hotels and enjoys a
superb location on the Kärnterstrasse between the Opera House and St.
Stephen's. **Pros:** location hard to beat; **Cons:** no air-conditioning; busy
area, at times noisy. $ *Rooms from: €300* ⊠ *Kärntnerstrasse 32–34,
1st District* 🕾 *01/51577* ⊕ *www.austria-trend.at/asw* 🔖 *120 rooms, 8
suites* 🍽 *No meals.*

$$$$ 🏨 **Do&Co.** Inside the glass-and-stone Haas House, which reflects St.
HOTEL Stephen's Cathedral in its facade, you'll discover this unique boutique
hotel. **Pros:** elegant ambience; most lavish breakfast in town. **Cons:** glass
walls in bathroom might bother more modest guests. $ *Rooms from:
€350* ⊠ *Stephansplatz 12, 1st District* 🕾 *01/241–880* ⊕ *www.doco.com*
🔖 *41 rooms, 2 suites* 🍽 *Breakfast.*

$$$ 🏨 **The Guesthouse.** Smack behind the Albertina and the Staatsoper, this
HOTEL authentically Austrian boutique hotel is an absolutely delightful addi-
Fodor'sChoice tion to the Vienna lodging scene, with fabulous views of the heart of
★ the Innere Stadt. **Pros:** peaceful, invigorating atmosphere; staff is top-
notch; pet-friendly; free loan of iPad, loaded with tourist information.
Cons: standard rooms are a tad small. $ *Rooms from: €230* ⊠ *Fueh-
richgasse 10-a* 🕾 *01/512–1320* ⊕ *www.theguesthouse.at* 🔖 *37 rooms,
2 suites* 🍽 *No meals.*

$$$$ 🏨 **Hotel Sacher.** One of Europe's legends, originally founded by Franz
HOTEL Sacher, chef to Prince Metternich—for whom the famous chocolate cake
Fodor'sChoice was invented—this hotel dates from 1876 but has delightfully retained
★ its old-world atmosphere-*mit-Schlag* while also providing luxurious,
modern-day comfort. **Pros:** master chef Werner Pichlmaier; location
directly behind the Opera House could hardly be more central; ratio
of staff to guests is more than two to one; Vienna's most sumptuous
hotel. **Cons:** cramped elevator; booking by phone can be frustrating;
the Sacher is such a welcoming world some may never exit the front
door to do their sightseeing. $ *Rooms from: €435* ⊠ *Philharmoniker-
strasse 4, 1st District* 🕾 *01/514–560* ⊕ *www.sacher.com* 🔖 *130 rooms,
22 suites* 🍽 *No meals.*

$$ 🏨 **Pension Nossek.** A family-run establishment on the upper floors of
HOTEL a 19th-century apartment building, the Nossek lies at the heart of
Vienna's pedestrian and shopping area. **Pros:** perfect location; family
oriented; friendly staff. **Cons:** a little drab in appearance. $ *Rooms
from: €125* ⊠ *Graben 17, 1st District* 🕾 *01/533–7041* ⊕ *www.pension-
nossek.at* 🔖 *30 rooms* 🍽 *Breakfast.*

$$$ 🏨 **Pertschy Hotel.** Housed in the former Palais Cavriani, this B&B just
B&B/INN off the Graben is about as central as you can get. **Pros:** hard-to-beat
location; family run and friendly. **Cons:** rooms facing street are noisy.
$ *Rooms from: €184* ⊠ *Habsburgergasse 5, 1st District* 🕾 *01/534–490*
⊕ *www.pertschy.com* 🔖 *55 rooms* 🍽 *Breakfast.*

$$ 🏨 **Radisson Blu Style Hotel.** Behind the hotel's Art Nouveau facade,
HOTEL London interior designer Maria Vafiadis has paid tribute to Viennese
Fodor'sChoice Art Deco, and the result is über-stylish yet comfortable. **Pros:** excel-
★ lent rates online; central location; quiet area of old city. **Cons:** small

CLOSE UP

Lodging Alternatives

APARTMENT RENTALS

If you want a home base that's roomy enough for a family and comes with cooking facilities, consider a furnished rental. Home-exchange directories sometimes list rentals as well as exchanges.

Vienna Residence. The city's largest portal for short-term serviced apartments has properties all over town. [$] *Rooms from:*

€100 ☎ 01/307–222 ⊕ www. viennaresidence.com.

BED-AND-BREAKFASTS

BedandBreakfast.com. This company advertises a dozen bed-and-breakfast establishments in Vienna, some of them with rates well below €100. [$] *Rooms from:* €85 ⊕ www.bedandbreakfast.com/vienna-austria.html.

4

---

reception area (with oddly low reception desks); not all room rates include breakfast. [$] *Rooms from: €149* ✉ *Herrengasse 12, 1st District* ☎ *01/227–800* ⊕ *www.radissonblu.com/stylehotel-vienna* 🛏 *78 rooms* 🍴 *Multiple meal plans.*

$$$ **Wandl.** The restored facade identifies this 300-year-old house that
HOTEL has been in family hands as a hotel since 1854, and you couldn't find a better location, tucked behind St. Peter's Church, just off the Graben. **Pros:** top location; quiet square; helpful staff. **Cons:** rooms can get stuffy in summer. [$] *Rooms from: €220* ✉ *Petersplatz 9, 1st District* ☎ *01/534–550* ⊕ *www.hotel-wandl.com* 🛏 *138 rooms* 🍴 *Breakfast.*

ACROSS THE DANUBE: THE SECOND DISTRICT

$ **Gal Apartments Vienna.** These spacious, modern apartments with fully
RENTAL equipped kitchens are in Leopoldstadt, Vienna's trendy 2nd District,
FAMILY and are within walking distance of the city center. **Pros:** enormous rooms; lower rates for longer stays; trendy neighborhood. **Cons:** no a/c. [$] *Rooms from: €89* ✉ *Grosse Mohrengasse 29, 2nd District/Leopoldstadt* ☎ *0650/561–1942* ⊕ *www.apartmentsvienna.net* 🛏 *12 apartments* 🍴 *No meals.*

$ **Hotel Vienna Downtown Franz.** Brother hotel to its sister "Sissi"—six
HOTEL blocks away—this member of the Meininger budget hotel chain offers
FAMILY the same hip style and out-for-fun clientele, but has room rates that are about €20 higher (these can be bargained lower, depending on daily availability). **Pros:** rare underground parking on-site; decent breakfast bar; easy to make new friends. **Cons:** only two elevators; rooms ready only at 3 pm. [$] *Rooms from: €100* ✉ *Rembrandtstrasse 21, 2nd District/Leopoldstadt* ☎ *720/882–065* ⊕ *www.meininger-hotels.com* 🛏 *131 rooms* 🍴 *No meals.*

$ **Hotel Vienna Downtown Sissi.** Part of the popular Meininger chain of
HOTEL budget hotels, this was the first of three to open in Vienna, all offering
FAMILY hip design, plugged-in clientele, and some of the best deals in town. **Pros:** rare underground parking on-site; decent breakfast bar; sociable. **Cons:** only two elevators; 15-minute walk to city center. [$] *Rooms from:*

€70 ✉ *Schiffamtsgasse 15, 2nd District/Leopoldstadt* ☎ *720/882–066* 🌐 *www.meininger-hotels.com* 🛏 *102 rooms* 🍴 *No meals.*

$ B&B/INN 🏨 **The Rooms.** With no two rooms alike, this tranquil, tiny guesthouse north of the Danube exudes an exotic aura, and the charming, friendly, and ever-so-helpful owners are ready to assist when needed. **Pros:** excellent breakfast; friendly vibe; home-away-from-home feel. **Cons:** outside center; accomodations differ greatly in size. [$] *Rooms from: €110* ✉ *Schlenthergasse 17, 22nd District/Donaustadt* ☎ *01/066–4431–6830* 🌐 *www.therooms.at* 🛏 *4 rooms* 🍴 *Breakfast* [M] *U1/Kagran.*

$$$$ HOTEL Fodor's Choice ★ 🏨 **Sofitel Vienna Stephansdom.** Minimalist luxury can be a contradiction, but at the Sofitel it's pulled off with supreme elegance, and here, on the border of the 2nd District, it's paired with outstanding city skyline views. **Pros:** outstanding views; incredible restaurant; sumptuous beds. **Cons:** monochromatic palate can feel cold to some; deep bathtubs can be difficult to maneuver. [$] *Rooms from: €500* ✉ *Praterstrasse 1, 2nd District/Leopoldstadt* ☎ *01/906–160* 🌐 *www.sofitel.com/Vienna* 🛏 *156 rooms, 26 suites* 🍴 *Breakfast* [M] *U4 or U1/Schwedenplatz.*

THE WESTERN CITY CENTER: BURGTHEATER AND BEYOND

$ B&B/INN 🏨 **Benediktushaus.** You can stay in this guesthouse of a monastery, in the heart of Vienna, without following the dictum *ora et labora* (pray and work), though you will get to see how the monks live by the credo. **Pros:** superb location; good value; excellent breakfast spread. **Cons:** reception hours limited in summer; surcharge for one-night stays. [$] *Rooms from: €99* ✉ *Freyung 6a, 1st District* ☎ *01/534–98900* 🌐 *www.benediktushaus.at* 🛏 *21 rooms* 🍴 *Breakfast.*

$$$$ HOTEL Fodor's Choice ★ 🏨 **Park Hyatt.** After much anticipation, Vienna's newest luxury hotel opened its grand doors in summer 2014, revealing the great care that was taken to preserve the integrity and historical significance of the elegant building, the former HQ of a leading bank. **Pros:** fabulous ambience; remarkable location. **Cons:** mirrors, mirrors, everywhere. [$] *Rooms from: €425* ✉ *Am Hof 2, 1st District* ☎ *01/2274–1234* 🌐 *www.vienna.park.hyatt.com* 🛏 *108 rooms, 35 suites* 🍴 *No meals.*

EAST OF THE RINGSTRASSE: STADTPARK AND KARLSPLATZ

$$$$ HOTEL Fodor's Choice ★ 🏨 **Das Triest.** Transformed by Sir Terence Conran into an ultrasleek ocean liner, this design hotel was once a postal-coach station on the route between Vienna and the Italian port city of Trieste; the original cross vaulting remains in the lounges and in some suites. **Pros:** lovely courtyard garden; famed bar; quiet surroundings. **Cons:** a bit out of the hub. [$] *Rooms from: €299* ✉ *Wiedner Hauptstrasse 12, 4th District/Wieden* ☎ *01/589–180* 🌐 *www.dastriest.at* 🛏 *56 rooms, 16 suites* 🍴 *Breakfast.*

$$$$ HOTEL 🏨 **Imperial.** One of the landmarks of the Ringstrasse, this hotel has exemplified the grandeur of imperial Vienna ever since it was built. **Pros:** discreet, unpretentious staff; excellent restaurant and café. **Cons:** some rooms are on the small side; bathrooms can be tiny. [$] *Rooms from: €465* ✉ *Kärntnerring 16, 1st District* ☎ *01/501–100* 🌐 *www.luxurycollection.com/imperial* 🛏 *107 rooms, 31 suites* 🍴 *Breakfast.*

$$$$ HOTEL **The Ring.** Following the trend toward smaller boutique properties, this luxury lodging takes its place alongside some of Vienna's opulent grand hotels. **Pros:** the best vodka bar in Vienna; good last-minute deals. **Cons:** the price; Wi-Fi can be slow; trams frequently thunder around the block. [$] *Rooms from: €425* ✉ *Kärntner Ring 8, 1st District* ☎ *01/221–220* 🌐 *www.theringhotel.com* 🛏 *60 rooms, 8 suites* 🍴 *No meals.*

$$ B&B/INN **Spiess & Spiess.** Considered by many to be the best B&B in Vienna, this small, family-run inn offers comfortable, spacious, and exquisitely furnished rooms. **Pros:** hot breakfast cooked by the proprietor; spacious rooms; easy access to public transportation. **Cons:** not in city center; two rooms lack a/c. [$] *Rooms from: €130* ✉ *Hainburgerstrasse 19, 3rd District/Landstrasse* ☎ *01/714–8505* 🌐 *www.spiess-vienna.at* 🛏 *9 rooms* 🍴 *Breakfast.*

4

SOUTH OF THE RINGSTRASSE: THE MUSEUMSQUARTIER

$$$ HOTEL Fodor's Choice ★ **25hours Hotel Wien.** A circus theme predominates at this marvelously bohemian addition to the city's lodging scene, each room containing extraordinary and exceptionally illustrated wallpaper of old-time big-top themes by German artist Olaf Hajek and deliciously quirky vintage furnishings. **Pros:** fun atmosphere; excellent staff; killer views. **Cons:** rooftop area gets overcrowded. [$] *Rooms from: €150* ✉ *Lerchenfelder Strasse 1–3, 7th District/Neubau* ☎ *01/5215–1830* 🌐 *www.25hours-hotels.com/wien* 🛏 *185 rooms, 34 suites* 🍴 *No meals.*

$$$ HOTEL **Altstadt.** When contemporary-arts patron Otto E. Wiesenthal hired premier Italian architect Matteo Thun to revamp this lodging, the results were exquisitely-decorated, sensuous chambers oozing atmosphere from the Vienna era of Freud and Klimt. **Pros:** good value; huge rooms; excellent staff; amazing private art collection; breakfast and afternoon tea included in room rate; all non-smoking. **Cons:** some stairs to climb to small reception area; outside the city center. [$] *Rooms from: €175* ✉ *Kirchengasse 41, 7th District/Neubau* ☎ *01/526–33–990* 🌐 *www.altstadt.at* 🛏 *42 rooms* 🍴 *Breakfast.*

$$$ HOTEL **Das Tyrol.** On a bustling Mariahilferstrasse corner, this small, luxurious hotel is a good choice for those who want to be next door to the MuseumsQuartier and near some fun shopping, too. **Pros:** great online deals; good location. **Cons:** rooms differ greatly in size. [$] *Rooms from: €259* ✉ *Mariahilferstrasse 15* ☎ *01/587–5415* 🌐 *www.das-tyrol.at* 🛏 *30 rooms* 🍴 *Breakfast.*

$$$$ HOTEL **Le Méridien Vienna.** The supercool "art and tech" lobby here, adorned with Mies van der Rohe–style sofas and ottomans and nouvelle fluorescent-light panels, is a fine introduction to a stylish and truly pampering stay in the heart of the city. **Pros:** next door to the museums; complimentary minibar. **Cons:** lacks "Vienna" character. [$] *Rooms from: €419* ✉ *Opernring 13, 1st District* ☎ *01/588–900* 🌐 *www.lemeridienvienna.com* 🛏 *269 rooms, 25 suites* 🍴 *No meals.*

$$ HOTEL **Park Royal Palace Vienna.** Within walking distance of Vienna's most beautiful park, this newer property brings a touch of modernity to the area around the Schönbrunn Palace. **Pros:** beautiful setting; sleek, modern style. **Cons:** Not directly in the center. [$] *Rooms from: €130* ✉ *Schlossallee 8, 14th District/Penzing* ☎ *01/89110* 🌐 *www.*

austria-trend.at/hotel-park-royal-palace-vienna/en 🗺 *212 rooms, 21 suites* ⦿ *No meals* Ⓜ *U4/Schönbrunn.*

$$$ 🛏 **Sans Souci Hotel.** Hip trying to outdo hip is the force behind this recent
HOTEL boutique addition to the hotel scene. **Pros:** nice summer terrace; great location near Mariahilferstrasse's trendy shops and within the MuseumsQuartier. **Cons:** beige and wood color schemes are a bit bland; minimum six nights for apartments. Ⓢ *Rooms from: €254* ✉ *Burggasse 2, 7th District* ☎ *01/522–2520* ⊕ *www.sanssouci-wien.com* 🗺 *60 rooms, 3 suites, 2 apartments* ⦿ *Breakfast.*

WEST OF THE RINGSTRASSE: PARLAMENT AND CITY HALL

$$ 🛏 **Pension Zipser.** With an ornate facade and a gilt-trimmed coat of
HOTEL arms, this 1904 house sits in the picturesque Josefstadt neighborhood of small cafés, bars, and shops and is steps from the J streetcar line to the city center. **Pros:** quiet area; some good bargains on select dates. **Cons:** rather bare inside; far from the city center. Ⓢ *Rooms from: €129* ✉ *Langegasse 49, 8th District/Josefstadt* ☎ *01/404–540* ⊕ *www.zipser. at* 🗺 *55 rooms* ⦿ *Breakfast.*

$$ 🛏 **Rathaus Wine & Design.** The friendliest staff and what might be the
HOTEL best breakfast buffet in town—see to it that your schedule allows you to savor the spread—make this exclusive boutique hotel a worthwhile choice. **Pros:** top-notch staff; unbeatable breakfast (served until 11 weekdays, noon weekends); penthouse has its own terrace—book way ahead. **Cons:** awkward spiral stairs from street; off the tourist track. Ⓢ *Rooms from: €165* ✉ *Langegasse 13, 8th District/Josefstadt* ☎ *01/400–1122* ⊕ *www.hotel-rathaus-wien.at* 🗺 *39 rooms, 1 penthouse* ⦿ *Multiple meal plans.*

$$$$ 🛏 **Ritz-Carlton.** Another Ringstrasse Palace to open its doors as a luxe
HOTEL downtown hotel, the Ritz Carlton came on the scene in 2012, complete with all the fineries you'd expect from the brand, including ceiling frescoes and open fireplaces in the poshest of its suites. **Pros:** rooftop terrace is a choice spot to watch the sun set over the city. **Cons:** Wi-Fi not free in the rooms. Ⓢ *Rooms from: €325* ✉ *Schubertring 5–7, 1st District* ☎ *01/311–88, 01/311–88111 reservations* ⊕ *www.ritzcarlton.com/en/ properties/vienna/default.htm* 🗺 *202 rooms, 45 suites* ⦿ *Breakfast.*

NIGHTLIFE AND PERFORMING ARTS

Updated
by Patti
McCracken

The arts in Vienna are not just for tourists. Locals enthusiastically partake of their city's rich cultural offerings, and there are many tantalizing choices, so it's probably good sense to do some planning ahead.

Do you want to time warp back to the 18th century at Mozart concerts featuring bewigged musicians in the opulent surroundings at Schönbrunn Palace? Or perhaps you'd like to cheer the divas at the grandest of grand opera at the Staatsoper, dive into the splendor of an evening concert of Strauss waltzes, or enjoy a trombone troupe at a *Jazzkeller*? Maybe a baroque opera in a stunning avant-garde setting at the Theater an der Wien (where Beethoven's *Fidelio* premiered in 1805)? The choices are endless during the regular season, which runs from September to June.

But Austria is not only about the classics, as it proudly proved to the world when Austrian singer Conchita Wurst won the 2014 Eurovision Song Contest. In summer, Vienna turns into a festival town. ImPulsTanz for modern dance enthusiasts has a rich variety of performances and venues, and for some the chamber music festival, held amid 18th-century frescoes at the Laudon Water Palace, is too enticing to pass up. The abundance of choices will leave you feeling spoiled. While the upper crust discuss opera singer Anna Netrebko's most recent performance, hipsters will flock to Flex for some of the city's best live acts.

One word of caution: the city's culture vultures dress for the occasion. Never take your coat inside the theater or the opera. (Vienna's performance halls do have coat checks.)

PLANNING

WHAT'S ON NOW?
A monthly printed program, the *Wien-Programm,* distributed by the city tourist board and available at any travel agency or hotel, gives an overview of what's going on in the worlds of opera, concerts, jazz, theater, and galleries, and similar information is posted on billboards and fat advertising columns around the city.

The film schedules in the daily newspapers *Der Standard* and *Die Presse* list foreign-language film showings; *OmU* means original language with German subtitles. The English-language online daily *Austrian Times* (⊕ *www.austriantimes.at*) lists a smattering of cultural happenings.

LATE-NIGHT TRANSPORTATION
During the week, subways and trams run until about midnight. On Friday and Saturday nights, U-Bahn subway lines run 24 hours a day at 15-minute intervals.

TOP EXPERIENCES

Catch an avant-garde opera. Anybody can go to the Staatsoper. Theater an der Wien bills itself as a "new opera house" and lives up to this claim with muscular performances of 20th- and 21st-century works.

Put on your ball gown. There is no other place on earth where women can live out their Cinderella fantasies in such a spectacular way. Balls in historic palaces take place in January and February, and summer balls abound. Don't be surprised, however, if you see women donning fur coats on their extravagant evenings out.

Enjoy a musical extravaganza. Over the past three decades, Vienna has garnered a reputation as a top spot for musicals, with local talent bringing Habsburg melodrama alive to the sounds of pop tunes.

Explore the smaller theaters. Scan the listings of *Wien Programm* to find performances of kitsch-free Viennese music by Die Strottern at Theater am Spittelberg, or a monologue by Elfriede Jelinek at Burgtheater's small stage at Kasino am Schwarzenbergplatz.

Hit the festivals. Vienna serves as a musical gateway to the East. Get a taste of Eastern European and Middle Eastern music at festivals such as Salam Orient and the annual Klezmore showdown, or attend Europe's largest open-air music festival in June, the Donauinselfest.

TICKETS

With a city as music mad and opera crazy as Vienna, it's not surprising to learn that the bulk of major performances are sold out in advance, but, with thousands of seats to be filled every night, you may luck out.

Albertinaplatz Tourist Information. Last-minute tickets for theater, musicals, or cabaret are available on a first-come, first-served basis daily between 2 and 5 inside the main tourist information office on Albertinaplatz. Here the theater-ticket company Jirsa sells same-day tickets for up to half off. Cash only. ⊠ *Albertinaplatz, corner of Maysedergasse, 1st District.*

Bundestheaterkassen. The State Theater Booking Office (Bundestheaterkassen), sells tickets for the Akademietheater, Staatsoper, Volksoper, and Burgtheater. Tickets for the Staatsoper go on sale two months in advance, and Volksoper tickets are available one month before the date of performance. You can visit the box office or call the (frequently busy) phone line, but you can also purchase tickets online, where you have the added advantage of putting your name on the waiting list for "standby" tickets to sold-out performances. ⊠ *Operngasse 2, 1st District* ☎ *01/514–44–7810* ⊕ *www.bundestheater.at* ☉ *Sept.–June, weekdays 8–6, weekends 9–noon; July and Aug., weekdays 10–4.*

Liener Brünn. Among the city's ticket agencies, the most trusted is Liener Brünn. It charges a 25% markup for seats. ⊠ *Augustinerstrasse 7, 1st District* ☎ *01/533–0961* ⊕ *www.viennafirsttickets.com* ☉ *Weekdays 9:30–5, Sat. 9:30–noon.*

NIGHTLIFE

With its swanky bars and clubs, Vienna is humming with nighttime activity. Teenagers congregate at the Bermuda Triangle south of St. Stephen's Cathedral, while hipsters meet in cafés and bars around MuseumsQuartier and the Naschmarkt. In recent years, the viaducts underneath the U6 subway line between Thaliastrasse and Nussdorferstrasse have been transformed into restaurants, bars, and clubs. A lively bar and club scene has also taken root at the Donaukanal across from Schwedenplatz, and Motto am Fluss is still holding its own against the competition.

Every year at the end of August, punkers, indie rockers, and world musicians blast their tunes during the Gürtel Night Walk. If you're in town, just stroll along the avenue from one bar to the next and enjoy the indoor and outdoor performances.

BALLS

Have you ever wondered why Vienna's young people still sway to melodies composed 150 years ago? The city's ball culture is carefully nurtured, and almost everybody between the ages of 16 and 19 attends a dancing school. On your strolls through the inner city, peek in at Elmayer's on Bräunerstrasse to see young couples practice the quadrille for the next Carnival extravaganza.

Among the 300 balls that are held in January and February, several welcome the public. Prices vary widely, and go as high as €600. Starting at 8 or 9 pm, these "full dress" events last until 3 or 4 am.

See the box Stepping Out in Three-Quarter Time in this chapter.

BARS, LOUNGES, AND NIGHTCLUBS

Nightlife has blossomed with a profusion of vibrant and sophisticated bars, clubs, and lounges. Many of the trendy people head to the clubs around the Naschmarkt area, then move on to nearby Mariahilferstrasse for dancing. The Freihaus Quarter sizzles with cafés and shops.

Café Carina. In a cavernous subway station, Café Carina is dazzling in dingy. Carina is very off-beat, artistic, and action-packed—anything can happen, from an air-guitar competition to an evening of 1980s hits. On weekends expect it to be packed. ⊠ *Josefstädterstrasse 84 at Stadtbahnbogen, 8th District/Josefstadt* ☎ *01/406–4322* Ⓜ *U6/ Josefstädterstrasse.*

Johnnys. Near the Naschmarkt, Johnny's brings a little Irish flair to the area. Good beer, inexpensive meals, quiz nights, and live music make this pub a popular hangout. ⊠ *Schleifmühlgasse 11, 4th District/Wieden* ☎ *01/587–1921* Ⓜ *U4/Kettenbrückengasse.*

Motto am Fluss. This hippest spot in town, this place resembles a sleek ocean liner gliding down the Danube Canal. The bar is all glass and chrome, lending it an ultramodern feel. Silver spheres dangle from the ceiling like drops of mercury. The outdoor terrace is the perfect spot

CLOSE UP

Stepping Out in Three-Quarter Time

Ever since the 19th-century Congress of Vienna—when pundits joked "The city dances, but it never gets anything done"—Viennese extravagance and gaiety have been world-famous. Fasching, the season of Carnival, was given over to court balls, opera balls, masked balls, chambermaids' and bakers' balls, and a hundred other gatherings, many held within the glittering interiors of Baroque theaters and palaces. Presiding over the dazzling evening gowns and gilt-encrusted uniforms, towering headdresses, flirtatious fans, "Wine, Women, and Song," *Die Fledermaus,* "Blue Danube," hand kissing, and gay abandon was the baton of the waltz emperor, Johann Strauss. White-gloved women and men in white tie would glide over marble floors to his heavenly melodies. They still do. Now, as in the days of Franz Josef, Vienna's old three-quarter-time rhythm strikes up anew each year at New Year's Eve and continues through Carnival, or Fasching.

During January and February as many as 40 balls may be held in a single

evening. Many events are organized by a professional group, including the Kaiserball (Imperial Ball), Philharmonikerball (Ball of the Philharmonic Orchestra), Kaffeesiederball (Coffee Brewers' Ball), the Zuckerbaeckerball (Confectioners' Ball), or the Opernball (Opera Ball). The latter is the most famous—some say too famous. This event transforms the Vienna Opera House into the world's most beautiful ballroom (and transfixes all of Austria when shown live on national television). The invitation reads *"Frack mit Dekorationen,"* which means that ball gowns and tails are usually required for most events (you can always get your tux from a rental agency) and women mustn't wear white (reserved for debutantes). But there's something for everyone these days, including the "Ball of Bad Taste" or "Wallflower Ball." The zaniest might be the Life Ball, sponsored by a charity raising funds for people with HIV. After your gala evening, finish off the morning with a *Katerfrühstuck—*hangover breakfast—of goulash soup.

5

to enjoy the breezes off the water. ⊠ *Schwedenplatz 2, 1st District* ☎ *01/25–225–11* ⊕ *www.motto.at/mottoamfluss.*

Passage. In a former underground walkway between the Hofburg palace and the Kunsthistorisches Museum, Passage is one of the trendiest clubs in the city. A state-of-the-art lighting system and futuristic interior come together in a blush-hued bar and a sizzling-blue dance room. You can spot the celebrities while sipping superbly mixed cocktails. ⊠ *Ringstrasse at Babenbergerstrasse, 1st District* ☎ *01/961–6677* ⊕ *www.clubpassage.at* Ⓜ *U2/MuseumsQuartier.*

Volksgarten Club. Back in 1870, Viennese used to come to the Volksgarten to waltz, drink champagne, and enjoy the night air in a candlelit garden. Today it's a *diskothek,* where locals flock to go clubbing, mostly to house and party music. ⊠ *Burgring 1, 1st District* ☎ *01/532–4241* Ⓜ *U2/3 MuseumsQuartier.*

DANCE CLUBS

Café Leopold. In the MuseumsQuartier, this café is hidden inside the large, white cube that is the Leopold Museum. Tables are scattered outside on the plaza at night. There are regular DJ lineups on Friday and Saturday, alongside video installations by young experimental filmmakers. ⊠ *Leopold Museum, Museumsplatz 1, 1st District* ☎ *01/523–6732* Ⓜ *U2 or U3/MuseumsQuartier.*

Club Schikaneder. In the middle of the Freihaus Quarter, the Schikaneder serves as both an independent, experimental movie theater and a very popular bar filled with the city's *künstlers und kunstlerinnen.* It screens one or two films daily, hosts art exhibits, and offers first-class DJ lineups. ⊠ *Margaretenstrasse 22–24, 4th District/Wieden* ☎ *01/585–2867* Ⓜ *U1, U2, or U4/Karlsplatz.*

Club U im Otto-Wagner-Café. "U" stands for underground, and Club U im Otto-Wagner-Café sits below one of the two Jugendstil pavilions that Otto Wagner built when designing Vienna's subway. This means that the disco is very easy to find. One of the best dance halls for alternative music, it has outdoor seating, live music, a great atmosphere, and excellent DJs who turn this place into a real Soul City most nights. ⊠ *Karlsplatz, Künstlerhauspassage, 1st District* ☎ *01/505–9904* Ⓜ *U1, U2, or U4/Karlsplatz.*

Flex. Considered the top venue for indie music in the city, Flex has a sound system unparalleled in Vienna. Top indie bands from across Europe showcase here, and the DJ lineup is considered by insiders to be the best in town. ⊠ *Donaukanal, Abgang Augartenbrücke, 1st District* ☎ *01/533–7525* Ⓜ *U1, U2, or U4/Karlsplatz.*

Fluc. One of the leaders in the resurgence of nightlife in Vienna's second district, the Fluc attracts world-famous DJs, who praise the small venue as one of the best in Europe. ⊠ *Praterstern 5, 2nd District/Leopoldstadt* ☎ *01/218-28-24* ⊕ *www.fluc.at.*

Pratersauna. Famous for its unisex bathrooms, outdoor pool, and several floors of entertainment, Pratersauna has become Vienna's most popular club—particularly in summer. Considered by many to be the best club in town, this location is cool. When you need a break from the dance floor, take in the art exhibits. ⊠ *Waldsteingartenstraße 135, 2nd District/Leopoldstadt* ☎ *01/729–1927.*

JAZZ CLUBS

In the last few decades, Austria has produced some great jazz talents. World-renowned saxophonist Wolfgang Puschnig, for example, holds a professorship at Vienna's Music University. He and his colleagues have inspired young musicians who can be found performing in the city's many jazz clubs.

Jazzland. In a cellar under St. Ruprecht's church, this is the granddaddy of Vienna's jazz clubs. Thanks to the pioneering work of the club's founder, Axel Melhardt, Austrian jazz musicians have grooved with the best American stars. The club also serves excellent, inexpensive, and authentic cuisine. ✉ *Franz-Josefs-Kai 29, 1st District* ☎ *01/533–2575.*

Porgy & Bess. In the heart of the Innere Stadt, Porgy & Bess has become a fixed point in the national and international jazz scene. ✉ *Riemergasse 11, 1st District* ☎ *01/512–8811.*

PERFORMING ARTS

Vienna learned long ago that a thriving arts scene is a boon to tourism, so it lends its support to everything from grand opera to intimate cabaret performances. As a result, artists from around the world have also settled in the city. That's why in addition to waltzes you can enjoy such varied fare as Greek *rembetiko* and Turkish Sufi music. Anyone who knows a bit of German should attend a performance at such major theaters as the Burgtheater and the Theater in der Josefstadt. Ever since Tanzquartier took up residence in the MuseumsQuartier, aficionados of contemporary dance have been able to enjoy avantgarde performances.

DANCE

As they live in the city of waltzes, the Viennese hold both ballet and contemporary dance especially dear. When the MuseumsQuartier was opened in 2001, the powers that be made sure to include space for dance performances, rehearsals, and classes.

Dance performances at the Staatsoper and Volksoper feature both classic and contemporary choreography. Dancers from both houses belong to the Vienna State Ballet under the direction of Manuel Legris, former star of the Paris Ballet.

ImPulsTanz (*Vienna International Dance Festival*). Europe's biggest contemporary dance festival takes place in venues large and small all over the city between mid-July and mid-August. The Vienna International Dance Festival—30 years old in 2014—attracts some of the world's leading companies, so it's no surprise that many Viennese schedule their summer vacations so as not to miss it. Recent years have brought stars like Alaine Platel, Mathilde Monnier, Ultima Vex, La La La Human Steps, and Marie Chouinard. ☎ *01/523–5558* ⊕ *www.impulstanz.com.*

Tanzquartier Wien (*DanceQuarter Vienna*). A small revolution has been brewing on the modern dance front, thanks to Tanzquartier Wien, Austria's foremost center for contemporary dance performances. The season runs from September to June and is followed by the so-called Factory Season, when the center concentrates solely on the projects presented in its dance studios. ✉ *Museumsplatz 1, 7th District/Neubau* ☎ *01/581–3591* ⊕ *www.tqw.at.*

FILM

Vienna has a thriving film culture, with many viewers seeking original rather than German-dubbed versions. If you're here October 25–November 7, make sure to check out Europe's oldest Viennale Film Festival (⊕ *www.viennale.or.at*), which draws crowds of nearly 100,000 to the city's historic movie palaces and showcases films by national and international directors.

Artis International. Around the corner from Tuchlauben, the Artis has six screens showing the latest blockbusters three to four times a day. ⊠ *Shultergasse 5, 1st District* ☎ *01/535–6570.*

Burg Kino. Carol Reed's Vienna-based classic *The Third Man*, with Orson Welles and Joseph Cotton, is screened every day except Wednesday. Hollywood's latest releases are usually shown here in the original English version. ⊠ *Opernring 19, 1st District* ☎ *01/587–8406.*

Haydn. One of the city's original movie theaters, this family-run place shows blockbuster movies in 3-D on three screens. ⊠ *Mariahilferstrasse 57, 6th District/Mariahilf* ☎ *01/587–2262.*

Filmmuseum. In the Albertina Museum, the Filmmuseum has one of the most ambitious and sophisticated schedules around, with a heavy focus on English-language films. It's closed July to September. A stylish bar serving drinks and snacks spills out onto the street. It's open until well past midnight. To celebrate its 50th anniversary (2014), the museum is hosting an array of lectures, retrospectives and film series throughout the year. ⊠ *Augustinerstrasse 1, 1st District* ☎ *01/533–7054* ⊕ *www.filmmuseum.at.*

Votiv Kino. This artsy theater usually features more alternative fare, with most movies shown in their original language with German subtitles. From October to June the Votiv-Kino offers a leisurely Sunday brunch-feature film package, *Filmfrühstück*, for €14.50 ⊠ *Währingerstrasse 12, 9th District/Alsergrund* ☎ *01/317–3571.*

GALLERIES

Contemporary art museums are springing up in cities all across Austria, and Vienna is not the least among them. You can find cutting-edge art and design in and around the MuseumsQuartier complex. The Freihaus-Quartier, in the 4th District, is where some of the most exciting contemporary galleries in town have set up shop, appropriately within range of the Secession Pavilion. The more traditional art galleries are still grouped around the Dorotheum auction house in the city center.

Bäckerstrasse4. With this gallery, owner Gabriele Schober has successfully established a way for young artists to display their works. Student works are submitted to an international jury, and the winner gets an exclusive show for two months. ⊠ *Bäckerstrasse 4, 1st District* ☎ *0676/555–1777.*

Brotfabrik (*Bread Factory*). A former bread factory is now the site of one of Vienna's newest contemporary art venues. Ateliers, galleries, showrooms, and artists' in residence studios are set up inside, making it akin to an urban artists' colony. It showcases some of the country's premier artists, as well as its up-and-comers. For art lovers, Brotfabrik is a must-see. ⊠ *Absberggasse 27, 10th District* ☏ *01/982–3939* ⊕ *www.loftcity.at.*

Gallery Christine Koenig. This is one of the most influential of the Schleifmülgasse galleries. ⊠ *Schleifmülgasse 1a, 4th District/Wieden* ☏ *01/585–7474* ⊕ *www.christinekoeniggalerie.com.*

Galerie Feichtner. Opposite Vienna's House of Music, Lucas Feichtner's gallery radiates with the bold colors of huge contemporary, abstract, and decorative artworks. The two-story gallery holds roughly seven exhibitions a year. National and international artists like Hubert Schmalix, Petar Mirkovic, Robert F. Hammerstiel, and David Smyth are included. Photo, video, and art installations can be seen regularly. ⊠ *Seilerstätte 19, 1st District* ☏ *01/512–0910.*

Gallery Georg Kargl. Most of the contemporary galleries in the Freihaus-Quartier are along Schleifmühlgasse. This one, in a former printing shop, shows art that sidesteps categorization and is a must for serious collectors. ⊠ *Schleifmühlgasse 5, 4th District/Wieden* ☏ *01/585–4199* ⊕ *georgkargl.com.*

Gallery Krinzinger. A presence at cutting-edge art fairs around the world, this gallery has been going strong since the 1970s, when it pushed Vienna Actionism. Its Krinzinger Projects are among the most important blips on the contemporary Austrian art radar screen. The gallery is close to the MuseumsQuartier. ⊠ *Schottenfeldgasse 45, 7th District* ☏ *01/513–3006* ⊕ *galerie-krinzinger.at.*

MUSIC

Vienna is one of the world's foremost music centers. Contemporary music gets its due, but it's the classics—the works of Beethoven, Brahms, Haydn, Mozart, and Schubert—that draw the Viennese public and make tickets to the Wiener Philharmoniker the hottest of commodities. Vienna is home to four full symphony orchestras: the great Wiener Philharmoniker (Vienna Philharmonic), the outstanding Wiener Symphoniker (Vienna Symphony), the broadcasting service's ORF Symphony Orchestra, and the Niederösterreichische Tonkünstler. There are also hundreds of smaller groups, from world-renowned trios to chamber orchestras.

Although the well-known mid-May to mid-June Wiener Festwochen (Vienna Festival) signals the official end of the concert season, the rest of the summer nowadays brims with musical performances, particularly in the Theater an der Wien.

Deutschordenskloster. The most enchanting place to hear Mozart in Vienna (or anywhere, for that matter) is the exquisite 18th-century Sala Terrena of the Deutschordenskloster. In this tiny room—it seats no more than 50 people—a chamber group in historic costumes offers concerts in a jewel box overrun with rococo frescoes in the Venetian style. The concerts—offered Thursday, Friday, and Sunday at 7:30

and Saturday at 6—are scheduled by the nearby Mozarthaus. Said to be the oldest concert hall in Vienna, the Sala Terrena is part of the German Monastery, where, in 1781, Mozart worked for his despised employer, Archbishop Colloredo of Salzburg. ⊠ *Singerstrasse 7, 1st District* ☎ *01/911–9077* ⊕ *www.mozarthaus.at.*

Festsaal. For a grand evening of Strauss and Mozart in imperial surroundings, head to the Wiener Hofburgorchester concerts given in the Hofburg Palace's mammoth 19th-century Festsaal. Performances are offered Tuesday through Saturday between May and October. ⊠ *Hofburg Palace, Heldenplatz, 1st District* ☎ *01/587–2552* ⊕ *www. hofburgorchester.at.*

Konzerthaus. A three-minute walk from the Musikverein is the Konzerthaus, home to three performance halls: the Grosser Konzerthaussaal, Mozartsaal, and Schubertsaal. The first is a room of magnificent size, with red velvet and gold accents. The calendar of Grosser Konzerthaussaal is packed with goodies, including the fabulous early-music group Concentus Musicus Wien and concerts of the Wiener Philharmoniker and the Wiener Symphoniker. ⊠ *Lothringerstrasse 20, 1st District* ☎ *01/242–200* ⊕ *www.konzerthaus.at.*

Musikverein. The city's most important concert halls are in the 1869 Gesellschaft der Musikfreunde, better known as the Musikverein. This magnificent theater holds six performance spaces, but the one that everyone knows is the venue for the annual New Year's Day Concert—the Goldene Saal (Gold Hall). It was designed by the 19th-century Danish architect Theophil Hansen, a passionate admirer of ancient Greece who festooned it with an army of gilded caryatids. The smaller Brahmssal is even more sumptuous—a veritable Greek temple with lots of gilding and green malachite. The avant-garde Gläserne, Hölzerne, Metallene, Steinerne Säle (Glass, Metal, Wooden, and Stone Halls) make fitting showcases for contemporary music. In addition to being the main venue for the Wiener Philharmoniker and the Wiener Symphoniker, the Musikverein hosts many of the world's finest orchestras. ⊠ *Bösendorferstrasse 12A, 1st District* ☎ *01/505–8190* ⊕ *www.musikverein.at.*

Wiener Festwochen. Although the well-known mid-May to mid-June Vienna Festival, the Wiener Festwochen, signals the end of the primary season, the rest of the summer music scene, from mid-July to mid-August, nowadays brims with activities, particularly in the Theater an der Wien. ☎ *01/589–22–11* ⊕ *www.festwochen.at.*

Wiener Kursalon. If the whirling waltzes of Strauss are your thing, head to the Johann Strauss concerts at the Wiener Kursalon, a majestic palacelike structure built in the Italian Renaissance Revival style in 1865 and set in Vienna's sylvan Stadtpark. Here, in gold-and-white salons, the Salonorchester Alt Wien performs concerts of the works of "Waltz King" Johann Strauss and his contemporaries. ⊠ *Johannesgasse 33, 1st District* ☎ *01/513–2477* ⊕ *www.strauss-konzerte.at.*

Wiener Sängerknaben (*Vienna Boys' Choir*). The beloved Vienna Boys' Choir, known here as the Wiener Sängerknaben, isn't just a set of living "dolls" out of a Walt Disney film (remember the 1962 movie *Almost*

Angels?). Its pedigree is royal, and its professionalism such that the choir regularly appears with the best orchestras around the world. The troupe was founded by Emperor Maximilian I in 1498, but with the demise of the Habsburg Empire in 1918 it was on its own, subsidizing itself by giving public performances starting in the 1920s. When the troupe lost its imperial patronage, it traded in court costume for the current charming costumes, then the height of fashion (a look even sported by Donald Duck, who was also born in that era).

From mid–September to late June, the apple-cheeked lads sing Mass at 9:15 am Sunday in the Hofburgkapelle. Written requests for seats should be made at least six weeks in advance. Tickets are also sold at ticket agencies and at the box office (open Friday 11–1 and 3–5). General seating costs €7, prime seats in the front of the church nave €35. Standing room is free. ■TIP➔ Note that only the 10 side-balcony seats allow a view of the choir. On Sunday at 8:45 am any unclaimed tickets are sold. If you miss hearing the choir at a Sunday Mass, you may be able to catch them in a more popular program in the Musikverein. ✉ *Hofmusikkapelle, Hofburg-Schweizerhof, 1st District* ☎ *01/533–9927* ⊕ *www.wsk.at.*

MuTh. MuTh (a play on the words Music and Theater) is the new concert hall and permanent home of the world-famous Vienna Boys' Choir, opened in December 2012 in Vienna's second district. The 400-seat theater has become the official music center inside the Augarten, the oldest Baroque garden in Vienna. In the "MuTh," the Vienna Boys' Choir performs music that ranges from classical to world music to pop. The vast stage has some of the finest acoustics in Vienna and is equipped with an orchestra pit, specially designed seating, and distinctive acoustic panels. The building itself combines a unique mix of Baroque and modern architecture and includes a cafe, shop, and seminar room, where musical education and other performances takes place. ✉ *Am Augartenspitz 1* ⊕ *www.muth.at.*

OPERA AND OPERETTA

Austria's handling of political scandals had led some to call it an "operetta state." It's small wonder that this antiquated art form is still cherished in musical theaters such as the Volksoper, albeit in a tongue-in-cheek manner. Although the Viennese officially boast of opera productions at the Staatsoper, many secretly prefer light-hearted operettas. Expect grand opera with all the attendant pomp and circumstance at the Staatsoper. In addition to offering operas that are just as satisfying as those at the Staatsoper, the Volksoper strikes just the right balance between operetta, musicals, and dance performances.

Letztes Erfreuliches Operntheater. What would *La Traviata* be like with two soloists and a piano? Or how about a *Tosca* where you can join in the chorus? Stefan Fleischhacker's Letztes Erfreuliches Operntheater (L.E.O. for short) offers marvelously funny and entertaining miniature performances of grand opera that are appropriate for audiences of all ages. For a small donation bread and wine are available. ✉ *Ungargasse 18, 3rd District/Landstrasse* ☎ *01/712–1427* ⊕ *www.theaterleo.at.*

Raimundtheater. The Raimundtheater is home to long-running musicals and shows from local and international producers. ☒ *Wallgasse 18, 6th District/Mariahilf* ☎ *01/58885 tickets, 01/588–301010 information* ⊕ *www.musicalvienna.at.*

Ronacherer. Extensively restored in recent years, the Ronacherer presents the latest musical smash hits from Broadway, including a German-language production of *Mama Mia!* ☒ *Seilerstätte 9, 1st District* ☎ *01/588–850* ⊕ *www.musicalvienna.at.*

Staatsoper (*State Opera House*). One of the world's great opera houses, the Staatsoper has been the scene of countless musical triumphs and a center of unending controversy over how it should be run and by whom. (When Lorin Maazel was unceremoniously dumped as head of the opera not so many years ago, he pointed out that the house had done the same thing to Gustav Mahler almost a century earlier.) A performance takes place virtually every night from September to June, drawing on the vast repertoire of the house, with emphasis on Mozart, Verdi, and Wagner. Guided tours are given year-round. ☒ *Opernring 2, 1st District* ☎ *01/514–440* ⊕ *www.wiener-staatsoper.at.*

Theater an der Wien. This beautiful rococo-style historic theater located in Mariahilf is more than 200 years old. It was used and abused for decades as a contemporary musical venue, but now the building—which is closely linked to Beethoven, who lived here—has renewed its role as an opera house, attracting an international crowd. It's open year-round and hosts a premiere nearly every month. The selection of works performed here is tremendous, including Janáček, Prokofiev, Britten, Handel, Monteverdi, Rossini, and Bach. ☒ *Linke Wienszeile 6, 6th District/Mariahilf* ☎ *01/58885 tickets, 01/588–301010 information* ⊕ *www.theater-wien.at.*

Volksoper. Opera, operetta, and ballet are performed at the Volksoper, just on the outer edge of the Innere Stadt at Währingerstrasse and Währinger Gürtel. Prices here are significantly lower than at the Staatsoper, and performances can be every bit as rewarding. This theater has a packed calendar, with offerings ranging from the grandest opera, such as Mozart's *Don Giovanni*, to an array of Viennese operettas, including Johann Strauss's *Die Fledermaus,* to Broadway musicals (*Guys and Dolls* a recent addition to the repertoire). Most operas and musicals are sung in German. The opera house is at the third stop on streetcar Nos. 41, 42, and 43, which run from Schottentor, U2, on the Ring. ☒ *Währingerstrasse 78, 9th District/Alsergrund* ☎ *01/513–1513* ⊕ *www.volksoper.at.*

THEATER

Opera and classical music get all the attention, but theater is also very popular among Vienna's residents. Tickets to the Burgtheater, one of the world's top German-language theaters, can be hard to come by.

Burgtheater. One of the leading German-language theaters in the world, the Burgtheater's repertoire frequently mixes German classics with more modern and controversial pieces. Particulary notorious are the works of Elfriede Jelinek, who won the 2004 Nobel Prize for Literature. ⊠ *Dr.-Karl-Lueger-Ring 2, 1st District* ☎ *01/514–444–4140* ⊕ *www.burgtheater.at.*

Akademietheater. The Burg's smaller house, the Akademietheater, draws on much the same group of actors for classical and modern plays, but performances are in a more relaxing setting. ⊠ *Lisztstrasse 1, 3rd District/Landstrasse* ☎ *01/514–444–145* ⊕ *www.bundesttheater.at.*

Kammerspiele der Josefstadt. The newly renovated theater offers a season of modern dramas and comedies. ⊠ *Rotenturmstrasse 20, 1st District* ☎ *01/42–700–359* ⊕ *www.josefstadt.org.*

FAMILY **Marionettentheater Schloss Schönbrunner.** Historical recordings of Mozart's *Magic Flute* and other favorites are on the program at this magnificent puppet theater in Schönbrunn Palace. These outstanding performances fill a whole evening and are definitely not just for kids. ⊠ *Schönbrunn Palace, Schönbrunner Schloss-Strasse 47, 13th District/Hietzing* ☎ *01/817–3247* ⊕ *www.marionettentheater.at.*

Theater in der Josefstadt. The Theater in der Josefstadt stages classical and modern works year-round in a space once run by the great producer and teacher Max Reinhardt. The theater had, of late, been seeming to gather layers of dust, but happily Director Herbert Föttinger has restored its reputation for more avant-garde and daring productions. ⊠ *Josefstädterstrasse 26, 8th District/Josefstadt* ☎ *01/42–700–300* ⊕ *www.josefstadt.org.*

Vienna's English Theater. For English-language theater—mainly classic comedies and dramas—head for this cozy and charming venue. The season runs early September to early July. ⊠ *Josefsgasse 12, 8th District/Josefstadt* ☎ *01/402–1260* ⊕ *www.englishtheatre.at.*

Volkstheater. Dramas and comedies are presented here. ⊠ *Neustiftgasse 1, 7th District/Neubau* ☎ *01/523–3501–0* ⊕ *www.volkstheater.at.*

SHOPPING

Updated
by Patti
McCracken

Upscale Vienna has gone über upscale as it debuts its brand new haut monde shopper's delight, Goldenes Quartier, or Golden Quarter, in the heart of the heart of the Innere Stadt. The exclusive shopping area is on the extension of the Kohlmarkt, between Tuchlauben, Bognergasse, and Am Hof, where the five-star Park Hyatt hotel opened in 2014. Flagship stores such as Prada, Saint Laurent, Bottega Venetta, and Louis Vuitton are just a few among the many that will entice all manner of serious shoppers. Visitors can stroll easily along, as the area has been turned into a pedestrian zone.

In the pedestrian-only streets of Kärntnerstrasse, Graben, and Kohlmarkt, shopaholics can readily give into their passion. Sleekly cut dresses and intricately crafted jewelry beckon from the windows of shops formerly occupied by purveyors to His Imperial Majesty. Even the Swedish clothing store H&M presents itself in exclusive garb. On Graben near St. Stephen's Cathedral, it has found a home in the mahogany-clad building that was once home of the department store of Braun & Co. Where baronesses once bought fur muffs, tattooed teens now rummage for cheap T-shirts. Luxury brands such as Hermès, Burberry, and Cartier have set up shop on or around Kohlmarkt, the street leading up to the Hofburg.

As you walk along Michaelerplatz, in front of the imperial palace, be sure to explore the little passageway next to the Michaeler Church. You'll find a few wonderful shops selling precious stones and silverware. If you want to venture farther afield, explore Mariahilferstrasse, Vienna's best-known shopping mile outside of the city center. Much of this shop-heavy area has been turned into a "shared space zone"—part of it now pedestrian-only—making it very friendly to shoppers. Running from MuseumsQuartier to the new BahnhofCity Wien shopping mall (the refurbished Westbahnhof train station), it's peppered with such department stores as Peek & Cloppenburg, Gerngross, and La Stafa. Lindengasse, which runs parallel to Mariahilferstrasse, is bustling with young designers who sell their wares in little boutiques. The creativity continues on nearby Kirchengasse and Burggasse.

SHOPPING PLANNER

HOURS

Outside the city center, shops are generally open weekdays from 9 am to 6 pm and on Saturday from 9 am to noon. On the busy shopping thoroughfares, most shops stay open until 8 pm during the week and 5 pm on Saturday. Stores are closed on Sunday and public holidays.

TAXES

Visitors from non-EU countries may claim a refund of Austria's value-added tax for goods costing more than €75. Ask your sales clerk to fill out a Global Blue tax-free form and to staple the original receipt to it. When you're leaving the country, bring your purchase and tax-free form to the customs counter. The officer will stamp your slip and you can obtain the refund from one of the airport banks.

Alternately, you can receive your refund at more than 700 refund points around the world or send the form to Global Blue and have the money transferred to your bank account. If you want to use this method, ask the sales clerk for a Global Blue envelope.

SALES

You should definitely haggle over prices at the flea markets. The biggest sale day of the year is Boxing Day (December 26), the first business day after Christmas, when nearly everything in the city is half price. Look for signs reading *ausverkauf* (sale), aktion (action), or angebote (special offer) in shop windows. Deep discount sales are in January and July.

SHOPPING DISTRICTS

The **Kärntnerstrasse, Graben,** and **Kohlmarkt**—the latter home to the new Goldenes Quartier (Golden Quarter)—are pedestrian areas in the Inner City that claim to have the best shops in Vienna. For some items, such as jewelry, they're probably some of the best anywhere. The side streets in this area have shops selling antiques, art, clocks, jewelry, and period furniture. A collection of attractive small boutiques can also be found in the **Palais Ferstel** passage at Freyung 2 in the 1st District.

Gumpendorferstrasse, in the 6th District, is rapidly turning into one of the hippest shopping destinations in town, with small boutiques, trendy hairstylists, and great eateries. Then there's the 7th District, Neubau, which is starting to compete for the title of hippest of all. On Neubaugasse, Kirchengasse, Lindengasse, and the quaint Mondscheingasse, fashionistas can find unique clothing, jewelry, and footwear in lovely little boutiques. Also in the 7th District, on **Spittelberggasse** between Burggasse and Siebensterngasse, are small galleries and handicrafts shops.

Vienna's **Naschmarkt** (between Linke and Rechte Wienzeile, starting at Getreidemarkt) is one of Europe's great and most colorful food and produce markets. Stalls open at 6 am, and the pace is lively until about 6 pm. Saturday is the big day, though, when farmers come into the city to sell at the back end of the market. Also on Saturday is a huge flea market at the Kettenbrückengasse end. The Naschmarkt is closed Sunday. Christmas is the time for the tinselly **Christkindlmarkt** (Rathausplatz in front of City Hall). In protest of its commercialization, smaller markets specializing in handicrafts have sprung up on such traditional spots as Am Hof, the Freyung, and in front of the Schönbrunn and Belvedere palaces.

TOP SHOPPING EXPERIENCES

Let the taste linger. Fill your bags with some edible delicacies, such as artisanal chocolates from Meinl am Graben (try some with poppy seeds and apricot brandy), small chocolate-rum-punch cubes from the shop at Hotel Sacher (even tastier than the classic torte), miniature chocolates from Altmann & Kühne on Graben, and a bottle of Styrian pumpkin-seed oil or Zweigelt wine from supermarkets like Billa or Merkur.

Serve in style. Once back home, you need to serve your goodies. Check out delicate Augarten china in Spiegelgasse near Graben or the green-striped Gmunden ceramics in Stadiongasse in the 1st District.

Dress like an Austrian. Treat yourself to an Austrian dirndl at Gexi Tostmann's shop on Schottengasse or a *trachten* jacket at Loden Plankl on Michaelerplatz. If you consider wearing these garments a bit silly, think again: even Klimt model Emilie Flöge wore them when she vacationed in the Alps. Complement your look with some gold-plated enamel jewelry at Frey Wille on Stephansplatz.

Haunt the flea markets. The best deals on the Naschmarkt flea market can be found at 6 am on Saturday. Avoid the elaborate stalls of the antiques dealers and check out what regular folks have scattered about on the pavement next to the subway. Who knows, maybe you'll discover Emilie Flöge's long-lost necklace or sugar tray.

VIENNA SHOPPING REVIEWS

Shopping listings are organized by neighborhood.

THE EASTERN CITY CENTER: STEPHANSDOM AND MEDIEVAL VIENNA

ANTIQUES

Gallery Dr. Sternat. Just around the corner from the Opera House, this is one of the most traditional art galleries, with a focus on fine Austrian paintings, Viennese bronzes, Thonet furniture, and beautiful Biedermeier pieces. ⊠ *Lobkowitzplatz 1, 1st District* ☏ *01/512–20–63.*

BOOKS

Frick. Some of the best business in art history and guidebooks on Vienna and Austria is done here. The staff is helpful, and bargains can often be found in the trays at the door. There are a few branches around the city, including a larger shop at Graben 27. ⊠ *Kärntnerstrasse 31, 1st District* ☏ *01/513–7364.*

Morawa. This could be the best stocked bookstore in Vienna, with titles on everything under the sun. Thankfully, help is always at hand if you can't find that specific one you're looking for. The magazine and newspaper section is impressive. ⊠ *Wollzeile 11, 1st District* ☏ *01/513–7513.*

CERAMICS, GLASS, AND PORCELAIN

Berger. Crafting made-to-order ceramics for his customers for 40 years, Herr Berger has now been joined in the business by his daughter Lisa. How about a hand-crafted ceramic stove made to measure for your alpine chalet, or a decorative wall plate blooming with a hand-painted flowering gentian? ⊠ *Weihburggasse 17, 1st District* ☎ *01/512–1434* ⊕ *www.berger-ofen.at.*

Lobmeyr. Nearly 200 years old, this shop is world renowned for its exquisite glassware. One of its collections is housed in the Metropolitan Museum of Art (MOMA) in New York and its chandeliers have graced opera houses (including New York's Metropolitan Opera) and private homes for centuries. This is one of the only stores left in Vienna that retains its interior of imperial glory, yet allows the cutting edge of design to enter its realm. (See the breathtakingly beautiful black rococo mirrors by Austrian designer Florian Ladstätter). Even if you're not buying, head upstairs to the second-floor glass museum. ⊠ *Kärntnerstrasse 26, 1st District* ☎ *01/512–0588.*

CLOTHING: AUSTRIAN

Giesswein. Dirndls and *trachten* (the typical Austrian costume with white blouse, print dress, and apron) for toddlers to ladies, and cute hand-embroidered cardigans for the kids, are all found here, with some of the best traditional clothing in town. ⊠ *Kärntnerstrasse 5–7, 1st District* ☎ *01/512–4597.*

CLOTHING: MEN'S

Sir Anthony. For the classic look, this is the place. A second location is nearby at the Ringstrassen Gallerien. ⊠ *Kärntnerstrasse 21–23, 1st District* ☎ *01/512–6835.*

Sturm am Parkring. Come here for dapper suits for well-dressed men. ⊠ *Parkring 2, 1st District* ☎ *1/706–4600* ⊕ *www.sturm-parkring.at.*

CLOTHING: WOMEN'S

Schella Kann. Fashionistas make a beeline for the flagship store of this Austrian designer/national treasure. Extravagant and trendy, these are clothes you never want to take off. ⊠ *Spiegelgasse 15, 1st District* ☎ *01/513–2287* ⊕ *www.schellakann.com.*

Sisi. The collection at Sissy Schranz' boutique is a charming take on the nostalgic styles donned in the days of beloved Empress Sisi. Soon after the shop first opened its doors in 2010, the local press announced "The Queen Has New Clothes." Austria's best designers are showcased here, including Susanne Bisovsky (she studied with Vivienne

---

CHRISTKINDLMÄRKTE

Vienna keeps the Christmas flame burning perhaps more brightly than any other metropolis in the world. Here, during the holiday season, no fewer than nine major *Christkindlmärkte* (Christmas Markets) proffer their wares, with stands selling enough wood-carved Austrian toys, crèche figures, and Tannenbaum ornaments to tickle anybody's mistletoes. Many of the markets have food vendors selling *Glühwein* (mulled wine) and *Kartoffelpuffer* (potato patties).

Westwood) and Mothwurf. Accessories, jewelry, and hats round out the offerings. ⊠ *Annagasse 11, 1st District* ☎ *1/513–05–18* ⊕ *www.sisi-vienna.at.*

DEPARTMENT STORES

Peek & Cloppenburg. British star architect Sir David Chipperfield designed the six-story P & C store. With the longest facade on the Kärntnerstrasse, huge windows, and almost a complete lack of ornamentation, it can't be missed. Find the best-known fashion labels, as well as inexpensive off-the-rack garb. Shop to the grooves of a live DJ every Saturday from 11 am to 6 pm at the Mariahilferstrasse location. ⊠ *Kärntnerstrasse 29, 1st District* ☎ *01/890–4888* ⊕ *www.peek-cloppenburg.at.*

Steffl. One of Vienna's most prominent department stores, Steffl stocks just about everything. It's moderately upscale without being overly expensive. ⊠ *Kärntnerstrasse 19, 1st District* ⊕ *www.steffl-vienna.at.*

GALLERIES

Bel Etage. This gallery has wonderful works by Josef Hoffmann, Dagobert Peche, and other Wiener Werkstätte masters, all of which entice onlookers to spend more than just time here. ⊠ *Mahlerstrasse 15, 1st District* ☎ *01/512–2379.*

GIFTS AND SOUVENIRS

Alt-Österreich. Are you looking for a vintage postcard, a hand-carved walking stick, a classic record, or even an old photograph of the Opera House from before the war? Head to Alt-Österreich—its name translates as "Old Austria"—and you'll find that this treasure trove has just about everything dealing with that time-burnished subject. ⊠ *Himmelpfortgasse 7, 1st District* ☎ *01/512–12–96.*

Petit Point Kovalcec. For that Alt Wien flourish, choose a needlepoint handbag, pill box, or brooch from one of the oldest shops in the city center—family run for nearly a hundred years. ⊠ *Kärntnerstrasse 16* ☎ *01/512–4886.*

JEWELRY

A. E. Köchert. One of Vienna's purveyors to the imperial court, A. E. Köchert has been Vienna's jeweler of choice for nearly two centuries. Almost 150 years ago Empress Elisabeth ordered some diamond-studded stars from here to adorn her legendary auburn hair (so long she could sit on it). Those stars are more fashionable than ever since Köchert started reissuing them. And if you're ever in need of a crown, Köchert will craft your very own. ⊠ *Neuer Markt 15, 1st District* ☎ *01/512–5828.*

Bucherer. For one of the finest selections of watches head to this store, where the gold- and diamond-jewelry selections are also top-notch. ⊠ *Kärntner Strasse 2, 1st District* ☎ *1/512–6730.*

Juwelier Heldwein. In 2013, this established Vienna jeweler added the iconic Madrid brand Carrera y Carrera to the range of jewelry, watches, silverware, and gifts that it's been offering to its customers since 1865. ⊠ *Graben 13, 1st District* ☎ *1/512–5781* ⊕ *www.heldwein.com.*

Reingold. One of the newer fine jewelry shops in old Vienna, Reingold quickly established itself as a premier site for jewelry design, specializing in fine diamond and pearls and refined silver, as well as red, white, and yellow gold. ⊠ *Kärntnerstrasse 16, 1st District* ☎ *1/512–71–03* ⊕ *www.reingold.at.*

MUSIC

EMI. Helpful sales assistants are at the ready if you're looking for any special titles at EMI—one of the big mainstays for classical music. The selections run the gamut from ethno to pop. ⊠ *Kärntnerstrasse 30, 1st District* ☎ *01/512–3675.*

VIENNA'S ANTIQUE ROWS

You'll find the best antiques shops in the 1st District, many clustered close to the Dorotheum auction house, along the Dorotheergasse, Stallburggasse, Plankengasse, and Spiegelgasse. There are also interesting shops in the 8th District, where prices are considerably lower than those in the center of town. Wander up Florianigasse and back down Josefstädterstrasse, being sure not to overlook the narrow side streets.

THE INNER CITY CENTER: BAROQUE GEMS AND VIENNA'S SHOPWINDOWS

6

ANTIQUES

Dorotheum. Founded as a pawnshop more than 300 years ago, the Palais Dorotheum is rapidly becoming one of the world's leading auction houses. The place is intriguing, with goods ranging from elegant furs to antique jewelry to period paintings and furniture auctioned almost daily. Information on how to bid is available in English. On the second floor, art and antiques are for immediate sale. Browse without hassle here. ⊠ *Dorotheergasse 17, 1st District* ☎ *01/515–600.*

Kulcsar Antiques. This is your best bet for some of the finer collectibles. Peter Kulcsar's special focus is on silverware, watercolors, and objets d'art. ⊠ *Spiegelgasse 19, 1st District* ☎ *01/512–7267.*

BOOKS

Freytag & Berndt. If you're planning a hiking holiday in Austria, stock up on the necessary maps at Freytag & Berndt, the best place for maps and travel books. ⊠ *Wallnerstrasse 3, 1st District* ☎ *01/533–8685.*

Wolfrum. Art-book lovers will adore Wolfrum. If you have money to burn, you can also spring for a Schiele print or special art edition to take home. ⊠ *Augustinerstrasse 10, 1st District* ☎ *01/512–5398.*

CERAMICS, GLASS, AND PORCELAIN

Albin Denk. If you want to enter an old-fashioned interior that is little changed from the time when Empress Sisi shopped here, Albin Denk is the place. The shop entrance is lined with glass cases and filled with a wonderful, if kitschy, army of welcoming porcelain figurines. ⊠ *Graben 13, 1st District* ☎ *01/512–4439.*

Augarten. The best china in town can be found at this flagship store, designed by Philipp Bruni, which has a sleek, modern design that shines a contemporary light on the traditional side of historic porcelain products. ⊠ *Spiegelgasse 3, 1st District* ☎ *01/512–1494.*

Swarovski. Ireland has its Waterford, France its Baccarat, and Austria has Swarovski, purveyors of some of the finest cut crystal in the world. You'll find your typical collector items and gifts here, but also high-style fashion accessories (Paris couturiers now festoon their gowns with Swarovski crystals the way they used to with ostrich feathers), crystal figurines, and home accessories. This flagship store is a cave of coruscating crystals that gleam and glitter. Breathtakingly beautiful window displays change monthly. ⊠ *Kärntnerstrasse 24, 1st District* ☎ *01/324–0000.*

CLOTHING: AUSTRIAN

Loden-Plankl. The Austrians take special pride in their traditional cloth-ing–*trachten*–and think naught of the kitschy von Trapp clan when doing so. *Lederhosen* and *dirndls* are worn at festivals and special occa-sions, and men's and women's *trachtenjacken* are worn in daily attire. Perhaps the best place to purchase traditional clothing is at Loden-Plankl, which stocks hand-embroidered jackets and *lederhosen* for kids. The building, opposite the Hofburg, is a centuries-old treasure. ⊠ *Mi-chaelerplatz 6, 1st District* ☎ *01/533–8032.*

CLOTHING: MEN'S

Grandits. This men's shop has a great selection from Armani, Boss, Joop, Ralph Lauren, Versace, and Zegna, all displayed in a stylish ambience. ⊠ *Rotenturmstrasse 10, 1st District* ☎ *01/512–6389.*

CLOTHING: WOMEN'S

Mondrean. This concept store brings a touch of Hollywood to Vienna. With more than 60 trendsetting labels from which to choose (Dekker, Rare, Vic Beckham, Exoal, local designer Niko Fechter and many more), you can match your outfit with all the right accessories: shades, bags, perfume, and jewelry. Even the music is produced in-house. ⊠ *Dorotheergasse 13, 1st District* ☎ *01/533–7312* ⊕ *www. mondrean.at.*

Mühlbauer Headwear. Skilled milliners produce unconventional headwear for this boutique. Klaus Mühlbauer and his sister Marlies design hats that have conquered the international market—over half what they make goes abroad. With stars like Brad Pitt, Meryl Streep, Madonna, and Yoko Ono as clients, you know everything in the shop is of the highest quality. ⊠ *Seilergasse 10, 1st District* ☎ *01/512–2241* ⊕ *www. muehlbauer.at.*

FLEA MARKETS

Am Hof. On Friday and Saturday from March to early November, an outdoor arts-and-crafts, collectibles, and flea market takes place on Am Hof. It's open 10 am to 6 pm.

Danube Canal art and antiques market. From early May to late Septem-ber, an outdoor art and antiques market springs up along the Danube Canal underneath the Salztorbrücke. The merchandise, including a lot of books, is slightly better quality than elsewhere. It's open Saturday from 2 to 8 pm and Sunday from 10 am to 8 pm.

Antique Shopping at the Dorotheum

Dorotheum. If you're looking for something truly special—an 18th-century oil portrait or a real fur, a rococo mirror or a fine silk fan, a china figurine or sterling-silver spoon, an old map of the Austrian Empire or even a stuffed parrot—the one place that may have the answer is the Dorotheum, Vienna's fabled auction house. Have you ever wanted to see how the Austrian aristocracy once lived, how their sumptuous homes were furnished? Well, don't bother with a museum—you can inspect their antique furnishings, displayed as if in use, for free, and without the eagle eyes of sales personnel following your every move. This was the first imperial auction house (*oops*, pawnshop), established in 1707 by Emperor Joseph I. Occupying the former site of the Dorothy Convent (hence the name), the Dorotheum has built up a grand reputation.

The neo-baroque building was completed in 1901 and deserves a walk-through (you can enter from Spiegelgasse and exit on Dorotheer-gasse) just to have a look, even if you only admire the gorgeous stuccoed walls and palatial interiors, or peek into the glass-roofed patio stocked with early-20th-century glass, furniture, and art. With more than 600 auctions a year, this has become one of the busiest auction houses in Europe. There are auctions held frequently throughout the week, though not Saturday, and it's closed Sunday. And if you don't fancy bidding for something, there are sale areas on the ground and second floors where loads of stuff can simply be bought off the floor. ⊠ *Dorotheergasse 17, 1st District* ☎ *01/515–600* ⊕ *www.dorotheum.at.*

6

GIFTS AND SOUVENIRS
Souvenir in der Hofburg. Fancy a collection of composers' busts? Schubert, Mozart, Beethoven, Haydn, and the rest of the gang can be had at Souvenir in der Hofburg. While you're at it, you might want to go for a ceramic figure of a Lipizzaner stallion, too. It may not be an Augarten original, but it's certainly more affordable. ⊠ *Hofburgpassage 1 and 7, 1st District* ☎ *01/533–5053.*

JEWELRY
Pomellato Boutique. In Vienna's prestigious new "Golden Quarter," this fine jewelry store opened in late 2013 and offers a unique collection of precious stones and silver. ⊠ *Tuchlaubenhof 7A, 1st District* ☎ *1/905–2324* ⊕ *www.pomellato.com.*

MUSIC
Arcadia. In case you bump into Plácido Domingo or Anna Netrebko, you can buy that picture postcard here so you can have it autographed. Arcadia, in the Opera House, stocks a grand selection of the latest CD releases from the operatic world, and quite a few classic rarities, too. ⊠ *Staatsoper, Opernring 2, 1st District* ☎ *01/513–9568.*

SHOES

Think!. This Austrian company is known worldwide for its yummy, trendy, well-crafted leather shoes for men and women. ⊠ *Bauernmarkt 1, 1st District* ☎ *1/815–8508–1371* ⊕ *dealer.thinkshoes.com.*

TOYS

Kober. Emperor Franz Josef in his horse-drawn carriage, the infantry cheering him on, and the Prussian emperor to meet him at the battlefield—here at Kober you can find all the historic tin soldiers you'll ever need to relive the eventful last years of the empire. If you prefer something a little less military, go for the full Johann Strauss Orchestra. ⊠ *Wollzeile 16/Schulerstrasse 11, 1st District* ☎ *01/533–6018.*

Spielzeugschachtel. The name means toy box, and this shop is one of the better toy boxes in the city. Parents with a passion for educational games love this place, and there are also loads of all other kinds of games to choose from, many made of that rarest of 21st-century materials, good old wood. ⊠ *Rauhensteingasse 5, 1st District* ☎ *01/512–4994.*

ACROSS THE DANUBE: THE SECOND DISTRICT
BOOKS

Lhotzky Literaturbuffet. With a roster of readings and presentations, and an offer of food and drink, Lhotzky's is a café and bookstore in one. ⊠ *Rotensterngasse 2, 2nd District/Leopoldstadt* ☎ *01/276–4736* ⊕ *www.literaturbuffet.com.*

CLOTHING: WOMEN'S

Song. This former fur factory in Vienna's 2nd District has been transformed into a fashion temple. The stylish interior design is by architect Gregor Eichinger. A lover of the avant-garde styles, the Korean-born Song combines the finest glamour labels (Balenciaga, Margiela) with contemporary elegance from young designers (Hartmann Nordenholz). Shop for fashion, bags, shoes, and furniture. Don't miss the Saturday "check out room" sale, where everything sells at half price. ⊠ *Praterstrasse 11–13, 2nd District/Leopoldstadt* ☎ *01/532–2858* ⊕ *www.song.at.*

FOOD

Kaas am Markt. Local cheeses, meats, and breads, fresh farm produce, and handmade specialty items look and taste delicious. Stop by for a good hearty snack or a three-course meal at lunch—if you get there soon enough. Inside there's enough room for only a few tables. ⊠ *Karmelitermarkt 33–36, 2nd District/Leopoldstadt* ☎ *0699/181–406–01* ⊕ *www.kaasammarkt.at.*

THE WESTERN CITY CENTER: BURGTHEATER AND BEYOND
ANTIQUES

Palais Kinsky. Check out this auction house for fabulous paintings and antiques. There are only about six auctions a year, and viewings are just one week prior to sale, so keep an eye on its website for news. ⊠ *Freyung 4, 1st District* ☎ *01/532–4200* ⊕ *www.imkinsky.com/en.*

CHRISTKINDLMÄRKTE

Altwiener Christkindlmarkt. This festive season market is held on one of Vienna's biggest squares. ⊠ *Freyung, 1st District* ☎ *01/270–2156.*

CLOTHING: AUSTRIAN

Tostmann. Fancy having your very own tailor-made Austrian dirndl? Tostmann is the place to fulfill your wishes. ⊠ *Schottengasse 3A, 1st District* ☏ *01/533–5331.*

EAST OF THE RINGSTRASSE: STADTPARK AND KARLSPLATZ

CHRISTKINDLMÄRKTE

Karlsplatz Christkindlmärkte. The Christmas market at Karlsplatz has some of the more refined stands in town, selling homemade wares. ⊠ *Karlsplatz, 4th District/Wieden.*

CLOTHING: MEN'S

Collins Hüte. This is one of the best sources for such accessories as scarves, gloves, and hats, including wide-brimmed sombrero (for that glaring summer sun on the slopes at Lech). ⊠ *Opernpassage, 1st District* ☏ *01/587–1305* ⊕ *www.collins-hats.at.*

SOUTH OF THE RINGSTRASSE: THE 6TH AND 7TH DISTRICTS

CHRISTKINDLMÄRKTE

Spittelberg Christkindlmärkte. The cognoscenti love this artsy market, held in Spittelberg's enchanting Biedermeier quarter. ⊠ *Burggasse and Siebensterngasse, 7th District/Spittelberg.*

CLOTHING: WOMEN'S

Ina Kent. Formerly known as Affair de Coeur, Ina Kent showcases exquisite, exclusive handbags. A second location is at Siebensternstrasse 50, also in the 7th District. ⊠ *Neubaugasse 34, 7th District/Neubau* ☏ *0699/19–54–10–90* ⊕ *www.inakent.com.*

Arnold's. This appealing boutique stocks a wide range of sought-after international brands and labels for urban fashionistas, like Happy Socks and Edwin. You'll also find dresses by Vienna's "most wanted designers," Maiko & Kawayan. ⊠ *Siebensterngasse 52, 7th District/Spittelberg* ☏ *01/923–1316.*

Art Point. Russian designer Lena Kvadrat treats Viennese hipsters to cutting-edge fashion, unveiling two collections each year. ⊠ *Neubaugasse 35, 7th District/Neubau* ☏ *01/522–0425* ⊕ *www.artpoint.eu.*

Be a Good Girl. At this eclectic boutique in the Neubau district, shoppers will find a mix of books, accessories and clothes, and a wide range of brands, including Barbara i Gongini, Don't Shoot the Messengers, Irina Rohpeter, and Pleasure Principle, to name a few. ⊠ *Westbahnstrasse 5A, 7th District/Neubau* ☏ *01/524–4728* ⊕ *www.beagoodgirl.com.*

Bisovsky. Haut couture and prêt-à-porter are by appointment only in Susanne Bisovsky's Neubau district studio. Email ahead for an appointment. ⊠ *Seidengasse 13/6, 7th District/Neubau* ⊕ *www.bisovsky.com.*

Ebenberg. Using materials that are friendly to the earth and its inhabitants is an important principle for Laura Ebenberg, who, besides her own creations, presents some very wearable silky, slinky fashion. Art exhibits held on-site are an added bonus. ⊠ *Neubaugasse 4, 7th District/Neubau* ☏ *06991/528–7226.*

6

Lena Hoschek. One of the shooting stars of Austria's fashion industry, Lena Hoschek finds inspiration in traditional styles. She uses floral fabrics to create petticoat dresses, blouses, and outfits worn by pop stars and celebrities. Singer Katy Perry is just one of many who love her figure-hugging fashions. This shop is in the 7th District, but for tailor-made clothes, visit her studio at Längenfeldgasse 27 in the 12th District. ⊠ *Gutenberggasse 17, 7th District/Neubau* ☎ *01/5030–9200* ⊕ *www.lenahoschek.com.*

Nachbarin. European avant-garde fashion can be found here, where select labels include Veronique Leroy, Anita Moser, and Elena Ghisellini. ⊠ *Gumpendorferstrasse 17, 6th District/Mariahilf* ☎ *01/587–2169* ⊕ *www.nachbarin.co.at.*

Nfive. Neutral, unadorned walls are as minimalist as the fashion on sale. American Vintage, Velvet, Cacharel, Best Behavior, Tigers of Sweden and many more labels are on offer. A men's clothing department is also on site, so head here with the fashion-conscious significant other. ⊠ *Neubaugasse 5, 7th District/Neubau* ☎ *01/523–8313* ⊕ *www.nfive.at.*

Pregenzer. Designer fashions, shoes, and gadgets by Jutta Pregenzer, Moncler, American Vintage, and Girbaud can be found here. ⊠ *Schleifmühlgasse 4, 4th District/Wieden* ☎ *01/586–5758* ⊕ *www.pregenzer. com.*

Printa. Trendy women's clothing, handbags, accessories and home decorations are sold here, along with posters and prints. ⊠ *Lindengasse 22, 7th District/Neubau* ☎ *1/890 48 83* ⊕ *printa.hu.*

Shu!. If you have a shoe fetish, this is your store. You'll find just the right footwear—be it extravagant, chic, practical, or just plain comfortable—in all shapes and sizes. Alberto Fermani, Blundstones, Doucal's, and Vic Matié are among the international designers represented. Contemporary art exhibitions are held here regularly. ⊠ *Neubaugasse 34, 7th District/Neubau* ☎ *01/523–1449* ⊕ *www.shu.at.*

Ulliko. Straight lines, practical cuts, and bold reds, black, and white—outfits reminiscent of the '60s style made popular by Mary Quant—are all strikingly beautiful. Ullrike Kogelmüller, known as Ulliko, does her designs here and has her fashions manufactered locally. ⊠ *Kirchengasse 7, 7th District/Neubau* ☎ *0699/128–43–922* ⊕ *www.ulliko.com.*

Flo Vintage. For preloved fashions, enter the world of Vintage Flo, where you'll find pieces from 1880 to 1980: that pearl-embroidered Charleston dress you always wanted, or a fabulous antique kimono. Besides bags, shoes, and jewelry, there are hats and even sheer silk stockings. ⊠ *Schleifmühlgasse 15A, 4th District/Wieden* ⊕ *www. flovintage.com.*

Wabisabi. Local designer Stefanie Wippel creates breezy, easy-to-wear pieces that flatter any figure. Choose any style to be made up there and then. ⊠ *Lindengasse 20, 7th District/Neubau* ☎ *0644/54–51–280* ⊕ *www.alle-tragen-wabi-sabi.at.*

DEPARTMENT STORES

Grüne Erde. The name translates as Green Earth, and this shop specializes in organic household goods, ecologically sound furniture and tableware, natural cosmetics, and "fashion with responsibility"—created using natural materials and manufactured with sustainability. ✉ *Mariahilferstrasse 11, 6th District/Mariahilf* ☎ *07615/203410* ⊕ *www.grueneerde.com.*

FLEA MARKETS

Flohmarkt am Naschmarkt. In back of the Naschmarkt, stretching along the Linke Wienzeile from the Kettenbrückengasse U4 subway station, you'll find the city's most celebrated flea market. It offers a staggering collection of items, ranging from serious antiques to plain junk. It's held every Saturday, rain or shine, from 6:30 am to 6 pm.

GIFTS AND SOUVENIRS

Gabarage. Old skis become coat stands, bowling pins turn into vases, traffic signs are transformed into lamps, and garbage bins find new lives as chairs at fabulously off-beat Gabarage. A clear conscience is guaranteed when you shop here. ✉ *Schleifmühlgasse 6, 4th District/Wieden* ☎ *01/585-7632* ⊕ *www.gabarage.at.*

HOUSEHOLD ITEMS AND FURNITURE

Werkbank. From charming, homespun knickknacks to painted skateboards hanging as wall art, Werkbank should be among the stops for the trend-conscious. ✉ *Breitegasse 1, 7th District/Neubau* ☎ *650/524–8136* ⊕ *www.werkbank.cc.*

SHOPPING MALLS

Bahnhof City Wien West. The city's newest mall is located at the refurbished and restyled former Westbahnhof train station. Nearly 100 shops selling clothes, sporting goods, electronics, and more can be found here, along with a food court. ✉ *Mariahilferstrasse, 6th District/Mariahilf* ⊕ *www.bahnhofcitywienwest.at.*

WEST OF THE RINGSTRASSE: PARLIAMENT AND CITY HALL

ANTIQUES

Rauminhalt. Specializing in European furniture, lamps, and objets d'art from the 1940s to today, this superb gallery has a particularly eye-catching collection of sandy-colored African berber rugs and sleek Pierre Jeanneret mid-20th-century modern tables and chairs. Exhibitions held regularly. ✉ *Schleifmühlgasse 13, 4th District/Wieden* ☎ *01/650–4099–892* ⊕ *www.rauminhalt.at.*

BOOKS

Babette's. More than 2,000 cookbooks from every corner of the world are piled on every conceivable space in Bernadette Wörndl's shop. Exotic aromas linger in the air—Wörndl is skilled at creating superb dishes, which she serves herself at the counter. Spices are also for sale, and cooking classes are held regularly. ✉ *Schleifmühlgasse 17, at Mühlgasse, 4th District/Wieden* ☎ *01/585–5165* ⊕ *shop.babettes.at/de.*

CHRISTKINDLMÄRKTE

Rathausplatz Christkindlmärkte. The biggest holiday market is the one on Rathausplatz, in front of the Gothic fantasy that is Vienna's city hall.

SCHÖNBRUNN PALACE, PARK, AND ZOO

CHRISTKINDLMÄRKTE

Schönbrunn Christkindlmärkte. All the glitter and gilt of the season frames the market held at the Habsburgs' Schönbrunn. ⊠ *Schönbrunn Palace, Schönbrunner-Schloss-Strasse, 13th District/Hietzing.*

VIENNA WOODS, LAKE NEUSIEDL, AND THE DANUBE RIVER

Updated
by Patti
McCracken

The area along the Danube and around Vienna is drenched in history. Composers like Johann Strauss were inspired by the woodlands and river, and Joseph Haydn and Anton Bruckner both lived in the region and left their traces. A trip here unfolds like a treasured picture book. Roman ruins, medieval castles, and Baroque monasteries perch precariously above the river. This is where the Nibelungs—later immortalized by Wagner—caroused operatically, and where Richard the Lionheart was locked in a dungeon and held to (a substantial) ransom for nearly two years.

Passenger boats can take you along the Danube on pleasure cruises that stop at quaint villages. Aside from the Danube, water sports are on offer in the Neusiedl Lake area, where Viennese go to escape the city. Biking both in the lake area and along the Danube is becoming increasingly popular, and the nearby town of Baden, a favorite haunt of Beethoven, offers superb postpedaling spa relaxation.

In the towns and hamlets throughout the region, time seems to be on pause. Colorful 17th- and 18th-century buildings now serve as hotels and inns, with old-fashioned charm and well-made traditional food that invites you to sit outdoors and savor the countryside. No one is in a hurry here. But not everything is old-fashioned. A little exploring, especially in the vineyards around Neusiedl Lake, will turn up eateries pushing the envelope with modern cuisine, matched with top-notch local wines. Time suddenly leaps forward in Linz, which has a few notable modern buildings punctuating the skyline along with its churches and castle, which itself is a blend of baroque with modern steel and glass.

ORIENTATION AND PLANNING

GETTING ORIENTED

The northeastern part of Austria has quite a diverse geography, with the practically untouched Vienna Woods to the southwest of the capital and the Weinviertel (Wine District) stretching northeast to the border. Along with hearty food, the region produces some remarkable wines, many of which inexplicably never travel beyond the borders. The diverse area has wooded hills as well as one of Europe's largest lakes. The lifeblood of the region is the Danube, which originates in Germany's Black Forest and empties into the Black Sea. The Romans used to say, "Whoever controls the Danube controls all Europe." That may no longer be true, but the scenery is still something to behold.

Vienna Woods. Taking a trip to the spa town of Baden means following the Vienna Woods' southern trail past ancient monasteries, fertile plains, and bucolic vineyards. Unlike other major metropolitan areas,

TOP REASONS TO GO

Baden. Spend an afternoon discovering the attractive spa and casino town of Baden.

Leisurely bike rides. Pedal through the flat plains surrounding Neusiedl Lake, stopping to explore scenic hamlets and dine on fresh fish from the lake.

The Melk Abbey. Magnificent Benedictine Baroque splendor leaves you breathless. The enormous edifice, stately royal rooms, lovely library, and golden, glittering church are incomparable.

Linz. As the saying goes, "It begins in Linz." Designated a Cultural Capital of Europe 2009, the capital of the province of Upper Austria has awakened to a new future, taking a leading role in contemporary art, style, and design.

Wachau Valley. Travel in tranquility by boat or bike between the historic towns of Krems and Melk and experience the Danube Valley's most picturesque and verdant vistas.

Vienna has yet to suffer from suburban sprawl, so the countryside is right outside its door.

The Weinviertel. North of Vienna, the rolling hills, vineyards, and pleasant rural vistas invite visitors to experience a slow-moving, almost dreamy kind of lifestyle, different from the Austria of cliché; this is the region that was for years the least developed, least modern part of the country.

Neusiedl Lake Area. The natural preserve at this lake is where storks come in the thousands to feed. Music lovers will want to make the pilgrimage to Eisenstadt, where the great composer Joseph Haydn (1732–1809) was in the employ of Prince Esterházy.

Along the Danube River. Dürnstein, Krems, and many other small medieval towns offer a peaceful respite to the wandering traveler. Wine taverns abound, and good home cooking in quaint restaurants is a perfect way to end the day. Travel through picturesque vineyards and orchards to the mighty Melk Abbey. Pass by ruins of old castles, or stop and hike through the woods for a closer look at the remnants. The views across the Danube will reward you for your toil.

Linz. Austria's third-largest city basks in amazing cutting-edge design. You can experience exciting insights into the latest technology at one of its incredible museums.

PLANNING

WHEN TO GO

Most of the regions around Vienna and along the Danube are best seen in the temperate months between mid-March and mid-November; not much is offered for winter sports and a number of hotels as well as sites close in the winter. The glorious riverside landscape takes on a fairy-tale quality when apricot and apple trees burst into blossom, late April to mid-June. Others might prefer the early- to mid-autumn days, when the vineyards on the terraced hills turn reddish-blue and a bracing chill settles on the Danube. From mid-September until the beginning of October, the Bruckner Festival in Linz joins forces with Ars Electronica, combining the classic with the contemporary. Seasons notwithstanding, crowds jam the celebrated abbey at Melk; you're best off going first thing in the morning, before the tour buses arrive, or at midday, when the throngs have receded. No matter when you come, be sure to try some fruit in a Linzer torte (a filling of brandy-flavored apricots, raspberries, or plums under a latticed pastry crust), a treat as rich and satisfying as the scenic wonders of the Danube Valley itself.

GETTING HERE AND AROUND

To get to the area between Linz and Weinviertel you can fly into the airport in Vienna or take a EuroCity train to Vienna or Linz. Once here, driving is the most convenient and scenic way to explore the region, especially if you're visiting the smaller towns and villages. If you don't want to drive, opt for the train—rather than a bus—for the main routes and longer distances. Local trains that stop at every station take a long time to get anywhere, but if you have a lot of time to spare, train rides can be fun.

AIR TRAVEL

The northern part of Eastern Austria is served by Vienna's international airport at Schwechat, 19 km (12 miles) southeast of the city center.

The Blue Danube Airport Linz is a good alternative to Vienna's Schwechat Airport if you want to start your journey in calmer surroundings. Located just 15 minutes from the city center by car or train, the airport is serviced regularly by Lufthansa, Austrian Airlines, and several low-cost airlines.

Airport Information Graz Airport (*GRZ*). ✉ *Kalsdorferstrasse, Graz* ☎ *0316/2902–0.*

BIKE TRAVEL

Bicycling is enormously popular in the flatlands around Neusiedl Lake. There are places that rent bikes in Neusiedl am See and Rust. Many hotels in the area also offer rentals, though some offer this only to their guests. ⇨ *See the individual towns for information.*

BOAT TRAVEL

You can take a day trip by boat from Vienna or Krems and explore one of the stops, such as Dürnstein or Melk. Boats run from May to late September. There are two boat companies that ply the Danube. ⇨ *For full information on cruises offered by the Blue Danube Schifffahrt/DDSG (Vienna to Dürnstein) and Brandner Schifffahrt (Krems to Melk), see Danube River Cruises under Tours.* Along this stretch of the river, bridges are few and far between. Old-fashioned tow ferries, attached to cables stretched across the river, allow a speedy crossing for people, cars, and bikes for a small fee.

BUS TRAVEL

Frequent scheduled bus service runs between Vienna and Baden, departing across from the Opera House in Vienna to the center of Baden. Connections are available to other towns in the area. Blaguss Reisen connects Vienna to towns in Eastern Austria. Buses run by the Austrian railroad system and those run by the Austrian postal service cover the area thoroughly for short distances, although services are sometimes infrequent in the less populated areas. If you link them together, bus routes will get you to the main points in this region, assuming you have the time. You can book bus tours in Vienna or Linz by calling central bus information, *listed below.*

Bus Information Blaguss Reisen ☎ *01/610 90–0* ⊕ *www.blaguss.at.*
Central bus information ☎ *01/71101.*

CAR TRAVEL

To reach Baden and the surrounding villages by car, take the A2 autobahn south in the direction of Graz, getting off in Baden and taking Route 210 west.

The Weinviertel is accessed by major highways but not by autobahns. Follow signs to Prague, taking Route E461 toward Mistelbach and Poysdorf if you want to go northeast.

The A4 autobahn is a quick way to reach the Carnuntum region. If you're going east to Carnuntum, follow signs to the A23 and the airport (Schwechat).

The A3 goes from Vienna and Eisenstadt. Route 10 from Vienna to Neusiedl Lake in Burgenland is the preferred scenic alternative to the A4 autobahn.

The main route along the north bank of the Danube is Route 3; along the south bank, there's a choice between the autobahn Route A1 and a collection of lesser roads. Roads are good and well marked, and you can switch over to the A1 autobahn, which parallels the general east–west course of the Danube Valley route. Car rental is best in Vienna or Linz.

TRAIN TRAVEL

The train system is excellent, and reliable trains run frequently from Vienna's Schnellbahn stations to most of the destinations around Vienna. The main east–west train line cuts through the Vienna Woods; the main north–south line out of Vienna traverses the eastern edge of the Vienna Woods. Trains leave Vienna Central Station regularly for Baden.

You can get from Wien-Nord/Praterstern to the Weinviertel, where you can connect to buses running between the small villages.

The Schnellbahn No. 7 running from Wien-Mitte (Landstrasser Hauptstrasse) stops at Petronell, with service about once an hour. Carnuntum is about a 10-minute walk from the Petronell station. Trains go on to Hainburg, stopping at Bad Deutsch-Altenburg.

Trains depart from Vienna Central Station frequently for the one-hour ride to Neusiedl am See.

Regional rail tracks run parallel to the north and south banks of the Danube, and while trains reach all the larger towns and cities in the region, they miss the smaller towns of the Wachau Valley along the

Danube's south bank. You can combine rail and boat transportation along this route, taking the train upstream and crisscrossing your way back on the river.

Train Information **ÖBB—National Train Information** ☏ *05/1717* ⊕ *www.oebb.at.* **ÖBB—Österreichisches Bundesbahn** ☏ *05/1717* ⊕ *www.oebb.at.*

ESSENTIALS
TOURS

The Vienna Woods is one of the standard routes offered by the sightseeing-bus tour operators in Vienna. These short tours give only a quick taste of the region; if you have more time, investigate further.

One-day tours to Neusiedl Lake usually include a boat ride. Tours from Vienna also take you to Melk and back by bus and boat. These tours usually run about eight hours, with a stop at Dürnstein. Bus tours operate year-round except as noted, but the boat runs only April–October. For details, check with your hotel or with Cityrama Sightseeing. Another good option is Vienna Sightseeing Tours.

Cityrama Sightseeing. In addition to its city tours, this company offers the Donau-Panorama tour, which heads out into the Vienna Woods and brings you back into the city by boat. The duration of the tour is 3½ hours and it is offered from mid-April to mid-October, with daily departures at 2:45 pm. ⊠ *Opernpassage Top 3, Vienna* ☏ *01/504 7500* ⊕ *www.cityrama.at* 🎫 *€44.*

Vienna Sightseeing Tours. A four-hour trip out into the Vienna Woods includes the Helenental Valley, Mayerling, Heiligenkreuz Abbey, and the Seegrotte, where you take a boat ride on the huge subterranean lake. Tours run year-round, daily from mid-April to early October, then Tuesday and Thursday–Saturday the rest of the year, departing from SüdTyroler Platz at 9:45 am (arrive 30 minutes before departure). You can get a shuttle to the departure point from the State Opera. ⊠ *Weyringergasse 28–30, Vienna* ☏ *01/712–4683–0* ⊕ *www.viennasightseeingtours.com* 🎫 *€49 (includes entrance to attractions).*

VISITOR INFORMATION

For information on Lower Austria, call the Niederösterreich Tourismus in Vienna. Local tourist offices in the Vienna Woods, including those in Baden, are generally open weekdays. The Weinviertel region also has several tourist centers. The regional tourist information office for Burgenland province is the Burgenland Tourismus. There are helpful local *Fremdenverkehrsämter* (tourist offices), listed in the individual towns. If you plan on seeing many museums, galleries, and castles in Lower Austria—including in Vienna, the Vienna Woods, Melk, Krems, and the Weinviertel—consider getting the Niederösterreich-Card (Lower Austria Card) for €54, which allows free entry to more than 300 sites and offers a host of discounts on concerts, rail travel, and accommodations. It's available at tourist information offices, Raiffeisen banks, tobacco shops, and online at ⊕ www.niederoesterreich-card.at.

Tourist Information **Burgenland Tourismus** ⊠ *Johann Permayer-Strasse 13, Eisenstadt* ☏ *02682/63384–0* ⊕ *www.burgenland.info.* **Lower Austria** ⊠ *St. Pölten* ☏ *02742/9000–9000* ⊕ *www.niederoesterreich.*

at. **Niederösterreich-Card** ☎ *01/535–05–05* ⊕ *www.niederoesterreich-card.at.* **Steirische Tourismus** ⊠ *St. Peter–Hauptstrasse 243, Graz, Styria* ☎ *0316/4003–0* ⊕ *www.steiermark.com.* **Upper Austria** ⊠ *Freistaedter Strasse 119, Linz* ☎ *0732/221022* ⊕ *www.oberoesterreich.at.* **Wachau** ⊠ *Schlossgasse 3, Spitz an der Donau* ☎ *02713/300–60060* ⊕ *www.donau.com.* **Waidhofen an der Ybbs** ⊠ *Schlossweg 2, Waidhofen/Ybbs* ☎ *07442/511255* ⊕ *www.waidhofen.at.* **Weinviertel** ⊠ *Kolpingstrasse 7, Poysdorf* ☎ *02552/3515* ⊕ *www.weinviertel.at.* **Wienerwald** ⊠ *Hauptplatz 11, Purkersdorf* ☎ *02231/62176* ⊕ *www.wienerwald.info.*

RESTAURANTS

With few exceptions, food in this region is on the simple side. The basics are available in abundance: roast meats, customary schnitzel variations, game (in season), fresh vegetables, and standard desserts such as *Palatschinken* (crepes filled with jam or nuts, topped with chocolate sauce) and *Apfelstrüdel*. However, imaginative cooking is beginning to spread, and most places have fresh fish and other lighter fare. Look for at least one vegetarian course on the menu.

Around Neusiedl Lake the local Pannonian cooking, strongly influenced by neighboring Hungary, showcases such spicy dishes as *gulyas* (goulash) flavored with paprika. You'll also find fresh fish, goose, game, and an abundance of fresh local vegetables. Along the Danube, restaurants make the most of the river view. Simple *Gasthäuser* are everywhere, but better dining is more often found in country inns. Restaurants, whether sophisticated and stylish or plain and homey, are often rated as much by their wine as by their chefs' creations.

Dining in the countryside is a casual affair. Meal times are usually from noon to 2 for lunch and from 6 to 10 for dinner. It's rare to find a restaurant that serves all afternoon, so plan ahead. It's a good idea to reserve a table, especially for Sunday lunch, which is a popular time for families to get together. As in Vienna, tipping is usually rounded up to the nearest euro. When in doubt, tip 5%.

HOTELS

Although there are some luxury hotels in Linz and a few castle-hotels along the Danube, in general accommodations in the countryside are no frills. That said, the region has become much more heavily traveled than it was a generation ago, and many lodgings have been upgraded and restyled to attract the growing number of guests. Establishments are family-run, and there is usually somebody on staff who speaks English. You'll probably have to carry your own bags, and sometimes climb stairs in older buildings. Booking ahead is a good idea, as most places have relatively few rooms, particularly rooms with private baths. The standard country pillows and bed coverings are down-filled, so if you're allergic to feathers ask for blankets. Accommodations in private homes are cheaper still, and these bargains are usually identified by signs reading "*zimmer frei*" (room available) or "*frühstückspension*" (bed-and-breakfast).

Some hotels offer half-board, with dinner in addition to buffet breakfast. The half-board room rate is usually an extra €15–€30 per person. Occasionally, quoted room rates for hotels already include half-board accommodations, though a discounted rate is generally offered if you prefer not to take the evening meal. Inquire when booking. Room rates include taxes and service, and usually breakfast—although this is likely to be little more than bread or rolls with slices of ham and cheese. In summer, nights are generally cool, but days can get uncomfortably hot. Most older hotels don't have air-conditioning, and rooms can get stuffy; whenever possible, see the room before checking in.

WHAT IT COSTS IN EUROS			
$	**$$**	**$$$**	**$$$$**
RESTAURANTS	under €12	€12–€17	€18–€22	over €22
HOTELS	under €100	€100–€135	€136–€175	over €175

Restaurant prices are per person for a main course at dinner. Hotel prices are for a standard double room in high season, including taxes and service.

VIENNA WOODS

Pass through the legendary Vienna Woods bordering Vienna on the west. The hills are skirted by vineyards forming a "wine belt," which also follows the valleys south of Vienna. You can tour this area easily in a day, either by car or by public transportation, or you can spend the night in Baden to allow for a more leisurely exploration of Mayerling, Heiligenkreuz, and any other towns and villages along the way.

BADEN

38 km (24 miles) southwest of Vienna.

The Weinstrasse brings you to the serenely elegant spa town of Baden. Since antiquity, Baden's sulfuric thermal baths have attracted the ailing and the fashionable from all over the world. When the Romans came across the springs, they dubbed the town Aquae; the Babenbergs revived it in the 10th century; and with the visit of the Russian czar Peter the Great in 1698, Baden's golden age began. Austria's Emperor Franz II spent 31 successive summers here. Later in the century Emperor Franz Josef was a regular visitor, his presence inspiring many of the regal trappings the city still displays. It was in Baden that Mozart composed his "Ave Verum"; Beethoven spent 15 summers here and wrote large sections of his Ninth Symphony and *Missa Solemnis* when he lived at Frauengasse 10; Franz Grillparzer wrote his historical dramas here; and Josef Lanner, both Johann Strausses (father and son), Carl Michael Ziehrer, and Karl Millöcker composed and directed many of their waltzes, marches, and operettas here.

GETTING HERE AND AROUND

A streetcar was built in the 19th century for the sole purpose of ferrying the rich Viennese from their summer homes in Baden to the opera in Vienna—the last stop is directly in front of the opera house. The modern streetcar still winds its way through Vienna's suburbs on its 50-minute journey to Baden, though things only start to get scenic

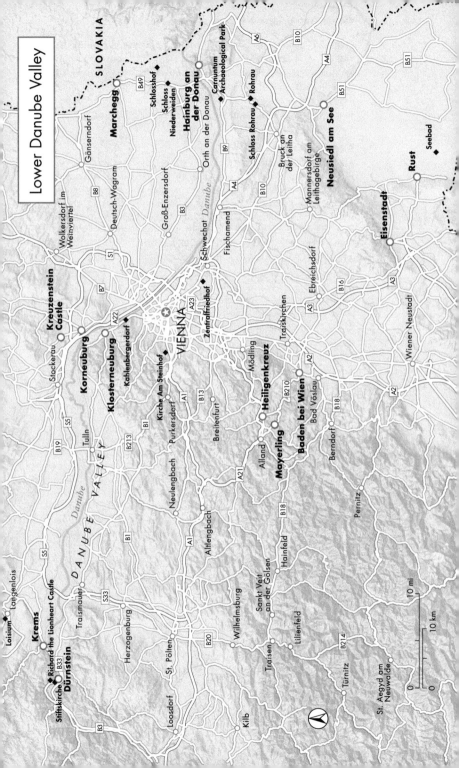

Lower Danube Valley

SLOVAKIA

Danube

VIENNA

DANUBE VALLEY

Langenlois
Loisium ♦
Krems
Richard the Lionheart Castle
Stiftskirche B33
Dürnstein

Stockerau
Kreuzenstein Castle
Korneuburg
Klosterneuburg
Kahlenbergerdorf ♦
Kirche Am Steinhof ♦

Gänserndorf
Marchegg
Schlosshof ♦
Schloss Niederweiden
Hainburg an der Donau
Carnuntum Archaeological Park
Schloss Rohrau ♦ Rohrau ♦
Orth an der Donau

Neusiedl am See
Seebad ♦
Rust
Seebad ♦
Eisenstadt

Wolkersdorf im Weinviertel
Deutsch-Wagram
Groß-Enzersdorf
Schwechat
Fischamend
Bruck an der Leitha
Mannersdorf am Leithagebirge
Ebreichsdorf
Wiener Neustadt

Zentralfriedhof ♦
Mödling
Traiskirchen
Bad Vöslau
Berndorf
Pernitz

Heiligenkreuz
Baden bei Wien
Mayerling
Alland
Purkersdorf
Breitenfurt
Neulengbach
Altlengbach
Hainfeld
Sankt Veit an der Gölsen
Lilienfeld
Türnitz
St. Aegyd am Neuwalde

Tulln
Traismauer
Herzogenburg
St. Pölten
Loosdorf
Kilb
Wilhelmsburg
Traisen

A6 B10 B51 B49 B9 A4 B10 B16 A3 A2 B18 B214 B20 B3 B1 A1 B13 A21 B18 A2 B210 A23 A22 B7 B8 B3 S1 S5 B19 B213 S33 B33

10 mi
10 km
0   0

about 25 minutes before Baden, when the car passes through the wine villages. A faster option is to take the train. It's about a half hour from Westbahnhof, and most trains are double-deckers (so you can sit up top and have a great view of the countryside).

ESSENTIALS

Tourist Information Baden ⊠ *Brusattiplatz 3* ☎ *02252/22600–600* ⊕ *www.tourismus.baden.at.*

EXPLORING

Arnulf Rainer Museum. A former 19th-century bathhouse—one that Emperor Franz Josef frequented on his visits to Baden—was converted in 2009 to a museum highlighting Austria's internationally renowned abstract artist Arnulf Rainer, now in his eighties. Exhibits also include other contemporary greats, including Damien Hirst. Rainer's work has been displayed in the Museum of Modern Art in New York and other noteworthy world-class museums. ⊠ *Josefsplatz 5* ☎ *02252/209–19–611* ⊠ *€6* ⊗ *Weekdays 10–5, weekends 10–3.*

Badener Puppen und Spielzeugmuseum (*Doll and Toy Museum*). Children of all ages will enjoy this enchanting museum, which has four rooms with dolls dating from the late 1700s to the 1950s, alongside other exhibits. ⊠ *Erzherzog Rainer-Ring 23* ☎ *02252/41020* ⊠ *€3.50* ⊗ *Tues.–Fri. 4–6, weekends and holidays 2–6.*

Beethoven Haus. Known locally and affectionately as Beethoven's *"Haus der Neunten"*—Ninth House—since he composed his Ninth Symphony while living at this address. In the spring of 2014, workers were delighted to discover works of art and belongings dating to the time when the musical master lived there, and a full restoration of the residence has begun. ⊠ *Rathausgasse 10* ☎ *02252/86800–231* ⊠ *€3.50* ⊗ *Tues.–Fri. 3–6, weekends 10–noon and 3–6.*

Casino. The ornate Casino—with a bar, restaurant, and gambling rooms—still includes traces of its original 19th-century touches, but has been enlarged and, in the process, overlaid with glitz rivaling that of Las Vegas. Evening attire is expected, and jackets are available on loan at the coat check. Casual dress is only acceptable in the Jackpot Casino. ⊠ *Kaiser Franz-Ring 1–3, Kurpark* ☎ *02252/44496–444* ⊠ *Free; guests have the option of several packages that combine food, beverages, and welcome chips* ⊗ *Casino daily 3 pm–4 am; Jackpot Casino daily 1 pm–4 am.*

Kurpark. One of the biggest draws to Baden, outside of the spa, is the vast, lovely, sloping Kurpark almost smack in the middle of town. It was created back in 1792 for Austria's beloved Empress Maria Theresa. But as her highness only occasionally made her way to this Vienna outpost, the locals were free to enjoy it themselves, and they've been doing so ever since. In summer the park is in full flush: concerts are held each weekend afternoon under the 100-year-old music pavilion, and operettas are performed at the arena (it's fitted with a glass dome, which comes out when it rains.) ■TIP➔ The Grand Casino and Kurtheater are located in the park—enticing indoor venues during wintry or bad weather. ⊠ *Kaiser Franz-Ring.*

WHERE TO EAT AND STAY

$$ ✕ **Rudolfshof.** Enjoy a walk through the Kurpark, where you'll find this
AUSTRIAN 19th-century hunting lodge. The fine restaurant serves traditional dishes
from the region, including Wiener and chicken schnitzel, pork fillet and
venison stew. The excellent wines served are local vintages, particularly
St. Laurent, Zweigelt, and Blauer Portugieser. Stop for a meal or just
take a break with coffee and cake. On weekends with clear air and
good weather, the grand vistas across the hills from the terrace mean
it's hard to get a table. $ *Average main: €13* ⊠ *Am Gamingerberg 5*
☎ *02252/209–2030* ⊕ *www.rudolfshof.at* ☉ *Closed Tues. and early
Jan.–early Mar.; also closed Wed. Oct.–early Jan. and early Mar.–Apr.
30. No dinner Mon.*

$$ ⊡ **Krainerhütte.** About 5 km (3 miles) from Baden, this typical Alpine
HOTEL house (think lots of balconies and natural wood) has an almost Scan-
dinavian feel thanks to its sleek, modern rooms. **Pros:** beautiful location; great for hiking or outdoor seminars. **Cons:** often gets booked up.
$ *Rooms from: €170* ⊠ *Helenental 41, Heiligenkreuz* ☎ *02252/445–
110* ⊕ *www.krainerhuette.at* ⇄ *62 rooms* ⓘ *Breakfast.*

$$ ⊡ **Schloss Weikersdorf.** On beautiful grounds, this restored Imperial cas-
HOTEL tle is minutes from the town center, on the edge of a vast public park.
Pros: helpful staff; beautiful surroundings; sometimes offers special last-
minute rates. **Cons:** rooms vary greatly in size; can feel crowded; air
conditoning available only in the Residenz wing. $ *Rooms from: €169*
⊠ *Schlossgasse 9–11* ☎ *02252/48301* ⊕ *www.hotelschlossweikersdorf.
at* ⇄ *88 rooms, 12 suites* ⓘ *Breakfast.*

MAYERLING

11 km (7 miles) northwest of Baden, 29 km (18 miles) west of Vienna.

Scenic Route 210 takes you through the quiet Helenental valley west
of Baden to Mayerling—the scene of a tragedy that is still passionately
discussed and disputed by Austrians at the slightest provocation. On the
snowy evening of January 29, 1889, the 30-year-old Habsburg heir and
Emperor Franz Josef's only son, Crown Prince Rudolf, and his 17-year-
old mistress, Baroness Marie Vetsera, met a violent and untimely end
at the emperor's hunting lodge. Most historians believe it was a sui-
cide pact between two desperate lovers, because the pope had refused
an annulment to Rudolf's unhappy marriage to Princess Stephanie of
Belgium. There are those, however, who feel Rudolf's pro-Hungarian
political leanings might be a key to the tragedy. Given information
gleaned from private letters that have more recently come to light, it is
also possible Rudolf was hopelessly in love with a married woman and
killed himself in despair, taking Marie Vetsera with him. In his grief, the
bereaved emperor had the hunting lodge where the tragedy occurred
torn down and replaced by a rather nondescript Carmelite convent.
Mayerling remains remote: the village is poorly signposted, but tourists
(and some organized tours) still find their way there.

GETTING HERE AND AROUND

Take Route 210 west from Baden through the Helenental valley to reach
Mayerling. From Vienna, take the A21 motorway.

7

WHERE TO STAY

$$$$ ⊞ **Hanner.** The spacious rooms here are filled with light and flush with
HOTEL   natural wood, exuding on overall contemporary flare. **Pros:** unparalleled dining; beautiful rooms; gorgeous surroundings. **Cons:** lacks traditional charm. $ *Rooms from: €248* ⊠ *Mayerling 1* ☎ *02258/2378*
⊕ *www.hanner.cc* ↝ *20 rooms* ⦿| *Breakfast.*

HEILIGENKREUZ

4 km (2½ miles) west of Mayerling, 14 km (9 miles) west of Mödling.

GETTING HERE AND AROUND

From Vienna, take the A21 to Exit 23 for Heiligenkreuz. From Baden
follow scenic Route 210.

EXPLORING

Heiligenkreuz. In the southern section of the Vienna Woods, this magnificent Cistercian abbey was founded in 1135 by Leopold III. Until
a few years ago it was a little-known place of contemplative worship
and prayer, but then the monks recorded a Gregorian chants CD (the
Cistercians are a singing order), and the chart buster rocketed the quiet
abbey to international fame.

The church itself is lofty and serene, with beautifully carved choir stalls
topped with busts of Cistercian saints. The great treasure here is the
relic of the cross that Leopold V is said to have brought back from
his crusade in 1188. It's open only for group tours, and they must be
arranged in advance; sightseeing companies often include the abbey on
their tours, but it's also worth checking the minimum group size—you
may be able to get enough people together. ⊠ *Heiligenkreuz 1, Heiligenkreuz im Wienerwald* ☎ *02258/8703* ⊕ *www.stift-heiligenkreuz.
org* ▨ *Group tours only, €8 per person* ☉ *Daily 9–11:45, 1:30–5:30.*

THE WEINVIERTEL

Luckily, Austria's Weinviertel (Wine District) has been largely neglected
by the "experts," and its deliciously fresh wines reward those who enjoy
partaking of the grape without the all-too-frequent nonsense that goes
with it. The Weinviertel is bounded by the Danube on the south, the
Thaya River and the Czech border on the north, and the March River
and Slovakia to the east. No well-defined line separates the Weinviertel
from the Waldviertel to the west; the Kamp River valley, officially part
of the Waldviertel, is an important wine region. A tour by car, just for
the scenery, can be made in a day. You may want two or three days to
savor the region and its wines, which are generally on the medium-dry
side. Don't expect to find here the elegant facilities found elsewhere in
Austria; prices are low by any standard, and village restaurants and
accommodations are mainly *Gasthäuser* that meet local needs. This
means that you'll be rubbing shoulders with the country folk over your
glass of wine or beer.

MARCHEGG

43 km (27 miles) east of Vienna.

This tiny corner of the lower Weinviertel is known as the Marchfeld, for the fields stretching east to the March River that form the border with Slovakia. In this region—known as the granary of Austria—two elegant baroque castles are worth a visit; while totally renovated, these country estates have lost none of their gracious charm over the centuries.

GETTING HERE AND AROUND

From Vienna, take the E58 motorway to Petronell and change to B49, which goes directly to Marchegg. Trains go from Vienna Central Station several times daily.

EXPLORING

FAMILY

Fodor's Choice

★

Schlosshof. A true Baroque gem, this castle is shining even more brilliantly since the completion of extensive restorations. The product of that master designer and architect Johann Lukas von Hildebrandt, who in 1732 reconstructed the square castle into an elegant U-shape building, the Schloss opens up on the eastern side to a marvelous Baroque formal garden that gives way toward the river. The famed landscape painter Bernardo Bellotto, noted for his Canaletto-like vistas of scenic landmarks, captured the view before the reconstruction. His three paintings were used as a guide for restoring the gardens to their baroque appearance. The castle was once owned by Empress Maria Theresa, mother of Marie Antoinette. You can visit the suite the empress used during her royal visits, faithfully re-created down to the tiniest details, as well as the two-story chapel in which she prayed. For kids there's a manor farm with a menagerie and petting zoo featuring exotic wild animals and old breeds of gentle pets. The complex includes a restaurant and pâtisserie, both with indoor and outdoor seating. Guided tours and audio tours of the castle and the garden are available in English, but it's also possible to saunter around the buildings and grounds on your own. The castle is about 8 km (5 miles) south of Marchegg. Enjoy the panoramic view (you can see Bratislava from here). If you come in winter, you can enjoy the charming Adventmarkt (market) set up on the sprawling grounds. ⊠ *Schlosshof* ☎ *02285/200–000* ⊕ *www.schlosshof.at* 🎫 *€12 (includes castle, grounds, and manor farm); audio or guided tour €3.*

Schloss Niederweiden. Three kilometers (nearly two miles) southwest of Schlosshof is Schloss Niederweiden, on the outskirts of the village of Engelhartstetten. Designed as a hunting lodge in 1694 by Fischer von Erlach, this jewel was subsequently owned in turn by Prince Eugene and Empress Maria Theresa, who added a second floor and the mansard roof. The castle fell into disrepair after World War II, but was completely renovated in the 1980s and contains a photo exhibit of the region's castles and the Imperials who lived in them. ⚠ **Be aware that the space is often rented out for private celebrations and polo matches.** Tours are in German only. ⊠ *Engelhartstetten* ☎ *02285/20000* ⊕ *www.schlosshof. at/cms_neu/index.php?page=schloss-niederweiden* 🎫 *€3; free with Schlosshof admission* ☉ *Early Apr.–early Nov., weekends 10–6.*

7

CARNUNTUM AND HAINBURG AN DER DONAU

32 km (20 miles) east of Vienna.

Until a few years ago, the village of Carnuntum was a yawning backwater on the Austrian plain and, along with its bigger neighbor, Hainburg, was the last stop before the Iron Curtain. But the fall of the wall turned the main road into a major throughway connecting East to West. The development of the Carnuntum archaeological complex and the rise of the Donau-auen National Park, protecting the last remaining intact wetlands in central Europe, turned this once-forgotten region into a significant destination for travelers.

GETTING HERE AND AROUND

From Vienna, take the E58 motorway east directly to Petronell-Carnuntum. By train, take the S7, a local service that departs from Wien-Mitte/Landstrasse or Wien-Nord/Praterstern; it stops at both Petronell and Bad Deutsch-Altenburg. The tiny village of Rohrau, Joseph Haydn's birthplace, is 5 km (3 miles) south of Petronell, on Route 211.

EXPLORING

Carnuntum. The remains of the important Roman legionary fortress and civil town of Carnuntum, which once numbered 55,000 inhabitants, extend about 5 km (3 miles) along the Danube from the tiny village of Petronell to the next town of Bad Deutsch-Altenburg. The recent discovery here of an ancient school of gladiators delighted archaeologists and significantly raised Carnuntum's stature, and rightfully so. Visitors can tour the grounds, which include two amphitheaters (the first one seating 8,000) and the foundations of former residences, reconstructed baths, and trading centers—some with mosaic floors. The ruins are quite spread out, with the impressive remains of a Roman arch, the **Heidentor** (Pagans' Gate), a good 15-minute walk from the main excavations in Petronell. You can experience what Roman life was like circa 380 AD in the elegantly furnished Villa Urbana. Many of the excavated finds are housed at the Museum Carnuntinum at Bad Deutsch-Altenburg. The star of the collection is a carving of Mithras killing a bull. Guided tours in English are available in July and August at noon; otherwise they are in German only. ⊠ *Hauptstrasse, Petronell* ☎ *02163/33770* ⊕ *www.carnuntum.co.at* 🖾 *€11; guided tour €3 each for main site and Museum Carnuntinum* ☉ *Mid-Mar.–mid-Nov., daily 9–5 (last admission 4).*

Museum Carnuntinum. Many of the finds from excavations at Carnuntum are housed 4 km (2½ miles) northeast of Petronell in the village of Bad Deutsch-Altenburg. The pride of the collection is a carving of Mithras killing a bull. ⊠ *Badgasse 40–46, Bad Deutsch-Altenburg* ☎ *2165/62480–13* 🖾 *€11 (part of the Archaeological Park Carnuntum)* ☉ *mid-March.–mid-Nov. daily 9–5.*

Kulturfabrik. A hundred years after the 1683 Turkish invasion that wiped out the town, the construction of the Imperial Royal Tobacco Factory brought Hainburg back to life. In the 21st century, a "culture factory" has been opened on the grounds. Kulturfabrik is part of the Petronell-Carnuntum Archaeological complex. Mostly used for conventions and seminars, it houses a small exhibit of Roman ruins, as well as gift store, and the spectacular panoramic views of the Danube from the second-floor café are a real treat. ✉ *Kulturplatz 1, Hainburg* ☎ *01263/3377–799* ⊕ *www.carnuntum.co.at* 🖾 *€7.50* ⊗ *Mon.–Sat. 9–4; call to check hrs.*

Rohrau. Just 5 km (3 miles) south of Petronell, this tiny village was the birthplace of Joseph Haydn, and the quaint, reed-thatched cottage where the composer, son of the local blacksmith, was born in 1732 is now a small museum. You'll see a pianoforte he is supposed to have played, as well as letters and other memorabilia. The furnishings are homey, if a bit spartan. After Haydn gained worldwide

WEINSTRASSE CYCLING

A great way to see Carnuntum and the towns along the Danube is by bicycle. Bike routes are well marked, extensive, and in excellent condition. Many shops in Vienna rent bikes, and some hotels have bikes available to their guests. For the most part, you can take a bike free of charge on the local and regional trains, which makes it easy to explore a larger area. And you'll be in good company: weekend cycle tours along the Danube are popular with the Viennese.

renown, he is said to have returned to his native Rohrau and knelt to kiss the steps of his humble home. Concerts are occasionally held on the grounds. The house may be closed for renovations, so check before visiting. ✉ *Obere Hauptstrasse 25, Rohrau* ☎ *02164/2268* ⊕ *www.haydngeburtshaus.at* 🖾 *€5* ⊗ *Tues.–Sun. 10–4.*

Schlossberg Castle Ruins. These castle ruins are easily approached on foot, and the views from the top are lovely, but it's equally appealing for its long and illustrious history. During the 11th century, Hainburg was a fortified town on the far eastern front of the Holy Roman Empire, and in 1252, Przemsyl Ottaker, King of Bohemia, married Duchess Margarethe of Austria here, a union designed to considerably expand his kingdom. The castle had been built not long before that with part of the ransom received from the capture in Dürnstein of King Richard the Lionheart. The Schloss was attacked many times, most severely by the 1683 Turkish invasion, which also took the lives of 8,000 residents, nearly the entire community. Each summer the town hosts "Burgspiele Hainburg," where open-air plays (often Shakespeare) are performed (in German) on the castle grounds. ✉ *Schlossbergstrasse, Hainburg* 🖾 *Free* ⊗ *Always accessible.*

Schloss Rohrau. This cream-and-beige palace is where Haydn's mother worked as a cook for Count Harrach. The palace has one of the best private art collections in Austria, with an emphasis on 17th- and 18th-century Spanish and Italian painting. ✉ *Rohrau* ☎ *02164/225318* ⊕ *www.schloss-rohrau.at* 🖾 *€10* ⊗ *Easter–Nov. 1, Tues.–Sun. 10–5.*

Stadtmuseum Wienertor. The imposing "Vienna Gate" still represents the entrance to the medieval town of Hainburg on the Danube, and many a bus and tractor and steady snake of cars still eke through its passage. The town is encircled by remarkably well-preserved 13th-century walls, including 12 towers and gates, including the Wienertor, which is the largest extant medieval gate in Europe. In 1683, the Turks devastated the town, leaving only a handful of survivors, including composer Josef

Haydn's grandfather, who as a small boy scrambled up a chimney and hid from the marauders. Climb up inside the Wienertor, now a museum, and see an impressive supply of weaponry left behind by the invaders—clearly in a hurry to get to Vienna—as well as a stockpile from other ancient wars. A view out the narrow window offers a charming look down at the winding main street and the church steeple. ✉ *Wienerstrasse 1, Hainburg* ☎ *02165/62111* 🌐 *www.wienertor.at* 🎫 *€4* 🕒 *May–Oct. Sun. noon–7.*

WHERE TO STAY

$ HOTEL 🏨 **Hotel Altes Kloster.** Adjacent to the new Kulturfabrik (see Exploring) and just around the corner from where little Joseph Haydn used to have his music lessons, this former monastery retains all its historic serenity regardless of this new incarnation. **Pros:** live piano music in the restaurant/café adds to the atmosphere. **Cons:** carpeting in rooms may aggravate allergies. [$] *Rooms from: €110* ✉ *Fabrikplatz 1a, Hainburg an der Donau* ☎ *02165/64020* 🌐 *www.alteskloster.at* 🛏 *52 rooms* 🍴 *Breakfast.*

NEUSIEDL LAKE AREA

In the north part of the Burgenland region, Neusiedl Lake occupies a strange world. One of the largest lakes in Europe, it is the Continent's only true steppe lake—a bizarre body of warm brackish water. Underground springs feed it, but when they fail it dries up, which last happened in the 1860s. Currently the water is not more than about 7 feet deep at any spot; its many shallower sections make it possible (but still hazardous) to wade across the lake. Its depth has varied dramatically, however, at times nearly engulfing the villages on its banks. Most of its 318-square-km (124-square-mile) surface area is in Austria, but the southern reaches extend into Hungary.

What really sets Neusiedl Lake apart is the thick belt of tall reeds—in some places more than a mile wide—that almost completely encircles it. This is the habitat of large and varied flocks of birds (more than 250 species) that nest near the water's edge. The lake is also a magnet for anglers, boaters, and windsurfers; other activities include swimming and, along its banks, bicycling.

Through a partnership deal, many hotels in the area offer the Neusiedler See Card ("*see*" means lake), valid for the duration of your stay, for free. From April through October it provides free or reduced admissions to main attractions and tours as well as free parking and use of public transportation.

The beach in Neusiedl am See makes the town a big draw in the summer. The town also has some ruins and a Trinity Column to check out, but history buffs will be more satisfied elsewhere in the area. The Burgenland state capital, Eisenstadt, due to its long association with the noble Esterházy family offers the most in terms of historical sightseeing—a castle, opulent churches, museums, a Jewish quarter, and a cemetery. If you want to get away from the crowds, try the town of Rust. With just 1,700 inhabitants, it is Austria's smallest administrative district and prides itself on its winemaking tradition, the keystone of the local economy. The small size of the town makes it a snap to get into the countryside on marked paths for Nordic walking.

NEUSIEDL AM SEE

51 km (32 miles) southeast of Vienna.

At the north end of the lake for which it is named, is a pleasant resort town with good facilities. Direct hourly commuter trains from Vienna have made it very popular, so you won't be alone here. To reach the lake, where you can rent small boats, swim, or just laze on the beach, follow the main street for three blocks east of the Hauptplatz and turn right on Seestrasse. In the town itself, visit the ruins of the 13th-century hill fortress, Ruine Tabor, and the 15th-century parish church near the town hall.

BICYCLING AROUND NEUSIEDL

The flat plains around Neusiedl Lake, with their tiny hamlets and unspoiled scenery, are perfect for leisurely bicycling. Practically every village has a bike-rental shop (*Fahrradverleih* or *Radverleih*), but on weekends demand is so great that it's a good idea to reserve in advance. A bike route encircles the lake, passing through Hungary (you can shorten the route by taking the ferry between Illmitz beach and Mörbisch). Bike route maps are available at tourist offices.

GETTING HERE AND AROUND

Trains leave from Vienna Central Station frequently every day. By car, take the A4 motorway east to the A50 and then B51, following the signs for Neusiedl am See.

ESSENTIALS

Tourist Information **Neusiedl am See Tourismusbüro** ✉ *Untere Hauptstrasse 7* ☎ *02167/2229* 🌐 *www.neusiedlamsee.at.*

WHERE TO EAT AND STAY

$$$ MEDITERRANEAN 🍴 **Nyikospark.** On the main street of Neusiedl, this well-regarded upscale eatery is ill marked, but worth the trouble to search for (it's on the left side about halfway down as you're driving through town from north to south). One side of the unique glass-and-wood structure opens onto an inviting terrace, shaded by canvas stretched between chestnut trees. Begin with a starter of organic sheep cheese and watercress puree. Continue with big, tender roasted duck or glazed calf's liver. Top it off with a peach yogurt tart. The Gasthaus now includes five bright, spacious apartments, which share a common kitchen. [$] *Average main: €18* ✉ *Untere Hauptstrasse 59* ☎ *02167/40222* 🌐 *www.nyikospark.at* 🕘 *Closed Mon. and Tues.*

$$$ HOTEL 🏨 **Hotel Wende.** This sprawling three-story hotel complex is close to the lake and has more than standard amenities, whether you want to get a massage or rent bicycles and set off on the path that begins at its doorstep. **Pros:** friendly and knowledgeable staff; spacious lobby; very good location. **Cons:** little charm. [$] *Rooms from: €180* ✉ *Seestrasse 40* ☎ *02167/8111* 🌐 *www.hotel-wende.at* 🛏 *104 rooms* 🕘 *Closed Christmas week and the first 2 weeks in Feb.* 🍽 *Breakfast.*

7

RUST

Fodor'sChoice ★ *14 km (9 miles) south of Purbach, 28 km (17½ miles) southwest of Neusiedl am See.*

Picturesque Rust, a UNESCO World Cultural Heritage site, is easily the most popular village on the lake for the colorful pastel facades of its houses and for lake sports. Tourists flock here in summer to see storks nesting atop the Renaissance and Baroque houses in the well-preserved historic center. ■ TIP→ **Be sure to look for Steckerl, a delicious local fish caught from Neusiedl Lake and grilled barbecue-style with spices. It's available in most restaurants, but only in the hot months of summer.**

GETTING HERE AND AROUND

By car from Eisenstadt take Route B52 east about 12 km (7½ miles). Bus service is also available from Eisenstadt.

ESSENTIALS

Bike Rentals **Schneeberger** ✉ *Rathausplatz 15* ☎ *02685/6442.*

Tourist Information **Tourismusbüro Rust** ✉ *Conradplatz 1* ☎ *02685/502* 🌐 *www.rust.at.*

EXPLORING

Fischerkirche (*Fishermen's Church*). The restored Gothic Fischerkirche is off the west end of the Rathausplatz. Built between the 12th and 16th centuries, it is surrounded by a defensive wall and is noted for its 15th-century frescoes and an organ from 1705. The church sometimes has classical concerts. Tours are available but must be arranged in advance. ✉ *Conradplatz 1* ☎ *02685/295, 0676/970–3316* 🎫 *€2, €4 with tour* 🕒 *June–Aug., Tues.–Fri. and Sun. 11–1 and 3–5, Sat. 11–1, 3–5 and 7–9; Apr.–May, Sept., and Oct., Tues.–Sat. 11–noon and 2–3 (to 4 Sun.).*

Seebad. A causeway leads through nearly a mile of reeds to the Seebad beach and boat landing, where you can take a sightseeing boat either round-trip or to another point on the lake. You can also rent a boat, swim, or enjoy a waterside drink or snack at an outdoor table.

Weingut Feiler-Artinger. This is one of several local, family-run wineries. ✉ *Hauptstrasse 3* ☎ *02685/237.*

WHERE TO EAT AND STAY

$$$ AUSTRIAN 🍴 **Rusterhof.** A lovingly renovated burgher's house—the town's oldest—at the top of the main square houses an excellent and imaginative restaurant. Light natural woods and vaulted ceilings set the tone in a series of smaller rooms; in summer there's an outside garden. The menu depends on what's fresh, and might include grilled fish or Weiner schnitzel made with organic veal. Finish with apple strudel or marzipan. The complex also includes four comfortable apartments. Under the same management is the Burgerhaus at Hauptstrasse 1, with another 10 modern, spacious apartments. [$] *Average main: €21* ✉ *Rathausplatz 18* ☎ *02685/6162* 🌐 *www.hotelbuergerhaus-rust.at* 🕒 *Tues.–Sun. noon–2 pm and 6–10 pm* 🕒 *Closed Mon.* 🍽 *Breakfast.*

$ AUSTRIAN 🍴 **Schandl.** The Schandl family of Rust is one of the best-known wine growers of the Neusiedl Lake area; their devotees come for wine tastings and stay for dinner. For good, simple food to go along with their excellent wine, join the locals at this popular *Heurige* (wine tavern). The buffet offers a selection of sausages, salads, cheeses, and pickles, as well as a few hot dishes that change daily. You can also order entrées from the menu, such as roast pork with sauerkraut or soft cheese wrapped in bacon. There's a pleasant courtyard for outdoor dining in summer. $ *Average main: €10* ✉ *Hauptstrasse 20* ☎ *02685/265* ⊕ *www.schandlwein.com* ☾ *Mon. and Wed.–Fri. 4–midnight; Sat.– Sun. 11 am–midnight. Closed Tues. and mid-Nov.–mid-Mar. No lunch weekdays.*

$$ **Sifkovits.** Rooms in this charming
HOTEL hotel run by the Tomschitz family are small but comfortable and tastefully decorated, and the location close to the lake and a block away from Rust's busy center is ideal. **Pros:** spacious, welcoming lobby; quiet rooms; large park behind the hotel. **Cons:** rooms facing street are sometimes noisy. $ *Rooms from: €122* ✉ *Am Seekanal 8* ☎ *02685/276* ⊕ *www.sifkovits.at* ⇄ *34 rooms* ☾ *Closed Dec.–mid-Mar.* ❙❍❙ *Breakfast.*

BOATING ON NEUSIEDL

You can hire boats (*Bootsvermietung* or *Bootsverleih*) around Neusiedl Lake. Expect to pay about €6 per hour for a rowboat, €7 for a pedal boat, and €12–€20 for an electric boat; sailboat prices vary widely. There are several businesses in the area:

Baumgartner (✉ *Neusiedl am See* ☎ *02167/2782*).

Knoll (✉ *Podersdorf* ☎ *02177/2431*).

Ruster Freizeitcenter (✉ *Rust* ☎ *02685/595*).

NIGHTLIFE AND PERFORMING ARTS

Römersteinbruch. Between Rust and Eisenstadt, outside the tiny village of St. Margarethen, is Römersteinbruch, a delightful rock quarry used for outdoor opera performances for six or seven weeks in July and August. It's one of the three largest outdoor opera venues in Europe, seating 7,000 nightly. The opera changes annually—usually a work by Verdi, or Bizet's *Carmen,* with a Passion play running every fifth year. Performances also include a dazzling fireworks display. Ticket prices range from €43 to €90. It's a good idea to bring a seat cushion, if possible, to soften the metal chairs. Bus trips from Vienna and back to see performances can be arranged through several tour agencies. Daytime tours of the quarry (in German) are possible from April to October. ☎ *02680/2188* ⊕ *www.roemersteinbruch.at.*

EISENSTADT

22 km (14 miles) northwest of Mörbisch, 48 km (30 miles) south of Vienna, 26 km (16¼ miles) west of Wiener Neustadt.

Burgenland's provincial capital, Eisenstadt, is a really small town. Nevertheless, it has an illustrious history and enough sights to keep you busy for a half, if not quite a full, day. Although the town has existed since at least the 12th century, it only became at all significant in the 17th century, when it became the seat of the Esterházys, a princely Hungarian family that traces its roots to Attila the Hun. The original Esterházy made his fortune by marrying a succession of wealthy landowning widows. Esterházy's support was largely responsible for the Habsburg reign in Hungary under the Dual Monarchy. At one time the family controlled a far-flung agro-industrial empire, and it still owns vast forest resources. The composer Joseph Haydn lived in Eisenstadt for some 30 years while in the service of the Esterházy family. When Hungary ceded Burgenland to Austria after World War I, its major city, Sopron, elected to remain a part of Hungary, so in 1925 tiny Eisenstadt was made the capital of the new Austrian province.

Eisenstadt's main draw is the former palace, Schloss Esterházy, and the tourist office can tell you about its other attractions, including the Museum of Austrian Culture, the Diocesan Museum, the Fire Fighters Museum, Haydn's little garden house, and an assortment of churches.

GETTING HERE AND AROUND

Eisenstadt is connected to Vienna and Neusiedl am See by train and to places throughout Burgenland by bus. By car from Rust, take Route B52 west past St. Margarethen and Trausdorf to the capital.

ESSENTIALS

Contacts **Eisenstadt Tourismus** ⊠ *Glorietteallee 1* ☎ *02682/67390* ⊕ *www.eisenstadt.at.*

EXPLORING

Bergkirche. At the crest of Esterházystrasse perches the Bergkirche, an ornate Baroque church that includes the strange *Kalvarienberg,* an indoor Calvary Hill representing the Way of the Cross with life-size figures placed in small grottos along an elaborate path. At its highest point, the trail reaches the platform of the belfry, offering a view over the town and this section of Burgenland. The magnificent wooden figures were carved and painted by Franciscan monks more than 250 years ago. The main part of the church contains the tomb of Joseph Haydn, who died in 1809 in Vienna. ⊠ *Josef Haydn Platz 1* ☎ *02682/62638* ⊕ *www.haydnkirche.at* ☑ *€3* ☉ *Apr.–Oct., daily 9–5; Nov.–Mar., by appointment.*

Haydn Museum. The composer lived in the simple house on a street that now bears his name—Joseph Haydn-Gasse—from 1766 until 1778. Now the Haydn Museum, it contains several first editions of his music and other memorabilia. The house itself, and especially its flower-filled courtyard with the small back rooms, is quite delightful. ⊠ *Joseph Haydn-Gasse 19–21* ☎ *02682/719–3900* ⊕ *www.haydnhaus. at* ☑ *€4.50* ☉ *Apr.–May, Tues.–Fri. 9–5, Sun. 10–5; June–Nov., Mon.–Sat. 9–5, Sun. 10–5.*

Landesmuseum Burgenland (*Burgenland Provincial Museum*). This museum brings the history of the region to life with displays on such diverse subjects as Roman culture and the area's wildlife. There's a section on the rich musical heritage of the area, including a memorial room to the composer Franz Liszt, along with more relics of the town's former Jewish community. ⊠ *Museumgasse 1–5* ☎ *02682/719–4000* ⊕ *landesmuseum-burgenland.at* ☑ *€5.50* ☉ *Mid-Feb.–May, Tues.–Sat. 9–5, Sun. and holidays 10–5; June–mid-Nov., Mon.–Sat. 9–5, Sun and holidays 10–5; mid-Nov–Dec. 23, Mon.–Fri. 9–5, holidays 10–5.*

Österreichisches Jüdisches Museum (*Austrian Jewish Museum*). Wertheimergasse and Unterbergstrasse were boundaries of the Jewish ghetto from 1671 until 1938. During that time Eisenstadt had a considerable Jewish population; today the Österreichisches Jüdisches Museum recalls the experience of Austrian Jews throughout history. A fascinating private synagogue in the complex survived the 1938 terror and is incorporated into the museum. ⊠ *Unterbergstrasse 6* ☎ *02682/65145* ⊕ *www.ojm. at* ☞ *€4* ⊙ *May–Oct., Tues.–Sun. 10–5; Nov.–Apr., by appointment and for groups of 10 or more only, Mon.–Thurs. 9–4, Fri. 9–1.*

> **HAYDN FULLY AT REST**
>
> Composer Joseph Haydn's body was returned to Eisenstadt for burial at the request of Prince Esterházy in 1821. The head, however, had been stolen by phrenologists and eventually became the property of the Gesellschaft der Musikfreunde, a Viennese musical society. A new marble tomb was built for Haydn in 1932 at Eisenstadt's Bergkirche, but the head was not returned until 1954. In the meantime a substitute head had been placed with the remains. Both skulls are now in the marble tomb.

Fodor's Choice ★ **Schloss Esterházy.** The former palace of the ruling princes reigns over the town. Built in the baroque style between 1663 and 1672 on the foundations of a medieval castle and later modified, it is still owned by the Esterházy family, who lease it to the provincial government for use mostly as offices. The Esterházy family rooms are worth viewing, and the lavishly decorated **Haydn Room,** an impressive concert hall where the composer conducted his own works from 1761 until 1790, is still used for presentations of Haydn's works, with musicians often dressed in period garb. The hall is one of several rooms on a guided tour (in English on request if there are at least 10 people) that lasts about 30 minutes. The cellar has a large **wine museum** with 700 objects including a massive wine barrel and historical grape press. A tour of the **princess's apartment** was added in 2012 and includes objects relating to three royal women. The **park** behind the Schloss is pleasant for a stroll or a picnic, and in late August it's a venue of the Burgenland wine week—Eisenstadt hosts the "Festival of 1,000 Wines"—and there's a two-hour tour on wine and culture at the palace. It ends with a tasting. Inquire at the information desk. ⊠ *Esterházy Platz* ☎ *02682/719–63004* ⊕ *www.schloss-esterhazy.at* ☞ *€9 for guided tour of family rooms; €7 for wine museum; €9 for princess's apartment* ⊙ *Apr.–mid-Nov., daily 9–6; mid-Nov.–Mar., Fri.–Sun. 9–5.*

WHERE TO EAT AND STAY

$$$$
ECLECTIC
Fodor's Choice ★
✕**Taubenkobel.** Consistently ranked as one of the top restaurants in Austria, the "Dovecote" is a rambling, elegantly restored 19th-century farmhouse 5 km (3 miles) from Eisenstadt in the village of Schützen. Owner-chef Walter Eselböck and his wife, Evelyne, have created a series of strikingly beautiful dining rooms. The seasonally changing menu has featured dishes such as saddle of lamb with mangold blossoms and asparagus in saffron sauce. A variety of packages pair multiple courses with wines; some also include an overnight stay in the connected hotel. The former stables and outbuildings have been

converted to 12 luxurious, unique bedrooms with wooden beams and cathedral ceilings. $ *Average main: €98* ⊠ *Hauptstrasse 33, Schützen am Gebirge* ☎ *02684/2297* ⊕ *www.taubenkobel.com* ⚒ *Reservations essential* ☉ *Closed Mon., Tues., and Jan.–Feb. 15.*

$$ ⊡ **Gasthof Ohr.** Personal service is the hallmark of this family-run hotel
HOTEL   and restaurant, an easy 10-minute walk from the town center. **Pros:** attractive rooms; good food. **Cons:** no real lobby; very expensive Wi-Fi; only "komfort class" rooms have air-conditioning. $ *Rooms from: €122* ⊠ *Rusterstrasse 51* ☎ *02682/62460* ⊕ *www.hotelohr.at* ⤳ *39 rooms* ☉ *Restaurant is closed Mon. and from Nov.–Apr. on Sun. afternoon as well* ⦿ *Breakfast.*

$$ ⊡ **Hotel Burgenland.** This sprawling hotel in the town center has every-
HOTEL   thing you'd expect in a first-class establishment, and the friendly staff goes out of its way to assist guests. **Pros:** well-equipped, modern hotel. **Cons:** business-hotel atmosphere. $ *Rooms from: €170* ⊠ *Franz Schubertplatz 1* ☎ *02682/6960* ⊕ *www.hotel-burgenland.at* ⤳ *80 rooms, 8 suites* ⦿ *Breakfast.*

NIGHTLIFE AND PERFORMING ARTS

Haydn Festival. Eisenstadt devotes much cultural energy to one of its favorite sons. In the first half of September it plays host to the annual Haydn Festival in the Esterházy Palace and other venues. Many of the concerts are by renowned performers, and admission prices vary with the event. Other concerts featuring the works of Joseph Haydn run from mid-May to early October. Contact the Haydnfestspiele office in Schloss Esterházy or the local tourist office. ☎ *02682/61866–0* ⊕ *www.haydnfestival.at.*

EN
ROUTE   Heading southwest from Eisenstadt brings you to the waist of Burgenland, the narrow region squeezed between Lower Austria and Hungary. The leading attraction here is Forchtenstein; take Route S31 for 20 km (12½ miles) to Mattersburg, then a local road 3 km (2 miles) west.

ALONG THE DANUBE RIVER

The loveliest stretches of the Danube's Austrian course run from the outskirts of Vienna through the narrow defiles of the Wachau to the Nibelungengau—the region where the mystical race of dwarfs, the Nibelungs, are supposed to have settled, at least for a while.

The gentle countryside south of the Danube and east of Linz is crossed by rivers that rise in the Alps and eventually feed the Danube. In this prosperous country of light industry and agriculture, there's little remaining evidence that the area was heavily fought over in the final days of World War II. From 1945 to 1955 the River Enns marked the border between the western (U.S., British, and French) and eastern (Russian) occupation zones. The great attraction here is a string of Baroque-era abbeys, including the incomparable Stift Melk, set above the Danube.

KLOSTERNEUBURG

13 km (8 miles) northwest of Vienna.

This moderate-size town, with forest mixed in between the houses, seems much farther from the big city than just a few miles. In antiquity the area was a Roman fort, and its modern habitation began in the 11th century.

GETTING HERE AND AROUND

Commuter trains from Vienna's Franz-Josefs-Bahnhof and buses from the Heiligenstadt station leave frequently for the short trip. By car, follow Route B14.

ESSENTIALS

Tourist Information Klosterneuburg Tourismus ⊠ *Niedermarkt 4* ☎ *02243/32038* ⊕ *www.klosterneuburg.net.*

EXPLORING

OFF THE BEATEN PATH

Kahlenbergerdorf. Near Klosterneuburg and just off the road tucked under the Leopoldsberg promontory is this charming little vintners' village, an excellent spot to stop and sample the local wines. You're just outside the Vienna city limits here, which accounts for the crowds (of Viennese, not international visitors) on weekends.

Sammlung Essl. Somewhat alarmingly, this contemporary art museum resembles a sports center from the outside, but it's well worth venturing inside. The building was designed by Heinz Tesar specifically to showcase art created after 1945, and the permanent collection includes works by such regional artists as Maria Lassnig, Hermann Nitsch, and Arnulf Rainer. Changing exhibitions also focus on contemporary artists. To get to the museum from Vienna, take the pink-and-blue shuttle bus from Albertinaplatz 2 (outside Café Mozart); it runs daily (except Monday) at 10, noon, 2, and 4, returning at 11, 1, 3, and 6. The bus is free only if you purchase a ticket to the museum on board. ⊠ *An der Donau–Au 1* ☎ *02243/370–5015–0* ⊕ *www.sammlung-essl.at* ⊡ *€9; free Wed. 6–9* ⊙ *Tues.–Sun. 10–6, Wed. 10–9.*

Fodor's Choice ★

Stift Klosterneuburg. The great Augustinian abbey Stift Klosterneuburg dominates the town. The structure has undergone many changes since the abbey was established in 1114, most recently in 1892, when Friedrich Schmidt, architect of Vienna's City Hall, added neo-Gothic embellishments to its two identifying towers. Klosterneuburg was unusual in that until 1568 it housed both men's and women's religious orders. In the abbey church look for the carved-wood choir loft and oratory and the large 17th-century organ. Among Klosterneuburg's treasures are the beautifully enameled 1181 Verdun Altar in the Leopold Chapel, stained-glass windows from the 14th and 15th centuries, Romanesque candelabra from the 12th century, and gorgeous ceiling frescoes in the great marble hall. In an adjacent outbuilding there's a huge wine cask over which people slide; the exercise, called *Fasslrutsch'n,* takes place during the Leopoldiweinkost, the wine tasting around St. Leopold's Day, November 15. The **Stiftskeller,** with its atmospheric underground rooms, serves standard Austrian fare and wine bearing the Klosterneuberg label. The **Treasury** features an imperial crown. There are several

Upper Danube Valley

different tours available covering religious artifacts, imperial rooms and treasures, winemaking, and the garden. Guided tours are in German; audio guides are available for some of the tours. ⊠ *Stiftsplatz 1* ☎ *02243/411–0* ⊕ *www.stift-klosterneuburg.at* 🎟 *Tours €10.50 or €16.50 for one-day ticket including multiple tours* ⊙ *May–mid-Nov. daily 9–6; mid-Nov.–Apr. 10–5.*

KORNEUBURG

18 km (11 miles) northwest of Vienna.

Aside from Burg Kreuzenstein, a castle a short distance outside the town, Korneuburg has a few attractions, including sections of a town wall, a Trinity column, and a Pied Piper well, to justify a brief stopover or drive-through on the way to Krems.

GETTING HERE AND AROUND

Commuter trains go frequently from Vienna's Praterstern station. To see the castle, go to the Leobendorf-Burg Kreuzenstein stop. By car from Vienna, take the A22 to Exit 16, and then follow Route B3.

EXPLORING

Fodor's Choice
★

Burg Kreuzenstein. Castle lovers, prepare yourself. Seemingly lifted from the pages of a German fairy tale, Burg Kreuzenstein, bristling with storybook turrets and towers, might have made Albrecht Dürer drop his sketch pad. Sitting atop a hillside 3 km (2 miles) beyond Korneuburg along Route 3, "Castle Cross-stone" is, in fact, a 19th-century architectural fantasy built to conjure up "the last of the knights"—Emperor Maximilian I himself. Occupying the site of a previously destroyed fort, the enormous structure was built by Count Nepomuk Wilczek between 1879 and 1908 to house his collection of late-Gothic art objects and armor, including the "Brixner Cabinet" dating from 15th-century Salzburg. Using old elements and Gothic and Romanesque bits and pieces, the castle was carefully laid out according to the rules of yore, complete with a towering Burgtor, "kennel" corridor (where attackers would have been cornered), Gothic arcades, and tracery parapet walls. The Burghof courtyard, with its half-timbered facade and Baltic loggia, could be a stand-in for a stage set for Wagner's *Tannhäuser*. Inside, the medieval thrills continue with rooms full of armaments, a festival and banquet hall, a library, a stained-glass chapel (available for weddings), vassal kitchens, and the Narwalzahn, a room devoted to hunting trophies (if you've ever wanted to see a "unicorn horn," here's your chance). Guided tours are available on the hour.

A group of falconers keeps peregrine falcons and other birds of prey near the castle grounds. ■ TIP➔ Eagles and falcons take flight, hunt, and return to their trainer's arm with the catch at least twice a day, taking part in a sport that goes back nearly 4,000 years. Shows, which run from April through October, are scheduled every day (except Monday) at 11 am and 3 pm and on Sunday at 11 am and 2 and 4 pm. Tickets cost €7.50 each.

It is possible to reach Kreuzenstein from Vienna via the suburban train (S-Bahn) to Leobendorf, followed by a ¾-hour hike up to the castle.

Until recently, the town of Korneuburg was the center of Austrian ship-building, where river passenger ships, barges, and transfer cranes were built to order for Russia, among other customers. Stop for a look at the imposing neo-Gothic city hall (1864), which dominates the central square and towers over the town. ⊠ *Leobendorf bei Korneuburg* ☎ *0664/422–53–63, 01/283–0308 falconer* ⊕ *www.kreuzenstein.com* 🖃 *€10* ⊗ *Apr.–Oct. Mon.–Sat. 10–4, Sun. 10–5.*

KREMS

10 km (6 miles) west of Haitzendorf, 80 km (50 miles) northwest of Vienna.

Krems marks the beginning (when traveling upstream) of the Wachau section of the Danube. The town is closely tied to Austrian history; here the ruling Babenbergs set up a dukedom in 1120, and the earliest Austrian coin was struck in 1130. In the Middle Ages Krems looked after the iron trade, while neighboring Stein traded in salt and wine. Now, according to Austrian law, any town that houses a jail must receive massive funding for the arts. Thus, charming Krems is fat with culture, starting with its Arts Mile. Besides a number of galleries and eateries, it includes the Karikaturmuseum, the Kunsthalle krems, the Frohner Museum (dedicated to the late Austrian graphic artist and painter), and the Lower Austria literature center.

The area is also at the center of a thriving wine-producing area, but Krems is most famed for the cobbled streets of its Altstadt (Old Town), which is virtually unchanged since the 18th century. The lower Old Town is an attractive pedestrian zone, while up a steep hill (a car can be handy) you'll find the upper Old Town, with its Renaissance Rathaus and a parish church that is one of the oldest in Lower Austria.

GETTING HERE AND AROUND

By car from Vienna, take the A22 to the Knoten Floridsorf exit, then follow the S5 to Krems. Trains from Vienna's Franz-Josefs-Bahnhof to Krems take a little over an hour.

ESSENTIALS

Tourist Information **Krems/Stein** ⊠ *Utzstrasse 1* ☎ *02732/82676* ⊕ *www.krems.info.*

EXPLORING

Karikaturmuseum (*Caricature Museum*). More than 250 works from the 20th century to the present can be viewed here, including a large collection of English-language political satire and caricature. Don't expect much on comic books and animation; the emphasis here is on political and satirical drawings. ⊠ *Steiner Landstrasse 3a* ☎ *02732/908020* ⊕ *www.karikaturmuseum.at* 🖃 *€10* ⊗ *Daily 10–6.*

Kunsthalle Krems. An old tobacco factory is now a showcase for art by both known and unknown artists from the 19th to 21st centuries. Notable examples include Martha Jungwirth and Gregor Schmoll. ⊠ *Franz-Zeller-Platz 3* ☎ *02732/908010* ⊕ *www.kunsthalle.at* 🖃 *€10* ⊗ *Tues.–Sun. and holiday Mon. 10–6.*

Loisium. About 10 km (6 miles) north of Krems, Langenlois is home to the Loisium, a sleek, ultramodern complex of shops with a hotel and spa, a comprehensive selection of wines, sparkling wines, and other delectables from the area. The labyrinthian wine cellar takes more than an hour to tour and has 15 stops. The hotel also has a restaurant featuring international cuisine. Top producers include Hirsch, Loimer, and Bründlmayer, the maker of one of Austria's best sparkling wines, chardonnay, *Alte Reben* (old-vine) Grüner Veltliner, and Riesling of exceptional character. ⊠ *Kornplatz, Langenlois* ⊕ *www.loisium.at* 🎫 *€11.50 for a tour of the wine cellar with an audio guide and one tasting.*

Weinstadt Museum Krems. A 14th-century former Dominican cloister now serves as this museum, displaying artworks from the municipal collections, archaeological finds, and items relating to winemaking. A modern gallery shows more recent works. ⊠ *Körnermarkt 14* 🕾 *02732/801–567* ⊕ *www.weinstadtmuseum.at* 🎫 *€5* 🕙 *mid-Apr.–mid June, Wed.–Sun. 11–6; mid-June–late-Oct., daily.*

WHERE TO EAT AND STAY

$$
AUSTRIAN

✕ **Jell.** In the heart of the medieval Altstadt, this storybook stone cottage run by Ulli Amon-Jell (pronounced "Yell") is a cluster of cozy rooms with lace curtains, dark-wood banquettes, candlelight, and Biedermeier knickknacks on the walls. Wild mushroom omelet, pasta with forest fruits, cabbage lasagne, and lamb chops with an olive-Parmesan crust are typical dishes. There are always lighter fish and vegetarian dishes on the menu, but the chef's motto is "None goes home hungry from my tavern." In summer book ahead for a table under the grape arbor in the small, secluded outdoor dining area. Ask the waitstaff about the preserves, sauces, and other jarred delicacies for sale. 🖇 *Average main: €14* ⊠ *Hoher Markt 8–9* 🕾 *02732/82345* ⊕ *www.amon-jell.at* 🖎 *Reservations essential* 🕙 *Tue.–Fri. 10–2:30 and 6–11, weekends 10–2* 🕙 *Closed Mon. and first two weeks in July. No dinner weekends.*

$$$$
AUSTRIAN

✕ **Zum Kaiser von Österreich.** At this landmark in Krems's Old City district, you'll find excellent regional cuisine along with an outstanding wine selection (some of these vintages come from the backyard). The inside rooms are bright and pleasant, and the outside tables in summer are even more inviting. Owner-chef Haidinger, awarded a toque from Gault Millaut, learned his skills at Bacher, across the Danube in Mautern, so look for refined fish dishes along with specialties such as potato soup and roast shoulder of lamb with scalloped potatoes. Local ingredients such as fish from the Danube are used whenever possible. 🖇 *Average main: €25* ⊠ *Körnermarkt 9* 🕾 *0800/400–171–052* 🖷 *02732/860–014* ⊕ *www.kaiser-von-oesterreich.at* 🖎 *Reservations essential* 🕙 *Closed Sun.–Mon., last 2 weeks in July and first week in Aug. No lunch.*

$
B&B/INN

🏨 **Alte Post.** The oldest inn in Krems, which for almost 140 years was a mail-route post house, is centered on an adorable Renaissance-style courtyard topped with a flower-bedecked, arcaded balcony and storybook mansard roof. **Pros:** excellent restaurant with large portions. **Cons:** old-fashioned; most rooms have shared shower and toilet facilities. 🖇 *Rooms from: €85* ⊠ *Obere Landstrasse 32* 🕾 *02732/822–76* ⊕ *www. altepost-krems.at* 🖙 *23 rooms* 🕙 *Closed Dec.–Mar.* 🍽 *Breakfast.*

7

DÜRNSTEIN

4 km (2½ miles) west of Stein, 90 km (56 miles) northwest of Vienna, 34 km (21¼ miles) northeast of Melk.

If a beauty contest were held among the towns along the Wachau Danube, chances are Dürnstein would be the winner—as you'll see when you arrive along with droves of tourists. The town is small; leave the car at one end and walk the narrow streets. The main street, Hauptstrasse, is lined with picturesque 16th-century residences.

■ TIP➜ **The trick is to overnight here—when the day-trippers depart, the storybook spell of the town returns.** The top night to be here is the summer solstice, when hundreds of boats bearing torches and candles sail down the river at twilight to honor the longest day of the year—a breathtaking sight best enjoyed from the town and hotel terraces over the Danube. In October or November the grapes from the surrounding hills are harvested by volunteers from villages throughout the valley—locals garnish their front doors with straw wreaths if they can offer tastes of the new wine, as members of the local wine cooperative, the Winzergenossenschaft Wachau.

GETTING HERE AND AROUND

Dürnstein is 8 km (5 miles) west of Krems on Route B3. Buses go from Krems/Donau Bahnhof at least once an hour in the daytime.

ESSENTIALS

Tourist Information Dürnstein ⊠ *Dürnstein No. 132* 🖀 *02711/200* ⊕ *www.duernstein.at.*

EXPLORING

Richard the Lionheart Castle. After taking in the Stiftskirche, head up the hill, climbing 500 feet above the town, to the ruins of the famous Richard the Lionheart Castle—known locally as Ruine Dürnstein—where Leopold V held Richard the Lionheart of England, captured on his way back home from the Crusades. Leopold had been insulted, so the story goes, by Richard while they were in the Holy Land and when the English nobleman was shipwrecked and had to head back home through Austria, word got out—even though Richard was disguised as a peasant—and Leopold pounced. In the tower of this castle, the Lionheart was imprisoned (1192–93) until he was located by Blondel, the faithful Minnesänger (troubadour). It's said that Blondel was able to locate his imprisoned king when he heard his master's voice completing the verse of a song Blondel was singing aloud—a bit recycled in Sir Walter Scott's *Ivanhoe* (and the Robert Taylor MGM film). Leopold turned his prisoner over to the emperor, Henry VI, who held him for months longer until ransom was paid by Richard's mother, Eleanor of Aquitaine. The rather steep 30-minute climb to the ruins will earn you a breathtaking view up and down the Danube Valley and over the hills to the south.

Stiftskirche. Set among terraced vineyards, the town is landmarked by its gloriously Baroque Stiftskirche, dating from the early 1700s, which sits on a cliff overlooking the river. This cloister church's combination of luminous blue facade and stylish Baroque tower is considered the most beautiful of its kind in Austria. ⊠ *Grübelgasse.*

CLOSE UP

Grape Expectations

The epitome of Austrian viticulture is found in the Wachau, those few precious kilometers of terraced vineyards along the north bank of the Danube River. There are few nicer ways to spend an afternoon than to travel to the fabled wineries of the valley and sample the golden nectar coaxed from the vines. It's usually possible to stop in and meet the winemaker, who will be happy to pour you a taste from the latest vintage and share some of the secrets of the trade. A late-spring drive through enchanting villages like Dürnstein, when the apricots are in blossom, is an experience not easily forgotten.

Here you can discover some of the finest white wines in Europe. The elegant, long-lived Rieslings are world-renowned, but the special glory of Austria is the Grüner Veltliner, an indigenous grape that can produce anything from simple *Heurigen* thirst-quenchers to wines of a nobility that rival the best of Burgundy.

The area has its own unique three-tiered classification system, ranging from the young, fresh Steinfeder and medium-bodied Federspiel to the rich, ripe Smaragd. Some of the already legendary vintners include Toni Zöhrer, F.X. Pichler, Prager, Knoll, and Hirtzberger, as well as the exemplary cooperative of the Freie Weingärtner Wachau.

Straddling both sides of the Danube is the Kremstal, centering on the medieval town of Krems, the hub of the area's wine trade. The range of grape varieties expands here to include intensely fragrant Traminer, Grauburgunder (more familiar as Pinot Gris), and even some full-bodied reds from Cabernet Sauvignon and Pinot Noir. To sample some of these wines, you may be tempted to make an excursion to one of the nearby wineries like Nigl, Salomon, Malat, or Zöhrer. Toni Zöhrer runs vineyard tours—his wines have been among the most successful in recent challenges.

Venturing farther from the Danube takes you through lush, rolling hills to the Kamptal, the valley that follows the winding course of the gentle Kamp River. Here is another premium wine region, this one dominated by Langenlois, the country's largest wine-producing town.

After you've had your fill of wine tasting, you might want to relax over a good meal at one of these distinguished wineries. Several have very nice restaurants on-site, including Jamek, near Dürnstein.

For more information on Wachau wineries, visit 🌐 www.vinea-wachau.at.

7

WHERE TO EAT AND STAY

$$$$ AUSTRIAN

🍴 **Loibnerhof.** It's hard to imagine a more idyllic frame for a memorable meal, especially if the weather is fine and tables are set out in the fragrant apple orchard. One of the oldest restaurants in the area, its kitchen offers inventive variations on regional themes: Wachau fish soup, crispy roast duck, and various grilled fish specialties. The house is famous for its *Butterschnitzel*, an exquisite variation on the theme of ground meat (this one's pan-fried veal with a touch of pork). To reach Loibnerhof, look for the Unterloiben exit a mile east of Dürnstein. [$] *Average main: €25* ✉ *Unterloiben 7* ☎ *02732/82890–0* 🌐 *www.*

loibnerhof.at ⌕ *Reservations essential* ⊘ *Closed Mon.–Tues. and early Jan.–mid-Feb.*

$$$

B&B/INN

⊡ **Richard Löwenherz.** Built up around the former church of a vast 700-year-old convent, this noted inn overlooks the Danube. **Pros:** river view; über-romantic; spacious guest rooms; specializes in package tours for cyclists. **Cons:** rooms can get hot in summer; no elevator. ⓢ *Rooms from:* €189 ⊠ *Dürnstein 8* ☎ *02711/222* ⊕ *www.richardloewenherz.at* ⤳ *37 rooms* ⊘ *Closed Nov.–Easter or mid–Apr.* ⍾ *Breakfast.*

$

B&B/INN

⊡ **Sänger Blondel.** Nearly under the shadow of the Baroque spire of Dürnstein's parish church, this *Gasthof-Pension* welcomes you with a lovely, sunny-yellow, flower-bedecked facade. **Pros:** great value for money; beautiful garden; quiet area. **Cons:** no elevator; outdated room style; Wi-Fi access only on the ground floor. ⓢ *Rooms from:* €103 ⊠ *Dürnstein 64* ☎ *02711/253–0* ⊕ *www.saengerblondel.at* ⤳ *15 rooms, 1 suite* ⊘ *Closed mid-Nov.–mid-Mar.* ⍾ *Breakfast.*

$$$

HOTEL

⊡ **Schloss Dürnstein.** Once the preserve of the princes of Starhemberg, this 17th-century early-Baroque castle on a rocky terrace with exquisite views over the Danube is one of the most famous hotels in Austria. **Pros:** indoor and outdoor pools; exquisite views from the terrace. **Cons:** no air-conditioning; not all rooms have high-speed Internet. ⓢ *Rooms from:* €229 ⊠ *Dürnstein 2* ☎ *02711/212* ⊕ *www.schloss.at* ⤳ *47 rooms* ⊘ *Closed Nov.–Mar.* ⍾ *Breakfast.*

MELK

22 km (13 miles) east of Ybbs an der Donau, 33 km (21 miles) southwest of Krems.

One of the most impressive sights in all of Austria, the abbey of Melk is best approached in mid- to late afternoon, when the setting sun ignites the abbey's ornate Baroque yellow facade. As you head eastward paralleling the Danube, the abbey, shining on its promontory above the river, comes into view. It easily overshadows the town, but remember that the riverside village of Melk itself is worth exploring. A self-guided tour (in English, from the tourist office) will point you toward the highlights and the best spots from which to photograph the abbey.

GETTING HERE AND AROUND

By car from Krems follow the signs on Route B3 to the Melk exit. A bus goes from Krems/Donau Bahnhof to the center of Melk. Train travel from Linz is possible with a change at St. Pölten.

ESSENTIALS

Tourist Information Melk ⊠ *Babenbergerstrasse 1* ☎ *02752/52307–410.*

EXPLORING

Fodor'sChoice
★

Stift Melk (*Melk Abbey*). By any standard, this is a baroque-era masterpiece. Part palace, part monastery, part opera set, Melk is a magnificent vision thanks greatly to the upward-reaching twin towers capped with Baroque helmets and cradling a 208-foot-high dome, and a roof bristling with Baroque statuary. Symmetry here beyond the towers and dome would be misplaced, and much of the abbey's charm is due to the way the early architects were forced to fit the building to the rocky outcrop that forms its base. Erected on the site of an ancient Roman fort, used by Napoléon as his Upper Austrian redoubt, exploited as the setting for part of Umberto Eco's *Name of the Rose,* and still a working monastery, the Benedictine abbey has a history that extends back to its establishment in 1089. The glorious building you see today is architect Jakob Prandtauer's reconstruction, completed in 1736, in which some earlier elements are incorporated. A tour of the building includes the main public rooms: a magnificent library, with more than 100,000 books, nearly 2,000 manuscripts, and a superb ceiling fresco by the master Paul Troger; the **Marmorsaal,** whose windows on both sides enhance the ceiling frescoes; and the glorious **Stiftskirche** (abbey church) of Saints Peter and Paul, an exquisite example of the baroque style. The **Stiftsrestaurant** (closed Jan.–mid-Mar.) offers standard fare, but the abbey's excellent wines elevate a simple meal to a lofty experience—particularly on a sunny day on the terrace. There is also a café in the garden pavilion. From April through October, you're free to wander on your own, but from November through March, visitors must book a tour ahead of time in order to see the abbey. ✉ *Abt Berthold Dietmayr-Strasse 1* ☎ *02752/555–232* 🌐 *www.stiftmelk.at* 🎟 *€10; with tour €12* 🕒 *May–Sept., daily 9–5:30; Mar., Apr., and Oct. daily 9–4:30; Ticket office closes 30 mins before abbey closing. Guided tours in English May–Oct., daily at 11 and 3; Nov.–Apr., open for guided tours only and must be booked in advance.*

WHERE TO EAT AND STAY

$ HOTEL 🏨 **Hotel zur Post.** Here in the center of town you're in a typical village hotel with the traditional friendliness of family management. **Pros:** close to the abbey; friendly and accommodating; in-house sauna and infrared cabin; free bicycle loan. **Cons:** parking area behind the hotel is small; noise from the abbey's bells can be intrusive. [$] *Rooms from: €110* ✉ *Linzer Strasse 1* ☎ *02752/52345* 🌐 *www.post-melk.at* 🛏 *22 rooms, 5 suites* 🕒 *Closed Jan.–mid-Feb.* 🍴 *Breakfast.*

7

LINZ: "RICH TOWN OF THE RIVER MARKETS"

48 km (22 miles) northwest of Baumgartenberg, 130 km (81 miles) northeast of Salzburg, 185 km (115 miles) west of Vienna.

The capital of Upper Austria—set where the Traun River flows into the Danube—has a fascinating Old City core and an active cultural life. Once known as the "Rich Town of the River Markets" because of its importance as a medieval trading post, it is today the center of Austrian steel and chemical production, both started by the Germans in 1938. Linz is also a leader in computer technology; every September the city hosts the internationally renowned Ars Electronica Festival, designed to promote artists, scientists, and the latest technical gadgets. A city where past and present collide, Linz has Austria's largest medieval square and one of the country's most modern multipurpose halls, the Brucknerhaus, which is used for concerts and conventions.

Linz can cast a spell, thanks to the beautiful old houses on the Hauptplatz; a Baroque cathedral with twin towers and a fine organ over which composer Anton Bruckner once presided; and its "city mountain," the

Pöstlingberg, with a unique railroad track to the top. Mozart often stayed here as his family relentlessly traveled up and down Europe, most notably in November 1783, when he was a guest of Count Johann Thun-Hohenstein at Thun Palace. Today extensive redevelopment, ongoing restoration, and the creation of traffic-free zones and bicycle paths through the city continue to transform Linz. ■ TIP➜ **If you will be in Linz for a day or more, consider purchasing the Linz Card, available at the Tourist Office at Hauptplatz 1, some museums, and in most hotels.** Valid for public transportation and free entry into several museums, including the Ars Electronica Center, the card also provides discounts on entry to the zoo, botanical gardens, St. Florian's Abbey, and other venues. It includes deals on Segway tours, casino chips, and a river cruise. The card comes in one-day (€15) and three-day (€25) versions. The three-day card also includes a round-trip on the Pöstlingberg Railway.

GETTING HERE AND AROUND

Linz is served mainly by Austrian Airlines, Lufthansa, Air Berlin, and Ryanair. Regular flights connect with Vienna, Berlin, Düsseldorf, Frankfurt, Stuttgart, and London-Stansted. The Linz airport is in Hörsching, about 12 km (7½ miles) southwest of the city. Buses run between the airport and the main train station according to flight schedules.

Fast trains connect German cities via Passau with Linz.

The city center is easy to manage on foot. The heart of the city—the Altstadt (Old City)—has been turned into a pedestrian zone; either leave your car at your hotel or use the huge parking garage under the main square in the center of town. Distances are not great, and you can take in the highlights in the course of a two- or three-hour walking tour.

Easy-to-use trams take visitors to sites of interest not directly in the city center. If in doubt grab a cab; there are many taxi stands in Linz.

From Linz the delightful LILO (Linzer Lokalbahn) interurban line makes the run up to Eferding. A charming narrow-gauge line meanders south to Waidhofen an der Ybbs.

ESSENTIALS

Airport Information LILO (Linzer Lokalbahn) ☎ 7272/2232–0, 7612/795–201 ⊕ www.linzer-lokalbahn.at. Linz Blue Danube airport ☎ 07221/600–0 ⊕ www.flughafen-linz.at. ÖBB—Österreichisches Bundesbahn ☎ 05/1717 ⊕ www.oebb.at.

Tourist Information Linz ✉ Hauptplatz 1 ☎ 0732/7070–2009 ⊕ www.linz.at. Linz Card ⊕ www.linz.at.

EXPLORING LINZ

TOP ATTRACTIONS

FAMILY **Ars Electronica Museum.** Just across the Nibelungen Bridge from the Hauptplatz, this futuristic museum allows visitors to try out all kinds of modern gadgets. In the 3-D cinema room you can fly over Renaissance cathedrals or explore ancient civilizations. Other exhibits delve into the latest developments in robotics and the origins of the universe. Instructions for all exhibits are in English. Allow at least a whole morning

DANUBE RIVER CRUISES

A cruise up the Danube to the Wachau Valley is a tonic in any season. A parade of storybook-worthy sights—fairy-tale castles-in-air, medieval villages, and Baroque abbeys crowned with "candle-snuffer" cupolas—unfolds before your eyes. Remember that it takes longer to travel north: the trip upstream to Krems, Dürnstein, and Melk will be longer than the return back to Vienna, which is why many travelers opt to return to the city by train, not boat. Keep your fingers crossed: rumor has it that on some summer days the river takes on an authentic shade of Johann Strauss blue.

Blue Danube Schifffahrt/DDSG. The main company offering sightseeing cruises is based in Vienna. Boats depart from the company's piers at Handelskai 265 (by the Reichsbrücke Bridge) There are thematic and brunch cruises as well, and you can also get trips from Krems to Melk. The ticket office is at the Vienna piers (take the U-Bahn line U1 to Vorgartenstrasse). ⊠ Friedrichstrasse 7, Vienna ☎ 01/588–800 ⊕ www. ddsg-blue-danube.at ⊠ €19.90 one way, €26 round-trip, with a possible €1 surcharge for rising fuel prices ⊙ Apr. 1–18 and mid-Sept.–late Oct., 12:30 and 4; mid-Apr.–mid-May, 12:30, 1:30, 4, and 5; mid-May–mid-Sept., 12:30, 1:30, 4, 5, and 6. Krems–Melk: mid- to end Apr., 10:15; May–early Oct., 10:15, 1:15, and 3:45; early–late Oct., 10:50.

Brandner Schifffahrt. Another way to cruise the Danube is to leapfrog ahead by train from Vienna to Krems. A short walk takes you to the Schiffstation Krems piers, where river cruises run by Brandner Schifffahrt from April through October depart at 10:05 am for a ride to glorious Melk Abbey and Dürnstein. Other options include special day and evening cruises with oompah band concerts, wine cruises, and the like. There is an occassional "crime cruise" (in German) with a murder mystery to be solved. ⊠ Ufer 50, Wallsee ☎ 07433/2590–21 ⊕ www.brandner. at ⊠ €23.70 one way.

or afternoon to experience all the cybersites. When you need a break, visit the Cubus Café Restaurant Bar on the third floor for refreshments and a spectacular view overlooking the Danube and Lentos museum. ⊠ Hauptstrasse 2 ☎ 0732/72720 ⊕ www.aec.at ⊠ €8 ⊙ Tues., Wed., and Fri. 9–5, Thurs. 9–9, weekends 10–6.

Lentos. Taking its name from the ancient Celtic settlement that was the origin of the city of Linz, this contemporary art museum hugs the banks of the Danube on the Altstadt side of the river. Designed by Zürich architects Weber and Hofer, its long, low-slung "shoe-box" gray-glass structure picks up the reflection of the water and, at night, lit in shimmering blue or red, really stands out. The collection contains an impressive number of paintings by Austrian Secession artists Klimt, Schiele, and Kokoschka, along with works by other artists, including sculptures by Alfred Hrdlicka and one of those famous silkscreen portraits of Marilyn Monroe by Andy Warhol. All in all, the museum has about 1,500 artworks, more than 10,000 sketches, and nearly 1,000 photographs. The excellent restaurant has an outdoor terrace with beautiful views of the river. ⊠ *Ernst-Koref-Promenade 1* ☎ *070/7070–3600–0* ⊕ *www. lentos.at* ☜ *€8* ⊙ *Tues.-Sun., 10–6 (to 9 Thurs.).*

Neuer Dom (*New Cathedral*). In 1862 the bishop of Linz engaged one of the architects of Cologne cathedral to develop a design for a grand cathedral in the French neo-Gothic style to accommodate 20,000 worshipers, at that time one-third of the population of Linz. According to legend, the tower was not to be higher than that of St. Stephen's in Vienna. The result was the massive 400-foot tower, shorter than St. Stephen's by a scant 6½ feet. The cathedral contains gorgeous stained-glass windows and offers organ recitals. ⊠ *Herrenstrasse 26* ☎ *0732/946100* ☜ *Free* ⊙ *Mon.–Sat. 7:30–7, Sun. 8–7:15.*

Pillar to the Holy Trinity. One of the symbols of Linz is the 65-foot Baroque column in the center of the Hauptplatz. Made in 1723 from white Salzburg marble, the memorial offers thanks from an earthly trinity—the provincial estates, city council, and local citizenry—for deliverance from the threats of war (1704), fire (1712), and plague (1713). ■ TIP→ **From March through October there's a flea market here each Saturday (except holidays), from 7 to 2, and a farmers' market each Tuesday and Friday from 9 to 2.** ⊠ *Hauptplatz.*

Pöstlingberg. When you want to escape the hustle and bustle of Linz, just hop on the **Pöstlingbergbahn,** an electric railway, for a scenic ride up to the famous mountain belvedere, the Pöstlingberg. The narrow-gauge marvel has been making the 16-minute journey since 1898, and today it the line extends to Hauptplatz. Europe's steepest non-cog mountain railway gains 229 meters (750 feet) in elevation in a journey of roughly 4 km (2½ miles), with neither pulleys nor cables to prevent it from slipping, tackling a gradien tof nearly 1:10. In summer the old open-bench cars are used. On a clear day the view from the top of the Postlingberg is superb, with the city and the wide sweep of the Danube filling the foreground and the snowcapped Alps on the horizon. With a glass of chilled white wine in hand, drink in the grand vista over Linz and the Danube from the terrace of the **Pöstlingberg-Schlössl** restaurant, at the top of Linz's "city mountain." There are also cafés and beer gardens at the summit, along with the **Church of the Seven Sorrows of the Virgin** (Sieben Schmerzen Mariens), an immense and opulent twin-towered Baroque pilgrimage church (1748) visible for miles as a Linz landmark. Also on the mountain is the **Märchengrotte (Fairy-Tale Grotto) Railroad.** A **museum** with an original carriage from the Pöstlingbergbahn and an interactive mockup of the driving controls is at the former ticket office in Landgutstrasse 19. ■ TIP→ **Halfway up is the Linz Zoological Garden and a children's petting zoo.** ☎ *0732/7801–7002* ⊕ *www.linzag.at* ☜ *€3.50 one way, €5.80 round-trip* ⊙ *Trains run every 30 mins: Mon.–Sat. 6 am–10 pm (last return 10:30 pm), Sun. 7:30 am–10 pm (last return 10:30 pm); from Nov.–Mar. the last train runs at 8 pm (last return 8:30 pm).*

Schlossmuseum Linz (*Linz Castle*). The massive four-story building on Tummelplatz was rebuilt by Friedrich III around 1477, literally on top of a castle that dated from 799. Note the **Friedrichstor** (the Frederick Gate), with the *A.E.I.O.U.* monogram (some believe it stands for the Latin sentence meaning "All Earth pays tribute to Austria") and two interior courtyards. This is widely known as one of the best provincial museums in the country. The interior of the castle is well worth a visit, with a 17th-century inlaid walnut portal from Schloss Hartheim, historical musical instruments (including Beethoven's Hammerklavier), re-creations of rooms from 19th-century Austrian homes, fine 19th-century portraits, and landscapes by Dutch and Austrian artists, as well as weaponry, coins, and ceramics. An incongruous steel-and-glass southern side with exhibits on nature and technology was added in 2009 to replace a building section that was destroyed by fire in 1800. ⊠ *Tummelplatz 10* ☎ *0732/774–419* ⊕ *www.schlossmuseum. at* ⊠ *€6.50* ⊙ *Tues., Wed., and Fri. 9–6, Thurs. 9–9, weekends 10–5.*

WORTH NOTING

Alter Dom (*Old Cathedral*). Hidden away off the Graben, a narrow side street off the Taubenmarkt above the Hauptplatz, is this Baroque gem (1669–78), where the striking feature is its single nave with side altars. Anton Bruckner was the organist here from 1856 to 1868. ⊠ *Domgasse 3* ⊕ *www.dioezese-linz.at* ⊙ *Daily 7–7.*

Altes Rathaus (*Old City Hall*). At the lower end of the main square, the original 1513 building was mostly destroyed by fire and replaced in 1658–59. Its octagonal corner turret and lunar clock, and some vaulted rooms, remain, and you can detect traces of the original Renaissance structure on the Rathausgasse facade. The present exterior dates from 1824. The approach from Rathausgasse 5, opposite the Kepler Haus, leads through a fine, arcaded courtyard. On the facade here you'll spot portraits of Emperor Friedrich III, the mayors Hoffmandl and Prunner, the astronomer Johannes Kepler, and the composer Anton Bruckner. The building houses a museum dedicated to the history of Linz and a rather odd museum of dentistry. ⊠ *Hauptplatz.*

Bischofshof (*Bishop's Residence*). This impressive mansion, which dates from 1721, was the residence of Mozart's friend Count Herberstein, who was later appointed Bishop of Linz, and is one of the the city's most impressive Baroque buildings. It was designed by Jakob Prandtauer, the architectural genius responsible for the glorious Melk and St. Florian abbeys. The building still serves as the bishop's residence and ecclesiatical offices. ⊠ *Herrenstrasse and Bischofstrasse.*

FAMILY **Grotto Railway** (*Grottenbahn*). More than 100 years old, the "Dragon Express" hasn't aged one bit, and still runs through a colorful imaginary world full of dwarfs and other displays at the top of the **Pöstlingberg.** ⊠ *Am Pöstlingberg* ☎ *0732/3400–7506* ⊕ *www.linz.at* ⊠ *€5* ⊙ *Mar.– May and Sept.–Nov., daily 10–5; June–Aug., daily 10–6.*

Karmelitenkloster. This magnificent Baroque church on Landstrasse was modeled after St. Joseph's in Prague. It underwent an extensive renovation in 2008. ⊠ *Landstrasse 33* ☎ *0732/770217* ⊙ *Weekdays 7–noon and 3–6:30; Sun. 6:15–noon and 3–6:45. From noon to 3, only the entry (narthex) is open.*

Kepler Haus. The astronomer Johannes Kepler lived here from 1612 to 1622, and the first printing shop in Linz was established in this house in 1745. The interior is generally closed to the public, but there are occasional lectures and events. ⊠ *Rathausgasse 5* ⊕ *www.kepler-salon.at.*

Kremsmünsterhaus. Emperor Friedrich III is said to have died here in 1493. The building was done over in Renaissance style in 1578–80, and a story was added in 1616, with two turrets and onion domes. There's a memorial room to the emperor here; his heart is entombed in the Linz parish church, but the rest of him is in St. Stephen's cathedral in Vienna. The traditional rooms house one of Linz's best restaurants, Herberstein. ⊠ *Altstadt 10.*

Landhaus. The early-Renaissance monastery adjoining the **Minoriten-kirche** is now the Landhaus, with its distinctive tower, seat of the provincial government. Look inside to see the arcaded courtyard with the Planet Fountain (honoring Johannes Kepler, the astronomer who taught here when it was the city's college) and the Hall of Stone on the first floor, above the barrel-vaulted hall on the ground floor. This hall, the Steinerner Saal, was probably the setting for a noted concert given by the Mozart children in October 1762 (from which Count Pálffy hurried back to Vienna to spread the word about the musical prodigies). For a more extensive look at the interior, inquire at the local tourist office about its scheduled guided tours. The beautiful Renaissance doorway (1570) is of red marble. ⊠ *Klosterstrasse 7.*

Minoritenkirche. At the end of Klosterstrasse, this church was once part of a monastery. The present building dates from 1752 to 1758 and has a delightful rococo interior with side-altar paintings by Kremser Schmidt and a main altar by Bartolomeo Altomonte. Mozart probably worshipped here when he stayed at the Thun Palace across the way. ⊠ *Klosterstrasse 7* ☎ *0732/7720–11364* ☾ *Apr.–Oct., daily 8–4; Nov.–Mar., daily 8 am–11 am.*

Mozart Haus. This three-story Renaissance town house, actually the Thun Palace, has a later baroque facade and portal. Mozart arrived here with his wife in 1783 to meet an especially impatient patron (Mozart was late by 14 days). As the composer forgot to bring any symphonies along with him, he set about writing one and completed the sublime Linz Symphony in the space of three days. The palace now houses private apartments, but the courtyard, which can be entered from Altstadt 17, around the corner, has a café. ⊠ *Klostergasse 20.*

Nordico. At the corner of Dametzstrasse and Bethlehemstrasse you'll find the city museum, dating from 1610. Its collection follows local history from pre-Roman times to the mid-1880s. ⊠ *Dametzstrasse 23* ☎ *0732/7070–1912* ⊕ *www.nordico.at* ☞ *€6.50* ☾ *Tues.–Sun. 10–6 (until 9 Thurs.).*

Seminarkirche (*Seminary Church*). Dating from 1725, this yellow-and-white Baroque treasure has an elliptical dome designed by Johann Lukas von Hildebrandt, who also designed its high altar. It was commissioned by the Order of the German Knights. ⊠ *Harrachstrasse 7* ☎ *0732/771205* ☾ *Daily 7–5.*

Stadtpfarrkirche. This city parish church dates from 1286 and was rebuilt in baroque style in 1648. The tomb in the right wall of the chancel contains Frederick III's heart and entrails (the corpse is in Vienna's St. Stephen's Cathedral). The ceiling frescoes are by Altomonte, and the figure of Johann Nepomuk (a local saint) in the chancel is by Georg

Raphael Donner, with grand decoration supplied by the master designer Hildebrandt. ⊠ *Pfarrplatz 4* ☎ *0732/7761–200* ☉ *Daily 8:30–6.*

Ursulinenkirche. The towers at this Baroque church are one of the identifying symbols of Linz. Inside is a blaze of gold and crystal ornamentation. Note the Madonna figure wearing a hooded Carmelite cloak with huge pockets, used to collect alms for the poor. ⊠ *Landstrasse 31* ☎ *0732/7610–3151* ☉ *Daily 7:30–6.*

WHERE TO EAT

$$$$ ✕ **Herberstein.** Tucked in the historic Kremsmünsterhaus you'll find an
EUROPEAN elegant and popular restaurant with a 1960s-retro look, defined by cozy tables, muted lighting, and attractive stonework. The cuisine is Austrian with a slice of Asia, as evidenced by the selection of wok dishes, not to mention the sushi bar. Main courses include mouthwatering variations of fish, such as the pan-fried salmon trout with saffron rice and cardamom-orange sauce. On Saturday, a romantic "Dinner for 2," including a four-course meal, aperitif, and bottle of wine, is offered for €115. If the weather is fine, you can opt to sit outside in the inviting, enclosed *Hof* (courtyard). $ *Average main: €26* ⊠ *Altstadt 10* ☎ *0732/786161* ⊕ *www.herberstein-linz.at* ⌁ *Reservations essential* ☉ *Mon.–Sat. 4 pm–4 am* ☉ *Closed Sun. No lunch.*

$$ ✕ **Promenadenhof.** The atmosphere is that of a spacious, contemporary
AUSTRIAN Gasthaus, with a fabulous roofed garden filled with flowers. The cellar is open for you to pick your own wine, available by the glass from open bottles. The varied menu of regional cuisine is reasonably priced and has a touch of the Mediterranean. Plenty of vegetarian meals are available, but go for the *Tafelspitz* (boiled beef) if you like really good beef. Desserts include Pear Hélène and an apple-walnut parfait. Service is excellent. The place is easy to find; just look for the theater in the heart of the Altstadt. $ *Average main: €13* ⊠ *Promenade 39* ☎ *0732/777661* ⊕ *www.promenadenhof.at* ☉ *Closed Sun.*

$ ✕ **Schloss Café.** A more pleasant spot for casual dining in Linz can hardly
EUROPEAN be imagined, tucked into the side of the town's landmark castle and affording lordly views of the Danube and the opposite bank. Tables are set outside under shady trees and take full advantage of the scenery, but it's alluring inside as well, thanks to the smart red-leather banquettes and modern artwork. The menu offers reasonably priced lunch specials as well as typical café fare. When weather permits, there is an outdoor grill. Zipfer beer is on tap, and wines from the Danube Valley are featured. A more upscale eatery called Schlossberg 1a is in the new wing of the castle. $ *Average main: €11* ⊠ *Tummelplatz 10* ☎ *6641/303–705.*

$ ✕ **Traxlmayr.** Proud with the patina of age, this is one of Austria's great
CAFÉ old-tradition coffeehouses and the only one of its kind in Upper Austria. You can linger all day over a single cup of coffee, reading the papers in their bentwood holders, and then have a light meal. There is a nonsmoking section inside, and in summer you can sit outside on the terrace and watch passersby. Ask for the specialty, *Linzertorte* (almond cake with jam) with your coffee, or try the homemade *Apfelstrudel*. $ *Average main: €5* ⊠ *Promenade 16* ☎ *0732/773353* ⊕ *www.cafe-traxlmayr. at* ⊟ *No credit cards.*

$$ AUSTRIAN 🍴 **Verdi Einkehr.** The trendy, less pricey bistro alternative to Verdi—a noted Linz dinner restaurant—shares the same house and kitchen. The rooms are done in rustic chic, with stone fireplaces, chintz-covered chairs, and lots of polished wood. There is also a terrace for summer dining. Delights are many, ranging from braised veal shoulder to a tartlet of octopus. If you don't have a car, you'll need a taxi to get here. It's set in Lichtenberg, about 3 km (2 miles) north of the town center, off Leonfelderstrasse. You must specify that you want to be seated in the Einkehr. [$] *Average main: €15* ✉ *Pachmayrstrasse 137* ☎ *0732/733005* ✍ *Reservations essential* ⏲ *Closed Sun. and Mon. No lunch.*

SWEET TOOTH?

The cuisine of the Danube Valley usually runs along traditional lines, but the desserts are often brilliant inventions. First among these is the celebrated fruit-filled Linzer torte. Less well-known are Linzer Augen, jam-filled cookies. A specialty found only in the Wachau region of the Danube Valley is the *Wachauer Semmel*, a freshly baked roll that is crisped golden on the outside and dense and chewy inside.

WHERE TO STAY

$ HOTEL 🏨 **Arcotel Nike.** Right next door to the Brucknerhaus concert hall and a good 10-minute walk from the Altstadt, this modern, relatively uninspiring high-rise on the banks of the Danube is a practical option for concertgoers. **Pros:** modern rooms, some with a view; spacious spa area. **Cons:** lacks charm. [$] *Rooms from: €95* ✉ *Untere Donaulände 9* ☎ *0732/76260* 🌐 *www.arcotel.at* 🛏 *171 rooms, 3 suites* 🍽 *No meals.*

$$ HOTEL 🏨 **Landgraf.** Set in a turn-of-the-century redbrick building, this ultra-chic hotel with large rooms is next door to the Ars Electronica Museum and just a five-minute walk across the bridge from the Altstadt. **Pros:** spacious rooms; very trendy interior; secured parking available (fee). **Cons:** busy area; can get noisy at night. [$] *Rooms from: €130* ✉ *Hauptstrasse 12* ☎ *0732/700712* 🌐 *hotellandgraf.com* 🛏 *32 rooms, 3 suites* 🍽 *Breakfast.*

$$ HOTEL 🏨 **Wolfinger.** A 500-year-old former nunnery, the centrally located Wolfinger has been a hostelry since the late 1700s, and that gives the interior some real charm. **Pros:** great location for museums and restaurants; charming rooms; very helpful and friendly staff. **Cons:** creaking floorboards; old fittings in some rooms; a few rooms share bathrooms. [$] *Rooms from: €126* ✉ *Hauptplatz 19* ☎ *0732/773291–0* 🌐 *www.hotelwolfinger.at* 🛏 *49 rooms, 1 suite* 🍽 *Breakfast.*

$ HOTEL 🏨 **Zum Schwarzen Bären.** The birthplace of the renowned Mozart tenor Richard Tauber (1891–1948), the "Black Bear" is a traditional house filled with memorabilia on a quiet side street in the center of the Old City, a block from the pedestrian zone. **Pros:** quiet location; some rooms have waterbeds; on-site underground parking. **Cons:** restaurant closed on weekends. [$] *Rooms from: €69* ✉ *Herrenstrasse 9–11* ☎ *0732/772477–0* 🌐 *www.linz-hotel.at* 🛏 *48 rooms, 2 suites* 🍽 *Breakfast.*

NIGHTLIFE AND PERFORMING ARTS

Linz is far livelier than even most Austrians realize. The local population is friendlier than that of either Vienna or Salzburg, and much less cliquish. And Linz hasn't lagged behind other Austrian cities in developing its own fashionable neighborhood, known as the Bermuda Triangle. Around the narrow streets of the Old City (Klosterstrasse, Altstadt, Hofgasse) are dozens of fascinating small bars and lounges; as you explore, you'll probably meet some Linzers who can direct you to the current "in" location.

NIGHTLIFE

Josef. This hopping establishment has its own home-brewed beer on tap, light snacks, and hearty regional dishes, and is open every day from 11 am until very late. ⊠ *Landstrasse 49* ☎ *0732/773165* ⊕ *www.josef.co.at.*

Landgraf Hotel. A good starting point, where both the young and the more mature will feel comfortable, is the below-stairs, fanciful, Moroccan-style bar in the Landgraf Hotel, which is just across the bridge from the Altstadt and open Tuesday–Saturday from 6 pm until the wee hours. ⊠ *Hauptstrasse 12* ⊕ *www.landgraf.at/cafe.*

Linz Casino. In the Hotel Schillerpark, and with a formal dress code, the casino has roulette, blackjack, poker, and slot machines, and the complex includes a bar and the Rouge et Noir restaurant. A passport ID is required for admission. Garage parking is available for €2. The less formal Jackpot Casino does not require a jacket and tie. A coupon on entry allows you to get €25 in welcome chips, and other deals give discounts on food and beverages combined with chips. ⊠ *Rainerstrasse 2–4* ☎ *0732/654–4870* ⊕ *www.casinos.at* 🎫 *Free* ⊙ *Daily 3 pm–3 am; Jackpot Casino from 11 am.*

PERFORMING ARTS

Brucknerhaus. A vast array of concerts and recitals are presented in the noted Brucknerhaus, the modern hall on the south bank of the Danube. From early to late September it's home to the International Bruckner Festival. The venue also hosts some events for Ars Electronica, a festival that explores art, science, and society. ⊠ *Untere Donaulände 7* ☎ *0732/775230* ⊕ *www.brucknerhaus.at* ⊙ *Box office: Sept.–June, weekdays noon–6:30, Sat. 10–1; July and Aug. Mon.–Sat. 10–1.*

Linz Opera Company. The talented Linz opera company often mounts venturesome works and productions. Most performances are in the Landestheater, with some in the Brucknerhaus.

The tourist office can give you details of theater performances and concerts.

SHOPPING

Linz is a good place to shop; prices are generally lower than those in resorts and the larger cities, and selections are varied. The major shops are found in the main square and the adjoining side streets, in the old quarter to the west of the main square, in the pedestrian zone of the Landstrasse and its side streets, and in the Hauptstrasse of Urfahr, over the Nibelungen Bridge across the Danube.

Flea Market. Everything from clothing to china is sold at the Flea Market, open every Saturday from 7 to 2 on the Hauptplatz (main square) from March through early November. In the winter, it moves to the square in front of the Neues Rathaus (New Town Hall) on Hauptstrasse. Check with the tourist office about other flea markets.

O. Ö. Heimatwerk. This is a good option if you're looking for local handmade goods and good-quality souvenirs. You'll find silver, pewter, ceramics, fabrics, and some clothing. ⊠ *Landstrasse 31* ☎ *0732/773–3770* ⊕ *ooe.heimatwerk.at.*

ANTIQUES

For antiques, head for the Old City and these shops on the side streets around the main square.

Dorotheum Auction House. At this state-run sale room, auctions take place on varying days—the website includes an auction calendar—but it's open to the public for viewing on weekdays from 9 to 5. ⊠ *Fabrikstrasse 26* ☎ *0732/773132–0* ⊕ *www.dorotheum.com.*

Ferdinand Saminger. Come here for antique paintings and objets d'art. ⊠ *Waldeggstrasse 20* ☎ *0732/654081.*

Kunst-Haus Dr. Pastl. This auction house is known throughout Linz for the great selection of sculpture and 18th-century paintings. ⊠ *Wischerstrasse 26* ☎ *0699/117221–44* ⊕ *www.pastl.com.*

Otto Buchinger. This is the place to go for modern drawings and 19th-century furniture and artworks. ⊠ *Bethlehemstrasse 5* ☎ *0732/770117* ⊕ *www.buchinger-austria.com.*

Richard Kirchmayr. There's a tempting collection of paintings and furniture here. ⊠ *Bischofstrasse 3a* ☎ *0732/797711* ☉ *Wed.–Fri., 10–noon and 3–6; Sat. 10:30–1.*

JEWELRY

There are two superior places in the city center to shop for elegant jewelry at reasonable prices.

Atelier Almesberger. Individual, handmade pieces at this shop catch the eye. ⊠ *Hofgasse 7* ☎ *0732/790561* ⊕ *www.donausteindesign.com.*

Juwelier Mayrhofer. Find upscale jewelry without the upscale price here. ⊠ *Hauptplatz 22* ☎ *0732/775649* ⊕ *www.juwelier-mayrhofer.com.*

Le Clou. For nice, less costly jewelry and souvenirs, check out this place. ⊠ *Landstrasse 17–25* ☎ *0732/782980* ⊕ *www.leclou.at.*

SPORTS AND THE OUTDOORS

BICYCLING

Cyclists appreciate the relatively level terrain around Linz, and within the city there are 200 km (125 miles) of marked cycle routes. Cycling at slow speeds is also allowed in the city's pedestrian zones. The international Donauradweg, or Danube Cycling Path, runs from Germany through Linz and to the Black Sea. Get bike maps from the tourist office.

Donau Touristik. Rent bikes here, or book a guided cycling tour along the Danube River. Bikes rented in Linz can be returned at several points along the Danube Cycling Path. ✉ *Lederergasse 4–12* ☎ *0732/2080* ⊕ *www.donaureisen.at.*

Linzer Schweben. If you prefer to glide and not pedal take the two- to three-hour Segway tour for €54 organized by Linzer Schweben that leaves from the Tourist Information Office. There is a half hour of training before the tours. ✉ *Hauptplatz 1* ☎ *0732/7070–2009* ⊕ *linzerschweben.at.*

TICKETS

Kartenbüro Pirngruber. Buy tickets here for special sports events. The office is open weekdays 9–6 and Saturday 9–1. ✉ *Landstrasse 34* ☎ *0732/772–833* ⊕ *www.pirngruber.com.*

TWO EXCURSIONS FROM LINZ

Many travelers find Linz the most practical point of departure for visits to nearby towns, which are filled with noteworthy Gothic and Baroque sights. You'll be dazzled by masterworks of the Austrian Baroque and the great abbey of St. Florian, in the town of the same name. Steyr—a gorgeous, Gothic-flavored market town once home to the great composer Anton Bruckner—merits a trip or an overnight.

ST. FLORIAN

Fodor's Choice ★ **Stift St. Florian** (*St. Florian Abbey*). Built to honor the spot on the river Enns where St. Florian was drowned by pagans in 304 (he is still considered the protector against fire and flood by many Austrians), the Stift St. Florian over the centuries came to comprise one of the most spectacular Baroque showpieces in Austria, landmarked by three gigantic "candle-snuffer" cupolas. In 1686 the Augustinian abbey was built by the Italian architect Carolo Carlone, then finished by Jakob Prandtauer. More a palace than anything else, it is centered on a mammoth **Marmorsaal** (Marble Hall)—covered with frescoes honoring Prince Eugene of Savoy's defeat of the Turks—and a sumptuous library filled with 140,000 volumes. In this setting of gilt and marble, topped with ceiling frescoes by Bartolomeo Altomonte, an entire school of Austrian historiographers was born in the 19th century. Guided tours of the abbey begin with the magnificent figural gateway, which rises up three stories and is covered with symbolic statues. The Stiegenhaus, or Grand Staircase, leads to the upper floors, which include the **Kaiserzimmer,** a suite of 13 opulent salons (where you can see the "terrifying bed" of Prince Eugene, fantastically adorned with wood-carved figures of captives). The tour includes one of the great masterworks of the Austrian Baroque, Jakob Prandtauer's **Eagle Fountain Courtyard,** with its richly sculpted figures. In the over-the-top **abbey church,** where the ornate surroundings are somewhat in contrast to Bruckner's music, the Krismann organ (1770–74) is one of the largest and best of its period, and Bruckner used it to become a master organist and composer. ■ TIP→ **From mid-May through mid-October, you can attend a 25-minute organ concert, held on Sunday, Monday, and Wednesday–Friday at 2:30.** Another highlight is the **Altdorfer Gallery,** which contains several masterworks by Albrecht Altdorfer, the leading master of the 16th-century Danube School and ranked with Dürer and Grunewald as one of the greatest northern

7

painters. ⊠ *Stiftstrasse 1* ☏ *07224/8902–0* ⊕ *www.stift-st-florian.at* ☞ *€8.50 for tour; €4.50 for concert* ☉ *One-hour tours: May–Sept., daily at 11, 1, and 3.*

STEYR

Austrian Christmas Museum. In a Gothic building on Michaelerplatz, the Austrian Christmas Museum houses the world's largest private collection of antique Christmas-tree decorations. There are more than 10,000 ornaments created out of glass, porcelain, metal, and many other materials. In addition, there are more than 200 parlor dolls, dollhouses, and doll tea cozies from the Biedermeier era to post–World War II. A thoroughly eccentric Viennese lady named Elfriede Kreuzberger collected this treasure and decided that Steyr was the right place to deposit her hoard. There's also a cute, tiny, single-seater train that takes you up two floors, past Nativity scenes, to the attic and its angel workshop. ⊠ *Michaelerplatz 2* ☏ *07252/80659, 07252/53229 tourist board* ☞ *€3, combination train and museum €6.50* ☉ *Late Nov.–early Jan., daily 10–5. For visits outside these dates call Steyr tourist board.*

Museum Industrielle Arbeitswelt (*Industrial Museum*). Set in former riverside factories, this museum recalls the era when Steyr was a major center of iron making and armaments production; hunting arms are still produced here, but the major output is powerful motors for BMW cars, including some assembled in the United States. Interactive installations and exhibitions make for a worthwhile visit. ⊠ *Wehrgrabengasse 7* ☏ *07252/77351* ⊕ *www.museum-steyr.at* ☞ *€5* ☉ *Tues.–Sun. 9–5.*

Steyrertalbahn. This narrow-gauge vintage railroad, wanders 17 km (10½ miles) from Steyr through the countryside on Sundays in June and weekends from July to the end of September. It also runs a holiday service on select days from late November to January 5. ☏ *0664/5087664, 07257/7102* ⊕ *www.steyrtalbahn.at* ☞ *€10 one way.*

▌**OFF THE BEATEN PATH**

Waidhofen an der Ybbs. Well worth a slight detour from the more traveled routes, this picturesque river town (30 km [18 miles] east of Steyr) developed early as an industrial center, where Styrian iron ore was turned into swords, knives, sickles, and scythes. These weapons proved successful in the defense against the invading Turks in 1532; marking the decisive moment of victory, the hands on the north side of the town tower clock remain at 12:45. In 1871 Baron Rothschild bought the collapsing castle and assigned Friedrich Schmidt, architect of Vienna's City Hall, to rebuild it in neo-Gothic style. The castle offers a selection of picnic lunches (with the option of keeping the basket) and rents bicycles. Stroll around the two squares in the Altstadt to see the Gothic and Baroque houses and to the Graben on the edge of the Old City for the delightful Biedermeier houses and churches and chapels.

SALZBURG

Updated by
Erin Snell

"All Salzburg is a stage," Count Ferdinand Czernin once wrote. "Its beauty, its tradition, its history enshrined in the grey stone of which its buildings are made, its round of music, its crowd of fancy-dressed people, all combine to lift you out of everyday life, to make you forget that somewhere far off, life hides another, drearier, harder, and more unpleasant reality." Shortly after the count's book, *This Salzburg*, was published in 1937, the unpleasant reality arrived; but having survived the Nazis, Salzburg once again became one of Austria's top cultural draws.

Art lovers call it the Golden City of High Baroque; historians refer to it as the Florence of the North or the German Rome; and music lovers know it as the birthplace of one of the world's most beloved composers, Wolfgang Amadeus Mozart (1756–91). If the young Mozart was the boy wonder of 18th-century Europe and Salzburg did him no particular honor in his lifetime, it is making up for it now. Since 1920 the world-famous Salzburger Festspiele (Salzburg Festival), the third-oldest on the continent, has honored "Wolferl" with performances of his works by the world's greatest musicians.

Ironically, many who come to this golden city of High Baroque may first hear the instantly recognizable strains of music from the film that made Salzburg a household name: from the Mönchsberg to Nonnberg Convent, it's hard to go exploring without hearing someone humming "How Do You Solve a Problem Like Maria?" A popular tourist exercise is to make the town's acquaintance by visiting all the sights featured in that beloved Hollywood extravaganza, *The Sound of Music,* filmed here in 1964. Just like Mozart, the von Trapp family—who escaped the Third Reich by fleeing their beloved country—were little appreciated at home; Austria was the only place on the planet where the film failed, closing after a single week's showing in Vienna and Salzburg. It's said that the Austrian populace at large didn't cotton to a prominent family up and running in the face of the Nazis.

ORIENTATION AND PLANNING

GETTING ORIENTED

Salzburg lies on both banks of the Salzach River, at the point where it's pinched between two mountains, the Kapuzinerberg on one side, the Mönchsberg on the other. In broader view are many beautiful Alpine peaks.

Salzburg's rulers pursued construction on a grand scale ever since Wolf-Dietrich von Raitenau began his regime in the latter part of the 16th century. At the age of only 28, Wolf-Dietrich envisioned "his" Salzburg to be the Rome of the Alps, with a town cathedral grander than St. Peter's, a Residenz as splendid as a Roman palace, and his private Mirabell Gardens flaunting the most fashionable styles of Italianate horticulture. After he was deposed by the rulers of Bavaria, other cultured prince-archbishops took over. Johann Ernst von Thun and Franz Anton von Harrach commanded the masters of Viennese baroque, Fischer von Erlach and Lukas von Hildebrandt, to complete Wolf-Dietrich's vision. The result is that Salzburg's many fine buildings blend into a harmonious whole. Perhaps nowhere else in the world is there so cohesive a flowering of baroque architecture.

But times change and the Salzburgians with them. It is not surprising to learn that Salzburg is now home to one of the most striking museums: the Museum der Moderne. The avant-garde showcase stands on the very spot where Julie Andrews "do-re-mi"-d with the von Trapp brood; where once the fusty Café Winkler stood atop the Mönchsberg mount, a modern, cubical museum of cutting-edge art now commands one of the grandest views of the city.

The Altstadt: In Mozart's Footsteps. Salzburg is the only city in the world with 1,300 years of continuous music history, which you can experience in concert halls, churches, restaurants and bars, and even outdoors in city squares.

Around Fortress Hohensalzburg. The showstopping medieval fortress is an attraction on its own, but it also offers sweeping Salzburg views.

North of the River Salzach. Here you can simultaneously enjoy outstanding old and new architecture and beautiful nature, from gardens to the hills.

8

PLANNING

GETTING HERE AND AROUND
AIR TRAVEL
Salzburg Airport, 4 km (2½ miles) west of the city center, is Austria's second-largest international airport. There are direct flights from London and other European cities to Salzburg, but from the United States you would have to fly to Munich and take the 90-minute train ride to Salzburg. You can also take a bus, run by Salzburger Mietwagenservice. Taxis are the easiest way to get downtown from the Salzburg airport; the ride costs around €15–€18 and takes about 20 minutes. City Bus No. 2, which makes a stop by the airport every 15 minutes, runs down to Salzburg's train station (about 20 minutes). Bus No. 8 runs directly to the city center.

BOAT TRAVEL
For a magically different vantage point, take a round-trip boat ride along the endlessly scenic Salzach River, departing at the Markartsteg in the Altstadt from April until October. The boat journeys as far south as Hellbrunn Palace (depending on the water level). In June, July, and August you can also take the cruise as you enjoy a candlelight dinner—the real dessert is a floodlit view of Salzburg.

BUS TRAVEL

A tourist map (available from tourist offices in Mozartplatz and the train station) shows all bus routes and stops; there's also a color-coded map of the public transportation network, so you should have no problem getting around. Virtually all buses and trolleybuses (O-Bus) run via Mirabellplatz and/or Hanuschplatz. Single-trip bus tickets bought from the driver cost €2.50. Multiple-use tickets, available at tobacconists (*Tabak-Trafik*), ticket offices, and tourist offices, are much cheaper. You can buy five single-trip tickets for €1.70 each (not available at tourist offices) or a 24-hour ticket, which costs €5.50 on the bus or €3.40 at tobacconists and ticket offices.

CAR TRAVEL

If driving, the fastest routes into Salzburg are the autobahns. From Vienna (320 km [198 miles]), take A1; from Munich (150 km [93 miles]), A8 (also known in Germany as E11); from Italy, A10. The only advantage to having a car in Salzburg itself is that you can get out of the city for short excursions. The Old City on both sides of the river is a pedestrian zone, and the rest of the city, with its narrow, one-way streets, is a driver's nightmare.

TRAIN TRAVEL

You can get to Salzburg by rail from most European cities. Salzburg Hauptbahnhof is a 20-minute walk from the center of town in the direction of Mirabellplatz. The bus station and the suburban train station are at the square in front. A taxi to the center of town should take about 10 minutes and cost €10. The Deutsche Bahn "Bayern Ticket" allows travel on all regional trains to Salzburg and is the most economical choice at €22 for one and €38 total for up to five people traveling together.

TOURS

The Old City, composed of several interconnecting squares and narrow streets, is best seen on foot. Salzburg's official licensed guides offer a one-hour walking tour (€9) through the Old City every day at 12:15, and a 1½-hour tour (€10) every day at 2, which start in front of the Information Center at Mozartplatz 5. A Salzburg Card reduces the fee.

Several local companies conduct 1½- to 2-hour city tours. The tours are by minibus, since large buses can't enter the Old City, and briefly cover the major sights, including Mozart's birthplace, the festival halls, major squares, churches, and the palaces at Hellbrunn and Leopoldskron. Bob's Special Tours is well known to American visitors—the company offers a 10% discount to Fodor's readers who book directly with them (not through their hotel). Salzburg Panorama Tours and Salzburg Sightseeing Tours offer similar tours.

To reach spots buses can't, ride along with one of Fraulein Maria's two daily 3½-hour bicycle tours (€26).

Bob's Special Tours. Bob's small vans allow access to the narrow streets of Salzburg that lumbering buses can't maneuver. Explore the city, nearby mountain regions, or *The Sound of Music* filming highlights on daily and seasonal tours. Experienced, multilingual guides are available. ✉ *Rudolfskai 38* ☎ *0662/849511* ⊕ *www.bobstours.com* 🔁 *Daily and seasonal tours €45–€90; private tours €90 per hour.*

TOP REASONS TO GO

The view from Fortress Hohensalzburg. Ascend to the fortress on the peak and see what romantic visitors in the 19th century enjoyed so much—the soul-stirring combination of gorgeous architecture in a stunning natural location.

A pilgrimage to the Rome of the North. See the magnificent Baroque churches built not only to honor God but also to document the importance of the ruling prince-archbishops during the 17th century.

Concerts, operas, and more. Feel the spirit of 1,300 years of musical history as you listen to the music of Wolfgang Amadeus Mozart, arguably the greatest Western composer who ever lived, in the Marble Hall of Mirabell Palace. World-class talent in a wide array of genres populates Salzburg's numerous music festivals, handcrafted marionettes perform well-known operas, and stunning, reverberant choral music accompanies a Mass or concert at many of the gorgeous churches. You'll run out of time, not options, in Salzburg.

Medieval city. After exploring the Altstadt's grand churches and squares, cross the river Salzach to take in the completely different atmosphere of the narrow, 16th-century Steingasse, where working people once lived, and shops, galleries, and clubs now beckon.

Rulers' delights. Drive, bike, walk, or take the boat out to Schloss Hellbrunn, a Renaissance-inspired pleasure palace with trick fountains, a lush, green lawn perfect for picnics, and the gazebo that witnessed so much wooing in *The Sound of Music.*

8

FAMILY **Fräulein Maria's Bicycle Tours.** Ride through the streets of Salzburg singing the soundtrack favorites and learn a surprising amount of the city's history with fellow movie and musical fans on these "Sound of Music"–themed small group bicycle tours. Guides share the von Trapp family cheer rain or shine with riders of all ages and abilities—inclement weather gear, tandem bikes, children's bikes, trailers, and baby seats are offered at no additional cost. Feeling adventurous? Try the full-day 25-km (16-mile) bike tours of Mondsee in Salzburg's Lake District. ✉ *Mirabellplatz 4* ☎ *0650/3426297* ⊕ *www.mariasbicycletours.com* 🎫 *Sound of Music Tour €26; Lake Tour €59* ☞ *Rain or shine.*

Salzburg Panorama Tours. One of the most reliable, respected tour companies in the area, offering a variety of themes and ways to become acquainted with Salzburg and the surrounding areas, either by bus, on foot, or in a luxurious private car. The "Original Sound of Music Tour" hits the movie location highlights and includes much about the city itself. Experts introduce the modern masterpieces of the UNESCO World Heritage City during the walking "PanoramARCHITECTour." Bus pick-up available at several local hotels; the website gives details. ✉ *Schrannengasse 2/2* ☎ *0662/883211* ⊕ *www.panoramatours.com* 🎫 *From €19.*

Salzburg Sightseeing Tours. One of the oldest tour companies in the city, Salzburg Sightseeing Tours offers prepackaged programs including the best of the city, *Sound of Music* locations, and nearby Alpine highlights, or custom tours. Their yellow hop-on, hop-off buses stop at the most famous Salzburg landmarks, with informative recorded audio guides between stops. The complete circuit (without getting off) takes an hour. ■ TIP→ **All tickets include free access to all local Salzburg buses, as well as the Gaisberg Bus (No. 151)** ✉ *Mirabellplatz 2* ☎ *0662/881616* ⊕ *www.welcome-salzburg.at* 🖃 *Hop on, hop off €16; "Sound of Music" €35; other tours from €18* ⊙ *Hop on, hop off: daily 9:15–4:45, every 30 min; "Sound of Music": daily 9:30 and 2:00.*

VISITOR INFORMATION
There are no information centers at the major highways. The Salzburg information on Mozartplatz is open April–October, at the Advent weekends, daily 9–6; and November–March, Monday–Saturday 9–6.

ESSENTIALS
Airport Contacts Flughafen München (MUC) ☎ *089/975-00* ⊕ *www.munich-airport.de.* **Salzburg Airport (SZG)** ✉ *Innsbrucker Bundesstrasse 95* ☎ *0662/8580-0* ⊕ *www.salzburg-airport.com.* **Salzburger Mietwagenservice (SMS)** ✉ *Wasserfeldstraße 24A* ☎ *0622/8161-0* ⊕ *www.flughafentransfer.at/index_e.php.*

Bus Contacts Salzburger Verkehrsverbund (*Main ticket office*). ✉ *Schrannengasse 4* ☎ *0662/632900* ⊕ *www.svv-info.at/en.*

Taxis Radio Cab ☎ *0662/8111.*

Train Information ÖBB ☎ *05/1717* ⊕ *www.oebb.at.* **Salzburg Hauptbahnhof** ✉ *SüdTyrolerplatz 1* ☎ *05/1717-4.*

Visitor Info Tourist Information at Train Station ✉ *Salzburg Hauptbahnhof, SüdTyrolerplatz 1* ☎ *0662/88987-340* ⊕ *www.salzburg.info/en/.* **Salzburg City Tourist Office** ✉ *Mozartplatz 5* ☎ *0662/88987-330* ⊕ *www.salzburginfo.at.*

EXPLORING SALZBURG

Getting to know Salzburg is not too difficult, because most of its sights are within a comparatively small area. The Altstadt (Old City) is a compact area between the jutting outcrop of the Mönchsberg and the Salzach River. The cathedral and interconnecting squares surrounding it form what used to be the religious center, around which the major churches and the old archbishops' residence are arranged (note that entrance into all Salzburg churches is free). The Mönchsberg cliffs emerge unexpectedly behind the Old City, crowned to the east by the Hohensalzburg Fortress. Across the river, in the small area between the cliffs of the Kapuzinerberg and the riverbank, is the Steingasse, a narrow medieval street where laborers, craftsmen, and traders served the salt mining industry and travelers coming in and out of the region's important mercantile hub. Northwest of the Kapuzinerberg lies Mirabell Palace and its manicured gardens.

It's best to begin by exploring the architectural and cultural riches of the Old City, then go on to the fortress. Afterward, cross the river to inspect the other bank. Ideally, you need two days to do it all. An alternative, if you enjoy exploring churches and castles, is to go directly up to the fortress, either on foot or by returning through the cemetery to the funicular railway.

■ TIP→ If you are doing this spectacular city in just one day, consider taking a walking tour run by city guides; one sets out every day at 12:15 pm from the tourist information office, **Information Mozartplatz,** at Mozart Square (closed on some Sundays during off-season). There are also escorted bus and bicycle tours through the city (*see Tours*).

THE ALTSTADT: IN MOZART'S FOOTSTEPS

Intent on becoming a patron of the arts, the prince-archbishop Wolf-Dietrich lavished much of his wealth on rebuilding Salzburg into a beautiful and Baroque city in the late 16th and early 17th centuries. In turn, his grand townscape came to inspire the young Joannes Chrysostomus Wolfgangus Amadeus (Theophilus) Mozart. In fact, by growing up in the center of the city and composing already at five years of age, Mozart set lovely Salzburg itself to music. He was perhaps the most purely Austrian of all composers, a singer of the smiling Salzburgian countryside, of the city's Baroque architecture. So even if you're not lucky enough to snag a ticket to a performance of *The Marriage of Figaro* or *Don Giovanni* in the Haus für Mozart, you can still appreciate what inspired his melodies just by strolling through his streets.

Ever since the 1984 Best Film Oscar-winner *Amadeus* (remember Tom Hulse as "Wolfie"?), the composer has been the 18th-century equivalent to a rock star. Born in Salzburg on January 27, 1756, he crammed a prodigious number of compositions into the 35 short years of his life, many of which he spent in Salzburg (he moved to Vienna in 1781). Indeed, the Altstadt revels in a bevy of important sights, ranging from his birthplace on the Getreidegasse to the abbey of St. Peter's, where the composer's *Great Mass in C Minor* was first performed. As you tour the composer's former haunts, why not listen to Papageno woo Papagena through your headphones?

TOP ATTRACTIONS

Alter Markt (*Old Market*). Right in the heart of the Old City is the Alter Markt, the old marketplace and center of secular life in past centuries. The square is lined with 17th-century middle-class houses, colorfully hued in shades of pink, pale blue, and yellow ocher. Look in at the old royal pharmacy, the **Hofapotheke,** whose ornate black-and-gold rococo interior was built in 1760. Inside, you'll sense a curious apothecarial smell, traced to the shelves lined with old pots and jars (labeled in Latin). These are not just for show: this pharmacy is still operating today. You can even have your blood pressure taken—but preferably not after drinking a *Doppelter Einspänner* (black coffee with whipped cream, served in a glass) in the famous Café Tomaselli just opposite. In warm weather the café's terrace provides a wonderful spot for watching the world go by as you sip a *Mélange* (another coffee specialty, served with frothy milk), or, during the summer months, rest your feet under the shade of the chestnut trees in the Tomaselli garden at the top end of the square. Next to the coffeehouse you'll find the **smallest house in Salzburg;** note the slanting roof decorated

Salzburg

Alter Markt **18**
Dom Quartier **26**
Dreifaltigkeitskirche **5**
Festspielhaus **20**
Festungsbahn **33**
Fortress Hohensalzburg **34**
Franziskanerkirche **24**
Friedhof St. Sebastian **8**
Geteidegasse **15**
Glockenspiel **27**

Kapuzinerberg Hill **9**
Kollegienkirche **19**
Marionettentheater **4**
Mirabellgarten **2**
Mirabell Palace **1**
Mönchsberg Elevator **11**
Mozart Audio
Visual Collection **6**
Mozart Geburtshaus **16**
Mozart Wohnhaus **7**
Mozarteum **3**

Mozartplatz **28**
Mozart Geburtshaus **16**
Museum der Moderne **12**
Nonnberg Convent **30**
Petersfriedhof **32**
Pferdeschwemme **14**
Rathaus **17**
Residenz **25**
Rupertinum **22**

Salzburg Museum **29**
Spielzeugmuseum **13**
Steingasse **10**
Stiftkirche St. Peter **31**
Toscaninihof **23**
Wiener
Philharmoniker-Gasse **21**

KEY

i *Tourist information*

with a dragon gargoyle. In the center of the square, surrounded by flower stalls, is the marble **St. Florian's Fountain,** dedicated in 1734 to the patron saint of firefighters.

Dom (*Cathedral*). When you walk through the arches leading from Residenzplatz into **Domplatz,** it's easy to see why Max Reinhardt chose it in August of 1920 as the setting for what has become the annual summer production of Hugo von Hofmannsthal's *Jedermann* (*Everyman*). The plaza is one of Salzburg's most beautiful urban set pieces. In the center rises the Virgin's Column, and at one side is the cathedral, considered to be the first early Italian Baroque building north of the Alps. Its facade is of marble, its towers reach 76 meters (250 feet) into the air, and it holds 10,000 people. There has been a cathedral on this spot since the 8th century, but the present structure dates from the 17th century. The cathedral honors the patron saint of Salzburg, St. Rupert, who founded Nonnberg Abbey around 700, and also the Irish St. Virgil, the founder of the first cathedral consecrated in 774, whose relics lie buried beneath the altar. Archbishop Wolf-Dietrich took advantage of the old Romanesque-Gothic cathedral's destruction by fire in 1598 to demolish the remains and make plans for a huge new structure facing onto the Residenzplatz to reaffirm Salzburg's commitment to the Catholic cause. His successor, Markus Sittikus, and the new court architect, Santino Solari, started the present cathedral in 1614; it was consecrated with great ceremony in 1628 during the Thirty Years' War. The church's simple sepia-and-white interior, a peaceful counterpoint to the usual Baroque splendor, dates from a later renovation. To see remains of the old cathedral, go down the steps from the left-side aisle into the crypt where the archbishops from 1600 on are buried. Mozart's parents, Leopold and Anna-Maria, were married here in 1747. Mozart was christened, the day after he was born, at the 14th-century font here, and he served as organist from 1779 to 1781. Some of his compositions, such as the *Coronation Mass,* were written for the cathedral. ■TIP➜ On Sunday and all Catholic holidays, Mass is sung at 10 am—the most glorious time to experience the cathedral's full splendor. This is the only house of worship in the world with five independent fixed organs, which are sometimes played together during special church-music concerts. Many of the church's treasures are in a special museum on the premises, entry to which now offers visitors access to the corridors that once only the Archbishops walked, linking the five historic landmarks overlooking the Domplatz. ✉ *Domplatz 1a* ☎ *0662/8047–1870* ⊕ *www.kirchen.net/dommuseum* ✆ *Museum €6* ⊘ *Late May–late Oct., Mon.–Sat. 10–5; Sun. and holidays 11–6.*

Fodor'sChoice
★ **DomQuartier.** For the first time since the early 1800s, you can look down on the original heart of Salzburg as once only the powerful Archbishops could, as you walk the top-floor corridors surrounding the Domplatz that connect the Residenz (palace), Dom (cathedral), and St. Peter's Abbey. Admission grants access to resplendent museums in each location. Sunny weather offers expansive views of the city and the interior walkways make it an appealing option for one of Salzburg's frequent rainy days. ✉ *Residenzplatz 1/Domplatz 1a* ☎ *0662/80–42–21–09* ⊕ *www.domquartier.at* ✆ *€12* ⊘ *July and Aug., daily 10–5; Sept.–June, Wed.–Mon. 10–5.*

Getreidegasse. For centuries, this has been the main shopping street in the Old City center. According to historians, the name means "trade street"—not "grain street," as many believe. Today you'll find elegant international fashion houses, traditional Austrian clothiers, familiar international brands, and a delicious ice cream shop, all with intricate wrought-iron signs conforming to Salzburg's strict Old City conservation laws. Besides coming to shop, crowds flock to this street because at No. 9 is Mozart's birthplace, the **Mozarts Geburtshaus.** In summer, the street is densely packed with people. You can always escape for a while through one of the many arcades—mostly flower bedecked and opening into delightful little courtyards—that link the Getreidegasse to the river and the Universitätsplatz. At No. 37 you'll find the glamorous Goldener Hirsch hotel—just look for its filigree-iron sign showing a leaping stag with gilded antlers. ■ TIP→ **The Goldener Hirsch's interiors are marvels of Salzburgian** *gemütlichkeit,* **so, if you're appropriately attired, you may wish to view the lobby and enjoy an aperitif in its gorgeous bar, the watering hole of chic Salzburg.** The southern end of Getreidegasse becomes Judengasse, once the heart of the city's Medieval Jewish community, which is also packed with shops and galleries festooned with more of Salzburg's famous wrought-iron signs.

Glockenspiel. The famous carillon tower is perched on top of the **Neue Residenz** (New Residence), Prince-Archbishop Wolf-Dietrich's government palace. The carillon is a later addition, brought from today's Belgium in 1695 and finally put in working order in 1704. The 35 bells play classical tunes (usually by Mozart or Haydn) at 7 am, 11 am, and 6 pm—with charm and ingenuity. From Easter to October, the bells are immediately followed by a resounding retort from perhaps the oldest mechanical musical instrument in the world, the 200-pipe "Bull" organ housed in the Hohensalzburg Fortress across town. Details about the music selections are listed on a notice board across the square on the corner of the Residenz building. ✉ *Mozartplatz 1.*

Mönchsberg Elevator. Just around the corner from the Pferdeschwemme horse fountain, at Anton-Neumayr Platz, you'll find the Mönchsberg elevator, which carries you up through solid rock not only to the **Museum der Moderne** but also to wooded paths that are great for walking and gasping—there are spectacular vistas of Salzburg. In summer this can be a marvelous—and quick—way to escape the tiny crowded streets of the Old City. ✉ *Gstättengasse 13* 🚡 *Round-trip €3.20, one way €2* ⊙ *Oct.–June, Thurs.–Tues. 8–7, Wed. 8 am–9 pm; July–Aug., daily 8 am–9 pm.*

Museum der Moderne. Enjoying one of Salzburg's most famous scenic spots, the dramatic museum of modern and contemporary art reposes atop the sheer cliff face of the Mönchsberg. The setting was immortalized in *The Sound of Music*—this is where Julie and the kids start warbling "Doe, a deer, a female deer." Clad in minimalist white marble, the museum (2004) was designed by Friedrich Hoff Zwink of Munich. It has three exhibition levels, which bracket a restaurant with a large terrace—now, as always, the place to enjoy the most spectacular view over the city while sipping a coffee. Collection highlights include graphics and paintings by Austrian and international artists, including Oskar

Kokoschka and Erwin Wurm, with a focus on large-scale installations and sculptural works. Visit in the evening to see the city illuminated. ✉ *Mönchsberg 32* ☎ *0662/84–22–20–401* ⊕ *www.museumdermoderne. at* ⬚ *€8* ⊗ *Tues.–Sun. 10–6, Wed. 10–8.*

Residenz. At the very heart of Baroque Salzburg, the Residenz overlooks the spacious Residenzplatz and its famous fountain. The palace in its present form was built between 1600 and 1619 as the home of Wolf-Dietrich, the most powerful of Salzburg's prince-archbishops. The Kaisersaal (Imperial Hall) and the Rittersaal (Knight's Hall), one of the city's most regal concert halls, can be seen, along with the rest of the magnificent **State Rooms** on a self-guided tour as part of the new **DomQuartier** (⇨ *see separate listing*) collaboration. Of particular note are the frescoes by Johann Michael Rottmayr and Martino Altomonte depicting the history of Alexander the Great. Upstairs on the third floor is the **Residenzgalerie,** a princely art collection specializing in 17th-century Dutch and Flemish art and 19th-century paintings of Salzburg. On the state-room floor, Mozart's opera *La Finta Semplice* premiered in 1769 in the Guard Room. Mozart often did duty here, as, at age 14, he became the first violinist of the court orchestra (in those days, the leader, as there was no conductor). Today the reception rooms of the Residenz are often used for official functions, banquets, and concerts, and might not always be open to visitors. The palace courtyard has been the lovely setting for Salzburg Festival opera productions since 1956—mostly the lesser-known treasures of Mozart. ✉ *Residenzplatz 1* ☎ *0662/840451–0* ⊕ *www.residenzgalerie. at* ⬚ *€14.50 for both museums; €6 art collection only* ⊗ *Daily 10–5, except Easter week and during the summer festival.*

Fodor's Choice ★ **Salzburg Museum** (*Neugebäude*). The biggest "gift" to Mozart was the opening—one day shy of his 250th birthday, on January 26, 2006—of an exhibition entitled "Viva! Mozart" in Salzburg's mammoth 17th-century **Neue Residenz** (New Residence). The setting is splendid. This building was Prince-Archbishop Wolf-Dietrich's "overflow" palace (he couldn't fit his entire archiepiscopal court into the main Residenz across the plaza), and as such, it features 10 state reception rooms that were among the first attempts at a *stil Renaissance* in the North. Highlights of the archaeological collection include Hallstatt Age relics, remains of the town's ancient Roman ruins, and the famous Celtic bronze flagon found earlier this century on the Dürrnberg near Hallein, 15 km (10 miles) south of Salzburg. Pride of place is given to the spectacular **Sattler Panorama,** one of the few remaining 360-degree paintings in the world, which shows the city of Salzburg in the early 19th century. Also here is the original composition of "Silent Night," composed by Franz Gruber in nearby Oberndorf in 1818. ✉ *Mozartplatz 1* ☎ *0662/620808–700* ⊕ *www.salzburgmuseum.at* ⬚ *€7* ⊗ *Tues., Wed., Fri.–Sun. 9–5, Thurs. 9–8.*

Stiftkirche St. Peter (*Collegiate Church of St. Peter*). The most sumptuous church in Salzburg, St. Peter's is where Mozart's famed *Great Mass in C Minor* premiered in 1783, with his wife, Constanze, singing the lead soprano role. Wolfgang directed the orchestra and choir and also played the organ. During every season of the city's summer

8

music festival in August, the work is performed here during a special church-music concert. The porch has beautiful Romanesque vaulted arches from the original structure built in the 12th century; the interior was decorated in the voluptuous late-baroque style when additions were made in the 1770s. Note the side chapel by the entrance, with the unusual crèche portraying the Flight into Egypt

> **GET CARDED**
>
> Consider purchasing the Salzburg Card. SalzburgKarten are good for 24, 48, or 72 hours for €26–€41, and allow no-charge entry to most museums and sights, use of public transportation, and special discount offers. Children under 15 pay half.

and the Massacre of the Innocents. Behind the Rupert Altar is the "Felsengrab," a rock-face tomb where—according to a legend—St. Rupert himself was originally buried. To go from the sacred to the profane, head for the abbey's legendary Weinkeller restaurant, adjacent to the church. ⌧ *St. Peter Bezirk* ☎ *0662/844576–87* 🔁 *Free* ⊙ *Apr.–Sept., daily 6:30 am–7 pm; Oct.–Mar., daily 6:30–6.*

WORTH NOTING

Festspielhaus (*Festival Hall Complex*). With the world-famous Salzburg Festival as their objective, music lovers head for the Hofstallgasse, the street where the three festival theaters are located. Arrow-straight and framing a grand view of the Fortress Hohensalzburg, the street takes its name from the court stables once located here. Now, in place of the prancing horses, festivalgoers promenade along Hofstallgasse during the intervals of summer performances, showing off their suntans and elegant attire. ■ **TIP→ If you want to see the inside of the halls, it's best to go to a performance, but guided tours are given and group tours can be booked on request.** The first theater is the **Haus für Mozart** (House for Mozart), formerly the Kleines Festspielhaus, or Small Festival Hall. The massive lobby frescoes by Salzburg painter Anton Faistauer welcome 1,600 patrons to world-class Lied (song) recitals and smaller scale operas. The center ring is occupied by the famous **Grosses Festspielhaus** (Great Festival Hall), leaning against the solid rock of the Mönchsberg. Opened in 1960, it seats more than 2,150. In recent times the Grosses Festspielhaus, nicknamed the Wagner Stage because of headline-making productions of the *Ring of the Nibelungs*, has been the venue for spectacular operas and concerts by the world's top symphony orchestras and soloists. Stage directors are faced with the greatest challenge in the third theater, the **Felsenreitschule** (the Rocky Riding School), the former Summer Riding School, which—hewn out of the rock of the Mönchsberg during the 17th century by architect Fischer von Erlach—offers a setting that is itself more dramatic than anything presented on stage. Max Reinhardt made the first attempt at using the Summer Riding School as a stage in 1926. With its retractable roof it gives the impression of an open-air theater; the three tiers of arcades cut into the rock of the Mönchsberg linger in the mind of fans of *The Sound of Music* film, for the von Trapps were portrayed singing "Edelweiss" here in their last Austrian concert. (In fact, the 1950 Festival farewell by the Trapp Family

Singers, conducted by Franz Wasner, was given in the Mozarteum and at the cathedral square.) The theaters are linked by tunnels (partially in marble and with carpeted floors) to a spacious underground garage in the Mönchsberg. ⊠ *Hofstallgasse 1* ☎ *0662/849097* ⊕ *www. salzburgfestival.at* 🎫 *Guided tours €5* ⊙ *Group tours: Jan.–May and Oct.–Dec. 20, daily at 2; June and Sept., daily at 2 and 3:30; July and Aug., daily at 9:30, 2, and 3:30.*

Franziskanerkirche (*Franciscan Church*). The graceful, tall spire of the Franciscan Church stands out from all other towers in Salzburg; the church itself encompasses the greatest diversity of architectural styles. There was a church on this spot as early as the 8th century, but it was destroyed by fire. The Romanesque nave of its replacement is still visible, as are other Romanesque features, such as a stone lion set into the steps leading to the pulpit. In the 15th century the choir was built in Gothic style, then crowned in the 18th century by an ornate red-marble and gilt altar designed by Austria's most famous baroque architect, Johann Bernhard Fischer von Erlach. Mass—frequently featuring one of Mozart's compositions—is celebrated here on Sunday at 9 am. ⊠ *Franziskanergasse 5* ☎ *0662/843629–0* 🎫 *Free* ⊙ *Daily 6:30 am–7 pm.*

Kollegienkirche (*Collegiate Church*). Completed by Fischer von Erlach in 1707, this church, sometimes called the Universitätskirche, is one of the purest examples of Baroque architecture in Austria. Unencumbered by rococo decorations, the modified Greek cross plan has a majestic dignity worthy of Palladio. Recent massive renovations have restored this church to its gleaming white glory. ⊠ *Universitätsplatz* ☎ *0662/841–32–772* ⊙ *Closed.*

Mozartplatz (*Mozart Square*). In the center of the square stands the statue of Wolfgang Amadeus Mozart, a work by sculptor Ludwig Schwanthaler unveiled in 1842 in the presence of the composer's two surviving sons. It was the first sign of public recognition the great composer had received from his hometown since his death in Vienna in 1791. The statue, the first for a non-noble person in old Austria, shows a 19th-century stylized view of Mozart, draped in a mantle, holding a page of music and a copybook. A more appropriate bust of the composer, modeled by Viennese sculptor Edmund Heller, is found on the Kapuzinerberg.

Mozarts Geburtshaus. This three-story homage to Salzburg's prodigal son offers fascinating insights into the life and works of W.A. Mozart, with carefully curated relics of his youth, listening rooms, and designer's models of famous productions of his operas. As an adult, the great composer preferred Vienna to Salzburg, complaining that audiences in his native city were no more responsive than tables and chairs. Still, home is home, and this was Mozart's—when not on one of his frequent trips abroad—until the age of 17. Mozart was born on the third (in American parlance, the fourth) floor of this tall house on January 27, 1756, and his family lived here in the front apartment, when they were not on tour, from 1747 to 1773. As the child prodigy composed many of his first compositions in these rooms, it is fitting

8

Mozart: Marvel and Mystery

"Mozart is sunshine." So proclaimed Antonín Dvořák—and how better to sum up the prodigious genius of Wolfgang Amadeus Mozart (January 27, 1756, to December 5, 1791)? Listening to his Rococo orchestrations, his rose-strewn melodies, and his insouciant harmonies, many listeners seem to experience the same giddiness as happiness. Scientists have found Mozart's music can cause the heart to pound, bring color to the cheeks, and provide the expansive feeling of being thrillingly alive. Yet, Mozart must have sensed how hard it is to recognize happiness, which is often something vaguely desired and not detected until gone. It is this melancholy undertow that makes Mozart modern—so modern that he is now the most popular classical composer, having banished Beethoven to second place. Shortly after *Amadeus* won the 1984 Oscar for best film—with its portrayal of Mozart as a giggling, foul-mouthed genius—*Don Giovanni* began to rack up more performances than *La Bohème*. The bewigged face graces countless "Mozartkugeln" chocolates, and Mostly Mozart festivals pay him homage. But a look behind the glare of the spotlights reveals that this blond, slightly built tuning-fork of a fellow was a quicksilver enigma.

Already a skilled pianist at age three, the musical prodigy was dragged across Europe by his father Leopold to perform for empresses and kings. In a life that lasted a mere 35 years, he spent 10 on the road—a burden that contributed to making him the first truly *European* composer. Growing up in Salzburg, the *Wunderkind* became less of a *Wunder* as time went by. Prince-Archbishop

Hieronymus von Colloredo enjoyed dissing his resident composer by commanding him to produce "table music" with the same disdainful tone he commanded his chef's dinner orders. Being literally forced to sit with those cooks, Mozart finally rebelled. In March 1781 he married Constanze Weber and set out to conquer Vienna.

Hated by Mozart's father, Constanze is adored today, since we now know she was Mozart's greatest ally. Highly repressed by stuffy Salzburg, Mozart came to like his humor glandular (he titled one cantata "Kiss My XXX") and his women globular, a bill Constanze adequately filled. She no doubt heartily enjoyed the fruits of his first operatic triumph, the naughty *Abduction from the Seraglio* (1782). His next opera, *The Marriage of Figaro* (1786), to no one's surprise, bombed. Always eager to thumb his nose at authority, Mozart had adapted a Beaumarchais play so inflammatory in its depiction of aristos as pawns of their own servants, it soon helped ignite the French Revolution. In revenge, wealthy Viennese gave a cold shoulder to his magisterial *Don Giovanni* (1787). Mozart was relegated to composing, for a lowly vaudeville house, the now immortal *Magic Flute* (1790), and to ghosting a *Requiem* for a wealthy count. Sadly, his star only began to soar after a tragic, early death. But in company with fellow starblazers Vincent van Gogh and Marilyn Monroe, we assume he must be enjoying the last laugh.

—Robert I.C. Fisher

and touching to find Mozart's tiny first violin on display. ⊠ *Getreidegasse 9* ☎ *0662/844-313* ⊕ *www.mozarteum.at* ☜ *€7; combined ticket for Mozart residence and birthplace €12* ⊘ *Sept.–June, daily 9–5:30; July and Aug., daily 9–8.*

Petersfriedhof (*St. Peter's Cemetery*). Eerie but intimate, this is the oldest Christian graveyard in Austria, in the present condition dating back to 1627. Enclosed on three sides by elegant wrought-iron grilles, Baroque arcades contain chapels belonging to Salzburg's old patrician families. The graveyard is far from mournful: the individual graves are tended with loving care, decorated with candles, fir branches, and flowers—especially pansies (because the name means "thoughts"). In Crypt XXXI is the grave of Santino Solari, architect of the cathedral; in XXXIX that of Sigmund Haffner, a patron for whom Mozart composed a symphony and named a serenade. The final communal Crypt LIV (by the so-called catacombs) contains the body of Mozart's sister Nannerl and the torso of Joseph Haydn's younger brother Michael (his head is in St. Peter's church). The cemetery is in the shadow of the Monchsberg mount; note the early Christian tombs carved in the rock face. ⊠ *3 Sankt-Peter-Bezirk* ☎ *0662/844576–0* ⊘ *Daily dawn–dusk.*

Pferdeschwemme (*Horse Pond*). If Rome had fountains, so, too, would Wolf-Dietrich's Salzburg. The city is studded with them, and none is so odd as this monument to the equine race. You'll find it if you head to the western end of the Hofstallgasse to find Herbert-von-Karajan-Platz, named after Salzburg's second-greatest musical son, the legendary conductor and music director of the Salzburg Festival for many decades. On the Mönchsberg side of the square is the Pferdeschwemme—a royal trough, constructed in 1695, where prize horses used to be cleaned and watered; as they underwent this ordeal they could delight in the frescoes of their pin-up fillies on the rear wall. The Baroque monument in the middle represents the antique legend of the taming of a horse, Bellerophon and his mount, Pegasus. ⊠ *Herbert-von-Karajan-Platz.*

Rathaus (*Town Hall*). Where Sigmund-Haffner-Gasse meets the Getreidegasse you will find the Rathaus, an insignificant building in the Salzburg skyline—no doubt reflecting the historical weakness of the burghers vis-à-vis the Church, whose opulent monuments are evident throughout the city. On the other hand, this structure is a prime example of the Italian influence in Salzburg's architecture. Originally this was a family tower (and the only one still remaining here), but it was sold to the city in 1407. ⊠ *Rathausplatz and Kranzlmarkt.*

Rupertinum. For a refreshing break from churches and gilded treasures of yore, don't miss the chance to see changing exhibitions of modern graphic art and interactive special exhibits on display in this lovely early-Baroque era building, part of Salzburg's **Museum der Moderne.** Stop for a delicious slice of *Topfentorte* (an airy, fresh-cheese cake) or *Apfelstrudel mit Obers* (apple strudel with whipped cream) in the street level **Café Sarastro.** ⊠ *Wiener-Philharmoniker-Gasse 9* ☎ *0662/842220–451* ⊕ *www.museumdermoderne.at* ☜ *€6* ⊘ *Tues. and Thurs.–Sun. 10–6, Wed. 10–8.*

FAMILY **Spielzeugmuseum** (*Toy Museum*). On a rainy day this is a delightful diversion for both young and old, with an interactive collection of dolls, teddy bears, model trains, and wooden sailing ships. Special Punch and Judy–style *"Kasperltheater"* puppet shows leave everyone laughing. Performance days change, so call ahead or check the website. ⊠ *Bürgerspitalplatz 2* ☎ *0662/620808–300* ⊕ *www.salzburgmuseum.at* 🗨 *€4* ⊙ *Tues.–Sun., daily 9–5.*

Toscaninihof (*Arturo Toscanini Courtyard*). The famous Italian maestro Arturo Toscanini conducted some of the Salzburg Festival's most legendary performances during the 1930s. Throughout the summer months the courtyard of his former festival residence is a hive of activity, with sets for the stage of the "House for Mozart" being brought in through the massive iron folding gates.

Wiener Philharmoniker-Gasse. Leading into Max-Reinhardt-Platz at the head of the grand Hofstallgasse, this street was named after the world-famous Vienna Philharmonic Orchestra in recognition of the unique contribution it has made annually to the Salzburg Festival, playing for most opera productions and for the majority of orchestral concerts. ■ TIP→ **The street blossoms with an open-air food market every Saturday morning; there is also a fruit-and-vegetable market on Universitätsplatz every day except Sunday and holidays.**

AROUND FORTRESS HOHENSALZBURG

According to a popular saying in Salzburg, "If you can see the fortress, it's just about to rain; if you can't see it, it's already raining." Fortunately there are plenty of days when spectacular views can be had of Salzburg and the surrounding countryside from the top of this castle.

TOP ATTRACTIONS

FAMILY **Fortress Hohensalzburg.** Founded in 1077, the Hohensalzburg is Salzburg's acropolis and the largest preserved medieval fortress in Central Europe. Brooding over the city from atop the Festungsberg, it was originally founded by Salzburg's Archbishop Gebhard, who had supported the pope in the investiture controversy against the Holy Roman Emperor. Over the centuries the archbishops gradually enlarged the castle, using it originally only sometimes as a residence, then as a siege-proof haven against invaders and their own rebellious subjects. The exterior may look grim, but inside there are lavish state rooms, such as the glittering **Golden Room,** the **Burgmuseum**—a collection of medieval art—and the **Rainer's Museum,** with its brutish arms and armor. Politics and Church are in full force here: there's a torture chamber not far from the exquisite late-Gothic **St. George's Chapel** (although the implements on view came from another castle and were not used here). The 200-pipe organ from the beginning of the 16th century, played during the warmer months daily after the carillon in the Neugebäude, is best heard from a respectful distance, as it is not called "the Bull" without reason. ■ TIP→ **Climb up the 100 tiny steps to the Recturm, a grand lookout post with a sweeping view of Salzburg and the mountains.** Children will love coming here, especially as some rooms of the castle are now given over to a special exhibition, the **Welt der Marionetten,** which offers a fascinating view into the world of marionettes—a great preview of the treats in store at the nearby Marionettentheater.

To reach the fortress, walk up the zigzag path that begins just beyond the Stieglkeller on the Festungsgasse. You don't need a ticket to walk the footpath; sturdy shoes are recommended. Visitor lines to the fortress can be long, so try to come early. The "Fortress Card" includes funicular round-trip, entrance to

> ### RIDING IN STYLE
>
> One of the most delightful ways to tour Salzburg is by horse-drawn carriage. Most of Salzburg's Fiaker are stationed in Residenzplatz, and cost €40 for 20 minutes, €80 for 50 minutes. During the Christmas season, large, decorated, horse-drawn carts take people around the Christmas markets.

fortress and an audio guide. ⊠ *Mönchsberg 34* ☎ *0662/842430–11* ⊕ *www.salzburgmuseum.at* 🎟 *€7* ☉ *Jan.–Apr. and Oct.–Dec., daily 9:30–5; May–Sept., daily 9–7.*

Festungsbahn (*funicular railway*). More than 110 years old, the Festungsbahn (funicular railway), behind St. Peter's Cemetery, is the easy way up to the Fortress Hohensalzburg (advisable with young children). ⊠ *Festungsgasse 4* ☎ *0662/4480–9750* ⊕ *www.festungsbahn.at* 🎟 *€11.30 round-trip (includes all museums); €6.50 one-way ride down* ☉ *Oct.–Apr., daily 9–5; May, June, and Sept., daily 9–8; July and Aug., daily 9 am–10 pm.*

Nonnberg Convent. Just below the south side of the Fortress Hohensalzburg—and best visited in tandem with it—the Stift Nonnberg was founded right after 700 by St. Rupert, and his niece St. Erentrudis was the first abbess (in the archway a late-Gothic statue of Erentrudis welcomes the visitor). ■**TIP→ Spend the extra €0.50 to illuminate the frescoes just below the steeple. They are some of the oldest in Austria, painted in the Byzantine style during the 10th century.** The church is more famous these days as "Maria's convent"—both the one in *The Sound of Music* and that of the real Maria. She returned to marry her Captain von Trapp here in the Gothic church (as it turns out, no filming was done here— "Nonnberg" was re-created in the film studios of Salzburg-Parsch). Each evening in May at 7 the nuns sing a 15-minute service called Maiandacht in the old Gregorian chant. Their beautiful voices can be heard also at the 11 pm Mass on December 24. Parts of the private quarters for the nuns, which include some lovely, intricate woodcarving, can be seen by prior arrangement. ⊠ *Nonnberggasse 2* ☎ *0662/841607–0* ☉ *Fall–spring, daily 7–5; summer, daily 7–7.*

NORTH OF THE RIVER SALZACH

Across the River Salzach in the Neustadt (New Town) area of historic Salzburg, Mirabell Palace and Gardens, the Landestheater, the Mozart Residence and the Mozarteum, the Church of the Holy Trinity, and the Kapuzinerkloster perched atop the Kapuzinerberg are worth a visit, as well as is the celebrated Salzburg Marionette Theater. If you want to see the most delightful Mozart landmark in this section of town, the Zauberflötenhäuschen—the mouthful used to describe the little

The Hills Are Alive...

Few Salzburgers would publicly admit it, but *The Sound of Music*, Hollywood's interpretation of the trials and joys of the local von Trapp family, has become their city's most eminent emissary when it comes to international promotion. The year after the movie's release, international tourism to Salzburg jumped 20%, and soon *The Sound of Music* was a Salzburg attraction. In the meantime the Salzburg Marionette Theater shows its own fairy-tale version, and the Landestheater has produced the musical.

Perhaps the most important *Sound* spin-offs are the tours offered. Besides showing you some of the film's locations (usually very briefly), these four-hour rides have the advantage of giving a very concise tour of the city. The buses generally leave from Mirabellplatz; lumber by the "Do-Re-Mi" staircase at the edge of the beautifully manicured Mirabell Gardens; pass by the hardly visible Aigen train station, where in reality the Trapps caught the escape train; and then head south to Schloss Anif. This 16th-century water castle, which had a cameo appearance in the opening scenes of the film, is now in private hands and not open to the public.

First official stop for a leg-stretcher is at the gazebo in the manicured park of Schloss Hellbrunn at the southern end of the city. Originally built in the gardens of Leopoldskron Palace, it was brought out here for photo ops. This is where Liesl von Trapp sings "I Am Sixteen Going on Seventeen" and where Maria and the Baron woo and coo "Something Good." The simple little structure is the most coveted prize of photographers. The bus then drives by other private palaces with limited visiting rights: Schloss Frohnburg; and Schloss Leopoldskron, with its magical water-gate terrace, adorned with rearing horse sculptures and site of so many memorable scenes in the movie. The bus continues on to Nonnberg Convent at the foot of the daunting Hohensalzburg fortress, then leaves the city limits for the luscious landscape of the Salzkammergut. You get a chance for a meditative walk along the shore of the Wolfgangsee in St. Gilgen before the bus heads for the pretty town of Mondsee, where, in the movie, Maria and Georg von Trapp were married at the twin-turreted Michaelerkirche.

Tour guides are well trained and often have a sense of humor, which they use to gently debunk myths about the movie. Did you know, for example, that Switzerland was "moved" 160 km (100 miles) eastward so the family could hike (and sing) over the mountains to freedom? It all goes to show that in Hollywood, as in Salzburg and its magical environs, almost anything is possible.

For tour details, see Planning.

Sound of Salzburg Dinner Show. If you don't mind a healthy dose of cheese with your dinner theater, you can hum along to those unforgettable songs from the *Sound of Music*, traditional Salzburg folksongs, and a medley of Austrian operettas between courses of your traditional Austrian meal in the Medieval cellar of the K+K am Waagplatz. Daily from May to October. The cost of the dinner show is €49–€69; without dinner it's €33. ⊠ *Am Waagplatz 2* ☎ *0662/2310–5800, 0699/1024–8666* ⊕ *www.soundofsalzburg.info.*

summerhouse where he finished composing *The Magic Flute*—can be viewed when concerts are scheduled in the adjacent Mozarteum.

TOP ATTRACTIONS

Friedhof St. Sebastian (*St. Sebastian's Cemetery*). Memorably re-created for the escape scene in *The Sound of Music* on a Hollywood soundstage, this final resting place for many members of the Mozart family, in the shadows of St. Sebastian's Church, is one of the most peaceful spots in Salzburg. Prince-Archbishop Wolf-Dietrich commissioned the cemetery in 1600 to replace the old cathedral graveyard, which he planned to demolish. It was built in the style of an Italian *campo santo* (sacred field), with arcades on four sides, and in the center of the square he had the Gabriel Chapel, an unusual, brightly tiled Mannerist mausoleum, built for himself; he was interred here in 1617 (now closed to visitors). Several famous people are buried in this cemetery, including the medical doctor and philosopher Theophrastus Paracelsus, who settled in Salzburg in the early 16th century (his grave is by the church door). Around the chapel is the grave of Mozart's widow, Constanze, her second husband, Georg Nikolaus Nissen, and probably also the one of Genoveva Weber, the aunt of Constanze and the mother of Carl Maria von Weber (by the central path leading to the mausoleum). According to the latest research, Mozart's father, Leopold, came to rest in the unmarked community grave here, too. If the gate is closed, enter through the back entrance around the corner in the courtyard. ⌂ *3 Sankt-Peter-Bezirk* ☉ *Daily 9–6.*

Kapuzinerberg Hill. Directly opposite the Mönchsberg on the other side of the river, Kapuzinerberg Hill is crowned by several interesting sights. By ascending a stone staircase near Steingasse 9, you can start your climb up the peak. At the top of the first flight of steps is a tiny chapel, **St. Johann am Imberg**, built in 1681. Farther on are a signpost and gate to the **Hettwer Bastion,** part of the old city walls. ■ TIP➔ **Hettwer Bastion is one of the most spectacular viewpoints in Salzburg.** At the summit is the gold-beige **Kapuzinerkloster** (Capuchin Monastery), originally a fortification built to protect the one bridge crossing the river. It is still an active monastery and thus cannot be visited, except for the church. The road down—note the Stations of the Cross along the path—is called Stefan Zweig Weg, after the great Austrian writer who rented the **Paschingerschlössl** house (on the Kapuzinerberg to the left of the monastery) until 1934, when he left Austria after the Nazis had murdered chancellor Dollfuss. As he was one of Austria's leading critics and esthetes, his residence became one of the cultural centers of Europe. Continue along to the northeast end of the Kapuzinerberg road for a well-earned meal with a stunning 180-degree view from the garden of the **Franziskischlössl Wirtzhaus.**

FAMILY **Marionettentheater** (*Marionette Theater*). The Salzburger Marionettentheater is both the world's greatest marionette theater and—surprise!—a sublime theatrical experience. Many critics have noted that viewers quickly forget the strings controlling the puppets, which assume lifelike dimensions and provide a very real dramatic experience. While it plays many enchanting fairy tales, the Marionettentheater is identified above all with Mozart's operas, which seem particularly suited to the

8

skilled puppetry; a delightful production of *Così fan tutte* captures the humor of the work better than many stage versions, and the shortened version of *Die Zauberflöte* is particularly charming. All productions are accompanied by historic recordings and are subtitled in several languages. The theater itself is a rococo concoction. The company is famous for its world tours, but is usually in Salzburg during the summer and around major holidays. ⊠ *Schwarzstrasse 24* ☎ *0662/872406* ⊕ *www.marionetten.at* 🎟 *€18–€35* ⊙ *Salzburg season May–Sept., Christmas, Mozart Week (Jan.), Easter. Box office Mon.–Sat. 9–1 and 2 hrs before performance.*

FAMILY
Fodor's Choice
★

Mirabellgarten (*Mirabell Gardens*). While there's a choice of entrances to the Mirabell Gardens—from the Makartplatz (framed by the statues of Roman gods), the Schwarzstrasse, and Mirabell Square—you'll want to enter from the Rainerstrasse and head for the Rosenhügel (Rosebush Hill): you'll arrive at the top of the steps where Julie Andrews and her seven charges showed off their singing ability in *The Sound of Music*. This is also an ideal vantage point from which to admire the formal gardens and one of the best views of Salzburg, as it shows how harmoniously architects of the Baroque period laid out the city. The center of the gardens—one of Europe's most beautiful parks, partly designed by Fischer von Erlach as the grand frame for the Mirabell Palace—is dominated by four large groups of statues representing the elements water, fire, air, and earth, and designed by Ottavio Mosto, who came to live in Salzburg from Padua. A bronze version of the winged horse Pegasus stands in front of the south facade of the palace in the center of a circular water basin. The most famous part of the Mirabell Gardens is the **Zwerglgarten** (Dwarfs' Garden), which can be found opposite the Pegasus fountain. Here you'll find 12 statues of "Danubian" dwarves sculpted in marble—the real-life models for which were presented to the bishop by the landgrave of Göttweig. Prince-Archbishop Franz Anton von Harrach had the figures made for a kind of stone theater below. The **Heckentheater** (Hedge Theater) is an enchanting natural stage setting that dates from 1700. ⊠ *Mirabellplatz 4* ⊙ *Daily 7 am–8 pm.*

Mirabell Palace. The "Taj Mahal of Salzburg," Schloss Mirabell was built in 1606 by the immensely wealthy and powerful Prince-Archbishop Wolf-Dietrich for his mistress, Salomé Alt, and their 15 children. It was originally called Altenau in her honor. Such was the palace's beauty that it was taken over by succeeding prince-archbishops, including Markus Sittikus (who renamed the estate), Paris Lodron, and finally, Franz Anton von Harrach, who brought in Lukas von Hildebrandt to give the place a baroque facelift in 1727. A disastrous fire hit in 1818, but happily, three of the most spectacular set-pieces of the palace—the Chapel, the Marble Hall, and the Angel Staircase—survived. The Marble Hall is now used for civil wedding ceremonies, and is regarded as the most beautiful registry office in the world. Its marble floor in strongly contrasting colors and its walls of stucco and marble ornamented with elegant gilt scrollwork are splendid. The young Mozart and his sister gave concerts here, and he also composed *Tafelmusik* (Table Music) to accompany the prince's meals. ■**TIP**→ Candlelight chamber music concerts in the Marble Hall provide an ideal combination of performance and

CYCLING IN SALZBURG

As most Salzburgers know, one of the best and most pleasurable ways of getting around the city and the surrounding countryside is by bicycle. Find bike and E-bike rental points along the Salzach, and visit local bookstores for maps of the extensive network of cycle paths. Check out the interactive map at www.stadt-salzburg.at/radlkarte to plan your trip. The

most delightful ride in Salzburg? The **Hellbrunner Allee** from Freisaal to Hellbrunn Palace is an enjoyable run, taking you past Frohnburg Palace and a number of elegant mansions on either side of the tree-lined avenue. The more adventurous can go farther afield, taking the **Salzach cycle path** north to the village of Oberndorf, or south to Golling and Hallein.

atmosphere. The magnificent marble Angel Staircase was laid out by von Hildebrandt and has sculptures by Georg Rafael Donner. The staircase is romantically draped with white marble putti, whose faces and gestures reflect a multitude of emotions, from questioning innocence to jeering mockery. The very first putto genuflects in an old Turkish greeting (a reminder of the Siege of Vienna in 1683). Outdoor concerts are held at the palace and gardens May through August, Sunday mornings at 10:30 and Wednesday evenings at 8:30. ⊠ *Mirabellplatz 4* ☎ *0662/889–87–330* 🖫 *Free* ☉ *Weekdays 8–6.*

FAMILY **Mozart Wohnhaus** (*Mozart Residence*). The Mozart family moved from its cramped quarters in Getreidegasse to this house on the Hannibal Platz, as it was then known, in 1773. Wolfgang Amadeus Mozart lived here until 1780, his sister Nannerl stayed here until she married in 1784, and their father, Leopold, lived here until his death in 1787. The house is accordingly referred to as the Mozart Residence, signifying that it was not only Wolfgang who lived here. During the first Allied bomb attack on Salzburg in October 1944, the house was partially destroyed, but was reconstructed in 1996. Mozart composed the "Salzburg Symphonies" here, as well as all five violin concertos, church music and some sonatas, and parts of his early operatic masterpieces, including *Idomeneo.* Take the informative audio tour for an introduction to the museum's interesting collection of musical instruments (for example, his own pianoforte) in the Dance Master Hall that are still played during frequent chamber concerts, as well as books from Leopold Mozart's library, family letters, and portraits. One room offers an informative multimedia show and wall-size map with more personal details about Mozart, like his numerous travels across Europe. Bring along your camera to capture a fun, virtual step into a family portrait at the end of the tour. ⊠ *Makartplatz 8* ☎ *0662/874227-40* ⊕ *www.mozarteum.at* 🖫 *Mozart residence €7, combined ticket for Mozart residence and birthplace €12* ☉ *Sept.–June, daily 9–5:30; July and Aug., daily 9–8.*

8

Steingasse. This narrow medieval street, walled in on one side by the bare cliffs of the Kapuzinerberg, was originally the ancient Roman entrance into the city from the south. The houses stood along the riverfront before the Salzach was regulated. Nowadays it's a fascinating mixture of shops and nightclubs, but with its tall houses the street still manages to convey an idea of how life used to be in the Middle Ages. The **Steintor** marks the entrance to the oldest section of the street; here on summer afternoons the light can be particularly striking. House No. 23 on the right still has deep, slanted peep-windows for guarding the gate. House No. 31 is the birthplace of Josef Mohr, the poet of "Silent Night, Holy Night" fame (not No. 9, as is incorrectly noted on the wall).

WORTH NOTING

Dreifaltigkeitskirche (*Church of the Holy Trinity*). The Makartplatz—named after Hans Makart, the most famous Austrian painter of the mid-19th century—is dominated at the top (east) end by Fischer von Erlach's first architectural work in Salzburg, built 1694–1702. It was modeled on a church by Borromini in Rome and prefigures von Erlach's Karlskirche in Vienna. Dominated by a lofty, oval-shape dome—which showcases a painting by Michael Rottmayr—this church was the result of the archbishop's concern that Salzburg's new town was developing in an overly haphazard manner. The church interior is small but perfectly proportioned, surmounted by its dome, whose trompe l'oeil fresco seems to open up the church to the sky above. ⊠ *Dreifaltigkeitsgasse 14* ☎ *0662/877495* ☉ *Mon.–Sat. 6:30–6:30, Sun. 8–6:30.*

Mozart Audio Visual Collection. In the same building as the Mozart Wohnhaus (Residence), this is an archive of thousands of Mozart recordings as well as films and video productions, all of which can be listened to or viewed on request. ⊠ *Makartplatz 8* ☎ *0662/883454–81* ⊕ *www.mozarteum.at* ✉ *Free* ☉ *Mon., Tues., and Fri. 9–1, Wed. and Thurs. 1–5, closed on holidays.*

Stiftung Mozarteum. Organizer of the important Mozart Week held every January and the new, forward-looking Dialogue Festival held during the first week of December, the Stiftung Mozarteum is the center for scholarly research and continued support of Mozart's life and works. The libraries, containing rare editions and significant publications, are open to the public. Thousands flock here for its packed calendar of important concerts (⇨ *see also Nightlife and Performing Arts*). ⊠ *Schwarzstrasse 26* ☎ *0662/88940–21* ⊕ *www.mozarteum.at.*

WHERE TO EAT

Salzburg has some of the best—and most expensive—restaurants in Austria, so if you happen to walk into one of the Altstadt posh establishments without a reservation, you may get a sneer worthy of Captain von Trapp. Happily, the city is plentifully supplied with pleasant eateries, offering not only good, solid Austrian food (not for anyone on a diet), but also exceptional Italian dishes and newer-than-now *neue Küche* (nouvelle cuisine) delights. There are certain dining experiences that are quintessentially Salzburgian, including restaurants perched on the town's peaks that offer "food with a view"—in some cases, it's too bad the food isn't up to the view—or rustic inns that offer "Alpine evenings" with entertainment. Some of the most distinctive places in town are the fabled hotel restaurants, such as those of the Goldener Hirsch or the "S'Nockerl," the cellar of the Hotel Elefant.

For fast food, Salzburgers love their broiled-sausages street stands. Some say the most delicious fare is found at the Balkan Grill at Getreidegasse 33 (its recipe for spicy Bosna sausage has always been a secret). **■ TIP→ For a quick lunch on weekdays, visit the market in front of the Kollegienkirche—a lot of stands offer a large variety of boiled sausages for any taste, ranging from mild to spiced.**

In the more expensive restaurants the set menus give you an opportunity to sample the chef's best; in less expensive ones they help keep costs down. Note, however, that some restaurants limit the hours during which the set menu is available. Many restaurants are open all day; otherwise, lunch is served from approximately 11 to 2 and dinner from 6 to 10. In more expensive restaurants it's always best to make a reservation. At festival time most restaurants are open seven days a week, and have generally more flexible late dining hours.

WHAT IT COSTS IN EUROS

	$	$$	$$$	$$$$
AT DINNER	under €12	€12–€17	€18–€22	over €22

Prices are per person for a main course at dinner.

8

THE ALTSTADT

$ AUSTRIAN 🍴 **Augustinerbräu.** One of the largest beer cellars in Europe, the celebrated Augustinerbräu is at the north end of the Mönchsberg. You can even bring your own food—a relic of the old tradition that forbade breweries from serving meals in order to protect the status of restaurants. Pick up a stone jug of strong, frothy beer and sit in the gardens or at a dark-wood table in one of the large refectory halls. Shops in the huge monastery complex sell a vast array of salads, breads, and pastries, as well as sausage and spit-roasted chicken. If you don't feel up to cold beer, there's an old copper beer warmer in the main hall. During Advent and Lent a special beer is offered, with the blessing of past popes, one of whom commented, "Drinking does not interrupt fasting." [$] *Average main: €10* ✉ *Augustinergasse 4* ☎ *0662/431246* 💳 *No credit cards* 🕒 *No lunch.*

$ HOT DOG 🍴 **Balkan Grill.** Known simply as "The Bosna Grill," this tiny sausage stand has become a cult destination for locals and international travelers. Find the long line of hungry people in the tiny passageway between the busy Getreidegasse and the Universitätsplatz to try this Bulgarian-inspired, Salzburg-born specialty: two thin, grilled bratwurst sausages in a toasted white bread bun, topped with chopped onions, fresh parsley, and a curry-based seasoning mixture that's been a secret since the owner, Zanko Todoroff, created it more than 50 years ago. **■ TIP→ In winter, join the locals by taking your warm Bosna next door and enjoying it**

BEST BETS FOR SALZBURG DINING

Fodor'sChoice ★	**Best by Price**	Daxlueg, p. 224
		Die Weisse, p. 225
Brunnauer im Magazin, $$$$, p. 219	$	
		$$$
Café Tomaselli, $, p. 219	Café Tomaselli, p. 219	
	Glüxfall, p. 222	Carpe Diem, p. 219
	Krimpelstätter, p. 222	Stiftskeller St. Peter, p. 223
	Zum Fidelen Affen, p. 225	
		$$$$
	$$	Brunnauer im Magazin, $$$$, p. 219
	Blaue Gans, p. 218	Pfefferschiff, p. 225

with a cup of the famous Punsch (orange liquor-spiked punch) from Sporer, the Austrian specialty liquor shop. $ *Average main: €3* ✉ *Getreidegasse 33* ☎ *0662/841483* ▤ *No credit cards* ☉ *Closed Sun.*

$$ ✕ **Bärenwirt.** Regionally sourced, top-quality ingredients elevate tradi-
AUSTRIAN tional Austrian dishes in this inviting *Wirtshaus*. Since 1663 locals have shared mugs of beer from the neighboring Augustiner Kloster Mülln brewery in these warmly lighted, wood-paneled rooms, adorned with traditional Salzburg-style heating ovens and cushioned benches. Request a table in the cozy main floor side room and enjoy the juicy *Backhendl* (breaded, fried chicken) as an entrée or salad with Styrian pumpkin seed oil dressing, Wiener schnitzel (veal or pork), cheesy *Kasnocken*, and beef goulash with a "bear-size" dumpling. Seasonal specialties highlight springtime *Spargelzeit* (asparagus) and the fall wild game hunt. Sip housemade schnapps before enjoying *Kaiserschmarren* (a fluffy pancake shredded, pan-fried with roasted plums, topped with powdered sugar). $ *Average main: €14* ✉ *Müllner Hauptstrasse 8* ☎ *0662/422404* ⊕ *www.baerenwirt-salzburg.at* ⟐ *Reservations essential.*

$$ ✕ **Blaue Gans.** In a 500-year-old building with vaulted ceilings and win-
AUSTRIAN dows looking out onto the bustling Getreidegasse, the restaurant of the Blaue Gans Hotel offers innovative, modern interpretations of traditional Austrian cooking. The fresh flavors are evident in dishes like the house-smoked *Lachsforelle* (salmon trout) and perfectly prepared beef carpaccio. There are always vegetarian choices. Ask your server for suggestions from the expertly selected Austrian and German wine list. The modern elegance extends to the setting, and the service is top-notch. Peer into the building's history through the dining room's glass floor, which reveals an old cellar, site of the oldest inn in Salzburg, mentioned in documents from the 15th century. $ *Average main: €15* ✉ *Blaue Gans Hotel, Getreidegasse 41–43* ☎ *0662/842491–0* ⟐ *Reservations essential* ☉ *Closed Sun.*

$$$$
MODERN
EUROPEAN
Fodor's Choice
★
╳ **Brunnauer im Magazin.** His time served behind the line of many of Salzburg's most recognized establishments has taught award-winning chef Richard Brunnauer the traditions of quality Austrian cuisine, and the elegant preparation of his hand-picked, seasonal, never-frozen ingredients entice a strong local connoisseur crowd. The repurposed World War II bunker, carved into the side of the Mönchsberg, creates an intimate and unique setting in the cleverly lighted main Kaverne dining room. The chef has forged tight relationships with his suppliers—hunters, fishermen, mushroom gatherers, and even grandmother backyard berry gardeners—so you benefit from the very best Styrian beef tartare, Tauern lamb, Alpine char, and Marchfeld white asparagus. A glass from the extensive wine list is best enjoyed in the fresh-air courtyard. $ *Average main: €30* ⊠ *Augustinergasse 13A* ☏ *0662/841584–20* ⊕ *www.magazin.co.at/de/brunnauer-im-magazin-salzburg* ⌕ *Reservations essential* ☉ *Closed Sun. and Mon.*

$$
EUROPEAN
╳ **Café 220°.** Whether you're craving a stellar late breakfast (served until 2 pm) or you're on the hunt for a carefully crafted espresso, you'll want to put this lively café on your daytime itinerary. The husband-and-wife team infuse care and quality into each step, from farm to cup, which takes them around the world to meet growers. They roast the beans in small batches at their own Salzburg *roasthaus*. Brunch dishes taste as good as they look—the "Green Yellow Red" scramble with housemade warm basil bread is a flavorful and hearty choice. Lunch offerings include soups paired with fluffy quiche and pan-fried chanterelles over leafy greens. $ *Average main: €14* ⊠ *Chiemseegasse 5* ☏ *0662/827881* ⊕ *www.220grad.com* ☉ *Closed Sun. and Mon. No dinner.*

$
AUSTRIAN
Fodor's Choice
★
╳ **Café Tomaselli.** This inn opened its doors in 1705 as an example of that new-fangled thing, a "Wiener Kaffeehaus" (Vienna coffeehouse). It was an immediate hit. Enjoying its 11 types of coffee was none other than Mozart's beloved, Constanze, who often dropped in, as her house was just next door. The Tomasellis set up shop here in 1850, becoming noted "Chocolatmachers." Feast on the famous "Tomaselliums Café" (mocha, Mozart liqueur, and whipped cream) and the large selection of excellent homemade cakes, tarts, and strudels. Inside, it's all marble, wood, and walls of 18th-century portraits. In summer the best seats are on the flower-bedecked terrace and at the pretty "Tomaselli-Kiosk" on the square. $ *Average main: €10* ⊠ *Alter Markt 9* ☏ *0662/844488–0* ⊕ *www.tomaselli.at* ⊟ *No credit cards.*

$$$
AUSTRIAN
╳ **Carpe Diem.** Dietrich Mateschitz (who also invented the Red Bull energy drink) together with Jörg Wörther put their heads together to create something unique: small dishes—both savory and sweet—served in "cones." Pickled perch with artichokes and asparagus tips arrives in a polenta cone, while a potato cone bursts with prime beef with creamed spinach and horseradish. Mix and match to create a delicious meal; be prepared to have your bill add up quickly. You can either sit inside in the barlike atmosphere or, in summer, on the open terrace. $ *Average main: €21* ⊠ *Getreidegasse 50* ☏ *0662/848800* ⊕ *www. carpediemfinestfingerfood.com* ⌕ *Reservations essential.*

8

Where to Eat and Stay in Salzburg

KEY

⊢⊢ Rail lines

𝒊 Tourist information

① Hotels

❶ Restaurants

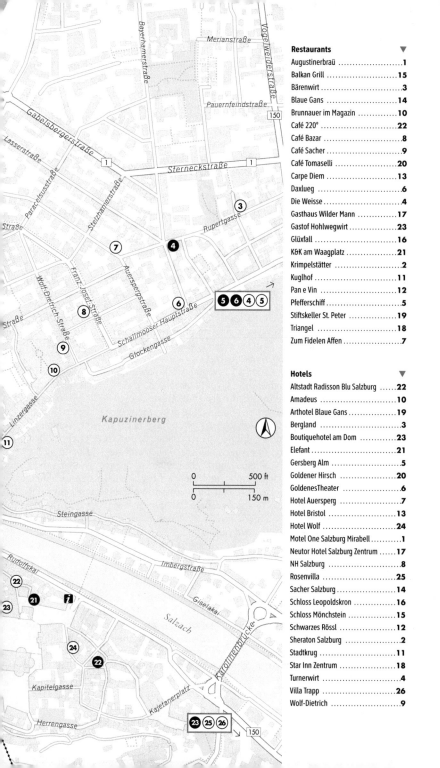

Restaurants ▼

Augustinerbräu **1**
Balkan Grill **15**
Bärenwirt **3**
Blaue Gans **14**
Brunnauer im Magazin **10**
Café 220° **22**
Café Bazar **8**
Café Sacher **9**
Café Tomaselli **20**
Carpe Diem **13**
Daxlueg **6**
Die Weisse **4**
Gasthaus Wilder Mann **17**
Gastof Hohlwegwirt **23**
Glüxfall **16**
K&K am Waagplatz **21**
Krimpelstätter **2**
Kuglhof **11**
Pan e Vin **12**
Pfefferschiff **5**
Stiftskeller St. Peter **19**
Triangel **18**
Zum Fidelen Affen **7**

Hotels ▼

Altstadt Radisson Blu Salzburg **22**
Amadeus **10**
Arthotel Blaue Gans **19**
Bergland **3**
Boutiquehotel am Dom **23**
Elefant **21**
Gersberg Alm **5**
Goldener Hirsch **20**
GoldenesTheater **6**
Hotel Auersperg **7**
Hotel Bristol **13**
Hotel Wolf **24**
Motel One Salzburg Mirabell **1**
Neutor Hotel Salzburg Zentrum **17**
NH Salzburg **8**
Rosenvilla **25**
Sacher Salzburg **14**
Schloss Leopoldskron **16**
Schloss Mönchstein **15**
Schwarzes Rössl **12**
Sheraton Salzburg **2**
Stadtkrug **11**
Star Inn Zentrum **18**
Turnerwirt **4**
Villa Trapp **26**
Wolf-Dietrich **9**

$ MODERN EUROPEAN 🍴 **Glüxfall.** Chef Fleischhacker, one of Salzburg's most respected chefs, has passed the torch of his renowned Pfefferschiff restaurant to his sous-chef and found new inspiration in this creative city-center café-cum-late-night bar that is already winning awards. The personalized, choose-your-own-breakfast-adventure menu (served until 2 pm) lets you savor several beautifully prepared, whimsically presented small dishes without encroaching on your date's plate. Mix and match two, four, or six sweet-and-savory choices: venison carpaccio with lingonberry chutney; heart-shape waffle with sour cherry sauce; nonalcoholic bloody mary shooter with a salmon canapé. After 2 pm a smaller menu comes into play until late. Sit in the leafy inner courtyard for a peaceful urban escape. [$] *Average main: €10* ✉ *Franz-Josef-Kai 11* ☎ *0662/265017* 🌐 *www.gluexfall.at* ✍ *Reservations essential* 🕒 *Closed Mon. and Tues. No dinner Sun. (except during festival).*

$$ AUSTRIAN 🍴 **K&K am Waagplatz.** This old house was once the domicile of the Freysauff family, who counted among their close friends Leopold Mozart, the composer's father. Its cellar, the downstairs section of the restaurant, is still called the Freysauff (but don't be misled—this translates into "free drinks"). The restaurant is particularly pleasant, with white-linen tablecloths, candles, flowers, and windows opening onto the street, with a lovely outdoor seating area in summer. Menu selections consist of local fish, mouthwatering steaks, traditional Austrian dishes, and game in season. [$] *Average main: €17* ✉ *Waagplatz 2* ☎ *0662/842156* 🌐 *www.kuk.at.*

$ AUSTRIAN 🍴 **Krimpelstätter.** About a 15-minute walk downriver from the Altstadt in the Mülln neighborhood, you'll often find Festival artists celebrating after their shows in this lovely 1548 *Gasthaus* (pub). They come for the traditional Salzburg cooking: the delicious *Schott* (cheese) soup, or the potato goulash with chunks of country ham, spinach dumplings in brown butter, or original Wiener schnitzel, and freshly tapped beer from the neighboring Augustinerbräu. The centuries-old building has fetching vaulted ceilings, leaded-glass windows, heavy wooden tables, and homespun decorations, and there's a big shady garden for dining in summer, rather close to the busy cross-town intersection, but offering a lovely view of the Gaisberg. [$] *Average main: €12* ✉ *Müllner Hauptstrasse 31* ☎ *0662/432274* 🌐 *www.krimpelstaetter.at* 🕒 *Closed Sun. and Mon. Sept.–end July.*

$ AUSTRIAN 🍴 **Kuglhof.** In Maxglan, a famous Austrian "farmer's village," now part of the city tucked behind the Mönchsberg and next to the Stiegl Brewery (best reached by taxi), Alexander Hawranek perfects Old Austrian specialties by giving them a nouvelle touch. The setting is your archetypal black-shuttered, yellow-hue, begonia-bedecked Salzburgian farmhouse, oh-so-cozily set with a tile oven, mounted antlers, embroidered curtains, and tons of *gemütlichkeit.* The menu is seasonal, so you might not be able to enjoy the signature *Beuschl* (calf's lungs) with dumplings. Best bet for dessert is the *Apfelschmarrn,* sliced pancake with apples. In summer opt for a table out in the shady garden. [$] *Average main: €12* ✉ *Kuglhofstrasse 13* ☎ *0662/832626* 🌐 *www.kuglhof.at* 🕒 *Closed Mon. and Tues.*

$$ ITALIAN 🍴 **Pan e Vin.** This tiny trattoria has only a handful of tables but it offers some lovely Italian specialties. Feel the spirit of the city called the "Rome of the North" here: burnt-sienna walls are lined with wine bottles, colorful ceramic plates, and Italian dry stuffs, and the chef cooks in full view. The upstairs restaurant of the same name has a more extensive menu, but it's also much more expensive. Fish lovers will appreciate Azzurro, the recent addition to the Pan e Vin trio of restaurants in one building. [$] *Average main: €16* ✉ *Gstättengasse 1* ☎ *0662/844666-14* 🌐 *www.panevin.at* 🕒 *Closed Sun. and Mon.*

ON THE MENU

Many restaurants favor the *neue Küche*—a lighter version of the somewhat heavier traditional specialties of Austrian cooking, but with more substance than nouvelle cuisine. Salzburgers also have a wonderful way with fish—often a fresh catch from the nearby lakes of the Salzkammergut. Favorite fish dishes are usually *gebraten* (fried). The only truly indigenous Salzburg dish is *Salzburger Nockerln*, a snowy meringue of sweetened whisked egg whites with a little bit of flour and sugar.

$$$ AUSTRIAN 🍴 **Stiftskeller St. Peter.** Legends swirl about the famous St. Peter's Beer Cellar. Locals claim that Mephistopheles met Faust here, others say Charlemagne dined here, and some believe Columbus enjoyed a glass of its famous Salzburg Stiegl beer just before he set sail for America in 1492. But there is no debating the fact that this place—first mentioned in a document dating back to 803—is Austria's oldest restaurant. Choose between the stately, dark-wood-panel Prälatenzimmer (Prelates' Room) or one of several less formal banqueting rooms. Elegantly presented Austrian standards and international dishes made with top quality ingredients fill the menu. [$] *Average main: €22* ✉ *St. Peter Bezirk 4* ☎ *0662/841268–0* 🌐 *www.haslauer.at* 🕒 *No lunch.*

$$ AUSTRIAN 🍴 **Triangel.** See and be seen among the Salzburg Festival glitteratti in Triangel's large outdoor seating area, or cozy up in the intimate dining room of this organic farming–focused Austrian restaurant. You can't go wrong with "absolutely Styrian" *Oma's Schweinsbraten* (owner Franzi's grandmother's roast pork belly recipe) and that pounding coming from the back room tells you that the Wiener schnitzel is a properly prepared choice. [$] *Average main: €15* ✉ *Wiener Philharmonikergasse 7* ☎ *0662/84–22–29* 🌐 *www.triangel-salzburg.co.at* ✍ *Reservations essential* 🕒 *Closed Mon.*

$ AUSTRIAN 🍴 **Gasthaus Wilder Mann.** Find a true time-tinged feel of an old Salzburg Gasthaus, right down to a huge ceramic stove next to wooden chairs that welcomed generations of locals as they tucked into enormous plates of *Bauernschmaus* (Farmer's Feast): roast pork, ham, sausage, sauerkraut and a massive dumpling. Pair it with a frothy-headed mug of the hometown "liquid bread"—Stiegl beer—from the oldest private brewery in Austria. The "Wild Man's" namesake fountain statue originally stood at the top of the Griesgasse, and can now be found in the small grassy park across from the Festival Hall—his cheeky portrait still welcomes guests at the restaurant's entryway. When this inn opened its doors in 1884, it became one of the most important burgher houses in the Altstadt, and it continues to be a popular choice for the Lederhosen crowd. [$] *Average main: €11* ✉ *Getreidegasse 20* ☎ *0662/841787* 🌐 *www.wildermann.co.at* 🕓 *Closed Sun.*

AROUND FORTRESS HOHENSALZBURG

$$ AUSTRIAN 🍴 **Gasthof Hohlwegwirt.** It's worth a detour on the way to Hallein along the B159 Salzachtal-Bundesstrasse about 10 km (6 miles) south of Salzburg to dine at this inviting inn, run by the same family for more than 130 years. Enjoy the cooking, the wine cellar filled with more than 100 different vintages, and the unmistakable atmosphere of this *stile Salzburg* house with its nicely decorated salons. Chef Ernst Kronreif uses his mother's recipes for the delicious *Butternockerlsuppe* (soup broth with buttered dumplings), the *Kalbsbries* (calf's sweetbreads), or the *Salzburger Bierfleisch* (beef boiled in beer)—all Salzburgian classics and yet always so up to date. [$] *Average main: €15* ✉ *Salzachtal-Bundesstrasse Nord 62, Hallein-Taxach* ☎ *06245/82415–0* 🌐 *www.hohlwegwirt.at* ✍ *Reservations essential* 🕓 *Closed Sun. evening–Tues. at noon, except during summer festival.*

NORTH OF THE RIVER SALZACH

$ CAFÉ 🍴 **Café Bazar.** Sip a *melange* under the shade of the leafy trees at this people-watching coffeehouse institution on the Salzach River. Marlene Dietrich, Max Reinhardt, Hugo von Hofmannsthal, Arturo Toscanini, and Seiji Ozawa are just a few of the famous faces to grace the terrace, and well-known locals make the "*Bussi links und Bussi rechts*" air-kiss rounds before settling into dark-wood chairs at the small marble tables. Wood panels reach to the lofty recessed ceilings in the main dining area. Salads, soups, and toasted ham-and-cheese sandwiches served with ketchup satisfy savory cravings; homemade Topfen- and Apfelstrudel beckon from the glass case of housemade tortes. [$] *Average main: €7* ✉ *Schwarzstrasse 3* ☎ *0662/874278* 🌐 *www.hotel-brandstaetter.com/en-salzburg-cafe-bazar.htm.*

$$ AUSTRIAN 🍴 **Café Sacher.** Red-velvet banquettes, sparkling chandeliers, and lots of gilt mark this famous gathering place, a favorite of well-heeled Salzburgers and an outpost of the celebrated Vienna landmark. It's a perfect choice for a leisurely afternoon pastry. The most popular choice is the famous housemade chocolate Sachertorte, but there is also a large variety of irresistible cakes. Don't pass up the coffee, which is second to none. Full meals are also served, and the restaurant offers a no-smoking room. [$] *Average main: €12* ✉ *Schwarzstrasse 5–7* ☎ *0662/889770* 🌐 *www.sacher.com.*

$$ AUSTRIAN 🍴 **Daxlueg.** If you really want to enjoy food with a view, drive 3 km (2 miles) north along the B1 Linzer Bundesstrasse to Mayrwies and turn right up through the woods. Here you can take in a view of Salzburg from the mountainside perch of this former Rupertialm (St. Rupert's Pasture), a famous scenic lookout even in Mozart's time. Owned by St. Peter's Monastery, this restaurant allures with the romantic charm of an Alpine chalet. Seasonal specialties of the region top the bill: not only venison and fried trout but heavenly garnishes—cress, elder blossoms, herbs from the meadows, raspberries, blueberries, *Schwammerl* (mushrooms) fresh out of the forest, cheese from goat and sheep. For breakfast, you need to make reservations at least the day before; lunch

and dinner reservations are recommended but not compulsory. $ *Average main: €13* ✉ *Daxluegstrasse 5, Hallwang-Esch* ☏ *0662/665800* ⊕ *www.daxlueg.at* ⚑ *Reservations essential.*

$$
AUSTRIAN

✕ **Die Weisse.** This *Weissbierbrauerei* combines the original charm of one of Salzburg's most historic breweries and adds a high ceilinged, wood paneled modern bar to satisfy the many locals who consider it to be the ultimate private retreat (so much so that from Wednesday through Saturday it's best to make a reservation). The beer garden really hits the spot on a hot summer day, but all year long you can savor traditional Bavarian style *Weisswurst* (veal sausages with sweet mustard) as well as the usual array of tempting Salzburg delights. $ *Average main: €17* ✉ *Rupertgasse 10* ☏ *0662/8722460* ⊘ *Closed Sun.*

$$$$
ECLECTIC

✕ **Pfefferschiff.** The "Pepper Ship" is one of the most acclaimed restaurants in Salzburg—though it's 3 km (2 miles) northeast of the center. It's in a pretty, renovated rectory, dated 1640, adjacent to a pink-and-cream chapel. The new owner and head chef, the right-hand man of award-winning chef and former owner, Klaus Fleischhacker, still makes you feel pampered in the country-chic atmosphere, adorned with polished wooden floors, antique hutches, and tabletops laden with fine bone china and Paloma Picasso silverware. The menu changes seasonally. A taxi is the least stressful way of getting here, but if you have your own car, drive along the north edge of the Kapuzinerberg toward Hallwang and then Söllheim. $ *Average main: €30* ✉ *Söllheim 3* ☏ *0662/661242* ⊕ *www.pfefferschiff.at* ⚑ *Reservations essential.*

$
AUSTRIAN

✕ **Zum Fidelen Affen.** The name means "At the Faithful Ape," which explains the monkey motifs in this popular Gasthaus dominated by a round copper-plated bar and stone pillars under a vaulted ceiling. Besides the beer on tap, the kitchen offers tasty Austrian dishes, such as *Schlutzkrapfen*, handmade cheese ravioli with a light topping of chopped fresh tomatoes, or a big salad with jucy *Backhendl* (breaded, fried chicken). Locals know this is a great value in a fun atmosphere, so it's often crowded; be sure to arrive early or book ahead. $ *Average main: €10* ✉ *Priesterhausgasse 8* ☏ *0662/877361* ⚑ *Reservations essential* ⊘ *Closed Sun. No lunch.*

8

WHERE TO STAY

It's difficult for a Salzburg hotel not to have a good location—you can find a room with a stunning view over the Kapuzinerberg or Gaisberg or one that simply overlooks a lovely Old City street—but it's possible. Salzburg is not a tiny town, and location is important. It's best to be near the historic city center; it's about a mile from the railway station to historic Zentrum (center), right around the main bridge of the Staatsbrücke. The Old City has a wide assortment of hotels and pensions, but there are few bargains. Also note that many hotels in this area have to be accessed on foot, as cars are not permitted on many streets. If you have a car, you may opt for a hotel or converted castle on the outskirts of the city. Many hostelries are charmingly decorated in *Bauernstil*—the rustic look of Old Austria; the ultimate in peasant-luxe is found at the world-famous Hotel Goldener Hirsch.

If you're looking for something really cheap (less than €50 for a double), clean, and comfortable, stay in a private home, though the good ones are all a little way from downtown.

The tourist information offices don't list private rooms; try calling Eveline Truhlar of **Bob's Special Tours** (☎ 0662/849–5110), who runs a private-accommodations service.

If you're planning to come at festival time (July and August), you must book as early as possible; try to reserve at least two months in advance. Prices soar over the already high levels—so much so that during the high season a hotel may edge into the next-higher price category.

Room rates include taxes and service charges. Many hotels include a breakfast in the room rate—check when booking—but the more expensive hostelries often do not. A property that provides breakfast and dinner daily is known as *halb pension,* and one that serves three meals a day is *voll pension.* If you don't have a reservation, go to one of the tourist information offices or the accommodations service (*Zimmernachweis*) in the railway station.

WHAT IT COSTS IN EUROS				
	$	**$$**	**$$$**	**$$$$**
FOR TWO PEOPLE	under €120	€120–€170	€170–€270	over €270

Prices are for a standard double room in high season, including taxes and service

THE ALTSTADT

$$$$
HOTEL
🖼 **Altstadt Radisson Blu Salzburg.** "Venerable" describes this 1372 building, one of the city's oldest inns, and its buff-pink facade with iron lanterns is an impressive riverside landmark. **Pros:** central location; expansive river views; generous breakfast buffet. **Cons:** inconvenient location if you have a car; chain-hotel feel; noisy; only mobile air-conditioning units on request. $ *Rooms from: €341* ⊠ *Judengasse 15/ Rudolfskai 28* ☎ *0662/848–5710* ⊕ *www.austria-trend.at/ass* ↩ *42 rooms, 20 suites* ⦿| *Breakfast.*

$$$
HOTEL
🖼 **Arthotel Blaue Gans.** The sleek, contemporary style of "The Blue Goose" boutique art hotel counters the building's 400-year-old pedigree and offers guests a stellar location at the top of the main shopping street and steps away from the Grosses Festspielhaus. **Pros:** spacious rooms; near the sights; close to shopping. **Cons:** on a noisy street. $ *Rooms from: €239* ⊠ *Getreidegasse 43* ☎ *0662/842–4910* ⊕ *www.blauegans. at* ↩ *35 rooms* ⦿| *Breakfast.*

$$
HOTEL
🖼 **Boutiquehotel am Dom.** Tucked away on a tiny street near Residenzplatz, this small boutique hotel in a 14th-century building offers stylish, comfortable rooms, some with oak-beam ceilings. **Pros:** rustic atmosphere; well-kept rooms, AC throughout. **Cons:** few amenities; off-site parking. $ *Rooms from: €140* ⊠ *Goldgasse 17* ☎ *0662/842–765* ⊕ *www.amdom.at* ↩ *15 rooms* ☉ *Closed 2 wks in Feb.* ⦿| *Breakfast.*

$$$$
HOTEL
🖼 **Elefant.** An old, historic favorite, The Elefant offers great stories, cozy rooms, modern touches, a fantastic central location, and delicious traditional Austrian meals at the on-site restaurant and bar. **Pros:** lots

BEST BETS FOR SALZBURG LODGING

Fodor's Choice ★	**Best by Price**	$$$
Goldener Hirsch, $$$$, p. 227	$	Hotel Auersperg, p. 228
Hotel Auersperg, $$$, p. 228	Turnerwirt, P. 230	Schloss Leopoldskron, p. 229
Sacher Salzburg, $$$$, p. 229	Villa Trapp, p. 230	$$$$
Schloss Leopoldskron, $$$, p. 229	$$	Goldener Hirsch, p. 227
Villa Trapp, $, p. 230	Boutiquehotel am Dom, p. 226	Hotel Bristol, p. 228
	Gersberg Alm, p. 228	Sacher Salzburg, p. 229
	Hotel Wolf, p. 227	Schloss Mönchstein, p. 227

of history; excellent location. **Cons:** some rooms are cramped; difficult to access with a car. $ *Rooms from: €278* ⊠ *Sigmund-Haffner-Gasse 4* ☎ *0662/843–3970* ⊕ *www.elefant.at* ⊅ *31 rooms* ⦵*Breakfast.*

$$$$
HOTEL
Fodor's Choice
★

🔲 **Goldener Hirsch.** Celebrities from Picasso to Pavarotti have favored the "Golden Stag" for its legendary *Gemütlichkeit* (cozy atmosphere), patrician pampering, and adorable interiors. **Pros:** unbeatable location; top-notch dining; charm to spare. **Cons:** noisy neighborhood; €35 a day for valet parking. $ *Rooms from: €585* ⊠ *Getreidegasse 37 / Herbert-von-Karajan-Platz 5* ☎ *0662/80840* ⊕ *www.goldenerhirsch.com* ⊅ *64 rooms, 5 suites* ⦵*No meals.*

$$
B&B/INN

🔲 **Hotel Wolf.** The embodiment of Austrian Gemütlichkeit, just off Mozartplatz, the small, family-owned, in-the-center-of-everything Wolf offers spotlessly clean and cozy rooms in a rustic building from the year 1429. **Pros:** plenty of atmosphere; in a historic house. **Cons:** parking is a problem; no a/c or fans. $ *Rooms from: €120* ⊠ *Kaigasse 7* ☎ *0662/843–4530* ⊕ *www.hotelwolf.com* ⊅ *15 rooms* ☾ *Closed early Feb.–early Mar.* ⦵*Breakfast.*

$$
HOTEL

🔲 **Neutor Hotel Salzburg Zentrum.** A two-minute walk from the Old City, next to the historic tunnel that plows through the Mönchsberg, and directly in front of a stop on several bus lines, this basic hotel has location and transportation covered. **Pros:** excellent location; easy access to public transportation; children ages eleven and under are free. **Cons:** on a busy street; very dated interior no a/c. $ *Rooms from: €165* ⊠ *Neutorstrasse 8* ☎ *0662/844–1540* ⊕ *www.schwaerzler-hotels.com* ⊅ *89 rooms* ⦵*Breakfast.*

$$$$
HOTEL

🔲 **Schloss Mönchstein.** With gorgeous gardens and hiking trails, it's little wonder the 19th-century naturalist Alexander von Humboldt called this retreat outside the city center a "small piece of paradise." **Pros:** luxurious rooms; lovely views; extensive and exclusive spa; feels far from the city. **Cons:** outside of city center; need a car to get around. $ *Rooms*

8

from: €450 ✉ Mönchsberg Park 26 ☎ 0662/848–5550 🌐 www.monchstein.at/en 🛏 9 rooms, 15 suites ⏲ Closed Feb. 🍴 Breakfast.

NORTH OF THE RIVER SALZACH

$$$ HOTEL **Amadeus.** If you're wondering why the hotel has Mozart's middle name, this 500-year-old, rather ramshackle yet charming house is not far from the St. Sebastian church and cemetery where many members of his family are booked for an eternal stay. **Pros:** huge breakfast; historic house. **Cons:** church bell next door goes off every quarter hour, and though it stops at 11 pm, it's a noisy alarm clock at 5 am. [$] *Rooms from: €190 ✉ Linzergasse 43–45 ☎ 0662/871–401 🌐 www.hotelamadeus.at 🛏 23 rooms 🍴 Breakfast.*

$$ B&B/INN **Bergland.** A 10-minute walk from the train station, this cheerful, pleasant, fourth-generation family-owned pension offers modern, comfortable rooms with breakfast included in the price. **Pros:** quiet location; 12 free parking spots; very good value; totally no-smoking. **Cons:** long walk to the center; basic accommodations. [$] *Rooms from: €145 ✉ Rupertgasse 15 ☎ 0662/872–318 🌐 www.berglandhotel.at 🛏 18 rooms ⏲ Closed end Oct.–Nov. 🍴 Breakfast.*

$$ HOTEL **Gersberg Alm.** A picture-perfect Alpine chalet on the lofty perch of the Gersberg, high above Salzburg, this hotel is less than 15 minutes by car from the center of the city. **Pros:** beautiful location; pleasant rooms. **Cons:** outside the city. [$] *Rooms from: €139 ✉ Gersberg 37 ☎ 0662/641–257 🌐 www.gersbergalm.at 🛏 44 rooms 🍴 Breakfast.*

$$$ HOTEL FAMILY Fodor's Choice ★ **Hotel Auersperg.** A lush, green oasis is tucked between the two buildings that comprise the Auersperg: the hotel, built in 1892 by the noted Italian architect Ceconi, and its neighboring "villa." **Pros:** historic hotel; family-friendly; great breakfast; hidden urban oasis; free iPad and bicycle use. **Cons:** on a busy intersection. [$] *Rooms from: €205 ✉ Auerspergstrasse 61 ☎ 0662/88944 🌐 www.auersperg.at 🛏 51 rooms 🍴 Breakfast.*

$$$$ HOTEL **Hotel Bristol.** There is little wonder that this pale-yellow palace, just across the river from the Alstadt and with stunning historic detail and fine artwork, has attracted an impressive roster of royal and celebrity guests. **Pros:** some fantastic views; charming accommodations; elegant restaurant. **Cons:** not in the old city; lower floor rear rooms lack view. [$] *Rooms from: €395 ✉ Makartplatz 4 ☎ 0662/873–557 🌐 www.bristol-salzburg.at 🛏 48 rooms, 12 suites ⏲ Closed Feb. and Mar. 🍴 Breakfast.*

$$ HOTEL **GoldenesTheater.** Close enough to the top of the Linzergasse shopping district and the theaters in the Neustadt but far enough to offer a respite from the summer crowds, this simple hotel is a decent value choice. **Pros:** close to Linzergasse shops; quiet terrace; helpful staff; air-conditioned. **Cons:** on a busy street; some rooms are quite dated; garage parking extra. [$] *Rooms from: €159 ✉ Schallmooser Hauptstrasse 13 ☎ 0662/881–6810 🌐 www.gt-hotel-salzburg.com 🛏 60 rooms 🍴 Breakfast.*

$ HOTEL **Motel One Salzburg Mirabell.** This simple, no frills, freshly modern hotel is a 15-minute walk from all that the historic city has to offer. **Pros:** riverfront location; close to city and train station; budget friendly; booking possible without credit card. **Cons:** few extras; no room safe; small bathrooms. [$] *Rooms from: €86* ✉ *Elisabethkai 58* ☎ *0662/885200* 🌐 *www.motel-one.com/en/hotels/salzburg* 🛏 *119 rooms* 🍴 *No meals.*

$$$ HOTEL 🏨 **NH Salzburg.** Part of a Spanish hotel chain, this pretty building is in a nice location, around the corner from Linzergasse (the shopping street leading to the Salzach River) and five minutes away from the beautiful Mirabell Gardens. **Pros:** in a historic setting; tasty breakfast; underground parking on-site. **Cons:** noisy common areas; charge for children ages 3 and up. [$] *Rooms from: €215* ✉ *Franz-Josef-Strasse 26* ☎ *0662/882–0410* 🌐 *www.nh-hotels.com* 🛏 *140 rooms* 🍴 *Breakfast.*

$$ B&B/INN 🏨 **Rosenvilla.** A haven of peace and tranquility, this family owned, upscale bed-and-breakfast is across the Salzach River from the Altstadt. **Pros:** quiet location; tasteful rooms, parking included. **Cons:** long walk to downtown. [$] *Rooms from: €165* ✉ *Höfelgasse 4* ☎ *0662/621–765* 🌐 *www.rosenvilla.com/en-rosenvilla-imprint.shtml* 🛏 *15 rooms* 🍴 *Breakfast.*

$$$$ HOTEL FAMILY Fodor's Choice ★ 🏨 **Sacher Salzburg.** On the Salzach River, this mammoth hotel has attracted guests from the Beatles and the Rolling Stones to Hillary and Chelsea Clinton, but the owners, the Gürtler family, will ensure that even if you don't have a Vuitton steamer trunk you'll feel welcome. **Pros:** some great views; delicious buffet breakfast; plenty of dining options. **Cons:** gets overcrowded during festival. [$] *Rooms from: €403* ✉ *Schwarzstrasse 5–7* ☎ *0662/88977* 🌐 *www.sacher.com* 🛏 *88 rooms, 25 suites* 🍴 *No meals.*

$$$ HOTEL Fodor's Choice ★ 🏨 **Schloss Leopoldskron.** Expansive grounds surround this historic palace immortalized in *The Sound of Music*, and the smart, freshly renovated rooms are surprisingly modest in price. **Pros:** idyllic, peaceful location; *Sound of Music* memorabilia; great value; a few free bicycles with picnic baskets available. **Cons:** no bus connection; no on-site restaurant and few nearby dining options. [$] *Rooms from: €180* ✉ *Leopoldskronstrasse 56–58* ☎ *0662/839–830* 🌐 *www.schloss-leopoldskron.com* 🛏 *55 rooms, 12 suites* 🍴 *Breakfast.*

$ HOTEL 🏨 **Schwarzes Rössl.** Once a favorite with Salzburg regulars, this traditional Gasthof now serves as student quarters for most of the year, but is well worth booking when available. **Pros:** near city center. **Cons:** few amenities. [$] *Rooms from: €100* ✉ *Priesterhausgasse 6* ☎ *0662/874–426* 📠 *01/401–7620* 🌐 *www.academiahotels.at* 🛏 *51 rooms* 🕑 *Closed Oct.–June* 🍴 *Breakfast.*

$$$$ HOTEL 🏨 **Sheraton Salzburg.** With the lovely Mirabell Park and Gardens virtually at its back door, this modern hotel tastefully blends in with the Belle Epoque buildings that surround it. **Pros:** spacious rooms; outstanding breakfast. **Cons:** often filled with conferences; chain-hotel feel. [$] *Rooms from: €450* ✉ *Auerspergstrasse 4* ☎ *0662/889–990* 🌐 *www.sheraton.at* 🛏 *163 rooms* 🍴 *Breakfast.*

$$$$ HOTEL 🏨 **Stadtkrug.** Snuggled under the monument-studded Kapuzinerberg and a two-minute walk from the bridge leading to the center of the Altstadt, the Stadtkrug (dated 1353) hits an idyllic, romantic, and quiet vibe, thanks to its mountainside setting. **Pros:** good location; lots of charm; helpful staff. **Cons:** on a busy street. [$] *Rooms from: €350* ✉ *Linzergasse 20* ☎ *0662/873–5450* 🌐 *www.stadtkrug.at* 🛏 *34 rooms* 🍴 *Breakfast.*

$$ ⊡ **Star Inn Zentrum.** Behind the Mönchsberg, this no-frills hotel stands
HOTEL   close to the center of the historic section, and if you want to fit in a
quiet morning stroll through the area, this is a decently priced option.
Pros: excellent location; close to public transportation, **Cons:** front
rooms on a busy street; spartan, outdated rooms. $ *Rooms from: €140*
⊠ *Hildmannplatz 5* ☎ *0662/846–846* ⊕ *www.starinnhotels.com* ⤴ *86
rooms* ¶ *Breakfast.*

$ ⊡ **Turnerwirt.** In the former farmer's village of Gnigl, now on Salz-
HOTEL   burg's outskirts, this is a quaint complex of buildings. **Pros:** family-
run friendliness; lots of charm. **Cons:** outside city center; no elevator;
dated. $ *Rooms from: €84* ⊠ *Linzer Bundesstrasse 54* ☎ *0662/640–630*
⊕ *www.turnerwirt.at* ⤴ *62 rooms* ¶ *Breakfast.*

$ ⊡ **Villa Trapp.** Stay at the home of the real von Trapp family in the
B&B/INN   southern suburb of Aigen, where each of the 22 comfortable rooms
Fodor's Choice   has been dedicated to the family member that once lived there. **Pros:**
★   quiet location. **Cons:** far outside the city center. $ *Rooms from: €100*
⊠ *Traunstraße 34* ☎ *0662/630–860* ⊕ *www.villa-trapp.cc* ⤴ *22 rooms,
6 suites* ¶ *Breakfast.*

$$$ ⊡ **Wolf-Dietrich.** Little touches like afternoon coffee and cake make this
HOTEL   small, family-owned hotel across the river from the Altstadt an invit-
ing choice. **Pros:** elegantly decorated rooms; nice views. **Cons:** nearby
church bells ring constantly. $ *Rooms from: €230* ⊠ *Wolf-Dietrich-
Strasse 7* ☎ *0662/871–275* ⊕ *www.salzburg-hotel.at* ⤴ *32 rooms, 8
suites* ¶ *Breakfast.*

NIGHTLIFE AND PERFORMING ARTS

NIGHTLIFE

Music in Salzburg is not just *Eine Kleine Nachtmusik*. The city's nightlife is livelier than it is reputed to be. The "in" areas include the "Bermuda Triangle" (Steingasse and Imbergstrasse) and Kaigasse; young
people tend to populate the bars and discos around Gstättengasse and
Rudolfskai.

Salzburg loves beer, and has some of the most picturesque Bierkeller
in Austria. The Augustinerbräu is a legendary Munich-style beer hall.

Fodor's Choice   **Augustinerbräu.** One of the largest beer cellars in Europe and the only one
★   of its kind in Austria, the celebrated Augustinerbräu serves its 10-week
aged Märzen—using the same recipe since 1621—directly from wooden
kegs into your overflowing stoneware mug at this sprawling, historic
landmark at the north end of the Mönchsberg. With communal, dark-
wood tables and beautifully restored chandeliers, the halls overflow
with cheerful locals, and outside, where massive chestnut trees shade the
sprawling garden, you'll find a complete cross-section of Salzburg society. Advent and Lent offer special beers, because the Catholic Church
decreed that "drinking does not interrupt fasting." ⊠ *Lindhofstrasse 7*
☎ *0662/431246* ⊕ *www.augustinerbier.at* ⊙ *Weekdays 3–11, weekends
and holidays 2:30–11* ☞ *Brewery tours by appointment, afternoon on
weekdays. Call or register online. €13.90 per person.*

Fridrich. This cozy little bar on the narrow Steingasse serves well-crafted drinks, an extensive selection of Austrian wines, antipasti, cold smoked locally caught fish, and small portions of savory Austrian favorites like *Faschierte Laibchen* (finely minced meatballs) with bread and pickles; and *Krautfleckerl* (square pasta with caramelized onions, shredded white cabbage, sweet wine and cumin). Eclectic music runs the gamut from Tarantino soundtracks to Italian music to jazz. In summer, the garden's open until midnight. ⊠ *Steingasse 15* ☎ *0662/87–62–18* ⊕ *www. gastlokal-fridrich.at* ⊗ *Closed Wed. Sept.–June.*

Glüxfall. Venture through the unassuming riverfront exterior and find a sophisticated alternative to the nearby raucous, smoky bar and club scene in Glüxfall's evening incarnation as a late-night cocktail and wine bar with a deliciously tempting menu and an illuminated inner courtyard. Menu highlights from Salzburg's famous Chef Fleischhacker include several choices of Flammkuchen (wood-fired, thinly rolled dough covered with crème fraîche and seasonal toppings) from his wife's native Black Forest region. Cocktail Wednesdays and Happy Hour Thursdays draw a lively crowd. ⊠ *Franz-Josef-Kai 11* ☎ *0662/265017* ⊕ *www. gluexfall.at* ⊗ *Closed Sun. after 4 pm (except during festival).*

Stieglkeller. Sample the selections of this hometown-pride brew under the shade of chestnut trees as you watch the sun set over the rooftops and steeples of the Old City. The noted local architect Ceconi devised this sprawling place around 1901. The Keller is partly inside the Mönchsberg hill, so its cellars guarantee the quality and right temperature of the drinks. It's a great place to stop for lunch, an afternoon *Jause* (snack) or an evening *Prost* with friends, though beware: climbing up the relatively steep incline is easier than stumbling down after a few *Grosses* (large beers). ⊠ *Festungsgasse 10* ☎ *0662/842681–0* ⊕ *www.stieglkeller. at* ⊗ *Closed Feb.*

8

PERFORMING ARTS

Before you arrive in Salzburg, do some advance research to determine the city's music schedule for the time you will be there, and make reservations; if you'll be attending the summer Salzburg Festival, this is a must. After you arrive in the city, any office of the Salzburg Tourist Office and most hotel concierge desks can provide you with schedules for all the arts performances held year-round in Salzburg, and you can find listings in the daily newspaper, *Salzburger Nachrichten.*

The Advent season transforms this picture-perfect city into an even more magical wonderland. Music fills the streets of the Old City during the Christmas markets. Warm up with a cup of *Glühwein* (mulled wine) from one of the numerous wooden stands and find the nearest festively attired brass ensemble for a lovely free concert.

To experience a true local tradition, get tickets to one of several Adventsingen performances. Folk singers, choral ensembles, children's choirs, traditional instrument ensembles, and actors weave music and theater into the Advent season. The stories and songs are typically in local dialect, which can be difficult for even High German speakers to understand, but the atmosphere and experience are worth it.

The spiritual surroundings of the St. Andrew's Church on Mirabell Square offer the perfect atmosphere for the performances by Salzburger Advent (⊕ *www.salzburgeradvent.at*). Salzburg Advent Singing (⊕ *www.salzburgeradventsingen.at*) in the Great Festival Hall is the largest event of the season.

THE SALZBURG MUSIC FESTIVAL

Salzburger Festspiele. The biggest event on the calendar—as it has been since it was first organized by composer Richard Strauss, producer Max Reinhardt, and playwright Hugo von Hofmannsthal in 1920—is the world-famous Salzburger Festspiele. The main summer festival is usually scheduled for the middle of July through the end of August. In addition, the festival presents two other major annual events: the Easter Festival (early April), and the Pentecost Baroque Festival (late May).

The most star-studded events—featuring the top opera stars and conductors such as Franz Welser-Möst and Nikolaus Harnoncourt—have tickets ranging from €55 to €420; for these glamorous events, first-nighters still pull out all the stops—summer furs, Dior dresses, and white ties stud the more expensive sections of the theaters. Other performances run from €10 to €220, with lesser prices for events outside the main festival halls, the **Grosses Festspielhaus** (Great Festival Hall) and the **Haus für Mozart** (House for Mozart), located shoulder to shoulder on the grand promenade of Hofstallgasse. This street, one of the most festive settings for a music festival, is especially dazzling at night, thanks to the floodlighted Fortress Hohensalzburg, which hovers on its hilltop above the theater promenade. Behind the court stables first constructed by Wolf-Dietrich in 1607, the *Festspielhäser* (festival halls) are modern constructions—the Grosses Haus was built in 1960 with 2,200 seats—but are actually "prehistoric," being dug out of the bedrock of the Mönchsberg mountain. There are glittering concerts and operas performed at many other theaters in the city. You can catch Mozart concertos in the 18th-century splendor of two magnificent state rooms in which the composer himself once conducted: the Rittersaal of the Residenz and the Marble Hall of the Mirabell Palace. Delightful Mozart productions are offered by the Salzburger Marionetten Theater. In addition, many important concerts are offered in the two auditoriums of the Mozarteum.

■ TIP→ Since you must order your tickets as early as possible, make your decisions as soon as the program comes out (usually in the middle of November). Many major performances are sold out two or three months in advance, as hordes descend on the city to enjoy staged opera spectacles, symphony concerts by the Vienna Philharmonic and other great orchestras, recitals, church oratorios, and special evenings at the Mozarteum year after year.

Tickets to the Summer, Easter, and Whitsun Festivals can be purchased directly at the box office (across the street from the Great Festival Hall against the Mönchsberg), at your hotel, or, most conveniently, on the festival website. ⊠ *Hofstallgasse 1* ☎ *0662/8045–500 for summer festival, 0662/8045–361 for Easter festival* ⊕ *www.salzburgfestival.at*.

EVENING MUSIC ABOUNDS

Salzburg is most renowned for the Salzburger Festspiele. But much of Salzburg's special charm can be best discovered and enjoyed off-season. Music lovers face loads of riches, including chamber concerts held in Mirabell Palace and the Fortress, as well as bountiful sacred music choices at the cathedral or any of the other churches offering impressive backdrops. Salzburg concerts by the Mozarteum Orchestra and the Camerata are now just as popular as the Vienna Philharmonic's program in the Musikverein in Vienna. The Landestheater season runs from September to June. And no one should miss the chance to be enchanted and amazed by the skill and artistry of the Salzburg Marionetten Theater.

Polzer. Since 1946, this agency has been selling tickets for the Salzburg Festival and other events in and around Austria. ⊠ *Residenzplatz 3* ☎ *0662/8969* ⊕ *www.polzer.com* ⊗ *Closed Sun. and Mon., except during Festival.*

Salzburg Ticket Service. This service provides tickets for a wide array of Salzburg area concerts, theater performances, and sightseeing tours. ⊠ *Mozartplatz 5* ☎ *0662/840310* ⊕ *www.salzburgticket.com.*

MUSIC

There is no shortage of concerts in this most musical of cities. Customarily, the Salzburg Festival hosts the Vienna Philharmonic, and the Berlin Philharmonic is in residence during the Easter Festival, but other orchestras can be expected to take leading roles as well. The Kulturvereinigung fills the Festival Hall during the fall and winter with more top-notch concerts and operas. In addition, there are the Pentecost Baroque Festival, Mozart Week (late January), Salzburg Cultural Days (October), and the Dialogues Festival (December). Mozart Week offers many musical gems; in recent seasons Daniel Barenboim, Pierre Boulez, and Nikolaus Harnoncourt have conducted the Vienna Philharmonic, while Sir John Eliot Gardiner, Rene Jacobs, and Marc Minkowski led other world-renowned orchestras. The Palace Concerts and the Fortress Concerts are year-round solo and chamber music mainstays. Find experimental works in the black box theater at the ArgeKultur.

Mozarteum. Two institutions share the address in this building finished just before World War I—the International Foundation Mozarteum, set up in 1870, and the University of Music and Performing Arts, founded in 1880. Scholars come here to research in the **Bibliotheca Mozartiana,** the world's largest Mozart library (for research only; public access allowed with advance registration). The Mozarteum also organizes the annual Mozart Week festival in January and the forward-looking Dialogues festival in December, selecting two composers each year, one contemporary and another historic, to intermingle with Mozart works, aiming to spark conversation and bring

8

fresh perspectives to the pieces. Many important concerts are offered from October to June in its two recital halls, the Grosser Saal (Great Hall) and the Wiener Saal (Vienna Hall).

Behind the Mozarteum, sheltered by the trees of the Bastiongarten, is the famous **Zauberflötenhäuschen**—the little summerhouse rumored to be the place where Mozart composed parts of *The Magic Flute*, with the encouragement of his frantic librettist, Emanuel Schikaneder, who finally wound up locking the composer inside to force him to complete his work. The house has more former addresses than most Salzburgers, having been moved numerous times around Salzburg after being donated to the Mozarteum by Vienna's Prince Starhemberg. It is much restored: back in the 19th century, the faithful used to visit it and snatch shingles off its roof and later it was damaged during World War II bombings. The house can generally be viewed only when concerts are offered in the adjacent Grosser Saal. ⊠ *Schwarzstrasse 26* ☎ *0662/88940–0* ⊕ *www.mozarteum.at* ⊙ *Summerhouse: only during Grosser Saal concerts.*

Salzburger Festungskonzerte. The concerts are presented in the grand Prince's Chamber at Festung Hohensalzburg and often include works by Mozart. A special candlelight dinner and concert-ticket combo is offered. ⊠ *Festung Hohensalzburg* ☎ *0662/825858* ⊕ *www. mozartfestival.at* ▨ *€33–€39.*

Salzburger Kulturvereinigung. World-class guest orchestras and Salzburg's own Mozarteum Orchestra appear in the Grosses Festspielhaus and the Great Hall of the Mozarteum during the fall and winter under the auspices of the Salzburg Cultural Association. If you visit over *Sylvester* (New Year's Eve), you can experience the Austrian tradition of the brass-and-wind-powered New Year's Concert. They also created Salzburg Cultural Days, filling the autumn off-season with top talent and exciting performances. ⊠ *Waagplatz 1A* ☎ *0662/845346–0* ⊕ *www. salzburgfestival.at.*

Salzburger Schlosskonzerte. Classical soloists and chamber ensembles perform in more than 230 concerts each year in the legendary Marmorsaal (Marble Hall) at **Mirabell Palace,** where Mozart performed. Concerts begin at 8:00 pm and last 1½ hours. ⊠ *Mirabell Palace, Mirabelplatz* ☎ *0662/848586* ⊕ *www.salzburger.schlosskonzerte.at* ▨ *€29–€35* ⊙ *Box office at Theatergasse 2, daily 9–2; Mirabell Palace box office open from 7 pm on concert days.*

OPERA

Landestheater. This neo-baroque gem seats 750 and from September to June offers a varied schedule of opera, theater and ballet, with Mozart always in the repertoire and recent expansion into daring new works. Productions slated for 2014/2015 include *The Magic Flute, The Sound of Music,* Austrian operetta *Im Weissen Rössl,* and *The Nutcracker* ballet. You may place ticket orders by telephone Monday and Saturday 10–2, Tuesday–Friday 10–5. ⊠ *Schwarzstrasse 22* ☎ *0662/871–51–221* ⊕ *www.salzburger-landestheater.at.*

Salzburger Festspiele. Eyes from all corners of the world are on this city during the Salzburger Festspiele, which mounts a full calendar of magnificently produced operas every summer, and even more during the Easter (April) and Whitsun (May) festivals. These performances are held in the Grosses Festspielhaus (Great Festival Hall), the Haus für Mozart (House for Mozart), the Landestheater, the Felsenreitschule, the Mozarteum, and numerous other smaller venues, where lieder recitals and chamber works predominate. ⊠ *Hofstallgasse 1* ⊕ *www.salzburgerfestspiele.at* ✆*€25–€400. Other box offices are allowed to add 20% to the ticket price.*

FAMILY
Fodor'sChoice
★

Salzburger Marionettentheater. This delightful, acclaimed cultural institution is devoted to opera, with a particularly renowned production of *Così fan tutte* to its credit. The Marionettentheater not only performs operas by Mozart, but also goodies by Rossini, the younger Strauss, Offenbach, Humperdinck, Mendelssohn (who wrote the music for the troupe's delightful show devoted to William Shakespeare's *A Midsummer Night's Dream),* and a fairy-tale version of *The Sound of Music,* all accompanied by historic recordings. Performances are staged during the first week of January, during Mozart Week (late January), from May through September, and December 26 through January 7. ⊠ *Schwarzstrasse 24* ☎ *0662/872406* ⊕ *www.marionetten. at* ✆*€18– €35* ☉ *Box office: Mon.–Sat. 9–1 and for 2 hrs before the performance.*

THEATER

ARGEkultur. The heart of Salzburg's contemporary art and culture scene beats at this modern, multipurpose performance venue. Its black box theater and small performance hall host envelope-pushing experimental music concerts, modern dance performances, Austrian cabaret evenings, and theater pieces. The Open Mind Festival (November) and the MotzArt Cabaret Festival (February) keep the winter months alive. ⊠ *Ulrike-Gschwandtner-Strasse 5* ☎ *0662/848784* ⊕ *www.argekultur.at.*

Jedermann (Everyman). This morality play, by Hugo von Hofmannsthal, is famously performed annually (in German) in the front courtyard of the cathedral. It begins with a rousing Medieval parade of performers through the streets of the Altstadt, spilling onto the stage for a colorful, intense, and moving presentation of the allegorical story of wealthy, selfish Jedermann's final journey before death. Few of the thousands packing the plaza are unmoved when, at the height of the banquet, church bells around the city ring out and the voice of Death is heard calling "Jedermann—Jedermann—Jed-er-*mann*" from the Franziskanerkirche tower, followed by echoes of voices from other steeples and from atop the Fortress Hohensalzburg. An unforgettable experience. ⊠ *Domplatz.*

SHOPPING

For a small city, Salzburg has a wide spectrum of stores. The specialties are traditional clothing, like lederhosen and loden coats, jewelry, glassware, handicrafts, confectionary, dolls in native costume, Christmas decorations, sports equipment, and silk flowers. A *Gewürzsträussl* is a bundle of whole spices bunched and arranged to look like a bouquet of flowers (try the markets on Universitätsplatz). This old tradition goes back to the time when only a few rooms could be heated, and people and their farm animals would often cohabitate on the coldest days. You can imagine how lovely the aromas must have been—so this spicy room freshener was invented.

At Christmas there is a special **Advent market** on the Domplatz and the Residenzplatz, offering regional decorations, from the week before the first Advent Sunday until December 26, daily 9–8. Stores are generally open weekdays 10–6, and many on Saturday 10–5. Some supermarkets stay open until 7:30 on Thursday or Friday. Only shops in the railway station, the airport, and near the general hospital are open on Sunday.

> ## SHOPPING STREETS
>
> The most fashionable specialty stores and gift shops are found along Getreidegasse and Judengasse and around Residenzplatz. Linzergasse, across the river, is less crowded and good for more practical items. There are also interesting antiques shops in the medieval buildings along Steingasse and on Goldgasse.

THE ALTSTADT
ANTIQUES
A.E. Köchert. As the imperial court jeweler and personal jeweler to Emperor Franz Josef I, the Köchert goldsmiths have crafted such world-renowned treasures as the Austrian Imperial Crown and the diamond stars adorning Empress Sisi's hair in her famous portrait. Today's sixth generation creates modern pieces using traditional techniques, replicas of the "Sisi Stars," and offers stunning antique jewelry in the firm's small Salzburg outpost. ⊠ *Alter Markt 15* ☏ *0662/843398* ⊕ *www. koechert.com.*

Antiquitäten Hiko-Antik. Tucked behind the Gstättentor archway, this family-run antiques shop offers myriad small and medium-size pieces spanning all epochs, with a focus on Austrian folk art, religious artifacts, and jewelry, perfect for stowing in your already bulging suitcase. ⊠ *Gstättengasse 2* ☏ *0664/2002004* ⊕ *www.hiko-antik.at.*

Internationale Messe für Kunst und Antiquitäten. The annual art and antiques fair takes place from Palm Sunday to Easter Monday in the staterooms of Salzburg's Residenz. ⊠ *Residenzplatz 1* ☏ *01/587–12–93* ⊕ *www. artantique-residenz.at* ☜ *€13.*

Madero CollectorsRoom. It's worth a short trip around the southeast tip of the Mönchsberg into Nonntal to discover the impressive collection of mid-20th-century furniture, contemporary design pieces, and delicate porcelain and glassware; all celebrating the tradition of European craftsmanship and offered at a variety of price levels. The shop has been garnering increasing international praise and recognition, so visit while it's still a relatively hidden gem. ⊠ *Nonntaler Hauptstr. 10/1* ☏ *0662/844–008* ⊕ *www.madero.at.*

CONFECTIONARY AND SCHNAPPS

Konditorei Fürst. If you're looking for the kind of *Mozartkugeln* (chocolate marzipan confections) you can't buy at home, try the store that claims to have invented them in 1890. It still produces the candy by hand according to the original, secret family recipe. Stock up on the *Bach Würfel* (coffee, nut and chocolate truffle) and other delicacies at one of its four locations while you're in town—Konditorei Fürst does not offer overseas shipping. ✉ *Brodgasse 13* ☎ *0662/843759–0* ⊕ *www. original-mozartkugel.com.*

Konditorei Schatz. Salzburg locals have relied on this small family-owned bakery since 1877 to satisfy their cravings for *Cremeschnitte* (vanilla custard cream between puff pastry layers), *Rigo-Jancsi* (Hungarian chocolate sponge cake, chocolate mousse, and chocolate glaze), *Himbeer-Obers-Souffle* (strawberry cream soufflé), apple strudel, and other mouthwatering selections from their 30 to 50 daily cakes and pastries. ✉ *Schatz passageway, Getreidegasse 3* ☎ *0662/842792* ⊕ *www.schatz-konditorei.at.*

Sporer. Leave room in your suitcase for a few bottles from the excellent selection of house brands and locally produced distilled Austrian Schnapps, liqueurs, brandies, festive punch, spirits, and wines at this fourth-generation family-owned shop and tavern. Locals look forward to the Christmas markets so they can warm up from the inside with their annual fix of orange-flavored *Sporer Punsch,* which you can purchase year-round in the store. Chat with the friendly owners and regular customers at the small bar while you sample the wares. ✉ *Getreidegasse 39* ☎ *0662/845431* ⊕ *www.sporer.at* ☉ *Closed Sun. and holidays.*

CRAFTS

Christmas in Salzburg. Rooms of gorgeous Christmas-tree decorations, notably an abundance of hand-painted blown egg ornaments for all holidays, fill this charming year-round shop. ✉ *Judengasse 11* ☎ *0662/846784.*

Fritz Kreis. Explore the finely crafted, hand-etched, traditionally blown glass pieces in this specialty shop. ✉ *Sigmund-Haffner-Gasse 14* ☎ *0662/841–323* ⊕ *www.glaskunstkreis.com.*

Gehmacher. Find chic European-traditional to modern-style home design and accessories at this centrally located shop. ✉ *Alter Markt 2* ☎ *0662/845506–0* ⊕ *www.gehmacher.at.*

SOUVENIR SWEETS

Mozartkugeln, candy balls of pistachio marzipan rolled in nougat cream and dipped in dark chocolate, which bear a miniportrait of Mozart on the wrapper, are omnipresent in Salzburg. Those handmade by Konditorei Fürst cost more but can be purchased individually. In hot summer months, ask for a thermos bag to prevent melting. You can find mass-produced products like those from Mirabell—500,000 pieces every day—or from the German competitor Reber almost everywhere. Discounts are easy to find in supermarkets or duty-free shops at the airport.

8

Salzburger Heimatwerk. Salzburg ladies choose fabrics for their custom-made *Dirndln* from the store's floor-to-ceiling wall of colorful linen, silk, and cotton; and they outfit their homes with locally produced ceramics, hand-stenciled linens, and regional cookbooks at good prices. ⊠ *Residenzplatz 9* ☎ *0662/844110* ⊕ *www.salzburgerheimatwerk.at.*

TRADITIONAL CLOTHING

Dschulnigg. This is a favorite among elegant Salzburgers for *Trachten*, the traditional Austrian costume including Lederhosen and Dirndl (region-specific dresses with white blouse, printed skirts, and apron). You can also get high-quality field and hunting gear and unique home decorations. ⊠ *Griesgasse 8, corner of Münzgasse* ☎ *0662/842376–0* ⊕ *www.jagd-dschulnigg.at.*

Jahn-Markl. Admire the traditional craftsmanship of the leather clothing and other goods here, some made to order. ⊠ *Residenzplatz 3* ☎ *0662/842610* ⊕ *www.jahn-markl.at.*

Madl am Grünmarkt. Flair and elegance distinguish the traditional Austrian designs here. ⊠ *Universitätsplatz 12* ☎ *0662/845457* ⊕ *www.madlsalzburg.at.*

NORTH OF THE RIVER SALZACH
TRADITIONAL CLOTHING

Lanz. A good selection of loden coats and *Dirndln* in the signature "Lanz cut" can be found at this famous Salzburg *Trachten* maker, known for leading the modern revival of traditional Austrian clothing. ⊠ *Schwarzstrasse 4* ☎ *0662/874272* ⊕ *www.lanztrachten.at.*

EXCURSIONS FROM SALZBURG

Gaisberg and Untersberg. Salzburg's "house mountains" are so called because of their proximity to the city settlements. You can take the bus to the summit of the Gaisberg, where you'll be rewarded with a spectacular panoramic view of the Alps and the Alpine foreland. The Untersberg is the mountain Captain von Trapp and Maria climbed as they escaped the Nazis in *The Sound of Music*. In the film they were supposedly fleeing to Switzerland; in reality, the climb up the Untersberg would have brought them almost to the doorstep of Hitler's retreat at the Eagle's Nest above Berchtesgaden. A cable car from St. Leonhard, about 13 km (8 miles) south of Salzburg, takes you 6,020 feet up to the top of the Untersberg for a breathtaking view. In winter you can ski down (you arrive in the village of Fürstenbrunn and taxis or buses take you back to St. Leonhard); in summer there are a number of hiking routes from the summit. ⊠ *Doktor-Friedrich-Oedl-Weg 2, St. Leonhard* ✠ *In summer the Albus "Gaisberg Bus" No. 151 (0662/424–000–0) leaves hourly from Mirabellplatz: weekdays 10:03–4:03, Sat. 9:58–3:58, Sun. and holidays 10:01 to 4:01; the journey takes about a half hour* ☎ *06246/72477* ⊕ *www.untersberg. net* 🚠 *Round-trip €20* ⊘ *Mid-Dec.–Feb., daily 9–4; Mar.–June and Oct., daily 8:30–5; July–Sept., daily 8:30–5:30.*

Hallein. The second-largest town of the region, 15 km (10 miles) south of Salzburg, Hallein was once famed for its caves of "white gold"—salt. "Hall" is the old Celtic word for salt, and this treasure was mined in the neighboring Dürrnberg mountain. You can get to Hallein by regular bus, by car along the B159 Salzachtal-Bundesstrasse, or by bicycle alongside the River Salzach. Once in Hallein, you can follow the winding paths of the oldest salt mine in the world at the **Salzwelten** and pay your respects to Franz Gruber, the composer of "Silent Night," who lies in the only grave still extant next to the town's parish church.

Keltenmuseum (*Museum of the Celts*). To learn all about Hallein, head to the Keltenmuseum, where more than 30 rooms explore the history of the region's Celtic settlements (before the birth of Christ). In the three staterooms more than 70 oil paintings show the working conditions of the salt mines and the salina. ⊠ *Pflegerplatz 5* ☏ *06245/80783* 🎫 *€6* ⊙ *Daily 9–5.*

Oberndorf. This little village 21 km (13 miles) north of Salzburg has just one claim to fame: it was here on Christmas Eve, 1818, that the world-famous Christmas carol "Silent Night," composed by the organist and schoolteacher Franz Gruber to a lyric by the local priest, Josef Mohr, was sung for the first time. The church was demolished and replaced in 1937 by a tiny commemorative chapel containing a copy of the original composition (the original is in the Salzburg Museum), stained-glass windows depicting Gruber and Mohr, and a Nativity scene. ∎**TIP➔** **Every December 24 at 5 pm, a traditional performance of the carol—two male voices plus guitar and choir—in front of the chapel is the introduction to Christmas.** You can get to Oberndorf by the local train (opposite the main train station), by car along the B156 Lamprechtshausener Bundesstrasse, or by bicycle along the River Salzach.

Heimatmuseum. About a 10-minute walk from the village center along the riverbank, the local Heimatmuseum, opposite the chapel, documents the history of the carol. ⊠ *Stille-Nacht-Platz 7* ☏ *06272/4422–0* 🎫 *€2.50* ⊙ *March–Jan. daily 9–4; during the Advent daily 9–6.*

FAMILY
Fodor's Choice
★

Schloss Hellbrunn (*Hellbrunn Palace*). Just 6½ km (4 miles) south of Salzburg, the Lustschloss Hellbrunn was the prince-archbishops' pleasure palace. It was built early in the 17th century by Santino Solari for Markus Sittikus, after the latter had imprisoned his uncle, Wolf-Dietrich, in the fortress. The castle has some fascinating rooms, including an octagonal music room and a banquet hall with a trompe-l'oeil ceiling. Hellbrunn Park became famous far and wide because of its **Wasserspiele**, or trick fountains. In the formal gardens (a beautiful example of the Mannerist style) owners added an outstanding mechanical theater that includes exotic and humorous fountains spurting water from strange places at unexpected times. You will probably get doused (bring a raincoat). A visit to the gardens is highly recommended: nowhere else can you experience so completely the realm of fantasy in which the grand Salzburg archbishops indulged. The **Monatsschlösschen**, the old hunting lodge (built in one month), contains an excellent folklore museum. Following the path over the hill you find the **Steintheater** (Stone Theater), an old quarry made into

8

the earliest open-air opera stage north of the Alps. The former palace deer park has become a **zoo** featuring free-flying vultures and Alpine animals that largely roam unhindered. You can get to Hellbrunn by Bus 25, by car on Route 159, or by bike or on foot along the beautiful Hellbrunner Allee past several 17th-century mansions. On the estate grounds is the little gazebo filmed in *The Sound of Music* ("I am 16, going on 17")—the doors are now locked because a devotee once tried to repeat the movie's dance steps, leaping from bench to bench, and managed to fall and break a hip. ✉ *Fürstenweg 37, Hellbrunn* ☎ *0662/82–03–72–0* ⊕ *www.hellbrunn.at* 🎟 *Tour of palace and water gardens €9.50* ☉ *Apr. and Oct., daily 9–4:30; May, June, and Sept., daily 9–5:30; July and Aug., daily 9–6; evening tours July and Aug., daily on the hr 7, 8, and 9.*

EASTERN ALPS

Updated by
Rob Freeman

The entire Eastern Alps region is a feast of dramatic countryside, with breathtaking scenery and mountainous terrain that offers great winter sports opportunities. Here, majestic peaks, many well over 9,750 feet, soar above slow-moving glaciers that give way to sweeping Alpine meadows ablaze with wildflowers in spring and summer. Long, broad valleys (many names have the suffix -au, meaning "water-meadow") are basins of rivers that cross the region between mountain ranges, sometimes meandering, sometimes plunging.

The land is full of ice caves and salt mines, deep gorges and hot springs. Tourism thrives through the towns and villages, with resorts such as Heiligenblut, in the shadow of the Grossglockner, Austria's highest mountain, a major draw for hikers and climbers. Wherever you go, you'll find a range of good lodging, solid local food, and friendly folk. Western Carinthia and Salzburg province are dotted with quaint villages that have charming churches, lovely mountain scenery and access to plenty of outdoor action—from hiking and fishing in summer to skiing in winter.

ORIENTATION AND PLANNING

GETTING ORIENTED

Austria's Eastern Alps straddle four provinces: Carinthia, East Tyrol, Salzburg, and Styria. Imposing mountain ranges ripple through the region, isolating Alpine villages whose picture-postcard perfection has remained unspoiled through the centuries. The mountainous terrain makes some backtracking necessary if you're interested in visiting the entire area, but driving through the spectacular scenery is part of the appeal of touring the region.

Across the Grossglockner Pass. There is a thrill every hundred yards along this scenic route, but your first will be sighting Heiligenblut, one of Austria's most captivating towns, at the foot of the Grossglockner.

Mountain Spas and Alpine Rambles. Mountain magic and healing waters abound in this traditional and historic area.

PLANNING

WHEN TO GO

Snowy conditions can make driving a white-knuckle experience but winter also brings extensive, superb skiing throughout the region—and somewhat cheaper than the better-known resorts in Tyrol. In summer the craggy mountain peaks and lush meadows provide challenge and joy to hikers, while spelunkers head into the bowels of the behemoths.

TOP REASONS TO GO

Drive the Grossglockner Highway. As long as weather conditions permit, this panoramic road is one of Austria's most spectacular mountain passes and an absolute must.

Take pictures at Heiligenblut. Of all the picture-book images in the country, this jewel of a photo-op town has to be the winner, with its slender church steeple and gorgeous mountain backdrop.

Head to the lake at Velden. There is a decided Mediterranean feel to this upscale lakeside town, where heavily wooded hills slope gently down to the Worthersee, and the lakeshore is lined by hotels and the fabulous villas of Austria's rich and famous—not to mention the casino.

Ski at Bad Kleinkirchheim. The province of Carinthia's best-known and most fashionable ski resort is home to the greatest downhill racer of all time, Franz Klammer. Join him—or follow in his tracks—on the slopes.

Eisriesenwelt. Literally translated to "the giant ice world," this wonder of nature is, in fact, one of the biggest ice caves in the world—don't miss this unforgettable experience.

"Take the cure" at Bad Gastein. This is, perhaps, the most famous of all Alpine mountain spas.

Placid lakes and meandering mountain streams attract anglers for some of the best fishing to be found in the country.

GETTING HERE AND AROUND

Driving is by far the preferred means of seeing this area; the roads are good, and you can stop to picnic or just to marvel at the scenery. There is a cost to driving these roads, though, as tunnels, passes, and panoramic roads often have tolls. Bus travel is also a relatively hassle-free option.

AIR TRAVEL

The busiest airport in the Eastern Alps region is the Mozart airport in Salzburg, larger and with more connections than the one in Carinthia at Klagenfurt. Both have frequent connections to other Austrian cities and points in Europe, but neither has scheduled overseas direct flights.

BUS TRAVEL

As is typical throughout Austria, where trains don't go, the buses do, though some side routes are less frequently covered. Coordinating your schedule with that of the buses is not as difficult as it sounds. Austrian travel offices are helpful in this regard, or bus information is available in Klagenfurt and Salzburg. The Postbus network is extensive throughout Austria, with services remaining reliable even through adverse weather, including heavy snow. You can take the Postbus 650/651 from the Zell am See train station up and over the mountains to the Grossglockner glacier at Kaiser-Franz-Josefs-Höhe, a 2½-hour trip. The bus runs twice a day from late June to the end of September. There's also a connecting bus from the glacier to Heiligenblut twice a day, so you can start the route from there, too.

Bus Information Post Bus ☎ *0810/222–333–55, 0463/31523–61 in Carinthia* ⊕ *www.postbus.at.*

CAR TRAVEL

If you're coming from northern Italy, you can get to the Eastern Alps from Villach on the E55/A13 in Italy, which becomes the A2 and then the A10; from Klagenfurt, farther east in Carinthia, taking the A2 autobahn is quickest. The fastest route from Salzburg is the A10 autobahn, but you'll have to take two tunnels into account at a total cost of €11 (Tauern- and Katschbergtunnel). In summer on certain weekends (especially during Germany's official holidays), the A10 southbound can become one very long parking lot, with hour-long waits before the tunnels. Taking the normal road over the passes, although long, is a very attractive option, but you won't be the only person who thought of it. A good alternative to the busy Tauern Highway is the Tauern Motorail link, connecting Bad Gastein with Carinthia (Mallnitz) through an 8-km (5-mile) tunnel. It's a 20-minute ride and cars are transported from one side to the other by train while passengers ride in a proper carriage. One way costs €17, round-trip €30. Prices are per car, including all passengers. If coming from abroad, don't forget to buy the autobahn vignette (sticker) for Austria (⇨ *Driving in Travel Smart Austria*).

> **SALZBURGERLAND CARD**
>
> The SalzburgerLand Card includes admission to thermal baths (including Bad Gastein) and museums, trains and cable-car rides, a 24-hour Salzburg-City card, and more—190 attractions in all. It's definitely worth the money if you plan to do more than a couple of activities in the area. A six-day card costs €59, and cards can be purchased from May till October 26. ⊕ *www.salzburgerlandcard.com.*

ROAD CONDITIONS

Be aware that the Grossglockner High Alpine Highway is closed from the first heavy snow (mid-November or possibly earlier) to mid-May or early June. Though many of the other high mountain roads are kept open in winter, driving them is nevertheless tricky and you may even need wheel chains.

TRAIN TRAVEL

Salzburg is the main hub for visiting the Eastern Alps, with frequent rail service from Vienna. Bad Gastein is also connected to Vienna, but with fewer direct trains; to get to Zell am See you must change trains in Salzburg. Most of the towns in the Eastern Alps are reachable by train, but the Grossglockner is reachable in a practical sense only by road.

If your onward travel plans from the Eastern Alps point you in the direction of Vienna, or you plan to travel to Carinthia after flying into Vienna, keep in mind the route via the **Semmering Railway**. It is now a section of rail travel that is part of the Austrian network, but the 41 km (25 miles) that is still called the Semmering is probably the most spectacular regular guage train journey you will ever take. And it has been in constant use for 160 years. Built between 1848 and 1854, it traverses high mountain terrain between Gloggnitz, southwest of Vienna, to Murzzuschlag over the Semmering Pass. It's commonly referred to as the world's first true mountain railway and a marvel of civil engineering. It features 14 tunnels, 16 viaducts (some of them two stories), more than 100 curved stone bridges and 11 small iron ones. It's possible to incorporate traveling this wonder on your way to or from Vienna and Klagenfurt, Heiligenblut or Zell am See. Get information about tickets and timetable from ÖBB (Austrian Railways).

Train Information **Österreichisches Bundesbahn** ☎ *05/1717* ⊕ *www.oebb.at.*

VISITOR INFORMATION

For information about Carinthia, contact Kärntner Tourismus. The central tourist board for East Tyrol is OstTyrol Information. For information about Salzburg Province, contact Salzburger Land Tourismus. The main tourist bureau for Styria is Steiermark Information.

Many individual towns have their own *Fremdenverkehrsamt* (tourist office); they are listed under the specific towns.

Tourist Information **Kärntner Tourismus** ☎ *0463/3000* ⊕ *www.carinthia. at.* **OstTyrol Information** ✉ *Maria-Theresien-Strasse 55, Innsbruck, Tyrol* ☎ *0512/7272* ⊕ *www.Tyrol.at.* **Salzburger Land Tourismus** ✉ *Wiener Bundesstrasse 23, Postfach 1, Hallwang bei Salzburg* ☎ *0662/6688–0* ⊕ *www. salzburgerland.com.* **Steiermark Information** ✉ *St. Peter-Hauptstrasse 243, Graz, Styria* ☎ *0316/4003* ⊕ *www.steiermark.com.*

RESTAURANTS

Although this region contains fine restaurants—in fact, two of the country's top dozen dining establishments are here—most of the dining in the small towns of the Eastern Alps will take place in *Gasthöfs* or *Gasthäuses*—chalet-style country hotels and inns with flower-decked balconies and overhanging eaves. Note that in many cases such inns are closed in the off-season, particularly November and possibly April or May.

HOTELS

This part of Austria is relatively inexpensive, except for the top resort towns of Bad Gastein and Zell am See. Even there, budget accommodations are available outside the center of town or in pensions. Note that room rates include taxes and service and almost always breakfast (except in the most expensive hotels) and one other meal, which is usually dinner. *Halb pension* (half-board), as this plan is called, is de rigueur in most lodgings. However, most will offer a breakfast-buffet-only rate if requested. Most hotels provide in-room phones and TVs. A few of the smaller hotels still take no credit cards, or if they do, will add a surcharge of between 3% and 5%. In the prominent resorts summer prices are often as much as 50% lower than during ski season.

WHAT IT COSTS IN EUROS			
	$	$$	$$$	$$$$
RESTAURANTS	under €12	€12–€17	€18–€22	over €22
HOTELS	under €100	€100–€135	€136–€175	over €175

Restaurant prices are per person for a main course at dinner. Hotel prices are for a standard double room in high season, including taxes and service.

ACROSS THE GROSSGLOCKNER PASS

This is the excursion over one of the longest and most spectacular highways through the Alps, the Grossglockner High Alpine Highway, which is a true engineering marvel. To explore this region from Salzburg head south on the A10 highway and take Route 311 to enter the valley to Zell am See. Go south over the Grossglockner Highway to Heiligenblut. (The trip can be done by car or bus.) If the Grossglockner road is closed due to weather conditions, you must drive west of Zell am See to Mittersill toward Lienz via the 5-km (3-mile) Felbertauern toll tunnel (€11 one-way) under the Tauern mountains. Exiting the tunnel, continue on Route 107 to Heiligenblut.

ZELL AM SEE

108 km (67 miles) southwest of Salzburg.

This lovely lakeside town got its name from the monks' cells of a monastery founded here in about 790. It has excellent skiing and is busy throughout the winter. But it is now also one of Austria's most popular summer destinations, with an idyllic setting that's hard to beat, and the town can get very crowded in the peak season of July and August. If you want to stay in the town center, booking well ahead of time is strongly advised.

Interestingly, Zell am See has also become one of Europe's top vacation destinations for people from the Middle East, and some Middle Eastern airlines have heavily increased their services into Vienna to meet this demand. The town faced considerable controversy after a booklet was issued by the city authorities in early summer 2014 offering "cultural advice" to visitors—it pointed out that Austrian shopkeepers don't expect customers to haggle over prices, and that eating on the floor in hotel rooms is very much a no-no. Visitors were advised not to wear burkas and to "adopt the Austrian mentality." It added: "Here the colour black symbolises mourning, and is rarely worn in daily life. In our culture, we are accustomed to look into the smiling face of the person opposite us in order to gain a first impression and establish mutual trust." The town's mayor claimed that the number of women wearing a full burka has been causing friction with locals. Some hotels criticize the booklet, saying it unfairly stigmatizes Arab visitors, while many see the matter as a fascinating example of how the spread of global tourism can bring interesting cultural interaction.

GETTING HERE AND AROUND
Enter the Pongau valley from the A10 highway from Salzburg by taking Exit 47 Pongau/Bischofshofen to merge onto Route B311, Bruckner Bundesstrasse.

ESSENTIALS
Tourist Information Zell am See ⌗ *Brucker Bundesstrasse 1A* ☎ *06542/770* ⊕ *www.zellamsee-kaprun.com.*

EXPLORING

Pinzgauer Railroad. This romantic narrow-gauge train winds its way under steam power on a two-hour trip through the Pinzgau, following the Salzach River valley westward 54 km (34 miles) to Krimml. Nearby are the famous Krimmler waterfalls, with a 396-meter (1,300-foot) drop, which you can see from an observation platform or explore close at hand if you don't mind a steep hike. Be sure to take a raincoat and sneakers. A one-day ticket is included with a SalzburgerLand Card. ☎ *06542/40600* 🌐 *www.pinzgauer-lokalbahn.info* 🎫 *Round-trip €18.20.*

St. Hippolyt Pfarrkirche (*parish church*). Unusually fine statues of St. George and St. Florian can be found on the west wall of the splendid Romanesque St. Hippolyt Pfarrkirche, built in 1217. The tower was added about two centuries later, and the church itself was beautifully renovated in 1975. ✉ *Stadtplatz.*

Schloss Rosenberg. In the town center, visit the very handsome 16th-century Schloss Rosenberg, which now houses the Rathaus (town hall). ✉ *Brucker Bundestrasse 2.*

Schmittenhöhe. A cable car will take you virtually from the center of Zell am See up to the Schmittenhöhe, at 1,967 meters (6,453 feet), for a far-reaching panorama that takes in the peaks of the Glockner and Tauern granite ranges to the south and west and the very different limestone ranges to the north. You can have lunch at the Berghotel at the top. Four other cable-car trips are available up this mountain, part of the ski lift system in the winter but open in the summer for walkers and mountain bikers.

Thumersbach. Several locations offer up stunning vistas of the town and its environs. On ground level, take a boat ride to the village of Thumersbach, on the opposite shore, for a wonderful reflected view of Zell am See.

Vogtturm. This ancient tower, built in the 11th century, now houses a museum of folklore, with old costumes and artifacts. ✉ *Stadtplatz* ☎ *0664/586–2706* 🎫 *€3.30* 🕒 *May–Oct., Mon., Wed., and Fri. 1:30–5:30.*

Votter's Fahrzeugmuseum (*Votter's Vehicle Museum*). Beautiful (and not so beautiful) cars and motorcycles from the 1950s, '60s, and '70s are on display here, including the remarkable one-person Messerschmitt Bubble Car and other, dare we say more appealing, automobiles. Altogether, the museum has more than 170 exhibits. ✉ *Schlossstrasse 32, Kaprun* ☎ *0699/1717–1342* 🌐 *www.oldtimer-museum.at* 🎫 *€8* 🕒 *Daily 10–6.*

9

WHERE TO EAT

$$ AUSTRIAN 🍴 **Restaurant Zum Hirschen.** In the hotel of the same name, the restaurant is in a charming typically Austrian stube—all wood-paneled and cozy—and serves regional specialties and international cuisine. It has been awarded 13 Gault Millau points for menu selections such as pork fillet in an herb and bacon crust, and braised veal with a cream sauce and small dumplings. They offer a daily three-course lunch menu for €22.50. It's popular with the locals, which makes for a good atmosphere. [$] *Average main: €14* ✉ *Dreifaltigkeitsstrasse 1* ☎ *06542/774–0* 🌐 *www.hotel-zum-hirschen.at.*

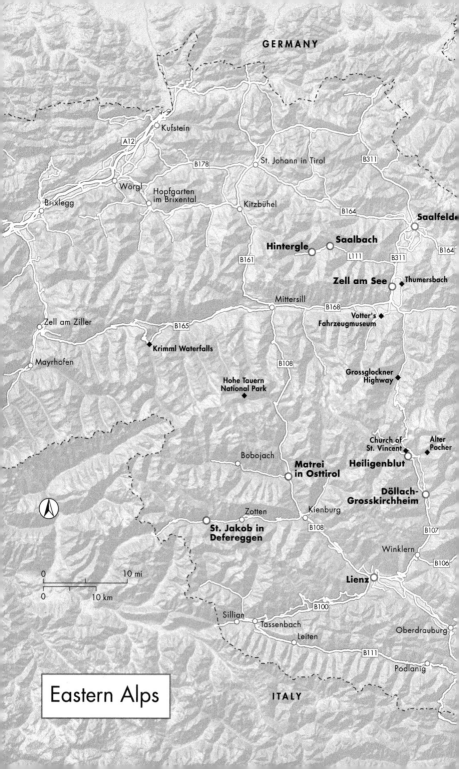

Eastern Alps

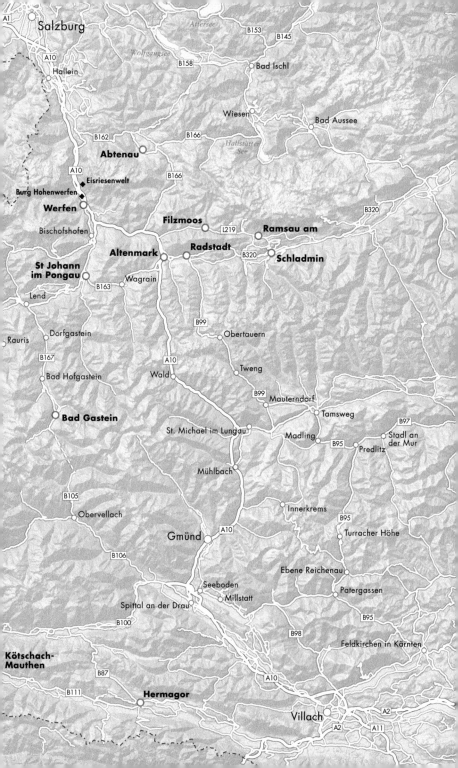

$$ AUSTRIAN 🍴 **Steinerwirt1493.** As the name suggests, the Steinerwirt dates back almost as far as Columbus's discovery of the New World. It is family run, and its newest generation of owners and staff have brought modernity to the cuisine while maintaining the original Alpine flair. The authentic atmosphere makes the place a favorite for locals and travelers alike. The roast pork served with bread dumplings and red cabbage and the *tafelspitz* (slow cooked beef with creamed spinach and a horseradish and chive sauce) are excellent. Ask for wine recommendations to make your experience complete—particular thought has been given to selecting the most interesting wines from Austria. [$] *Average main: €13* ✉ *Dreifaltigkeitsgasse 2* ☎ *06542/72502* 🌐 *www.steinerwirt.com.*

WHERE TO STAY

$$$ HOTEL FAMILY 🏨 **Grand Hotel Zell am See.** In the style of the great turn-of-the-century resort hotels, this palatial lake house is the best-located address in Zell am See, with direct beach access and wonderful lake views. **Pros:** great location; big standard rooms; kids' club for ages 3–10 and other kid-friendly services. **Cons:** some rooms face noisy railroad; rooms with a view are more expensive. [$] *Rooms from: €220* ✉ *Esplanade 4–6* ☎ *06542/788* 🌐 *www.grandhotel-zellamsee.at* 🛏 *116 rooms, 17 suites* 🍽 *Multiple meal plans.*

$$$$ HOTEL Fodor's Choice ★ 🏨 **Salzburgerhof.** The well-located five-star hotel, styled like an oversize chalet, stands out with its lovely courtyard garden, a natural swimming pool, and the best spa in the area. **Pros:** the region's best place to stay; top-notch staff; big standard rooms; free Wi-Fi. **Cons:** rooms at rear of building are near railroad tracks; standard rooms do not face garden. [$] *Rooms from: €310* ✉ *Auerspergstrasse 11* ☎ *06542/7650* 🌐 *www.salzburgerhof.at* 🛏 *35 rooms, 35 suites* 🕒 *Closed Nov.* 🍽 *All meals.*

$$$ B&B/INN 🏨 **Schloss Prielau.** Attentive host Annette Mayer takes care of her guests in this fairy-tale castle, with its turreted towers and striped shutters. **Pros:** eye-popping architecture; very personal feeling; private lake beach is only five minutes' walk. **Cons:** 20-minute walk to town; no elevator; no Internet access in rooms. [$] *Rooms from: €180* ✉ *Hofmannsthalstrasse 12* ☎ *06542/729–110* 🌐 *www.schloss-prielau.at* 🛏 *7 rooms, 2 suites* 🕒 *Closed Nov.* 🍽 *Breakfast.*

$$ HOTEL 🏨 **Steinerwirt1493.** Redesigned by Austrian architects in a minimalistic and modern style that distances itself from the local Alpine kitsch, this centrally located boutique hotel has a lot to offer. **Pros:** cultural programs; in the center of Zell am See; DVD player in room. **Cons:** no swimming pool. [$] *Rooms from: €138* ✉ *Dreifaltigkeitsgasse 2* ☎ *06542/72502* 🌐 *www.steinerwirt.com* 🛏 *26 rooms, 2 suites* 🕒 *Closed mid-Nov.–mid-Dec. and mid-Mar.–mid-June* 🍽 *Multiple meal plans.*

NIGHTLIFE

The emphasis in Zell is more on drinking than on dancing, but the scene does change periodically.

B17. One of the "in" places, this bar near the lake has an appropriate aircraft hangar atmosphere (the B17 was an aircraft, otherwise known as the Flying Fortress). Good drinks selection, good atmosphere, and good (mostly) classic rock. ✉ *Salzmannstrasse 2, Zell am See* ☎ *06542/47424.*

Crazy Daisy. This restaurant-café and dance pub is in the center of town. It has legendary status among skiers and boarders, and a great summertime scene on the terrace, plus regular live music. ⊠ *Salzmannstrasse 8* ☎ *06542/725260* ⊕ *crazy-daisy.at.*

SPORTS AND THE OUTDOORS
BICYCLING
The area around Zell am See is ideal for bicycling. From April to October, bike tours run from south of Zell am See up to St. Johann and Salzburg via the Tauern cycle route.

Adventure Service. Mountain-bike tours, Segway tours, and other outdoor activities are available. ⊠ *Steinergasse 5–7* ☎ *06542/73525* ⊕ *www.adventureservice.at.*

Sport Achleitner. If you left your wheels at home, you can rent some here for €12 per day for a city bike or €20 for a mountain bike. Renting by the week is more economical. ⊠ *Postplatz 2* ☎ *06542/73581* ⊕ *www. sport-achleitner.at.*

FISHING
The lake's tranquil waters offer fine fishing, and many hotels in the area have packages for avid anglers.

Strandbad. Boats are for hire at the Strandbad and other lakeside locations.

SKIING
Zell am See-Kaprun. There's good skiing on the slopes immediately above the town. Most of the runs are intermediate, but there are good areas for beginners too, and experts will find some steepish, sweeping runs on which to have fun if not be truly tested. Towering over Zell am See, the Schmittenhöhe has tree-lined runs that will feel familiar to Colorado and New England skiers. Kitzsteinhorn mountain, which rises to 10,499 feet above Kaprun, offers year-round glacier skiing and was the first glacier ski area in Austria. Together these mountains offer 57 lifts, with 130 km (80 miles) of prepared slopes. In addition, there are more than 200 km (124 miles) of cross-country trails and eight ski schools. ☎ *06542/770 tourist office* ⊕ *www.zellamsee-kaprun.com/winter.*

WATER SPORTS
Boating—from paddle-boating to sailing—and swimming are excellent on the uncrowded Zeller See.

Wasserskischule Thumersbach. Powerboats are restricted on many Austrian lakes, but there is this waterskiing school at Thumersbach. ⊠ *Strandbad, Lindenallee, Thumersbach* ☎ *0664/2068506.*

GROSSGLOCKNER HIGHWAY

The Grossglockner Highway is 46 km (29 miles) long.

One of the best-known roads in the Alps, the Hochalpenstrasse—rising to more than 2,438 meters (8,000 feet) and negotiating 36 hairpin bends, with spectacular views the whole way—leads you deep into the Hohe Tauern National Park. The highway is generally open from May through November, but only during daylight hours. There's a toll of €34.

GETTING HERE AND AROUND

From Zell am See head south toward Bruck an der Grossglocknerstrasse, and continue on the B107. After the toll station in Ferleitern on the north side of the Grossglockner peak, the highway begins its many hairpin turns and continues to Heiligenblut.

ESSENTIALS

Tourist Information Grossglockner Hochalpenstrasse ⊠ *Rainerstrasse 2, Salzburg* ☎ *0662/873673–0* ⊕ *www.grossglockner.at.*

EXPLORING

Grossglockner   Hochalpenstrasse (*Grossglockner High Alpine Highway*). This is the excursion over the longest and most spectacular highway through the Alps. The

> ### HERCULES WAS HERE
>
> Before the Grossglocknerstrasse was built, there had been no passage anywhere between the Brenner Pass and the Radstädter Tauern Pass (more than 160 km [100 miles] apart) leading over these mountains, nor was it on record that there had ever before been a regularly used route across the barrier at this point. Yet when the engineers who built the High Alpine Highway were blasting for the Hochtor tunnel, they found, deep in the bowels of a mountain, a Roman statuette of, appropriately, Hercules.

road was completed in 1935, after five years of labor by 3,200 workers. From Heiligenblut the climb begins up the Carinthian side of the Grossglockner Mountain. The peak itself—at 3,801 (12,470 feet) the highest point in Austria—is to the west. The Grossglocknerstrasse twists and turns as it struggles to the 2,551-meter (8,370-foot) Hochtor, the highest point on the through road and the border between Carinthia and Salzburg Province.

A side trip on the Edelweiss-Strasse leads to the scenic vantage point at the **Edelweissspitze**. It's an unbelievable view out over East Tyrol, Carinthia, and Salzburg, including 19 glaciers and 37 peaks rising above the 2,926-meter (9,600-foot_ mark. The rare white edelweiss—the von Trapps sang its praises in *The Sound of Music*—grows here. Though the species is protected, don't worry about the plants you get as souvenirs; they are cultivated for this purpose. ■TIP➡ **It is strictly forbidden to pick a wild edelweiss (or several other plant species) should you happen to come across one.**

You can get somewhat closer to Grossglockner peak than the main road takes you by following the highly scenic but steep Gletscherstrasse westward up to the Gletscherbahn on the Franz-Josef-Plateau, where you'll be rewarded with absolutely breathtaking views of the Grossglockner peak and surrounding Alps, of the vast glacier in the valley below, and, on a clear day, even into Italy. ☎ *0662/873673 road information* ⊕ *www.grossglockner.at* 🖃 *€29 per vehicle for a one-day pass, €45 per vehicle for 30-day pass* ☉ *Early May–late Oct., 6 am–7:30 pm.*

Hohe Tauern National Park. This is one of the most varied and unspoiled landscapes on the planet—high Alpine meadows, deep evergreen woods, endless spiraling rock cliffs, and glacial ice fields—and at 1,786 square km (690 square miles) it's the largest national park of central Europe. It touches on three provinces (Salzburg, Carinthia, and Tyrol) and includes the Grossglockner mountain group. The Grossglockner Hochalpenstrasse passes through the park. The hardier traveler may want to spend a few days hiking and lodging at any one of several refuges, where you may occasionally be treated to very rustic, homemade victuals (cheeses and hams). ⊕ *www.hohetauern.at.*

HEILIGENBLUT

Fodor'sChoice *54 km (34 miles) south of Zell am See.*

★ One of the most photographed places in the country, Heiligenblut remains one of Austria's most picturesque Alpine villages. With the majestic Grossglockner—Austria's highest mountain—for a backdrop, the town cradles the pilgrimage church of St. Vincent. Nowhere else does a steeple seem to find such affirmation amid soaring peaks. Some say the best time to experience this little slice of Alpine nirvana is after a leisurely dinner at one of the many Gasthöfs, gazing out at the starry firmament over the Hohe Tauern range. Others relish standing around an early morning fire used by hikers setting out to conquer the mighty foothills of the Grossglockner peaks. It's the famed mountain-climbing school and climbing and skiing possibilities (there are 40 peaks higher than 3,048 meters [10,000 feet] here) that draw flocks of all-out active types.

GETTING HERE AND AROUND

You can get to Heiligenblut from Zell am See via the Grossglockner pass or via Lienz. In winter, buses run from Heiligenblut to the nearby ski areas.

ESSENTIALS

Tourist Information Heiligenblut ⊠ *Hof 4* ☎ *04824/2001* ⊕ *www.heiligenblut.at.*

EXPLORING

OFF THE
BEATEN
PATH

Alter Pocher. This 16th-century-style *Goldgräberdorf* (gold-mining town) was built upon historic gold mines in the Fleiss valley. The Hohe Tauern was considered one of the most important gold-mining regions of its day, and gold was mined near Heiligenblut from the 14th century until the turn of the 20th century. Many caves were created through grueling labor by thousands of miners over this period, under the most arduous conditions (of course, the owners of the mines themselves lived comfortable and rich lives). Alter Pocher, 10 minutes from Heiligenblut and more than 1,800 meters (5,906 feet) above sea level, showcases the lives of the miners who dug for gold here for so many centuries; the *freilichtmuseum* (open-air museum) gives an insight into their living conditions.

Gold panning. If you get struck by gold fever, you can try panning for gold in the Fleiss stream. From mid-June through September, you can buy a ticket for an excursion in the town at the Tourist Office. It's the only gold mining village in the Alps and has been rebuilt to its original state. The price includes a visit to the museum, a guided tour and the necessary equipment, and—if you're lucky enough to pan a small nugget—a permit to take home your finds. ☎ *04824/24655* ⊕ *www. heiligenblut.at* ☜*€12* ☾ *June–Sept., daily 10–5 (weather permitting).*

9

Church of St. Vincent. According to local legend, St. Briccius, after obtaining a vial of the blood of Jesus, was buried by an avalanche, but when his body was recovered the tiny vial was miraculously found hidden within one of the saint's open wounds. The town gets its name, Heiligenblut (Holy Blood), from this miraculous event. Today the relic is housed in the Sakramenthäuschen, the chapel of this small but beautiful Gothic church. Completed in 1490 after more than a century of construction under the toughest conditions, the church is marked by its soaring belfry tower. Sublimely, the sharply pointed spire finds an impressive echo in the conical peak of the Grossglockner. St. Vincent's contains a beautifully carved late-Gothic double altar nearly 36 feet high, and the Coronation of Mary is depicted in the altar wings, richly carved by Wolfgang Hasslinger in 1520. The region's most important altarpiece, it imparts a feeling of quiet power in this spare, high church. The church also has a noble crypt and graveyard, the latter sheltering graves of those lost in climbing the surrounding mountains. ☎ *04824/2700.*

WHERE TO STAY

$$$ B&B/INN 🏨 **Chalet-Hotel Senger.** A peaceful location and great views makes this farmhouse chalet a great choice. **Pros:** romantic feel; great place for honeymooners. **Cons:** 10-minute walk to town. [$] *Rooms from: €212* ✉ *Hof 23* ☎ *04824/2215* 🌐 *www.romantic.at* 🛏 *9 rooms, 10 suites* 🕒 *Closed 1 wk after Easter–June and Oct.–mid-Dec.* 🍴 *Multiple meal plans.*

$$$ HOTEL FAMILY 🏨 **Glocknerhof.** This wooden chalet in the center of the village offers old-fashioned charm and modern amenities. **Pros:** pleasant atmosphere; friendly staff; many extras included in the price; kids' activities and services include on-staff nanny; eco-friendly. **Cons:** some rooms on the small side. [$] *Rooms from: €214* ✉ *Hof 6* ☎ *04824/2244* 🌐 *www.glocknerhof.info* 🛏 *50 rooms* 🕒 *Closed May–mid-June, Oct., and Nov.* 🍴 *Multiple meal plans.*

$$$ HOTEL 🏨 **Hotel Lärchenhof.** This charming hotel is a true *panoramagasthof*—a guesthouse with spectacular views. **Pros:** good spa; gourmet meals; quiet location. **Cons:** some double rooms are on the small side. [$] *Rooms from: €230* ✉ *Hof 70* ☎ *04824/2262* 🌐 *www.ski-heiligenblut.at* 🛏 *23 rooms* 🍴 *Multiple meal plans.*

$$$ HOTEL FAMILY 🏨 **Hunguest Hotel Heiligenblut.** This small family-friendly hotel, a short distance from the town center, runs its own kindergarten on weekdays, where you can leave the kids while you hit the slopes. **Pros:** perfect for families; lots of activities; mountain views. **Cons:** not a place for peace and quiet; sauna is small; views from the rooms vary. [$] *Rooms from: €172* ✉ *Winkl 46* ☎ *04824/4111* 🌐 *www.hotel-heiligenblut.at/* 🛏 *97 rooms, 17 suites* 🕒 *Closed Easter–May and Oct.–Dec.* 🍴 *Multiple meal plans.*

SPORTS AND THE OUTDOORS

HIKING AND MOUNTAIN CLIMBING

This is a hiker's El Dorado during summertime, with more than 240 km (150 miles) of marked pathways and trails in all directions. There are relatively easy hikes to the Naturlehrweg Gössnitzfall-Kachlmoor (1½ hours), Wirtsbauer-Alm (two hours), and the Jungfernsprung (one hour), which ends atop a 152-meter (500-foot) cliff above the Mölltal.

Guided Tours. Enjoyable group or private guided tours are run by the national park service. These could include walks to the foot of the Grossglockner to see surefooted ibex in their natural habitat jumping about on seemingly sheer rock walls; a hike to the Pasterze Glacier, the largest in Austria; or the recently opened walk to the Mollschlucht gorge, much of it a *via ferrata* route—not for the faint-hearted. ☎ *04824/2700 national park programs office* ✉ *From €8 for short group tour; from €130 per person for private one- to three-day tours.*

Heiligenblut Climbing Park. The park has a high-rope course, climbing wall, children's playground, and restaurant. The new via ferrata has two routes of varying levels of difficulty, which take you along spectacular waterfalls and cliffs. The high-rope course is at the Gasthof Sonnblick, where the Brandstatter family can give information and make bookings. ✉ *Hof 21* ☎ *04824/21310* ⊕ *www.sonnblick-heiligenblut.at* ✉ *€20* ⊙ *May–Sept., 10–4.*

MOUNTAIN SPAS AND ALPINE RAMBLES

Glaciers, hot springs, luxurious hotels, and tranquil lakes are the enticing combinations this Austrian region serves up superlatively. Gold and silver mined from the mountains were the source of many local fortunes; today glittering gold jewelry finds many buyers in the shops of Bad Gastein's Kaiser Wilhelm Promenade. To set off on this trip, head south from Salzburg on the A10 and take the Bischofshofen exit toward St. Johann im Pongau, which gets you to Route 311 and, 17 km (11 miles) later, the Route 167 junction. From Zell am See, head east on Route 311 to pass Bruck, continue through Taxenbach to Lend, and turn south at the intersection of Route 167.

BAD GASTEIN

54 km (34 miles) southeast of Zell am See.

Though it traces its roots all the way back to the 15th century, this resort, one of Europe's leading spas, gained renown only in the 19th century, when VIPs from emperors on down to impecunious philosophers flocked to the area to "take the cure." Today Bad Gastein retains much of its allure. The stunning setting—a mountain torrent, the Gasteiner Ache, rushes through the town—adds to the attraction. Much of the town has a solid though timeworn elegance, and some of the aging buildings are in need of a spruce-up. But the old buildings still dominate the townscape, giving it a wonderful feeling of substance and history. The baths themselves, however, are state-of-the-art, as evidenced by the massive **Felsentherme Gastein** and the nearby **Thermalkurhaus.**

A special tradition in Bad Gastein is the old pagan *Perchtenlaufen* processions in January of every fourth year (the next is scheduled for 2018): people wearing huge and intimidating masks and making lots of noise chase the winter away, bringing good blessings for the new year. However, it can be an excuse for excessive drinking by some costume-wearing youths, who may cross the line to unruliness.

9

GETTING HERE AND AROUND

Bad Gastein is serviced by many rail lines, with many expresses running from Salzburg and Klagenfurt. You can also reach the town by bus from Salzburg.

ESSENTIALS

Tourist Information Bad Gastein Tourist Office ⊠ *Tauernplatz 1* ☎ *06432/3393-114* ⊕ *www.gastein.com.*

WHERE TO EAT

$ ✕ **Bellevue Alm.** Idyllically set on the east side of the Stubnerkogel,
AUSTRIAN directly on the ski slope, this Alpine hut is one of the oldest in Europe,
Fodor's Choice remarkably well preserved, with wooden interiors and a huge open
★ fire. Wooden parlors and a big terrace, with a spectacular view over Bad Gastein, invite visitors in for a substantial meal, followed by a couple of drinks after a hike or long skiing day. Try the roasted *Hörnchen* (a kind of pasta) with liverwurst hash and endive potato salad, or one of the desserts, such as *Kaiserschmarrn* (chopped up pancakes served with fruit compote, usually apple or plum) or *Schwarzbeernocken* (blackberry or blueberry dumplings). You'll need a car or taxi to get here; in winter you can ski in or take the restaurant's own chair lift. ■ TIP→ **Reservations are highly recommended during winter, when it's a popular après-ski spot.** For the complete Alpine experience, they also have 12 nice rooms. $ *Average main: €11* ⊠ *Bellevue-Alm-Weg 6* ☎ *06434/3881* ⊕ *www.bellevue-alm.com* ⊟ *No credit cards* ☉ *Closed Nov.*

$ ✕ **Jägerhäusl.** With green wood paneling and a red timber ceiling, the
AUSTRIAN restaurant is strangely stylish. Right in the old-town center, it has a garden and cozy wooden parlors. Traditional Austrian fare is its forte, but pizza is on the menu too. Try the *Jägerhauspfandl* (grilled pork tenderloin and mushroom cream sauce with roast potatoes) or pumpkin-, game-, or duck-based seasonal specialties. $ *Average main: €11* ⊠ *Kaiser-Franz-Josef-Str. 9* ☎ *06434/20254* ☉ *Closed Nov.*

WHERE TO STAY

$$ ⬚ **Alpenblick.** Perched high above the town, the Alpenblick has a sweep-
HOTEL ing view of the valley, and is an ideal base for skiers, hikers, and anyone who wants a quiet stay away from the town center. **Pros:** free transportation to hotel; laid-back vibe; family owned. **Cons:** 15-minute walk to town and a bit steep on your way back; not a great bar. $ *Rooms from: €120* ⊠ *Kötschachtalerstrasse 17* ☎ *06434/20620* ⊕ *www.alpenblick-gastein.at* ↜ *40 rooms* ☉ *Closed Nov.–mid-Dec.* ⑩ *Multiple meal plans.*

$$$ ⬚ **Haus Hirt Alpine Spa Hotel.** This stylish Alpine lodge, on a hillside
HOTEL about a half mile from the town center, has good amenities for families,
FAMILY spectacular views, and a style that cleverly combines Alpine traditional with contemporary-chic. **Pros:** complimentary tea and apples; organic breakfast buffet; free transportation. **Cons:** spa and pool are small and can get packed during winter, a 20-minute walk to town. $ *Rooms from: €240* ⊠ *Kaiserhofstraße 14* ☎ *06434/2797* ⊕ *www.haus-hirt.com* ↜ *32 rooms, 9 suites* ☉ *Closed Nov.* ⑩ *Multiple meal plans.*

$$$ ⬚ **Hotel Miramonte.** A somewhat retro-style hotel, with original 1950s
HOTEL and '60s elements, is a chic retreat that caters well to the sophisticated

traveler, from mostly spacious bedrooms with balconies to high-quality meals. **Pros:** big sundeck; friendly staff; special dietary requirements (vegetarian and vegan) available upon request. **Cons:** no swimming pool; limited parking; 15-minute walk to center of Bad Gastein. $ *Rooms from: €182* ✉ *Reitlpromenade 3* ☎ *06434/2577* 🌐 *www.hotelmiramonte.com* 🛏 *36 rooms* 🕒 *Closed Nov.* 🍴 *Multiple meal plans.*

$$$ HOTEL FAMILY 🏨 **Hoteldorf Grüner Baum.** Well away from the center of town, in a remote and peaceful little "secret" valley, the Grüner Baum feels like a tiny village in itself, made up of several buildings, amid meadows and woodlands. **Pros:** great deals in summer; big standard rooms; children 14 and under stay free (including meals) in parents' room. **Cons:** gets busy during holiday season; must go outside to get to main building. $ *Rooms from: €266* ✉ *Kötschachtal* ☎ *06434/2516–0* 🌐 *www.hoteldorf.com* 🛏 *60 rooms, 20 suites* 🕒 *Closed Nov.* 🍴 *Multiple meal plans.*

NIGHTLIFE

Grand Hotel de l'Europe casino. Baccarat, blackjack, roulette, and slot machines are all available at the casino. A passport is required. ✉ *Kaiser-Franz-Josef-Strasse 14* ☎ *06434/2465* 🕒 *Mid-July–Sept. and Dec. 25–Mar., daily 7 pm–3 am.*

SPORTS AND THE OUTDOORS

Bad Gastein will keep guests entertained with all sorts of events from snowboarding competitions to llama trekking (popular with families). You will not be bored.

HIKING

Stubnerkogel Cable Car. Take the Stubnerkogel gondola lift 2.2 km (1½ miles) above sea level, where spectacular views over the Gastein Valley will take your breath away. A suspension bridge will make you go weak in the knees, and the modern Panorama platform guarantees a view of the Grossglockner. In summer, many hikes are possible from here, while in winter the cable car is used to access the ski slopes. One round-trip is included with the SalzburgerLand Card. ☎ *06434/232–2415* 🎫 *€21 round-trip.*

SKIING

Although not as well known to outsiders as other resorts, the Gastein Valley is very popular with Austrians. There are a number of ski areas here, with a free shuttle bus running between them. The main access to the Bad Gastein area is by the Stubnerkogelbahn gondola and it's possible to link with the Bad Hofgastein sector at Angertal. Sportgastein, quite exposed and with a remote feel, and Graukogel, with some protected wooded runs, are both above Bad Gastein and are not linked with any of the other sectors. Graukogel is delightful and all too often foolishly ignored by visitors—it's a great place for family skiing, with super views and a good mountain restaurant. Farther down the valley is the Dorfgastein area, which links with Grossarl on the far side of the Kreuzkogel. All in all, the valley has good and varied skiing for all levels, including a wealth of intermediate runs, but there are also a few challenges to be found. There are 43 ski lifts, and all the sectors have decent rental shops. You can get information on skiing conditions in all the areas from the tourist office.

ST. JOHANN IM PONGAU

43 km (27 miles) north of Bad Gastein.

St. Johann has developed into a full-fledged year-round resort, with its own small local ski area and a more extensive ski network starting 4 km (2½ miles) away. The area is favored by cross-country and intermediate-level downhill skiers, as the gentle slopes provide a decent variety of runs.

GETTING HERE AND AROUND

St. Johann im Pongau is on Route B311 east of Zell am See or south of Salzburg, taking Exit 47 from the A10.

ESSENTIALS

Tourist Information **St. Johann im Pongau** ✉ *Ing. Ludwig Pech Strasse 1* ☎ *06412/6036* 🌐 *www.sanktjohann.com.*

EXPLORING

Liechtensteinklamm. Traveling from Bad Gastein along Route 311, turn east toward Schwarzach in Pongau, where the road heads north, to find, between Schwarzach and St. Johann, the Liechtensteinklamm, the deepest (305 meters [1,000 feet]), narrowest (3.8 meters [12½ feet]), and most spectacular gorge in the Eastern Alps. At its far end is a 200-foot waterfall. A tour on a wooden walkway criss-crossing the gorge takes about one hour. Admission is included with SalzburgerLand Card. The gorge may be closed in extreme weather conditions. ☎ *06412/6036* 🌐 *www.liechtensteinklamm.at* 🎟 *€4.50* ⏲ *Early May–Sept., daily 8–6; Oct., daily 9–4.*

Perchtenlauf. Every four years during the first week of January, the people of St. Johann, like the Bad Gasteiners, celebrate Perchtenlauf, which can be poetically translated to mean "away with winter's ghost." Taking to the streets, they ring huge cowbells and wear weird masks and costumes to drive away evil spirits. Overenthusiastic—meaning inebriated—participants can also drive away some spectators, who find their antics a little intimidating. St. Johann is on the rail network connecting Munich, Klagenfurt, and Salzburg.

Pongau Domkirche (*Cathedral*). The huge, twin-spired *Pfarrkirche* (parish church), built in 1861 in neo-Gothic style, is known locally as the Pongau Domkirche—a mammoth structure that rises quite majestically out of the townscape.

WHERE TO STAY

$$$ HOTEL FAMILY 🏨 **Sporthotel Alpenland.** Expansive and spacious, this hotel is centrally located. **Pros:** good food; plenty for the children to do. **Cons:** it can feel too busy when tour groups are in. [$] *Rooms from: €182* ✉ *Hans-Kappacher-Strasse 7–9* ☎ *06412/7021–0* 🌐 *www.alpenland-sporthotels.com* 🛏 *137 rooms* 🍴 *Multiple meal plans.*

SPORTS AND THE OUTDOORS

SKIING

A huge conglomerate of 25 ski villages has joined together under the Ski Amade marketing umbrella so that on one lift pass skiers and snowboarders have access to more than 270 lifts and 860 km (535 miles) of runs. Ski Amade embraces the Salzburger Sportwelt region, Schladming-Dachstein, the Gastein Valley, the Grossarl Valley and Hochkonig. St. Johann in Pongau remains the ski capital of the region called Salzburger Sportwelt, which showcases 100 lifts and more than 350 km (217 miles) of well-groomed slopes. St. Johann has 14 ski lifts, including several cable cars. But most of the villages are joined only for promotion purposes and retain their individuality and separate identities.

Tourismusverband St. Johann. This is a good contact for information on skiing in the area. ✉ *Hauptplatz, St. Johann, Tyrol* ☎ *06412/6036* 🌐 *www.sanktjohann.com.*

FILZMOOS

36 km (22 miles) east of St. Johann im Pongau.

One of the most romantic villages in Austria, Filzmoos is still something of a well-kept secret. Though skiing in the nearby Dachstein mountains is excellent, the relatively inexpensive winter resort (which is part of the Salzburger Sportwelt ski area) has yet to be fully discovered by foreign tourists. During the summer months meandering mountain streams and myriad lakes attract anglers eager for trout, while hikers come to challenge the craggy peaks.

Filzmoos calls itself a "balloon village," not only for the International Hot Air Balloon Week every January, but because hot-air balloon trips are a popular attraction for visitors and a great way to see the spectacular region.

GETTING HERE AND AROUND

Head south on the A10 highway and take Exit 60-Eben onto Filzmooserstrasse-L219.

ESSENTIALS

Tourist Information Filzmoos ✉ *Filzmoos 50* ☎ *06453/8235* 🌐 *www.filzmoos.at.*

WHERE TO EAT AND STAY

$$$$ AUSTRIAN Fodor's Choice ★ 🍴 **Hubertus.** Every last detail, from romantic furnishings to the doting service, is done to perfection here, making this restaurant the best in the area. Chef Johanna Maier's way with trout is exquisite, but don't overlook the game, roast poultry, or veal sweetbreads. Finish with *topfenknödel* (cream cheese dumpling), a house specialty. Frau Maier offers cooking courses several times each month—call for dates. The restaurant is within the equally plush and inviting hotel of the same name. [$] *Average main: €25* ✉ *Am Dorfplatz 1* ☎ *06453/8204* 🌐 *www.johannamaier.at* ✍ *Reservations essential* ⏲ *Closed mid-Apr.–mid-May and mid-Oct.–mid-Dec. No lunch.*

$$ HOTEL 🏨 **Alpenkrone.** From the balconies of this hotel above the town center you'll have a great view of the surrounding mountains. **Pros:** great value; friendly staff; wonderful location; lovely indoor pool. **Cons:** steep climb from town. [$] *Rooms from: €132* ✉ *Filzmoos 133* ☎ *06453/8280–0* 🌐 *www.alpenkrone.com* 🛏 *58 rooms* ⏲ *Closed Easter–mid-May and mid-Oct.–mid-Dec.* 🍽 *Multiple meal plans.*

9

EN
ROUTE

Salzburger Dolomitenstrasse (*Salzburg Dolomites Highway*). From Filzmoos, rejoin Route 99/E14 again at Eben im Pongau. Here you can take the A10 autobahn north to Salzburg if you're in a hurry. But if you have time for more majestic scenery and an interesting detour, continue about 4 km (2½ miles) on Route 99/E14, and turn north on Route 166, the Salzburger Dolomitenstrasse, for a 43-km (27-mile) swing around the Tennen mountains. ■TIP➜ Be careful, though, to catch the left turn onto Route 162 at Lindenthal; it will be marked to Golling. Head for Abtenau.

WERFEN

Fodor's Choice
★

17 km (10 miles) north from St. Johann im Pongau.

The small size of Werfen, adorned with 16th-century buildings and a lovely Baroque church, belies its importance, for it's the base for exploring three extraordinary attractions: the largest and most fabulous ice caverns in the world; one of Austria's most spectacular castles; and a four-star culinary delight, Obauer. These riches place Werfen on a par with many larger and more highly touted Austrian cities.

GETTING HERE AND AROUND
Werfen is close to the A10 highway; take Exit 43 and follow the signs to the town. Many trains from Salzburg stop here.

ESSENTIALS
Tourist Information **Werfen** ⊠ *Markt 24* ☎ *06468/5388* ⊕ *www.werfen.at.*

EXPLORING
Burg Hohenwerfen. From miles away you can see Burg Hohenwerfen, one of the most formidable fortresses of Europe (it was never taken in battle), which dates from 1077. Though fires, reconstructions, and renovations have altered the appearance of the imposing fortress, it still maintains its medieval grandeur. Hewn out of the rock on which it stands, the castle was called by Maximilian I a "plume of heraldry radiant against the sky." Inside, it has black-timber-beamed state rooms and an enormous frescoed Knights' Hall. It even has a torture chamber. Eagles, falcons, and other birds of prey swoop dramatically above the castle grounds, adding considerably to the medieval feel. In a varied history, it has been used as a prison and a police training center. Now the castle harbors Austria's first museum of falconry, and the birds of prey are rigorously trained. Special shows with music, falconry, and performers in period costume are held at least twice a month; call ahead for dates and times. ⊠ *Burgstrasse* ☎ *06468/7603* ⊕ *www.salzburg-burgen. at* 🎫 *€10.50, including tour and birds-of-prey performance; €3.50 for lift* ☉ *Apr., Tues.–Sun. 9:30–4; May–July 22 and Aug. 18–Sept., daily 9–5; July 23–Aug. 17, daily 9–6; Oct.–Nov., daily 9:30–4. Birds-of-prey performance: Apr.–July 22 and Aug. 18–Nov., daily 4, 11:15, and 3:15; July 23–Aug. 17, 11:15, 2:15, and 4:30.*

OFF THE
BEATEN
PATH

Eisriesenwelt (*Ice Caves*). The "World of the Ice Giants," houses the largest known complex of ice caves, domes, galleries, and halls in Europe. It extends for some 42 km (26 miles) and contains a fantastic collection of frozen waterfalls and natural formations. Drive to the rest house, about halfway up the hill, and be prepared for some seriously scenic vistas. Then walk 15 minutes to the cable car, which takes you to a point about 15 minutes on foot from the cave, where you can take a 1¼-hour guided tour. The entire adventure takes about half a day. And remember, no matter how warm it is outside, it's below freezing inside, so bundle up, and wear appropriate shoes. You must be in good shape, as there are 700 steps, but there's a restaurant with a terrace and a view where you can recover after the tour. ✉ *Eishohenstrasse 30, Throwing* ☎ *06468/5248* 🌐 *www.eisriesenwelt.at* 🎫 *€22, including cable car* ⏲ *Cave: May–Oct., daily from 9, last cave tour 3:45 (4:45 July and Aug.); visitor center: daily 8–3 (4 July and Aug.); last cable car ascent 3:20 (4:20 July and Aug.)*

Transportation. You can also take a bus to the cable car from the Werfen train station. Buses run at 8:20 am, 10:20 am, 12:20 pm and 2:20 pm, or upon request. ☎ *06468/5293.*

WHERE TO EAT AND STAY

$$$$ CONTEMPORARY Fodor's Choice ★

🍴 **Obauer.** Among Austria's top dining spots, Obauer is presided over by the brothers Karl and Rudolf, who share chef-de-cuisine responsibilities. Thanks to their flair, this has become a culinary shrine, especially for Salzburgers and Germans. Trout strudel with Veltliner sauce, Werfen lamb with parsley pesto and lamb salami, stuffed zucchini blossoms with wild thyme and mushrooms—any of these specialties might top the nightly bill of fare and are highly recommended. The cuisine is creative, and local delights and herbs are deftly mixed with nouvelle garnishes, many inspired by the brothers' far-flung travels. **■ TIP→ For a complete experience book one of Obauer's 11 chic and modern guest rooms and suites and enjoy a legendary breakfast in the morning.** [$] *Average main: €30* ✉ *Markt 46* ☎ *06468/52120* 🌐 *www.obauer.com* ✍ *Reservations essential.*

$ HOTEL

🏨 **Hotel-Garni Erzherzog Eugen.** You can't miss this hot-pink hotel with window boxes trailing garlands of geraniums, as it's smack in the middle of town. **Pros:** budget rates; friendly staff; generous breakfasts. **Cons:** often booked up in advance. [$] *Rooms from: €95* ✉ *Markt 38* ☎ *06468/5210–0* 🌐 *www.obauer-krieger.at* 🛏 *12 rooms* 🍽 *Breakfast.*

SALZKAMMERGUT

Updated by
Erin Snell

Remember the exquisite opening scenes of *The Sound of Music*? Castles reflected in water, mountains veiled by a scattering of downy clouds, flower-strewn valleys dotted with cool blue lakes: a view of Austria as dreamed up by a team of Hollywood's special-effects geniuses—so many thought. But, no, except for the bicycle ride along the Mondsee, those scenes were filmed right here, in Austria's fabled Salzkammergut region.

The Lake District of Upper Austria, centered on the region called the Salzkammergut (literally, "salt estates"), presents the traveler with stunning sights: soaring mountains and needlelike peaks; a glittering necklace of turquoise lakes; forested valleys populated by the *Rehe* (roe deer) immortalized by Felix Salten in *Bambi*—this is Austria at its most lush and verdant. Some of these lakes, like the Hallstätter See, remain quite unspoiled, partly because the mountains act as a buffer from busier, more accessible sections of the country. Another—historic—reason relates to the presence of the salt mines, which date back to the Celtic era; with salt so common and cheap nowadays, many forget it was once a luxury item mined under strict government monopoly, and the Salzkammergut was closed to the casually curious for centuries, opening up only after Emperor Franz Josef made Bad Ischl—one of the area's leading spa towns (even then, studded with *salt*water swimming pools)—his official summer residence in 1854.

A favorite passion for Austrians is *das Wandern*, or hiking. The Lake District has many miles of marked trails, with lovely stretches around Bad Ischl—which alone has more than 100 km (62 miles) of trails—and the mountains in the Hallstatt area. Cycling, popular among locals and visitors, offers an athletic way to see miles of landscape at a human pace. Within this pastoral perfection you can stay in age-old *Schloss*-hotels or modern villas, dine in fine restaurants, and shop for the linens, ceramics, woodcarvings, and painted glass of the region.

ORIENTATION AND PLANNING

GETTING ORIENTED

To the west of Bad Ischl are the best known of all the Salzkammergut's 76 lakes—the Wolfgangsee and the Mondsee (*See* is German for "lake"). Not far to the southeast of these lakes lies one of Austria's loveliest spots, Gosau am Dachstein. Here the Gosau lakes are backdropped by a spectacular sight that acts as a landmark for many leagues: the Dachstein peak. Another scenic wonder is the storybook village of Hallstatt, huddled between mountain and lake.

Whether you start out from Salzburg or set up a base in Bad Ischl—the heart of the Lake District—it's best to take in the beauties of the

Salzkammergut in perhaps two separate courses: first around the Fuschlsee, Mondsee, the Wolfgangsee, and Bad Ischl; then southwest to Gosau am Dachstein and back to the Hallstätter See.

Fuschl, St. Wolfgang, and Bad Ischl. Between its romantic lakes surrounded by Alpine peaks, this region is perfect for both water sports in summer and skiing in winter. The charming Bad Ischl's old-fashioned buildings document the town's importance in the days of the Habsburgs.

Gosau and Hallstatt. The sight from atop the Dachstein mountain range gives the impression of being on top of the world. The picturesque towns in this region are full of Austrian folklore and tradition, and have inspired many composers, painters, and poets.

PLANNING

WHEN TO GO
Year-round, vacationers flock to the Lake District, but late fall is not the best time to visit the region. It could be rainy and cold, and many sights are closed or operate on a restricted schedule. By far the best months are July and September. August sees the countryside overrun with families on school holidays and music lovers from the nearby Salzburg Music Festival (even so, who can resist a visit to Bad Ischl on August 18, when Emperor Franz Josef's birthday is still celebrated). Others like to visit Hallstatt for its annual procession across the lake, held on Corpus Christi day (weather permitting, around the last weekend in May, or the Sunday after)—a Catholic, and therefore, national holiday all over Austria. December finds several small picturesque markets in the villages around the Wolfgangsee and traditional *Adventsingen* concerts in churches throughout the region.

GETTING HERE AND AROUND
AIR TRAVEL
By air, the Lake District is closer to Salzburg than to Linz. The Salzburg airport is about 53 km (33 miles) from Bad Ischl, heart of the Salzkammergut; the Linz airport (Hörsching) is about 75 km (47 miles).

CAR TRAVEL
Driving is by far the easiest and most convenient way to reach the Lake District; traffic is excessive only on weekends (although it can be slow on some narrow lakeside stretches). From Salzburg you can take Route 158 east to Fuschl, St. Gilgen, and Bad Ischl or the A1 autobahn to Mondsee. Coming from Vienna or Linz, the A1 passes through the northern part of the Salzkammergut; get off at the Steyrermühl exit or the Regau exit and head south on Route 144/145 to Gmunden, Bad Ischl, and Bad Goisern. Remember: gasoline is expensive in Austria.

TRAIN TRAVEL
The geography of the area means that rail lines run mainly north–south. Where the trains don't go, buses do, so if you allow enough time you can cover virtually all the area by public transportation. The main bus routes through the region are Bad Ischl to Gosau, Hallstatt, Salzburg, and St. Wolfgang; Mondsee to St. Gilgen and Salzburg; St. Gilgen to Mondsee; Salzburg to Bad Ischl, Mondsee, St. Gilgen, and Strobl.

10

TOP REASONS TO GO

Fairy-tale landscape: The lakes and mountains resemble the pictures in a children's book.

Bad Ischl: This town, where the rich and famous have long come for the healing waters, was Emperor Franz Josef's summer retreat in the 19th century.

Cradle of culture: Vienna and Salzburg may get all the credit, but the composers who made those cities cultural capitals came to this part of Austria to hear the music in the air.

Sports abound: Everyone knows about the region's great ski resorts, but there is an endless array of summer sports as well.

TOURS

Daylong tours of the Salzkammergut, offered by Salzburg Sightseeing Tours and Salzburg Panorama Tours, whisk you all too quickly from Salzburg to St. Gilgen, St. Wolfgang, Fuschl and Mondsee.

Salzburg Sightseeing Tours. A four-hour tour of the Salzkammergut (Fuschl, St. Gilgen, St. Wolfgang) leaves from Mirabellplatz in Salzburg daily at 2, and the price includes a boat trip on Lake Wolfgang (May–Oct.). Half- and full-day guided tours are also available upon request. ⊠ *Mirabellplatz 2, Salzburg* ☎ *0662/881616* 🖶 *0662/878776* ⊕ *www.salzburg-sightseeingtours.at* 🎫 *Salzkammergut tour €37.*

Salzburg Panorama Tours. Tours through the Salzkammergut depart from Salzburg and include a four-hour tour and five-hour lake district tour (both depart daily at 2). Private guided tours also available. Bookings must be made online up to 24 hours prior to departure, or call the bus terminal for last-minute reservations. ⊠ *Schrannengasse 2/2, Salzburg* ☎ *0662/883211 office, 0662/874029 bus terminal* ⊕ *www.panoramatours.com* 🎫 *From €40.*

VISITOR INFORMATION

Most towns in the Salzkammergut have their own *Tourismusverband* (tourist office), which is listed in the specific towns. The main tourist offices for the provinces and regions covered in this chapter are Salzkammergut and Upper Austria. Upper Austria and the Salzkammergut comprise the backbone of the Dachstein range.

ESSENTIALS

Bus Information ÖBB/Postbus ☎ *05/1717–4* ⊕ *www.oebb.at.*

Medical Assistance St. Johannsspital-Landeskrankenhaus ⊠ *Müllner Hauptstrasse 48, Salzburg* ☎ *0662/4482–0* ⊕ *www.salk.at.*

Train Information ÖBB—Österreichisches Bundesbahn ☎ *05/1717–4* ⊕ *www.oebb.at.*

Visitor Information **Salzkammergut Tourist Information Office** ⊠ *Salinen-platz 1, Bad Ischl* ☏ *06132/26909-0* ⊕ *www.salzkammergut.at.* **Upper Austria Tourist Information Center** ⊠ *Freistädterstraße 119, Linz* ☏ *0732/221022* ⊕ *www.oberoesterreich.at.*

RESTAURANTS

Culinary shrines are to be found around Mondsee. However, in many of the towns of the Salzkammergut, you'll find country inns with dining rooms but few independent restaurants, other than the occasional simple *Gasthäuser.*

HOTELS

In the grand old days, the aristocratic families of the region would welcome paying guests at their charming castles. Today most of those castles have been, if you will, degentrified: they are now schools or very fine hotels. But you needn't stay in a castle to enjoy the Salzkammergut—there are also luxurious lakeside resorts, small country inns, even guesthouses without private baths; in some places the *Herr Wirt,* his smiling wife, and his grown-up children will do everything to make you feel comfortable. Although our hotel reviews cover the best in every category, note that nearly every village, however small, also has a *Gasthaus* or village inn; the ubiquitous *Hotel-* or *Gasthof zur Post* is usually a solid choice. Many hotels offer half-board, with dinner in addition to buffet breakfast included in the price (although the most expensive hotels will often charge extra for breakfast). The half-board room rate is usually an extra €15–€30 per person. Occasionally quoted room rates for hotels already include half-board accommodations, though a "discounted" rate is usually offered if you prefer not to take the evening meal. Inquire when booking. Happily, these hotels do not put their breathtakingly beautiful natural surroundings on the bill.

WHAT IT COSTS IN EUROS				
	$	**$$**	**$$$**	**$$$$**
RESTAURANTS	under €12	€12–€17	€18–€22	over €22
HOTELS	under €100	€100–€135	€136–€175	over €175

Restaurant prices are per person for a main course at dinner. Hotel prices are for a standard double room in high season, including taxes and service. Higher prices (inquire when booking) prevail for any meal plans.

10

FUSCHLSEE, ST. WOLFGANG, AND BAD ISCHL

The mountains forming Austria's backbone may be less majestic than other Alps at this point, but they are also considerably less stern; glittering blue lakes and villages nestle safely in valleys without being constantly under the threatening eye of an avalanche from the huge peaks. Here you'll find what travelers come to the Lake District for: elegant restaurants, Baroque churches, meadows with green space and privacy, lakeside cabanas, and forests that could tell a tale or two.

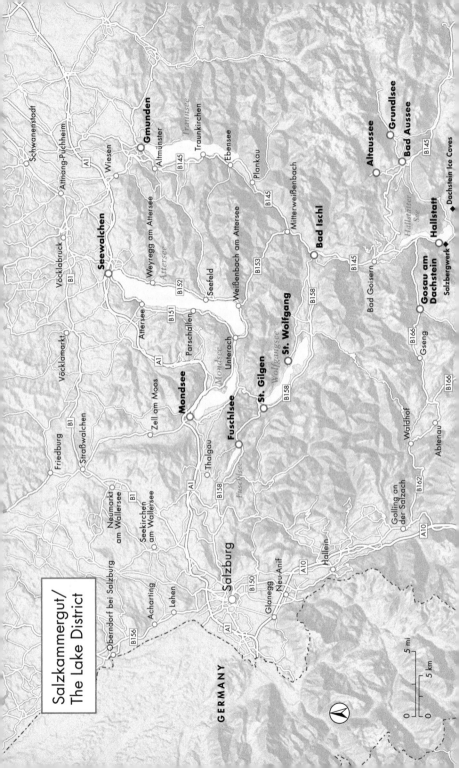

Salzkammergut/
The Lake District

GERMANY

Schwanenstadt

Attnang-Puchheim

Wiesen

A1

Gmunden

Traunkirchen

Traunsee

Altmünster

B145

Ebensee

Plankau

Mitterweißenbach

Grundlsee

Altaussee

Bad Aussee

B145

Dachstein Ice Caves

Vöcklabruck

B1

Seewalchen

Weyregg am Attersee

Attersee

Seefeld

Weißenbach am Attersee

B145

B153

Bad Ischl

B145

Bad Goisern

Hallstätter See

Hallstatt

Gosau am Dachstein

Salzbergwerk

Vöcklamarkt

Attersee

B152

B151

Parschallen

Mondsee

Unterach

St. Wolfgang

B158

Gseng

B166

Waldhof

B166

Vöcklabruck

A1

Zell am Moos

Mondsee

Fuschlsee

St. Gilgen

Wolfgangsee

B158

Abtenau

B162

Friedburg

B1

Straßwalchen

Thalgau

Fuschlsee

Golling an
der Salzach

A10

Neumarkt
am Wallersee

B1

A1

B158

Oberndorf bei Salzburg

Acharting

Lehen

Seekirchen
am Wallersee

Salzburg

B150

Glanegg
Neu-Anif

A10

Hallein

B56

GERMANY

A1

5 mi

5 km

0

0

FUSCHLSEE

20 km (12 miles) east of Salzburg.

Nothing powered by more than a trolling motor is allowed on the crystalline waters of the peaceful alpine Lake Fuschl, and the emperor's Schloss Fuschl overlooking vintage wooden rowboats, swan couples, and wooden chalets still forms an enduring, enchanting scene. The stillness is not frozen in time, however. Energy drink powerhouse Red Bull is headquartered here, and you can often spot its sponsored athletes and pilots practicing in the area. It's also an easy escape for Salzburgers who are looking for nearby wooded hikes and a refreshing swim on a hot summer day.

GETTING HERE AND AROUND

From Salzburg, take Route 158 east. Be prepared for heavy traffic on summer weekends and holidays. Postbus 150 (toward Bad Ischl Bahnhof or St. Gilgen Busbahnhof) takes about 40 minutes from Salzburg's main station or the Mirabellplatz stop to the center of Fuschl am See, with intermediate stops including Schloss Fuschl and the public beach (*Strand*). On weekdays the bus runs once to twice per hour, 5:55 am–11 pm; on weekends and holidays it's hourly, 8:15–8:15.

ESSENTIALS

Tourist Information **Fuschlsee** ✉ *Dorfplatz 1, Fuschl am See* ☎ *06226/8384* 🌐 *fuschlsee.salzkammergut.at.*

WHERE TO EAT AND STAY

$$ ITALIAN 🍴 **Edenbergers Café Am See.** Come for the crispy-crusted pizza and stay for the view—Edenbergers' wooden pier extending from the lakeside terrace aims directly at the sun's path as it sets between the mountains overlooking the Fuschlsee. Italian and regional Austrian dishes round out the menu, all with a focus on locally sourced ingredients, including char from the lake. The well-selected Austrian wine list and full cocktail bar keeps locals chatting till the wee hours. ■ **TIP→ The demand for a seat on the terrace can be high during the high season, so come early, order a Hugo, sit on the dock and cool your feet in the water while you wait for your table.** [$] *Average main: €14* ✉ *Seestrasse 15, Fuschl am See* ☎ *0662/68220–11* 🌐 *www.edenberger.at* ✍ *Reservations essential* ⏲ *Closed Mon. No lunch weekdays.*

$$$$ RESORT 🏨 **Schloss Fuschl.** Modern luxury intermingles with historical elegance in this expansive lakeside castle resort and spa. **Pros:** fairy-tale atmosphere; exemplary service; lots of extras; secluded retreat. **Cons:** far from the city; need a car; pricey. [$] *Rooms from: €330* ✉ *Schlossstrasse 19, Hof bei Salzburg* ☎ *06229/22530* 🌐 *www.schlossfuschlsalzburg.com/en* 🛏 *110 rooms, 7 suites, 6 chalets* 🍽 *Breakfast.*

ST. WOLFGANG

Fodor's Choice *19 km (12 miles) east of St. Gilgen, 50 km (31 miles) east of Salzburg.*
★ The town has everything: swimming and hiking in summer, cross-country skiing in winter, and natural feasts for the eye at every turn. Here you'll find yourself in the Austria of operetta fame. Indeed, St. Wolfgang became known around the world thanks to the inn called the **Weisses Rössl,** which was built right next to the landing stage in 1878. It featured prominently in a late-19th-century play that achieved fame as an operetta by Ralph Benatzky in 1930. Ironically, the two original playwrights, Gustav Kadelburg and Oskar Blumenthal, had another, now destroyed, Weisses Rössl (along the road from Bad Ischl to Hallstatt) in mind. In the years following World War II the composers Samuel Barber and Gian Carlo Menotti spent summer vacations here, too.

GETTING HERE AND AROUND
A lovely way to enter the picture-book town of St. Wolfgang is to leave your car at Strobl, at the southern end of the Wolfgangsee, and take one of the steamers that ply the waters of the lake. Strobl itself is a delightful village but not as fashionable as St. Wolfgang; if you prefer a quiet vacation base, this may be its attraction for you. Between St. Wolfgang and Strobl, the Wolfgangsee retains its old name of "Abersee." The earliest paddleboat on the lake is still in service, a genuine 1873 steamer called the *Kaiser Franz Josef.* Service is regular from May to mid-October, and on the Advent weekends. The view of the town against the dramatic mountain backdrop is one you'll see again and again on posters and postcards. If you decide to drive all the way to town, be prepared for a crowd. Unless your hotel offers parking, you'll have to park on the fringes of town and walk a short distance, as the center is a pedestrian-only zone.

ESSENTIALS
Tourist Information Wolfgangsee ⊠ *Au 140* ☎ *06138/8003*
⊕ *www.wolfgangsee.at.*

EXPLORING
Wallfahrtskirche St. Wolfgang (*Pilgrimage Church*). You shouldn't miss seeing Michael Pacher's great altarpiece in the 15th-century Wallfahrtskirche, one of the finest examples of late-Gothic woodcarving to be found anywhere. This 11-meter (36-foot) masterpiece took 10 years (1471–81) to complete. The paintings and carvings on this winged altar were used as an *Armenbibel* (a Bible for the poor)—illustrations for those who couldn't read or write. You're in luck if you're at the church on a sunny day, when sunlight off the nearby lake dances on the ceiling in brilliant reflections through the stained-glass windows. Visit the Wolfgangsee Tourist Office website for a list of frequent concerts in the sanctuary and *Pfarramt* (rectory). ⊠ *Maria Bühel Strasse* ☽ *May–Sept., daily 9–5; Oct.–Apr., daily 10–4; altar closed to view during Lent.*

Schafberg. From the end of April to mid-October, and on the Advent weekends (weather permitting), the historic steam train trip from St. Wolfgang to the 1,768-meter (5,800-foot) peak of the Schafberg offers a great chance to survey the surrounding countryside from what is

OFF THE
BEATEN
PATH

ON THE MENU

Fresh, local lake fish is on nearly every menu in the area, so take advantage of the bounty. The lakes and streams are home to several types of fish, notably trout, carp, and perch. They are prepared in numerous ways, from plain breaded (*gebacken*), to smoked and served with *Kren* (horseradish), to fried in butter (*gebraten*). Look for *Reinanke*, a mild whitefish straight from the Hallstättersee. Sometimes at country fairs and weekly markets you will find someone charcoaling fresh trout wrapped in aluminum foil with herbs and butter: it's worth every euro. *Knödel*—bread or potato dumplings sometimes filled with either meat or jam—are a tasty specialty. Desserts are doughy as well, though *Salzburger Nockerl*, a sabayon-based soufflé, consists mainly of sugar, beaten egg whites, and air. And finally, keep an eye out for seasonal specialties: spring is *Spargelzeit* (white asparagus time) in summer restaurants often serve chanterelle mushrooms (*Eierschwammerl*) with pasta, and in October it's time for delicious venison and game during the *Wildwochen* (game weeks).

acclaimed as the "belvedere of the Salzkammergut lakes." The mountain is also a hiker's paradise–take advantage of one-way train tickets for a less strenuous afternoon. Pause for refreshments at one of two inns on the peak. On a clear day you can almost see forever—at least as far as the Lattengebirge mountain range west of Salzburg. Crowds waiting for trains are likely, so start out early to get a seat by a window for the best view; call the ticket office to reserve a spot at your preferred departure time. ☎ *06138/2232–0* ⊕ *www.schafbergbahn.at/en_uk.html*

Schafbergbahn. The steam train itself is a curiosity dating from 1893, and does not run in bad weather. Buy tickets on the train and allow at least a good half day for the outing. ☎ *06138/2232–0* 🖷 *06138/2232–9705* ⊕ *www.schafbergbahn.at* 💶 *€22 for either the mountain or valley trip, €32 for both* ☉ *Late Apr.–mid-Oct., daily 9:15–5:10 (hourly service).*

WHERE TO STAY

$$$ **Cortisen am See.** A large chalet-style structure with a glowing yellow
B&B/INN facade, "At the Court" has become one of St. Wolfgang's most stylish and comfortable hotels. **Pros:** in the center of the village; a quiet place to relax; unique atmosphere **Cons:** front rooms face busy street. 💲 *Rooms from: €170* ✉ *Markt 15* ☎ *06138/2376* ⊕ *www.cortisen.at* 🛏 *20 rooms, 12 suites* ⏺ *Some meals.*

$ **Gasthof Zimmerbräu.** This pleasant, rustic, and central Gasthof began
B&B/INN four centuries ago as a brewery and opened its doors to guests in 1895, and though it's not directly on the lake, it does maintain its own bathing cabana on the shore. **Pros:** central; all rooms with balconies; reasonable rates; pretty views. **Cons:** not on the lake; noisy until evening. 💲 *Rooms from: €79* ✉ *Markt 89* ☎ *06138/2204* ⊕ *www.zimmerbraeu.com* 🛏 *25 rooms* ☉ *Closed mid-Jan.–Feb. and mid-Oct.–mid-Nov.* ⏺ *Some meals.*

$$$ **Landhaus zu Appesbach.** Secluded, quiet, and offering excellent ser-
HOTEL vice, this old ivy-covered manor hotel is tucked away from the hubbub

10

of the village and offers sailboats and rowboats to enjoy the direct lake access. **Pros:** peaceful atmosphere; quiet location; excellent service. **Cons:** need a car to get around; some rooms are more modern than others. [$] *Rooms from: €210* ✉ *Au 18* ☎ *06138/2209* 🌐 *www.appesbach.com* 🛏 *26 rooms* 🕒 *Closed end Oct.–mid-Nov. and Dec. 23–end Apr.* 🍴 *Some meals.*

$$$ HOTEL 🏨 **Weisses Rössl.** Family-owned since the 1800s, the "White Horse" guest rooms and apartments, in nine connected houses, are full of the country charm, flowered fabrics, and quaint furniture brought to the big screen in the movie version of the idyllic Austrian operetta of the same name. **Pros:** cozy rooms; excellent location; outstanding breakfast. **Cons:** very touristy; noisy location. [$] *Rooms from: €236* ✉ *Markt 74* ☎ *06138/23060* 🌐 *www.weissesroessl.at* 🛏 *94 rooms* 🕒 *Closed end Feb.–end Mar.* 🍴 *Some meals.*

NIGHTLIFE AND THE ARTS

Free brass-band concerts are held on the Marktplatz in St. Wolfgang every Saturday evening at 8:30 in May, and on both Wednesday and Saturday at 8:30 pm from June to September. Folk events are usually well publicized with posters (if you're lucky, Benatzky's operetta *Im Weissen Rössl* might be on the schedule). The Wallfahrtskirche hosts a weekly series of International Church Concerts in July and August, putting their two wonderful organs on proud display. Not far from St. Wolfgang, the town of Strobl holds a Day of Popular Music and Tradition in early July—"popular" meaning brass band, and "tradition" being *Tracht,* the local costume. Check with the regional tourist office for details. Water plane landings, a real acrobatics by the Flying Bulls (locally based energy drink giant Red Bull's team of pilots and airplanes), and international vintage plane flights draw celebrities who liven the slow pace of St. Wolfgang during the second week of July for the Scalaria Air Challenge.

BAD ISCHL

56 km (35 miles) east of Salzburg, 16 km (10 miles) southeast of St. Wolfgang.

Many travelers used to think of Bad Ischl primarily as the town where Zauner's pastry shop is located, to which connoisseurs drove miles for the sake of a cup of coffee and a slice of *Guglhupf,* a lemon sponge cake studded with raisins and nuts. Pastry continues to be the best-known drawing card of a community that symbolizes, more than any other place except Vienna itself, the Old Austria of resplendent uniforms and balls and waltzes and operettas.

Although the center is built up, the town is charmingly laid out on a peninsula between the Rivers Traun and Ischl. Bad Ischl was the place where Emperor Franz Josef chose to establish his summer court, and it was here that he met and fell in love with his future empress, the troubled Sisi, though his mother had intended him for Sisi's elder sister. Today you can enjoy the same sort of pastries *mit Schlag* (whipped cream) that the emperor loved. Afterward, you can hasten off to the town's modern spa, one of the best known in Austria.

You'll want to stroll along the shaded **Esplanade,** where the pampered and privileged of the 19th century loved to take their constitutionals, usually after a quick stop at the **Trinkhalle,** a spa pavilion in high 19th-century Austrian style, still in the middle of town on Ferdinand-Auböck-Platz.

GETTING HERE AND AROUND

Bad Ischl is accessed easily via various routes. From St. Wolfgang, backtrack south to Strobl and head eastward on Route 158. To get to the town directly from Salzburg, take the A1 to Mondsee, then Routes 151 and 158 along the Wolfgangsee and the Mondsee. There are many buses that depart hourly from Salzburg's main train station; you can also travel by train via the junction of Attnang-Puchheim or Stainach-Irdning (several transfers are required)—a longer journey than the bus ride, which is usually 90 minutes. There are also many regular bus and train connections between Gmunden and Bad Ischl.

ESSENTIALS

Tourist Information Bad Ischl ⊠ *Auböckplatz 5* ☎ *06132/277570* ⊕ *www.badischl.at.*

EXPLORING

Kaiservilla. In Bad Ischl the quickest way to travel back in time to the gilded 1880s is to head for the mammoth Kaiservilla, the imperial-yellow (signifying wealth and power) residence, which looks rather like a miniature Schönbrunn: its ground plan forms an "E" to honor the empress Elisabeth. Archduke Markus Salvator von Habsburg-Lothringen, great-grandson of Franz Josef, still lives here, but you can tour parts of the building to see the ornate reception rooms and the surprisingly modest residential quarters (through which sometimes even the archduke guides visitors with what can only be described as a very courtly kind of humor). It was at this villa that the emperor signed the declaration of war against Serbia, which officially marked the start of World War I. The villa is filled with Habsburg and family mementos, none more moving than the cushion, on display in the chapel, on which the head of Empress Elisabeth rested after she was stabbed by an Italian assassin in 1898. ⊠ *Kaiserpark* ☎ *06132/23241* ⊕ *www.kaiservilla.at* ⊠ *€13.50; grounds only €4.50* ⊙ *May–Sept., daily 9:30–5; Apr.–Oct., Dec. Advent weekends and Dec. 26–early Jan., daily 10–4; early Jan.–Mar., Wed. 10–4.*

Museum der Stadt Bad Ischl. Fascinating is the only word to describe this museum, which occupies the circa-1880 Hotel Austria—the favored summer address for Archduke Franz Karl and his wife Sophie (from 1834 on). More momentously, the young Franz Josef got engaged to his beloved Elisabeth here in 1853. After taking in the gardens (with their Brahms monument), explore the various exhibits, which deal with the region's salt, royal, and folk histories. Note the display of national folk costumes, which the emperor wore while hunting. From December until the beginning of February, the museum shows off its famous *Kalss Krippe,* an enormous mechanical Christmas crèche. Dating from 1838, it has about 300 figures. The townsfolk of Ischl, in fact, are famous for their Christmas "cribs," and you can see many of them in tours of private houses opened for visits after Christmas until January 6. ⊠ *Esplanade 10* ☎ *06132/30114* ⊕ *www.stadtmuseum.at* ⊠ *€5.20* ⊙ *Mon., Tues. and Thurs.–Sun. 10–5; Wed. 2–7.*

10

Photo Museum. Don't overlook the small but elegant "marble palace" built near the Kaiservilla for Empress Elisabeth, who used it as a teahouse; this now houses a photography museum. The permanent collection offers an interesting overview of the history of analog photography, with a nice tribute to Empress Elizabeth. The marriage between Franz Josef and Elisabeth was not an especially happy one; a number of houses bearing women's names in Bad Ischl are said to have been quietly given by the emperor to his various lady friends (such as Villa Schratt, given to Katharina Schratt, the emperor's nearly official mistress). You'll first need to purchase a ticket to the museum to enter the park grounds. ✉ *Kaiserpark* ☎ *06132/24422* 🌐 *www.landesmuseum.at/ueber/die-haeuser/photomuseum-bad-ischl* 🎫 *Museum €2 Kaiserpark €4.50* 🕒 *Apr., daily 10–4; May–Oct., daily 9:30–5.*

Stadtpfarrkirche St. Nikolaus. In the center of town, St. Nikolaus parish church graces Ferdinand-Auböck-Platz. It dates back to the Middle Ages, but was enlarged to its present size during Maria Theresa's time in the 1750s. The decoration inside is in the typically gloomy style of the Franz Josef era (note the emperor's family portrayed to the left above the high altar). Anton Bruckner used to play on the old church organ. ✉ *1 Kirchengasse.*

Villa Lehár. A steady stream of composers followed the aristocracy and the court to Bad Ischl. Anton Bruckner, Johannes Brahms (who composed his famous *Lullaby* here as well as many of his late works, and whom Gustav Mahler visited here), Johann Strauss the Younger, Carl Michael Ziehrer, Oscar Straus, and Anton Webern all spent summers here, but it was the Hungarian-born Franz Lehár, composer of *The Merry Widow,* who left the most lasting musical impression—today, Bad Ischl's summer operetta festival always includes one Lehár work. With the royalties he received from his operettas, he was able to settle into the sumptuous Villa Lehár, in which he lived from 1912 to his death in 1948. Now a museum, it contains a number of the composer's fin-de-siècle period salons, which can be viewed only on guided tours. ✉ *Lehárkai 8* ☎ *06132/26992* 🌐 *www.stadtmuseum.at/hg_leharvilla.php* 🎫 *€5.20* 🕒 *May–Sept., daily 10–5.*

WHERE TO EAT AND STAY

$ CAFÉ Fodor's Choice ★

🍴 **Café Zauner.** If you haven't been to Zauner, you've missed a true highlight of Bad Ischl. There are two locations, one on the Esplanade overlooking the River Traun (open only in summer) and the other a few blocks away on Pfarrgasse. **TIP→ The desserts—particularly the house creation, Zaunerstollen, a chocolate-covered confection of sugar, hazelnuts, and nougat—have made this one of Austria's best-known pastry shops.** Emperor Franz Josef used to visit every day for a Guglhupf, a lemon sponge cake. [$] *Average main: €6* ✉ *Pfarrgasse 7* ☎ *06132/23310–20* 🌐 *www.zauner.at.*

$ AUSTRIAN

🍴 **Rettenbachmühle.** A shady walk of about 20 minutes east from Bad Ischl's town center follows a brook and deposits you at the leafy gardens of this former farmhouse, where the owners swear that this was the very locale where the *Kaiserschmarrn* was born. The name literally translates to "emperor's nonsense," but many consider it to

CLOSE UP

Landscape as Muse

For nearly two centuries the Salzkammergut Lake District has been a wellspring of inspiration to great artists and composers. Richard Strauss, Gustav Klimt, and Franz Léhar are just a few of the greats who ventured here to holiday and, as souvenirs of their trips, left behind immortal symphonies and paintings.

It was in the 19th century that the region was discovered. French philosopher Jean Jacques Rousseau's "back to nature" theories and the Romantic movement of the 19th century made tourism fashionable. And the Salzkammergut was opened for the first time to visitors (previously, the "salt-mine" region was a private preserve of the Habsburgs).

Following the example of Emperor Franz Josef and other royals, painters and poets soon began flocking to this region to enjoy the "simple life." The region's spas also attracted aristos by the boatload. Archduke

Rudolf—brother of the emperor and pupil of Beethoven (for whom the composer wrote his *Missa solemnis*)— was the first Habsburg to enjoy the cure in Bad Ischl. The sensitive souls of the composers of the Romantic era were highly attracted by the beauty of the landscape. Little wonder that listeners can hear its reflection in the music written here: listen to the scherzo movement of Gustav Mahler's Third Symphony and you'll know where its cuckoo-theme and wistful post horn come from. Then when the Salzburg Music Festival hit its stride in the 1930s, many of the great artists involved—Hugo von Hofmannsthal and Richard Strauss among them— liked to escape to summerhouses in the hills after performing in town. Just as Johannes Brahms used to walk over a meadow on a sunny day or through a silent forest, or climb a mountain to renew mind and spirit, they followed his example and footsteps. So should you.

be the most delicious dessert in Austria—a raisin-studded pancake covered with powdered sugar. It makes for a lovely time to stop here to enjoy this treat along with an afternoon coffee. But it's not just pancakes here—delicious traditional Austrian entrées entice both locals and visitors, so be sure to make a reservation. $ *Average main: €11* ✉ *Hinterstein 6* ☎ *06132/23586* ⚭ *Reservations essential* ☉ *Closed Mon. and Tues.*

$ ⚏ **Goldener Ochs.** The "Golden Ox" is in a superb location in the town
HOTEL   center, with the sparkling River Traun a few steps away. **Pros:** great value; close to the sites; modern rooms; private wellness spa. **Cons:** traffic noise in front rooms. $ *Rooms from: €61* ✉ *Grazerstrasse 4* ☎ *06132/23529* ⊕ *www.goldenerochs.at* ⚈ *48 rooms* ⦿ *Multiple meal plans.*

NIGHTLIFE AND PERFORMING ARTS

The main musical events of the year in the Salzkammergut are the July and August operetta festivals held in Bad Ischl.

Kongress- und Theaterhaus. Schmaltz and waltz fill the Kongress- und Theaterhaus during the summer Lehár Festival. Operetta and classic musical theater lovers flock to Bad Ischl during July and August for favorite standards like *The Merry Widow* and *My Fair Lady*. Tickets are sold online, at local tourist offices, and on-site. Pre-sales for the upcoming season begin in October. ⊠ *Kurhausstrasse 8* ☎ *06132/23839* ⊕ *www.leharfestival.at* ✉ *Tickets from €26–€80*

Lehár Festival. To buy tickets to performances ahead of time, contact the Lehár Festival offices in the Kongress und Theaterhaus. ⊠ *Kurhausstrasse 8* ☎ *06132/23839.*

GOSAU AND HALLSTATT

It's hard to imagine anything prettier than this region of the Salzkammergut, which takes you into the very heart of the Lake District. The great highlight is Gosau am Dachstein—a beauty spot that even the least impressionable find hard to forget. But there are other notable sights, including Hallstatt and the Dachstein Ice Caves.

GOSAU AM DACHSTEIN

Fodor's Choice ★ *67 km (42 miles) southeast of Salzburg, 10 km (6 miles) west of the Hallstättersee.*

Lovers of scenic beauty should not leave the Hallstatt region without taking in Gosau am Dachstein, considered the most beautiful spot in Austria by 19th-century travelers but unaccountably often overlooked today.

Instead of driving around the area, it's worthwhile to take a serious walk (about 2½ hours, depending on your speed), departing from the tourist information office not far from the crossroads known as the Gosaumühle. Passing by churches, the road follows the valley over the meadows. From Gosauschmied Café on, it's a romantic way through the forest to the first Gosau lake, the Vorderer Gosausee (Front Gosau Lake), which is the crown jewel, some 8 km (5 miles) to the south of the village itself. Beyond a sparkling, almost fjordlike basin of water rises the amazing Dachstein massif, majestically reflected in the lake's mirrorlike surface. Aside from a restaurant and a gamekeeper's hut, the lake is undefiled by man-made structures. At the right hour—well before 2:30 pm, when due to the steepness of the mountain slopes, the sun is already withdrawing—the view is superb. Then you may choose to endure the stiff walk to the other two lakes set behind the first and not as spectacularly located (in fact, the third is used by an electric power station and therefore not always full of water, yet it remains the closest place from which to view the glittering Dachstein glacier). Hiking to the latter two lakes will take about two hours. You can also take a cable car up to the Gablonzer Hütte on the Zwieselalm (you might consider skiing on the Gosau glacier); or tackle the three-hour hike up to the summit of the Grosser Donnerkogel.

At day's end, head back for Gosau village, settle in at one of the many Gasthöfe (reserve ahead) overhung with wild gooseberry and rosebushes (or stay at one of Gosau's charming *Privatzimmer* accommodations). Cap the day off with a dinner of fried *Schwarzrenterl*, a delicious regional lake fish. To get to Gosau, travel north or south on Route 145, turning off at the junction with Route 166, and travel 36 km (20 miles) east through the ravine of the Gosaubach River.

GETTING HERE AND AROUND

This lovely spot is 10 km (6 miles) west of the Hallstätter See, just before the Gschütt Pass: you travel either by bus (eight daily from Bad Ischl to Gosau) or car. The village makes a good lunch stop, and, with its many Gasthöfe and pensions, could be a base for your excursions.

ESSENTIALS

Tourist Information **Gosau am Dachstein** ✉ *Tourismusverband Dachstein, Gosau 547* ☎ *06136/8295* 🌐 *www.dachstein-salzkammergut.at.*

WHERE TO EAT AND STAY

$$$ AUSTRIAN 🍴 **Kirchenwirt.** Adjacent to Gosau's pretty parish church, this inn is evidence of the venerable tradition of locating town restaurants next to houses of worship (on Sunday farmers would attend the service then head for the nearest table and discuss the past week's events). Mentioned in town records as early as 1596, the inn here has now been much restored and built up in typical modern Alpine style of natural wood, mounted antlers, hunter greens, and bright reds. The current hosts, the Peham family, provide a rich breakfast buffet, and best bets for other meals include broth with strudel of minced meat, homemade noodles with cheese and white cabbage salad, and plums with vanilla ice cream and whipped cream. In August the inn hosts some festive concerts with a traditional *Trachtenmusikkapelle,* a brass band dressed in folkloric costume. [$] *Average main: €21* ✉ *Gosau 2* ☎ *06136/8196* 🌐 *www.kirchenwirt-peham.at.*

$$ HOTEL 🏨 **Hotel Koller.** One of the most charming hotels in Gosau, the peaked gables and weather vanes of this 1850s-era villa give a fairy-tale aura when seen from its pretty park. **Pros:** cheerful interiors; pretty views. **Cons:** half-board is required. [$] *Rooms from: €135* ✉ *Pass-Gschütt-Strasse 353* ☎ *06136/8841* 🌐 *www.hotel-koller.com* 🛏 *17 rooms* ⏲ *Closed Nov. and 1 month around Easter (dates vary)* 🍽 *Some meals.*

HALLSTATT

Fodor's Choice ★ *89 km (55 miles) southeast of Salzburg, 19 km (12 miles) south of Bad Ischl.*

As if rising from Swan Lake itself, the town of Hallstatt is the subject of thousands of travel posters. "The world's prettiest lakeside village" perches precariously on what seems the smallest of toeholds, one that nevertheless prevents it from tumbling into the dark waters of the Hallstättersee. Down from the steep mountainside above it crashes the Mühlbach waterfall, a sight that can keep you riveted for hours. Today, as back when—Emperor Franz Josef and his Elisabeth took an excursion here on the day of their engagement—the town is a magnet for tourists, and accordingly a bit too modernized, especially considering that Hallstatt is believed to be the oldest community in Austria. More than 1,000 graves of prehistoric men have been found here, and it has been such an important source of relics of the Celtic period that this age is known as the Hallstatt epoch.

GETTING HERE AND AROUND

Arriving in Hallstatt is a scenic spectacle if you come by train, with the entire village arrayed on the other side of the lake; from the train station, a boat, the *Stefanie*, takes you across the Hallstättersee to the town, leaving every hour. You can take the train from Bad Ischl or via the Stainach-Irdning junction. To get to Hallstatt from Bad Ischl by car, head south on Route 145 to Bad Goisern (which also has curative mineral springs but never achieved the cachet of Bad Ischl). Just south of town, watch for signs for the turnoff to the Hallstättersee. Since the lake is squeezed in between two sharply rising mountain ranges, the road parallels the shore, with spectacular views. From Bad Ischl you can also take a half-hour bus ride to Hallstatt.

ESSENTIALS

Tourist Information **Hallstatt** ⊠ *Seestrasse 99* ☎ *06134/8208* ⊕ *www.oberoesterreich.at/hallstatt or www.hallstatt.net/home-en-US/.*

EXPLORING

Archaeological Excavation. A peek into the Celtic past is offered at the DachsteinSport Janu shop. A decade ago, its intention to put a new heating system in the cellar unexpectedly turned into a historical excavation when workmen found the remains of a Celtic dwelling, now on view to visitors. ⊠ *Seestrasse 50* ☎ *06134/8298* ⊕ *www.dachsteinsport. at/ausgrabungen/ueberblick.php* ☒ *Free* ⊗ *Mon.–Sat. 8–6.*

Fodor's Choice ★ **Dachstein Ice Caves.** This is one of the most impressive sights of the eastern Alps—vast ice caverns, many of which are hundreds of years old and aglitter with ice stalactites and stalagmites, illuminated by an eerie light. The most famous sights are the **Rieseneishöhle** (Giant Ice Cave) and the **Mammuthöhle** (Mammoth Cave), but there are other caves and assorted frozen waterfalls. The cave entrance is at about 6,500 feet, accessed via cable car and a hike (or you can hike all the way), but still well below the 9,750-foot Dachstein peak farther south. If you visit in August, you can enjoy the weekly Ice Sounds concert series under the Parsifal Dome of the Dachstein cave. Tickets for these special shows include a cave tour and dinner at the Erlebnisrestaurant Schönbergalm. ■TIP→ Be sure to wear warm, weatherproof clothing and good shoes; inside the caves it is very cold, and outside the slopes can be swept by chilling winds. Start before 2 pm to see both caves. ⊠ *34 Winkl, Obertraun* ✛ *From Hallstatt, take the scenic road around the bottom of the lake to Obertraun; then follow the signs to the cable car (Dachstein-seilbahn). From the cable-car landing, a 15-minute hike up takes you to the entrance (follow signs "Dachsteineishöhle")* ☎ *05/0140* ⊕ *www. dachstein-salzkammergut.com/en/* ☒ *Giant Ice or Mammoth Cave €29, combined ticket €35; cable car €28 round trip; Ice Sounds tickets €62* ⊗ *Mammoth Cave: late May–late Oct., daily 10:15–2:30. Giant Ice Cave: May–Oct. 15, daily 9:20–4.*

Michaelerkirche (*St. Michael's*). The Hallstatt market square, now a pedestrian area, is bordered by colorful 16th-century houses and this 16th-century Gothic church, which is picquesuely situated near the lake. Within, you'll find a beautiful winged altar, which opens to reveal nine 15th-century paintings. The *Karner* (charnel house) beside the church is a rather morbid but regularly visited spot. Because there was little space to bury the dead over the centuries in Hallstatt, the custom developed of digging up the bodies after 12 or 15 years, piling the bones in the sun, and painting the skulls. Ivy and oak-leaf wreaths were used for the men, alpine flowers for the women, plus names, dates, and often the cause of death. The myriad bones and skulls are now on view in the charnel house, also known as the *"Beinhaus"* (bone house), in the back of the cemetery, which has a stunning setting overlooking the lake. Each year at the end of May the summer season kicks off with the Fronleichnahm (Corpus Christi) procession, which concludes with hundreds of boats out on the lake. ⊠ *Pfarre Hallstatt.*

Museum Hallstatt. Most of the early relics of the Hallstatt era are in Vienna (including the greatest Iron-Age totem of them all, the Venus of Willendorf, now a treasure of Vienna's Naturhistorisches Museum), but some are here in the local museum. ⊠ *Seestrasse 56* ☎ *06134/828015* ⊕ *www.museum-hallstatt.at* ☞ *€8* ⊗ *May–Sept., daily 10–6; Apr. and Oct., daily 10–4; Nov.–Mar., Wed.–Sun. 11–3.*

Salzbergwerk. Salt has been mined in this area for at least 4,500 years, and the Hallstatt mines of the Salzberg (not "burg") mountain are the oldest in the world. These "show mines" are in the Salzbergtal valley, accessed either by paths from the village cemetery or, much more conveniently, via a funicular railway that leaves from the southern end of the village. From the railway a 10-minute walk takes you to a small-scale miner's train (tall people, beware), which heads deep into the mountain. Inside, you can famously slide down the wooden chutes once used by the miners (watch out, or you'll get a bad case of "hot pants") all the way down to an artificial subterranean lake, once used to dissolve the rock salt. At the entrance to the mines you'll find an Iron Age cemetery and a restaurant. ■ **TIP →** **Buy a "Salzerlebnis" (Salt Adventure) combination ticket from the ÖBB (Austrian Railway) that offers an all-inclusive value fare for travel to, from, and within Hallstatt, as well as the salt mine tour.** ⊠ *Salzbergstrasse 21* ☎ *06132/200–2490* ⊕ *www.salzwelten.at* ☞ *Funicular €7 one way, €13 round-trip; mine and tour €19; combination ticket for cable car and salt mines €24* ⊗ *Late Apr.–end Aug., daily 9:30–4:30; Sept. and Oct., daily 9:30–3* ☞ *No children under 5 years.*

Schifffahrt Boat Trips. The same company that ferries train passengers across the lake to Hallstatt also runs three other vessels offering boat tours around the lake via Obertraun to the south (50 minutes) or Obersee to the north (80 minutes). You can also link boat trips with hiking along the shore between pick-up points. ⊠ *Am Hof 126* ☎ *06134/8228* ⊕ *www.hallstattschifffahrt.at* ☞ *South lake trip: €5.50 one way, €8.50 round-trip. North lake trip: €5.50–6.50 one way, €10 round-trip. Full day unlimited ride pass: €17. Bikes: €3* ⊗ *May–Sept. south lake trip: daily at 11, 1, 2, 3, and 4:10; north trip: daily at 10:30, 1:30, and 3:30 (weather permitting).*

10

WHERE TO STAY

$ ⬚ **Bräugasthof.** With an idyllic lakeside perch, this former 16th-century
B&B/INN brewery (*Bräugasthof*), offers distinctive charm. **Pros:** cozy rooms;
lakefront setting. **Cons:** noisy during the day. $ *Rooms from: €105*
✉ *Seestrasse 120* ☎ *06134/8221* ⊕ *www.brauhaus-lobisser.com* ↦ *8
rooms* ⦿ *Breakfast.*

$$ ⬚ **Grüner Baum.** Glowing with a daffodil-yellow facade, sitting directly
HOTEL on the shore of the lake, and at the foot of a picture-perfect square, this
traditional inn is one of Hallstatt's most memorable accommodations.
Pros: on the lake; pretty views; newly renovated. **Cons:** simple break-
fast. $ *Rooms from: €158* ✉ *Marktplatz 104* ☎ *06134/8263* ⊕ *www.
gruenerbaum.cc* ↦ *20 rooms* ⦿ *Closed late Oct.–Apr.* ⦿ *Some meals.*

SPORTS AND THE OUTDOORS
ADVENTURE SPORTS
Outdoor Leadership. If you're ready for a true Alpine adventure, just
name your fear factor—from family-friendly to daredevil—and Heli
and Anja Putz's company has you covered, with a full team of skilled
outdoor guides ready to take you kayaking, canyoning, climbing, raft-
ing, paragliding or skiing throughout the Salzkammergut. These experts
know the mountains and caves like they're walking through their own
backyards, and they personally created many of the half- and full-day
routes that they offer. All necessary equipment is meticulously main-
tained and available for rent. ✉ *Steinach 4, Bad Goisern* ☎ *6135/6058*
⊕ *www.outdoor-leadership.com* ⏎ *Half day €68, full day €98.*

BOATING
Sport Zopf. The lakes of the Salzkammergut are excellent for canoeing
because most prohibit or limit powerboats. Try canoeing on the Hall-
stätter See. Sport Zopf delivers canoes, kayaks, and equipment directly
to the lakes and rivers nearby. ✉ *Obere Marktstraße 6, Bad Goisern*
☎ *06135/8254* ⊕ *www.abenteuersport.zopf.co.at.*

HIKING
There are many great hiking paths around Hallstatt; contact the local
tourist office for information about the path along the Echerntal to
Waldbachstrub past pleasant waterfalls, or the climb to the Tiergarten-
hütte, continuing on to the Wiesberghaus and, two hours beyond, the
Simony-Hütte, spectacularly poised at the foot of the Dachstein glacier.
From here, mountain climbers begin the ascent of the Hoher Dachstein,
the tallest peak of the Dachstein massif.

CARTHINA AND GRAZ

Updated by
Lizzy Randle
Williams

While lesser-known than the mountainous terrain of Tyrol or the culture-rich cities of Vienna and Salzburg, the southern provinces of Carinthia and Styria with its capital Graz—located directly above Italy and Slovenia and 2½ hours by train from Vienna—beckon visitors with spectacular mountain ranges, abundant forests, and glass-clear lakes.

Art lovers gravitate to such architectural landmarks as the Romanesque Gurk Cathedral, a host of Baroque town halls, and the medieval fantasy of the 9th-century castle Hochosterwitz. The provinces' summer season is custom tailored for bicycling, fishing, hiking, and water sports.

The area has a rich history and a distinguished musical past, and the sophistication and beauty of Graz may surprise you.

ORIENTATION AND PLANNING

GETTING ORIENTED

Carinthia is protected in the northwest by the vast Hohe Tauern range and the impossibly high and mighty Grossglockner. Along its northern borders are the bulky Nockberge National Park and the massive crests of the Noric mountain range, and to the east are the grassy meadows on the slopes of the Saualpe and Koralpe. Completing the circle in the south and bordering Slovenia and Italy are the steep, craggy Karawanken mountains and Carnic Alps. Lying serenely in the valleys between these rocky mountains are the long, meandering Drau and Gail rivers and more than 100 lakes, including the best known and largest, the Wörther See, as well as the Ossiacher See and Faaker See.

Klagenfurt toward the Gurktal Region. On the eastern end of Wörther See, the region's biggest lake, the Carinthian capital Klagenfurt prides itself on its charming city center and mellow lifestyle. The unspoiled Gurktal region attracts both hikers and art lovers. Blessed with verdant forests and Romanesque architecture, the northeastern corner of Carinthia enchants visitors with its pristine landscape.

Graz. Austria's second-largest city headlines as one of Europe's best preserved Renaissance town centers, dating to an era when Graz, not Vienna, was the capital. Italian architects, in fact, came to Graz to gain design experience and shaped the city with their exquisite building skills. Located in the Grazer basin and crossed by the Mur River, Graz has now turned into a lively meeting point for art and culture. The surrounding countryside boasts vineyards, thermal spas, and mountains.

TOP REASONS TO GO	

The Wörther See. In summer, this area turns into Austria's version of the Hamptons. Pleasure-seekers check into mansions-turned-hotels, boat on the crystalline lake, and party until the wee hours.

Burg Hochosterwitz. Walt Disney drew the inspiration for Snow White from this magnificent castle on top of a mountain. Not even the Turks were able to pass through its 14 gates.

Gurk Cathedral. Supported by 100 marble pillars, the most splendid of all the region's Romanesque churches features the original chair of St. Hemma. When women sit in it,

they supposedly have a nice surprise nine months later.

Graz. The UNESCO city of design, a fresh and young creative city, offers an all-year-round cultural program with events for all tastes.

Museum in a Palace. Actually there are four museums—plus the gorgeous Prunkräume (staterooms) in Graz's Schloss Eggenberg, itself a museum piece that sheds light on Austria's past.

Rogner Bad Blumau. A natural spring-water resort, a two-hour train ride northeast of Graz, is designed by artist Friedensreich Hundertwasser.

PLANNING

WHEN TO GO

Because of the bulwark of mountains that protect it from the cold winds of the north, the Carinthian and Styrian climate is milder than that of the rest of Austria, and it also boasts more sunshine. Consequently, the lakes maintain an average summer temperature of between 75°F and 82°F.

To see the province in its best festive dress of blue and emerald lakes framed by wooded hills and rocky peaks, and also do some swimming, come between mid-May and early October. Early spring, when the colors are purest and the crowds not yet in evidence, and fall, are perhaps the best times for quiet sightseeing. Christmas in Graz and Klagenfurt is a visual spectacle, with whole sections of the cities turned into a Christmas market. Winter in the area is an enigma: the Semmering mountains mark the eastern tail end of the Alps—north of the divide can be overcast and dreary while the area to the south basks in sunshine.

FESTIVALS

Lovers of classical music will enjoy Carinthischer Sommer, a festival in July and August with a heavy emphasis on sacred and chamber music. The Musikforum Viktring near Klagenfurt brings together world-renowned classical, electronic, and jazz artists. Through the summer and early fall, villages big and small celebrate their patron saints. These festivals are called Kirtag and feature music, dance, horseback-riding competitions, and lots of wine and beer. The Styriarte festival in Graz, from June to July, has classical music on the program. The Styrian Autumn festival, a celebration of contemporary art in October, or the

Spring festival, an electronic-music event, are just two examples of the many events taking place in Graz throughout the year.

GETTING HERE AND AROUND

AIR TRAVEL

Klagenfurt–Wörther See airport, just northeast of Klagenfurt, is served by Austrian, Lufthansa, and German low-cost carrier TUIfly airlines. Several flights daily connect the provincial capital with Vienna and Frankfurt, Germany. In summer, charter flights will take you from here to several popular Mediterranean tourist destinations.

The northern part of Eastern Austria is served by Vienna's international airport at Schwechat, 19 km (12 miles) southeast of the city center.

Graz has its own international airport at Feldkirchen, just south of the city, with flights to and from many major European cities, like London, Paris, and Berlin. Austrian Airlines, FlyNiki, and Lufthansa are the most ubiquitous carriers there.

Airport Information Graz Airport (*GRZ*). ✉ *Kalsdorferstrasse, Graz* ☎ *0316/2902–0.*

CAR TRAVEL

If you are driving, the most direct route from Vienna is via the Semmering mountain pass through Styria to Graz and on to Klagenfurt. Or take the heavily traveled A2 from Vienna to Graz and farther south. From Salzburg, the A10 autobahn tunnels beneath the Tauern range and the Katschberghöhe to make a dramatic entry into Carinthia, although the parallel Route 99, which runs "over the top," is the more scenic route. A pretty alternative here that leads you straight into the Nock Mountains or Gurk Valley is to leave the A10 at St. Michael after the Tauern Tunnel, head toward Tamsweg, and then take Route 97 through the Mur Valley; at Predlitz the pass road begins its climb over the steep Turracherhöhe into the Nock Mountains. The fork to Flattnitz, the most scenic way into the Gurk Valley, is at Stadl. Several mountain roads cross over from Italy, but the most traveled is Route 83 from Tarvisio.

TRAIN TRAVEL

As in all of Austria, post-office or railway (*Bundesbahn*) buses go virtually everywhere, but you'll have to allow plenty of time and coordinate schedules carefully so as not to get stranded in some remote location.

The main rail line south from Vienna parallels Route 83, entering Carinthia north of Friesach and continuing on to Klagenfurt and Villach. From Salzburg, a line runs south, tunneling under the Tauern mountains and then tracing the Möll and Drau river valleys to Villach. The main international north–south route connecting Vienna and northeastern Italy runs through Graz and is traversed by EuroCity trains from Munich and Salzburg.

Services on the main routes are fast and frequent. Trains depart from Vienna Meidling Station every two hours to Graz for a 2½-hour ride. The new train station, Hauptbahnhof (Central Train Station), officially opened in October2014.

Train Information ÖBB—National Train Information ☎ *05/1717* ⊕ *www.oebb.at.*

TOURS

The official tourist office for the province is Kärnten Werbung in Velden. The Kärnten Card costs €34, works between April and October, and includes access to more than 100 museums, attractions, lifts, and other sites of interest in the province. Many hotels offer the card to their guests for free for the duration of their stay.

ESSENTIALS

Visitor Information Kärnten Werbung ⊠ *Velden* ☎ *04274/521000* ⊕ *www.kaernten.at.*

RESTAURANTS

Through much of Carinthia you'll discover that, other than simple *Gasthäuser* (wine taverns), most dining spots are not independent establishments but belong to country inns. Carinthia's peasant tradition is reflected in its culinary specialties, such as *Kärntner Käsnudeln* (giant ravioli stuffed with a ricotta-like local cheese, and a whisper of mint), *Sterz* (polenta served either sweet or salty), and *Hauswürste* (smoked or air-cured hams and sausages, available at butcher shops).

Styria, bordering on Slovenia, has a hearty cuisine with Slavic overtones; a typical dish is *Steirisches Brathuhn* (roast chicken turned on a spit). The intensely nutty *Kürbiskernöl* (pumpkinseed oil) is used in many soup and pasta dishes, as well as in salad dressings, or to top off vanilla ice cream.

HOTELS

Accommodations range from luxurious lakeside resorts to small inns, and even include guesthouses without private baths. Accommodations in private homes are cheaper still. These bargains are usually identified by signs reading "Zimmer frei" (room available) or "Frühstückspension" (bed-and-breakfast). Summers are never too hot, and it cools off delightfully at night, which means that most hotels are not equipped with air-conditioning. Some hotels offer half-board, which includes dinner in addition to buffet breakfast (although most $$$$ hotels will charge extra for breakfast). The half-board room rate is usually an extra €15–€30 per person. Occasionally quoted room rates for hotels already include half-board accommodations, though a "discounted" rate is usually available if you prefer not to take the evening meal. Inquire when booking.

WHAT IT COSTS IN EUROS			
$	**$$**	**$$$**	**$$$$**
RESTAURANTS under €12	€12–€17	€18–€22	over €22
HOTELS under €100	€100–€135	€136–€175	over €175

Restaurant prices are per person for a main course at dinner. Hotel prices are for a standard double room in high season, including taxes and service. Higher prices (inquire when booking) prevail for any meal plans.

KLAGENFURT TOWARD THE GURKTAL REGION

Heading north from Klagenfurt you enter genuine, rural, Austrian countryside. Small villages, farms, wide pastures, and forests unfold while driving over smooth hills. Burg Hochosterwitz, perched on a steep hill, can be seen from far away. A popular place of pilgrimage is Gurk Cathedral, a Romanesque basilica from the 12th century and an important building full of European religious art. Friesach, a medieval town, and one of the oldest in Carinthia, is another highlight on this route.

KLAGENFURT

329 km (192 miles) southwest of Vienna, 209 km (130 miles) southeast of Salzburg.

Klagenfurt became the provincial capital in 1518, so most of the delightful sites here date from the 16th century or later. However, a group of attention-getting Carinthian architects has also breathed new life into old buildings. The town is an excellent base for excursions to the rest of Carinthia. In the city center you can't miss the *Lindwurm,* Klagenfurt's emblematic dragon with a curled tail, which adorns the fountain on Neuer Platz (New Square). Legend has it that the town was founded on this spot, where the beast was destroyed by resident peasants back in days of yore (but the notion of Klagenfurt's dragon became more intriguing when the fossilized cranium of a prehistoric rhinoceros was found nearby).

GETTING HERE AND AROUND

If you come from Italy, Klagenfurt can be reached via the southern highway, A2, which continues all the way to Graz and Vienna. Coming from Salzburg take the A10, via Villach. It's well connected by railway from Salzburg and Vienna. Several buses serve the route daily from Graz. A system of public buses connects Klagenfurt and its surroundings. Centrally located Heiligengeistplatz is the major bus hub. Bus tickets can be purchased from the driver (€1.90). Take bus No. 10 or No. 20 to explore the Wörther See. Klagenfurt itself is compact and easy to explore on foot.

ESSENTIALS

Bike Rentals **Impulse Radverleih Klagenfurt** ✉ *Durchlassstrasse 44* ☎ *0463/418937* ⊕ *www.impulse.co.at.*

Tourist Information **Klagenfurt** ✉ *Neuer Platz 1* ☎ *0463/537–2223* ⊕ *www.klagenfurt-tourismus.at.*

EXPLORING

Alter Platz. The old town square of Klagenfurt, or Alter Platz, is still the center of the city. Brightly colored buildings with baroque facades dating from the 12th century frame this pedestrian meeting area. A Trinity Column dating from 1680 (which represents God, Jesus Christ, and the Holy Spirit) now stands in the Alter Platz. These columns were built all over Europe as a thanks to God from the people for having survived the Plague that killed nearly 25 million Europeans during the Middle Ages. The brightly colored yellow building is the old town hall. ✉ *Alter Platz.*

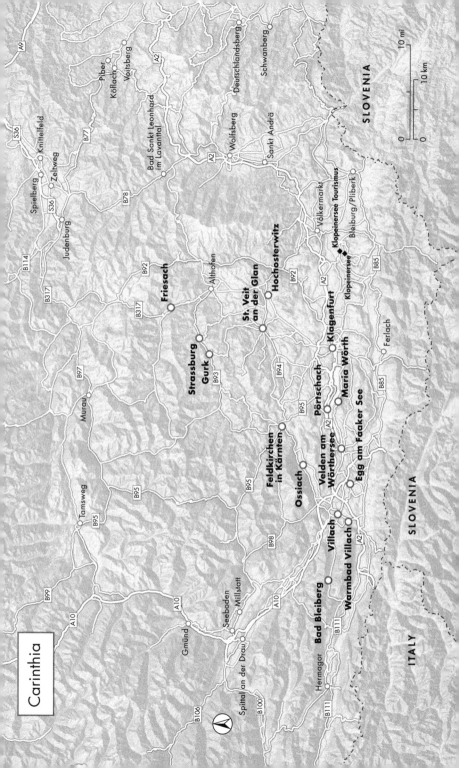

Domkirche (*Cathedral*). South of Neuer Platz (take Karfreitstrasse) is the Domkirche, completed as a Protestant church in 1581, given over to the Jesuits and reconsecrated in 1604, and finally declared a cathedral in 1787. The 18th-century side-altar painting of St. Ignatius by Paul Troger, the great Viennese rococo painter and teacher, is a fine example of the qualities of transparency and light he introduced to painting. ⊠ *Domplatz.*

OFF THE BEATEN PATH

Klopeinersee. With water temperatures averaging 28°C (82°F) from spring to fall, this lake is a popular spot for sunbathing. Surrounded by gentle mountains, it's a little over 1½-km (1-mile) long and 1-km (½-mile) wide, and motorboats are not allowed. To reach the Klopeinersee, take the west Völkermarkt/Tainach exit from the A2 autobahn and follow signs to the lake. It's about a 30-minute drive east of Klagenfurt. ⊠ *Klopein.*

Klopeinersee Tourismus. For information on lakeside hotels and pensions, contact Klopeinersee Tourismus. ⊠ *Klopeiner Strasse 5* ⊕ *www. klopeinersee.com.*

Landhaus (*District government headquarters*). One of the most notable sights of the city is the Landhaus, with its towers and court with arcaded stairways. It was completed in 1590, and at the time formed a corner of the city wall. The only interior on view is the dramatic **Grosser Wappensaal** (Great Hall of Heraldry), which contains 665 coats of arms of Carinthia's landed gentry and on the ceiling a stirring rendition of the Fürstenstein investiture ceremony portrayed by Fromiller, the most important Carinthian painter of the Baroque period. ∎**TIP**➔ **The Gasthaus im Landhaushof, on the ground floor, is well worth a stop for lunch.** ⊠ *Landhaushof 1* ☏ *463/577–570* ⊕ *www. landesmuseum-ktn.at* ☜ *€3* ⊙ *Apr.–Oct., weekdays 9–4, Sat. and holidays 9–2.*

FAMILY **Minimundus.** From Klagenfurt, bypass the autobahn and instead take Villacher Strasse (Route 83) to the Wörther Lake, Austria's great summer resort area. You'll pass by the entrancing Minimundus, literally "miniature world," with around 150 1:25 scale models. These are of such structures as the White House, the Taj Mahal, the Eiffel Tower, and the Gur-Emir Mausoleum from Uzbekistan, all built when possible from the original materials. Net proceeds support needy children and families in Carinthia. ⊠ *Villacher Strasse 241* ☏ *0463/211940* ⊕ *www.minimundus.at* ☜ *€13, family tickets avaliable* ⊙ *Apr. daily 9–6; May, June, and Sept., daily 9–7; Aug., Mon. 9 am–10 pm, Wed. 9 am–11 pm, Tues., Fri., weekends 9–8.*

Museum Moderner Kunst Kärnten. This museum displays works by modern and contemporary artists. It pays special attention to avant-garde artists with roots in Carinthia. Maria Lassnig, Arnulf Rainer, and Bruno Gironcoli, some of the heavyweights of post–World War II art, hail from the region. The museum also fosters the young art scene by showing works by emerging artists such as Hans Schabus and Heimo Zobernig. ⊠ *Burggasse 8* ☏ *050/53616252* ⊕ *www.mmkk.at* ☜ *€5* ⊙ *Tues.–Sun. 10–6, Thurs. 10–10.*

OFF THE BEATEN PATH

Pyramidenkogel. On the shore of the Wörthersee, a winding 5-km (3-mile) road ascends to the 850-meter (2,790-foot) observation tower, the Pyramidenkogel; take its elevator up to its three platforms and you can see out over half of Carinthia. ⊠ *Keutschach Am See* ⊕ *www.pyramidenkogel.info* ⓢ *€6* ☉ *Apr. and Oct., daily 10–6; May and Sept., daily 9–7; June, daily 9–8; July and Aug., daily 9–9.*

FAMILY **Reptilien Zoo.** Adjacent to Minimundus is the Reptilien Zoo, featuring crocodiles, cobras, rattlesnakes, and several kinds of hairy spiders, as well as colorful fish from the nearby Wörther Lake. ⊠ *Villacher Strasse 237* ☎ *0463/23425* ⊕ *www. reptilienzoo.at* ⓢ *€13* ☉ *Summer 8–6; winter 10–5; Nov. closed.*

> **FRESH CATCHES**
>
> Carinthia is full of lakes and rivers that abound with carp, pike, perch, eel, bream, crawfish (in a rather short season), and, best of all, a large variety of trout. The most popular way of serving Austrian brook trout and rainbow trout is *blau* (blue), the whole fish simmered in a court bouillon and served with drawn butter. Or try it *Müllerin*—sautéed in butter until a crisp brown. In summer, try *kalte Räucherforelle* (cold smoked trout) with lemon or horseradish as a delicate hors d'oeuvre.

St. Egyd. North of Neuer Platz (go along Kramergasse for two blocks, then angle left to the Pfarrplatz) is the parish church of St. Egyd, with its eye-catching totem-pole bronze carving by Austrian avant-garde artist Ernst Fuchs in the second chapel on the right. In the next chapel is the crypt of Julian Green (1900–98), the noted French-born American novelist whose works include *The Closed Garden* and *The Other One*. He perceived the city as a sanctuary of peace in the world and decided he wanted to be buried here. ⊠ *Pfarrhofgasse 4.*

WHERE TO EAT

$$$ ✕ **Bar-Bistro 151.** A haunted-house chandelier on the front porch of
CONTEMPORARY this sprawling establishment leads the way to 1930s-style salons with crimson accent walls, sofas, gilt sconces, naughty modern art, petite low-light table lamps, and a fireplace (with a video monitor of a fire playing). The restaurant is a haven for trendsetters, so you may want to don your best duds. Best bets include the seasonal cream of asparagus soup with a generous amount of crayfish, the butter-knife-tender filet mignon, and the delicate duck ravioli. The bistro is five minutes by car outside of town along the way to the Wörther See. ⓢ *Average main: €19* ⊠ *Höhenweg 151* ☎ *0463/281653* ⌕ *Reservations essential* ☉ *Closed Sun.*

$ ✕ **Bierhaus zum Augustin.** This rustic brewery is in one of the oldest build-
AUSTRIAN ings in Klagenfurt and attracts a mixed and lively clientele. The excellent beer produced here pairs perfectly with the local cuisine. If the weather permits, try to get a place in the lovely courtyard. Its convenient location in the city center makes it a popular meeting place; be prepared for a crowd. ⓢ *Average main: €9* ⊠ *Pfarrhofgasse 2* ☎ *0463/513–992* ☉ *Closed Sun.*

$$$ ✕ **Dolce Vita.** Small and exclusive, this tucked-away establishment in
MEDITERRANEAN the city center offers cutting-edge Austrian cuisine with an Italian slant. Though the tiny peach-color interior is appealing, the secluded

garden is the real draw. Your meal begins with a colorful sampling of soups arranged like an artist's palette: saffron potato, white asparagus, and gazpacho. Frequent offerings include the Venetian *sarde in saor* (sardines in a sweet-and-sour sauce) or the silky tagliatelle with prosciutto and asparagus. The restaurant uses organic products and locally caught fish in dishes like turbot fillet with foie gras and artichokes. Be sure to save room for homemade ice cream. $ *Average main: €22* ⊠ *Heuplatz 2* ☎ *0463/55499* ⚐ *Reservations essential* ⊙ *Weekdays 11–3, and from 6 pm* ⊙ *Closed weekends.*

$ ✕ **Hamatle.** Like a little family-owned farmhouse in the center of the
AUSTRIAN city, this homey establishment just off the Villacher Ring is the place to go for Kärntner Käsnudeln, a Carinthian specialty resembling large, round ravioli. They're light as a feather and delicately stuffed with your choice of spinach, cheese, or minced beef. Schnitzels and other Austrian specialties are also featured. On Saturday, the restaurant serves its signature Schweinsbraten, pork roast with slow-cooked sauerkraut. The sommelier is well informed about Austrian wines. $ *Average main: €11* ⊠ *Linsengasse 1* ☎ *0463/555700* ⊙ *Closed Mon.*

$$ ✕ **Maria Loretto.** Gorgeous is the word to describe this spot's perch,
SEAFOOD which offers a view over the Wörther See and makes a fitting backdrop for some of the area's best seafood. This former villa offers several romantic dining rooms in champagne and red tones, or you can sit outdoors on the wraparound terrace overlooking the glistening water. Don't miss the appetizer of delicate trout caviar and smoked salmon on crispy toast points, then try the grilled calamari or *Seeteufel* medallions (monkfish drizzled with garlic butter). For dessert, try the sinfully good Grand Marnier parfait. You'll need a taxi to get here. $ *Average main: €17* ⊠ *Lorettoweg 54* ☎ *0463/24465* ⊕ *www.restaurant-maria-loretto.at* ⚐ *Reservations essential* ⊙ *Warm food daily 11–10 in July and Aug.* ⊙ *Closed Tues.*

$$ ✕ **Ristorante Michelangelo.** Don't be fooled by the Klagenfurt's proximity
ITALIAN to Italy. Most eateries claiming to serve authentic Italian cuisine don't have it quite right. For the real deal, take the trip out of the town center to Michelangelo. Come for the welcoming environment and stay for a three-course menu or the pasta *alla Norma,* a Sicilian specialty with eggplant and salted ricotta. A favorite is the sea bass baked in salt crust. There are many vegetarian options, including the wood-oven-baked pizzas. Local families crowd the place on weekends. $ *Average main: €13* ⊠ *St. Veiter Strasse 181* ☎ *0463/481–889* ⊕ *www.ristorante-michelangelo.at* ⊙ *Tues.–Sun. 11:30 am–midnight; closed Mon.*

WHERE TO STAY

$$ ⬚ **Arcotel Moser Verdino.** With a facade of dusky rose and wrought-iron
HOTEL balconies, this central hotel has been around for more than a century. **Pros:** state-of-the-art amenities; comfortable mattresses; free Wi-Fi. **Cons:** not enough parking; expensive breakfast if not in your room rate. $ *Rooms from: €156* ⊠ *Domgasse 2* ☎ *0463/578780* ⊕ *www.moserverdino.at* ⤳ *68 rooms, 3 suites* ⊙ *Breakfast.*

$ ⬚ **City Hotel zum Domplatz.** Just a few steps from the center's main
HOTEL square, this convenient little hotel is a good choice for leisure or business travelers on a budget. **Pros:** quiet courtyard; good breakfast;

complimentary tea and apples. **Cons:** no elevator; no meals other than breakfast. [$] *Rooms from: €80* ✉ *Karfreitstrasse 20* ☎ *0463/54320* 🌐 *www.cityhotel-klagenfurt.at* 🛏 *12 rooms* 🍴 *Breakfast.*

$$ HOTEL **Sandwirth.** Once *the* watering hole of Klagenfurt society, the Sandwirth now features streamlined furniture and innovative works of art that recast vintage landscape photographs in a new light, while retaining the 19th-century yellow facade. **Pros:** ideal for large conference groups; friendly staff. **Cons:** lobby is used for conference coffee breaks at times; no parking. [$] *Rooms from: €140* ✉ *Pernhartgasse 9* ☎ *0463/56209* 🌐 *www.sandwirth.at* 🛏 *96 rooms, 4 suites* 🍴 *Breakfast.*

$$ HOTEL **Seepark Hotel.** Designed by a group of young Austrian architects, this hotel attracts business and leisure travelers alike, thanks to its position on the shores of the Wörther See. **Pros:** five-minute walk to Wörther See; modern design; lake views from third floor and higher. **Cons:** small pool; no outdoor pool; out of town. [$] *Rooms from: €150* ✉ *Universitätsstrasse 104* ☎ *0463/204–4990* 🌐 *www.seeparkhotel.at/hotel.html* 🛏 *142 rooms.*

NIGHTLIFE AND PERFORMING ARTS

NIGHTLIFE

For a true after-hours scene in Klagenfurt, head for the Pfarrplatz-Herrengasse area, where you'll find a number of intimate bars and cafés.

Palais Egger Helldorff. For some of the best mixed drinks in town, visit the discreetly marked Palais Egger Helldorff, once the palace where Napoléon camped out during the French occupation in 1797. Within its courtyard are two hip bars and a trendy Mexican restaurant. ✉ *Herrengasse 12* ⏱ *Tues.–Sun. 8 pm–4 am.*

PERFORMING ARTS

Stadttheater Klagenfurt. A large variety of operas, operettas, plays, and ballets are performed year-round at the Stadttheater in Klagenfurt, an inviting art nouveau building designed by the famous theater architects Helmer and Fellner of Vienna and completed in 1910. The box office is open Monday–Saturday, 9–6. ✉ *Theaterplatz 4* ☎ *0463/54064* 🌐 *www.stadttheater-klagenfurt.at.*

HOCHOSTERWITZ

31 km (19 miles) south of Friesach.

GETTING HERE AND AROUND

From Klagenfurt, head northeast on St. Veiterstrasse and merge onto S37. The castle is well signposted and can be seen from far away.

EXPLORING

FAMILY Fodor's Choice ★ **Hochosterwitz.** The year 860 marks when the name of this dramatic castle was first written. The castle of Hochosterwitz crowns the top of a steep, isolated outcropping, looking as if it has just emerged from the pages of a fairy tale. It was in this castle that the forces of "Pocket-Mouthed Meg"—Margarethe Maultasch—were tricked by two slaughtered oxen dropped onto the heads of its soldiers. Those inside the fortress were starving, but the strategy succeeded, and, dispirited by such apparent proof of abundant supplies, the Tyrolese abandoned the siege. The most recent fortifications were added in the late 1500s against invading Turks; each of the 14 towered gates is a small fortress unto itself. Inside, there's an impressive collection of armor and weaponry plus a café-restaurant in the inner courtyard. There's a glass elevator (accommodating wheelchairs) from a point near the parking-lot ticket office. The hike up the rather steep path to Hochosterwitz adds to the drama. Your reward at the summit is spectacular vistas from every vantage point. Get to the castle on the back road from Treibach or via Route 83/E7. ⊠ *Hochosterwitz 1, Launsdorf* ☎ *04213/34597* ⊕ *www.burg-hochosterwitz.com* 🖃 *€12* ⊘ *Apr.–Oct., 10–5; May–Sept., 9–6.*

GURK

47 km (29 miles) north of Klagenfurt.

Gurk is located in central Carinthia in the Gurk Valley, surrounded by high mountain meadows and magnificent forests. The actual center of the valley is characterized by the two mighty towers of the cathedral.

GETTING HERE AND AROUND

Take the Klagenfurter Schnellstrasse S37, at Pöckstein, and turn left onto Gurktalstrasse B93.

EXPLORING

Dom (*Cathedral*). Gurk's claim to fame is its massive Romanesque Dom topped by two onion cupolas and considered the most famous religious landmark in Carinthia. It was founded in the 11th century by Hemma, Countess of Zeltschach, who after losing her two sons and husband decided to turn to religious works. She had two oxen tied before a cart and let them walk until they stopped on their own. At that spot she founded a cloister and gave all her belongings to the church for building a cathedral. Construction on the cathedral itself began in 1140 and ended in 1200. Hemma wasn't canonized until 1938. Her tomb is in the crypt, whose ceiling, and hence the cathedral itself, is supported by 100 marble pillars. The Hemma-Stein, a small green-slate chair from which she personally supervised construction, is also there and alleged to bring fertility to barren women. In the church itself, the high altar is one of the most important examples of early baroque in Austria. Note the *Pietà* by George Rafael Donner, who is sometimes called the Austrian Michelangelo. Be sure to visit the bishop's chapel, which features rare late-Romanesque and Gothic frescoes. At the end of August and in early September a concert series is held in the cathedral. Tours are restricted by church services, but in summer 90-minute tours are usually scheduled for 10:30, 1:30, and 3. ⊠ *Domplatz 11* ☎ *04266/82830* 🖃 *Short tour including crypt €4.60; long tour €7.50* ⊘ *Daily 9–5, Aug. 9–6, winter 10–4.*

FAMILY **Zwergenpark.** The Zwergenpark is a vast natural preserve filled with amusing garden statuary, consisting largely of typically about 1,000 Austrian-German garden gnomes; children can traverse the park via a miniature railway. ⊠ *Dr. Schnerichstrasse* ☎ *04266/8077* ⊕ *www.zwergenpark.com* 🖃 *€5* ⊘ *May–late June, daily 10–4; late June–late Aug., daily 10–6; late Aug–mid-Sept., daily 11–4.*

FRIESACH

22 km (13 miles) northeast of Gurk.

The oldest settlement in Carinthia, romantic Friesach is great for wandering. Friesach has many medieval marvels: be sure to stop in at the tourist office for information on all of them.

GETTING HERE AND AROUND

Take the Klagenfurter Schnellstrasse S37 coming from the south.

ESSENTIALS

Tourist Information **Friesach.** Freisach is the oldest town in Carinthia, first mentioned in an 860 deed. The town is peppered with red-roofed buildings encircled by an old stone wall. There is a well-preserved medieval town center and a Romanesque parish church, as well as Petersburg Castle, home to the Friesach City Muesum, which features exhibits on the town's history and culture. ✉ *Fürstenhofplatz 1* ☎ *04268/221340* 🌐 *www.friesach.at.*

EXPLORING

Dominican Monastery. This Dominican Monastery of St. Nikolaus von Myra is named after St. Nikolaus, the man who eventually led to the pop culture Saint Nick and to Santa Claus. The monastery is near the town's moat, and was rebuilt in 1673, though the church nearby dates from 1217. Take a moment to notice the stone statue of the Virgin Mary inside the monastery, and the massive crucifix. At the end of July a large medieval festival takes place in Freisach and the courtyard is the reenacted meeting place for dueling knights. ✉ *Stadtgrabengasse 5.*

Hauptplatz. It's easy to find the Hauptplatz (main square), with its old town hall and gleaming, multicolor pastel facades. As you stroll you'll discover aspects of the medieval-era town: beautiful stone houses, the double wall, and the towers, gates, and water-filled moat. ✉ *Hauptplatz, off Kirchgasse.*

Schloss Petersberg. From a footpath at the upper end of the main square, take a steep 20-minute climb up to the impressive remains of Schloss Petersberg to see the 12th- and 13th-century castle. The **Stadtmuseum** (city museum) displays the history of the oldest city in Carinthia. Additionally, make a stop to the **Petersbergkirche**, a Romanesque church first built in 1130. ✉ *North of Hauptplatz off Kirchgasse.*

Stadtpfarrkirche. The 12th-century Romanesque Stadtpfarrkirche (parish church) has some excellent stained glass in the choir.

WHERE TO STAY

$ HOTEL 🏨 **Friesacherhof.** Incorporated into a centuries-old building on the main square, this comfortable hotel has rather plain but well-kept rooms; those in front look out over the square and the Renaissance fountain and can be somewhat noisy. **Pros:** bargain rates; newly renovated rooms. **Cons:** front rooms can be noisy. [$] *Rooms from: €70* ✉ *Hauptplatz 4* ☎ *04268 2123* 🌐 *www.friesacherhof.at/* 🛏 *23 rooms* ⏲ *Closed Jan.* 🍴 *Multiple meal plans.*

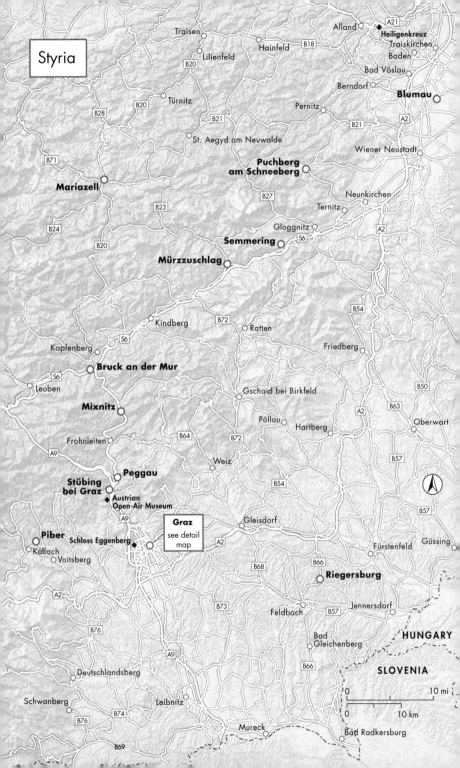

11

$ **Metnitztalerhof.** This delightful hotel has overlooked the medieval
HOTEL town square for more than 400 years. **Pros:** historic charm; in the center of town. **Cons:** some rooms have so-so views. $ *Rooms from: €100* ⊠ *Hauptplatz 11* ☎ *04268/25100* ⊕ *www.metnitzhof.at* ⤳ *27 rooms* ⊘ *Closed 2 wks in Nov.* ⦿ *Multiple meal plans.*

GRAZ

Fodor's Choice *200 km (125 miles) southwest of Vienna, 285 km (178 miles) southeast*
★ *of Salzburg.*

Austria's second-largest city, Graz is graceful, welcoming, and far from the usual tourist routes. Instead of visitors, it's the large university population that keeps the sidewalk cafés, trendy bars, and chic restaurants humming in the vibrant Altstadt. The modern-art museum, the Kunsthaus, has a startling biomorphic blue shape that looms over rooftops like some alien spaceship. Along with this, the annual Styriarte summer music festival has become one of the most prestigious cultural draws in the country, and the city opera theater now attracts top companies like the Bolshoi. Graz is far from the cultural backwater it once was; in fact, it was designated the 2003 "European Capital of Culture" and was appointed as UNESCO city of design in 2011.

With its skyline dominated by the squat 16th-century clock tower, this stylish city has a gorgeous and well-preserved medieval center whose Italian Renaissance overlay gives it, in contrast to other Austrian cities, a Mediterranean feel. The name Graz derives from the Slavic *gradec,* meaning "small castle"; there was probably a fortress atop the Schlossberg hill as early as the 9th century. By the 12th century a town had developed at the foot of the hill, which in time became an imperial city of the ruling Habsburgs. Graz's glory faded in the 17th century when the court moved to Vienna, but the city continued to prosper as the provincial capital of Styria, especially under the enlightened 19th-century rule of Archduke Johann.

In 1811, the archduke founded the Landesmuseum Joanneum, making it the oldest public museum in Austria. This museum complex, with 12 locations, has notable collections of art, archaeology, and armor, as well as fossils and folklife artifacts. An €11, 24-hour ticket allows you entry to all collections and exhibitions.

GETTING HERE AND AROUND

Streetcars and buses are an excellent way of traveling within the city. Single tickets (€2.10) can be bought from the driver or kiosks, and one-day and multiple-ride tickets are also available. All six streetcar routes converge at Jakominiplatz near the south end of the Old City. One fare may combine streetcars and buses as long as you take a direct route to your destination. Driving in the Graz city center is not advisable, because there are many narrow, one-way, and pedestrian streets and few places to park. In Graz, taxis can be ordered by phone.

If you're pressed for time, choose which part of the Old City you'd rather see: the lower section, with its churches, historical houses, and museums, or the upper town, with its winding wooded paths, famous clock tower, and the Schlossberg, the lookout point of the city. The best time to visit is between April and October, when the weather is at its most inviting.

WALKING TOURS

Guided walking tours of Graz in English and German are conducted daily at 2:30 from April to October, and on Saturday at 2:30 between November and March. The meeting point for these tours is Tourist Information at Herrengasse 16. The cost is €9.50.

ESSENTIALS

Bus Information Graz Airport (GRZ). ☎ 0316/2902172 ⊕ www. flughafen-graz.at. **Public Transport Graz** ☎ 0316/887–4224 ⊕ www.holding-graz.at/linien.html. **Taxis** ☎ 0316/889, 0316/889, 0316/2801.

Tourist Information Grazer Tourismus ✉ Herrrengasse 16, Graz, Styria ☎ 0316/8075 ⊕ www.graztourismus.at.

> ### EXCURSIONS
>
> The lush, wine-terraced area 30 minutes south of Graz is home to some of the best wineries in the country.
>
> **Graz Tourist Office.** The Graz tourist office offers city walking tours, as well as bus excursions on Saturday to see Styria. A favorite one is the trip to the southern Styrian wine region, where you can explore the local food and drink culture. Ask at the office for details. ☎ 0316/8075–0 ⊕ www. graztourismus.at.

EXPLORING GRAZ

TOP ATTRACTIONS

Burg. The scanty remains of this former imperial palace now house government offices. Most of this uninspired structure is from the 19th and 20th centuries, but two noteworthy vestiges of the original 15th-century stronghold remain: the **Burgtor** (palace gate), which opens into the sprawling **Stadtpark** (municipal park), and the unusual 49-step, 26-foot carved stone double-spiral **Gothic staircase** from 1494 to 1500, in the hexagonal tower at the far end of the first courtyard. While meandering around take note of the Spor, a statue of a seed, which represents the center of Graz. ✉ Hofgasse 15, Graz, Styria.

Domkirche. On the cathedral's south exterior wall is a badly damaged 15th-century fresco called the *Gottesplagenbild*, which graphically depicts contemporary local torments—the plague, locusts, and the Turks. Step inside to see the outstanding high altar made of colored marble, the choir stalls, and Konrad Laib's *Crucifixion* from 1457 (considered one of the top late-Gothic panel paintings of German-speaking Europe). The 15th-century reliquaries on either side of the triumphal arch leading to the choir were originally the bridal chests of Paola Gonzaga, daughter of Ludovico II of Mantua. The Baroque **Mausoleum** of Emperor Ferdinand II, who died in 1637, adjoins the cathedral. Its sumptuous interior is partly an early design by native son Fischer von Erlach, and his only work to be seen in Graz. ✉ Burggasse 3, Graz, Styria ☎ 0316/80750 ⌑ Domkirche free; mausoleum free ☉ Domkirche daily 11–dusk; mausoleum daily 10:30–12:30 and 1:30–4.

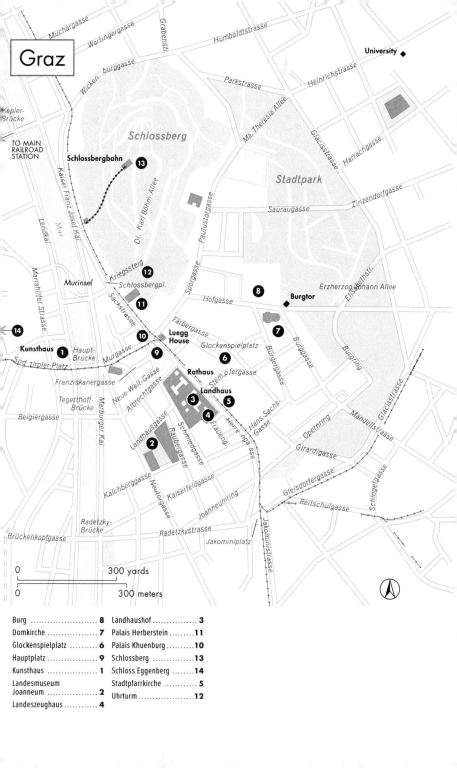

Graz

Muchargasse
Wartingergasse
Wicken burggasse
Grabenstr.
Humboldtstrasse
University ◆
Parkstrasse
Heinrichstrasse
Kepler-Brücke
TO MAIN RAILROAD STATION
Schlossberg
Ma. Theresia Allee
Glacisstrasse
Harrachgasse
Schlossbergbahn
Stadtpark
13
Dr. Karl Böhm Allee
Paulustorgasse
Zinzendorfgasse
Sauraugasse
Kaiser Franz Josef Kai
Mur
Lendkai
Murinsel
Kriegssteig
Schlossbergpl.
Sackstrasse
Sporgasse
Hofgasse
Erzherzog Johann Allee
Elisabethstr.
12
11
8
Burgtor ◆
Mariahilfer Strasse
Färbergasse
Luegg House
Glockenspielplatz
7
Burggasse
Burgring
14
Kunsthaus **1**
Haupt-Brücke
Stig tirpler-Platz
Murgasse
10
9
Rathaus
6
Burgergasse
Franziskanergasse
Neue-Welt-Gasse
Albrechtgasse
Landhausgasse
Raubergasse
Schmiedgasse
Landhaus
3
5
Fraueng.
Stempfergasse
Herre ngasse
Hans-Sachs-Gasse
Opernring
Mandellstrasse
Glacisstrasse
Tegetthoff-Brücke
Belgiergasse
Marburger Kai
2
4
Girardigasse
Schlögelgasse
Kalchberggasse
Neutorgasse
Kaiserfeldgasse
Joanneumring
Gleisdorfergasse
Reitschulgasse
Radetzky-Brücke
Brückenkopfgasse
Radetzkystrasse
Jakominiplatz
Jakoministrasse

0 ——— 300 yards
0 ——— 300 meters

Burg	8	Landhaushof	3
Domkirche	7	Palais Herberstein	11
Glockenspielplatz	6	Palais Khuenburg	10
Hauptplatz	9	Schlossberg	13
Kunsthaus	1	Schloss Eggenberg	14
Landesmuseum Joanneum	2	Stadtpfarrkirche	5
Landeszeughaus	4	Uhrturm	12

Glockenspielplatz. Every day at 11 am and 3 and 6 pm two mullioned windows open in the mechanical clock high above the square, revealing a life-size wooden couple, the man adorned in lederhosen, a tankard of beer in his upraised fist, accompanied by a dirndl-clad Austrian maiden. An old folk tune plays and they dance on the window ledges before returning to their hidden perch. The musical box was erected in 1905 by the owner of the house. Look into the courtyard at No. 5, which has an impressive 17th-century open staircase. The house at No. 7 has an arcaded Renaissance courtyard. ■TIP→ Have a typical Austrian meal right next door at Glöckl Bräu, where they brew their own beer. Every time a new barrel is opened, the bells above ring. ⊠ *Glockenspielplatz, Graz, Styria.*

> **GRAZ'S BERMUDA TRIANGLE**
>
> Mehlplatz is lined with historic houses and has a number of bars. This is popularly known as the Bermuda Triangle, because the university students have such a good time here that they "never come out again." In summer it's perfect for sipping a beer or wine while watching the passing crowd.

Hauptplatz (*Main Square*). This triangular area was converted from a swampy pastureland to a town square by traveling merchants in 1164; today it's the central meeting spot of Graz. In its center stands the **Erzherzog Johann Brunnen** (Archduke Johann Fountain), dedicated to the popular 19th-century patron whose enlightened policies did much to develop Graz as a cultural and scientific center. The four female figures represent what were Styria's four main rivers; today only the Mur and the Enns are still within the province. The **Luegg House,** at the corner of Sporgasse, is noted for its baroque stucco facade. On the west side of the square are Gothic and Renaissance houses. The spectacular, late-19th-century **Rathaus** (City Hall) totally dominates the south side. From the Neue-Welt-Gasse and Schmiedgasse you get a superb view of the Hauptplatz. ⊠ *Hauptpltatz, Graz, Styria.*

Kunsthaus. Across the River Mur from the Altstadt is a new modern-art museum nicknamed the "Friendly Alien"—and indeed, it does look like an alien ship landed smack in the middle of the town's medieval orange-tile, gabled roofs. Designed by London-based architects Peter Cook and Colin Fournier, with the aim of forging an interaction between the traditional landmarks of Graz and the avant-garde, it resembles a gigantic, blue, beached whale with spiky tentacles—which light up at night. Inside, the vast exhibition rooms are linked by escalators and spiraling walkways, with an open arena at the top offering spectacular views. There is no permanent collection here, only temporary exhibits of renowned modern artists. ■TIP→ Check out the gift shop on the ground floor. ⊠ *Lendkai 1, Graz, Styria* ☎ *0316/801–79–200* ⊕ *www. kunsthausgraz.at* ☜ €8 ☉ *Tues.–Sun. 10–6.*

NEED A BREAK? If you need a break after visiting Graz's many churches and museums, head to Murinsel island. It's actually not an island but a floating platform, designed by modernist artist Vito Acconci in 2003 in honor of the city's designation as the European Capital of Culture. You can access it below

11

the Kunsthaus, where a pedestrian walkway leads from the Haupt-Brucke bridge to the steel structure in the shape of a seashell. Murinsel includes a trendy café, amphitheater, and playground made of ropes. Mothers beware: your kids will love the ropes.

Landesmuseum Joanneum. The oldest public museum in Austria is a vast complex located between Neutorgasse, Kalchberggasse, and Raubergasse. The recently restructured Joanneum Quarter hosts the natural history collections, the Styrian state library, the Neue Galerie Graz and the multimedia collections. ⊠ *Joanneumsviertel, access Kalchberggasse, Graz, Styria* ☎ *0316/8017 9100* ⊕ *www.museum-joanneum.at* ☎ *€11. Ticket valid within 24 hrs for all other museums of Landesmuseum* ⊙ *Daily 10–5.*

Department of Geology and Paleontology. The holdings of the Department of Geology and Paleontology, which was founded in 1892, take you through 500 million years of Styrian geology. Shells and corals show that Styria was once a sea. Later fossils reveal its mammal inhabitants, now extinct. ☎ *0316/801-79-730.*

Mineralogy Collection. The Mineralogy Collection contains more than 13,000 minerals collected in Styria. ☎ *0316/801-79-740.*

Department of Zoology. The Department of Zoology includes more than 500,000 items and shows reconstructions of typical Styrian habitats with the animals that populate them. ☎ *0316/801-79-760.*

Botanic Collection. Started by Archduke Johann, Botanic Collection has grown to include more than 400,000 dried specimens. The main focus of the collection is on ferns and flowering plants; there are no greenhouses or gardens. ☎ *0316/801-79-750.*

FAMILY **Landeszeughaus.** With 32,000 items on display, the Styrian Armoury is the largest preserved arsenal in the world, and one of the biggest attractions in Graz. Built between 1642 and 1644 on behalf of the Styrian nobility, the four-story armory still contains the 16th- and 17th-century weapons intended for use by Styrian mercenaries in fighting off the Turks. Empress Maria Theresia closed the armory in 1749, due to extended periods of peace; however, it remained intact to illustrate the history of the area. The collection includes more than 3,000 suits of armor (some of which are beautifully engraved), thousands of halberds, swords, firearms, cannons, and mortars—some hanging off the ceiling, others projecting off the walls, and still more sitting on the floor. The sheer quantity of displays can be daunting, so thankfully the most unusual items are highlighted, sometimes in striking displays. ⊠ *Herrengasse 16, Graz, Styria* ☎ *0316/801-79-810* ☎ *€8* ⊙ *Apr.–Oct., Mon. and Wed.–Sun. 10–5; Nov.–Mar. admission only as part of a guided tour.*

Palais Herberstein. This 17th-century former city residence of the ruling princes houses the **Cultural History Collection**. In addition to a Baroque interior, the permanent collection of 35,000 items features items related to the political history of Graz and Styria. Palais Herberstein has a special focus on the "status symbols" that defined the time; and as visitors walk down a red carpet they question the equivalent in the world today. Temporary exhibitions focus on individual themes. ⊠ *Sackstrasse 16, Graz, Styria* ☎ *0316/801-79-810* ☎ *€8* ⊙ *Wed.–Sun. 10–5.*

FAMILY
Fodor's Choice
★

Schlossberg (*Palace Mountain*). The view from the summit of Graz's midtown mountain takes in all of the city and much of central Styria. A zigzagging stone staircase beginning at Schlossbergplatz leads to the top, but because it's 260 steps, you may prefer to use the Schlossbergbahn funicular railway (Kaiser-Franz-Josef-Kai 38) for €2.10, or an elevator, carved through the rock face, that leaves from Schlossbergplatz (€1.10). A romaneque castle, with touches of the gothic turned into a renaissance fortress, the Schlossberg is only a section of what one finds after making their way to the top of this sight. This is one of the few places not conquered by Napóleon. Atop the Schlossberg and a few steps east of the funicular station is the Glockenturm (bell tower), an octagonal structure from 1588 containing Styria's largest bell, the famous 4-ton Liesl, in the upper belfry. It resounds three times daily (7, noon, and 7) with 101 chimes. The Open-Air Theater, just yards to the north, is built into the old casements of the castle and has a sliding roof in case of rain. Both opera and theater performances are presented here in summer. Additionally one finds ruins of the older structure, and many a modern café to enjoy a beer or wine mixed with sparkling water. ⊠ *Am Schlossberg 1, Graz, Styria* ☎ *0316/887–405* ⊗ *Funicular Sun.–Wed. 9 am–midnight, Thurs.–Sat. 9 am–2 am; elevator 8 am–12:30 am.*

NEED A BREAK?

Aiola. Ailoa is a tiny bar, café and restaurant located at the top of the Schlossberg, the mountain fortress visible from anywhere in the city. The restaurant serves traditional Austrian breakfasts with a selection of bread, cheese, and meat and dinner entrées such as lamb and polenta and salmon with gnocchi and mushrooms. Relax under crisp, white, canvas umbrellas on an outdoor deck, or behind the disappearing glass walls that blend with the environment. Enjoy a glass of the local dry Rose Schilcher or a coffee with all of Graz spread out before you. ⊠ *Schlossberg 2, Graz, Styria* ☎ *0316/818797* ⊗ *Closed midnight–9am daily.*

FAMILY
Fodor's Choice
★

Schloss Eggenberg. This 17th-century palace is a UNESCO world heritage site on the very eastern edge of the city and is surrounded by a large park full of peacocks. Schloss Eggenberg is the largest Baroque palace in Styria. Enjoy a guided tour of the **Prunkräume** (state rooms), one of which is shows one of the few dipictions in the world of Osaka before 1615. Next, visit the gallery of traditional art, the collection of coins, and the Archaeology Museum. There is a lot to see here so stop by the outdoor café to take a rest, or wander through the park before enjoying your next museum. ⊠ *Eggenberger Allee 90, Graz, Styria* ☎ *0316/801–79–532* ⊠ *€8; park €2* ⊗ *Park and Gardens: Apr.–Oct. 8 am–7 pm, State-room tours Apr.–Oct., Tues.–Sun. 10, 11, noon, 2, 3, and 4, Alte Galerie, Archaeological Museum and Coin Cabinet: Apr.–Oct., Wed.–Sun. 10–5*

Prunkräume (*Staterooms*). Built around an arcaded courtyard lined with antlers, this fine example of the High Baroque style contains the gorgeous Prunkräume noted for their elaborate stucco decorations and frescoes. They can be visited on a guided tour only.

Alte Galerie (*Old Gallery*). A world-famous collection of art from the Middle Ages through the Baroque period can be found at the Alte Galerie. Among its treasures are works by Pieter Brueghel the Younger and both Hans and Lucas Cranach, the noted *Admont Madonna* wood carving from 1400, and a medieval altarpiece depicting the murder of Thomas à Becket. ☎ *0316/801–79–770*

Abteilung für Vor- und Frühgeschichte (*Archaeological Museum*). The holdings here include a remarkable collection of Styrian archaeological finds, including the small and rather strange Strettweg Ritual Chariot dating from the 7th century BC.

Uhrturm (*Clock Tower*). This most famous landmark is the symbol of Graz. As a special stop on the Schlossberg, it has the same open hours and route up the hill. It dates from the 16th century, though the first mention of the tower is from the 1200s. The clock has four giant faces that might at first confuse you—until you realize that the *big* hands tell the hour and the *small* hands the minutes. At the time the clock was designed, it only had the hour hand, therefore a smaller minute hand was added later. Nearby notice a statue of a watchdog—he is said to represent a dog who once saved the daughter of an Emperor from being kidnapped by a slighted lover. ⊠ *Schlossberg 3, Graz, Styria.*

WORTH NOTING

Landhaushof. The main wing of the Styrian provincial parliament house was built starting in 1557 by Italian Domenico dell'Allio in the Renaissance Lombard style. Through an archway off of Herrengasse, visitors can glimpse a magnificently proportioned three-floor courtyard, surrounding a bronze fountain and copper gargoyles dating from the 16th century. The striking Styrian coat of arms, which depicts a white panther on a green background, is painted as a mural on a nearby wall. ⊠ *Herrengasse 16, Graz, Styria.*

Palais Khuenburg. This was the birthplace in 1863 of Archduke Franz Ferdinand, heir to the throne of the Austro-Hungarian Empire. His assassination at Sarajevo in 1914 led directly to the outbreak of World War I. The palace is now home to the **Stadtmuseum** (City Museum), whose exhibits trace the history of Graz and includes an old-time pharmacy. ⊠ *Sackstrasse 18, Graz, Styria* ☎ *0316/872–7600* ⊕ *www.grazmuseum.at/* ☎ *€5* ⊘ *Wed.–Mon. 10–5.*

Stadtpfarrkirche. The spire of the city parish church is easily noticed on the main street of Graz. The church itself was built early in the 16th century from a 15th century chapel, and later received baroque touches and an 18th-century spire. Tintoretto's *Assumption of the Virgin* decorates the altar. Badly damaged in World War II, the stained-glass windows were replaced in 1953 by a Salzburg artist, Albert Birkle, who included portrayals of Hitler and Mussolini as malicious spectators at the scourging of Christ (left window behind the high altar, fourth panel from the bottom on the right). ⊠ *Herrengasse 23, Graz, Styria* ☎ *0316/829–684* ⊘ *Daily 7–7.*

WHERE TO EAT

$$ AUSTRIAN 🍴 **Altsteirische Schmankerlstub'n.** Arguably the best place to experience authentic Styrian cooking, this old Graz institution is reminiscent of a cozy country cottage. Salads are a must here, prepared with that Styrian specialty, *Kürbiskernöl,* pumpkinseed oil. Main courses include *Rinderschulterscherzl,* boiled beef with pumpkin puree and roasted potatoes, or chicken breast in a creamy herb sauce. A vegetarian menu, with choices like potato strudel with sour-cream dip and spaetzle sprinkled with leeks and cheese, is always offered. Often, every table in the Schmankerlstub'n is taken, so if you're alone, you may be asked if others could share your table. [$] *Average main: €14* ✉ *Sackstrasse 10, Graz, Styria* ☎ *0316/833211* 🌐 *www.schmankerlstube.at/* 💳 *No credit cards.*

$ CAFÉ 🍴 **Cafe Schwalbennest.** A tiny old house turned coffee shop in the center of the city, Cafe Schwalbennest serves traditional Austrian cakes such as homemade sweet poppy-seed and cheese-curd torte. Green shutters on a red facade make Cafe Schwalbennest easy to spot and there is an upstairs patio overlooking the river Mur, which runs through Graz; but beware, with only three tables upstairs it can be difficult to snag a spot! Also worth trying are the flavored hot chocolates made by the famous local chocolatre maker, Zotter. [$] *Average main: €4* ✉ *Franziskanerplatz 1, Graz, Styria* ☎ *0316/818892* 🌐 *cafe-schwalbennest.stadtausstellung.at/home* 💳 *No credit cards* 🕒 *Closed Mon.*

$$ AUSTRIAN Fodor's Choice ★ 🍴 **Die Herzl Weinstube.** Located in Mehlplatz, one of the oldest squares of Graz, the Die Herzl restaurant opened in 1934 and is known for both its tavernlike atmosphere and its traditional Austrian cuisine. Die Herzl feels a bit like a secret underground club for which you need a password to enter, though everyone is welcome.What's more, Die Herzl is actually above ground. Drink local Austrian white and red wines such as Grüner Veltliner and Welschriesling (white), or Zweigelt and Blauburger (red). Seasonal entrées (think asparagus and potato tart) are mixed with the typical Austrian dishes such as Gemischter Salat (a mix of cucumber, potato, and sauerkraut on lettuce) or the Gebackener Camembert, fried camembert cheese served with tart berry chutney. [$] *Average main: €13* ✉ *Prokopigasse 12/Mehlplatz, Graz, Styria* ☎ *0316/824 300* 🌐 *www.dieherzl.at.*

$ AUSTRIAN 🍴 **Gasthaus zur Alten Press.** Warm wooden parlors, romantic corners, and authentic Austrian cuisine define this rustic spot. Products are mainly local and seasonal, in keeping with the restaurant's slow-food philosophy. Pumpkin and dark-green pumpkinseed oil are prominent ingredients. Try the Schnitzel in a coat of pumpkinseeds with potatoes and field salad or homemade pasta with pumpkinseed pesto. Leave space for a dessert such as parfait with plum jam. The daily lunch menus are popular with locals, and the restaurant can get quickly packed. Smoking is allowed in some seating areas but there's a separate nonsmoking room. [$] *Average main: €11* ✉ *Griesgasse 8, Graz, Styria* ☎ *0316/719–770* 🌐 *www.zuraltenpress.at* 🕒 *Closed Sun. No dinner Sat.*

$$$$ ITALIAN 🍴 **Hofkeller.** With its vaulted ceiling and dark, gleaming wainscoting, the elegantly appointed Hofkeller offers the most innovative Italian cuisine in the city. The engaging waitstaff lets you linger over complimentary

appetizers—Gaeta olives, cheese sticks, fresh-baked breads, and a plate of Parma ham, which is thinly sliced before your eyes on a big oak table in the center of the room—before bringing the huge blackboard menu to your table. Look for the generous arugula salad with shaved Parmesan, pasta with salami and cherry tomatoes, and lightly fried John Dory atop a mound of grilled vegetables. Guests are invited to sample a wine before ordering by the glass. [$] *Average main: €25* ✉ *Hofgasse 8, Graz, Styria* ☎ *0316/832439* 🕒 *Noon–3, 6–10* 🕒 *Closed Sun.*

$$$$ AUSTRIAN

🍴 **Landhauskeller.** The magnificent centuries-old Landhaus complex, which houses Graz's provincial parliament and its armory, also includes a favorite traditional restaurant containing a labyrinth of charming old-world dining rooms set within the ancient arcaded Landhaus itself. Weather permitting, try to get a table in the historic courtyard. Styrian beef is the main event here, but there are lots of other tasty dishes to choose from. A five-course dinner option features seasonal specialties. [$] *Average main: €23* ✉ *Schmiedgasse 9, Graz, Styria* ☎ *0316/830276* 🕒 *Closed Sun.*

$ VEGETARIAN

🍴 **Mangolds.** In the block parallel to the Hotel Wiesler, this popular vegetarian restaurant offers tasty dishes served cafeteria-style. You can choose between at least five main courses plus salads and desserts (including whole-grain cakes.) Mangolds also serves freshly squeezed juice, wine, and coffee—the *Eiskaffee mit Schlag* (iced coffee with vanilla ice cream and whipped cream) is addictive. Reasonable prices make this a place for the cost- and health-conscious, especially students and young families. [$] *Average main: €8* ✉ *Griesgasse 11, Graz, Styria* ☎ *0316/718002* 🌐 *www.mangolds.at/* 💳 *No credit cards* 🕒 *Weekdays and Sat. 11–7* 🕒 *Closed Sun.*

$$$ AUSTRIAN

🍴 **Sacher.** Joining the expanding enterprise of Sacher cafés in Austria's most prominent cities, Graz's Sacher has an imperious location at the junction of the Hauptplatz and Herrengasse. It's everything you would expect from a Sacher Café—lots of gilt, crimson upholstery, sparkling chandeliers, and Viennese desserts, including the rich chocolate Sachertorte. If you're hungry for a meal, there are breakfast, lunch, and dinner specialties; try the Styrian *Almochsen* fillet (Alp steer) with seasonal vegetables, or one of the unrivaled desserts, like the nougat parfait with egg liquor. In the adjoining Sacher Wein-Snackbar you can choose tasty snacks to blend with a full-bodied Austrian white wine or champagne. [$] *Average main: €20* ✉ *Herrengasse 6, Graz, Styria* ☎ *0316/800500* 🕒 *Closed Sun.*

$ INTERNATIONAL

🍴 **Speisesaal.** The Hotel Wiesler's stylish dining room has become a popular meeting place for guests and nonguests alike. International comfort food from gazpacho to bacon burgers are served in this shabby-chic restaurant, which combines secondhand furniture with modern art. Unfinished walls and scratched, original wood panels—a graffiti-style piece of art by Josef Wurm—frame the room and set the mood. At times you may have to shout over your charcoal-grilled steak as DJs spin soul music. [$] *Average main: €11* ✉ *Grieskai 4–8, Graz, Styria* ☎ *0316/70660* 🌐 *www.hotelwiesler.com/en/speisesaal.html* 🕒 *No lunch.*

WHERE TO STAY

$$
HOTEL

Augartenhotel. A glass-and-chrome structure in the middle of a residential neighborhood, the Augarten has more than 400 pieces of art in every room and common area from the 1960s to works of current-day Austrians. **Pros:** free Internet; good food in top-rated Magnolia restaurant. **Cons:** a bit cold feeling; not in the city center. $ *Rooms from: €129* ✉ *Schönaugasse 53, Graz, Styria* ☎ *0316/20800* ⊕ *www.augartenhotel. at* ⌔ *51 rooms, 5 apartments* ⎆ *Breakfast.*

$$
HOTEL
Fodor'sChoice
★

Erzherzog Johann. Travelers who prefer a traditionally elegant city hotel will be happy with this historic establishment in a 16th-century building. **Pros:** central location; historical rooms; excellent café. **Cons:** rooms facing main street can be a bit noisy, limited parking in front of hotel. $ *Rooms from: €149* ✉ *Sackstrasse 3–5, Graz, Styria* ☎ *0316/811515* ⊕ *www.erzherzog-johann.com* ⌔ *55 rooms, 2 suites* ⎆ *Breakfast.*

$
HOTEL

Hotel Daniel. Located next door the train station, Hotel Daniel's young, fresh concept makes it *the* budget option in Graz. **Pros:** great design; good value. **Cons:** 10-minute walk from the city center; the outside looks a little run down. $ *Rooms from: €100* ✉ *Europaplatz 1, Graz, Styria* ☎ *0316/711–080* ⊕ *www.hoteldaniel.com* ⌔ *107 rooms.*

$$
HOTEL

Hotel Gollner. A popular hotel since the mid-1800s and family owned for four generations, the friendly Gollner is close to the Jakominiplatz and about a 10-minute walk from the Old City. **Pros:** family-owned property with personalized service; some rooms face the backyard. **Cons:** breakfast not included; not in the center of town. $ *Rooms from: €145* ✉ *Schlögelgasse 14, Graz, Styria* ☎ *0316/822521* ⊕ *www. hotelgollner.at* ⌔ *50 rooms, 4 apartments.*

$
HOTEL

Hotel Mariahilf. A comfortable hotel in the center of things, the Mariahilf is across the river from the Old City close to the Kunsthaus. **Pros:** quiet central location; modern rooms; good price. **Cons:** no restaurant; rooms on the third floor can get hot in summer. $ *Rooms from: €99* ✉ *Mariahilferstrasse 7–9, Graz, Styria* ☎ *0316/713163* ⊕ *www. hotelmariahilf.at* ⌔ *42 rooms, 3 suites* ⎆ *Breakfast.*

$
HOTEL

Hotel Pfeifer Kirchenwirt. An inn has stood on this lofty knoll since 1695, initially providing beds to those who made the pilgrimage to Mariatrost, the magnificent rococo, daffodil-yellow basilica next door. **Pros:** family run; quiet surroundings. **Cons:** no elevator to lobby; no staff to carry heavy bags; a bit far from the center of town. $ *Rooms from: €90* ✉ *Kirchplatz 9, Graz, Styria* ☎ *0316/391112–0* ⊕ *www. kirchenwirtgraz.com/* ⌔ *55 rooms* ⎆ *Breakfast.*

$
HOTEL

Hotel Wiesler. Five guesthouses were converted into Hotel Wiesler in 1870 where retro touches delight: Polaroid cameras are available for guests to use throughout their stay; vinyl records are available to rent; and a barbershop caters to male guests while serving up black Turkish coffee. **Pros:** variety of prices for every budget; spacious guest rooms with high ceilings; modern, arty feel. **Cons:** the downstairs restaurant can be too hip at night for everyone's taste; rooms facing the side street can be a bit dark. $ *Rooms from: €109* ✉ *Grieskai 4–8, Graz, Styria* ☎ *0316/70660* ⊕ *www.hotelwiesler.com* ⌔ *98 rooms* ⎆ *Breakfast.*

$$ Hotel   **Fodor's Choice** ★ **Hotel zum Dom.** Occupying the 18th-century Palais Inzaghi, the Dom has whimsically decorated rooms and works to combine the old history of Graz with the new modern style. **Pros:** great location; luxury in a historic building. **Cons:** some baths on the small side; noise from the street on weekends; breakfast not included. *$ Rooms from: €154 ✉ Bürgergasse 14, Graz, Styria ☎ 0316/824800 ⊕ www.domhotel.co.at ⌁ 29 rooms, 10 suites.*

$$ Hotel **Schlossberg Hotel.** Contemporary art meets antiquity and modern convenience at this town house tucked up against the foot of the Schlossberg, which was turned into a hotel in 1982. **Pros:** tastefully furnished rooms; pool with a view; great art. **Cons:** longer walk to center of city; make sure breakfast is included in your rate or be prepared to cough up an extra €17; front-desk staff can be quite rude. *$ Rooms from: €165 ✉ Kaiser-Franz-Josef-Kai 30, Graz, Styria ☎ 0316/80700 ⊕ www. schlossberg-hotel.at ⌁ 49 rooms, 4 suites, 8 apartments.*

NIGHTLIFE AND PERFORMING ARTS

NIGHTLIFE

Graz's after-hours scene is centered on the area around Prokopigasse, Bürgergasse, Mehlplatz, and Glockenspielplatz. Here you'll find activity until the early-morning hours.

Casino Graz. At the corner of Landhausgasse and Schmiedgasse in the Old City, Casino Graz offers French and American roulette, blackjack, baccarat, and punto banco. Entry is free, but you are required to buy chips for €25. You must bring a passport and be at least 21. Men are expected to wear a jacket and tie, though it is not required. *✉ Landhausgasse 10, Graz, Styria ☎ 0153/44050 ⊙ Daily 3 pm–late.*

PERFORMING ARTS

Graz, a major university town, has a lively, avant-garde theater scene known especially for its experimental productions. Its **Schauspielhaus,** built in 1825, is the leading playhouse, and there are smaller theaters scattered around town. It is also known for its opera, concerts, and jazz. Contact the tourist office for current offerings.

Opernhaus Graz. A 19th-century opera house, the Opernhaus Graz, with its resplendent rococo interior, is a showcase for young talent and experimental productions as well as more conventional works; it stages three to five performances a week during its late September to June season. Tickets are generally available until shortly before the performances, prices starting at €9; call for information, or stop by the office. *✉ Kaiser-Josef-Platz 10, Graz, Styria ☎ 0316/8000 ⊕ www.oper-graz.com.*

Springfestival Graz. This four-day festival during the last week of May, the largest of its kind in the country, serves as a showcase for Austrian alternative and underground music. Concerts take place across Graz in venues ranging from clubs to beaches to empty plots of land. Tickets can be purchased online in advance or during festival week at the various spots where performances take place. (A four-day pass costs €48, and a one-day ticket costs €15.70.) *✉ Graz, Styria ⊕ www.springfestival.at/.*

Styrian Autumn Festival. The annual Steirischer Herbst, or Styrian Autumn Festival, a celebration of the avant-garde with the occasional shocking piece in experimental theater, music, opera, dance, jazz, film, video, and other performing arts, is held in Graz from the end of September to the middle of October. ⊠ *Graz, Styria* ⊕ *www. steirischerherbst.at.*

Styriarte. The Styriarte festival (late June to mid-July) gathers outstanding classical musicians from around the world. Performances take place at the Helmut-List-Halle, with some at Schloss Eggenberg. The ticket office is located in the center of the city. ⊠ *Sackstrasse 17, Graz, Styria* ☎ *0316/825000* ⊕ *www.styriarte.com.*

SHOPPING

Graz is a smart, stylish city with great shopping. In the streets surrounding Hauptplatz and Herrengasse you'll find top designer boutiques and specialty shops. Be on the lookout for traditional skirts, trousers, jackets, and coats of gray and dark-green loden wool; dirndls; modern sportswear and ski equipment; handwoven garments; and objects of wrought iron. Take time to wander around the cobblestone streets of the Altstadt near the cathedral, where you'll come across several little specialty shops selling exotic coffees, wine, and cheese.

Käse- Nussbaumer. For a wide selection of wine and cheese, as well as hard-to-find Styrian cheese varieties, go to Käse-Nussbaumer, at Paradeisgasse 1, near the Hauptplatz. ⊠ *Paradeisgasse 1, Graz, Styria.*

Moser. This three-floored bookstore is at the end of Graz's main street, Herrengasse, near Jakominiplatz. Moser bustles with people buying postcards, CDs, children's books in multiple languages, and quirky gifts though not from local dealers. There is a large selection of English fiction and nonfiction on the ground floor, as well as cookbooks with Austrian cuisine written in English. ■ TIP→ **There is a basic no-frills coffee shop on the top floor, where shoppers can have a snack and peruse books before purchasing them.** ⊠ *Am Eisernen Tor 1, Graz, Styria* ☎ *0316/83 01 10* ⊙ *Closed Sun.*

Fodor's Choice **Steirisches Heimatwerk.** The Heimatwerk shop is associated with the local
★ folklore museum and stocks a good variety of regional crafts and luxuries. ⊠ *Sporgasse 23, Graz, Styria.*

THREE EXCURSIONS FROM GRAZ

BÄRNBACH

Church of St. Barbara. Bärnbach offers the amazing vision of the Church of St. Barbara; it was completely redone in 1988 by the late Austrian painter and architect Friedensreich Hundertwasser. The exterior is a fantasy of symbols in brilliant colors and shapes, including 12 towers representing all of the world's religions. A tour is available and must be booked in advance at the rectory costing €2 and lasting an hour. ⊠ *Kirchplatz, Piberstrasse 15, Bärnbach, Styria* ☎ *03142 62 581* 🖃 *Voluntary donation without tour* ⊙ *Daily 8–6.*

11

$ **Rogner Bad Blumau.** An overnight spa resort designed by Austrian
RESORT   artist Friedensreich Hundertwasser (his last name means 100 waters),
is about a two-hour train ride northeast of Graz, and is home to pool
after pool of mineral waters. **Pros:** breakfast plus lunch or dinner are
included in the room fee. **Cons:** Wi-Fi in lobby only. $ *Rooms from:
€110* ⊠ *Bad Blumau 100, Bad Blumau, Styria* ☎ *03383 5100* ⊕ *www.
blumau.com/* ↪ *312 rooms.*

STÜBING BEI GRAZ

FAMILY   **Austrian Open-Air Museum** (*Österreichisches Freilichtmuseum*). Blanket-
ing more than 100 acres of hilly woodland, the Austrian Open-Air
Museum is worth a visit. A fascinating collection of about 80 authentic farmhouses, barns, Alpine huts, working water mills, forges, and
other rural structures dating from the 16th century through the early
20th century has been moved to this site from seemingly every province of Austria. Buildings that otherwise would have been lost in the
rush to "progress" have been preserved complete with their original
furnishings. Most are open to visitors, and in several of them artisans
can be seen at work, sometimes in period costume. It is also possible
to have a guided tour in English. There is a restaurant and outdoor
café by the entrance. You can reach the Austrian Open-Air Museum
by car from Graz via Route 67 to Gratkorn, by train (15 minutes) to
Stübing and a 2-km (1½-mile) walk from there, or by municipal bus
(35 minutes) from Lendplatz directly to Freilichtmuseum Stübing.
⊠ *Gratweinerstrasse 134, Deutschfeistritz, Styria* ☎ *03124/53700*
⊕ *www.freilichtmuseum.at* 🎟 *€9.50* ⊗ *Apr.–Oct., daily 9–5; last
admission at 4.*

INNSBRUCK, TYROL, AND VORARLBERG

Updated by
Rob Freeman

The provinces of Tyrol and Vorarlberg make up the western tip of Austria with Innsbruck, the capital of Tyrol, the natural, historic, and economic center. These two provinces are so different from the rest of Austria that you might think you've crossed a border, and in a way you have. The frontier between Tyrol and the province of Salzburgerland to the east is defined by mountains; four passes routed over them are what make access possible. To the west of Tyrol lies Vorarlberg—"before the Arlberg," the mountain range straddling the border between the two provinces.

In winter you'll find masses of deep, sparkling powder snow and unrivaled skiing and tobogganing. You can also venture into the famous Arlberg ski resorts, cult destinations for skiers from all over the world. In summer, Bregenz, the historic state capital of Vorarlberg, becomes the "Summer Capital of Austria" when the Bregenz Festival opens with a performance by the Viennese Symphonic Orchestra. Thousands flock to see operas and musicals by Giuseppe Verdi or Leonard Bernstein—to name just two—which take place on a huge floating stage with Lake Constance (the Bodensee), and the Swiss mountains as a backdrop.

Like most other mountain peoples, the Tyroleans are proud and independent—so much so that for many centuries the natives of one narrow valley fastness had little communication with their "foreign" neighbors in the next valley.

Until a tunnel was cut through the Arlberg range, Vorarlberg was effectively cut off from the rest of the country in winter. The province has much in common with its neighbor, Switzerland. Both peoples are descended from the same ancient Germanic tribes that flourished in the 3rd century BC.

ORIENTATION AND PLANNING

GETTING ORIENTED

Innsbruck makes a good starting point for exploring western Austria. It's a city that preserves the charm of ancient times and has lots to offer: culture, stellar restaurants, and trendy nightclubs. But Tyrol's gorgeous geography precludes the convenient loop tour. You must go into the valleys to discover the charming villages and hotels, and a certain amount of backtracking is necessary. It will allow you to discover a cross-section of Tyrol's highlights: the old and the new, glossy resorts, medieval castles, and, always, that extraordinary scenery in these breathtaking valleys. On the western side of the Arlberg range, you have the wide-open spaces of Vorarlberg with Bregenz, a

TOP REASONS TO GO

The Ötz Valley. Outdoors enthusiasts love hiking through this region because of rich green pastures in summer and glittering expanses of white in winter.

Highly rated skiing areas. Known around the world for its extensive and in many cases fashionable ski villages, Tyrol often attracts celebrities and global glitterati to its resorts to experience the high-altitude good life, along with dedicated skiers keen to take on its challenging slopes.

Tyrolean Stuben. These warm and cozy wooden parlors, often found today in hotels and restaurants, are traditionally part of old farmhouses in Tyrol.

Bernstein in Bregenz. With the sun setting over Lake Constance and the Vienna Philharmonic Orchestra striking up the overture of *West Side Story* on the world's biggest floating stage, this is an unparalleled place to see an opera or a musical.

See four countries at once. Take the cable car up Pfänder, the mountain behind Bregenz; the views are incredible: Swiss mountains on your left, German rolling hills on your right, Liechtenstein to your left in the Rhine valley, Austria below your feet, and the glittering expanse of Lake Constance stretching 64km (40 miles) into the hazy distance.

Experience top hospitality in a top village. The Gasthof Post is a bit like Lech itself—full of charming understatement. Teatime in over-stuffed armchairs for all houseguests will keep you going until it's time for a delicious dinner. You'll never want to leave.

city the Romans built up with a harbor for warships, which today is used for cruise ships zigzagging across Lake Constance to Switzerland and Germany.

Tyrol is famous for the beauty of its valleys, radiating from Innsbruck at the center of it all. To the northeast you find one of Austria's most famous folk-music regions. On the road to Kitzbühel, the sunny valley has plenty of snow in winter and golf in summer. Upscale hotels and a renowned ski area make Kitzbühel the region's number one year-round vacation destination. To the west, in the very heart of Tyrol, the villages of Telfs and Imst are known for tradition and culture. Then there is the Ötz Valley, with its long trekking routes and outdoor facilities. The western part of Tyrol is a winter heaven: steep and challenging slopes along with well-trained instructors made St. Anton famous, whereas high in the mountains, in a valley toward the south, are the snow towns of Ischgl and Galtür.

And over the Arlberg range (or through it, via road and rail tunnels), you have the Vorarlberg, with the mountain villages of Lech and Zürs as havens for highly rated skiing and high-end, expensive hotels. On the other end of the spectrum is the Montafon region, a winter and summer destination for the more cost-conscious—especially families.

PLANNING

WHEN TO GO

The physical geography of the Tyrol and Vorarlberg makes them perfect for enjoying outdoor life year-round. Ski-crazy travelers descend on the resorts during the winter months; in summer, when the mountains are awash with wildflowers, campers' tents spring up like mushrooms in the valleys as hikers, spelunkers, mountain bikers, and climbers take advantage of the soaring peaks. High season for summer activities is July through August, while the skiing season begins in many resorts in late November or early December and can go on until early May in the higher ski areas. If you're in the Vorarlberg in summer be sure to stop in Bregenz, when the city comes to life with the Bregenzer Festspiele (Bregenz Music Festival). Also boat excursions to Switzerland and Germany are a must. You can even rent a boat and go out on the lake to do some fishing.

FESTIVALS

There is more here than the Bregenz festival. The annual Tyrolean calendar is packed with special events: the famous Schemenlaufen, a procession of carved wooden masks, held in February in Imst; the Fasching balls, which reach their peak at the end of February; the Hahnenkamm ski race and curling competition held in winter in Kitzbühel; the world-famous Gauder Fest at Zell am Ziller during the first weekend in May; the castle concerts and music and dance festivals in summer, primarily in Kufstein and Innsbruck; the ceremonial Almabtrieb in autumn, when the farmers bring their richly adorned cattle from mountain pastures down to the valley for the winter; and the many village harvest festivals in the fall throughout Tyrol.

GETTING HERE AND AROUND

AIR TRAVEL

All of Tyrol uses the Innsbruck Flughafen, the airport 3 km (2 miles) west of the capital, which is served by a number of international airlines including Austrian Airlines, British Airways, and Lufthansa. But for intercontinental flights the main gateway airports for Tyrol and Vorarlberg are Munich in Germany and Zurich in Switzerland.

Vorarlberg uses the intercontinental airport of Zurich, 120 km (75 miles) from Bregenz. Directly from the airport several Euro City express trains a day make the journey to Bregenz in 1½ hours on their way to Munich. There are also trains direct from Zurich airport to many stations in Tyrol. Munich is convenient for the eastern part of Tyrol, with rail and coach links.

AIRPORT TRANSFERS

From Innsbruck Flughafen, take the F Line bus into Innsbruck to the main train station (about 20 minutes). Get your ticket (€2) from the driver. Taxis into Innsbruck should take no more than 10 minutes, and the fare is about €15.

From Switzerland to Vorarlberg in winter, there are buses from the Zurich airport Friday, Saturday, and Sunday several times each day for Zürs and Lech. You can book the transfer through the airline Swiss.

BUS TRAVEL

Bus lines operated by the railroads and post office connect all the towns and villages not served by train, using vehicles with snow chains when necessary in winter. Even so, some of the highest roads can become impassable for a few hours. And except in the most remote areas, buses are frequent enough that you can get around.

In Innsbruck the deluxe ski buses that depart from the Landestheater on Rennweg, across from the Hofburg, are the most convenient way to reach the six major ski areas outside the city. A Club Innsbruck pass (free from the tourist office or your hotel if you spend one night or more) gives you complimentary transportation to the ski areas. Many hotels even provide shuttle service to the ski bus stop.

CAR TRAVEL

Driving is the best way to see Tyrol and Vorarlberg, since it allows you to wander off the main routes at your leisure. The autobahns are fastest, but for scenery you're best off on the byways, as you can stop and admire the view. But roads can be treacherous in winter. Cars are not allowed on some mountain roads in the Arlberg without chains, which you can rent from many service stations. If you are renting a car in the winter specify that you want winter tires. These will be sufficient to deal with fairly heavy snow on the road, although you will often be required to also carry snow chains. Roads with particularly attractive scenery are marked on highway maps with a parallel green line. To drive on Austria's autobahn, you will need a *vignette,* or sticker, available at almost all service stations. A 10-day sticker costs €8.50, for 60 days it's €24.80.

FERRY TRAVEL

From May to October, passenger ships of the Austrian railroad's Bodensee White Fleet connect Bregenz with Lindau, Friedrichshafen, Meersburg, and Konstanz on the German side of the lake. The Eurailpass and Austrian rail passes are valid on these ships. You must bring your passport.

TRAIN TRAVEL

Direct trains from Munich serve Innsbruck. From here on, the line follows the Inn Valley to Landeck and St. Anton, where it plunges into an 11-km (7-mile) tunnel under the Arlberg range, emerging at Langen in Vorarlberg, continuing to Bregenz, where you can change to the EuroCityExpress to Zurich (you can also change at Innsbruck for a more direct route to Zurich via Feldkirch) or go back to Munich via Bavaria. A line from Innsbruck to the south goes over the dramatic Brenner Pass (4,465 feet) into Italy.

Some of the most fascinating and memorable side trips can be made by rail. For example, two narrow-gauge lines steam out of Jenbach, one up to the Achensee, the other down to Mayrhofen in the Zillertal. From Innsbruck, the narrow-gauge Stubaitalbahn runs south to Telfes and Fulpmes.

PUBLIC TRANSPORT TRAVEL

As in other areas of Austria, having a car makes travel easy, but you can also use the area trains and buses to get around. In Bregenz a Bodensee-Pass includes the Swiss and German trains, as well as the Austrian lake steamers, all at half price, plus area trains, buses, and cable-car lifts; this pass comes in 7- and 15-day variations. Similar passes exist in Tyrol.

VISITOR INFORMATION

The headquarters for tourist information about Vorarlberg is in Bregenz. There is a branch office in Vienna. Other regional tourist offices (called either *Tourismusbüro, Verkehrsverein,* or *Fremdenverkehrsamt*) are found throughout the province using the contact information listed under particular towns. They are easily spotted—just look for the large "i" (for information) sign.

Tourist Information Austrian National Tourist Board ☎ 212/944–6880 in the U.S., 00800/400–200–00 ⊕ www.austria.info. **Tourist Information Vorarlberg** ✉ Bahnhofstrasse 14, Bregenz, Vorarlberg ☎ 05574/42525–0 ⊕ www.vorarlberg.at ✉ Tuchlauben 18, Vienna, Vorarlberg ☎ 01/535–7890.

ESSENTIALS

Airport Information Innsbruck Flughafen Airport (INN). ☎ 0512/22525 flight information ⊕ www.innsbruck-airport.com. **Swiss** ☎ 810/81–08–40 in Austria, 855/254–1842 in the U.S. ⊕ www.swiss.com.

Boat Information Bodensee White Fleet ☎ 05574/42868 ⊕ www.vorarlberg-lines.at.

Bus Information Postbus AG ☎ 01/71101 ⊕ www.postbus.at.

Train Information Österreichisches Bundesbahn ☎ 05/1717 information and reservations ⊕ www.oebb.at.

Emergency Services Ambulance ☎ 144. **Fire department** ☎ 122. **Police** ☎ 133.

RESTAURANTS

The gastronomic scene of Austria's westernmost provinces is as varied as its landscape: first-rate gourmet restaurants, traditional inns, rustic local taverns, as well as international chains and ethnic cuisine are all part of the mix. In small towns throughout the region restaurants are often the dining rooms of country inns, and there are plenty of these. Austria used to have a reputation for substantial but stereotypical dishes of meat, dumplings and sauerkraut, but things have changed considerably. Gourmet meals are available at many wonderful restaurants, often at much more reasonable prices than is typical of Europe's high-class dining scene. That said, in many villages you'll find inns catering largely to local farm workers, where the old favorites are still the order of the day—prepare to be filled rather than thrilled.

Most hotel restaurants will be closed in the off-season, usually November and April. In ski season breakfast is typically served early enough for you to hit the slopes in good time, and dinner is timed so that exhausted skiers can get an early night in preparation for the next day.

MOUNTAIN SPORTS

HIKING AND CLIMBING

Tyrol has an abundance of the more than 35,000 miles of well-maintained mountain paths that thread the country. Hiking is one of the best ways to experience the truly awesome Alpine scenery, whether you just want to take a leisurely stroll around one of the crystalline lakes mirroring the towering mountains or trek your way to the top of one of the mighty peaks. Mountain climbing is a highly organized activity in Tyrol, a province that contains some of the greatest challenges to devotees of the sport. The instructors at the Alpine School Innsbruck are the best people to contact if you want to make arrangements for a mountain-climbing holiday.

SKIING

Downhill was practically invented in **Tyrol**. Legendary skiing master Hannes Schneider took the Norwegian art of cross-country skiing and adapted it to downhill running. No matter where your trip takes you, world-class—and often gut-scrambling—skiing is available, from the glamour of Kitzbühel in the east to the imposing peaks of St. Anton am Arlberg in the west.

Close to the Arlberg Pass is **St. Anton**, which, at 4,300 feet, proudly claims to have one of the finest ski schools in the world. The specialty at St. Anton is piste skiing—enormously long runs studded with moguls (and few trees), some so steep and challenging that the sport is almost the equal of mountain climbing. In fact, this is the only place in Austria where you can heli-ski. It was here in the 1920s that Hannes Schneider started the school that was to become the model for all others.

A short bus ride to the top of the pass brings you to **St. Christoph**, at 5,800 feet. If you care to mingle with royalty on the lifts, the upscale ski villages of **Zürs** and **Lech**, on the Vorarlberg side of the pass, are likely for you.

Farther along the Inn is the Ötz Valley. From the Ötztal station you can go by bus to **Sölden**, a resort at 4,500 feet that has become almost as well known for its party scene as for its superb skiing. The up-and-comer of Austrian ski resorts is **Ischgl**, in the Paznaun Valley bordering Switzerland, where good snow and a long ski season are assured on high-altitude slopes with a top station at 9,422 feet. **Kitzbühel**, chic and *charmant*, is perhaps most famous for its "Ski Safari," a far-ranging system of ski lifts and trails, some floodlit at night, that allows you to ski for weeks without retracing your steps. **Alpbach** is one of the most popular resorts for families, with many not-too-challenging slopes and a reputation for being one of the most beautiful villages in Austria, full of heavily timbered traditional chalets surrounded by thickly wooded runs. The area east of Innsbruck is collectively known as the **Ski Welt** (Ski World), where the villages of **Soll, Ellmau, Scheffau, Itter, Going, Brixen im Thale, Westendorf, Hopfgarten,** and **Kelchsau** form Austria's largest linked skiing area dotted with cozy, welcoming mountain huts, also family-friendly. Innsbruck itself is at the center of a group of resorts easily reached by bus from the city; the best time to ski Innsbruck's slopes is January through March.

12

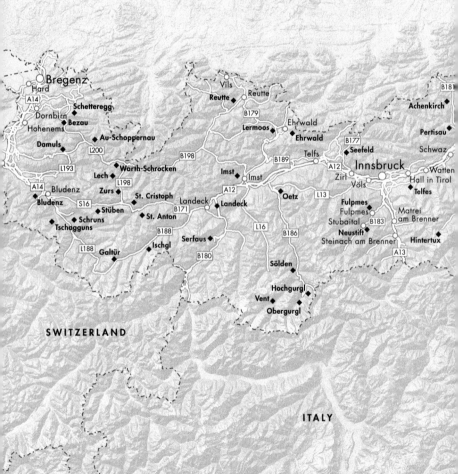

Ski Areas

GERMANY

Bregenz
Hard
A14
Schetteregg
Dornbirn
Bezau
Hohenems
Au-Schoppernau
Damuls
L200
L193
Warth-Schrocken
B198
Lech
L198
Zürs
A14 Bludenz
St. Cristoph
Bludenz
S16
Stüben
Landeck
Schruns
St. Anton
Tschagguns
B171
B188
Galtür
Serfaus
L188
Ischgl
B180

Vils
Reutte
Reutte
B179
Lermoos
Ehrwald
Ehrwald
B189
Telfs
B177
Seefeld
Schwaz
Imst
Imst
A12
Innsbruck
Zirl
A12
Watten
Oetz
Völs
Hall in Tirol
L13
Telfes
L16
Fulpmes
Fulpmes
B186
Matrei
am Brenner
Stubaital
B183
Neustift
Hintertux
Sölden
Steinach am Brenner
A13
Hochgurgl
Vent
Obergurgl

Achenkirch
B18
Pertisau

SWITZERLAND

ITALY

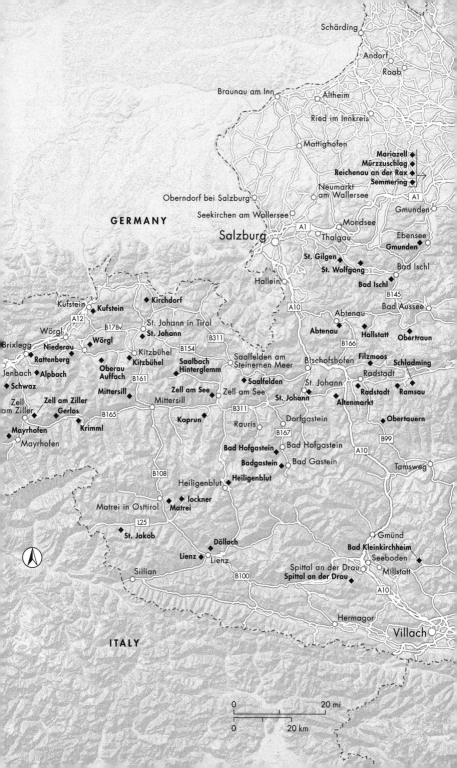

Restaurants range from grand-hotel dining salons to little *Wirtshäuser,* rustic restaurants where you can enjoy hearty local specialties such as *Tyroler Gröstl* (a skillet dish made of ham or pork, potatoes, and onions, with caraway seeds, paprika and parsley), *Knödel* (dumpling) soup, or *Schweinsbraten* (roast pork with sauerkraut), while sitting on highly polished (and rather hard) wooden seats. Don't forget to enjoy some of the fine Innsbruck coffeehouses, famous for their scrumptious cakes and cappuccino.

HOTELS

In Innsbruck travelers do not seem to stay long, so there is a fast turnover and, almost always, a room to be had. Some travelers opt to set up their base not in town but *overlooking* it, on the Hungerburg Plateau to the north perhaps, or in one of the nearby villages perched on the slopes to the south. In any case, the official **Innsbruck Reservation Center,** online at ⊕ *www.innsbruck.info* or ⊕ *www.ski-innsbruck.at,* offers a booking source for Innsbruck and the surrounding villages.

Innsbruck Reservations Office. If you arrive in Innsbruck without a hotel room, check with the Innsbruck Reservations Office. The downtown office, in the main tourist office in the Old City, is open weekdays 10–6 and Saturday 8–12:30. The main train station branch is open in summer daily and in winter Monday through Saturday 9–6. ⊠ *Burggraben 3, Innsbruck* ☎ *0512/562–0000* ⊕ *www.innsbruck.info.*

Book in advance if you're traveling in the region, especially Vorarlberg, in the winter high season and in July and August. Room rates include taxes and service and, almost always, a breakfast buffet. In the resort towns dinner will be included. *Halb pension* (half-board), as plans that include breakfast and dinner are called, is usually the best deal. Hotel rates vary widely by season, the off-peak periods being March–May and September–November. Most hotels take credit cards. Note that at the most expensive hotels in the resort towns of Zürs/ Lech, Kitzbühel, St. Anton, and Sölden, rooms can reach as high as €450 a night (or sometimes more). If you're out for savings, it's a good idea to find lodgings in small towns nearby rather than in the bigger towns or in the resorts themselves; local tourist offices can help you get situated, possibly even with accommodations in pensions (simple hotels) or *Bauernhöfe* (farmhouses). It's worth remembering that in Austria, cheap accommodations can still be of a very high standard, with large en-suite rooms of sparkling cleanliness.

⚠ Keep in mind that in hotel saunas and steam baths, nude people of both genders should be expected. Other patrons and management will often take great exception to guests who enter a sauna wearing a swimsuit. Children under certain ages are usually not admitted.

WHAT IT COSTS IN EUROS			
$	$$	$$$	$$$$
RESTAURANTS under €12	€12–€17	€18–€22	over €22
HOTELS under €100	€100–€135	€136–€175	over €175

Restaurant prices are per person for a main course at dinner. Hotel prices are for a standard double room in high season, including taxes and service. Higher prices (inquire when booking) prevail for any meal plans.

INNSBRUCK

190 km (118 miles) southwest of Salzburg, 471 km (304 miles) southwest of Vienna, 146 km (91 miles) south of Munich.

The capital of Tyrol is one of the most beautiful towns of its size anywhere in the world, owing much of its charm and fame to its unique location. To the north, the steep, sheer sides of the Alps rise, literally from the edge of the city, like a shimmering blue-and-white wall—an impressive backdrop for the mellowed green domes and red roofs of the baroque town tucked below. To the south, the peaks of the Tuxer and Stubai ranges undulate in the hazy purple distance.

Squeezed by the mountains and sharing the valley with the Inn River (Innsbruck means "bridge over the Inn"), the city is compact and very easy to explore on foot. Reminders of three historic figures abound: the local hero Andreas Hofer, whose band of patriots challenged Napoléon in 1809; Emperor Maximilian I (1459–1519); and Empress Maria Theresa (1717–80), the last two responsible for much of the city's architecture. Maximilian ruled the Holy Roman Empire from Innsbruck, and Maria Theresa, who was particularly fond of the city, spent a substantial amount of time here.

GETTING HERE AND AROUND

Innsbruck Airport is only minutes from Innsbruck city center and is linked by frequent bus service.

Direct trains serve Innsbruck from Munich, Vienna, Rome, and Zürich, and all arrive at the train station, Innsbruck Hauptbahnhof, at SüdTyrolerplatz. The station is outfitted with restaurants, cafés, a supermarket, and even a post office.

Innsbruck is connected by bus to other parts of Tyrol, and the bus terminal is beside the train station. In Innsbruck, most bus and streetcar routes begin or end at Maria-Theresien-Strasse, nearby Boznerplatz, or the main train station. One-way tickets cost €1.80 on the bus or streetcar, and you can transfer to another line with the same ticket as long as you continue in more or less the same direction in a single journey. You can get tickets from machines, or at slightly increased cost from the driver.

If you're driving, remember that the Altstadt (Old City) is a pedestrian zone. Private cars are not allowed on many streets, and parking requires vouchers that you buy from blue coin-operated dispensers found around parking areas. Fees are usually €0.50–€1 per half-hour.

In Innsbruck taxis are not much faster than walking, particularly along the one-way streets and in the Old City. Basic fare is €6.20 for the first 1.3 km (0.8 mile) and 1.90 per km after that, so that most rides within the city limits will amount to between €8.10 and €12. Innsbruck Taxi 4 You is a good option if you want to call a cab. For longer journeys, to a ski resort for example, from the train station or airport, there are set fares, but if you're prepared to haggle they are still highly negotiable, particularly on a quiet day when plenty of cabs are waiting in line. Let the driver know that you are aware of the alternatives available, such as train or bus.

Horse-drawn cabs, still a feature of Innsbruck life, can be hired at the stand in front of the Landestheater. Set the price before you head off; a half-hour ride will cost around €25.

Innsbruck's main tourist office is open daily 9–6. Tyrol's provincial tourist bureau, the Tyrol Werbung, is also in Innsbruck. The Österreichischer Alpenverein is the place to go for information on Alpine huts and mountaineering advice. It's open weekdays 8:30–6, Saturday 9–noon.

ESSENTIALS

Bus Information **Postbus AG** ☎ *0512/390–390–210* ⊕ *www.postbus.at.*

Taxi Information **City Taxis** ☎ *0512/292915, 0800/201148* ⊕ *www.taxi-292915.at.* **Innsbruck Taxi 4 You** ☎ *0676/607–8190* ⊕ *www.innsbruck-taxi4you.com.*

Train Information **Innsbruck Hauptbahnhof** ✉ *SüdTyroler Platz* ☎ *0512/930–000.* **Österreichische Bundesbahn** ☎ *051/1717* ⊕ *www.oebb.at.*

Visitor Information **Innsbruck Tourist Office** ✉ *Burggraben 3* ☎ *0512/5356–314* ⊕ *www.innsbruck.info.* **Österreichischer Alpenverein** ✉ *Wilhelm-Greil-Strasse 15* ☎ *0512/59547* ⊕ *www.alpenverein.at.* **Tyrol Werbung** ✉ *Maria-Theresien-Strasse 55* ☎ *0512/7272* ⊕ *www.Tyrol.at* or *www.Tyrolwerbung.at.*

TOURS

The red **Sightseer** bus, a service of the Innsbruck Tourist Office, is the best way to see the sights of Innsbruck without walking. It features a recorded commentary in several languages, including English. There are two routes, both beginning from Maria-Theresien-Strasse in the Old City, but you can catch the bus from any of the nine marked stops, and jump off and on the bus whenever you like. The ride is free with your Innsbruck Card (⇨ *See below for information)*, or buy your ticket from the driver or at the tourist office.

Guided walking tours of the Old City run by the tourist office start daily at 11 and 2 from the tourist office and highlight historic personalities and some offbeat features of Innsbruck.

EXPLORING INNSBRUCK

TOP ATTRACTIONS

Domkirche zu St. Jakob. Innsbruck's cathedral was built between 1717 and 1724 on the site of a 12th-century Romanesque church. Regarded as possibly the most important Baroque building in Tyrol, its main attraction is the painting of the Madonna by Lucas Cranach the Elder, dating from about 1530 and displayed above the high altar. The tomb, dating from 1620, of Archduke Maximilian III, Master of the Teutonic Knights, can be seen in the north aisle. ⊠ *Domplatz 6* ☎ *0512/5839–02* 🎟 *Free* 🕐 *Mon.–Sat. 10:15–6.30; Sun. 12:30–6:30, except during worship.*

Ferdinandeum (*Tyrolean State Museum Ferdinandeum*). The Tyrolean state museum houses Austria's largest collection of Gothic art, 19th- and 20th-century paintings, including works by Rembrandt, Brueghel, and Klimt. There are also musical instruments and medieval arms, along with special exhibitions. Here you'll find the original coats of arms from the Goldenes Dachl balcony. Chamber music concerts are offered throughout the year. ⊠ *Museumstrasse 5* ☎ *0512/59489–180* 🌐 *www.Tyroler-landesmuseen.at* 🎟 *€10 combined ticket with Zeughaus and Hofkirche* 🕐 *Tues.–Sun. 9–5.*

NEED A BREAK?

Kunstpause. Within the Ferdinandeum, Kunstpause, the "Art pause," offers breakfast, light meals, and a wine bar in elegant but relaxed surroundings. ⊠ *Museumstrasse 15* ☎ *512/572020* 🌐 *www.kunstpause.at* 🕐 *open 11:30–2, 6–10.*

Fodor's Choice ★

Goldenes Dachl (*Golden Roof*). Any walking tour of Innsbruck should start at the Goldenes Dachl, which made famous the late-Gothic mansion whose balcony it covers. In fact, the roof is capped with 2,657 gilded copper tiles, and its refurbishment is said to have taken nearly 31 pounds of gold. The house was built in 1420 for Frederick IV as the residence of the Tyrolean sovereign. The legend persists that he added the golden look to counter rumors that he was penniless, but the balcony was, in fact, added by Emperor Maximilian I in the late 15th century as a "royal box" for watching various performances in the square below. He had the roof gilded to symbolize the wealth and power of Tyrol, which had recently undergone massive financial reform. The structure was altered and expanded at the beginning of the 18th century, and now only the loggia and the alcove are identifiable as original. Maximilian is pictured in the two central sculpted panels on the balcony. In the one on the left, he is with his first and second wives, Maria of Burgundy and Bianca Maria Sforza of Milan; on the right, he is pictured with an adviser and a court jester. The magnificent coats of arms representing Austria, Hungary, Burgundy, Milan, the Holy Roman Empire, Styria, Tyrol, and royal Germany are copies. You can see the originals (and up close, too) in the Ferdinandeum. The Golden Roof building houses the **Maximilianeum,** a small museum that headlines memorabilia and paintings from the life of Emperor Maximilian I. The short video presentation about Maximilian is worth a look. ⊠ *Herzog-Friedrich-Strasse 15* ☎ *0512/5873–8029* 🎟 *€4* 🕐 *Oct.–Apr., Tues.–Sun. 10–5; May–Sept., daily 10–5.*

CLUB INNSBRUCK CARD

Pick up a free Club Innsbruck card at your hotel for no-charge use of ski buses and reduced-charge ski-lift passes. For big savings, buy the **all-inclusive Innsbruck Card,** which gives you free admission to all museums, mountain cable cars, the Alpenzoo, and Schloss Ambras, plus free bus and tram transportation, including bus service to nearby **Hall in Tyrol.** The card includes unlimited ride-hopping onboard the big red **Sightseer** bus, which whisks you in air-conditioned comfort to all of the major sights, and even provides recorded commentary in English and five other languages. Cards are good for 24, 48, and 72 hours at €33, €41, and €47 respectively, with a 50% discount for children ages 6 to 15, and are available at the tourist office, on cable cars, and in larger museums.

NEED A BREAK?

Kröll. The small bakery and café, a few steps from the Goldenes Dachl, offers homemade Strudel (sweet or savory fillings wrapped in a fine pastry) and Italian coffee specialties. The café opens at 6 am every day of the year. ✉ *Hofgasse 6* 🕾 *0512/574347.*

Imperial Palace (*Hofburg*). One of Innsbruck's most historic attractions is the Hofburg, or Imperial Palace, which Maximilian I and Archduke Sigmund the Rich commissioned to be built in late-Gothic style in the 15th century. Center stage is the **Giant's Hall**—designated a marvel of the 18th century as soon as it was topped off with its magnificent trompe-l'oeil ceiling painted by Franz Anton Maulpertsch in 1775. The rococo decoration and the portraits of Habsburg ancestors in the ornate white-and-gold great reception hall were added in the 18th century by the Empress Maria Theresa; look for the portrait of "Primal" (primrose)—to use the childhood nickname of the empress's daughter, Marie-Antoinette. On the first floor is the Alpine Club Museum, open daily all-year round from 9 to 5. ✉ *Rennweg 1* 🕾 *0512/587186* ⊕ *www.hofburg-innsbruck.at* 🎟 *€8* 🕑 *Daily 9–5 (to 7 pm Wed, Mar.–Aug.). Last admission half hour before closing. Tours daily at 11 and 2.*

Stadtturm. Down the street from the Goldenes Dachl, the City Tower was built in about 1460. It has a steep climb of 148 steps to the top, where the bulbous cupola was added in the 16th century, and from it there are magnificent views of the city and surrounding mountains. ✉ *Herzog-Friedrich-Strasse 21* 🕾 *0512/5615–00* 🎟 *€4* 🕑 *Oct.–May, daily 10–5; June–Sept., daily 10–8.*

WORTH NOTING
Annasäule. St. Anne's Column, erected in 1706, commemorates the withdrawal of Bavarian forces in the war of the Spanish Succession on St. Anne's Day (July 26) in 1703. Along with the Triumphal Arch, one of the two most important sights on Maria Theresien Strasse. From here there is a classic view of Innsbruck's Altstadt (Old City), with the glorious Nordkette mountain range in the background. ✉ *Maria-Theresien-Strasse.*

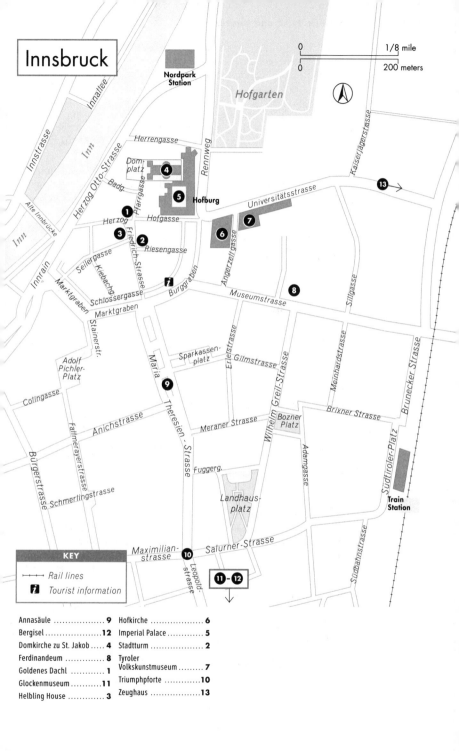

Innsbruck

Nordpark Station

Hofgarten

Innstrasse

Innallee

Innrain

Inn

Alte Innbrücke

Herzog Otto-Strasse

Herrengasse

Rennweg

Kaiserjägerstrasse

Dom platz

4

Badg.

Pfarrgasse

5 **Hofburg**

Universitätsstrasse

13

1

Herzog

Hofgasse

7

3

2

Riesengasse

6

Angerzellgasse

Friedrich-Strasse

Seilergasse

Kiebachg.

Schlossergasse

8

Burggraben

Museumstrasse

Sillgasse

Innrain

Marktgraben

Marktgraben

Stainerstr.

Sparkassen-platz

Erlerstrasse

Gilmstrasse

Meinhardstrasse

Brunecker Strasse

Adolf Pichler-Platz

Collingasse

Maria

9

Theresien - Strasse

Wilhelm Greil-Strasse

Anichstrasse

Meraner Strasse

Bozner Platz

Brixner Strasse

Südtiroler-Platz

Fallmerayerstrasse

Fuggerg.

Adamgasse

Train Station

Bürgerstrasse

Schmerlingstrasse

Landhaus-platz

KEY

⊢——⊣ *Rail lines*

i *Tourist information*

Maximilian-strasse

10

Salurner-Strasse

Leopold-strasse

11 – **12**

Südbahnstrasse

Annasäule **9**
Bergisel **12**
Domkirche zu St. Jakob **4**
Ferdinandeum **8**
Goldenes Dachl **1**
Glockenmuseum **11**
Helbling House **3**

Hofkirche **6**
Imperial Palace **5**
Stadtturm **2**
Tyroler
Volkskunstmuseum **7**
Triumphpforte **10**
Zeughaus **13**

0   1/8 mile

0   200 meters

Bergisel. This ski-jumping stadium towers over Innsbruck with a gloriously modern, concrete-and-glass observation deck and restaurant designed by world-celebrated architect Zaha Hadid. It opened in 2003, replacing the old stadium that no longer complied with modern requirements for ski jumping and crowd safety. There's a café at the base area, and if you're lucky you can have a beer while watching ski jumpers practice, even during the summer when they heavily water the slope. ⊠ *Bergiselweg 3* ☎ *0512/589259* ⊕ *www.bergisel.info* ⊠ *€9.50* ⊘ *Nov. 29–May 31, daily 10–5; June–Nov. 2, daily 9–6.*

Glockenmuseum. A visit to the 400-year-old Grassmayr Bell Foundry includes a fascinating little museum and sound chamber, which will give you an idea of how bells are cast and tuned. Guided tours in English can be arranged. ⊠ *Leopoldstrasse 53* ✛ *Take bus J, K, or S south to Grassmayrstrasse* ☎ *0512/59416–37* ⊕ *www.grassmayr.at* ⊠ *€6* ⊘ *Oct.–Apr., weekdays 9–5; May–Sept., weekdays 9–5, Sat. 9–5.*

Helbling House. Facing the Stadtturm is the dramatic blue and white Helbling House, originally a Gothic townhouse dating from the 15th century. In about 1730 the facade was decorated with late-Baroque stuccos by artists of the Wessobrunn school of decorative plasterers. ⊠ *Herzog-Friedrich-Strasse 10.*

Hofkirche (*Court Church*). Close by the Hofburg, the Court Church was built as a mausoleum for Maximilian I (although he is actually buried in Wiener Neustadt, south of Vienna). The emperor's ornate black-marble tomb is surrounded by 24 marble reliefs depicting his accomplishments, as well as 28 larger-than-life-size statues of his ancestors (real and imagined), including the legendary King Arthur of England. Freedom fighter Andreas Hofer is also buried here. Don't miss the 16th-century **Silver Chapel,** up the stairs opposite the entrance, with its elaborate altar and silver Madonna. The chapel was built in 1578 to be the tomb of Archduke Ferdinand II and his wife, Philippine Welser, the daughter of a rich and powerful merchant family. ▪TIP➜ **Visit the chapel for picture-taking in the morning; the blinding afternoon sun comes in directly behind the altar.** ⊠ *Universitätsstrasse 2* ☎ *0512/59489–511* ⊕ *www.hofkirche.at* ⊠ *€5; €10 combined ticket with Zeughaus and Ferdinandeum* ⊘ *Mon.–Sat. 9–5, Sun. 12:30–5.*

Tyroler Volkskunstmuseum (*Tyrolean Folk Art Museum*). In the same complex as the Hofkirche, this is regarded as the most important folk art museum in the Alpine region. Its wood-paneled parlors house furniture, including entire room settings from old farmhouses and inns, decorated in styles from Gothic to rococo. Other exhibits include costumes, farm implements, carnival masks, and fascinating Christmas cribs. ⊠ *Universitätsstrasse 2* ☎ *0512/594–89–511* ⊕ *www.tyroler-volkskunstmuseum. at* ⊠ *€6* ⊘ *Mon.–Sat. 9–5, Sun. and holidays 10–5.*

Triumphpforte. The Triumphal Arch was built in 1765 to commemorate both the marriage of emperor-to-be Leopold II (then Duke of Tuscany) and the death of Emperor Franz I, husband of Empress Maria Theresa. One side clearly represents celebration, and the other, tragedy. ⊠ *Salurner Strasse.*

Zeughaus. The late-Gothic secular building now housing the Zeughaus museum was the arsenal of Maximilian I. Displays include cartography, mineralogy, music, hunting weapons, coins, aspects of Tyrol's culture and the province's wars of independence. ✉ *Zeughausgasse* ☎ *0512/59489–11* 🌐 *www.tyroler-landesmuseen.at* 🎟 *€6, €10 combined ticket with Ferdinandeum and Hofkirche* ⏲ *Tues.–Sun. 9–6.*

WHERE TO EAT

$$$$ AUSTRIAN Fodor's Choice ★ 🍴 **Alfred Miller's Schoneck.** With fine views of the city, an atmospheric stube, and veranda and garden for summer dining, this is one of Innsbruck's most exquisite restaurants—with a Michelin star and an impressive 16 points from the Gault Millau. Occupying a former imperial hunting lodge, across the River Inn from the city center, this has been a magnet for lovers of fine dining since 1899. There's a two-course business lunch for around €19 (the Viennese goulash with fried egg or bouillabaisse with garlic bread are good choices, but the menu often changes daily). Evening menus are always a surprise on the day. [$] *Average main: €26* ✉ *Weiherburggasse 6* ☎ *0512/272728* 🌐 *www.wirtshaus-schoeneck.com* ⏲ *Closed Sun.–Tues.*

$$ AUSTRIAN 🍴 **Café Central.** Dark wooden paneling, crystal chandeliers, and the smell of coffee make this Viennese-style café a meeting point for intellectuals, artists, and students. International newspapers and magazines are available, as is a variety of cakes, pastries, and meals. Wrong city of course, but it feels like a scene from "The Third Man." You can have breakfast any time of day, or choose a meal from the daily menu. A typical small dish to sample is *Kasnocken* (cheese dumplings with brown butter); more substantial choices might include traditional boiled beef. Enjoy your cappuccino with live piano accompaniment every Sunday from October to April. In summer, there's also terrace seating. [$] *Average main: €15* ✉ *Central Hotel, Gilmstrasse 5* ☎ *0512/5920.*

$ ECLECTIC 🍴 **Cammerlander.** A bright and breezy spot along the Inn River, this place has a distinct Mediterranean feel about it. During the summer take a table if you can find one on the open terrace or in the cooler months in the glass-enclosed courtyard. The atmosphere is not rushed and you can order lunch well after 2 pm. Japanese-style noodle soups and pizzas (we recommend the one with arugula and Serrano ham) are some of the offerings. Vegan dishes are also available. Across the corridor you can let yourself be absorbed by the Latin rhythms of the adjacent Tapabar, and there's a Mexican eatery upstairs. [$] *Average main: €11* ✉ *Innrain 2* ☎ *0512/586–398* 🌐 *www.cammerlander.at.*

$$$$ INTERNATIONAL Fodor's Choice ★ 🍴 **Das Schindler.** Some say this is Innsbruck's current go-to gourmet experience, and its 14 Gault Millau points are a fine endorsement. In the heart of the old town, the restaurant likes to be known for its obsession with using local ingredients as much as possible, with farm-to-table distances kept to a minimum. Flavor enhancers and artificial additives are also demonized by chef de cuisine Thomas Knittl. Details of suppliers, farms, and even local hunting grounds for game are available for perusal. The interior is modern and the atmosphere is trendy. The barbecued lamb pairs well with the rosé from Brad Pitt and Angelina Jolie's

French vineyard. [$] *Average main: €26* ✉ *Maria-Theresien-Strasse 31* ☎ *0512/566969* 🌐 *www.dasschindler.at* ⏲ *Closed Sun.*

$$$ AUSTRIAN Fodor's Choice ★ 🍴 **Europastüberl.** Cuisine that is creative, yet draws on traditional recipes, is what you'll find at the Grand Hotel Europa's acclaimed dining room. It achieves the difficult feat of combining coziness with elegance, with carved wood alcoves—the typical Tyrolean Stüberl—harboring intimate tables dressed with white linens and flickering candles. For the last 20 years the signature dish has been Dover sole sautéed in butter—served by the same waiter for the entire time. Seasonal regional specialties, such as local game or house-made pastas, are recommended. Our favorite is *Tafelspitz*, an Austrian specialty of boiled beef and creamed spinach, with fresh horseradish. The four- to seven-course prix-fixe menus are good options for those who just cannot decide. The wine list includes a great selection of Austrian wines. [$] *Average main: €22* ✉ *SüdTyrolerplatz 2* ☎ *0512/5931* 🌐 *www.grandhoteleuropa.at.*

$$$ AUSTRIAN 🍴 **Goldener Adler.** This restaurant is as popular with locals as it is with travelers. The traditional dining rooms on the arcaded ground floor and the summer-only terrace are popular places to sit, the former more romantic and private and the latter good for people-watching. Start with a glass of *Sekt* (an Austrian sparkling wine) flavored with a dash of cassis—a kir royale—as you peruse the menu. The kitchen takes a modern approach to traditional dishes, so the pork medallions are topped with ham and Gorgonzola, and the veal steaks are ladled with a creamy herb sauce that's as steeped in flavor as the restaurant is steeped in history. [$] *Average main: €20* ✉ *Herzog-Friedrich-Strasse 6* ☎ *0512/5711.*

$ AUSTRIAN 🍴 **Hofgarten.** For many, this is *the* summer gathering place in Innsbruck, perhaps because it is so pleasant to eat and drink outdoors amid the beauty of the city's ancient and splendid park. Whether enjoying a beer and light meal on a sunny afternoon or celebrating with friends after a show at the nearby Landestheater, this is a fine place for chilling out and having fun. The place is popular with students, and on Tuesday they pack the place. Food service ends around 10:30 pm, but the place continues to get even more packed with revelers. [$] *Average main: €12* ✉ *Rennweg 6a* ☎ *0512/588871.*

$$$$ ECLECTIC 🍴 **Lichtblick.** This little restaurant's location on the seventh floor of the chic **Rathausgalerie** is as lofty as its reputation. The all-around glass of Lichtblick (which means "bright spot") provides you with sensational views of the Old City. The kitchen offers creative, captivating dishes made from fresh local ingredients. The menu changes often and the desserts are especially good. ■ **TIP→ If you're not lucky enough to get dinner reservations, score a table at the adjacent Café Bar Lounge 360.** [$] *Average main: €23* ✉ *Rathaus Gallery, Maria-Theresienstrasse 18* ☎ *0512/566550* ✍ *Reservations essential* ⏲ *Closed Sun.*

$ AUSTRIAN 🍴 **Markthalle.** This tidy indoor market offers plenty of farm-fresh produce, including a variety of cheeses, just-picked berries, and a wide choice of mushrooms. You'll also find pastas and other homemade delicacies. The central location makes this a good stop for an inexpensive lunch—basically a take-out, but with stand-up tables available to lounge against. Go to the bakery for your choice of breads and then browse the stalls to find your ideal fillings. Popular with students and office workers, always a good sign. $ *Average main: €5* ⊠ *Herzog-Siegmund-Ufer 1-3, Marktplatz* ☎ *0512/572562* ▭ *No credit cards* ⊗ *Closed Sun.*

$$ ✕ **Ottoburg.** This family-run restaurant offers excellent food and an
AUSTRIAN extraordinary location in an ancient landmark, built in 1180 as a city watchtower, with an abundance of historical charm. It's fun just to explore the rabbit warren of paneled rustic rooms named after emperors. Several of the bay-window alcoves in the shuttered house have great views of the main square, while others overlook the river. Try the *Tafelspitz*, an Austrian specialty of boiled beef served with vegetables and horseradish, or the *Pfandl*, a fillet of pork and a steak served in an old-fashioned pan. On a sunny day come early to get a table outside $ *Average main: €16* ⊠ *Herzog-Friedrich-Strasse 1* ☎ *0512/584338* ⊕ *www.ottoburg.at* ⊗ *Closed Mon.*

$$$$ ✕ **Pavillon.** In stark contrast to the surrounding stately buildings—it's
ECLECTIC between the Hofburg Palace and the National Theater—this two-story, gleaming glass box houses a café on the ground floor that serves small dishes during the day, with a more elaborate dining experience upstairs in the evening. A creative international menu demonstrates a dedication to local and seasonal ingredients. Low armchairs create a fashionable and comfortable atmosphere for this hip Innsbruck landmark. It's a café, it's a restaurant, it's a cocktail bar. $ *Average main: €28* ⊠ *Rennweg 4* ☎ *0512/257–000* ⊕ *www.der-pavilion.at* ⊗ *No dinner Mon. No breakfast Mon.–Sat.*

$$$ ✕ **Schwarzer Adler.** This intimate, romantic restaurant on the ground
AUSTRIAN floor of the Romantik Hotel Schwarzer Adler Hotel has leaded-glass windows and rustic embellishments—and in summer, dining on the rooftop terrace—offering the perfect backdrop for a memorable meal. The innovative cooks present a new menu every couple of months based on regional seasonal specialties. The year-round classics, such as the garlic soup with croutons, or three kinds of local dumplings served with sauerkraut, are delicious. The pictures on display are constantly changing, as the stubes house what is in effect an exhibition for local artists, with works for sale. $ *Average main: €22* ⊠ *Kaiserjägerstrasse 2* ☎ *0512/587109* ⊕ *www.deradler.com* ⊗ *No lunch.*

$$ ✕ **Seegrube.** If your plans include a Friday night stay in Innsbruck and
AUSTRIAN the weather is clear, try to book a table at this restaurant in the Seegrube cableway station at 2,000 meters (6,561 feet)—cuisine that is literally "haute." Reservations are needed, and dinner is served from 6. The last descent by cable car is at 11:30. The four-course dinner includes mostly Tyrolean specialties. The view of the city lights twinkling below makes a wonderful background for a romantic dinner. During the week the self-service buffet feeds hungry hikers. Alternatively, during July and August there is a jazz brunch every Sunday, served from 11. $ *Average main: €14* ⊠ *Höhenstrasse 145* ☎ *0512/303065* ⊕ *www.seegrube.at* ⊗ *Closed weekends.*

$$$ ✕ **Sitzwohl Restaurant-Bar.** Stylishly modern, with a functional yet warm
MEDITERRANEAN and intimate atmosphere, Sitzwohl has built up a solid reputation in a short time for superb cuisine, with the accent on Mediterranean and Tyrolean dishes. Chanterelle mushroom stew with dumplings or black

gnocchi with wild salmon and fennel are favorites. Run by Elisabeth Geisler and Irmgard Sitzwohl, it has been awarded 15 Gault Millau points. Lunchtime service is quick and efficient for business diners; the evenings are more relaxed. Chutneys, jams, and soups are available from the attached deli. $ *Average main: €20* ⊠ *Stadtforum, Gilmstrasse, Innsbruck* ☎ *512/562888* ⊕ *www.restaurantsitzwohl.at* ☉ *Closed Sun.*

$ ✕ **Thai-Li.** This Thai kitchen has quietly fashioned a reputation as one
THAI   of the best and most popular, yet very affordable, dining spots in the old town, just along from the Golden Roof. Thai-Li is short on elbow room but long on excellent food presented with elegance and efficiency. Come for lunch, when you can sit outside at the tables on the cobbled pavement. In the evening start with skewers of grilled chicken and pork, fried prawns, and vegetables with a range of dipping sauces. For a main course try one of the curry dishes, such as duck simmered in green curry. Beverages include a good selection of teas, coffees, and fruit juices. $ *Average main: €12* ⊠ *Marktgraben 3* ☎ *0512/562813* ⊕ *www. thaili.at* ☉ *Closed Mon.*

$$ ✕ **Weisses Rössl.** This is the oldest restaurant in Innsbruck and in the
AUSTRIAN   authentically rustic dining rooms, the hunting pedigree of these parts is reflected by arrays of antlers adorning the walls. This is not a vegetarian's natural habitat. It is, however, the right place for solid local standards, such as *Tyroler Gröstl*, a tasty hash, and Wiener schnitzel (veal, or pork if you prefer, cutlet), both of which taste even better on the outside terrace in summer. Ask about the specials that don't appear on the menu, such as wild game or freshly picked mushrooms. Because the place hosts regular local gatherings it can get quite lively, but all you have to do is request a table in one of the smaller stubes. $ *Average main: €13* ⊠ *Kiebachgasse 8* ☎ *0512/583057* ⊕ *www.roessl. at* ☉ *Closed Sun.*

WHERE TO STAY

$ ⛶ **Adlers.** One of Innsbruck's newest hotels, Adlers eclipses all with its
HOTEL   panoramic vistas, and every room in the striking, supermodern build-
Fodor's Choice   ing has floor-to-ceiling windows. **Pros:** best view in the city; handy for
★   train station. **Cons:** no on-site parking (but €15 a day parking close by); windows don't open. $ *Rooms from: €111* ⊠ *Bruneckerstasse 1* ☎ *0512/56–31–00* ⊕ *www.deradler.com* ⇆ *75 rooms* ⍩ *No meals.*

$$ ⛶ **Goldener Adler.** In the heart of the Old Innsbruck's pedestrian area,
HOTEL   this hotel is said to be one of Europe's oldest hotels, and since 1390 it
Fodor's Choice   has welcomed nearly every king, emperor, duke, or poet who passed
★   through Innsbruck. **Pros:** perfect location; free Internet; friendly and helpful staff. **Cons:** no spa; no on-site parking, but guests can enter pedestrian-only area to unload car, then park two minutes away for €10.90 per day. $ *Rooms from: €140* ⊠ *Herzog-Friedrich-Strasse 6* ☎ *0512/571–11110* ⊕ *www.goldeneradler.com* ⇆ *37 rooms* ⍩ *Multiple meal plans.*

$$$$ ⛶ **Grand Hotel Europa.** Opposite the train station, this five-star hotel has
HOTEL   long provided lodging to the celebrated and wealthy in richly appointed,
Fodor's Choice   extremely comfortable rooms since it opened in 1869. **Pros:** spacious
★   rooms; wonderful restaurant. **Cons:** on a busy square, although this

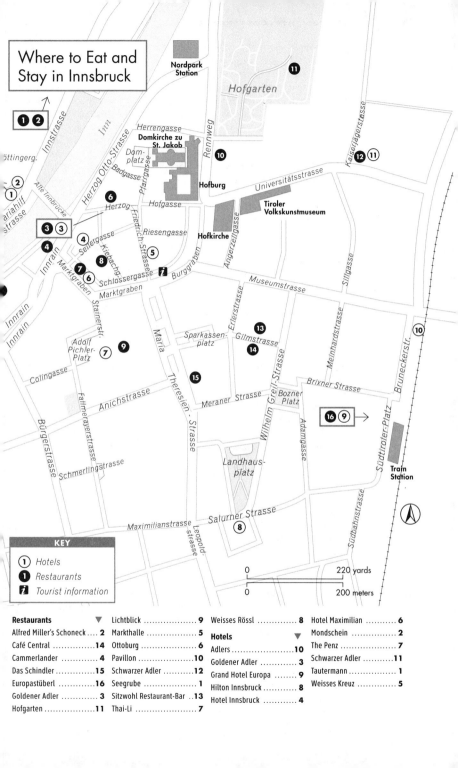

Where to Eat and Stay in Innsbruck

Nordpark Station

Hofgarten

Domkirche zu St. Jakob

Domplatz

Hofburg

Tiroler Volkskunstmuseum

Hofkirche

Adolf Pichler-Platz

Sparkassen-platz

Landhaus-platz

Train Station

| 0 | 220 yards |
| 0 | 200 meters |

KEY

(1) Hotels
(1) Restaurants
(i) Tourist information

Restaurants ▼
Alfred Miller's Schoneck **2**
Café Central **14**
Cammerlander **4**
Das Schindler **15**
Europastüberl **16**
Goldener Adler **3**
Hofgarten **11**
Lichtblick **9**
Markthalle **5**
Ottoburg **6**
Pavillon **10**
Schwarzer Adler **12**
Seegrube **1**
Sitzwohl Restaurant-Bar ..**13**
Thai-Li **7**
Weisses Rössl **8**

Hotels ▼
Adlers **10**
Goldener Adler **3**
Grand Hotel Europa **9**
Hilton Innsbruck **8**
Hotel Innsbruck **4**
Hotel Maximilian **6**
Mondschein **2**
The Penz **7**
Schwarzer Adler **11**
Tautermann **1**
Weisses Kreuz **5**

adds to the city vibe. $ *Rooms from: €260* ✉ *SüdTyrolerplatz 2* ☎ *0512/5931* 🌐 *www.grandhoteleuropa.at* 🛏 *117 rooms, 10 suites* 🍴 *Multiple meal plans.*

$$$ HOTEL 🏨 **Hilton Innsbruck.** Built in the 1970s as part of a 14-story complex that sits rather uncomfortably in this historic city, the Hilton nevertheless offers wonderful views and a full range of classic comforts. **Pros:** views; huge breakfast buffet. **Cons:** bland personality; chain-hotel feel. $ *Rooms from: €190* ✉ *Salurner Strasse 15* ☎ *0512/59350–2220* 🌐 *www.hilton.com* 🛏 *176 rooms* 🍴 *Breakfast.*

$$ HOTEL 🏨 **Hotel Innsbruck.** With an ideal location in the heart of Innsbruck, there's an efficient and functional slant here rather than any wow factor—until you look out the window. **Pros:** lovely sauna area; great location; family run. **Cons:** often has large groups and can have a conference hotel feel; the hotel is a warren and you might need a route map to find your room. $ *Rooms from: €160* ✉ *Innrain 3* ☎ *0512/59868–0* 🌐 *www.hotelinnsbruck.com* 🛏 *109 rooms* 🍴 *Multiple meal plans.*

$$ HOTEL 🏨 **Hotel Maximilian.** Clean, modern, almost stark lines within the vaulted interior of a historic building are immediately striking in this hotel, a couple of minutes from the center of the old town. **Pros:** great location; free Wi-Fi throughout and lots of English-language channels on TV; striking modern luxury. **Cons:** some will feel the Tyrol character has been abandoned along the way. $ *Rooms from: €160* ✉ *Marktgraben 7–9, Innenstadt* ☎ *0512/59967* 🌐 *www.hotel-maximilian.com* 🛏 *46 rooms* 🍴 *Breakfast.*

$$ HOTEL 🏨 **Mondschein.** Among the city's oldest houses stands this pink hotel, built in 1473, a warm and welcoming family-run Best Western facing the River Inn a few minutes from the center of the old town. **Pros:** very friendly staff; free on-site parking; riverfront location. **Cons:** some rooms can be noisy; courtyard rooms are dark and some areas are looking tired. $ *Rooms from: €129* ✉ *Mariahilfstrasse 6* ☎ *0512/22784* 🌐 *www.mondschein.at* 🛏 *34 rooms* 🍴 *Breakfast.*

$$$ HOTEL 🏨 **The Penz.** The ultramodern steel-and-glass architecture of this luxury hotel, designed by the renowned French architect Dominique Perrault and opened in 2002, is a striking contrast to the old town and has a purposeful, business feel that will make traveling executives feel right at home. **Pros:** sleek design; great breakfast; popular rooftop bar. **Cons:** no spa or sauna; some may find it all a bit sterile. $ *Rooms from: €200* ✉ *Adolf-Pichler-Platz 3* ☎ *0512/575657–0* 🌐 *www.thepenz.com* 🛏 *92 rooms, 2 suites* 🍴 *Breakfast.*

$ HOTEL Fodor's Choice ★ 🏨 **Schwarzer Adler.** The vaulted cellars of this 500-year-old building were once stables for Emperor Maximilian's horses; now they host glittering events in atmospheric surroundings, and the hotel attracts those in search of a romantic experience. **Pros:** lovely spa; romantic; every room is different. **Cons:** only one elevator; some rooms face busy street. $ *Rooms from: €108* ✉ *Kaiserjägerstrasse 2* ☎ *0512/587–109* 🌐 *www.deradler.com* 🛏 *40 rooms, 7 suites* 🍴 *Breakfast.*

$ HOTEL 🏨 **Tautermann.** This solid, red-shuttered house, a friendly, family-run hotel, is within a five-minute walk of the city center but is in a quiet area and offers a great value to anyone traveling on a budget. **Pros:** very quiet location on the fringes of the city; inexpensive rates; free parking.

Cons: basic breakfast; furnishings a little dated. $ *Rooms from: €80* ✉ *Stamserfeld 5* ☎ *0512/281–572* ⊕ *www.hotel-tautermann.at* ⇆ *32 rooms* |◯| *Breakfast.*

$

HOTEL

🔲 **Weisses Kreuz.** Quirky, endearing, and in an unrivaled position over ancient stone arcades in the pedestrian heart of the old town, this hotel begs you to fall in love with it—and you might, as long as you put character and atmosphere above slick service and cutting-edge amenities. **Pros:** good value; family-friendly. **Cons:** parking is a short walk away; not all rooms are air-conditioned. $ *Rooms from: €112* ✉ *Herzog-Friedrich-Strasse 31* ☎ *0512/59479–0* ⊕ *www.weisseskreuz.at* ⇆ *40 rooms* |◯| *Breakfast.*

NIGHTLIFE AND PERFORMING ARTS

PERFORMING ARTS

It's said that Tyrol has more bandleaders than mayors. Folklore shows at the **Messehalle** and other spots around the city showcase authentic Tyrolean folk dancing, yodeling, and zither music. The tourist office and hotels have details.

Festwochen der Alten Musik (*Festival of Early Music*). Between mid-July and late August, the Festival of Early Music highlights music from the 14th to 18th centuries, performed by many of Europe's finest musicians in such dramatic settings as Innsbruck's beautiful Schloss Ambras and the Hofkirche. In summer there are frequent brass-band (*Musikkapelle*) concerts in the old town. During the Renaissance and in the Baroque era, Innsbruck was one of Europe's most important centers for music, and this is the oldest existing festival for early music. ✉ *Burggraben 3* ☎ *0512/5710–32* ⊕ *www.altemusik.at.*

Internationaler Tanzsommer Innsbruck. The world's premiere dance companies have been coming to Innsbruck for more than 20 years for this international dance festival between the last week in June and mid-July. The world-renowned Dance Theatre of Harlem and the São Paulo Dance Company, as well as Maracana, Brazil's Grupo Corpo, and Sankai Juku all feature regularly. Visitors can join in dance workshops too. Tickets are available through the tourist office or the festival office. ✉ *Burggraben 3* ☎ *0512/561–561* ⊕ *www.tanzsommer.at.*

Kongresshaus. The original congress house was built by Archduke Leopold V in 1629 as the first free-standing opera house in the north of the Alps, and in the 19th century it was converted into the Dogana, or customs house. Destroyed during World War II, its remains were used to create this modern congress and events center in 1973. Concerts take place in the modern Saal Tyrol. ✉ *Rennweg 3* ☎ *0512/5936–0.*

Tiroler Landestheater. Innsbruck's principal theater is said to be the oldest German-speaking theatre. It was built in 1654 as the court opera house but totally renovated in the classical style in 1846 and modernized and extended in the 1960s. Both operas and operettas are presented in the main hall, usually starting at 7:30; plays and dance in the Kammerspiele start at 8. Obtain tickets at the box office or at the main tourist office. ✉ *Rennweg 2* ☎ *0512/52074–4* ⊕ *www.landestheater.at.*

NIGHTLIFE

Blue Chip. For dancing, this basement club on Landhaus Square is a leading hotspot and a magnet for students on Wednesday and the weekend. DJs are highly rated, house music the staple. ✉ *Wilhelm-Greil-Strasse 17* ☎ *0512/565050.*

Casino. The jazzy casino next to the Hilton Innsbruck offers blackjack, baccarat, roulette, poker, and plenty of slot machines, as well as a bar. You must present your passport to enter the casino. Special meal-plus-gambling-chips packages are available in conjunction with the Hilton. ✉ *Salurner Strasse 15* ☎ *0512/587040–0* ⊕ *www2.casinos.at/en/innsbruck* 🎫 *€22, exchangeable for €25 worth of chips; admission free for those not playing* ☉ *Daily 3 pm–3 am.*

Jimmy's Bar. This upstairs bar is wildly popular and has built up a jazz-loving clientele. In the winter it's something of an après-ski hangout. Lots of events, from guest DJs to jam sessions and party nights. ✉ *Wilhelm-Greil-Strasse 17* ☎ *0512/570473.*

Krahvogel. Known for its wide choice of beer—the drink of choice here rather than cocktails—Krahvogel is also something of a gastro-pub, with regional and international cuisine on offer. It's on one of Innsbruck's busiest shopping streets and attracts a good cross-section of customers, from tourists to local office workers and students. ✉ *Anichstrasse 12* ☎ *0512/580149.*

Piano Bar. Tiny, and exuding old-world charm, this bar is a favored hangout of local artists and has occasional live music. Devotees insist it has the best steaks in Austria, and the Wiener schnitzel is good too. It has a nice patio with an outdoor dining area. ✉ *Herzog-Friedrich-Strasse 5* ☎ *0512/571010* ⊕ *www.cafepiano.at.*

Tapabar. For Latin rhythms, Tapabar is the go-to place. On Wednesday there are flamenco lessons, and occasional live performances are a good warm-up for long nights of dancing. Good homemade tapas. ✉ *Marktplatz, Innrain 2* ☎ *0512/586398–43.*

SPORTS AND THE OUTDOORS

GOLF

Several hotels—Grand Hotel Europa in Innsbruck, Sporthotel Igls, Gesundheitszentrum Lanserhof at Lans, and the Geisler at Rinn—have special golfing arrangements.

Golf Course Innsbruck-Igls. Breathtaking views of surrounding mountains from the concentric, partly hilly fairways on an ascending plateau make this a special experience. About 9 km (5½ miles) outside Innsbruck, this club has two courses, an 18-hole championship course at Rinn and a 9-hole course at nearby Lans. Founded in 1935, it's among Austria's oldest. It's open April–November. ✉ *Oberdorf 11, Rinn* ☎ *05223/78734* ⊕ *www.golfclub-innsbruck-igls.at* 🎫 *€70 for 18 holes, €60 for 9 holes weekdays until Fri. at 10 am; €75 for 18 holes, €65 for 9 holes Fri. 10 am–Sun. €175 for 3 days' play; €275 for 5 days' play* 🏌 *Rinn: 18 holes, 6,622 yards, par 71; Lans: 9 holes, 5,056 yards, par 33.*

HIKING

Both easy paths and extreme slopes await hikers and climbers. From June to October holders of the Club Innsbruck card can take free, daily, guided mountain hikes. The tourist office has a special hiking brochure.

Alpine School Innsbruck. If you want to learn to rock climb, this is the place. ⊠ *In der Stille 1, Natters* ☏ *0512/546000–0* ⊕ *www.asi.at.*

Österreichischer Alpenverein. If you're already an experienced *Kletterer* (rock climber), check in with the Österreichischer Alpenverein. ⊠ *Wilhelm-Greil-Strasse 15* ☏ *0512/59547–0* ⊕ *www.alpenverein.at.*

SKIING

Around Innsbruck you'll find everything from the beginner slopes of the Glungezer to the good intermediate skiing of Axamer Lizum and Patscherkofel to the steep runs and off-piste skiing of Seegrube. Your Club Innsbruck membership card (free with an overnight stay in any Innsbruck hotel) includes transportation to the areas and reduced prices on a number of ski lifts. A Super Ski Pass covers all the ski areas of Innsbruck, the Stubai Glacier, Kitzbühel, and St. Anton, with 520 km (290 miles) of runs, 210 lifts, and all transfers. The Gletscher Ski Pass includes Innsbruck and the Stubai Glacier. There's year-round skiing on the Stubai Glacier, about 40 km (25 miles) from Innsbruck via the free ski shuttle bus (ask at your hotel). You can book your skiing needs, such as lift tickets, equipment rentals, and ski lessons, through the tourist office. Hotels have details on winter ski kindergartens.

Ski & Snowboardschule Innsbruck. You can book all skiing needs—lift tickets, equipment and lessons—here. You can book instructors through the Innsbruck Ski School and meet them at your hotel or one of the ski areas, or the school will arrange transportation (at extra cost). They can arrange days out, with instruction, at farther-flung resorts such as St. Anton, Ischgl, or Solden. One-on-one tuition starting at about €180 or €65 per person, per day for a group of four. The Innsbruck H.Q. is at the sports store, Die Boerse. ⊠ *Leopoldstrasse 4* ☏ *0512/581742–17* ⊕ *www.skischool-innsbruck.com.*

Snowboard Börse. This is a good place to rent ski and snowboard equipment, particularly as it's on-site at the Innsbruck Ski School, making it a one-stop for all your skiing needs. It's tucked into an alley just south of the Triumphpforte. ⊠ *Leopoldstrasse 4* ☏ *0512/581742–0* ⊕ *www.dieboerse.at.*

SWIMMING

Around Innsbruck there are plenty of lakes, but in town you have little choice other than pools, indoors and out.

Freischwimmbad Tivoli. Come here to swim under the sun with a panoramic view of the mountains. ⊠ *Purtschellerstrasse 1* ☏ *0512/502–7081.*

Hallenbad Amraser Strasse. If the weather goes south, try this turn-of-the-20th-century indoor swimming pool. ⊠ *Amraser Strasse 3* ☏ *0512/502–7051.*

Hallenbad Höttinger Au. This is a popular indoor swimming facility. ⊠ *Fürstenweg 12* ☏ *0512/502–7071.*

SHOPPING

The best shops are along the arcaded Herzog-Friedrich-Strasse in the heart of the Altstadt, and along its extension, Maria-Theresien-Strasse; and the adjoining streets Meraner Strasse and Anichstrasse. Innsbruck is the place to buy native Tyrolean clothing, particularly lederhosen (traditional brushed leather shorts and trousers) and loden (sturdy combed-wool jackets and vests). Look also for cut crystal and woodcarvings; locally handmade, delicate silver-filigree pins make fine gifts.

> ### INNSBRUCK'S SMALLEST SHOP
>
> **S'Speckladele.** Definitely worth a visit, this is the smallest shop in Innsbruck. With room for only two clients at a time, it sells delicious *Speck* (bacon) and other smoked meats produced by local organic farms. Enjoy a sandwich; you'll be tempted to take something home, but import rules on meat products are strict so check before you buy, or consume your purchases before you go home. ⊠ *Stiftgasse 4* ☎ *0512/588816.*

Christmas Market. For sheer holiday delight, nothing tops the traditional Christmas Market, which features wooden and glass handicrafts, Christmas-tree decorations, candles, and Tyrolean toys and loden costumes. The market stalls are set up around the giant, illuminated Christmas tree next to the Goldenes Dachl museum, in the heart of the Altstadt. ⊠ *Herzog-Friedrich-Strasse 15* ۞ *Open Nov. 23–Dec. 28.*

Galerie Thomas Flora. The droll graphics by Tyrolean artist Paul Flora on sale here provide much to smile at, and maybe you'll even find something to take home. ⊠ *Herzog-Friedrich-Strasse 5* ☎ *0512/577402.*

Hubertus Loden Steinbock. This is an outstanding source of dirndls, those attractive traditional costumes for women, with white blouses, dark skirts, and colorful aprons. It also has children's clothing. ⊠ *Sparkassenplatz 3* ☎ *0512/585092.*

Rathausgalerie. Innsbruck's swish, central, glass-roofed indoor mall is home to luxury boutiques and world-famous brand names. Here you can shop, eat, and drink in style. ⊠ *Maria-Theresien-Strasse* ⊕ *www.rathausgalerien.at.*

Rudolf Boschi. Reproductions of old pewterware, using the original molds when possible, are among the items you'll find here, along with locally produced, hand-decorated beer mugs with pewter lids. A second location, nearby, has mostly prints. ⊠ *Kiebachgasse 8* ☎ *0512/589224* ⊕ *www.boschi.at.*

S'Culinarium. At *the* shop to buy Austrian wine and liquor (Austria produces some very decent wine these days and always has produced wonderful schnapps and rum), you can try everything before you buy, and the talkative, friendly owner will be happy to advise. Some of the famous Rochelt schnapps may still be available, but supplies are limited since owner Gunter Rochelt's death. ⊠ *Pfarrgasse 1* ☎ *0512/574903* ⊕ *culinarium-signor.at.*

Swarovski Crystal Gallery. This dazzling gallery features mostly crystal from the world-renowned maker, whose headquarters is in nearby Wattens, east of Innsbruck. ☒ *Herzog-Friedrich-Strasse 39* ☎ *0512/573100* ⊕ *innsbruck.swarovski.com.*

Tyroler Heimatwerk. Make this your first stop for high-quality souvenirs. The extremely attractive shop carries textiles and finished clothing, ceramics, carved wooden chests, and some furniture, but don't expect a bargain. You can also have clothing made to order. ☒ *Meraner Strasse 2–4* ☎ *0512/582320* ⊕ *Tyroler.heimatwerk.at.*

12

THREE EXCURSIONS FROM INNSBRUCK

NORDPARK

FAMILY **Alpenzoo.** With its unusual collection of Alpine birds and animals, including endangered species, the zoo alone is worth the trip up the Hungerburg. Go by bus or take the funicular from its city center underground station, and get off at Alpenzoo. Or from the Markthalle bus terminal, buses marked "W" run every 30 minutes to the Alpenzoo between 9 am and 6 pm. ☒ *Weiherburggasse 37A, Innsbruck* ☎ *0512/292–323* ⊕ *www.alpenzoo.at* ☒ *€9; combined ticket with park-and-ride from city €11* ☼ *Apr.–Oct., daily 9–6; Nov.–Mar., daily 9–5.*

FAMILY **Nordpark Funicular.** This is a great way to travel from the city center to the Hungerburg Plateau, from where you can take the Nordkettenbahn Cableway to the top of the mountain for a commanding view of Innsbruck. The futuristic base station can be reached in five minutes by foot from the Goldenes Dachl. The Sightseer bus also takes you to the base station. ☒ *Rennweg, Innsbruck* ☎ *0512/293344* ⊕ *www.nordpark.com* ☒ *Funicular round-trip €6.80; cable-car round-trip €27; both are free with Innsbruck Card.*

SCHLOSS AMBRAS

Schloss Ambras. When Archduke Ferdinand II wanted to marry a commoner for love, the court grudgingly allowed it, but the newlyweds were forced to live outside the city limits. Ferdinand revamped a 10th-century castle for the bride, Philippine Welser, which was completed in 1556 and was every bit as luxe as what he had been accustomed to in town. Amid acres of gardens and woodland, it is an inviting castle with cheery red-and-white shutters on its many windows, and is home to a collection of armaments. The upper castle now houses rooms of noble portraits and the lower section has the collection of weaponry and armor. Be sure to inspect Philippine's sunken bath, a luxury for its time. Look around the grounds to see the fencing field and a small cemetery containing samples of earth from 18 battlefields around the world. ☒ *Schloss Strasse 20* ✛ *The castle is 3 km (2 miles) southeast of the city. By public transportation, take Tram 3 or 6 to Ambras (a short walk from the castle) or Route 1 on the Sightseer from Maria-Theresien-Strasse* ☎ *01/525–24–4802* ⊕ *www.khm.at/ambras* ☒ *Apr.–Oct., €10; Dec.–Mar., €7* ☼ *Sept., Oct., and Dec.–July, daily 10–5; Aug., daily 10–7.*

THE STUBAITAL VALLEY

The delightful Stubai Valley, less than 40 km (25 miles) long, is one of the most beautiful valleys in the Tyrol, with no fewer than 80 glistening glaciers (including the Stubai Glacier) and more than 40 towering peaks. The gondola lift up to the glacier is spectacular, and you can venture onto the glacier on marked walks. The higher slopes are open for skiing most of the summer too. If you just want to look, you can see the whole Stubaital in a full day's excursion from Innsbruck.

GETTING HERE AND AROUND

The narrow-gauge electric Stubaitalbahn can take you from the center of Innsbruck (on Maria-Theresien-Strasse and in front of the main train station), as well as from the station just below the Bergisel ski jump, as far as Fulpmes, partway up the valley. You can take the bus as far as Ranalt and back to Fulpmes, to see more of the valley, then return on the quaint rail line.

Autobusbahnof. Buses leave from Gate 1 of the Autobusbahnhof, just behind the train station at SüdTyroler Platz, about once an hour, and the tram-train leaves from there too. ⊠ *Maria-Theresien-Strasse, Innsbruck* ☎ *0512/5307–102.*

Stubaitalbahn ⊠ *Südbahnstrasse, Innsbruck* ☎ *0512/53070* ⊕ *www. stubaitalbahn.at.*

TYROL

The area north of the Kitzbüheler Alps and south of the German border, is a distillation of all things Tyrolean: perfectly maintained ancient farmhouses with balconies overflowing with flowers; people who still wear the traditional lederhosen and dirndls as their everyday attire; Alpine villages and medieval castles; and wonderfully kitschy winter resorts such as Kitzbühel and St. Johann.

The upper Inn Valley, from Innsbruck stretching up to the Swiss border, is beautiful countryside, particularly the narrow valleys that branch off to the south. Most visitors take Route 171 west from Innsbruck along the banks of the Inn, rather than the autobahn, which hugs the cliffs along the way. This is a region of family-run farms perched on mountainsides and steep granite peaks flanking narrow valleys leading to some of Austria's finest ski areas.

■TIP→ **Many of the Tyrol's finest folk musicians come from the beautiful Zillertal (Ziller Valley) so if you go, ask about live music programs.**

HALL IN TYROL

10 km (4 miles) east of Innsbruck.

A few minutes by road east of Innsbruck is what many assert to be the most beautiful town in Tyrol—ancient Hall, wonderfully preserved and with a historic center actually larger than that of Innsbruck. The town has a history of great prosperity—salt mining in the Middle Ages made it the most important commercial hub in the region at the time (the High German word *Hal* meant salt mine). The town received its municipal

charter in 1286, but even greater prestige was to come nearly 200 years later when the provincial mint was moved to the town. In 1486 a coin called the Thaler was minted here: say it quickly and you'll realize where the word *dollar* comes from. The U.S. currency originated in Hall.

GETTING HERE AND AROUND

From Innsbruck, take Highway A12 east. There is frequent bus service between Innsbruck and Hall on Route 4 (every 15 minutes), with a journey time of about 30 minutes. The Postbus system has frequent services linking Hall with the rest of Tyrol and beyond. Hall is also on the rail network.

ESSENTIALS

Visitor Information Hall in Tyrol ⊠ *Wallpachgasse 5, Hall in Tyrol* ☎ *05223/45544* ⊕ *www.hall-wattens.at.*

EXPLORING

Burg Hasegg and Hall Mint. Built to protect the salt mines and trade on the River Inn, Burg Hasegg was enlarged into a showpiece castle by Duke Siegmund and Emperor Maximilian I. Meanwhile, the first silver coin in Tyrol, the *taler*, emerged from the mint in the center of Hall. In 1567, Ferdinand II moved the mint to Burg Hasegg, and thereafter the fortunes of the mint and the castle became intertwined. In the 18th century 17 million Maria Theresia taler were minted here and became a valued currency throughout the world. Today, you can visit the mint museum—even mint your own coin—and climb to the top of the Mint Tower for splendid views. ⊠ *Burg Hasegg, Hall in Tyrol* ☎ *0680/553–2117* ⊕ *www.muenze-hall.at* ⊡ *€6; €4 for mint only* ⊗ *Apr.–Oct., daily 10–5; Nov.–Mar., Tues.–Sat. 10–5.*

Damenstift. Archduchess Magdelena, sister of Ferdinand II, founded the Damenstift Abbey, home of the silent order of Carmelite nuns, in 1567–69. The church front, with its four full-length fluted pilasters, is an example of the transition from the Renaissance to the Baroque style. Very few nuns remain, mostly elderly, but it is interesting to witness their silent and extensive devotions, and it's perfectly acceptable to do so. ⊠ *Unterer Stadtplatz, Hall in Tyrol* ⊡ *Free* ⊗ *No formal open hrs.*

Pfarrkirche St. Nikolaus. The Waldaufkapelle is the best known part of this 13th-century church, home to Florian Waldauf's rather gruesome collection of 45 skulls, said to be those of B-list saints. Waldauf was something of a fixer for Emperor Maximilian I at the beginning of the 16th century when, apparently looking for a hobby as he became wealthier, decided that scouring Europe for such relics to purchase would be a jolly pursuit. He was as pleased as punch, by all accounts, when he was able to open his prized collection to the public. Now each one rests on an embroidered cushion and, incongruously, is also given a headdress—it's all horribly fascinating. ⊠ *Pfarrplatz, Hall in Tyrol* ☎ *05223/57914* ⊕ *www.pfarre-hall.at* ⊡ *Free* ⊗ *Usually open.*

Fodor's Choice   **Wolfsklamm.** This is an exhilarating and spectacular, but very safe, climb
★   up through a gorge beside a raging torrent from the village of Stans, to the northeast of Hall, to the Benedictine monastery of St. Georgenberg. The climb, on walkways hewn from the mountainside and across bridges spanning the tumbling river and beside waterfalls—all protected

by railings—takes about 90 minutes and features 354 steps. At the top the monastery's sumptuously decorated Baroque church, precariously perched on a rocky peak, is worth a few minutes of your time. There is a decent restaurant there, too, with a terrace dizzily located above a sheer drop of several hundred feet. ⊠ *Stans* ☎ *05242/71435* ⊕ *www. silberregion-karwendel.com.*

WHERE TO STAY

$

HOTEL

🏨 **Garten Hotel Maria Theresia.** Built in solid, substantial, flower-bedecked chalet style, this is a family hotel to the core, and the Hofmann family is the epitome of true Tyrolean innkeeping and hospitality. **Pros:** prices are reasonable; superhospitable; excellent food. **Cons:** away from the prettiest, historic part of town. $ *Rooms from: €82* ⊠ *Reimmichlstrasse 25, Heiligkreuz, Hall in Tyrol* ☎ *05223/56313* ⊕ *www.gartenhotel.at* ⊅ *22 rooms, 2 suites* ⊙ *Breakfast.*

$

B&B/INN

🏨 **Gasthof Badl.** For a short stay, this gasthof can fit the bill at a budget price, offering a warm welcome and rooms that are sparkling clean, with all the comfort you need for an overnight or two. **Pros:** extremely friendly; low prices and comfortable. **Cons:** close to a noisy autobahn, so take a room on the river side. $ *Rooms from: €39* ⊠ *Haller Innbrucke 4, Ampass, Hall in Tyrol* ⊕ *www.badl.at* ⊅ *25 rooms* ⊙ *Breakfast.*

$

HOTEL

🏨 **Rettenberg Hotel.** Close to Hall in Tyrol and very handy for Innsbruck, this comfortable four-star hotel has had €2 million spent on developments and improvements, but remains a place where you can feel part of a small community and actually meet locals in the bar. **Pros:** reasonable prices; a chance to interact with Tyroleans; on-site spa, pool, and bowling alley. **Cons:** rooms at the front can be noisy in the morning as the community comes to life. $ *Rooms from: €59* ⊠ *Mühlbach 6, Kolkass-Weer* ☎ *05224/68124* ⊕ *www.kolsass.at* ⊅ *45 rooms* ⊙ *Breakfast.*

ZELL AM ZILLER

60 km (40 miles) southeast of Innsbruck, 25 km (16 miles) south of Jenbach.

Zell is the main town of the Zillertal, one of the many beautiful Alpine valleys of the Tyrol, and a real working community rather than just a resort. It is noted for its traditional 500-year-old Gauder Fest, and has also developed into a center of summer activities. You can choose to stay in one of a dozen hotels or bed-and-breakfast pensions at surprisingly reasonable cost. For although Zell is considered the valley's main town, the bigger-name resort, especially for skiing, is Mayrhofen, a little farther up the valley and somewhat more expensive. In Zell, families enjoy the Fun-arena, which has water glides and a roller coaster for kids, while adults can try rafting or paragliding.

GETTING HERE AND AROUND

From Innsbruck, take Highway A12 or Route 171. The B169 will lead you to the Ziller Valley. Kids—and quite a few adults—will love the old steam engine of the Zillertalbahn pulling a few historical cars from Jenbach train station up the Zillertal to Zell, and then on to Mayrhofen, twice a day.

EXPLORING

Fodor's Choice ★ **Gauder Fest.** The more than 500-year-old Gauder Fest is held on the first weekend in May. Thousands of visitors, many of them in traditional costume from Tyrol and other parts of Austria, pack the little market town for the colorful skits, music, and singing—and great quantities of *Gauderbier,* a strong brew created for the occasion. You can hear some of the country's best singing by the valley residents and listen to expert harp and zither playing, for which the valley is famous. Tradition runs strong here, so even if you can't make it in May, there are other festival opportunities: witness the Perchtenlaufen, processions of colorfully masked well-wishers going on the neighborhood rounds on January 5; the annual Almabtrieb is celebrated in the last September and first October days, when the cows, decorated with wreaths and bells, are herded back from the high Alpine pastures into the lower fields and barns. ⊕ *www.gauderfest.at.*

Krimml Waterfalls. The tiered Krimml falls plunge down in three stages, with a total drop of 1,247 feet, making it the highest waterfall in Austria and one of Austria's most popular natural attractions. A path ascends through the woods beside the falls, with frequent viewing points. By car or bus, it's 35 minutes from Zell am Ziller over the Gerlos Pass. ⊠ *Krimml* ☎ *06564/7212* ⊕ *www.wasserfaelle-krimml.at* ☞ *€8.80 (includes parking and waterpark); €3 to just walk the path beside the waterfall* ⊙ *May–Oct., daily 9.30–5.*

WHERE TO EAT

$$
AUSTRIAN
✕ **Hotel Gasthof Bräu.** The core of this frescoed building in the town center dates from the 16th century, but subsequent renovations have brought the five-story structure up to date. The three-room restaurant offers fine dining, with an emphasis on fish and game, and many ingredients come directly from the owner's own farm and fish ponds or from other local suppliers. Go for the trout! Make sure to taste the house beer from the on-site brewery, also the source of a special made-for-the-festival brew, *Gauderbier.* The "Bräu" also has some nice rooms. Book early if you want to reserve a room during the Gauder Fest. $ *Average main: €16* ⊠ *Dorfplatz 1* ☎ *05282/2313–0* ⊕ *www.hotel-braeu.at* ⊙ *Closed Apr. and mid-Oct.–mid-Dec.*

SPORTS AND THE OUTDOORS

ZIPLINING

Arena Skyliner. A development of the Flying Fox zipline concept, the Skyliner has four lines where you can hurtle along at 50 kph (31 mph) and get a bird's-eye view of the area (on Line 3 you are more than 61 meters (200 feet) above the ground). The meeting point is at the top station of the Gerlosstein cable car. Minimum and maximum weight restrictions apply—40 kilos (88 pounds) and 120 kilos (265 pounds) respectively. ⊠ *Dorfplatz 3a* ☎ *0664/44–19–283* ⊕ *www.zillertalerarena.com/en/zell/sommer/arena-skyliner.html* ☞ *€33* ⊙ *Late May–late Sept., daily at 9:15, 10:45, 1:15 (also 2:45 on request).*

KITZBÜHEL

12 km (7 miles) south of St. Johann, 71 km (44 miles) northeast of Gerlos.

Kitzbühel is indisputably one of Austria's most fashionable winter resorts, although the town boasts a busy summer season as well. "Kitz" offers warm-season visitors a hefty program of hiking, cycling, and golf, along with outdoor concerts and plays and a professional tennis tournament in July. In winter, many skiers are attracted by the famous Ski Safari—a carefully planned, clever combination of chairlifts, gondola lifts, draglifts and runs that lets you ski for more than 145 km (91 miles) without having to walk a single foot. Kitzbühel is in perpetual motion and is busy December through mid-April, notably at the end of January for the famed **Hahnenkamm** downhill ski race. At any time during the season there's plenty to do, from sleigh rides to fancy-dress balls. ■TIP➜ **In summer visitors are offered free guest cards, which provide free access or substantially reduced fees for various activities, such as tennis, riding, and golf.** The best swimming is in the nearby Schwarzsee.

GETTING HERE AND AROUND

From Innsbruck, take the autobahn A12 or B171 west to the town of Wörgl, then the B170 to Kitzbühel. From here you can travel south on the B161/B108 on the Felbertauernstrasse and through the Felbertauerntunnel to Matrei in OstTirol and Lienz.

ESSENTIALS

Visitor Information Kitzbühel. The tourist office in the center of Kitzbühel can help you book any activities and tours, and advise on weather conditions for hiking or climbing excursions. ✉ *Hinterstadt 18* ☎ *05356/66660* ⊕ *www.kitzbuehel.com.*

EXPLORING

Alpine Flower Garden Kitzbühel. Take the *gondolabahn* (cable car) up the Kitzbüheler Horn to this lovely garden at 1,981 meters (6,500 feet). Amid glorious mountain scenery you will see hundreds of varieties of Alpine flowers in their native habitat, including varieties from other parts of the world. Guided tours are offered daily at 11 from June to early September. ☎ *05356/62857* ✉ *Free; cable car: one way €17.10, round trip €20.60* ⊙ *Always accessible; cable car runs 8:45–5.*

Church of St. Catherine. Built around 1350, this church houses a Gothic winged altar dating from 1515.

St. Andrew's parish church. Built in the 16th century with proceeds from copper and silver mining, Kitzbühel itself is scenic enough, but among its pleasures are its churches. St. Andrew's parish church (1435–1506) has a lavishly rococo chapel, the Rosakapelle, and the marvelously ornate tomb (1520) of the Kupferschmid family.

WHERE TO EAT

$ ╳ **Gallo.** This contemporary Italian restaurant is quite a find. In the
ITALIAN pedestrian area, it's a good choice for a light meal or an afternoon cup of coffee. Sit on the sunny terrace and enjoy a pizza from the wood-burning oven while watching high society go by. Heartier dishes such as

risotto with arugula make for more substantial meals. $ *Average main: €12* ⊠ *Vorderstadt 12* ☎ *05356/65862* ⊟ *No credit cards.*

$$
AUSTRIAN
Fodor'sChoice
★

✕ **Hallerwirt.** In the small village of Aurach about 5 km (3 miles) south of Kitzbühel, Hallerwirt is known for its great Austrian cuisine and charm. Old wooden floors and a ceramic stove in the parlor lend a period flair to this 400-year-old farmhouse. A colorful mix of people gathers here, and young and old enjoy the easygoing vibe. The congenial hosts, Monika and Jürgen Stelzhammer, take time to give everyone some good wine suggestions. The friendly staff serves specialties such as Jerusalem artichoke soup and fillet of lamb. $ *Average main: €16* ⊠ *Oberaurach 4, Aurach bei Kitzbühel* ☎ *05356/64502* ⊕ *www. hallerwirt.at* ⌕ *Reservations essential* ☉ *Closed Mon.–Tues. and mid-Nov.–early Dec.*

$$$$
INTERNATIONAL

✕ **HeimatLiebe.** After a great day's hiking or skiing at Kitzbühel, celebrate your good fortune by putting yourself in the hands of head chef Andreas Senn and enjoying his Tyrolean cuisine par excellence at this Michelin-starred destination restaurant. The name means "Home Love," and it's certainly a romantic spot. The gourmet cuisine, skillfully blending traditional ideals with contemporary ideas and international influences, has brought accolades raining down on both the chef and the restaurant. An eight-course tasting menu at €145 includes delights such as foie gras with fennel and malt; king crab with celeriac and fermented onion; black cod with miso and wild broccoli; and Wagyu beef. The restaurant is not open in summer. $ *Average main: €35* ⊠ *Grand Spa Resort A-Rosa, Ried Kaps 7, Kitzbühel* ☎ *05356/656600* ⊕ *resort.a-rosa.de/ english/kitzbuehel/fine-food/gourmetrestaurant-heimatliebe/* ☉ *Closed Sun., Mon., and May–mid-Dec. No lunch.*

$
CAFÉ

✕ **Praxmair.** Après-ski can't begin early enough for the casually chic crowds that pile into this famous pastry shop for its *Krapfen* (something like jelly doughnuts and available throughout Austria in January and February). For locals the Praxmair is a meeting point for regular get-togethers, cabaret performances, and small events. The wood interior and a tiled stove give the special flair to this café. $ *Average main: €8* ⊠ *Vorderstadt 17* ☎ *05356/62646* ⊟ *No credit cards* ☉ *Closed Apr. and Nov.*

$$$$
AUSTRIAN
Fodor'sChoice
★

✕ **Tennerhof.** Elegant dress is not out of place and quiet conversations are the rule in this high-class restaurant, where Stefan Lenz and his creative team have been awarded 15 Gault Millau points and a Michelin star. Freshly picked herbs from the garden accompany almost every dish, from soup to sorbet, and dishes could scarce be more imaginative—roasted goose liver with mango ravioli and a reduction of cacao, for example. Local game is a passion, and food and wine are presented by well-trained, white-gloved staff in one of the four cozy parlors that make up the *Kupferstube.* From noon to 7 pm a smaller menu is available. $ *Average main: €27* ⊠ *Griesenauweg 26* ☎ *05356/63181* ⊕ *www.tennerhof.com* ⌕ *Reservations essential* ☉ *Closed Mon. and Tues., also Apr.–mid-May and mid-Oct.–mid-Dec.*

WHERE TO STAY

$$$$
HOTEL
Fodor'sChoice
★
Golf-Hotel Rasmushof. For myriad reasons, it's hard to imagine a better choice for a Kitzbühel stay than this superluxurious but informal and relaxed former farmstead, with unrivaled year-round proximity to outdoor activities. **Pros:** fabulous location; breathtaking views. **Cons:** dragging yourself away when it's time to leave. $ *Rooms from: €330* ✉ *Hermann Reisch Weg 15* ☎ *05356/65252* ⊕ *www.rasmushof.at* ⤴ *49 rooms, 11 suites* ⦿ *Multiple meal plans.*

$$$
B&B/INN
Fodor'sChoice
★
Hotel Villa Licht. With its name translating as "light," this luxurious B&B is certainly a luminous discovery, an outrageously cute Hansel-and-Gretel chalet where hospitality and attention to every detail are paramount. **Pros:** a short walk from town center; very quiet; close to skiing; lots of free parking. **Cons:** no restaurant, although plenty are close at hand. $ *Rooms from: €250* ✉ *Franz Reisch Strasse 8* ☎ *05356/62293* ⊕ *www.villa-licht.at* ⤴ *14 rooms, 3 suites, 3 apartments* ⦿ *Breakfast.*

$$$$
HOTEL
Fodor'sChoice
★
Tennerhof. Adored by the rich and famous, from the Duke of Windsor to Kirk Douglas, this Alpine Shangri-la, in a huge parklike garden, is at once rustic and glamorous, with gold chandeliers hung over country cupboards and silk-covered sofas next to shuttered windows. **Pros:** aristocratic flair; great breakfast; nice garden. **Cons:** a little way from the town center and the ski lifts, but there's a hotel shuttle. $ *Rooms from: €350* ✉ *Griesenauweg 26* ☎ *05356/63181* ⊕ *www.tennerhof.com* ⤴ *40 rooms* ⊗ *Closed Apr.–mid-May and mid-Oct.–mid-Dec.* ⦿ *Multiple meal plans.*

NIGHTLIFE

Ecco. A top nightspot, serving light food in an upscale setting, Ecco is known for its party atmosphere and friendly staff. ✉ *Hinterstadt 22* ☎ *05356/71300–20.*

Fünferl. In the Kitzbüheler Hof, this place is full of character and has many dedicated fans. It's good for late-evening cocktails and attracts a somewhat more mature clientele who want to hear themselves speak, and think. ✉ *Franz-Reisch-Strasse 1* ☎ *05356/71300–5.*

Jimmy's. A modern bar, occasionally with a DJ, Jimmy's might not be the most atmospheric bar in town, but it's a popular rendezvous point at the start of the evening before moving on elsewhere. ✉ *Vorderstadt 31* ☎ *05356/644–09.*

Kitzbühel Casino. In the center of the pedestrian area, much activity centers on the casino, which offers baccarat, blackjack, roulette, and one-armed bandits. There's a restaurant and bar, and no set closing time. A valid passport or driver's license is needed to enter the casino. ✉ *Hinterstadt 24* ☎ *05356/62300* ⤢ *Free* ⊗ *Daily from 3 pm.*

Londoner. Young people flock to this popular watering hole, one of the biggest name bars in town. It gets packed with fans and racers alike on big ski race days, and can be just too jammed to get in. People dancing on tables is not unknown. ✉ *Franz-Reisch-Strasse 4* ☎ *05356/71428.*

Stamperl. This is an established local favorite—it's been going strong for 40 years—and in winter it's very popular with the après-ski crowd; a place on the heated terrace is prized. It serves decent Tyrolean food until 10. ✉ *Franz-Reisch-Strasse 7* ☎ *05356/62555.*

12

Take Five. The dance-club crowd moves from place to place, but check out this hot spot in the center of Kitz. It has three bars and a spacious VIP area, and aims for a sophisticated atmosphere. ⊠ *Hinterstadt 22* ☏ *05356/71300–30.*

SPORTS AND THE OUTDOORS
GOLF

With 19 courses within an hour's drive, Kitzbühel may properly lay claim to being the golf center of the Alps. The Golf Alpin Pass offers special deals on greens fees; it's available at some hotels and golf clubs, or from the tourist office.

Golf Eichenheim. Heady views of soaring Alpine peaks surrounding the course are mixed with leafy fringed fairways to give this 18-hole PGA-rated venue a unique appeal. The name, "Oak Home," reflects the surroundings, and a round includes the opportunity to appreciate rare flora and fauna. If you work up a good appetite, the clubhouse includes a gourmet restaurant. ⊠ *Eichenheim 8–9* ☏ *05356/66615–560* ⊕ *www. eichenheim.com* ✉ *May €75, June and Oct. €80, July–Sept. €95–€100; 9 holes €40* ⅄ *18 holes, 6,092 yards, par 71.*

Golfclub Kitzbühel. A pretty course, the nine holes of the Golfclub Kitz-bühel wind between ancient trees and water hazards with a fabulous backdrop of Alpine grandeur. The slightly hilly terrain of the 9-hole course is set around the Grand Spa Resort A-Rosa, and resort guests receive a discount. There are plenty of water hazards, with two of the greens located on islands. The course, built in 1955, is open from May to October and has a handicap limit of 36. ⊠ *Ried Caps 3* ☏ *05356/63007* ⊕ *www.golfclub-kitzbuehel.at* ✉ *€82 for 18 holes, €48 for 9 holes* ⅄ *18 holes, 6,135 yards, par 70.*

Golf-Club Kitzbühel-Schwarzsee. Amazing views to the Wilder Kaiser mountain range and the Kitzbuheler Horn peak nearby help to make this 18-hole course a treat for the senses. The club was opened in 1989 after two years of preparation. The par-72 course is varied, with wide fairways. A big surprise is sprung at the par-3 16th hole—called the Mousetrap—which is played over a small ravine. The course is open from May to October, and holders of the Kitzbühel Guest Card get a 30% discount on weekdays and various multiround deals. ⊠ *Golfweg 35* ☏ *05356/66660–70* ⊕ *www.kitzbuehel.com/golf-schwarzsee* ✉ *May and June, €80 for 18 holes, €41 for 9 holes; July–Oct., €87 for 18 holes, €46 for 9 holes* ⅄ *18 holes, 6,675 yards, par 72.*

Rasmushof Golf Club. In winter this is the final slope of the famous Streif run of the fearsome Hahnenkamm World Cup downhill race, so the May–October golf course could scarcely be more spectacularly located. It is the course closest to the town center and belongs to the Rasmushof Hotel. The greens and fairways are in full view of the glorious old building's balconies and hotel guests receive special rates. ⊠ *Hermann Reisch Weg 15* ☏ *05356/65252* ⊕ *www.rasmushof.at* ✉ *€24 for 9 holes on weekdays, €30 on weekends; €34 for 18 holes on weekdays, €40 on weekends. Hotel guests: €18 per day for unlimited play* ⅄ *9 holes, 3,060 yards, par 54.*

12

SKIING

Kitzbühel is one of Austria's leading resorts and home to the Hahnen-kamm World Cup downhill, one of the most daunting events on the racing calendar. There are many easy slopes, too, and the ski network here is vast and spectacular, with many lovely mountain huts scattered over the slopes offering excellent food and drink to break the ski day—56 at the last count! There are 170 km (106 miles) of slopes and 53 ski lifts. Intersport Kitzsport has a number of shops in town with the latest equipment for rental, as does Sport 2000. There are 11 ski schools with more than 500 instructors at peak times. The tourist office website has full information.

SÖLDEN

28 km (18 miles) south of Ötz.

Sölden's newest addition to its already massive lift network is the "Black Blade," which carries eight at a time more than 2,987 meters (9,800 feet) to the Rettenbach glacier, completing the only lift system in Austria to boast skiing on three mountains more than 2,987 meters (9,800 feet) high. The view from any of the three peaks provides a panoramic 360-degree view of the mountains. Sölden's reputation as a wild, après-ski party town is well deserved, meaning that if you are searching for a tranquil, romantic ski holiday, or have small children, you may want to try the village of **Hochsölden**—on the slopes above town, where things are quieter—or search elsewhere.

GETTING HERE AND AROUND

From Innsbruck take the A12 west. Then take the B168 south to the Ötztal; after about 40 km (25 miles) you will reach the town of Sölden.

Leaving Sölden you can backtrack on the B168 north to the A12, or if you feel like some real hairpin Alpine driving, go south into Italy over the Timmelsjoch Pass.

ESSENTIALS

Visitor Information Sölden/Ötztal ✉ *Rettenbach 466* ☎ *05254/510–0.*

WHERE TO STAY

$$$$
HOTEL
🏨 **Aqua Dome Hotel and Spa.** Here you'll not only find what is reputed to be the finest spa in Tyrol, but also elegant guest rooms with balconies and stunning mountain views. **Pros:** spa is open late; lovely rooms; great food; nonalcoholic drinks in the minibar are complimentary. **Cons:** spa busy on weekends; too sprawling for some. 💲 *Rooms from: €280* ✉ *Oberlängenfeld 140, Längenfeld* ☎ *05253/6400* ⊕ *www.aqua-dome. at* 🛏 *168 rooms, 32 suites* ⊗ *Some meals.*

$$$$
HOTEL
🏨 **Central.** Huge arches and heavy wood beams set the mood at this five-star hotel that's substantial both in size and character, and it has superb spa and fitness amenities. **Pros:** great service; shuttle to the slopes; nice suites. **Cons:** slopes are not within walking distance. 💲 *Rooms from: €424* ✉ *Auweg 3* ☎ *05254/2260–0* ⊕ *www. central-soelden.at* 🛏 *109 rooms, 12 suites* ⊗ *Closed May–mid-July* ⊗ *Some meals.*

$$ 🏨 **Hotel Ritzlerhof.** Spectacularly located in the village of Sautens, on a
HOTEL　shelf in the hillside high above the Oetz Valley, the Ritzlerhof is single-
mindedly purposed toward meditational levels of peace and relaxation.
Pros: idyllic location; heated indoor and outdoor pools; high-quality
rooms; obsessionally peaceful. **Cons:** far from ski lifts, bars, and res-
taurants. *$ Rooms from: €130 ⊠ Ritzlerhof 1, Sautens, Sautens*
☎ 05252/62680 ⇥ 39 rooms, 5 suites ❍| Some meals.

$$$$ 🏨 **Liebe Sonne.** Skiers will be right next to the Giggijoch chairlift to
HOTEL　Hochsölden at this sprawling yellow complex, and the lift is open
all summer too, to give hikers and mountain bikers a flying start to
their day. **Pros:** spacious rooms; bustling atmosphere; nightlife nearby;
on-site stables for horseback riding. **Cons:** sometimes it can be too
bustling; expensive Wi-Fi. *$ Rooms from: €300 ⊠ Dorfstrasse 58*
☎ 05254/22030 ⊕ www.liebesonne.at ⇥ 51 rooms, 9 suites ⊘ Closed
May and June ❍| Multiple meal plans.

$$ 🏨 **Nature-Hotel Waldklause.** It's hard to tell where this hotel ends and the
HOTEL　countryside begins—floors are natural stone, rooms smell of applewood
Fodor's Choice　paneling, and some exterior walls are built around trees that couldn't be
★　felled. **Pros:** Pampered way to save the environment; guests can use the
nearby Aqua Dome spa. **Cons:** Not close to the mountain lifts. *$ Rooms*
from: €137 ⊠ Unterlangenfeld 190, Längenfeld ☎ 05253/5455 ⊕ www.
waldklause.at ⇥ 40 rooms, 15 suites ❍| Some meals.

NIGHTLIFE

The nightlife here varies from nonexistent to wild, depending on the
season. In winter the more than 85 bars, discos, pubs, and eateries are
packed, and many nightspots have live bands, but expect cover charges
of around €5.

Bierhimml Partyhaus. This is the most popular music bar hereabouts,
with a never-ending selection of beers and decent food. ⊠ *Dorfstrasse*
9 ☎ 05254/50112.

Fire & Ice. The dance floor is kept pumped by big-name DJs until 3 am
here. ⊠ *Dorfstrasse 58 ☎ 05254/2203.*

SPORTS AND THE OUTDOORS

CLIMBING

Wildspitze. The Ventertal valley burrows far into the Ötztal Alps, ending
in the tiny village of Vent, a popular resort center. In summer the village
is transformed into a base for serious mountain climbers experienced in
ice and rock climbing, who want to attempt the formidable Wildspitze
(12,450 feet) or other, even more difficult neighboring peaks. Hiring a
professional local guide is strongly advised. To reach Vent from Sölden,
turn off at the road marked to Heiligenkreuz. ⊠ *Vent.*

RAFTING

Vacancia Outdoor Tyrol. Everything you need to enjoy the area's wild
water can be found here, including guided rafting trips. They also organize canyoning, glacier walks, and special outdoor adventures for kids.
In winter you can secure skiing gear, lessons, and, again, children's programs. ⊠ *Dorfstrasse 11 ☎ 05254/3100 ⊕ www.vacancia.at.*

Western Tyrol

SKIING

Sölden is one of Austria's top skiing and snowboarding areas, with great snow through a long season because of its high-altitude slopes and two skiable glaciers. There are 150 km (93 miles) of slopes, with the top station at 10,660-feet, served by 33 lifts. The tourist office website has full information on ski instruction and equipment rental.

LANDECK

24 km (15 miles) southwest of Imst.

Landeck is a popular place to pause while traveling from Tyrol into Switzerland and Italy.

GETTING HERE AND AROUND

Coming from the Arlberg on the B516 near Landeck, you get onto the Autobahn A12 to Innsbruck. Or else you turn south onto the B180, which takes you to Switzerland and Italy.

ESSENTIALS

Visitor Information **Landeck** ✉ *Malserstrasse 10* ☎ *05442/65600.*

EXPLORING

Burg Landeck. The 13th-century castle dominates from its position above the town. Climb up and catch the superb views from this vantage point. ✉ *Schlossweg 2* ☎ *05442/63202* 🌐 *www.schlosslandeck.at* 🕒 *Apr.–Oct., Tues.–Sun. 2–6.*

Church of the Assumption. Take special note of the 16th-century winged altar in this 15th-century Gothic church.

WHERE TO STAY

$ B&B/INN 🏨 **Post–Gasthof Gemse.** Austrian *gemütlichkeit* abounds in this handsome family-run inn in the village of Zams. **Pros:** intimate feel; bargain rates. **Cons:** not luxurious; no spa services. [$] *Rooms from: €66* ✉ *Hauptplatz 1, Zams* ☎ *05442/63001* 🌐 *www.postgasthof-gemse.at* 🛏 *15 rooms* 💳 *No credit cards* 🕒 *Closed Easter–May and Nov.–mid.-Dec.* 🍴 *Multiple meal plans.*

$ HOTEL 🏨 **Schwarzer Adler.** Virtually in the shadow of the town castle, this 250-year-old traditional, family-run hotel offers solid comfort in typical Tyrolean style. **Pros:** generous breakfast buffet; secure storage for bicycles. **Cons:** bathrooms have a shower, but no tub; no on-site parking (town parking five minutes' walk away). [$] *Rooms from: €80* ✉ *Malser Strasse 8* ☎ *05442/62316* 🌐 *www.schwarzeradler.at* 🛏 *28 rooms* 💳 *No credit cards* 🕒 *Closed Nov.–mid-Dec.* 🍴 *Multiple meal plans.*

SPORTS AND THE OUTDOORS

HIKING

Zammer Lochputz. A deep, rocky gorge across the Inn River from Zams has been made accessible by a series of tunnels, steep metal stairways, and bridges. Open only between May and September, the gorge provides a refreshing half-hour hike, particularly on a hot summer day. ✉ *Zams* ☎ *05442–65600* 🌐 *www.zammer-lochputz.at* 🕒 *May–Sept.* 🕒 *Closed Oct.–Apr.*

ST. ANTON AM ARLBERG

22 km (15 miles) west of Landeck.

St. Anton is a particularly lovely town in summer, which has also become a fashionable season, but it really swarms with visitors at the height of the ski season. It is known as a cult destination for good skiers and boarders from around the world because of its extensive slopes full of character and challenge, and its huge amount of off-piste opportunities. But it's a high-profile destination and attracts the wealthy, the prominent, and, occasionally, the royal. Accommodations are not cheap, but there is a wide range of options, and if you shop around you can find somewhere to lay your head, particularly outside the center of the action, at a bearable price.

Thanks to an amazing system of cable cars, gondolabahns, chairlifts and T-bars, St. Anton grants skiers access to the Arlberg region's more than 300 km (186 miles) of marked runs. If you decide to take to the slopes, remember that skiing remains a serious business in St. Anton: this is a resort where skiers come in search of the steep and the deep, so choose your itinerary with care. Be aware of the different trail classifications in Europe—easy runs are marked blue on the trail map, medium is red, and difficult is black—but in places such as St. Anton a blue might be a red elsewhere and a red might easily be a black.

GETTING HERE AND AROUND

If you come from the east—from Innsbruck and Landeck—you either take Autobahn A12, then the B516, or you come on the B171. From the west from Bregenz you travel on Autobahn A14, which at the city of Bludenz becomes the B516. Near the village of Klösterle in summer you have to decide: continue on the B516 through the 14-km (8½-mile) Arlbergtunnel or travel over the pass on the B197 (1 mile) to St. Anton. If you're not in a hurry, go over the pass every time. This is high alpine country and the surroundings are fabulous.

ESSENTIALS

Visitor Information St. Anton am Arlberg ⊠ *Dorfstrasse 8* ☎ *05446/2269–0* ⊕ *www.stantonamarlberg.com.*

WHERE TO STAY

$$$ 🏨 **Anton Aparthotel.** If you're not looking for a quaint Tyrolean hotel,
HOTEL this wood-and-glass house—modern, casual, and almost Zen-like in its simplicity—could be the answer, right in front of the slopes and steps from the main ski lifts. **Pros:** contemporary architecture that some will find refreshing; funky vibe; central location. **Cons:** modern look not for devotees of the traditional; draws a party crowd and, inevitably, party noise. Ⓢ *Rooms from:* €200 ⊠ *Kandaharweg 4* ☎ *05446/2408* ⊕ *www. hotelanton.at* ⤽ *14 rooms, 3 apartments* ⵔⵔ *Breakfast.*

$$$ 🏨 **Brunnenhof.** A homely and intimate 300-year-old farmhouse, painted
HOTEL a distinctive yellow, in nearby St. Jakob, the Brunnenhof has character in abundance. **Pros:** Cozy and romantic; reasonable off-season prices. **Cons:** Shuttle bus needed to get to the skiing or bustling activity of St. Anton; not for those like to be in the mainstream. Ⓢ *Rooms from:* €220 ⊠ *St. Jakober Dorfstrasse 53* ☎ *05446/2293* ⊕ *www.arlberg.*

com/brunnenhof ↩ *9 rooms, 1 apartment* ⊘ *Closed May–June and Oct.–Nov.* ❄ *Breakfast.*

$$$$ ⬚ **Hotel Raffl's St. Antonerhof.** The
HOTEL Raffl family has created a distinctive and memorable hotel filled with antiques and art of all kinds. **Pros:** great location for skiers; well-trained staff. **Cons:** closed in summer; expensive. ⓢ *Rooms from: €450* ✉ *Arlbergstrasse 69* ☎ *05446/2910* ⊕ *www.antonerhof. at* ↩ *30 rooms, 6 suites* ⊘ *Closed mid-Apr.–Nov.* ❄ *Some meals.*

$$$$ ⬚ **Schwarzer Adler.** The beautifully
HOTEL frescoed facade of this ancient inn, which has been offering hospitality for nearly 450 years, hints at what you'll find inside: open fireplaces, Tyrolean antiques, and colorful Oriental carpets. **Pros:** very helpful and friendly staff; best bar in St. Anton; lovely building. **Cons:** can be loud on lively weekends. ⓢ *Rooms from: €416* ✉ *Dorfstrasse 35* ☎ *05446/22440* ⊕ *www. schwarzeradler.com* ↩ *71 rooms, 6 suites* ⊘ *Closed mid-Apr.–May, Oct., and Nov.* ❄ *Some meals.*

THE ORIGINAL SKI INSTRUCTOR

Modern ski techniques were first developed in the Vorarlberg by Hannes Schneider (1890–1955), a local who, as a young man, was supposed to follow in his father's footsteps as a cheese maker. Instead, he founded the first ski school in St. Anton in 1921. This "Arlberg School" method, developed by Schneider in the 1920s and 1930s, laid down the basic principles since followed by skiing courses the world over.

NIGHTLIFE AND THE ARTS

For some visitors to St. Anton the show, not the snow, is the thing. Most of the bars are in the pedestrian zone.

Bar Kandahar. Owned and run by Englishman Jonathan Verney, this is a popular spot for après-skiers in late afternoon, and in the early evening becomes a restaurant for a while, then morphs into the town's leading nightclub, with live music and guest DJs. ✉ *Sporthotel, Dorfstrasse 48* ☎ *05446/30260.*

Krazy Kanguruh. With its cellar disco and outside bar, this is a favorite gathering spot for après-skiers, but it's up on the slopes and after a couple of drinks and a bop, you'll still need to ski down the home run to town—which could be tricky. Skiers have been partying here since 1965, and a visit to St. Anton is not complete without at least one visit. ✉ *Moos 113* ☎ *05446/2633.*

Mooserwirt. Raucous, mindboggling, and legendary, the Mooserwirt, on the piste-side above St. Anton, has carved a reputation as one of skiing's most famous—or notorious—haunts. By all acounts, owner Eugen Scalet decided to "kill the cows and milk the tourists" by turning his parents' farmhouse into one of the world's rowdiest après-ski bars. He succeeded, but it's a wild and seductive way for visitors to be milked and the thousands who flock there love it, if they can get anyway near. It's said to sell the second-largest amount of beer annually of any bar in Austria. They have a boutique (soundproofed) hotel next door— the ultimate ski-in, ski-out. ✉ *Unterer Mooserweg 2* ☎ *05446/3588* ⊕ *www.mooserwirt.at.*

SPORTS AND THE OUTDOORS
SKIING

The *Skihaserl*, or ski bunny, as the beginner is called, usually joins a class on St. Anton's nursery slopes, where he or she will have plenty of often-distinguished company. Once past the Skihaserl stage, skiers go higher in the Arlberg mountains to the superlative runs at Galzig and the 9,100-foot Valluga above it. Check with your hotel or the ski-pass desks at the base of the Galzigbahn gondola about an **Arlberg Skipass,** which is good on cable cars and lifts in St. Anton and St. Christoph on the Tyrol side and on those in Zürs, Lech, Oberlech, and Stuben in Vorarlberg, as well as the resorts of Warth and Schrecken, to which Lech in now linked via a gondolabahn. For complete details on St. Anton's skiing facilities, contact the town's tourist office.

Skischule Arlberg. This is considered by some to be the Harvard of ski schools and its location is certainly fitting, since Arlberg is known as the cradle of skiing—the world's first properly organized ski school was opened here by ski pioneer Hannes Schneider. ☎ *05446/3411* ⊕ *www.skischool-arlberg.com.*

ISCHGL AND GALTÜR

67 km (42 miles) southeast of St. Christoph.

Ischgl, the best-known resort in the Paznaun Valley, has become as renowned for its party scene as for its excellent skiing—it links with the Swiss resort of Samnaun and has a wealth of high-altitude runs. In summer it's a popular health resort, with activities including hiking, climbing, and mountain biking. There are many high-profile events here, both summer and winter, including big-name rock concerts, mountain biking and culinary events, and one of Europe's leading snow sculpture (as opposed to ice sculpture) competitions.

Slightly higher up the valley is **Galtür,** equally popular as a winter-sports area, summer resort, and a base for mountain climbing. Although Galtür is a starting point for practiced mountaineers, many of the climbs up the Blue Silvretta are easy and lead to the half-dozen mountain huts belonging to the Alpenverein. Galtür and the Silvretta region inspired Ernest Hemingway's novella *Alpine Idyll*; the author spent the winter of 1925 here, and the town still remembers him.

You can get to Idalp, at 2,286-meter (7,500-feet), via the 4-km-long (2½-mile-long) Silvretta gondolabahn. The enchanting Paznaun Valley follows the course of the Trisanna River for more than 40 km (25 miles). The valley runs into the heart of the Blue Silvretta mountains, named for the shimmering ice-blue effect created by the great peaks and glaciers, dominated by the Fluchthorn 3,189 meters (10,462 feet) at the head of the valley.

GETTING HERE AND AROUND

From the B516 just west of Landeck, take the B188 into the Paznauntal (Paznaun Valley). After about 40 km (25 miles) you'll reach Ischgl. Another 13 km (8 miles) gets you to Galtür. Returning, you can either double back, or, if it's nice weather and you feel like some serious Alpine driving, head to the Silvretta-Hochalpen-strasse (Silvretta High Alpine Road). It takes you on many hairpin curves up to 2,134 meters (7,000 feet) and then down into the Montafonvalley in Vorarlberg. The cost for using the pass is €15 per car.

ESSENTIALS

Visitor Information **Ischgl** ✉ *Dorfstrasse 43* ☎ *05444/52660.*

EXPLORING

Alpinarium. Following an avalanche of catastrophic proportions on February 23, 1999, which took 31 lives and destroyed many centuries-old homes and guesthouses, the community of Galtür undertook a massive building project that resulted in the Alpinarium, a memorial, museum, conference center, café, indoor climbing hall, library, and, most significantly, a 345-meter-long (1,132-foot-long) wall built of steel and concrete designed to prevent such an accident from occurring again. On summer Saturdays, 10–4, the *Bauernmarkt* (farmers' market) sets up in front of the Alpinarium, bringing produce, cheese, meat, and specialty products. ✉ *Hauptstrasse 29c, Galtür* ☎ *05443/20000* 🌐 *www.alpinarium.at* 🎟 *€8* 🕒 *Museum: Tues.–Sun. 10–6.*

WHERE TO STAY

$$$ HOTEL 🏨 **Hotel Madlein.** Quirkiness reigns supreme at this luxurious hotel, from the minimalist lobby to the Zen-influenced guestrooms (although some retain Tyrolean wood paneling), and the two nightclubs. **Pros:** unique atmosphere; showbizzy vibe; escalator access to ski lift. **Cons:** expensive; no Tyrolean feel. [$] *Rooms from: €175* ✉ *Madleinweg 2* ☎ *05444/5226* 🌐 *www.madlein.com* 🛏 *74 rooms, 5 suites* 🍴 *Some meals.*

$$$$ HOTEL 🏨 **Hotel Rössle.** The oldest guesthouse in Galtür (as shown by a tax return record from 1600), the centrally located Rossle hotel overflows with Tyrolean charm. **Pros:** plenty of atmosphere; top-notch dining. **Cons:** for winter guests the lifts are a short ski bus ride away. [$] *Rooms from: €250* ✉ *Am Dorfplatz, Galtür* ☎ *05443/82320* 🌐 *www.roessle.com* 🛏 *32 rooms, 8 suites* 🍴 *Some meals.*

$$$ HOTEL 🏨 **Post Ischgl.** In the middle of the town's pedestrian area, an imposing facade fronts this 200-year-old haven of luxury and Tyrolean charm, with attractive rooms and a highly rated restaurant serving international and local cuisine. **Pros:** close to shops, pubs, and restaurants; luxurious. **Cons:** lively bar/nightclub means it can be noisy in ski season; in winter high season you can book only by the week. [$] *Rooms from: €260* ✉ *Dorfstrasse 47* ☎ *05444/5232* 🌐 *www.post-ischgl.at* 🛏 *73 rooms, 10 suites* 🍴 *Multiple meal plans.*

$$$$ HOTEL Fodor's Choice ★ 🏨 **Trofana Royal.** This is Ischgl's flagship hotel, elegant and romantic, and the only five-star superior in town. **Pros:** great location; large, impressive nightclub; après-ski bar. **Cons:** very expensive. [$] *Rooms from: €500* ✉ *Ischgl 334* ☎ *05444/600* 🌐 *www.trofana.at* 🛏 *102 rooms, 10 suites* 🍴 *Some meals.*

NIGHTLIFE AND PERFORMING ARTS

Ischgl has such a rousing nightlife that during the ski season it would be difficult not to find the après-ski and nightlife action.

Kuhstall. In the center of town, Kuhstall (meaning cowshed) in the winter is a heaving, rocking, ultrapopular après-ski bar, rustically themed. Sometimes it can be just too crowded to enter. ⊠ *Sporthotel Silvretta, Dorfstrasse 74* ☎ *05444/5223* ⊕ *www.kuhstall.at.*

Niki's Stadl. An Ischgl après-ski institution, this place is traditional, raucous, bizarre, and a must-visit. DJ Niki, who also owns the hotel of which the bar is a part, provides a mix of Europop and Tyrolean après-ski cheesy oompah-rock. The program includes videos of Niki in Arab dress hamming it up in Dubai, and singing marmottes being lowered from the ceiling. You have to be there. ⊠ *Piz Buin Hotel, Dorfstrasse* ☎ *05444/5300* ⊕ *www.nikis-stadl.com.*

Trofana Alm. It might feel like an ancient, timbered, converted barn, but this purpose-built adjunct to a five-star hotel is one of the most successful and slick après-ski bars in the Alps. Open from 3 pm, it switches at 7 pm from dance venue to romantic candle-lighted restaurant, then at 11 it's back to full-on nightclub and disco. Fabulous fun, if you can get in. ⊠ *Trofana Royal Hotel, Dorfstrasse 91, Ischgl* ☎ *05444/602.*

VORARLBERG

The Western Alps are a haven for those who love the great outdoors. It's also a region that provides getaway space and privacy—Ernest Hemingway came to Schruns to write *The Sun Also Rises.* In spring, summer, and fall, travelers delight in riding, tennis, swimming, and hiking the Montafon Valley, which is dominated by the "Matterhorn of Austria," the Zimba peak (2,643 meters [8,671 feet]), and is probably the most attractive of Vorarlberg's many tourist-frequented valleys. When the first snowflakes begin to fall, skiers head to the hills to take advantage of the Arlberg mountain range, the highest in the Lechtal Alps.

SCHRUNS-TSCHAGGUNS

10 km (6 miles) northeast of Brand, 60 km (39 miles) south of Bregenz.

Author Ernest Hemingway spent many winters at the Schruns–Tschagguns skiing area in the Montafon Valley. Today neither of the towns—across the Ill River from each other—is as fashionable as the resorts on the Arlberg, but the views over the Ferwall Alps to the east and the mighty Rätikon on the western side of the valley are unsurpassed anywhere in Austria. In winter the heavy snowfalls here provide wonderful skiing. In fact, many believe the fully integrated ski area to be seriously underrated. The snow record is good, the runs are interesting, and a renaissance of the area's winter status could be on the horizon. Many skiers head for Hochjoch-Zamang—the main peak at **Schruns**—to have lunch on the spectacularly sited sun terrace of the Kapell restaurant. Then it's on to Grabs-Golm over the river in **Tschagguns.** Others prefer the Silvretta-Nova run at Gaschurn and St. Gallenkirch. In summer, the heights are given over to climbers and hikers, the mountain streams to trout anglers, and the lowlands to tennis players.

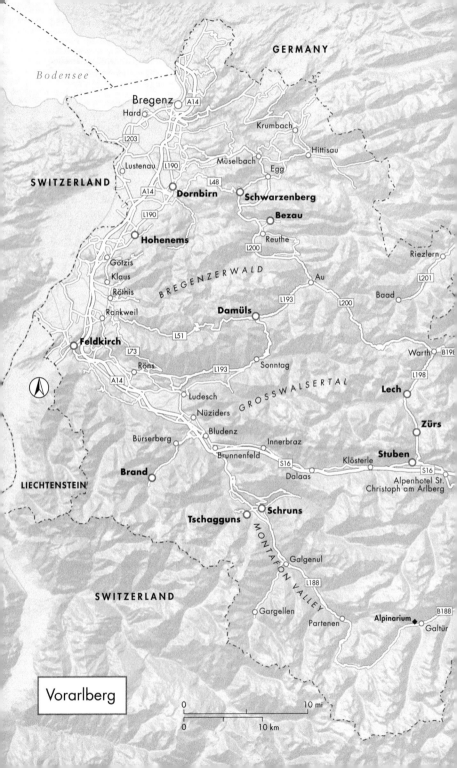

GETTING HERE AND AROUND

From Bregenz take the Autobahn A14 south. Soon after Bludenz take the B188 to the Montafoner Tal (Montafon valley). After about 8 km (5 miles) you reach Schruns–Tschagguns. If you want to experience Alpine driving after your visit to town, continue south on the B188 to the Silvretta-Hochalpenstrasse (Silvretta High Alpine Road) to the Bielerhöhe at 2,134 meters (7,000 feet), and then over many hairpin curves into Tyrol and the Paznaun Valley. The cost of using the pass is €15 per car. Attempt the drive only in ideal weather conditions and if you have good brakes; in winter the pass is closed.

Tourist Information **Montafon Valley** ✉ *Montafoner Strasse 21, Schruns* ☎ *05556/72253-0* 🌐 *www.montafon.at.*

WHERE TO EAT AND STAY

$ AUSTRIAN 🍴 **Gasthof Löwen.** Guests started eating here more than 500 years ago, and they have been doing so ever since. The old dining room has wood-paneled walls and ceiling and is the perfect setting in which to enjoy a *Zwiebelrostbraten* (steak with onions) and a good red wine. Unfortunately, the historic tables with the beautiful inlay work are not for sale. Ernest Hemingway certainly enjoyed his stays in "the old inn with the antlers in Tschagguns." There's folk music here every Thursday at 9 pm. You can ask the staff if one of the five guest rooms is available. The reception is in the Montafoner Hof, just across the street, which belongs to the same family. [$] *Average main: €11* ✉ *Kreuzgasse 4* ☎ *05556/7100-0* 🌐 *www.loewen-tschagguns.at* 🕒 *Closed Mon. and mid-June–mid-July.*

$$$$ HOTEL 🏨 **Löwen.** In the heart of Schruns this hotel looks (and is) huge, but inside the modern take on a traditional Austrian feel works well, with the rustic dark-wood theme of the exterior carried over elegantly into the comfortable modern rooms with balconies. **Pros:** spacious and luxurious; enormous spa, which includes a women-only section. **Cons:** a bit formal. [$] *Rooms from: €280* ✉ *Silvrettastrasse 8* ☎ *05556/7141* 🌐 *www.loewen-hotel.com* 🛏 *84 rooms, 1 suite* 🕒 *Closed mid-Apr.–mid-May and mid-Oct.–mid-Dec.* 🍽 *Some meals.*

$$$ HOTEL 🏨 **Montafoner Hof.** There's a lot of local flavor in this popular and welcoming family-run hotel in Tschagguns, where the owner's hunting credentials are reflected in the delicious traditional food in the restaurant. **Pros:** Austrian hospitality at its best; comfortable atmosphere and wonderful food; guided hunting trips possible for anyone with a license. **Cons:** after staying here, you will judge other hotels by this standard. [$] *Rooms from: €200* ✉ *Kreuzgasse 9, Tschagguns* ☎ *05556/71000* 🌐 *www.montafonerhof.com* 🛏 *48 rooms* 🕒 *Closed Apr., May, end of Nov.–mid-Dec.* 🍽 *Breakfast.*

SPORTS AND THE OUTDOORS

FISHING

The local mountain streams and rivers are full of fish. Licenses are available; ask the regional tourist office in Bregenz for detailed information on seasons and locations.

SKIING

Schruns is one of the skiing centers of the Montafon region, which also includes the Bartholomäberg, Gargellen, Gaschurn-Partenen, St. Gallenkirch/Gortipohl, Silbertal, and Vandans ski areas. They are together covered with a Montafon Ski Pass and comprise 65 lifts and 208 km (129 miles) of groomed runs. Ski pass prices are attractive here, €105 for a 2½-day adult pass, for example, with discounts for seniors and children. For details contact Montafon Tourism.

STUBEN

38 km (23 miles) northeast of Schruns, 24 km (15 miles) east of Bludenz.

Traveling from Feldkirch to the Arlberg Pass you'll come to the village of Stuben, poised right above the 14-km (8.6-mile) -long Arlberg Tunnel. From the beginning of December to the end of April the magnificent skiing makes Stuben popular among serious skiers—this is a smaller, quieter village steeped in skiing tradition and a draw for those looking for perhaps a more authentic Austrian experience. Stuben has skiing links with St. Anton and St. Christoph, and, by way of short ski-bus link, Lech and Zürs. For information on its skiing facilities, contact the Arlberg region tourist office.

GETTING HERE AND AROUND

Take the B516 from Bludenz near Klösterle, but do not go into the Arlberg Tunnel. Instead change to the B197 towards the Arlberg Pass. After 5 km (3 miles) you will reach Stuben. To get here by public transportation, take the train from either Innsbruck or Feldkirch to Langen am Arlberg and then a bus to Stuben.

Visitor Information **Arlberg region tourist office** ✉ *Dorf 2, Lech* ☎ *05583/2161–0* 🌐 *www.lech-zuers.at.*

WHERE TO STAY

$ HOTEL 🏨 **Hotel Arlberg Stuben.** If you're thinking of driving the Arlberg Pass or skiing its slopes, this hotel, on the road to the top, is a perfect choice, nestling on a grassy slope beneath the towering peaks. **Pros:** excellent location right on the pass road; good restaurant; inviting guest rooms. **Cons:** no elevator; front rooms can be slightly noisier. [$] *Rooms from: €100* ✉ *Arlbergstrasse 50* ☎ *05582/521* 🌐 *www.arlberg-stuben.at* 🛏 *18 rooms* ⏲ *Closed 3 wks in Nov.* 🍴 *Breakfast.*

ZÜRS

13 km (8 miles) north of Stuben, 90 km (56 miles) southeast of Bregenz.

The chosen resort of the rich and fashionable on this side of the Arlberg, Zürs is little more than a collection of large and seriously plush hotels. Perched at 1,707 meters (5,600 feet), it's strictly a winter-sports community; when the season is over, the hotels close. But Zürs is more exclusive than nearby Lech and certainly more, in an ultra-discreet fashion, than Gstaad or St. Moritz in Switzerland. Royalty and celebrities don't come here to promenade or to be seen. They come to enjoy a hedonistic lifestyle behind the often anodyne facade of their five-star hotel, and to ski on perfectly groomed slopes, nicely anonymous in helmet and sunglasses. Full board is required in most hotels, so there are relatively few "public" restaurants in town and little chance to dine around. But the hotel dining rooms are elegant; in some, jacket and tie are required in the evening. High standards were always part of the history of Zürs—the hotel Zürserhof was built by the aristocratic hotelier Count Tattenbach in the 1920s, and the first ski lift in Austria was constructed here in 1937.

CHAMPAGNE ON THE SLOPES

Accessed by the Trittkopf cable car, at the highest point of the Flexen Pass you'll find the Flexenhäsl (Little Flexen House), a very special little hut that can seat only 20. Here you can order up mouthwatering tidbits such as scampi with garlic butter and *Hirschwürstel* (venison sausage) with fresh horseradish sauce, washed down with a bottle of chilled Dom Pérignon. In the evening join in for piping-hot fondue *chinoise*. Reservations are essential (☎ *05583/4143*).

GETTING HERE AND AROUND

If you are coming from the west on the B516, make sure to take the B197 toward the Arlberg Pass after passing Klösterle (do not go into the Arlberg Tunnel). A few miles past Stuben follow the sign to the left toward Zürs/Lech on the B198. The Arlberg Pass is sometimes closed in winter after heavy snowfall, but the road to Zürs/Lech is rarely closed, with sections protected by avalanche balconies. Coming from the east from Innsbruck in winter, you may have to go through the Arlberg Tunnel and then use the B197/B198.

ESSENTIALS

Tourist Information Zürs ✉ *Lechtal Strasse* ☎ *05583/2245* 🌐 *www.lech-zuers.at.*

WHERE TO STAY

$$$$ HOTEL 🏨 **Sporthotel Edelweiss.** This 19th-century house may not be the most fashionable hotel in town, but it has the best nightlife and one of the best restaurants, which is a consideration if you're on meal-inclusive terms. **Pros:** new guest rooms; excellent restaurant. **Cons:** restaurant is closed Monday; some room decoration might be too busy for some. [$] *Rooms from: €300* ✉ *Lechtal Strasse 79* ☎ *05583/2662* 🌐 *www.edelweiss.net* 🛏 *63 rooms, 3 apartments* ⏲ *Closed mid-Apr.–Nov.* 🍴 *Some meals.*

$$$$ HOTEL 🏨 **Sporthotel Lorünser.** The hospitable elegance of this hotel draws royalty, including Princess Caroline of Monaco and Princess (formerly Queen) Beatrix of the Netherlands. **Pros:** discreet elegance; continued top quality. **Cons:** closed in summer. [$] *Rooms from: €400* ☎ *05583/22540* 🌐 *www.loruenser.at* 🛏 *56 rooms, 18 suites* ⏲ *Closed mid-Apr.–early Dec.* 🍴 *Some meals.*

$$$$ HOTEL FAMILY 🏨 **Zürserhof.** When celebrities seek privacy, they ensconce themselves in this world-famous hostelry resembling five huge interlinked chalets, a family-run house that has managed to preserve a certain intimacy. **Pros:** exclusivity and privacy; top luxury. **Cons:** the price you have to pay for exclusivity and top luxury. [$] *Rooms from: €650* ✉ *Zürs, Vorarlberg*

☎ *05583/2513–0* 🌐 *www.zuerserhof.at* 🛏 *104 rooms* 💳 *No credit cards* 🕒 *Closed mid-Apr.–Nov.* 🍴 *Breakfast.*

SPORTS AND THE OUTDOORS

SKIING

There are four main lifts out of the village: take the chairlift to Hexenboden (2,317 meters [7,600 feet]) or the cable car to Trittkopf (2,377 meters [7,800 feet]), with a restaurant and sun terrace; two chairlifts head up to Seekopf (2,134 feet [7,000 feet]) and the Zurzersee, where there is another restaurant. This mountain often gets huge snowfalls. ■ TIP→ **Skiers need to be particularly aware of avalanche conditions—check with the tourist office or your hotel before you hit the off-piste slopes.**

LECH

Fodor's Choice ★

4 km (2½ miles) north of Zürs, 90 km (56 miles) southeast of Bregenz.

Just down (literally) the road from Zürs, Lech is a full-fledged community—and one of the most fashionable in the Alps. But there are more hotels in Lech than in Zürs, better tourist facilities, bigger ski schools, more shops, and more nightlife. Hotel prices are nearly as high. Celebrities, captains of industry and royalty are often to be found in this very pretty Alpine village. Be sure to check with the hotel of your choice about meal arrangements; some hotels recommend that you take half-board, which is usually a good deal.

GETTING HERE AND AROUND

From Zürs go north on the B198 for 4 km (2½ miles) to Lech. In summer you can continue north on the B198 down to the town of Warth and Reutte in Tyrol, near the German border. You can't get to Zürs or Lech via rail; take the train to Langen am Arlberg station, then transfer to a bus or taxi.

ESSENTIALS

Tourist Information **Lech** ✉ *Dorf 2* ☎ *05583/2161–0* 🌐 *www.lech-zuers.at.*

WHERE TO STAY

$$$$ HOTEL Fodor's Choice ★

🏨 **Gasthof Post.** A *gemütlich* atmosphere enfolds in this blue-shuttered Relais & Chateaux chalet hotel, with murals, flower boxes, and a wood-paneled interior of extravagant luxury. **Pros:** refined, comfortable luxury in historic setting; antiques artfully displayed throughout the hotel; excellent restaurants; huge spa with in- and outdoor pools. **Cons:** if you can afford it, you'll never want to leave. [$] *Rooms from: €400* ✉ *Dorf 11* ☎ *05583/22060* 🌐 *www.postlech.com* 🛏 *43 rooms, 3 suites, 2 apartments* 🕒 *Closed May–mid-June, Oct., and Nov.* 🍴 *Breakfast.*

$$ HOTEL

🏨 **Pfefferkorn's Hotel.** A cozy yet spacious wood-paneled lobby makes you feel welcome the minute you enter the Pfefferkorn, and this warm, wood, Alpine style continues into many of the guest rooms. **Pros:** warm atmosphere; very attentive staff; great location close to the main lifts. **Cons:** rooms near the street on the lower floors can be noisy. [$] *Rooms from: €200* ✉ *Dorf 138* ☎ *05583/25250* 🌐 *www.pfefferkorns.net* 🛏 *19 rooms, 10 suites* 🕒 *Closed May, June, Oct., and Nov* 🍴 *Breakfast.*

12

$$$$
HOTEL
☐ **Romantik Hotel Krone.** Across the street from two of the main lifts, this family-managed, five-star hotel started life as a tavern in 1741 and is now providing hospitality of an altogether more luxurious variety. **Pros:** spacious lobby; excellent staff; delicious food; impressive spa. **Cons:** some rooms tend to be noisy, as the hotel is very close to the main street. $ *Rooms from: €320 ☒ House 13 ☎ 05583/2551 ⊕ www.romantikhotelkrone-lech. at* ⇌ *46 rooms, 10 suites* ☾ *Closed mid-Apr.–mid-June, Oct., and Nov.* *Multiple meal plans.*

> ### SAY KÄSE, PLEASE
>
> In the last two decades, cheese making has undergone a magnificent revival in the region. Farmers produce more than 30 varieties of *Käse*—from Emmental to beer cheese, Tilsit to red-wine cheese, and *Bergkäse* (mountain cheese) in dozens of varieties. Look for discreet *KäseStrasse* signs along the road, pointing you toward the region's elite cheese makers, or for the word *Sennerei*, which means Alpine dairy (⊕ www.kaesestrasse.at).

NIGHTLIFE AND PERFORMING ARTS

Lech has a lively après-ski and nightlife scene—not nearly as overt as nearby St. Anton or Ischgl, but partying is important to most Austrian ski villages, even ones as upscale as Lech. Prices vary from place to place, but in general a mixed drink will cost €9–€12.

Burg. The bar in the Burg hotel in Oberlech features live music most nights. ☒ *Oberlech 266, Lech, Tyrol* ☎ 05583/2291.

Goldener Berg. The bar at the Goldener Berg is usually a hot après-ski spot. ☒ *Goldener Berg, Oberlech 117, Lech, Tyrol* ☎ 05583/2205.

Krone Bar. The bar in the Krone Hotel (⇨ *Where to Stay, above*) opens at 9 pm and goes on until 2 or 3 am. ☒ *Lech 13, Lech, Tyrol.*

Pfefferkörndl. This is among the popular places in Lech for a mid-evening drink (starting at 9:30). ☒ *Pfefferkorn's Hotel, Lech, Tyrol* ☎ 05583/2525–429.

Tannberghof Bar. Activity continues in the late-afternoon at the ice-bar of the Tannbergerhof. ☒ *Dorf 111, Lech, Tyrol* ☎ 05583/2202–0 ⊕ *www. tannbergerhof.com.*

Umbrella. You can join the snacks-and-drinks crowd as early as 11 am at the outdoor and famed Umbrella bar at the Petersboden Sport Hotel at Oberlech. ☒ *Oberlech 278Lech, Tyrol* ☎ 05583/3232.

SPORTS AND THE OUTDOORS

SKIING

Lech is linked with Oberlech and Zürs, with more than 30 ski lifts and cable cars, all accessed by the regional ski pass, which allows skiers to take in the entire region, including Lech, Oberlech, Zürs, Stuben, St. Christoph, and St. Anton, as well as Warth and Schrocken, newly linked by lift to Lech. The area as a whole includes more than 90 cable cars and lifts (many of them with heated seats!), 260 km (161 miles) of groomed pistes, and 180 km (112 miles) of open slopes. In addition, there is a vast network of cross-country trails.

The ski pistes and open slopes in Lech are spread between 4,757 feet and 9,186 feet above sea level, including the slopes Rüfikopf, Madloch, and Mohnenfluh. Some 400 skiing instructors can help you master the craft here. Snowboarders have their own Fun Park, and there is a floodlit toboggan run and horse-drawn sleigh rides.

Lech-Zürs Tourist Office. For complete information on skiing facilities contact the Lech-Zürs Tourist Office on the main street in the center of Lech. ☎ *05583/2161–0* ⊕ *www.lech-zuers.at.*

BREGENZ

150 km (90 miles) west of Innsbruck, 660 km (409 miles) west of Vienna, 120 km (75 miles) east of Zurich, 193 km (120 miles) southwest of Munich.

Lying along the southeastern shore of the Bodensee (Lake Constance) with the majestic Pfänder as its backdrop, Bregenz is where Vorarlbergers themselves come to make merry, especially in summer. Along the lakeside beach and public pool, cabanas and cotton candy lure starched collars to let loose, while nearby an enormous floating stage is the open-air site for performances of grand opera and orchestral works (Verdi, Rimski-Korsakov, Strauss, and Gershwin are just some of the composers who have been featured). Bregenz is the capital of Vorarlberg, and has been the seat of the provincial government since 1819. The upper town has maintained a charming old-world character. The lower city is the vibrant part of town with pedestrian streets, shops, the train station, restaurants, and offices.

GETTING HERE AND AROUND

Fly into Zurich airport and take a Euro City Express train directly from the airport to Bregenz Main Station. The trip takes about 1½ hours.

The city of Bregenz runs a very efficient public bus line.

From Innsbruck you come through the Arlberg tunnel, from Germany on the autobahn, and from Switzerland on the autobahn via St. Gallen.

Taxi fares in Bregenz start at about €6, so taking one even a short distance can be expensive. Call to order a radio cab.

From Vienna it takes about 7½ hours by car, from Munich about 2½.

ESSENTIALS

Bus Information Bus ⊠ *Rathausstraße 4* ☎ *5574/410–01–833* ⊕ *www.stadtwerke-bregenz.at.*

Taxi Companies City Taxi ☎ *05574/65400.*

Visitor Information Visitor Information ⊠ *Poststr. 11, Dornbirn* ☎ *05572/3770330* ⊕ *www.vorarlberg.at.*

EXPLORING BREGENZ

TOP ATTRACTIONS

Martinsturm. This tower (1599–1602) has the largest onion dome in Central Europe, and was the first Baroque construction on Lake Constance. It has become a symbol of Bregenz. ⊠ *Martinsgasse 3b* ☉ *Daily, except Mon. Oct.–Apr.*

12

FAMILY

Fodor's Choice

★

Pfänder. A cable car takes you up to this 1,064-meter [3,491-foot] peak overlooking Bregenz, one of the most famous lookout points in the region, from which you can see four countries—Austria, Germany, Liechtenstein and Switzerland—and almost 240 Alpine peaks. It's a breathtaking view, with the city directly below on the shores of the Bedensee and the lake stretching for 64 km (40 miles) into the hazy distance. On your left lies the Rhine valley, and you can see the hills of Liechtenstein and Switzerland. Just across the water from Bregenz you'll notice the ancient and fascinating German island-city of Lindau in Bavaria, once a free state (a status it lost in 1802). The Pfänder restaurant is open June–mid-September. Children will enjoy a 30-minute circular hike to a small outdoor zoo with deer, Alpine goats, and wild boar. Admission is free. ☎ *05574/42160* ✉ *Cable-car round trip €11.40* ☉ *Dec.–Oct., daily 9–7; service on hr and half hr.*

Adlerwarte. Eagles and other birds of prey demonstrate their prowess in free flight May–September at 11 and 2:30. ☎ *0664/905–3040* ✉ *€5.*

WORTH NOTING

Altes Rathaus (*Old City Hall*). Amble on along Martinsgasse to Graf-Wilhelm-Strasse and the brightly shuttered Altes Rathaus, the old town hall. The ornate half-timber construction was completed in 1622. ⊠ *Rathausstrasse and Anton-Schneider-Strasse.*

Beckenturm. From the hill outside the church there is a wonderful view of the southwestern wall of the Old City, including the Beckenturm, the 16th-century tower once used as a prison and named after bakers imprisoned there for baking rolls that were too skimpy for the town fathers.

Bodensee White Fleet. The lake itself is a prime attraction, with boat trips available to nearby Switzerland and Germany. Don't forget to bring along your passport. The Bodensee White Fleet ferries offer several trip options. You can travel to the "flower isle" of Mainau or make a crossing to Konstanz, Germany, with stops at Lindau, Friedrichshafen, and Meersburg. The longest round-trip excursion is the Drei-Länder Rundfahrt, which includes stops in Germany and Switzerland. The ferries have different operating schedules, but most run only in the summer months. The Mainau excursion runs from May to mid-September. ⊠ *Vorarlberg Lines Bodenseeschiffahrt, Seestrasse 4* ☎ *05574/42868* ⊕ *www.bodenseeschifffahrt.at.*

Fodor's Choice

★

Bregenzer Festspiele. Bregenz is pleasant at any time of year, but the best time to visit is during the Bregenzer Festspiele (Bregenz Music Festival ⇨ *Nightlife and the Arts*) in July and August. Acclaimed artists from around the world perform operas, operettas, and musical comedies on the festival's floating stage, part of the Festspiel und Kongresshaus

(Festival Hall and Congress Center) complex. In front of the stage, the orchestra pit is built on a jetty, while the audience of 6,800 is safely accommodated on the 30-tier amphitheater built on dry land—a unique and memorable setting you are sure to enjoy. Reserve your tickets and hotels in advance, as performances and rooms sell out early. ⊕ *www. bregenzerfestspiele.com.*

City Wall. Remains of the ancient city wall are to the right of the tower on Martinsgasse. The coats of arms of several noble Bregenz families can still be seen on the house standing next to the wall's remains. ⊠ *Martinsgasse.*

Gasthof Kornmesser. To the right of the Nepomuk-Kapelle along Kornmarktstrasse is the Gasthof Kornmesser, built in 1720 and a gorgeous example of a Baroque town house. ⊠ *Kornmarktstrasse.*

Gesellenspital (*Journeymen's Hospital*). Behind the Altes Rathaus on Eponastrasse stands the former Gesellenspital; remnants of a fresco still visible on its wall depict St. Christopher, St. Peter, and a kneeling abbot. ⊠ *Eponastrasse.*

Gösser Braugaststätte. Behind the Seekapelle is the traditional Gösser Braugaststätte. ■ TIP➜ **This might be just the moment for a cool beer, a cup of coffee, or the daily vegetarian special. Try to get a table in the Zirbenstüble, with its beautifully carved wood-paneled walls and ceiling.** ⊠ *Anton-Schneider-Strasse 1.*

Herz-Jesu Kirche (*Sacred Heart Church*). Off Belrupstrasse, the Herz-Jesu Kirche was built in 1908 in brick Gothic style. The stained-glass windows by Martin Hausle are especially bright and colorful.

Kunsthaus. Vorarlberg now has its own modern art museum. Designed by Swiss architect Peter Zumtho, the steel-and-concrete building with etched-glass panels creates a feeling of space and light. Note the innovative feature of 8-foot openings between each story, which allows sunlight to enter the translucent glass through the ceiling. This marvel of design bathes each gallery in natural light in spite of concrete walls. ⊠ *Karl-Tizian-Platz* ☎ *05574/485–940* ⊕ *www.kunsthaus-bregenz.at* ▧ *€6* ☉ *Tues.–Sun. 10–6 (to 9 Thurs.).*

Künstlerhaus Thurn und Taxis. Owned by the princely Thurn und Taxis family until 1915, this building, erected in 1848, now contains a modern gallery. The **Thurn und Taxispark** contains rare trees and plants from around the world. ⊠ *Gallusstrasse 8* ⊕ *www.kuenstlerhaus-bregenz.at.*

Landesmuseum (*Provincial Museum*). Next door to the Theater am Kornmarkt, this museum houses relics from Brigantium, the Roman administrative city that once stood where Bregenz is today. Gothic and Romanesque ecclesiastical works are also on display in this turn-of-the-20th-century building. Guided tours are offered on weekends. ⊠ *Kornmarktplatz 1* ☎ *05574/46050* ⊕ *www.vorarlbergmuseum.at* ▧ *€9; guided tour €5. Various combined tickets with other attractions are available* ☉ *Sept.–mid-July, Tues.–Sun. 10–5 (to 9 Thurs.); mid-July–Aug. 31, daily 10–8 (to 9 Thurs.).*

Martinskirche. Next to the Stadtsteig, explore the interior of this tiny church for its fine 14th-century frescoes. ⊠ *Martinsplatz.*

Montfortbrunnen (*fountain*). In the center of Ehreguta Platz, the Mont-fortbrunnen is the scene of a ritual washing of wallets and change purses, when carnival jesters clean out their empty pockets and spin tales about the events of the previous year. The fountain honors the minnesinger Hugo von Montfort, who was born in the city in 1357. ⊠ *Ehreguta Platz.*

Nepomuk-Kapelle. Behind the post office is the distinctive circular Chapel of St. John of Nepomuk, built in 1757 to serve the city's fishermen and sailors. It has a richly decorated altar, and today the town's Hungarian community celebrates mass here. ⊠ *Kaspar Moosbrugger Platz.*

Parish Church of St. Gallus. The small parallel streets running uphill from Ehreguta Square roughly outline the boundaries of the town in the Middle Ages. Hidden around the corner of the building at the beginning of Georgen-Schilde-Strasse are the **Meissnerstiege** (Meissner steps), named after a local poet, that lead from the Old City to the parish church of St. Gallus. At the bottom of the steps, follow Schlossbergstrasse up the hill to the church, which combines Romanesque, Gothic, and rococo elements. The interior is decorated simply with pastel coloring instead of the usual excessive gilding. Empress Maria Theresa donated the money for the high altarpiece. You'll notice the monarch's features on one of the shepherdesses depicted there. ⊠ *Schlossbergstrasse.*

Post Office. Most of Bregenz's important sights can be seen in the course of a walk of about two hours. The town's neoclassical main post office was built in 1893 by Viennese architect Friedrich Setz. Because of the marshy conditions, the post office is built on wood pilings to prevent it from sinking. ⊠ *Seestrasse 5.*

Seekapelle (*Lake Chapel*). Next door to the Rathaus is the Seekapelle (Lake Chapel), topped with an onion dome. The chapel was put up over the graves of a band of Swiss whose 1408 attempt to incorporate Bregenz into Switzerland was repulsed. ⊠ *Rathausstrasse.*

Stadtsteig. Go left from Belrupstrasse onto Maurachgasse. Walking up Maurachgasse, you'll reach the Stadtsteig guarding the entrance to the Old City, which bears the emblem of a Celtic-Roman equine goddess (the original is now housed in the Landesmuseum (⇨ *above*). Inside the gate are the coats of arms of the dukes of Bregenz and the dukes of Montfort, the latter crest now the Vorarlberg provincial emblem. ⊠ *Maurachgasse.*

Theater am Kornmarkt. Just after the alley simply marked "theater" along Kornmarktstrasse you'll reach this theater, originally constructed in 1838, when Bregenz was still an important commercial port, as a grain storehouse; in 1954 the granary was converted into a 700-seat theater. ⊠ *Kornmarktstrasse.*

WHERE TO EAT

$
CAFÉ

✕ **Café Götze.** Locals frequent this small, unpretentious café, also a bakery, because it's known to have the best pastries in town. The location halfway between the waterfront and the Old City is convenient. $ *Average main: €5* ✉ *Kaiserstrasse 9* ☎ *05574/44523* ▭ *No credit cards* ⊘ *Closed Sun. and Oct. and Nov. No dinner.*

$
ECLECTIC

✕ **Gasthof Goldener Hirsch.** Allegedly the oldest tavern in Bregenz and close to the Old City, this rustic restaurant offers delicious traditional food and drinks in lively surroundings. Many say it's the best traditional Austrian eatery in town, great for *Tafelspitz* (slow-cooked beef with horseradish), and it also has good pasta dishes, including spicy spaghetti in a tomato, onion, bacon, and red pepper sauce. In spring, local asparagus is featured, and later in the year the menu focuses on game. You won't go wrong with the apricot dumplings for dessert. $ *Average main: €12* ✉ *Kirchstrasse 8* ☎ *05574/42815* ⊕ *www.hotelweisseskreuz.at/de-restaurant-goldener-hirsch.htm* ⊘ *Closed Tues. and 2 wks in Sept.*

$
TAPAS

✕ **Ilge-Weinstube Tapas Bar.** Austria meets Spain in this tapas bar housed in a 300-year-old building close to the heart of the old town. All the classics are there, Andalusian meatballs, dates wrapped in bacon and deep fried squid, but also prawns in sherry and garlic oil. A good selection of decent Spanish wines too. The atmosphere is lively, and it's popular with a young crowd but enjoyable for all. $ *Average main: €8* ✉ *Maurachgasse 6* ☎ *05574/43609* ⊘ *Closed Sun.*

$$$
INTERNATIONAL

✕ **Maurachbund.** Heino Huber, rated one of Austria's top five chefs, runs this elegant restaurant with a focus on home-style Austrian cuisine with a sophisticated twist—all ingredients are locally sourced if possible, and fish figures heavily. Dining here is an enjoyable, intimate experience. In summer you can choose to eat outside on the back terrace. Herr Huber and his wife run the nearby Deuring Schlossle gourmet hotel, as well as being responsible for the menu in the gourmet restaurant of a steamer on the Bodensee. $ *Average main: €20* ✉ *Maurachgasse 11* ☎ *05574/45029* ⊕ *www.maurachbund.at.*

$$
AUSTRIAN

✕ **Wirtshaus am See.** This half-timbered house with a gabled roof is right on the shore of Lake Constance, next to the floating stage used for the Bregenz Festival. The menu has the usual Austrian favorites, from schnitzel to *Zwiebelrostbraten* (a skirt steak topped with crispy fried onions), fresh fish, and a worthy wine list. Some dishes from Germany and Switzerland—which you can see without moving from your chair—are also offered. The main attraction here is the spectacular lake view. You can watch the steamers from the nearby harbor go by from the restaurant's extensive outdoor terrace. In winter the Chimney Room, with an open fire, is popular. $ *Average main: €15* ✉ *Seepromenade 2* ☎ *05574/42210* ⊕ *www.wirtshausamsee.at* ⊘ *Closed Jan. and Feb.*

12

WHERE TO STAY

$$$ HOTEL **Deuring-Schlössle.** This 400-year-old castle with its Baroque tower has inspired paintings by Turner and Schiele and is a charming and atmospheric place to stay, with a superb restaurant. **Pros:** a genuine castle, yet modern where needed; excellent kitchen. **Cons:** a bit far from the lower town, where the action is. [$] *Rooms from: €200* ✉ *Ehregutaplatz 4* ☎ *05574/47800* 🌐 *www.deuring-schloessle.at* 🛏 *13 rooms* 🍴 *Breakfast.*

$$ HOTEL **Schwärzler.** On the edge of town, the Schwärzler has the feeling of being in the country. **Pros:** spacious lobby and rooms; very attentive staff. **Cons:** on the edge of town; rooms toward the street are noisy; during the week it's mainly a business hotel. [$] *Rooms from: €150* ✉ *Landstrasse 9* ☎ *05574/4990* 🌐 *www.s-hotels.com* 🛏 *75 rooms* 🍴 *Breakfast.*

$$ HOTEL **Weisses Kreuz.** This traditional, family-run, turn-of-the-20th-century house is in a great central location, on the edge of the pedestrian zone, and is noted for its friendly staff. **Pros:** it's the traditional center of hospitality in Bregenz; renovated rooms; excellent restaurant; central location. **Cons:** front rooms look out onto a well-traveled street. [$] *Rooms from: €150* ✉ *Römerstrasse 5* ☎ *05574/4988–0* 🌐 *www.bestwestern.com* 🛏 *44 rooms* 🕒 *Closed Christmas week* 🍴 *Breakfast.*

NIGHTLIFE AND THE ARTS

Fodor's Choice ★ **Bregenzer Festspiele** (*Bregenz Music Festival*). The big cultural event in Bregenz is the Bregenzer Festspiele, held mid-July to late August, with the main stage a huge floating platform on the lake. For information and tickets, contact the festival office. Tickets are also available at the Bregenz tourist office. In the event of rain, the concert performance is moved indoors to the massive Festival Hall and Congress Center adjacent to the floating stage (it can accommodate at least 1,800 of the 6,800 seats usually available for performances on the floating lake stage). ✉ *Platz der Wiener Symphoniker 1* ☎ *05574/4076* 🌐 *www.bregenzerfestspiele.com*

Bodensee-Vorarlberg Tourismus. Travel and performance packages are available through Bodensee-Vorarlberg Tourismus. ✉ *Römerstr. 2* ☎ *05574/434430* 🌐 *www.bodensee-vorarlberg.com.*

Bregenzer Frühling. The cultural year starts with the spring music and dance festival that runs from March to May. ☎ *05574/4080* 🌐 *www.bregenzerfruehling.at.*

Tourist Office. Information and tickets are available through the tourist office in Bregenz. ✉ *Bahnhofstrasse 14* ☎ *05574/43443* 🌐 *www.bregenz.at.*

Casino. There's much activity at this gambling house, which opens at 3 pm and closes at 3 or 4 am. It offers table games, poker, and slot machines. The dress code demands appropriate clothing (no sportswear) and that men wear a jacket and tie (available for rent if you come casual). Bring your passport. ✉ *Platz der Wiener Symphoniker 3* ☎ *05574/45127* 🌐 *www.bregenz.casinos.at.*

Music Pavilion. Outdoor concerts are held during the summer months in this horseshoe-shape pavilion at the end of the promenade on the lake.

SPORTS AND THE OUTDOORS

BICYCLING

It's possible to cycle around Lake Constance in two to four days, traveling all the while on well-marked and -maintained paths (don't forget your passport). If this sounds too strenuous, parts of the route can be covered by boat. Rental bikes can be hired at local sports shops or at the train stations in Bregenz or Feldkirch; the tourist office can provide you with maps and details. Another cycling path, popular with families, follows the Rhine—a 70-km (43-mile) stretch from Bregenz south to Bludenz. Parts of the route are possible by train.

SKIING

Pfänder. There is some modest skiing on the Pfänder mountain, in Bregenz's backyard, which has a cable tramway and two drag lifts. The views are stunning from atop the peak, stretching as far as the Black Forest and the Swiss Alps. ⊠ *Steinbruchgasse 4* ☎ *05574/42160* ⊕ *www.pfaenderbahn.at*

Ski Runs. The runs are closed during the second and third week of November. ☎ *05572/42160* ⊕ *www.pfaenderbahn.at.*

WATER SPORTS

With the vast lake at its doorstep, Bregenz offers a variety of water sports, from swimming to fishing to windsurfing.

The Innsbruck Card. The Innsbruck Card is a bargain. It includes transport on bus and tram throughout the city and surrounding holiday villages, the Sightseer hop-on hop-off bus, lifts and cable cars, and entrance to museums and attractions. It costs €33 for 24 hours, €41 for 48 hours, and €47 for 72 hours, with a 50% discount for children up to 15. Details and how to buy on ⊕ *www.innsbruck.info.* ⊠ *Tyrol.*

Segelschule Lochau. You can learn to sail here, although a minimum of two weeks is required for a full course. ⊠ *Alte Fähre im Yachthafen, Marina, Lochau* ☎ *05574/52247* ⊕ *www.segelschule-lochau.com.*

UNDERSTANDING
AUSTRIA

AUSTRIA AT A GLANCE

CHRONOLOGY

WORDS AND PHRASES

MENU GUIDE

CONVERSIONS

AUSTRIA AT A GLANCE

FAST FACTS

Capital: Vienna

National anthem: "Land der Berge, Land am Strome" ("Land of Mountains, Land on the River")

Type of government: Federal republic

Administrative divisions: Nine states

Independence: 1156 (from Bavaria)

Constitution: 1920; revised 1929, reinstated 1945

Legal system: Civil law system with Roman law origin; judicial review of legislative acts by the Constitutional Court; separate administrative and civil/penal supreme courts

Suffrage: 18 years of age; universal; compulsory for presidential elections

Legislature: Bicameral Federal Assembly consists of Federal Council (62 members; members represent each of the states on the basis of population, but with each state having at least three representatives; members serve a five- or six-year term) and the National Council (183 seats; members elected by direct popular vote to serve four-year terms)

Population: 8.2 million

Literacy: 98%

Language: German (official nationwide), Slovene (official in Carinthia), Croatian (official in Burgenland), Hungarian (official in Burgenland)

Ethnic groups: Austrian 91%, former Yugoslavs 4% (includes Croatians, Slovenes, Serbs, and Bosnians), Turks 1.6%, German 0.9%, other or unspecified 2.4%

Religion: Roman Catholic 74%; other 17%; Protestant 5%; Muslim 4%

GEOGRAPHY AND ENVIRONMENT

Land area: 82,444 square km (31,832 square miles)

Terrain: Steep Alps in the west and south; mostly flat along the eastern and northern borders; at the crossroads of central Europe with many easily traversable Alpine passes and valleys

Natural resources: Antimony, coal, copper, graphite, hydropower, iron ore, lignite, magnesite, natural gas, oil, salt, timber, tungsten, uranium, zinc

Natural hazards: Avalanches, earthquakes, landslides

Environmental issues: Forest degradation caused by air and soil pollution; soil pollution results from the use of agricultural chemicals; air pollution results from emissions by coal- and oil-fired power stations and industrial plants and from trucks transiting Austria between northern and southern Europe

ECONOMY

Currency: Euro

GDP: $417.9 billion (2005 est.)

Major industries: Chemicals, communications equipment, construction, food, lumber and wood processing, machinery, paper and paperboard, vehicles and parts, tourism

Agricultural products: Cattle, dairy products, fruit, grains, lumber, pigs, potatoes, poultry, sugar beets, wine

Major export products: Chemicals, foodstuffs, iron and steel, machinery and equipment, metal goods, motor vehicles and parts, paper and paperboard, textiles

Major import products: Chemicals, foodstuffs, machinery and equipment, metal goods, motor vehicles, oil and oil products

DID YOU KNOW?

■ The Vienna Staatsoper is the site of the world's longest round of applause. For 90 minutes and 101 curtain calls, the crowd applauded Plácido Domingo for his performance in *Othello* in 1991.

CHRONOLOGY

ca. 800 BC Celts move into Danube Valley.

ca. 100 BC Earliest fortresses set up at Vindobona, now the inner city of Vienna. Roman legions, and Roman civilization, advance to Danube. Carnuntum (near Petronell, east of Vienna) is established about 30 years later as a provincial capital.

AD 180 Emperor Marcus Aurelius dies at Vindobona. Other Roman settlements include Juvavum (Salzburg) and Valdidena (Innsbruck).

ca. 400–700 The Danube Valley is the crossing ground for successive waves of barbarian invaders. Era of the events of the Nibelung saga, written down circa 1100.

ca. 700 Christian bishop established at Salzburg; conversion of pagan tribes begins.

791–99 Charlemagne, king of the Franks, conquers territory now known as Austria.

800 Pope Leo III crowns Charlemagne Emperor of the West.

ca. 800–900 Invasion of Magyars; they eventually settle along the Danube.

962 Pope John XII crowns Otto the Great, of Germany, emperor of the Holy Roman Empire, constituting the eastern portion of Charlemagne's realm. Neither holy, nor Roman, nor an empire, this confederation continued until 1806.

THE HOUSE OF BABENBERG

976 Otto II confers the eastern province of the Reich—Österreich, or Austria—upon the margrave Leopold of Babenberg.

1095–1136 Reign of Leopold III, later canonized and declared patron saint of Austria.

1156 Austria becomes a duchy. Duke Heinrich II makes Vienna his capital, building a palace in Am Hof.

1192 Leopold V imprisons King Richard the Lion-Hearted of England, who is on his way back from a crusade. Parts of Vienna and several town walls, particularly Wiener Neustadt, south of Vienna, are later built with the ransom money.

THE HOUSE OF HABSBURG

1273 Rudolf of Habsburg in Switzerland is chosen duke by the electors of the Rhine; his family rules for 640 years.

1282 Habsburgs absorb the land of Austria.

1365 University of Vienna founded.

1496 Maximilian's son, Philip, marries Juana of Castile and Aragon, daughter of Ferdinand and Isabella of Spain.

1519 Death of Maximilian; his grandson, Charles I of Spain, inherits Austria, Burgundy, and the Netherlands; he is elected Holy Roman Emperor as Charles V.

1521 Charles V divides his realm with his brother Ferdinand, who becomes archduke of Austria and the first Habsburg to live in the Hofburg in Vienna.

1529 Turks lay siege to Vienna.

1556 Charles V abdicates; Ferdinand becomes Holy Roman Emperor. A Catholic with many Protestant subjects, he negotiates the Peace of Augsburg, which preserves a truce between the Catholic and Protestant states of his realm until 1618.

1618–48 Thirty Years' War begins as a religious dispute but becomes a dynastic struggle between Habsburgs and Bourbons, fought on German soil by non-Germans. The Peace of Westphalia, 1648, gives Austria no new territory and reestablishes the religious deadlock of the Peace of Augsburg.

1683 Turks besiege Vienna; are routed by combined forces of Emperor Leopold I, the duke of Lorraine, and King Jan Sobieski of Poland. By 1699, armies led by Prince Eugene of Savoy drive the Turks east and south, doubling the area of Habsburg lands. The Turkish legacy: a gold crescent and a sack of coffee beans; Vienna's coffeehouses open for business.

1740 Last male Habsburg, Charles VI, dies; succession of his daughter Maria Theresa leads to attack on the Habsburg dominions; long-term rivalry between Austria and Prussia begins.

1740–80 Reign of Maria Theresa, a golden age, when young Mozart entertains at Schönbrunn Palace and Haydn and Gluck establish Vienna as a musical mecca. Fundamental reforms modernize the Austrian monarchy.

1780–90 Reign of Maria Theresa's son Joseph II, who continues her liberalizing tendencies by freeing the serfs and reforming the Church. Her daughter, Marie Antoinette, has other problems.

1806 Napoléon forces Emperor Franz II to abdicate, and the Holy Roman Empire is no more; Franz is retitled emperor of Austria and rules until 1835.

1814–15 The Congress of Vienna defines post-Napoleonic Europe; Austria's Prince Metternich (who had arranged the marriage between Napoléon and Franz II's daughter Marie Louise) gains territory and power.

1815–48 Rise of nationalism threatens Austrian Empire; as chief minister, Metternich represses liberal and national movements with censorship, secret police, and force.

1848 Revolutions throughout Europe, including Budapest, Prague, Vienna; Emperor Ferdinand I abdicates in favor of his 18-year-old nephew Franz Josef. Under his personal rule (lasting until 1916), national and liberal movements are thwarted.

1856–90 Modern Vienna is created and much of the medieval city torn down; the Waltz Kings, Johann Strauss father and son, dominate popular music. Sigmund Freud (1856–1939) begins his research on the human psyche in Vienna. By 1900 artistic movements include the Secession and Expressionism.

1866 Bismarck's Prussia defeats Austria in a seven-week war, fatally weakening Austria's position among the German states.

1867 In response to Hungarian clamor for national recognition, the Ausgleich, or compromise, creates the dual monarchy of Austria-Hungary with two parliaments and one monarch.

1889 Franz Josef's only son, Rudolf, dies mysteriously in an apparent suicide pact with his young mistress, Baroness Marie Vetsera.

1898 Empress Elisabeth is murdered in Geneva by an anarchist.

1914 June 28: Archduke Franz Ferdinand, nephew and heir of Franz Josef, is assassinated by a Serbian terrorist at Sarajevo in Bosnia-Herzegovina. By August 4, Europe is at war: Germany and Austria-Hungary versus Russia, France, and Britain.

1916 Death of Franz Josef.

THE REPUBLIC

1918 End of World War I; collapse of Austria-Hungary. Emperor Karl I resigns; Republic of Austria is carved out of Habsburg crown lands, while nation-states of the empire declare autonomy. Kept afloat by loans from the League of Nations, Austria adjusts to its new role with difficulty. Culturally it continues to flourish: Arnold Schoenberg's 12-tone scale recasts musical expression, while the Vienna Circle redefines philosophy.

1934 Dollfuss suppresses the Socialists and creates a one-party state; later in the year he is assassinated by Nazis. His successor, Kurt von Schuschnigg, attempts to accommodate Hitler.

1938 Anschluss: Hitler occupies Austria without resistance.

1945 Austria, postwar, is divided into four zones of occupation by the Allies; free elections are held.

1955 Signing of the Austrian State Treaty officially ends the occupation. Austria declares itself "perpetually" neutral.

1989 Austria becomes the first destination for waves of Eastern European emigrants as the borders are opened.

1990 Austria applies for membership in the European Union.

1999 Spearheaded by Jörg Haider, the anti-immigration and extremist Freedom Party is admitted to Austria's national cabinet, setting the government on a collision course with fellow members of the European Union, who subsequently issue economic and political sanctions against Austria.

2002 The Austrian government is in full upheaval. The status of the ÖVP coalition as the leading party in power is in doubt, with the SPÖ party coming to the fore. The leaders of the Freedom Party resign because of differences with Jörg Haider, who in the September elections becomes head of this party again, only to back down from taking over the leadership. Happily, the launch of euro notes and coins continues to be a tremendous success in Austria.

2004 Elfriede Jelinek wins the Nobel Prize for Literature, confirming her status as one of Austria's most important and controversial cultural figures. Her novels deal with sexual violence and oppression and right-wing extremism. After years of friction with the government, her plays are once again performed in her homeland. The revered and respected president of Austria, Dr. Thomas Klestil, dies of heart failure just days before his second four-year term expires in July. He is replaced by Dr. Heinz Fischer, a prominent member of the Socialist Party, who is elected in April. Pope John Paul II beatifies the last Austrian emperor, Karl I, who was against fighting in World War I. And Austria's most famous export since Mozart, Arnold Schwarzenegger, completes his first year as governor of California.

2008 Austria's resurgent far-right parties win 29 percent of the popular vote. A month later, however, their leader Jörg Haider is killed in a car crash, and two months after that a new coalition government made up of the center-left SPO and the conservative People's Party is sworn in. SPO leader Werner Faymann becomes chancellor.

2010 President Fischer reelected in April. Six months later, the far-right Freedom Party wins 26% of the vote in Vienna's municipal elections, putting it just behind the Social Democrats.

2011 Otto von Habsburg, the oldest son of the last Austrian emperor, is laid to rest in the Imperial Crypt in Vienna in a ceremony that recalled the splendor of the empire.

WORDS AND PHRASES

Austrian German is not entirely the same as the German sp[...]
many. Several food names are different, as well as a few ba[...]

Umlauts have no similar sound in English. An ä is pronoun[...]
An äu or eu is pronounced as "oy." An ö is pronounced [...]
your lips like an "O" while trying to say "E" and a ü is pronounced by
making your lips like a "U" and trying to say "E".

Consonants are pronounced as follows:
CH is like a hard H, almost like a soft clearing of the throat.
J is pronounced as Y.
Rs are rolled.
ß, which is written "ss" in this book, is pronouced as double S.
S is pronounced as Z.
V is pronounced as F.
W is pronounced as V.
Z is pronounced as TS.

An asterisk (*) denotes common usage in Austria.

ENGLISH	GERMAN	PRONUNCIATION

BASICS

ENGLISH	GERMAN	PRONUNCIATION
Yes/no	Ja/nein	yah/nine
Please	Bitte	**bit**-uh
May I?	Darf ich?	darf isch?
Thank you (very much)	Danke (vielen Dank)	**dahn**-kuh (**fee**-len dahnk)
You're welcome	Bitte, gern geschehen	**bit**-uh, gairn ge**shay**-un
Excuse me	Entschuldigen Sie	ent-**shool**-di-gen zee
What? (What did you say?)	Wie, bitte?	vee, **bit**-uh?
Can you tell me?	Können Sie mir sagen?	kunnen zee meer **sah**-gen?
Do you know _____?	Wissen Sie _____?	**viss**-en zee
I'm sorry	Es tut mir leid.	es toot meer lite
Good day	Guten Tag	**goo**-ten tahk
Goodbye	Auf Wiedersehen	owf **vee**-der-zane
Good morning	Guten Morgen	**goo**-ten **mor**-gen
Good evening	Guten Abend	**goo**-ten **ah**-bend
Good night	Gute Nacht	**goo**-tuh nahkt
Mr./Mrs.	Herr/Frau	hair/frow
Miss	Fräulein	**froy**-line

ENGLISH	GERMAN	PRONUNCIATION
Pleased to meet you.	Sehr erfreut.	zair air-**froyt**
How are you?	Wie geht es Ihnen?	vee **gate** es **ee**-nen?
Very well, thanks.	Sehr gut, danke.	sair goot, **dahn**-kuh
And you?	Und Ihnen?	oont **ee**-nen?
Hi!	*Servus!	**sair**-voos

DAYS OF THE WEEK

Sunday	Sonntag	**zohn**-tahk
Monday	Montag	**moan**-tahk
Tuesday	Dienstag	**deens**-tahk
Wednesday	Mittwoch	**mitt**-voak
Thursday	Donnerstag	**doe**-ners-tahk
Friday	Freitag	**fry**-tahk
Saturday	Samstag	**zahm**-stahk

USEFUL PHRASES

Do you speak English?	Sprechen Sie Englisch?	**shprek**-hun zee **eng**-glisch?
I don't speak German.	Ich spreche kein Deutsch.	isch **shprek**-uh kine doych
Please speak slowly.	Bitte sprechen Sie langsam.	bit-uh **shprek**-en zee **lahng**-zahm
I don't understand.	Ich verstehe nicht.	isch fair-**shtay**-uh nicht
I understand.	Ich verstehe.	isch fair-**shtay**-uh
I don't know.	Ich weiss nicht.	isch vice nicht
Excuse me/sorry.	Entschuldigen Sie.	ent-**shool**-di-gen zee
I am American/ British.	Ich bin Amerikaner(in)/ Engländer(in).	isch bin a-mer-i-**kahn**-er(in)/ **eng**-len-der(in)
What is your name?	Wie heissen Sie?	vee **high**-sen zee
My name is . . .	Ich heisse . . .	isch **high**-suh
What time is it?	Wieviel Uhr ist es?	**vee**-feel oor ist es
	*Wie spät ist es?	**vee** shpate ist es
It is one, two, three . . . o'clock.	Es ist ein, zwei, drei . . . Uhr.	es ist ine, tsvy, dry . . . oor

ENGLISH	GERMAN	PRONUNCIATION
Yes, please	Ja, bitte	yah **bi**-tuh
No, thank you	Nein, danke	**nine** dahng-kuh
How?	Wie?	vee
When?	Wann? (as conjunction, als)	vahn (ahls)
This/next week	Diese/nächste Woche	**dee**-zuh/**nehks**-tuh **vo**-kuh
This/next year	Dieses/nächstes Jahr	**dee**-zuz/**nehks**-tuhs yahr
Yesterday/today/tomorrow	Gestern/heute/morgen	**geh**-stern/**hoy**-tuh/**mor**-gen
This morning/afternoon	Heute morgen/nachmittag	**hoy**-tuh **mor**-gen/**nahk**-mit-tahk
Tonight	Heute Nacht	**hoy**-tuh nahkt
What is it?	Was ist es?	**vahss** ist es
Why?	Warum?	vah-**rum**
Who/whom?	Wer/wen?	vair/vehn
Who is it?	Wer ist da?	vair ist dah
I'd like to have . . .	Ich hätte gerne . . .	isch **het**-uh gairn
a room	ein Zimmer	ine **tsim**-er
the key	den Schlüssel	den **shluh**-sul
a newspaper	eine Zeitung	i-nuh **tsy**-toong
a stamp	eine Briefmarke	i-nuh **breef**-mark-uh
a map	eine Karte	i-nuh **cart**-uh
I'd like to buy . . .	ich möchte . . . kaufen	isch **merhk**-tuh **cow**-fen
cigarettes	Zigaretten	tzig-ah-**ret**-ten
How much is it?	Wieviel kostet das?	**vee**-feel **cost**-et dahss?
It's expensive/cheap	Es ist teuer/billig	es ist **toy**-uh/**bill**-ig
a little/a lot	ein wenig/sehr	ine **vay**-nig/zair
more/less	mehr/weniger	mair/**vay**-nig-er
Enough/too much/too little	genug/zuviel/zu wenig	geh-**noog**/tsoo-**feel**/tsoo **vay**-nig
I am ill/sick	Ich bin krank	isch bin krahnk

ENGLISH	GERMAN	PRONUNCIATION
I need . . .	Ich brauche . . .	isch **brow**-khuh
a doctor	einen Arzt	I-nen artst
the police	die Polizei	dee po-lee-**tsai**
help	Hilfe	**hilf**-uh
Fire!	Feuer!	**foy**-er
Caution/Look out!	Achtung!/Vorsicht!	**ahk**-tung/**for**-zicht
Is this bus/train/sub-way going to.?	Fährt dieser Bus/ dieser Zug/diese U-Bahn nach.?	fayrt **deez**-er buhs/ **deez**-er tsook/**deez**-uh **oo**-bahn nahk.
Where is.	Wo ist.	**vo** ist
the train station?	der Bahnhof?	dare **bahn**-hof
the subway station?	die U-Bahn-Station?	dee **oo**-bahn-**staht**-sion
the bus stop?	die Bushaltestelle?	dee **booss**-hahlt-uh-**shtel**-uh
the airport?	der Flugplatz?	dare **floog**-plats
	*der Flughafen	dare **floog**-hafen
the hospital?	das Krankenhaus?	dahs **krahnk**-en- house
the elevator?	der Aufzug?	dare **owf**-tsoog
the telephone?	das Telefon?	dahs te-le-**fone**
the rest room?	die Toilette?	dee twah-**let**-uh
open/closed	offen/geschlossen	**off**-en/ge-**schloss**-en
left/right	links/rechts	links/recktz
straight ahead	geradeaus	geh-**rah**-day-owws
Is it near/far?	Ist es in der Nähe/ist es weit?	ist es in dare **nay**-uh? ist es vite?

MENU GUIDE

ENGLISH	GERMAN
Entrées	Hauptspeisen
Homemade	Hausgemacht
Lunch	Mittagsessen
Dinner	Abendessen

ENGLISH	GERMAN
Dessert	Nachspeisen
Your choice	Önach Wahl
Soup of the day	Tagessuppe
Appetizers	Vorspeisen

BREAKFAST

Bread	Brot
Butter	Butter
Eggs	Eier
Hot	Heiss
Cold	Kalt
Caffeine-free coffee	Café Hag
Jam	Marmalade
Milk	Milch
Juice	Saft
Bacon	Speck
Lemon	Zitrone
Sugar	Zucker

SOUPS

Stew	Eintopf
Goulash soup	Gulaschsuppe
Chicken soup	Hühnersuppe
Potato soup	Kartoffelsuppe
Liver dumpling soup	Leberknödelsuppe
Onion soup	Zwiebelsuppe

FISH AND SEAFOOD

Trout	Forelle
Prawns	Garnele
Halibut	Heilbutt
Lobster	Hummer
Crab	Krabbe

ENGLISH	GERMAN
Salmon	Lachs
Squid	Tintenfisch
Tuna	Thunfisch
Turbot	Steinbutt

MEATS

Veal	Kalb
Lamb	Lamm
Beef	Rindfleisch
Pork	Schwein

GAME AND POULTRY

Duck	Ente
Pheasant	Fasan
Goose	Gans
Chicken	Hühner
Rabbit	Kaninchen
Venison	Reh
Turkey	Truthahn
Quail	Wachtel

VEGETABLES AND SIDE DISHES

Red cabbage	Rotkraut
Cauliflower	Karfiol
Beans	Bohnen
Button mushrooms	Champignons
Peas	Erbsen
Cucumber	Gurke
Cabbage	Kohl
Lettuce	Blattsalat
Potatoes	Kartoffeln
Dumplings	Knödel
French fries	Pommes frites

	ENGLISH	GERMAN
FRUITS		
	Apple	Apfel
	Orange	Orangen
	Apricot	Marillen
	Blueberry	Heidelbeere
	Strawberry	Erdbeere
	Raspberry	Himbeere
	Cherry	Kirsche
	Cranberry	Preiselbeere
	Grapes	Trauben
	Pear	Birne
	Peach	Pfirsich
DESSERTS		
	Cheese	Käse
	Crepes	Palatschinken
	Soufflé	Auflauf
	Ice cream	Eis
	Cake	Torte
DRINKS		
	Tap water	Leitungswasser
	With/without water	Mit/ohne wasser
	Straight	Pur
	Non-alcoholic	Alkoholfrei
	A large/small dark beer	Ein Krügel/Seidel Dunkles
	A large/small light beer	Ein Krügel/Seidel Helles
	Draft beer	Vom Fass
	Sparkling wine	Sekt
	White wine	Weisswein
	Red wine	Rotwein
	Wine with mineral water	Gespritz

CONVERSIONS

DISTANCE

KILOMETERS/MILES

To change kilometers (km) to miles (mi), multiply km by .621. To change mi to km, multiply mi by 1.61.

km to mi		mi to km	
1 =	.62	1 =	1.6
2 =	1.2	2 =	3.2
3 =	1.9	3 =	4.8
4 =	2.5	4 =	6.4
5 =	3.1	5 =	8.1
6 =	3.7	6 =	9.7
7 =	4.3	7 =	11.3
8 =	5.0	8 =	12.9

METERS/FEET

To change meters (m) to feet (ft), multiply m by 3.28. To change ft to m, multiply ft by .305.

m to ft		ft to m	
1 =	3.3	1 =	.30
2 =	6.6	2 =	.61
3 =	9.8	3 =	.92
4 =	13.1	4 =	1.2
5 =	16.4	5 =	1.5
6 =	19.7	6 =	1.8
7 =	23.0	7 =	2.1
8 =	26.2	8 =	2.4

TEMPERATURE

METRIC CONVERSIONS

To change centigrade or Celsius (C) to Fahrenheit (F), multiply C by 1.8 and add 32. To change F to C, subtract 32 from F and multiply by .555.

°F	°C
0	-17.8
10	-12.2
20	-6.7
30	-1.1
32	0
40	+4.4
50	10.0
60	15.5
70	21.1
80	26.6
90	32.2
98.6	37.0
100	37.7

WEIGHT

KILOGRAMS/POUNDS

To change kilograms (kg) to pounds (lb), multiply kg by 2.20. To change lb to kg, multiply lb by .455.

kg to lb		lb to kg	
1 =	2.2	1 =	.45
2 =	4.4	2 =	.91
3 =	6.6	3 =	1.4
4 =	8.8	4 =	1.8
5 =	11.0	5 =	2.3
6 =	13.2	6 =	2.7
7 =	15.4	7 =	3.2
8 =	17.6	8 =	3.6

GRAMS/OUNCES

To change grams (g) to ounces (oz), multiply g by .035. To change oz to g, multiply oz by 28.4.

g to oz		oz to g	
1 =	.04	1 =	28
2 =	.07	2 =	57
3 =	.11	3 =	85
4 =	.14	4 =	114
5 =	.18	5 =	142
6 =	.21	6 =	170
7 =	.25	7 =	199
8 =	.28	8 =	227

LIQUID VOLUME

LITERS/U.S. GALLONS

To change liters (L) to U.S. gallons (gal), multiply L by .264. To change U.S. gal to L, multiply gal by 3.79.

L to gal		gal to L	
1 =	.26	1 =	3.8
2 =	.53	2 =	7.6
3 =	.79	3 =	11.4
4 =	1.1	4 =	15.2
5 =	1.3	5 =	19.0
6 =	1.6	6 =	22.7
7 =	1.8	7 =	26.5
8 =	2.1	8 =	30.3

CLOTHING SIZE

WOMEN'S CLOTHING

US	UK	EUR
4	6	34
6	8	36
8	10	38
10	12	40
12	14	42

WOMEN'S SHOES

US	UK	EUR
5	3	36
6	4	37
7	5	38
8	6	39
9	7	40

MEN'S SUITS

US	UK	EUR
34	34	44
36	36	46
38	38	48
40	40	50
42	42	52
44	44	54
46	46	56

MEN'S SHIRTS

US	UK	EUR
14½	14½	37
15	15	38
15½	15½	39
16	16	41
16½	16½	42
17	17	43
17½	17½	44

MEN'S SHOES

US	UK	EUR
7	6	39½
8	7	41
9	8	42
10	9	43
11	10	44½
12	11	46

TRAVEL SMART VIENNA AND AUSTRIA

GETTING HERE AND AROUND

■ AIR TRAVEL

Flying time from New York to Vienna is eight hours; it's nine hours from Washington, D.C., and two hours from London. Airline and Airport Links.com has links to many of the world's airlines and airports. The Transportation Security Administration has answers for almost every security question that might come up.

Airlines and Airports Airline and Airport Links.com ⊕ www.airlineandairportlinks.com.

Airline Security Issues Transportation Security Administration ⊕ www.tsa.gov.

AIRPORTS

Austria's major air gateway is Vienna's Schwechat Airport, about 19 km (12 miles) southeast of the city. Salzburg Airport is Austria's second-largest airport, about 4 km (2½ miles) west of the center. Just south of Graz, in Thalerhof, is the Graz Airport. Two other airports you might consider, depending on where in Austria you intend to travel, are Bratislava's M. R. Stefanik international airport in neighboring Slovakia, and Munich Airport International in Germany, not far from Salzburg. Bratislava is about 80 kms (50 miles) east of Vienna and is the hub for RyanAir, a budget carrier with low-cost connections to several European cities. Frequent buses can take you from Bratislava airport to central Vienna in about an hour. Consider Munich if your primary destination is western Austria, Salzburg, or Innsbruck.

Airport Information Graz Airport (GRZ) ☎ 0316/2902–172 ⊕ www.flughafen-graz. at. M. R. Stefanik Airport (Bratislava, BTS) ☎ 421/233–0333–53 from outside of Slovakia ⊕ www.airport-bratislava.sk or www.bts. aero. Munich Airport International (MUC) ☎ 49/899–7500 from outside Germany ⊕ www.munich-airport.de. Salzburg Airport (SZG) ☎ 0662/85800 ⊕ www.salzburg-airport.

FODORS.COM CONNECTION

Before your trip, be sure to check out what other travelers are saying in Travel Ratings and Talk on www.fodors.com.

com. Schwechat Airport (Vienna, VIE) ☎ 01/70070 ⊕ www.viennaairport.com.

GROUND TRANSPORTATION AND TRANSFERS

The City Airport Train (CAT) provides service from Schwechat to downtown Vienna for €12 (one-way ticket, available at the CAT counter in the arrivals hall); the trip takes about 16 minutes. Travel into the city on the local S-Bahn takes about 25 minutes and costs €4.40 (ticket machines are on the platforms). City bus No. 2 runs every 10 minutes between both the city center and Salzburg's main train station and the airport; transfers cost €2.30. A taxi ride from the airport will be about €18. Schwechat Airport's website has information for all ground transfers.

Ground Transportation Contacts CAT ☎ 01/7909–100 ⊕ www.cityairporttrain. com. S-Bahn ⊕ www.schnellbahn-wien. at. Schwechat Airport ☎ 01/7007–22233 ⊕ www.viennaairport.com. Vienna Bus ☎ 01/7909–100 ⊕ www.wienerlinien.at.

FLIGHTS

Austria is easy to reach from the United States. Austrian Airlines, Austria's flagship carrier and a Lufthansa subsidiary, flies nonstop to Vienna from the United States, departing from New York's JFK airport and Washington Dulles. From Canada, Austrian flies direct from Toronto. Its membership to the Star Alliance means that cities serviced by United Airlines have good connecting service to Austria. Austrian Airlines has an excellent network of domestic flights linking

Vienna to regional cities like Salzburg and Graz. It's also possible to travel from North America with major U.S. carriers—including American, Delta, and United—but you'll be routed through a major European hub, such as London, Amsterdam, or Frankfurt, to Vienna. Leave plenty of time between connections (a minimum of three hours is ideal), as transfers at major airports inevitably take some time. Many international carriers also offer service to Vienna after stopovers at major European airports.

In addition to the major international carriers, European budget airlines, including RyanAir, Air Berlin, and its subsidiary, FlyNiki, offer low-cost flights from major cities around the Continent. These airlines are not normally recommended for connecting with transatlantic flights because of the occasional hassle of changing airports, but they provide a low-cost way of getting around. Although RyanAir has left some customers less than satisfied, Air Berlin and FlyNiki offer reliable service. They travel between Vienna, Graz, Linz, Klagenfurt, Salzburg, Innsbruck, and major hubs in Europe, Asia, Africa, the Caribbean, the United States, and Canada. More recently, German charter carrier Condor also added flights between Vienna and Las Vegas to its schedule, as did Canadian charter airline Air Transat (⊕ *www. airtransat.ca*), with planes flying from Montreal and Toronto to Vienna.

Within Austria, Austrian Airlines and its subsidiary Austrian Arrows, operated by Tyrolean Airways, offer service from Vienna to Linz, Salzburg, Klagenfurt, and Innsbruck; they also provide routes to and from points outside Austria.

Airline Contacts American Airlines
☎ *800/433-7300* ⊕ *www.aa.com.* **Austrian Airlines** ☎ *800/843-0002, 05/1717 within Austria* ⊕ *www.austrian.com.* **British Airways** ☎ *800/247-9297, 0844/493-0787 within the U.K., 01/795-67-567 within Austria* ⊕ *www.britishairways.com.* **Delta Airlines** ☎ *800/221-1212* ⊕ *www.delta.com.*

Lufthansa ☎ *800/645-3880, 0810/102-58-080 within Austria* ⊕ *www.lufthansa.com.* **United Airlines** ☎ *800/864-8331 for U.S. reservations, 800/538-2929 for international reservations* ⊕ *www.united.com.*

Smaller Airlines Air Berlin ☎ *0820/737-800 within Austria for €0.12/minute, 1-866/266-5588 toll-free from the U.S.* ⊕ *www.airberlin. com.* **Air Transat** ☎ *1-877/872-6728* ⊕ *www. airtransat.ca.* **Condor** ☎ *1-866/960-7915 from the U.S. and Canada* ⊕ *www.condor. com.* **Fly Niki** ☎ *0820/737-800 within Austria, €0.12/minute* ⊕ *www.flyniki.com.* **Ryanair** ☎ *0900/210-240 in German only, +44 871/246-0002 U.K. number for service in English* ⊕ *www.ryanair.com.*

▌BUS TRAVEL

Austria has an extensive national network of buses run by the national postal and railroad services. Where Austrian trains don't go, buses do, and you'll find the railroad and post-office buses (bright yellow for easy recognition) in even remote regions carrying passengers as well as mail. You can get tickets on the bus, and in the off-season there is no problem getting a seat; on routes to favored ski areas, though, reservations are essential during holiday periods. Bookings can be handled at the ticket office (there's one in most towns with bus service) or by travel agents. In most communities bus routes begin and end at or near the train station, making transfers easy. Increasingly, coordination of bus service with railroads means that many of the discounts and special tickets available for trains apply to buses as well. There are private bus companies in Austria, too. Buses in Austria run like clockwork, typically departing and arriving on time, even, astonishingly, in mountainous regions and during bad weather. Most operators on the information lines *below* speak English and, impressively, many of the drivers do, too.

Bus Information Blaguss Reisen
☎ *01/610900* ⊕ *www.blaguss.at/en.* **Colum-bus** ☎ *01/534–110* ⊕ *www.columbus-reisen.* *at.* **Dr. Richard Reisebusse** ☎ *01/331–00–335* ⊕ *www.richard.at.* **Post und Bahn** ☎ *05/1717* *customer service for postbuses and trains* ⊕ *www.postbus.at, www.oebb.at.*

∎ CAR TRAVEL

Carefully weigh the pros and cons of car travel before choosing to rent. If your plans are to see Vienna and one or two other urban destinations, you're better off taking the train, avoiding hassles, and saving money. Bear in mind that in addition to the not inconsiderable cost of renting, you'll have to pay for gasoline (which costs more than twice what it does in the United States) and frequent tolls. In addition, you might find yourself dealing with heavy traffic on the main roads. Added to that is the constant headache of finding a place to park. Central Vienna is completely restricted and the situation is not much better in the smaller cities.

On the other hand, if you have the time and your plan is a more leisurely tour of the country, including back roads and off-the-beaten-track destinations, then car rental is certainly an option. You'll have more freedom—and roads are mostly very well maintained, even in rural districts and mountainous regions. Bear in mind that if you're traveling in winter, your car should be fitted with winter tires and you should also carry snow chains. Even in summer you can come across sudden winterlike conditions on the high mountain passes.

Vienna is 300 km (187 miles) east of Salzburg and 200 km (125 miles) north of Graz. Main routes leading into the city are the A1 Westautobahn from Germany, Salzburg, and Linz and the A2 Südautobahn from Graz and points south.

GASOLINE

Gasoline and diesel are readily available, but on Sunday stations in the more out-of-the-way areas may be closed. Stations carry only unleaded (*bleifrei*) gas, both regular and premium (super), and diesel. If you're in the mountains in winter with a diesel, and there is a cold snap (with temperatures threatening to drop below -4°F [-20°C]), add a few liters of gasoline to your diesel, about 1:4 parts, to prevent it from freezing. Gasoline prices are the same throughout the country, slightly lower at discount and self-service stations. Expect to pay about €1.38 per liter for regular gasoline and slightly less for diesel. If you are driving to Italy, fill up before crossing the border, because gas in Italy is even more expensive. Oil in Austria is expensive, retailing at €14 or more per liter. If need be, purchase oil, windshield wipers, and other paraphernalia at big hardware stores. The German word for "receipt" is *Quittung* or *Rechnung*.

RENTING A CAR

Rates in Vienna begin at about €80 per day and €100 per weekend for an economy car with manual transmission. This includes a 21% tax on car rentals. Rates are more expensive in winter months, when a surcharge for winter tires may be added. Renting a car is cheaper in Germany, but make sure the rental agency knows you are driving into Austria and ask for the car to be equipped with the Autobahnvignette, an autobahn sticker for Austria. The answer will usually be that you have to buy your own vignette, which you can get from service stations near the border. Get your sticker, also known as a *Pickerl,* before driving to Austria (⇨ *See Rules of the Road section*). When renting an RV be sure to compare prices and reserve early. It's cheaper to arrange your rental car from the United States, but be sure to get a confirmation in writing of your quoted rate. Extremely big savings can often be made by renting from a company that has partnered with your chosen airline—airline websites will

CAR RENTAL RESOURCES		
LOCAL AGENCIES		
Megadrive Autovermietung GmbH, Erdbergerstrasse 202, A-1030 Vienna	01/054–124	www.megadrive.at
Autoverleih Buchbinder at all major Austrian airports	0810/007–010	www.buchbinder-rent-a-car.at
MAJOR AGENCIES		
Alamo	877/222–9075	www.alamo.com
Avis	800/331–1212	www.avis.com
Budget	800/527–0700	www.budget.com
Hertz	800/654–3131	www.hertz.com
National Car Rental	800/227–7368	www.nationalcar.com

have the link—or use Arguscarhire.com, which has connections with a range of car rental companies and often comes up with the best prices.

The age requirement for renting a car in Austria is generally 19 (the minimum age for driving a car in Austria is 18), and you must have had a valid driver's license for one year. There is no extra charge to drive over the border into Italy, Switzerland, or Germany, but there may be some restrictions for taking a rental into Slovakia, Slovenia, Hungary, the Czech Republic, or Poland. If you're planning on traveling east, it's best to let the agency know beforehand.

In Austria your own driver's license is acceptable. An International Driver's Permit (IDP; $15), while not strictly necessary, is a good idea; these international permits are universally recognized, and having one in your wallet may save you a problem with the local authorities. Check the AAA website (⊕ www.aaa.com) for more info.

ROAD CONDITIONS

Roads in Austria are excellent and well maintained—perhaps a bit too well maintained, judging by the frequently encountered construction zones on the autobahns. Secondary roads may be narrow and winding. Remember that in winter you will need snow tires and sometimes chains, even on well-traveled roads. It's wise to check with the automobile clubs for weather conditions, because mountain roads are often blocked, and ice and fog are hazards.

ROADSIDE EMERGENCIES

If you break down along the autobahn, a small arrow on the guardrail will direct you to the nearest emergency (orange-color) phones that exist along all highways. Austria also has two automobile clubs, ÖAMTC and ARBÖ, both of which operate motorist service patrols. Both clubs charge nonmembers for emergency service.

Emergency Services ARBÖ ☎ *01/891–21–0* ⊕ *www.arboe.at.* **ÖAMTC** ☎ *0810/120–120* ⊕ *www.oeamtc.at.*

No area or other code is needed for either number.

RULES OF THE ROAD

Tourists from EU countries may bring their own cars into Austria with no documentation other than the normal registration papers and their regular driver's license. A Green Card, the international certificate of insurance, is recommended for EU drivers and compulsory for others. All cars must carry a first-aid kit (including rubber gloves), a red warning triangle, and a yellow neon jacket to use in case of accident or breakdown. These are available at gas stations along the road, or at any automotive supply store or large hardware store.

The minimum driving age in Austria is 18, and children under 12 must ride in the back seat; smaller children require a car seat. Note that all passengers must use seat belts.

Drive on the right side of the road in Austria. Unmarked crossings, particularly in residential areas, are common, so exercise caution at intersections. Trams always have the right of way. No turns are allowed on red.

When it comes to drinking and driving, the maximum blood-alcohol content allowed is 0.5 parts per thousand, which in real terms means very little to drink. Remember when driving in Europe that the police can stop you anywhere at any time for no particular reason.

Unless otherwise marked, the speed limit on autobahns is 130 kph (80 mph), although this is not always strictly enforced. If you're pulled over for speeding, though, fines are payable on the spot, and can be heavy. On other highways and roads the limit is 100 kph (62 mph), 80 kph (49 mph) for RVs or cars pulling a trailer weighing more than 750 kilos (about 1,650 pounds). In built-up areas a 50-kph (31-mph) limit applies and is likely to be taken seriously. In some towns special 30-kph (20-mph) limits apply. More and more towns have radar cameras to catch speeders. Remember that insurance does not necessarily pay if it can be proven you were going above the limit when involved in an accident.

■ **TIP→** If you're going to travel Austria's highways, make absolutely sure your car is equipped with the **Autobahnvignette**, a little sticker with a highway icon and the Austrian eagle, or with a calendar marked with an **M** or a **W**. This sticker, sometimes also called a Pickerl, allows use of the autobahn. It costs €82.70 (valid for one year) and is available at gas stations, tobacconists, and automobile-club outlets in neighboring countries or near the border. Some

rental cars may already have them, but you need to check. You can also purchase a two-month vignette for €24.80, or a 10-day one for €8.50. Prices are for vehicles up to 3.5 tons and RVs. For motorcycles it's €32.90 for one year, €12.40 for two months, and €4.90 for 10 days. If you're caught without a sticker you may be subjected to extremely high fines. Get your Pickerl before driving to Austria from another country. Besides the Pickerl, if you are planning to drive around a lot, budget in a great deal of toll money: for example, the tunnels on the A10 autobahn cost €11, the Grossglockner Pass road will cost about €34 per car (you can buy a ticket for €10 for a second ride over the pass in the same calendar year and in the same car if you show the cashier the original ticket). Driving up some especially beautiful valleys, such as the Kaunertal in Tyrol, or up to the Tauplitzalm in Styria, also costs money—around €23 per car for the Kaunertal.

■ SHIP AND BOAT TRAVEL

For leisurely travel between Vienna and Linz, or eastward across the border into Slovakia or Hungary, consider taking a Danube boat. **DDSG Blue Danube Schifffahrt** offers a diverse selection of pleasant cruises, including trips to Melk Abbey and Dürnstein in the Wachau, a grand tour of Vienna's architectural sights from the river, and a dinner cruise, with Johann Strauss waltzes as background music. **Brandner Schifffart** offers the same kind of cruises between Krems and Melk, in the heart of the Danube Valley.

Most of the immaculate white-painted craft carry about 1,000 passengers each on their three decks. As soon as you get on board, give the steward a good tip for a deck chair and ask him or her to place it where you will get the best views. Be sure to book cabins in advance. Day trips are also possible on the Danube. You can use boats to move from one riverside community to the next. Along some sections, notably the Wachau, the only way to cross the river is to use the little shuttles (in the Wachau, these are special motorless boats that use the current to cross).

For the cruises up and down the Danube, the DDSG Blue Danube Steamship Company departs and arrives at Reichsbrücke near Vienna's Mexikoplatz. To reach the Reichsbrücke stop, you walk two blocks from the Vorgartenstrasse stop on the U1 subway toward the river. The DDSG stop is on the right side of the Reichsbrücke bridge. There is no pier number, but you board at Handelskai 265. Boat trips from Vienna to the Wachau run daily from May to September. The price is €23.70 one way and €28 round-trip. There are other daily cruises within the Wachau, such as from Melk to Krems. Other cruises, to Budapest, for instance, operate from April to early November. The website has dozens of options and timetables in English. For cruises from Krems to Melk, contact Brandner Schifffahrt. ⇨ *For more information, see the "Danube River Cruises" box in Chapter 7.*

Cruise Lines Brandner Schifffahrt
☎ 07433/259–021 ⊕ www.brandner.at. **DDSG/ Blue Danube Schifffahrt** ☎ 01/58880 ⊕ www.ddsg-blue-danube.at.

▌ TRAIN TRAVEL

Austrian train service is excellent: it's fast and, for Western Europe, relatively inexpensive, particularly if you take advantage of discount fares. Trains on the mountainous routes are slow, but no slower than driving, and the scenery is gorgeous. Many of the remote rail routes will give you a look at traditional Austria, complete with Alpine cabins tacked onto mountainsides and a backdrop of snowcapped peaks.

Austrian Federal Railways trains are identifiable by the letters that precede the train number on the timetables and posters. The IC (InterCity) or EC (EuroCity) trains are fastest. EN trains have

sleeping facilities. The EC trains usually have a dining car with fairly good food. The trains originating in Budapest have good Hungarian cooking. Otherwise there is usually a fellow with a cart serving snacks and hot and cold drinks. Most trains are equipped with a card telephone in or near the restaurant car.

The difference between *erste Klasse* (first class), and *zweite Klasse* (second class) on Austrian trains is mainly a matter of space. First- and second-class sleepers and couchettes (six to a compartment) are available on international runs, as well as on long trips within Austria. Women traveling alone may book special compartments on night trains or long-distance rides (ask for a *Damenabteil*). If you have a car but would rather watch the scenery than the traffic, you can put your car on a train in Vienna and accompany it to Salzburg, Innsbruck, Feldkirch, or Villach: you relax in a compartment or sleeper for the trip, and the car is unloaded when you arrive.

Allow yourself plenty of time to purchase your ticket before boarding the train. IC and EC tickets are also valid on D (express), E (*Eilzug*; semi-fast), and local trains. For information, unless you speak German fairly well, it's a good idea to have your hotel call for you. You may also ask for an operator who speaks English. You can reserve a seat for €3.50 (€3 online) up until four hours before departure. Be sure to do this on the main-line trains (Vienna–Innsbruck, Salzburg–Klagenfurt, Vienna–Graz, for example) at peak holiday times.

For train schedules from the Austrian rail service, the ÖBB, ask at your hotel, stop in at the train station and look for large posters labeled "*Abfahrt*" (departures) and "*Ankunft*" (arrivals), or log on to the website. In the Abfahrt listing you'll find the departure time in the main left-hand block of the listing and, under the train name, details of where it stops en route and the time of each arrival. There is also information about connecting trains and buses, with departure details. Working days are symbolized by two crossed hammers, which means that the same schedule might not apply on weekends or holidays. A little rocking horse sign means that a special playpen has been set up on the train for children.

There's a wide choice of rail routes to Austria, but check services first; long-distance passenger service across the continent is undergoing considerable reduction. There is regular service from London's St. Pancras station to Vienna via Brussels and Frankfurt; the fastest journey time is 13 hours, 55 minutes. An alternative is to travel via Paris, where you can change to an overnight train to Salzburg and Vienna. Be sure to leave plenty of time between connections to change stations. First- and second-class sleepers and second-class couchettes are available as far as Innsbruck. Although rail fares from London to these destinations tend to be much more expensive than air fares, the advantages are that you'll see a lot more of the countryside en route and you'll travel from city center to city center.

Information **ÖBB (Österreichische Bundesbahnen)** ☎ *05/1717* ⊕ *www.oebb.at.*

ESSENTIALS

■ ACCOMMODATIONS

You can live like a king in a real castle in Austria or get by on a modest budget. Starting at the lower end, you can find a room in a private house or on a farm, or dormitory space in a youth hostel. Next up the line come the simpler pensions, many of them identified as *Frühstückspensionen* (bed-and-breakfasts). Then come *Gasthäuser,* the simpler country inns. Fancier pensions in cities can often cost as much as hotels; the difference lies in the services they offer. Most pensions, for example, do not staff the front desk around the clock. Among the hotels, you can find accommodations ranging from the most modest, with a shower and toilet down the hall, to the most elegant, with every possible amenity. Increasingly, more and more hotels in the lower to middle price range are including breakfast with the basic room charge, but check when booking. Room rates for hotels in the rural countryside can often include breakfast and one other meal (in rare cases, all three meals are included). It's worth remembering that in Austria the cheaper option will usually still bring high standards. Most village *gasthofs* take great pride in providing sparkling cleanliness and a warm welcome—and you'll often find they have spacious rooms of great character.

Lodgings in Austria are generally rated from one to five stars, depending mainly on the facilities offered and the price of accommodations rather than on more subjective attributes like charm and location. In general, five-star properties are top of the line, with every conceivable amenity and priced accordingly. The distinctions get blurrier the farther down the rating chain you go. There may be little difference between two- and three-star properties except perhaps the price. In practice, don't rely heavily on the star system, and always try to see the hotel and room before you book. That said, lodging standards are generally very good, and

even in one- and two-star properties you can usually be guaranteed a clean room and a private bath.

These German words might come in handy when booking a room: air-conditioning (*Klimaanlage*); private bath (*Privatbad*); bathtub (*Badewanne*); shower (*Dusche*); double bed (*Doppelbett*); twin beds (*Einzelbetten*).

All hotels listed *in this guide* have private bath unless otherwise noted. *Prices in the reviews are the lowest cost of a standard double room in high season.*

Most hotels and other lodgings require you to give your credit-card details before they will confirm your reservation. If you don't feel comfortable emailing this information, ask if you can fax it (some places even prefer faxes). Get confirmation by email or in writing and have a copy of it handy when you check in.

Be sure you understand the hotel's cancellation policy. Some places allow you to cancel without any kind of penalty—even if you prepaid to secure a discounted rate—if you cancel at least 24 hours in advance. Others require you to cancel a week in advance or penalize you the cost of one night. Small inns and B&Bs are most likely to require you to cancel far in advance. Most hotels allow children under a certain age to stay in their parents' room at no extra charge, but others

ONLINE BOOKING RESOURCES		
Barclay International Group	800/845–6636	www.barclayweb.com
Interhome	800/882–6864	www.interhome.us
Villas and Apartments Abroad	212/213–6435	www.vaanyc.com
Villas International	415/499–9490 or 800/221–2260	www.villasintl.com

charge for them as extra adults; find out the cut-off age for discounts.

The Vienna Tourism Board has a hotel assistance service.

Contacts. Vienna Tourist Information ☎ 01/24555 ⊕ www.wien.info.

APARTMENT AND HOUSE RENTALS

Rentals are an important part of the accommodations mix in Austria, with one-, two- or four-week rentals becoming increasingly popular. Most of the rental properties are owned privately by individuals, and often the main rental organizers are simply the local tourist offices. For rental apartments in Vienna, check out ⊕ *www.apartment.at* or ⊕ *www.netland.at/wien.*

CASTLES

Schlosshotels und Herrenhäuser in Österreich, or "Castle Hotels and Mansions in Austria," is an association of castles and palaces that have been converted into hotels. The quality of the accommodations varies with the property, but many have been beautifully restored and can be a memorable alternative to standard hotels. The website is in English and has plenty of photos. The association also lists a smattering of castles in the Czech Republic, Hungary, Slovenia, Croatia, and Italy.

Information Schlosshotels und Herrenhäuser in Österreich ☎ 062/459–0123 ⊕ *www.schlosshotels.co.at.*

HOME EXCHANGES

With a direct home exchange you stay in someone else's home while they stay in yours. Some outfits also deal with vacation homes, so you're not actually staying in someone's full-time residence, just their vacant weekend place.

Exchange Clubs Home Exchange.com ☎ *800/877–8723* ⊕ *www.homeexchange. com* ✉ *$118 for a 1-year membership.* **HomeLink International** ☎ *800/638–3841* ⊕ *www.homelink.org* ✉ *From $89 for a 1-year membership.* **Intervac U.S.** ☎ *866/884–7567* ⊕ *www.intervac-homeexchange.com* ✉ *$99 for 1-year membership.*

Austria has more than 100 government-sponsored youth hostels, for which you need an HI membership card. Inexpensively priced, these hostels are run by the Österreichischer Jugendherbergsverband and are popular with the backpack crowd, so be sure to reserve in advance.

Information Hostelling International— USA ☎ *0240/650–2100* ⊕ *www.hiusa.org.* **Österreichischer Jugendherbergsverband** ☎ *01/533–5353* ⊕ *www.oejhv.at.*

■ COMMUNICATIONS

INTERNET

Most hotels in Austria have worked hard to upgrade their Internet offerings, and the majority will offer some form of Internet access for your laptop, sometimes still via a LAN line, but often with Wi-Fi. Occasionally these services are offered free of charge; sometimes you have to pay. Hotels that don't offer Internet access in the rooms will usually have a computer somewhere in their business center or lobby available for guests to check email. Outside of hotels there are some, but not many, Internet cafés (ask at your hotel). A good number of cafés offer Wi-Fi to customers.

Contacts Cybercafés. The website lists more than 4,000 Internet cafés worldwide. ⊕ *www.cybercafes.com.*

CLOSE UP

Local Do's and Taboos

CUSTOMS OF THE COUNTRY

Austrians are keen observers of social niceties, and there are strongly embedded cultural norms for guiding behavior in all sorts of public interactions, ranging from buying a piece of meat from the butcher (be extremely polite) to offering your seat on the metro to an elderly or physically challenged person. In general, always err of the side of extreme politeness and deference (particularly to age).

GREETINGS

Greetings are an important part of day-to-day interaction with strangers. On entering a shop, it's customary to say *Grüss Gott* or *Guten Tag*, "good day," to the shopkeeper. Don't forget to say *Auf Wiedersehen*, "good-bye," on leaving. Austrians do like their academic titles. PhDs go as "Frau/Herr Doktor;" those who have a master's degree are addressed as "Frau/Herr Magister."

OUT ON THE TOWN

In busy restaurants at lunchtime it's not uncommon to have to share a table with strangers. You're not expected to make conversation across the table, but you should at least offer a tip-of-the-hat *Grüss Gott* when sitting down and a farewell *Auf Wiedersehen* on leaving. When your neighbor's food arrives, turn and wish him or her *Mahlzeit*, literally "mealtime," the Austrian-German equivalent of "bon appétit." When it comes to table manners, there are a few departures from standard American practice (beyond how one holds a knife and fork). Toothpicks are sometimes found on restaurant tables, and it's normal to see people clean their teeth after a meal, discreetly covering their mouth with their free hand. Austria is a dog-loving society, and you will often find dogs accompanying their masters to restaurants.

If you have the pleasure of being invited to someone's home for a meal, it's customary to bring a small gift, like a bouquet of flowers, a box of chocolates, or a bottle of wine.

DRESS (OR UNDRESS) CODE

Austrians tend to be far more comfortable with public nudity than Americans. Women routinely remove their tops on public beaches and in saunas at hotels. Resorts with saunas are usually used in the buff by both sexes, and a towel is optional. In many spas it will cause offense if you wear a swimsuit in the sauna, bringing frowns from other users or even intervention by the management.

LANGUAGE

German is the official language in Austria. One of the best ways to avoid being an Ugly American is to learn a little of the local language—Austrians are usually delighted if you at least try to speak German. In larger cities and most resorts you will usually have no problem finding people who speak English; hotel employees in particular speak it reasonably well, and many young Austrians speak it at least passably. However, travelers do report that they often find themselves in stores, restaurants, and train and bus stations where it's hard to find someone who speaks English—so it's best to have some native phrases up your sleeve. Note that all public announcements on trams, subways, and buses are in German. Train announcements are usually given in English as well, but if you have any questions, try to get answers before boarding.

PHONES

The good news is that you can now make a direct-dial telephone call from virtually any point on earth. The bad news? You can't always do so cheaply. Calling from a hotel is almost always the most expensive option; hotels usually add huge surcharges to all calls, particularly international ones. In some countries you can phone from call centers or even the post office. Calling cards usually keep costs to a minimum, but only if you purchase them locally. Cell phone calls are nearly always a much cheaper option than calling from your hotel.

When calling Austria, the country code is 43. When dialing an Austrian number from abroad, drop the initial 0 from the local Austrian area code. For instance, the full number to dial for the Hotel Sacher in Vienna from America is 011 (international dial code) –43 (Austria's country code) –1 (Vienna's full city code is 01, but drop the 0) and –514–560 (the hotel number). All numbers given *in this guide* include the city or town area code.

CALLING WITHIN AUSTRIA

As the number of cell phones has risen in Austria, the number of coin-operated pay telephones has dwindled. If you find one, a local call costs from €0.14 to €0.60, depending on whether you call a landline or a cell phone. Most pay phones have instructions in English.

When placing a long-distance call to a destination within Austria, dial the local area codes with the initial zero (for instance, 0662 for Salzburg). Note that calls within Austria are one-third cheaper between 6 pm and 8 am on weekdays and from 1 pm on Saturday to 8 am on Monday.

For information about phone numbers inside and outside of Austria, dial 118–877. Most operators speak some English; if yours doesn't, you'll most likely be passed along to one who does.

CALLING OUTSIDE AUSTRIA

It costs more to telephone from Austria than it does to telephone to Austria. Although nearly everyone now uses their cell phone for all calls, international or otherwise, it is still possible to make inexpensive calls from some post offices, and you can get helpful assistance in placing a long-distance call; in large cities these centers at main post offices (*Hauptpostamt*) are open around the clock. To use a post office phone you first go to the counter to be directed to a certain telephone cabin; after your call you return to the counter and pay your bill. Faxes can be sent from post offices and received as well, but neither service is very cheap.

To make a collect call—you can't do this from pay phones—dial the operator and ask for an *R-Gespräch* (pronounced air-ga-*shprayk*). Most operators speak English; if yours doesn't, you'll be passed to one who does.

The country code for the United States is 1.

U.S. Phone Access Codes from Austria
AT&T Direct ☎ *800/331–0500 in the U.S, 916/843–4685 for 24/7 support outside the U.S.* ⊕ *www.att.com.* **MCI Verizon Worldwide Access** ☎ *800/999–762.*

CALLING CARDS

If you plan to make calls from pay phones, a Telecom Austria calling card is a convenience. You can buy calling cards with a credit of €10 or €15 at any post office or Telecom Austria shop, and they can be used at any public phone booth. Insert the card, punch in your access code, and dial the number; the cost of the call is automatically deducted from the card—note that the "credits" displayed is not usually the amount of money left on the card, but a different sort of counter. A few public phones in the cities also take American Express, Diners Club, MasterCard, and Visa credit cards.

MOBILE PHONES

In Austria a cell phone is called a *Handy*. If you have a GSM cell phone, you can probably use your phone abroad. Roaming fees are generally being dramatically reduced by most phone companies. As soon as you switch your phone on after arriving you are likely to get a message from your provider telling you exactly how much it will be to call home or to receive calls. It's almost always cheaper to send a text message than to make a call, because text messages have a very low set fee.

If you just want to make local calls, consider buying a new SIM card (note that your provider may have to unlock your phone for you to use a different SIM card) and a prepaid service plan in the destination. You'll then have a local number and can make local calls at local rates. If your trip is extensive, you could also simply buy a new cell phone in your destination, as the initial cost will be offset over time.

■ TIP→ If you travel internationally frequently, save one of your old cell phones or buy a cheap one on the Internet; ask your cell phone company to unlock it for you, and take it with you as a travel phone, buying a new SIM card with pay-as-you-go service in each destination.

If you want to use your own cell phone in Austria, first find out if it's compatible with the European 1800 GSM standard. Once in Austria, stop by a cell phone store, usually identifiable by the word "Handy" in the name, and purchase a prepaid SIM card (make sure your existing SIM card is unlocked). Prepaid cards start at around €15. Local calls are then billed at about €0.15 to €0.20 a minute. If you don't have a phone but want to use one here, look into buying a used phone. Rates are reasonable. Buy the prepaid card in the same way you would as if you were bringing in your own phone.

When dialing an Austrian "Handy" from abroad (generally 0676, 0699, or 0664), dial 00–43, then the number without the 0.

Contacts Cellular Abroad. This company rents and sells GMS phones and sells SIM cards that work in many countries. ☎ *800/287–5072* ⊕ *www.cellularabroad.com.* **Mobal.** You can rent cell phones and buy GSM phones (starting at $29) that will operate in 190 countries. Per-call rates vary throughout the world. ☎ *888/888–9162* ⊕ *www.mobal.com.* **Planet Fone.** Cell phones can be rented from $21, but the per-minute rates are expensive. ☎ *888/988–4777* ⊕ *www.planetfone.com.*

∎ EATING OUT

When dining out, you'll get the best value at simpler restaurants. Most post menus with prices outside. If you begin with the *Würstelstand* (sausage vendor) on the street, the next category would be the *Imbiss-Stube,* for simple, quick snacks. Many meat stores serve soups and a daily special at noon; a blackboard menu will be posted outside. Many cafés also offer lunch. *Gasthäuser* are simple restaurants or country inns. Austrian hotels have some of the best restaurants in the country, often with outstanding chefs. In the past few years the restaurants along the autobahns, especially the chain Rosenberger, have developed into very good places to eat (besides being, in many cases, architecturally interesting). Some Austrian chain restaurants offer excellent value for the money, such as the schnitzel chains Wienerwald and Schnitzelhaus and the excellent seafood chain Nordsee. You can also grab a quick sandwich made from a wide variety of scrumptious whole-wheat breads at bakery chains such as Anker, Felber, and Mann. With migration from Turkey and Northern Africa on the rise, thousands of small kebab restaurants have set up shop all over Austria, offering both Middle Eastern fare and sometimes pizza at a reasonable rate. The latest fad is the Asian noodle lunchbox, available at many sausage vendors.

■ TIP→ In all restaurants be aware that the basket of bread put on your table isn't free. Most of the older-style Viennese restaurants charge €0.70–€1.25 for each roll that is eaten, but more and more establishments are beginning to charge a per-person cover charge—anywhere from €1.50 to €5—which includes all the bread you want, plus usually an herb spread and butter. Tap water (*Leitungswasser*) in Austria comes straight from the Alps and is some of the purest in the world. Be aware, however, that a few restaurants in touristy areas are beginning to charge for tap water.

Austrians are manic about food quality and using agricultural techniques that are in harmony with the environment. The country has the largest number of organic farms in Europe, as well as some of the most stringent food-quality standards. An increasing number of restaurants use food and produce from local farmers, ensuring the freshest ingredients for their guests.

MEALS AND MEALTIMES

Besides the normal three meals—*Frühstück* (breakfast), *Mittagessen* (lunch), and *Abendessen* (dinner)—Austrians sometimes throw in a few snacks in between, or forego one meal for a snack. The day begins with an early continental breakfast of rolls and coffee. *Gabelfrühstück*, normally served a little later in the morning, is a slightly more substantial breakfast with eggs or cold meat. Lunch is usually served between noon and 2, although in some country districts where work, particularly agricultural, might start very early in the morning, you will see people eating lunch from 11 am. An afternoon *Jause* (coffee with cake) is taken at teatime. A light supper would traditionally be eaten between 6 and 9, but tending toward the later hour, and dinner in the evening, as the main meal of the day, is increasingly the norm. Many restaurant kitchens close in the afternoon, but some post a notice saying *durchgehend warme Küche,* meaning that hot food is available even between regular mealtimes. In Vienna some restaurants go on serving until 1 and 2 am, a tiny number also through the night. The rest of Austria is more conservative.

Unless otherwise noted, the restaurants listed *in this guide* are open daily for lunch and dinner.

PAYING

Prices in the reviews are the average cost of a main course at dinner or, if dinner is not served, at lunch.

⇨ *For guidelines on tipping see Tipping below.*

RESERVATIONS AND DRESS

Regardless of where you are, it's a good idea to make a reservation if you can. In some places it's expected. We mention reservations specifically only when they are essential (there's no other way you'll ever get a table) or when they are not accepted. For popular restaurants, book as far ahead as you can (often 30 days), and reconfirm as soon as you arrive. (Large parties should always call ahead to check the reservations policy.) We mention dress only when men are required to wear a jacket or a jacket and tie.

WINES, BEER, AND SPIRITS

Austrian wines range from unpretentious *Heurigen* whites to world-class varietals. Look for the light, fruity white *Grüner Veltliner*, intensely fragrant golden *Traminer*, full-bodied red *Blaufränkischer*, and the lighter red *Zweigelt*. Sparkling wine is called *Sekt*, some of the best coming from the Kamptal region northwest of Vienna. Some of the best sweet dessert wines in the world (Spätlesen) come from Burgenland. Austrian beer rivals that of Germany for quality. Each area has its own brewery and local beer, to which people are loyal. A specialty unique to Austria is the dark, sweet Dunkles beer. Look for Kaiser Doppelmalz in Vienna. Schnapps is an after-dinner tradition in Austria; many restaurants offer several varieties, and it is not uncommon for the management to offer a complimentary Schnapps at the end of a meal. One of the most popular is that made from the William pear, and given the nickname, a "little Willy."

▌ELECTRICITY

The electrical current in Austria is 220 volts, 50 cycles alternating current (AC); wall outlets take Continental-type plugs, with two round prongs.

Consider making a small investment in a universal adapter, which has several types of plugs in one lightweight, compact unit. Most laptops and cell phone chargers are dual voltage (i.e., they operate equally well on 110 and 220 volts), so require only an adapter. These days the same is true of small appliances such as hair dryers. Always check labels and manufacturer instructions to be sure. Don't use 110-volt outlets marked "for shavers only" for high-wattage appliances such as hair dryers.

Contacts Walkabout Travel Gear.
This company has a good coverage of electricity under "adapters."
⊕ www.walkabouttravelgear.com.

▌EMERGENCIES

On the street, some German phrases that may be needed in an emergency are: *Hilfe!* (Help!), *Notfall* (emergency), *Rettungswagen* (ambulance), *Feuerwehr* (fire department), *Polizei* (police), *Arzt* (doctor), and *Krankenhaus* (hospital).

Foreign Embassies Consulate of the U.S./ Passport Division ⊠ *Parkring 12a, 1st District, Vienna* ☎ *01/313–3975–35, 01/313–390 for after-hours emergencies* ⊕ *austria.usembassy. gov.* **Embassy of the United States** ⊠ *Boltzmanngasse 16, 9th District, Vienna* ☎ *01/31–339–0* ⊕ *austria.usembassy.gov.*

General Emergency Contacts Ambulance ☎ *144.* **Fire** ☎ *122.* **Police** ☎ *133.*

▌HEALTH

Travel in Austria poses no specific or unusual health risks. The tap water is generally safe to drink—in fact, Austrians are obsessed about water quality and it is some of the purest in the world. If in doubt, buy bottled water—available

everywhere. The only potential risk worth mentioning is tick-bite encephalitis, which is only a danger if you're planning to do extensive cycling or hiking in the backcountry.

OVER-THE-COUNTER REMEDIES

You must buy over-the-counter remedies in an *Apotheke*, and most personnel speak enough English to understand what you need. Try using the generic name for a drug, rather than its brand name. You may find over-the-counter remedies for headaches and colds less effective than those sold in the United States. Austrians are firm believers in natural remedies, such as homeopathic medicines and herbal teas.

SHOTS AND MEDICATIONS

No special shots are required before visiting Austria, but if you will be cycling or hiking through the eastern or southeastern parts of the country, get inoculated against encephalitis; it can be carried by ticks.

Health Warnings National Centers for Disease Control & Prevention (*CDC*). ☎ *800/232–4636 international travelers' health line* ⊕ *www.cdc.gov/travel.* **World Health Organization** (*WHO*). ⊕ *www.who.int.*

Contact Transportation Security Administration (*TSA*). ⊕ *www.tsa.gov.*

■ HOURS OF OPERATION

In most cities banks are open weekdays 8–3, Thursday until 5:30 pm. Lunch hour is from 12:30 to 1:30 pm. All banks are closed on Saturday, but you can change money at various locations, such as American Express (which has an office in Vienna open on Saturday from 9 to noon) and major train stations, open around the clock; changing machines are also found here and there in the larger cities.

Gas stations on the major autobahns are open 24 hours a day, but in smaller towns and villages you can expect them to close early in the evening and on Sunday. You can usually count on at least one station to stay open on Sunday and holidays in most medium-size towns, and buying gas in larger cities is usually not a problem.

Pharmacies (called *Apotheken* in German) are usually open from 9 to 6, with a midday break between noon and 2 pm. In each area of the city one pharmacy stays open 24 hours; if a pharmacy is closed, a sign on the door will tell you the address of the nearest one that's open. Call ☎ *01/1550* for names and addresses (in German) of pharmacies open that night.

In many villages and small towns shops still keep the custom of half-day closing one day a week, usually Tuesday or Wednesday, so don't be surprised to find an apparent ghost town on those days. Shops usually close at 12:30 pm and place the sign *Ruhetag* (rest day) in the window or door. Hotels sometimes follow suit—they will be open, but the front desk will not be manned and, typically, a welcome note will be left with your key. It is also common in country areas for shops to close from midday on Saturday until Monday morning.

HOLIDAYS

All banks and shops are closed on national holidays: New Year's Day; Jan. 6, Epiphany; Easter Sunday and Monday; May 1, May Day; Ascension Day (6th Thursday after Easter); Pentecost Sunday and Monday; Corpus Christi; Aug. 15, Assumption; Oct. 26, National Holiday; Nov. 1, All Saints' Day; Dec. 8, Immaculate Conception; Dec. 25–26, Christmas. Museums are open on most holidays, but are closed on Good Friday, Dec. 24 and 25, and New Year's Day. Banks and offices are closed on Dec. 8, but most shops are open.

■ MAIL

All mail goes by air, so there's no supplement on letters or postcards. Within Europe a letter or postcard of up to 20 grams (about ¾ ounce) costs €0.65; to the United States or Canada, it's €1.40. Up to 50 grams costs €1.30 for Europe and €2.05 for the United States or Canada. If in doubt, mail your letters from a post office and have the weight checked. The Austrian post office also adheres strictly to a size standard; if your letter or card is outside the norm, you'll have to pay a surcharge. Always place an airmail sticker on your letters or cards. Shipping packages from Austria to destinations outside the country can be expensive.

You can also have mail held at any Austrian post office; letters should be marked *Poste Restante* or *Postlagernd*. You will be asked for identification when you collect mail.

SHIPPING PACKAGES

For overnight services, Federal Express, DHL, and UPS service Austria; check with your hotel concierge for the nearest address and telephone number.

■ MONEY

ATMS AND BANKS

Your own bank will probably charge a fee for using ATMs abroad; the foreign bank you use may also charge a fee. Nevertheless, you'll usually get a better rate of exchange at an ATM than you will at a currency-exchange office or even when changing money in a bank. And extracting funds as you need them is a safer option than carrying around a large amount of cash.

■TIP→ PIN numbers with more than four digits are not recognized at ATMs in many countries. If yours has five or more, remember to change it before you leave.

Called *Bankomats* and fairly common throughout Austria, ATMs are one of the easiest ways to get euros. Cirrus and Plus locations are easily found throughout large city centers and even in small towns. Look for branches of one of the larger banks, including Bank Austria, Raiffeisen, BAWAG, or Erste Bank. These are all likely to have a bank machine attached somewhere nearby. If you have trouble finding one, ask your hotel concierge. Note, too, that you may have better luck with ATMs if you're using a credit card or debit card that's also a Visa or MasterCard rather than just your bank card.

ATM Locations Cirrus ☎ *1–800/627–8372* ⊕ *www.mastercard.us/cardholder-services/ atm-locator.html.* **Plus** ☎ *800/843–7587* ⊕ *www.visa.com.*

CREDIT CARDS

It's a good idea to inform your credit-card company before you travel, especially if you're going abroad and don't travel internationally very often. Otherwise, the credit-card company might put a hold on your card owing to unusual activity—not a good thing halfway through your trip. Record all your credit-card numbers—as well as the phone numbers to call if your cards are lost or stolen—in a safe place, so you're prepared should something go wrong. Both MasterCard and Visa have general numbers you can call (collect if you're abroad) if your card is lost, but you're better off calling the number of your issuing bank, since MasterCard and Visa usually just transfer you to your bank; your bank's number is usually printed on your card.

If you plan to use your credit card for cash advances, you'll need to apply for a PIN at least two weeks before your trip. Although it's usually cheaper (and safer) to use a credit card abroad for large purchases (so you can cancel payments or

be reimbursed if there's a problem), note that some credit-card companies *and* the banks that issue them add substantial percentages to all foreign transactions, whether they're in a foreign currency or not. Check on these fees before leaving home, so there won't be any surprises when you get the bill.

■TIP→ Before you charge something, ask the merchant whether or not he or she plans to do a dynamic currency conversion (DCC). In such a transaction the credit-card processor (shop, restaurant, or hotel, not Visa or MasterCard) converts the currency and charges you in dollars. In most cases you'll pay the merchant a 3% fee for this service in addition to any credit-card company and issuing-bank foreign-transaction surcharges.

Dynamic currency conversion programs are becoming increasingly widespread. Merchants who participate in them are supposed to ask whether you want to be charged in dollars or the local currency, but they don't always do so. And even if they do offer you a choice, they may well avoid mentioning the surcharges. The good news is that you *do* have a choice. And if this practice really gets your goat, you can avoid it entirely thanks to American Express; with its cards DCC simply isn't an option. However, many establishments in Europe prefer MasterCard or Visa to American Express because of the high commission that the latter charges.

Reporting Lost Cards American Express ☎ *800/992–3404 in U.S., 336/393–1111 collect from abroad* ⊕ *www.americanexpress. com.* **Diners Club** ☎ *800/234–6377 in U.S., 303/799–1504 collect from abroad* ⊕ *www. dinersclub.com.* **Discover** ☎ *800/347–2683 in U.S., 801/902–3100 collect from abroad* ⊕ *www.discovercard.com.* **MasterCard** ☎ *800/627–8372 in U.S., 636/722–7111 collect from abroad* ⊕ *www.mastercard.com.* **Visa** ☎ *800/847–2911 in U.S., 0800/200–288 collect from Austria* ⊕ *www.visa.com.*

CURRENCY AND EXCHANGE

Austria is a member of the European Union (EU) and its currency is the euro. Under the euro system there are eight coins: 1 and 2 euros, plus 1, 2, 5, 10, 20, and 50 euro cents. All coins have one side that has the value of the euro on it and the other side with a country's own national symbol. There are seven banknotes: 5, 10, 20, 50, 100, 200, and 500 euros. Banknotes are the same for all EU countries.

At this writing, the euro continues to hold strong against the U.S. dollar, and one euro was worth about $1.34.

Although fees charged for ATM transactions may be higher abroad than at home, Cirrus and Plus exchange rates are excellent, because they are based on wholesale rates offered only by major banks. Otherwise, the most favorable rates are through a bank. You won't do as well at exchange booths in airports or train and bus stations, in hotels, in restaurants, or in stores, although you may find their hours more convenient than the banks'.

■ TIP→ Even if a currency-exchange booth has a sign promising no commission, rest assured that there's some kind of huge, hidden fee (oh, that's right. The sign didn't say "no fee.") And as for rates, you're almost always better off getting foreign currency at an ATM or exchanging money at a bank.

Contacts **American Express** ☎ 888/412–6945 in U.S., 0800/232–340 collect in Austria to add value or speak to customer service ⊕ www.americanexpress.com.

Currency Conversion **Google**. For currency conversion just type in the amount you want to convert and an explanation of how you want it converted (e.g., "14 euros in dollars"), and then voilà. ⊕ www.google.com. **Oanda. com**. This site not only converts specific amounts, it also allows you to print out a handy table with the current day's conversion rates. ⊕ www.oanda.com. **XE.com**. This is a good currency-conversion website. ⊕ www. xe.com.

▮ PACKING

Austrians, particularly the Viennese, are dapper dressers. Packing "musts" include at least one nice shirt and sport coat for men and a casual but stylish dress or shirt and skirt combination for women. These will see you through nearly any occasion, from a decent dinner out on the town to a night at the opera. Note that Austrians dress nicely for the opera and the theater. Men should bring a nice pair of dress shoes, because this is a wardrobe staple to which the locals pay particular attention. As a general rule of thumb, the more expensive the shoes, the more respect you're likely to get. High on the list, too, would be comfortable walking or hiking shoes. Austria is a walking country, in cities and mountains alike. And because an evening outside at a *Heurige* (wine garden) may be on your agenda, be sure to take a sweater or light wrap; evenings tend to get cool even in the summer. Music lovers might consider toting those rarely used opera glasses; the cheaper seats, understandably, are usually far from the action (and standby tickets will have you craning your neck at the back). However, opera glasses are usually available for a modest fee.

If you are heading into the mountains, bring sunscreen, even in winter. Sunglasses are a must as well—make sure that they block lateral rays. Boots that rise above the ankle and have sturdy soles are best for hiking. Consider packing a small folding umbrella for the odd deluge, or a waterproof windbreaker. Mosquitoes can become quite a bother in summer around the lakes and along the rivers, especially the Danube. Bring or buy some good insect repellent.

SHIPPING LUGGAGE AHEAD

Imagine globe-trotting with only a carry-on in tow. Shipping your luggage in advance via an air-freight service is a great way to cut down on backaches, hassles, and stress—especially if your packing list includes strollers, car seats, and so on.

There are some things to be aware of, though. First, research carry-on restrictions; if you absolutely need something that isn't practical to ship and isn't allowed in carry-ons, this strategy isn't for you. Second, plan to send your bags several days in advance to U.S. destinations and as much as two weeks in advance to some international destinations. Third, plan to spend some money: it will cost at least $100 to send a small piece of luggage, a golf bag, or a pair of skis to a domestic destination, much more to places overseas. Some people use Federal Express to ship their bags, but this can cost even more than airfreight services. All these services insure your bag (for most, the limit is $1,000, but you should verify that amount); you can, however, purchase additional insurance for about $1 per $100 of value.

Contacts **Luggage Concierge** ☎ 800/288–9818 ⊕ www.luggageconcierge.com. **Luggage Free** ☎ 800/361–6871 ⊕ www.luggagefree.com.

▌ PASSPORTS AND VISAS

U.S. citizens need only a valid passport to enter Austria for stays of up to three months.

▌TIP➜ Before your trip, make two copies of your passport's data page (one for someone at home and another for you to carry separately). Or scan the page and email it to someone at home and/or yourself.

▌ RESTROOMS

Vienna has a scattering of public toilets that are suitably clean and cost about €0.50 to use. Metro stations invariably have decent public facilities. Public toilets are less common outside the big cities, but you can usually use the facilities of hotels and restaurants without too much fuss. It's courteous to purchase something in a bar or restaurant beforehand, but this is rarely a problem and nothing that can't usually be resolved with a smile and a *Danke*. Gas stations along highways usually have restrooms attached, and these are generally open to the public whether you purchase gas or not. Cleanliness standards vary, but are usually on the acceptable side.

Find a Loo **The Bathroom Diaries.** Flush with unsanitized info on restrooms the world over—each one located, reviewed, and rated. ⊕ www.thebathroomdiaries.com.

▌ SAFETY

Austrians are remarkably honest in their everyday dealings, and Vienna, given its size, is a refreshingly safe and secure city. That said, be sure to watch your purses and wallets in crowded spaces like subways and trams, and to take the standard precautions when walking at night along empty streets. The number of pickpocketing incidents has increased over the years. Be particularly careful if you're traveling with a bicycle. Here, as everywhere else, bikes routinely go missing. Always lock your bike firmly.

▌TIP➜ Distribute your cash, credit cards, IDs, and other valuables between a deep front pocket, an inside jacket or vest pocket, and a hidden money pouch. Don't reach for the money pouch once you're in public.

▌ TAXES

The Value Added Tax (V.A.T.) in Austria is 20% generally, but this is reduced to 10% on food and clothing and certain tourism services. If you are planning to take your purchases with you when you leave Austria (export them), you can get a refund. Wine and spirits are heavily taxed—nearly half of the sale price goes to taxes. For every contract signed in Austria (for example, car-rental agreements), you pay an extra 1% tax to the government, so tax on a rental car is 21%.

When making a purchase, ask for a V.A.T. refund form and find out whether the merchant gives refunds—not all stores do, nor are they required to. Have the form stamped like any customs form by customs officials when you leave the country, or if you're visiting several European Union countries, when you leave the EU. After you're through passport control, take the form to a refund-service counter for an on-the-spot refund (which is usually the quickest and easiest option), or mail it to the address on the form (or the envelope with it) after you arrive home. You receive the total refund stated on the form, but the processing time can be long, especially if you request a credit-card adjustment.

Global Refund is a Europe-wide service with 225,000 affiliated stores and more than 700 refund counters at major airports and border crossings. Its refund form, called a Tax Free Check, is the most common across the European continent. The service issues refunds in the form of cash, check, or credit-card adjustment.

V.A.T. Refunds Global Refund
⊕ *www.globalrefund.com.*

▌ TIME

The time difference between New York and Austria is six hours (so when it's noon in New York, it's 6 pm in Vienna). The time difference between London and Vienna is one hour; between Sydney and Vienna, eight hours (when it's noon in Sydney, it's 4 am in Vienna); and between Auckland and Vienna, 10 hours (when it's noon in Auckland, it's 2 am in Vienna).

Time Zones Time and Date.com
⊕ *www.timeanddate.com/worldclock.*

▌ TIPPING

Although virtually all hotels and restaurants include service charges in their rates, tipping is still customary, but at a level lower than in the United States. In very small country inns such tips are not expected but are appreciated. In family-run establishments, tips are generally not given to immediate family members, only to employees. Tip the hotel concierge only for special services or in response to special requests. Maids normally get no tip unless your stay is a week or more or service has been special. Big tips are not usual in Austrian restaurants, since 10% has already been included in the prices.

▌ TOURS

Guided tours are a good option when you don't want to do it all yourself. You travel along with a group (sometimes large, sometimes small), stay in prebooked hotels, eat with your fellow travelers (the cost of meals is sometimes included in the price of your tour, sometimes not), and follow a schedule. But not all guided tours are an if-it's-Tuesday-this-must-be-Belgium experience. A knowledgeable guide can take you places that you might never discover on your own, and you may be pushed to see more than you would have otherwise. Tours aren't for everyone, but they can be just the thing for trips to places where making travel arrangements is difficult or time-consuming (particularly when you don't speak the language). Whenever you book a guided tour, find out what's included and what isn't. A "land-only" tour includes all your travel (by bus, in most cases) in the destination, but not necessarily your flights to and from or even within it. Also, in most cases prices in tour brochures don't include fees and taxes. And remember that you'll be expected to tip your guide (in cash) at the end of the tour.

Among companies that sell tours to Austria, the following are nationally known, have a proven reputation, and offer plenty of options. The classifications used here represent different price categories, and you'll probably encounter these terms when talking to a travel agent or tour operator. The key difference is usually in accommodations. Note that each company doesn't schedule tours to Austria every year; check by calling.

Super-Deluxe Abercrombie & Kent
☎ *800/554–7016* ⊕ *www.abercrombiekent. com.* **Travcoa** ☎ *888/979–4044*
⊕ *www.travcoa.com.*

Deluxe **Globus** ☎ *866/755–858* ⊕ *www.globusjourneys.com.* **Maupintour** ☎ *800/255–4266* ⊕ *www.maupintour.com.*

First-Class **Brendan Tours** ☎ *800/421–8446* ⊕ *www.brendanvacations.com.* **Trafalgar Tours** ☎ *866/544–4434* ⊕ *www.trafalgartours.com.*

Budget **Cosmos** ☎ *800/276–1241* ⊕ *www.cosmos.com.* **Trafalgar Tours.** Trafalgar Tours (see above). ☎ *866/544–4434* ⊕ *www.trafalgartours.com.*

SPECIAL-INTEREST TOURS

BIKING

The Austrian national tourist information website, ⊕ *www.austria.info,* includes excellent sections on hotels that welcome cyclists, as well as some of the better-known tours and routes.

You can no longer rent a bike at train stations in Austria. The cost of renting a bike (21-gear) from a local agency is around €35 a day. Tourist offices have details (in German), including maps and hints for trip planning and mealtime and overnight stops that cater especially to cyclists. Ask for the booklet "Radtouren in Österreich" or go to the website ⊕ *www.radtouren.at.* There's also a brochure in English: "Biking Austria—On the Trail of Mozart" that provides details in English on the cycle route through the High Tauern mountains in Salzburg Province and neighboring regions in Bavaria (⊕ *www.mozartradweg.com*).

E-bikes are becoming increasingly popular and are widely available for rent. Small electric motors make cycling up hills easy and increase the range of routes you can tackle in a day. You still have to pedal and can choose how much input you want the motor to make. A network of battery stations—at shops, gas stations and even mountain huts—means you can exchange a waning battery for a fully charged one at suitable intervals.

■ TIP→ Most airlines accommodate bikes as luggage, provided they're dismantled and boxed.

Contacts **Austria Radreisen** ☎ *07712/5511–0* ⊕ *www.austria-radreisen. at.* **Backroads** ☎ *800/462–2848* ⊕ *www. backroads.com.* **Butterfield & Robinson** ☎ *866/551–9090 from the U.S., 800/678–1477 from other countries* ⊕ *www.butterfield.com.* **Euro-Bike Tours** ☎ *800/575–1540* ⊕ *www. eurobike.com.* **Mountain Bike Hotels.** This is a good resource for finding biking hotels. ☎ *0810/101818* ⊕ *www.austria.info.* **Pedal Power** ☎ *01/729–7234* ⊕ *www.pedalpower. at.* **VBT (Vermont Biking Tours)** ☎ *800/245–3868* ⊕ *www.vbt.com.*

CHRISTMAS/NEW YEAR'S

Contacts **Annemarie Victory Organization.** Annemarie Victory Organization is known for its spectacular "New Year's Eve Ball in Vienna" excursion. Annemarie Victory also organizes a "Christmas in Salzburg" trip, with rooms at the Goldener Hirsch and a side trip to the Silent Night Chapel in Oberndorf. Annemarie is Austrian—her family still owns a castle there—and says she can obtain the very best tickets for the balls. ☎ *212/486–0353* ⊕ *www. annemarievictory.com.* **Smolka Tours.** Festive holiday-season tours include concerts, gala balls, and the famous Christmas Markets of Vienna and Salzburg. ☎ *800/722–0057* ⊕ *www.smolkatours.com.*

ECO TOURS

Austria is a popular vacation spot for those who want to experience nature—many rural hotels offer idyllic bases for hiking in the mountains or lake areas. The concept of the *Urlaub am Bauernhof* (farm vacation), where families can stay on a working farm and children can help take care of farm animals, is increasingly popular throughout Austria. There are numerous outfitters that can provide information on basic as well as specialty farms, such as organic farms or farms for children, for people with disabilities, or for horseback riders.

Contacts **Austrian Tourist Board** ☎ *212/944–6880 in the U.S., 416/967–3381 in Canada* ⊕ *www.austria.info.* **Naturidyll Hotels.** You might have to get your search engine to translate the German-only, but you'll find a good choice of hotels that focus on nature, and plenty of photos to show what the accommodations look like. ☎ *01/867–3660– 16, 0800/80-18-400 reservations* ⊕ *www.naturidyll.at.*

Information on Farm Vacations Farmhouse Holidays in Austria. Based in Salzburg, this company has an English language website and online booking. ⊕ *www.farmholidays.com.* **Kärnten/Landesverband Urlaub auf dem Bauernhof.** This company is based in Carinthia and has an English language website. ⊕ *www. urlaubambauernhof.com.* **Oberösterreich/Das Land vor den Alpen.** An English-language website for farm vacations in Upper Austria. ☎ *050/69-02-1248* ⊕ *www.farmholidays. com.* **Salzburg/Das Land der Tradition** ☎ *0662/870-571-248* ⊕ *www.salzburg. farmholidays.com.* **Tyrol/Das Land der Berge** ☎ *05/9292-1172* ⊕ *www.bauernhof.cc.*

HIKING AND MOUNTAIN CLIMBING

With more than 50,000 km (about 35,000 miles) of well-maintained mountain paths through Europe's largest reserve of unspoiled landscape, the country is a hiker's paradise. Three long-distance routes traverse Austria, including the E-6 from the Baltic, cutting across mid-Austria via the Wachau valley region of the Danube and on to the Adriatic. Wherever you are in Austria, you will find shorter hiking trails requiring varying degrees of ability. Routes are well marked, and maps are readily available from bookstores, the Österreichische Alpenverein/ÖAV, and the automobile clubs.

If you're a newcomer to mountain climbing or want to improve your skill, schools in Salzburg province will take you on. Ask the ÖAV for addresses. All organize courses and guided tours for beginners as well as for more advanced climbers.

Tourist offices have details on hiking holidays; serious climbers can write directly to Österreichischer Alpenverein/ÖAV (Austrian Alpine Club) for more information. Membership in the club (€55, about $74) will give you a 30%–50% reduction on the regular fees for overnights in the 275 mountain refuges it operates in Austria and for huts operated by other mountain organizations in Europe. Membership also includes accident insurance for vacations of up to six weeks. Young people up to 25 and senior-citizen memberships have a reduced price.

Contacts Inn Travel. Though based in the U.K., this company is happy to arrange hiking and walking tours in Austria for clients from the U.S. ☎ *+44 1653/617001 from outside U.K.* ⊕ *www.inntravel.co.uk.* **Österreichischer Alpenverein** ☎ *0512/59547* ⊕ *www.alpenverein.at.*

▌ RESOURCES

ONLINE TRAVEL TOOLS

All About Austria "About Austria." This is a nice general overview of facts and figures. ⊕ *www.aboutaustria.org.* **Austria Tourist Office** ⊕ *www.austria.info.* **Train information** ⊕ *www.oebb.at.*

All About Salzburg For basic information: **Salzburg** ⊕ *www.salzburg.info.*

All About Vienna For basic information: **Vienna** ⊕ *www.wien.info.*

Here are some other top websites for Vienna:

Die Falter. It's mostly in German, but this site has excellent movie and restaurant reviews and comprehensive coverage of the city's "alternative" scene. ⊕ *www.falter.at.* **Die Presse.** In German only, this is the website of the city's leading serious newspaper. ⊕ *www. diepresse.at.* **Jirsa Tickets Wien.** This is the place for prebooking event tickets online. ⊕ *www.viennaticket.at/english.* **Museums-Quartier.** Visit this website for the scoop on what's happening in Vienna's trendy museum quarter. ⊕ *www.mqw.at.* **Wienerzeitung.** This newspaper site has an English translation. ⊕ *www.wienerzeitung.at.* **Wien Online.** This is the city government's official website. ⊕ *www.magwien.gv.at.*

INDEX

A

Abbeys, *25*
Carinthia and Graz, *293*
Innsbruck, Tyrol, and Vorarlberg, *338–339*
Salzburg, *213*
Vienna Woods, Lake Neusiedl, and the Danube Valley, *164, 175, 177, 182–183, 193–194*
Adlerwarte, *361*
Adventure sports, *280*
Air travel, *18, 382–383*
Carinthia and Graz, *284*
Eastern Alps, *243*
Innsbruck, Tyrol, and Vorarlberg, *312*
Salzburg, *197*
Salzkammergut, *265*
Vienna, *39–40*
Vienna Woods, Lake Neusiedl, and the Danube Valley, *156*
Akademie der Bildenen Künste, *83*
Albertina Museum, *53–54*
Alpenzoo, *335*
Alpinarium, *352*
Alpine Flower Garden Kitzbühel, *341*
Alte Schmiede, *50*
Alter Dom, *187*
Alter Markt, *201, 203*
Alter Platz, *286*
Alter Pocher, *253*
Altes Rathaus (Bregenz), *361*
Altes Rathaus (Linz), *187*
Altes Rathaus (Vienna), *58*
Am Hof, *54*
Andromeda Fountain, *58*
Annasäule, *322*
Antiques shops
Salzburg, *236*
Vienna, *142, 145, 147, 148, 151*
Vienna Woods, Lake Neusiedl, and the Danube Valley, *192*
Apartment and house rentals, *121, 390*
Archaeological Excavation, *278*
Architecture, *81*
Architekturzentrum Wien, *80*
Arnulf Rainer Museum, *162*
Ars Electronica Museum, *184–185*

Art galleries and museums
Carinthia and Graz, *288, 298, 301*
Innsbruck, Tyrol, and Vorarlberg, *321, 324, 362*
Salzburg, *204–205, 209*
Salzkammergut, *274*
Vienna, *53–54, 66, 70, 75, 76, 77–80, 83, 132–133, 144*
Vienna Woods, Lake Neusiedl, and the Danube Valley, *162, 175, 178, 185–186*
ATMs and banks, *396–397*
Augustinerbräu, *230*
Augustinerkirche, *62*
Austria Fountain, *69*
Austrian Christmas Museum, *194*
Austrian Open-Air Museum, *307*

B

Bad Gastein, *255–257*
Bad Ischl, *267, 272–276*
Baden, *160, 162–163*
Badener Puppen und Spielzeugmuseum, *162*
Balls, *128*
Banks, *396–397*
Bärnbach, *306–307*
Bars, lounges, and nightclubs, *128–129*
Basiliskenhaus, *50*
Beckenturm, *361*
Bed-and-breakfasts, *121*
Beer, *24, 230, 394*
Beethoven Haus, *162*
Beethoven Pasqualatihaus, *70*
Belvedere Palace, *71, 73*
Bergisel, *324*
Bergkirche, *172*
Bicycling, *25*
Eastern Alps, *251*
Innsbruck, Tyrol, and Vorarlberg, *366*
Salzburg, *215*
tours, *401*
Vienna, *40*
Vienna Woods, Lake Neusiedl, and the Danube Valley, *156, 167, 192–193*
Bischofshof, *187*
Blutgasse District, *52*
Boat and ferry travel, *386–387*
Innsbruck, Tyrol, and Vorarlberg, *313*

Salzburg, *197*
Vienna, *40*
Vienna Woods, Lake Neusiedl, and the Danube Valley, *156*
Boat tours and cruises
Eastern Alps, *251*
Innsbruck, Tyrol, and Vorarlberg, *361*
Salzkammergut, *279, 280*
Vienna Woods, Lake Neusiedl, and the Danube Valley, *185, 171*
Bodensee White Fleet, *361*
Böhmische Hofkanzlei, *58*
Bookstores, *142, 145, 148, 151*
Botany Collection, *299*
Bregenz, *360–366*
Bregenzer Festspiele, *361–362, 365*
Brunnauer im Magazin ✕, *219*
Burg, *296*
Burg Hasegg and Hall Mint, *338*
Burg Hohenwerfen, *260*
Burg Kreuzenstein, *177–178*
Burg Landeck, *348*
Burggarten, *62*
Burgtheater, *67*
Bus tours, *42, 320*
Bus travel, *383–384*
Eastern Alps, *243*
Innsbruck, Tyrol, and Vorarlberg, *313*
Salzburg, *198*
Vienna, *41*
Vienna Woods, Lake Neusiedl, and the Danube Valley, *157*
Business hours, *141, 396*

C

Café Central ✕, *67, 69*
Café Tomaselli ✕, *219*
Cafés and coffeehouses, *20, 104*
Canuntum, *166–168*
Car travel and rentals, *384–386*
Carinthia and Graz, *284*
Eastern Alps, *244*
Innsbruck, Tyrol, and Vorarlberg, *313*
Salzburg, *198*
Salzkammergut, *265*
Vienna, *40*
Vienna Woods, Lake Neusiedl, and the Danube Valley, *157*

Carinthia and Graz, 17, 282–307
dining, 285, 289–290, 300, 302–303
lodging, 285, 290–291, 293, 295, 303–304, 307
nightlife and the arts, 291, 304–305
price categories, 285
shopping, 306
tour operators, 285, 296
transportation, 284
visitor information, 285
when to go, 283
Casino, 162
Castle rentals, 390
Castles, 25
Carinthia and Graz, 291–292, 293
Eastern Alps, 247, 260
Innsbruck, Tyrol, and Vorarlberg, 335, 338, 348
Salzburg, 210–211
Vienna, 54
Vienna Woods, Lake Neusiedl, and the Danube Valley, 165, 167, 177–178, 180, 186–187
Cemeteries, 76, 209, 213
Ceramics shops, 143, 145–146
Cheese making, 359
Christkindlmärkte, 143, 148, 149, 152
Christmas/New Year's tours, 401
Church of St. Catherine, 341
Church of St. Vincent, 254
Churches. ⇨ See also Abbeys
Carinthia and Graz, 288, 289, 292, 293, 296, 301, 306–307
Eastern Alps, 247, 254, 258
Innsbruck, Tyrol, and Vorarlberg, 321, 324, 338, 341, 362, 363
Salzburg, 203, 207, 210, 213, 216
Salzkammergut, 270, 274, 278–279
Vienna, 50–51, 52, 56–57, 59, 62, 63, 70, 73–74, 84, 85–86
Vienna Woods, Lake Neusiedl, and the Danube Valley, 170, 172, 180, 186, 187, 188–189
City Wall (Bregenz), 362
Civic Armory, 54
Climate, 29, 155–156, 265, 283

Clothing shops
Salzburg, 238
Vienna, 143–144, 146, 148, 149–150
Club Innsbruck card, 322
Coffeehouses, 20, 104
Collection of Arms and Armor, 65
Collection of Historic Musical Instruments, 65
Colleges and universities, 83, 85
Column of Our Lady, 54
Communications, 390, 392–393
Confectionary shops, 237
Convents, 211
Conversions, 380
Copa Kagrana, 87
Crafts shops, 237–238
Credit cards, 11, 397
Cultural History Collection, 299
Currency, 398

D

Dachstein Ice Caves, 278
Damenstift, 338
Dance, 131
Dance clubs, 130
Danube River, 155, 174–183, 185
Danube Valley. ⇨ See Vienna Woods, Lake Neusiedl, and the Danube Valley
Das Schindler ✕, 325–326
Das Triest 🏨, 122
Demel, 54
Department of Geology and Paleontology, 299
Department of Zoology, 299
Department stores, 144, 151
Die Herzl Weinstube ✕, 302
Dinner theater, 212
Dining, 11, 19, 393–394
Austrian cuisine, 22–23, 190, 223, 271, 289, 359
Carinthia and Graz, 285, 289–290, 300, 302–303
Eastern Alps, 245, 247, 250, 256, 259, 261
Innsbruck, Tyrol, and Vorarlberg, 314, 318, 321, 322, 325–328, 340, 341–342, 355, 364
menu guide, 376–379
Salzburg, 216–225
Salzkammergut, 267, 269, 274–275, 277
tipping, 93

Vienna, 48, 51, 53, 67, 69, 80, 92–112
Vienna Woods, Lake Neusiedl, and the Danube Valley, 159, 163, 169, 170–171, 173–174, 179, 181–182, 189–190
DO & CO Albertina ✕, 102
Dom (Gurk), 292
Dom (Salzburg), 203
Dominican Monastery, 293
Dominikanerkirche, 52
Domkirche (Graz), 296
Domkirche (Klagenfurt), 288
Komkirche zu St. Jakob, 321
DomQuartier, 203
Dorotheum, 54, 147
Dreifaltigkeitskirche, 216
Dritt Mann Museum, 83
Dürnstein, 180–182

E

Eastern Alps, 16, 242–261
dining, 245, 247, 250, 256, 259, 261
lodging, 245, 250, 254, 256–257, 258, 261
nightlife and the arts, 250–251, 257
price categories, 245
sports and the outdoors, 251, 253, 254–255, 257, 258–259
tour operators, 255
transportation, 243–245
visitor information, 245
when to go, 242–243
Eco tours, 401–402
Eisenstadt, 171–174
Eisriesenwelt, 260–261
Electricity, 395
Emergencies, 395
road service, 385
Engel Apotheke, 54
Ephesus Museum, 65
Equestrian statue of Emperor Joseph II, 63
Erzherzog Johann 🏨, 304
Erzherzog Johann Brunnen, 298
Esplanade (Bad Ischl), 273
Ethnological Museum, 65
Etiquette, 391
Europastüberl ✕, 326
Exchanging money, 398

F

Fälschermuseum, 66
Felsentherme Gastein, 255

Festivals and seasonal events, 30
Carinthia and Graz, 283–284, 305–306
Eastern Alps, 258
Innsbruck, Tyrol, and Vorarlberg, 312, 331, 340, 361–362, 365
Salzburg, 206–207, 232
Salzkammergut, 275–276
Vienna, 93
Vienna Woods, Lake Neusiedl, and the Danube Valley, 174
Festspielhaus, 206–207
Festungsbahn, 211
Fiaker tours, 42
Film, 132
Filzmoos, 259–260
Finanzministerium, 52
Fischerkirche, 170
Fishing, 251, 355
Flea markets, 146, 151
Flexenhäsl ✕ , 357
Fodor, Eugene, 11
Fodor's ratings, 11
Food shops, 148
Fortress Hohensalzburg, 210–211
Fountains
Carinthia and Graz, 298
Innsbruck, Tyrol, and Vorarlberg, 363
Salzburg, 209, 239
Vienna, 58, 69
Franziskanerkirche, 207
Franziskischlössl Wirtzhaus, 213
Friedhof St. Sebastian, 213
Freihaus, 87
Friesach, 293, 295
Freud Haus, 84
Freyung, The, 69
Furniture shops, 151
Fuschlsee, 267, 269

G

Gaisberg, 238
Galtür, 351–353
Gardens
Innsbruck, Tyrol, and Vorarlberg, 341
Salzburg, 213, 214
Vienna, 62, 71
Gasometers, 86
Gasthaus Kornmesser, 362
Gasthof Post 🖫 , 358
Gauder Fest, 340
Getreidegasse, 204

Gift shops, 144, 147, 151
Glass shops, 143, 145–146
Globe Museum, 70
Glockenmuseum, 324
Glockenspiel, 204
Glockenspielplatz, 298
Gloriette, 86
Gold panning, 253
Goldener Adler 🖫 , 328
Goldener Hirsch 🖫 , 227
Goldenes Dachl, 321
Golf, 332, 344
Golf-Hote Rasmushof 🖫 , 343
Gosau am Dachstein, 276–277
Gösser Braugatstätte, 362
Graben, The, 55
Grand Hotel Europa 🖫 , 328, 330
Grand Hotel Wien 🖫 , 116
Graz. ⇨ See Carinthia and Graz
Griechenbeisl ✕ , 45, 48
Grosses Festspielhaus, 206–207
Grossglockner Hochalpenstrasse, 252
Grossglockner Highway, 251–253
Grossglockner Pass, 246–255
Grotto Railway, 187
Guesthouse, The 🖫 , 120
Gurk, 292

H

Haas-Haus, 59
Hainburg an der Donau, 166–168
Hall in Tyrol, 336, 338–339
Hall Mint, 338
Hallein, 238–239
Hallerwirt ✕ , 342
Hallstatt, 276, 277–280
Hauptplatz (Graz), 298
Hauptplatz (Friesach), 293
Haus der Musik, 48
Haus Für Mozart, 206
Haydn, Joseph, 83, 172, 173
Haydn Museum, 172
Health concerns, 395
Heidentor, 166
Heiligenblut, 253–255
Heiligenkreuz, 164
Heiligenkreuzerhof, 49, 53
Heimatmuseum, 239
Hebling House, 324
Heldenplatz, 65
Herz-Jesu Kirche, 362
Hettwer Bastion, 213

Hiking, 402
Eastern Alps, 254–255, 257
Innsbruck, Tyrol, and Vorarlberg, 315, 333, 348
Salzkammergut, 280
Himmelpfortgasse, 48
Hochosterwitz, 291–292
Hofapotheke, 201
Hofbibliothek, 62–63
Hofburg, The, 60–66
Hofburgkapelle, 63
Hofkirche, 324
Hofmobiliendepot, 83
Hofpavillon, 86
Hohe Tauern National Park, 252–253
Hoher Markt, 59
Holidays, 396
Home exchanges, 390
Horse carriage tours, 42, 211
Hotel Auersperg 🖫 , 228
Hotel Lamée 🖫 , 116
Hotel Sacher 🖫 , 120
Hotel Villa Licht 🖫 , 343
Hotel zum Dom 🖫 , 305
Hotels. ⇨ See also Lodging
price categories, 11, 115, 160, 226, 245, 267, 285, 319
House rentals, 121, 390
Housewear shops, 151
Houses of historic interest
Carinthia and Graz, 298
Innsbruck, Tyrol, and Vorarlberg, 321, 324, 325, 362, 363
Salzburg, 201, 203, 204, 207, 209, 213, 215
Salzkammergut, 273, 274
Vienna, 49, 50, 52, 56, 58, 59, 63–64, 65, 66, 69, 70, 75–76, 82, 83, 84, 85, 90
Vienna Woods, Lake Neusiedl, and the Danube Valley, 162, 187, 188
Hubertus ✕ , 259
Hundertwasserhaus, 75–76

I

Ice caves, 260–261, 278
Ice Dream Factory ✕ , 109–110
Imperial Palace, 323
In der Burg, 63
Innsbruck, Tyrol, and Vorarlberg, 17, 310–366
dining, 314, 318, 321, 322, 325–328, 340, 341–342, 355, 364

lodging, 318, 328–331, 339, 343, 345–346, 348, 349–350, 352, 355, 356, 357–359, 365
nightlife and the arts, 331–332, 343–344, 346, 350, 352–353, 359, 365
price categories, 319
shopping, 334–335, 344–345
sports and the outdoors, 315, 332–333, 340, 346, 348, 351, 355–356, 358, 359–360, 366
tour operators, 320, 361
transportation, 312–314
visitor information, 314
when to go, 312
Internet, 390
Ischgl, *351–353*
Itineraries, *26–28*

J

Jazz clubs, *130–131*
Jewelry shops, *144–145, 147, 192*
Johann Strauss the Younger's House, *66*
Josefsplatz, *63*
Joseph Haydn House, *83*
Jüdisches Museum der Stadt Wien, *55*
Jugendstil architecture, *76*

K

Kahlenbergerdorf, *175*
Kaiserappartements, *63–64*
Kaisergruft, *59*
Kaiserliche Schatzkammer, *64*
Kaiservilla, *273*
Kapuzinerberg Hill, *213*
Kapuzinerkloster, *213*
Karikaturmuseum, *178*
Karmelitenkloster, *187*
Karlskirche, *73–74*
Karlsplatz, *74–75*
Kärntnerstrasse, *55*
Keltenmuseum, *239*
Kepler Haus, *187*
Kirche Am Hof, *59*
Kirche Am Steinhof, *84*
Kitzbühel, *341–345*
Klagenfurt, *286–291*
Klopeinersee, *288*
Klosterneuburg, *175, 177*
Kohlmarkt, *55–56*
Kollegienkirche, *207*
Korneuburg, *177–178*
Krems, *178–179*
Kremsmünsterhaus, *188*

Krems, *178–179*
Kriminal Museum, *66*
Krimml Waterfalls, *340*
Kulturfabrik, *166–167*
Kunsthalle Krems, *178*
Kunsthalle Wien, *79–80*
Kunsthaus (Bregenz), *362*
Kunsthaus (Graz), *298*
Kunsthaus Wien, *76*
Kunsthistorisches Museum, *77–78*
Kunstkammer, *78*
Kurpark, *162*

L

Lake Neusiedl. *⇨ See* Vienna Woods, Lake Neusiedl, and the Danube Valley
Landeck, *348*
Landesmuseum (Bregenz), *362*
Landesmuseum Burgenland, *172*
Landesmuseum Joanneum, *299*
Landeszeughaus, *299*
Landhaus (Klagenfurt), *288*
Landhaus (Linz), *188*
Landhaushof, *301*
Language, *373–379, 391*
Lech, *358–360*
Lentos, *185–186*
Leopold Museum, *79*
Libraries, *62–63, 216*
Liechtensteinklamm, *258*
Linke Wienzeile 38 and 40, *82*
Linz, *155, 183–194*
Lodging, 11, 389–390
Carinthia and Graz, 285, 290–291, 293, 295, 303–304, 307
Eastern Alps, 245, 250, 254, 256–257, 258, 261
Innsbruck, Tyrol, and Vorarlberg, 318, 328–331, 339, 343, 345–346, 348, 349–350, 352, 355, 356, 357–359, 365
Salzburg, 225–230
Salzkammergut, 267, 269, 271–272, 275, 277, 280
Vienna, 114–124
Vienna Woods, Lake Neusiedl, and the Danube Valley, 159–160, 163, 164, 168, 169, 171, 174, 179, 182, 173, 190
Loisium, *179*
Looshaus, *56*
Luegg House, *298*
Luggage, *398–399*

M

Mail and shipping, *396*
Malls, *151*
Mammuthöhle, *278*
Marchegg, *165*
Marionettentheater, *213–214*
Martinskirche, *363*
Martinsturm, *361*
Maximilianeum, *321*
Mayerling, *163–164*
Meissnerstiege, *363*
Melk, *182–183*
Michaelerkirche (Hallstatt), *278–279*
Michaelerkirche (Vienna), *56*
Michaelerplatz, *56*
Mineralogy Collection, *299*
Minimudus, *288*
Minoritenkirche (Linz), *188*
Minoritenkirche (Vienna), *70*
Mirabell Palace, *214–215*
Mirabellgarten, *214*
Monatsschlösschen, *239–240*
Mönchsberg Elevator, *204*
Money matters, *11, 396–398*
Money saving tips, *19*
Montfortbrunnen, *363*
Mountain climbing, *402*
Eastern Alps, 254–255
Innsbruck, Tyrol, and Vorarlberg, 315, 346
Mozart, Wolfgang Amadeus, *49, 51, 68, 188, 204, 207, 208, 215, 216*
Mozart Audio and Visual Collection, *216*
Mozart Haus, *188*
Mozart Wohnhaus, *215*
Mozarthaus, *49*
Mozartplatz, *207*
Mozarts Geburtshaus, *204, 207, 209*
Museum Carnuntinum, *166*
Museum der Moderne, *204–205, 209*
Museum der Stadt Bad Ischl, *273*
Museum für Angewandte Kunst (MAK), *75*
Museum Hallstatt, *279*
Museum im Schottenstift, *70*
Museum Industrielle Arbeitswelt, *194*
Museum Moderner Kunst Kärnten, *288*
Museum Moderner Kunst Stiftung Ludwig, *79*

Museums. ⇨ *See also* Art galleries and museums; Houses of historic interest
architecture, 80
art fakes, 66
avalanche memorial, 352
bells, 324
botany, 299
caricature, 178
Carinthia and Graz, 288, 298, 299, 301
carriages, 90
cars and motorcycles, 247
Celtic settlements, 239
children's, 80
Christmas-tree decorations, 194
clocks, 58
crime, 66
in Eastern Alps, 247
ethnological, 65
folklore, 247
furniture, 83
geology and paleontology, 299
globes, 70
Haydn, 172
history, 75, 172, 188, 205, 273, 279, 299, 301
industry, 194
in Innsbruck, Tyrol, and Vorarlberg, 321, 324, 325, 352, 362
Jewish life, 55, 173
Maximilian I, 321, 325
mineralogy, 299
Mozart, 49, 216
music, 48, 65
natural history, 80, 299
photography, 274
Roman antiquities, 59, 65, 166–167, 362
in Salzburg, 204–205, 209, 210, 216, 239
Salzkammergut, 273, 274, 279
"Silent Night," 239
silver and tableware, 64
Styrian Armoury, 299
technology, 89, 184–185
Third Man, 83
toys, 162, 210
in Vienna, 48, 49, 53–54, 55, 58, 59, 64, 65, 66, 70, 75, 76, 77–80, 83, 89, 90
"Vienna Gate," 167–168
in Vienna Woods, Lake Neusiedl, and the Danube Valley, 162, 166–168, 172–173, 175, 178, 179, 184–187, 188, 194
weapons, 65
wine, 179
zoology, 299
MuseumsQuartier, 76–80, 82–84
Music, 21
Innsbruck, Tyrol, and Vorarlberg, 331, 361–362, 365
Salzburg, 232, 233–234
Salzkammergut, 275–276
Vienna, 130–131, 133–136
Music shops, 145, 147

N

Naschmarkt, 80
Nature-Hotel Waldklause 🏠, 346
Naturhistorisches Museum, 80
Nepomuk-Kapelle, 363
Neue Burg, 65
Neue Residenz, 204, 205
Neuer Dom, 186
Neusiedl am See, 169
Neusiedl Lake. ⇨ *See* **Vienna Woods, Lake Neusiedl, and the Danube Valley**
New Year's tours, 401
Nightlife and the arts
Carinthia and Graz, 291, 304–305
Eastern Alps, 250–251, 257
Innsbruck, Tyrol, and Vorarlberg, 331–332, 343–344, 346, 350, 352–353, 359, 365
Salzburg, 230–235
Salzkammergut, 272, 275–276
Vienna, 126–137
Vienna Woods, Lake Neusiedl, and the Danube Valley, 171, 174, 191
Nonnberg Convent, 211
Nordico, 188
Nordpark, 335
Nordpark Funicular, 335

O

Obauer ✕, 261
Oberndorf, 239
Opera and operetta
Innsbruck, Tyrol, and Vorarlberg, 361–362
Salzburg, 234–235
Salzkammergut, 275–276
Vienna, 57–58, 135–136
Österreichisches Jüdisches Museum, 173
Otto Wagner Houses, 82

P

Packing, 398–399
Palaces, 25
Carinthia and Graz, 296, 299, 300–301
Innsbruck, Tyrol, and Vorarlberg, 322
Salzburg, 214–215, 204, 205, 214–215, 239–240
Vienna, 52, 71, 71, 73, 75, 86, 88–90
Vienna Woods, Lake Neusiedl, and the Danube Valley, 173
Palais Ferstel, 69
Palais Hansen Kempinski Vienna 🏠, 117
Palais Harrach, 71
Palais Herberstein, 299
Palais Kinsky, 71
Palais Khuenburg, 301
Palmenhaus, 86
Parish Church of St. Gallus, 363
Park Hyatt 🏠, 122
Parks
Carinthia and Graz, 292
Eastern Alps, 252–253
Vienna, 66–67, 89
Vienna Woods, Lake Neusiedl, and the Danube Valley, 162
Parlament, 85
Paschingerschlössl, 213
Passports and visas, 399
Pastry shops, 101
Perchtenlauf, 258
Petersbergkirche, 293
Petersfriedhof, 209
Peterskirche, 56–57
Pfänder, 361
Pfarrkirche St. Nikolaus, 338
Pferdeschwemme, 209
Pillar to the Holy Trinity, 186
Pinzgauer Railroad, 247
Pongau Domkirche, 258
Porcelain shops, 143, 145–146
Post Office (Bregenz), 363
Pöstlingberg, 186
Pöstlingbergbahn, 186
Postsparkasse, 49
Prater, 66–67
Price categories, 11
Carinthia and Graz, 285
dining, 11, 19, 94, 160, 217, 245, 267, 285, 319
Eastern Alps, 245
Innsbruck, Tyrol, and Vorarlberg, 319

lodging, 11, 115, 160, 226, 245, 267, 285, 319
Salzburg, 217, 226
Salzkammergut, 267
Vienna, 94, 115
Vienna Woods, Lake Neusiedl, and the Danube Valley, 160
Public transit, 18, 41, 314
Pyramidenkogel, 289

R

Radisson Blu Style Hotel ☷, 120–121
Rafting, 346
Rathaus (Graz), 298
Rathaus (Salzburg), 209
Rathaus (Vienna), 85
Reptilien Zoo, 289
Residenz, 205
Restaurant Edvard ✕, 110
Restaurants. ⇨ *See also* Dining
price categories, 11, 19, 94, 160, 217, 245, 267, 285, 319
Restrooms, 399
Richard the Lionheart Castle, 180
Rickshaws, 42
Rieseneishöhle, 278
Ringstrasse, 71–86
River Salzach, 211, 213–216
Rohrau, 167
Roman ruins, 59, 166
Römermuseum, 59
Rottal Palace, 52
Rupertinum, 209
Ruprechtskirche, 57
Russian War Memorial, 75
Rust, 170–171

S

Sacher Salzburg ☷, 229
Safety, 399
St. Andrew's parish church, 341
St. Anton am Arlberg, 349–351
St. Egyd, 289
St. Florian, 193–194
St. George's Chapel, 210
St. Hippolyt Pfarrkirche, 247
St. Johann am Imberg, 213
St. Johann im Pongau, 258–259
St. Wolfgang, 267, 270–272
Salt mines, 279
Salzbergwerk, 279
Salzburg, 16, 196–240
dining, 216–225
excursions from, 238–240

exploring, 200–216
lodging, 225–230
nightlife and the arts, 230–235
price categories, 217, 226
shopping, 235–238
sports and the outdoors, 215
tour operators, 198–200, 211, 212
transportation, 197–198
visitor information, 200
when to go, 29
Salzburg Card, 206
Salzburg Museum, 205
Salzburg Music Festival, 232
Salzburgerhof ☷, 250
Salzburger Dolomitenstrasse, 260
Salzburger Marionettenthe-ater, 235
Salzburger Schlosskonzerte, 234
Salzkammergut, 17
dining, 267, 269, 274–275, 277
lodging, 267, 269, 271–272, 275, 277, 280
nightlife and the arts, 272, 275–276
price categories, 267
sports and the outdoors, 280
tour operators, 266, 279
transportation, 265
visitor information, 266–267
when to go, 265
Salzwelten, 239
Sammulung Essl, 175
Sattler Panorama, 205
Scale models, 288
Schafberg, 270–271
Schafbergbahn, 271
Schifffahrt Boat Trips, 279
Schloss Ambras, 335
Schloss Eggenberg, 300
Schloss Esterházy, 173
Schloss Hellbrunn, 239–240
Schloss Leopoldskron ☷, 229
Schloss Niederweiden, 165
Schloss Petersberg, 293
Schloss Rohrau, 167
Schloss Rosenberg, 247
Schlossberg, 300
Schlossberg Castle Ruins, 167
Schlosshof, 165
Schlossmuseum Linz, 186–187
Schmetterlinghaus, 62
Schmittenhöhe, 247
Schnapps, 237
Schönbrunn Palace, 86, 88–90
Schönbrunn Schlosspark, 89

Schönlaterngasse, 49
Schottenhof, 69
Schottenkirche, 70
Schruns-Tschagguns, 353, 355–356
Schubert's Birthplace, 85
Schwarzenberg Palace, 75
Schwarzenbergplatz, 75
Schwazer Adler ☷, 330
Schweizertor, 63, 66
Schweizerhof, 63
Secession Building, 82
Seebad, 170
Seekapelle, 363
Seminarkirche, 188
Shoe shops, 148
Shopping
Carinthia and Graz, 306
Innsbruck, Tyrol, and Vorarlberg, 334–335, 344–345
Salzburg, 235–238
Vienna, 140–152
Vienna Woods, Lake Neusiedl, and the Danube Valley, 191–192
Silberkammer, 64
"Silent Night" site, 239
Silver Chapel, 324
Skiing, 24, 32–33
Eastern Alps, 251, 257, 258–259
Innsbruck, Tyrol, and Vorarlberg, 315, 333, 345, 348, 350, 351, 356, 358, 359–360, 366
Smallest house in Salzburg, 201, 203
Sound of Music tours, 212
Snowboarding, 32–33
Sofitel Vienna Stephansdom ☷, 122
Sölden, 345–346, 348
Souvenir shops, 144, 147, 151, 237
Spanische Reitschule, 64–65
Spas, 255
Spielzeugmuseum, 210
Spittelberg Quarter, 83–84
Sports and the outdoors, 20–21, 24, 25, 32–33
Eastern Alps, 251, 253, 254–255, 257, 258–259
Innsbruck, Tyrol, and Vorarlberg, 315, 332–333, 340, 346, 348, 351, 355–356, 358, 359–360, 366
Salzburg, 215
Salzkammergut, 280

Vienna Woods, Lake Neusiedl, and the Danube Valley, 167, 169, 171, 192–193
Staatsoper, 57–58
Stadtmuseum (Graz), 301
Stadtmuseum Wienertor, 167–168
Stadtpark, 71
Stadtpfarrkirche (Friesach), 293
Stadtpfarrkirche (Graz), 301
Stadtpfarrkirche (Linz), 188–189
Stadtpfarrkirche St. Nikolaus, 274
Stadtsteig, 363
Stadtturm, 322
Steingasse, 216
Steirereck ✕, 108
Steirisches Heimatwerk (shop), 306
Stephansdom, 44, 48–53
Steyrertalbahn, 194
Stift Klosterneuburg, 175, 177
Stift Melk, 182–183
Stift St. Florian, 193–194
Stiftskirche (Dürnstein), 180
Stiftkirche St. Peter, 205–206
Stiftung Mozarteum, 216
Stock-im-Eisen, 60
Streetcar travel, 41
Stubaital Valley, 336
Stuben, 356
Stübing bei Graz, 307
Subway system, 41
Swimming, 251, 333
Symbols, 11

T

Taubenkobel ✕, 173–174
Taxes, 93, 141, 399–400
Taxis, 42
Technisches Museum, 89
Telephones, 392–393
Tennerhof ✕⬚, 342, 343
Theater, 136–137, 235, 331
Theater am Kornmarkt, 363
Theater buildings
Innsbruck, Tyrol, and Vorarlberg, 363
Salzburg, 206–207, 213–214
Salzkammergut, 276
Vienna, 57–58, 67
Thermalkurhaus, 255
Third Man Museum, 83
Third Man Portal, 71
Third Man tour, 72
Thumersbach, 247
Tickets, 127, 193

Tiergarten, 89–90
Time, 400
Timing the visit, 18, 29
Tipping, 93, 400
Tomb of the Archduchess Maria-Christina, 62
Topazz ⬚, 117
Toscaninihof, 210
Tours, 400–402
Carinthia and Graz, 285, 296
Eastern Alps, 255
Innsbruck, Tyrol, and Vorarlberg, 320, 361
Salzburg, 198–200, 211, 212
Salzkammergut, 266, 279
Vienna, 42–43
Vienna Woods, Lake Neusiedl, and the Danube Valley, 158, 185
Toy shops, 148
Train travel, 18, 387–388
Carinthia and Graz, 284
Eastern Alps, 244–245, 247
Innsbruck, Tyrol, and Vorarlberg, 313
Salzburg, 198, 211
Salzkammergut, 265, 270–271
Vienna, 42
Vienna Woods, Lake Neusiedl, and the Danube Valley, 157–158, 186, 187, 194
Transportation, 18, 382–388
Travel times, 18
Triumphpforte, 324
Trofana Royal ⬚, 352
Tschagguns, 353, 355–356
21er Haus, 75
Tyrol. ⇨ See Innsbruck, Tyrol, and Voralberg
Tyroler House, 90
Tyroler Volkskunstmuseum, 324
25hours Hotel Wien ⬚, 123

U

Uhrenmuseum, 58
Uhrturm, 301
Universität, 85
Universitätskirche, 51
Untersberg, 238
Ursulinenkirche, 189

V

Vienna, 16, 36–152
dining, 48, 51, 53, 67, 69, 80, 92–112
exploring, 44–90
lodging, 114–124

nightlife and the arts, 126–137
price categories, 94, 115
shopping, 140–152
tour operators, 42–43
transportation, 39–42, 126
visitor information, 43–44
when to go, 29
Vienna Boys' Choir, 63
"Vienna Gate," 167–168
Vienna Woods, Lake Neusiedl, and the Danube Valley, 16, 154–194
dining, 159, 163, 169, 170–171, 173–174, 179, 181–182, 189–190
lodging, 159–160, 163, 164, 168, 169, 171, 174, 179, 182, 173, 190
nightlife and the arts, 171, 174, 191
price categories, 160
shopping, 191–192
sports and the outdoors, 167, 169, 171, 192–193
tour operators, 158, 185
transportation, 156–158
visitor information, 158–159
when to go, 155–156
Villa Lehár, 274
Villa Trapp ⬚, 230
Visas, 399
Visitor information, 19, 402
Carinthia and Graz, 285
Eastern Alps, 245
Innsbruck, Tyrol, and Vorarlberg, 314
Salzburg, 200
Salzkammergut, 266–267
Vienna, 43–44
Vienna Woods, Lake Neusiedl, and the Danube Valley, 158–159
Vocabulary words, 373–379
Vogtturm, 247
Volksgarten, 71
Voralberg. ⇨ See Innsbruck, Tyrol, and Voralberg
Votivkirche, 85–86
Votter's Fahrzeugmuseum, 247

W

Wachau, The, 181
Wagenburg, 90
Waidhofen and der Ybbs, 194
Walking tours, 42–43, 296
Wallfahrtskirche St. Wolfgang, 270
Wasserspiele, 239

Water sports, *251, 366*
Waterfalls, *340*
Weather, *29, 155–156, 265, 283*
Websites, *402*
Weingut Feiler-Artinger, *170*
Weinstadt Museum Krems, *179*
Weinviertel, *155, 164–168*
Weisses Rössl, *270*
Werfen, *260–261*
When to go, *18, 29*

Wien Museum Karlsplatz, *75*
Wiener Philharmoniker-Gasse, *210*
Wine, *24, 111, 181, 394*
Wolfsklamm, *338–339*

Z

Zell am See, *246–247, 250–251*
Zel am Ziller, *339–340*

Zentralfriedhof, *76*
Zeughaus, *325*
Ziplining, *340*
ZOOM Kinder Museum, *80*
Zoos, *89–90, 289, 335*
Zum Schwarzen Kameel ✕, *103*
Zürs, *356–358*
Zwergenpark, *292*

PHOTO CREDITS

NOTES

NOTES

NOTES

Fodor's VIENNA & THE BEST OF AUSTRIA

Publisher: Amanda D'Acierno, *Senior Vice President*

Editorial: Arabella Bowen, *Editor in Chief*; Linda Cabasin, *Editorial Director*

Design: Tina Malaney, *Associate Art Director*; Chie Ushio, *Senior Designer*; Ann McBride, *Production Designer*

Photography: Jennifer Arnow, *Senior Photo Editor*; Jennifer Romains, *Photo Researcher*

Production: Linda Schmidt, *Managing Editor*; Evangelos Vasilakis, *Associate Managing Editor*; Angela L. McLean, *Senior Production Manager*

Maps: Rebecca Baer, *Senior Map Editor*; David Lindroth; Mark Stroud, Moonstreet Cartography, *Cartographers*

Sales: Jacqueline Lebow, *Sales Director*

Marketing & Publicity: Heather Dalton, *Marketing Director*; Katherine Punia, *Publicity Director*

Business & Operations: Susan Livingston, *Vice President, Strategic Business Planning*; Sue Daulton, *Vice President, Operations*

Fodors.com: Megan Bell, *Executive Director, Revenue & Business Development*; Yasmin Marinaro, *Senior Director, Marketing & Partnerships*

Copyright © 2015 by Fodor's Travel, a division of Random House LLC.

Writers: Rob Freeman, Patti McCracken, Nicholas K. Smith, Erin Snell, Lizzy Randle Williams

Editors: Kristan Schiller, Penny Phenix

Production Editor: Carrie Parker

2nd Edition

ISBN 978-1-101-87805-7

ISSN 2372-689X

SPECIAL SALES

This book is available at special discounts for bulk purchases for sales promotions or premiums. For more information, e-mail specialmarkets@penguinrandomhouse.com

PRINTED IN THE UNITED STATES OF AMERICA

10 9 8 7 6 5 4 3 2 1

ABOUT OUR WRITERS

Rob Freeman specializes in mountain sports on every continent. A former journalist at London's *Daily Mail*, he is a qualified ski instructor who now writes on travel and adventure for a variety of newspapers, magazines, and websites. As research for his book, *Snowfinder Austria,* he has skied almost every run—and visited an equal number of après-ski bars—at every main ski resort in Austria. He updated the Innsbruck, Tyrol, and Vorarlberg, Eastern Alps, and Travel Smart chapters for this edition.

Patti McCracken is a journalist and educator who has lived and worked in more than 25 countries across Central and Eastern Europe, the Balkans, the Caucasus, North Africa, and Southeast Asia. She is a former Knight International Press Fellow whose articles have appeared in *The Wall Street Journal, The San Francisco Chronicle, The Chicago Tribune, Smithsonian Magazine,* and *Afar,* among other publications. She lives in rural Austria with her Jack Russell terrier, Remi, and is currently at work on her first book, a historical nonfiction narrative. She updated the Exploring, Where to Eat, Where to Stay, Nightlife and the Arts, Shopping, and Vienna Woods, Lake Neusiedler, and the Danube River chapters for this edition.

When **Nicholas K. Smith** first traveled to Austria in 2005 with his then-girlfriend (now wife), he had no idea he'd one day be wiling away his days sipping *Wiener Melange* and finding pleasure in German words like *Gugelhupf.* Nick has been a Vienna resident since 2010; he now splits his time between English teaching and freelance journalism for outlets including Esquire.com, *GlobalPost, The Vienna Review,* and GlacierHub.com. He updated the Experience chapter for this edition.

A former Master's student at the prestigious Eastman School of Music, soprano and scribe **Erin Snell** moved from Chicago to Salzburg in 2012 to continue her professional opera-singing career. She has performed in North America at Santa Fe Opera, the Ravinia Festival, Utah Opera, and Central City Opera, as well as at recital halls throughout Europe including in London, Vienna, Salzburg, and Nürnberg. She divides her time among creative pursuits including singing, writing, and photography and can be found hiking the Alps when she's not touring with the opera. She updated the Salzburg chapter for this edition.

Lizzy Randle Williams has lived in Austria for the last two years; first, as a student at Smith College, studying history and the German language, and then again after graduating as an English teacher in a small Styrian town. She has also worked as a travel blogger for Eurail, documenting her travels using the train system throughout Europe. She updated the Carinthia and Graz chapter for this edition.